INSIGHT GUIDES

GREECE

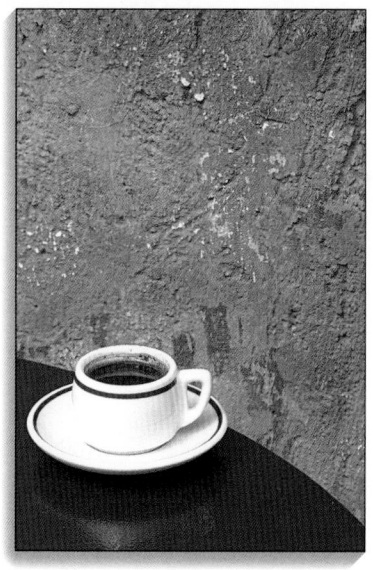

APA PUBLICATIONS L

Part of the Langenscheidt Publishing Group

INSIGHT GUIDE
GREECE

ABOUT THIS BOOK

Editorial

Project Editor
Maria Lord
Picture Editor
Steven Lawrence
Series Manager
Rachel Fox

Distribution

North America
Langenscheidt Publishers, Inc.
36–36 33rd Street 4th Floor
Long Island City, NY 11106
orders@langenscheidt.com

UK & Ireland
GeoCenter International Ltd
Meridian House, Churchill Way West
Basingstoke, Hampshire RG21 6YR
sales@geocenter.co.uk

Australia
Universal Publishers
1 Waterloo Road
Macquarie Park, NSW 2113
sales@universalpublishers.com.au

New Zealand
Hema Maps New Zealand Ltd (HNZ)
Unit 2, 10 Cryers Road
East Tamaki, Auckland 2013
sales.hema@clear.net.nz

Worldwide
Apa Publications GmbH & Co.
Verlag KG (Singapore branch)
38 Joo Koon Road, Singapore 628990
apasin@signet.com.sg

Printing

Insight Print Services (Pte) Ltd
38 Joo Koon Road, Singapore 628990
Tel: (65) 6865 1600. Fax: (65) 6861 6438

©2009 Apa Publications GmbH & Co.
Verlag KG (Singapore branch)
All Rights Reserved

First Edition 1987
Fifth Edition 2004
Updated 2008
Reprinted 2009

CONTACTING THE EDITORS

We would appreciate it if readers
would alert us to errors or out-
dated information by writing to:
Insight Guides, P.O. Box 7910,
London SE1 1WE, England.
insight@apaguide.co.uk

www.insightguides.com

The first Insight Guide pioneered
the use of creative full-colour photography in travel guides in 1970.
Since then, we have expanded our
range to cater for our readers' need
not only for reliable information about
their chosen destination but also for
a real understanding of the culture
and workings of that destination.
Now, when the internet can supply
inexhaustible (but not always reliable)
facts, our books marry text and pictures to provide those much more
elusive qualities: knowledge and
discernment. To achieve this,
they rely heavily on the authority of locally based writers
and photographers.

How to use this book

Insight Guide: Greece is structured
to convey an understanding of
Greece, its people and its culture,
as well as to guide readers through
its sights and everyday activities:

◆ To understand Greece, you need
to know something about its past.
The **Features** section covers the history and culture of the country.

◆ The main **Places** section is
a complete guide to all the
sights and areas worth
visiting. Places of interest are coordinated by
number with the maps.

◆ The **Travel Tips** listings
section provides a handy

point of reference for information on travel, hotels, restaurants, shops and more.

The contributors

This edition was put together by **Maria Lord**, an Insight Guides editor. She updated the chapters on Athens, Itháki, Kefalloniá and Zákynthos, and also wrote the feature on the Cycladic Bronze Age.

The Ancient, Byzantine and Ottoman history chapters were revised by **Jeffrey Pike**, who also did much editing work on the rest of the text. The Independent Greece chapter was revised by eminent historian **Professor Richard Clogg**.

Anthropologist **Dr David Sutton**, Assistant Professor at Southern Illinois University, wrote the sections on Modern Greece and Peoples and Identities. **Professor Gail Holst-Warhaft** of Cornell University contributed the chapters on Literature and Music and Dance.

The section on Food and Drink was written by **Aglaia Kremezi**, a highly respected food writer and consultant. Art historian and sculptor **Dr John Lord** wrote the wide-ranging chapter on Art and Architecture. **Danny Aeberhard**, a long-standing Insight travel writer, contributed the Flora and Fauna chapter.

Marc Dubin, a well-travelled Londoner and part-time resident of Sámos, updated the chapters on Rhodes, the Dodecanese, Northeast Aegean, Corfu, Paxí and Levkáda, as well as central Greece and Epirus. He also overhauled the Travel Tips, and contributed both the Geography essay and the information panel on the New Immigrants. The feature on Italian Architecture was written by **John Chapple**.

Crete and the Peloponnese were covered by writer, tour leader and botanist **Lance Chilton**. **Paul Hellander**, writer and historian, updated the chapters on Thessaloníki, Macedonia and Thrace, as well as the Argo-Saronic Islands, the Sporádes and Évia, and Samothráki. **Jeffrey Carson**, a long-time resident of Páros, wrote and updated the chapter on the Cyclades.

Photographers included **Gregory Wrona**, **Phil Wood**, **Terry Harris** and **Blaine Harrington**. The book was proofread by **Emma Sangster** and indexed by **Elizabeth Cook**. Thanks goes to **Marc Dubin** for the 2008 update, edited by **Alexia Georgiou**.

Map Legend

–·–	International Boundary
––––	Regional Boundary
–·–	National Park/Reserve
––––	Ferry Route
⊖	Border Crossing
✈ ✦	Airport: International/Regional
🚌	Bus Station
Ⓜ	Metro
❶	Tourist Information
⌂ † ⊤	Church/Ruins
†	Monastery
✡	Synagogue
☾	Mosque
∴	Archaeological Site
∩	Cave
🯱	Statue/Monument
★	Place of Interest
⌂ ⌂	Castle/Ruins
⚑	Beach

The main places of interest in the Places section are coordinated by number with a full-colour map (e.g. ❶), and a symbol at the top of every right-hand page tells you where to find the map.

CONTENTS

Maps

A map of Greece is also on
the inside front cover, and a
street plan of Athens is on
the inside back cover.

The Acropolis towers
above the market
place of Athens on a
white rocky platform

Insight on ...

Information panels

Travel Tips

◆ Full Travel Tips index
is on page 323

Places

THE BEST OF GREECE

Ancient sites steeped in history, sun-bleached islands or the cool mountain villages of the Zagória, Venetian forts and clifftop monasteries, hikes through river gorges, food, music and folklore – Here, at a glance, are our recommendations for your visit

TOP SIGHTS

- **The Parthenon, Athens.** Covered in scaffolding for the forseeable future, this treasure of Classical Athens' Golden Age still impresses. *See page 128.*
- **Metéora, Thessaly.** Half-a-dozen-plus frescoed Byzantine monasteries perched on otherworldly rock pinnacles in the Píndos foothills *See pages 174–5.*
- **Rhodes Old Town.** Among the best preserved medieval townscapes in the Mediterranean, a legacy of the

crusading Knights of St John and the Ottomans. *See pages 245–50.*
- **Delphi Sanctuary.** The ancients reckoned this oracle the centre of the world – with its striking setting at the base of Mount Parnassós. *See pages 167–8.*
- **Kérkyra Old Town, Corfu.** Venetian flair, domesticity and town planning at the far end of the Adriatic. *See pages 293–7.*
- **New Acropolis Museum, Athens.** Long awaited and though functionally designed, it does justice to its interesting exhibits. *See pages 130–31.*
  - **Monemvasiá.** First a Byzantine, later a Venetian, stronghold washed by the

sea on three sides, and its lower town still inhabited. *See pages 157–8.*
- **Mystrás.** At the base of Mount Taïgettos, the capital of the Morea Despotate – with frescoed palaces and monasteries – saw out the Byzantine twilight until 1460. *See pages 156–7.*
- **Ósios Loukás monastery.** The best 11th-century mosaics on view in Greece now that Néa Moní and Dáfni are closed. *See page 165.*
- **Santoríni.** Commercialised to within an inch of its life but still a must-see, especially

at sunset from a bar in Firá or Ía. *See pages 238–9.*
- **Hóra and Monastery of St John, Pátmos.** When the cruise-ship groups have left, enjoy this stunningly atmospheric hilltop village set around a labyrinthine monastery. *See pages 264–5.*
- **Mastic village, Híos.** Fortified settlements with gates, arcaded passageways, keep-towers and sombre-hued houses. *See pages 277–8.*

ABOVE: stunning Acropolis. **LEFT:** in the New Acropolis Museum **BELOW:** Santoríni.

BEST CASTLES

- **Acrocorinth.** A soaring rock with an ancient acropolis stippled with Ottoman monuments, wrapped in Byzantine, Frankish and Venetian walls. *See page 149.*
- **Methóni.** Venetian stronghold and waystation for pilgrims, with a moat, gates, and a causeway to the remote Boúrtzi tower. *See pages 161–2.*
- **Palamídi, Návplio.** Venetian citadel critical in the War of Independence and reached via hundreds of steps. *See page 151.*
- **Knights of St John Castle, Kós Town.** Well preserved, very easy to visit example of the crusading order's Dodecanese strongholds. *See page 260.*
- **Néo Froúrio, Kérkyra Town.** Intricately designed Venetian fort with ramps and tunnels, a café and superb views. *See page 293*
- **Mólyvos, Lesvos.** Great views over town and to Turkey – and summer performances in the courtyard. *See page 276.*

BEST WINES

- **Límnos, Ároma Ínou Drýinos.** Oak-aged, smokey-dry white.
- **Sámos, Samos Nectar or Anthemis.** Best in a series of fortified (14–15%), muscat-based dessert wines.
- **Thessaly/Macedonia border, Tsantali Rapsáni.** Easy drinking red from foot hills of Mt Ólympos.
- **Lésvos, Methymneos Red.** Velvety red born of a volcanic terrain.
- **Epirus, Zítsa Cooperative white wines.** Reliably light, dry, semi-sparkling.
- **Dráma region, Château Lazaridi.** Red or white high-quality blends.
- **Neméa, Ktima Papaïoannou.** Rich dark red, a medium-priced taverna staple.

BEST HIKES

- **Northern Kárpathos.** A maintained network of trails links local settlements to occupy keen hikers for a week – the route from Trístomo to Diafáni is the most spectacular. *See pages 253–5.*
- **Ascent of Mt Díkeos, Kós.** Easy, three-hour round-trip from Ziá village, with views over half the Dodecanese. *See page 261.*
- **Vikos Gorge, Zagória.** Beats Crete's Samarian Gorge for its unspoilt, riverine environment and the height of its cliffs. *See pages 186–90.*
- **Dimosári Gorge, southern Évvia.** Another canyon walk, mostly along an old and shady cobbled trail, emerging at a beach hamlet where pickup transport should be arranged. *See page 291.*
- **Mount Áthos, southern tip.** The route through the "hermit's desert" between Megístis Lávras and Osíou Grigoríou monasteries on the Holy Mountain, will hopefully survive the bulldozers. *See pages 207–8.*
- **Mount Pílio transect.** Partly cobbled paths, from Xouríhti to Kalá Nerá via Miliés, descend from forested glades to seaside olive groves. *See pages 173-4.*
- **Egiáli to Hóra, Amorgós.** Trekkers come to this island specially for this spectacular five-hour traverse with the sea on both sides. *See pages 237–8.*

TOP : Agías Triádos monastery, Metéora.
ABOVE LEFT: Methóni castle, surrounded by the sea. **LEFT:** grapes for easy-drinking wines.

BEST MUSEUMS

- **Iráklio Archeological Museum.** Recently renovated it showcases the best of Minoan art and artefacts. *See page 307.*
- **Ambelákia, George Schwartz Mansion.** Grand 18th-century mansion in Constantinopolitan style, with superb murals, hooded fireplaces, carved ceilings and panelling. *See page 174.*
- **Sámos Archeological Museum, Vathý.** One of the country's best collections of the Archaic era, with exquisite small objects (including wood and ivory) from the Hera sanctuary, culminating in an enormous *kouros*. *See page 282.*
- **Theophilos and Theriade Museums, Variá, Lésvos.** Two galleries in an olive grove: the first with over 50 works by naïve local artist Theophilos (1873–1934); the second, the finest modern art collection in Greece amassed by Theriade, Theophilos' patron. *See page 275.*
- **Jewish Museum of Thessaloníki.** Two millennia of Jewish life in the city documented with gravestones, costumes, archival photos and religious items that survived the 1917 fire and 1944 deportation. *See page 199.*

- **Peloponnesian Folklore Foundation, Návplio.** Costumes, embroideries, rural or household items from all over Greece, with exemplary labelling. *See page 151.*
- **Benáki Museum, Athens.** Arguably Athens' best museum, spanning the whole of Greek history. *See pages 137-8.*

ABOVE: Hellenic Festival performance at Herod Atticus theatre. **BELOW:** *kouros*, Sámos Archaeological Museum.

BEST FESTIVALS

See page 374.
- **Hellenic (Athens) Festival.** Going for well over half a century now, with big-name international artists from June to September. Most performances at Herod Atticus and Epidaurus theatres.
- **Pátra Carnival.** The liveliest and most organised of Greece's pre-Lenten events: floats. outrageous costumes, and parades.
- **Easter on Ýdra or Corfu.** Fishermen at Ýdra carry the Epitáfios into the water to bless the boats and ensure calm seas; while on Corfu, brass bands leave not a dry eye with their funeral hymns, and showers of old crockery thrown from windows bring luck.
- **15 August at Olympos, Kárpathos.** Tables for communal feasting in the streets, music on *lýra, laoúto* and *tsaboúna*, and not a bed to be had locally without reserving months in advance.
- **Thessaloníki Film Festival.** This star-studded October event, premiering both Greek and foreign works, is one of the most prestigious in Europe.
- **Rhodes Ecofilms.** Not just environmental documentaries, but new features, tributes and classic films from around the Mediterranean, Europe and Asia. Late June, free.
- **Lefkas International Folklore Festival.** The largest folkdance festival in Greece, with troupes from all over the world. Last full week of August.

OFF THE BEATEN TRACK

- **Néstos Valley, Thrace.** Follow this scenically wooded river valley by train or car to Stavroúpoli, a well-preserved vernacular village that is an alternative tourist centre. *See page 210.*
- **Préspa Lakes, west Macedonia.** Eerily scenic upland basin on the borders with Macedonia and Albania, with sleepy villages and good birdwatching. *See pages 203-4.*
- **Mathráki.** Most vegetated but depopulated of the isolated Diapóndia islets northwest of Corfu, with a fine, 3-km beach and basic facilities. *See page 297.*
- **Kímolos.** Perhaps the sleepiest of the Cyclades, with decent beaches in the south and an intriguing fortified *kástro-hóra*. *See page 236.*

- **Mt Smólikas.** Greece's second highest mountain range, separating Epirus and Macedonia, with two small lakes and excellent hiking. *See page 188.*
- **Néda Gorge, Peloponnese.** From the modern village of Figalía, below the temple of Vassae, a track threads through ancient Phigalia to the River Néda where it thunders underground. *See page 155.*
- **Gávdos islet, Crete.** Southernmost Greek territory, waking up to tourism, preserves unique ecosystems by the Libyan Sea. *See page 307.*
- **Gomáti dunes, Límnos.** Protected environment in the far north of the island with shallow waters, September sea lilies… and a proliferation of sun-loungers. *See pages 271–2.*

Top Right: try locally produced feta cheese and taste the difference. **Right:** Kímolos harbour.

BEST LOCAL SPECIALITIES

- **Pickled caper greens, Níssyros.** The "national shrub" of this volcanic islet gets the vinegar treatment, thorns and all.
- *Soumáda*, **Lefkáda.** A white syrup from bitter almonds, drunk diluted with cold water – this island's is the best.
- *Lakérda*, **Aegean-wide.** Bonito fillet slices soaked, pressed, then cured in salt – the finest *oúzo* partner.
- *Tsípouro*, **Thessaly or Sporades.** If you find *oúzo* too cloying try this clean grape-mash spirit. *See page 93.*
- *Kalatháki féta*, **Límnos.** Small drum-

shaped sheep-milk cheese. *See page 64.*
- **Genuine thyme honey.** Bare islands like Kálymnos make for the purest, dark and strongly aromatic.
- *Tsitsíravla*, **Pílio or Sporades.** Pickled wild pistachio shoots, gathered in spring – good on their own or as a salad topping.

MONEY-SAVING TIPS

Travel late May to late June, or opt for September. You won't have the full range of sea transport at your disposal, but air schedules are much the same as usual, hotel rates can come to little more than half of what they would be in high season, and both taverna food and service are better. *See pages 324–7.*

Book domestic air tickets well in advance. Both Aegean and Olympic

are now largely web-only airlines with tiered fare structures. Early birds can find seats much cheaper than a ferry cabin berth to the same island destination. *See pages 324–7.*

Book rental cars in advance, online if possible. Even in peak season it's possible to secure rates of under €150 per week from airports and major towns. *See page 328.*

Don't order expensive main courses. Instead , assemble a meal from *mezédes* (starters) such as *tyropitákia* (small cheese pastries) – six to eight of these dishes will satisfy most dining couples. *See pages 88–91 and 352–3.*

AN ANCIENT STORY

A heady mix of sun, sea and ancient sites bathed in brilliant
Aegean light, Greece has enchanted travellers for centuries

Modern Greece, which emerged in the 19th century from 500 years of Ottoman rule, lies in a rocky pile of peninsulas and islands at the bottom of the Balkans in the eastern Mediterranean, with a language and landscape redolent of its pre-eminent place in the development of the western world. History, drama, politics, philosophy: the words as well as the concepts have their roots here. Around its rugged terrain are the names of the city states which vied for supremacy in this region 2,000 years ago: Corinth, Sparta, Mycenae, Rhodes, Athens. And here too are Delphi, the Parthenon and Mount Olympos, forever associated with the ancient gods.

Whether you arrive in Greece by boat, train or plane, your first impression as you stretch your legs is likely to be of the sun. Glimmering on the water, reflecting off metal and glass, casting shadows, the Mediterranean sun is omnipresent. Like the flash of a hidden camera, the brilliant light catches you unawares and transfixes you.

From that minute, you seem effortlessly to become a part of the Greek landscape – blue sky above, white sand below, ancient ruins, olive groves, a wine festival… It is easy to fall in love with this radiant country, not least because so many of its 11 million people are emotionally open, unafraid of shedding a tear, either in sorrow or in joy. Many travellers first experience this passion in the warmth of the welcome they receive, and they may even feel a little uneasy at the exuberance of their hosts. Yet those travellers tend to return time after time – for the mirror-smooth Aegean Sea shimmering in the still of the morning, for the *kafenia* with their wooden, thatched chairs and rickety tables offering some shade from the blistering afternoon heat, and for the silvery green olive groves where the cicadas drone at evening time.

The country's membership of the European Union and its capital's hosting of the 2004 Olympic Games have done much to accelerate modernisation. But modern is less a synonym for homogeneous than it is in many other rapidly changing countries. A sense of history and a respect for tradition remain powerful, and most Greeks are proud to share their culture with visitors. The Greek word *xénos* means not only "stranger" but also "guest", and a fortunate *xénos* will be invited into a Greek family's house to be lavishly supplied with food and drink and questioned with genuine curiosity. The aim of this book is both to guide visitors around Greece and its islands and to preview what is likely to be an entirely captivating experience. ❑

PRECEDING PAGES: a back street on Ýdra; classic Cycladic architecture; a view on Santoríni. **LEFT:** old men in Tzermiado, Crete.

A DIVERSE LAND

*Mountains and caves, salt marshes and rainforest, blazing summers
and snow in winter – few countries have such varied landscape and climate*

People perceive Greece as a land where people eat oranges and the sun shines all the time, but it is equally accurate (if not more so) to describe it as a place where it rains a lot and apples figure largely in the diet. Greece is actually the most varied country in the Mediterranean, with habitats ranging from near-deserts to temperate rainforests, from salt marshes to alpine peaks.

The splintered outline of the southeastern Balkan peninsula is the result of the flooding of the Mediterranean basin, which occurred when a debris dam at the future Strait of Gibraltar gave way. Waters from the Atlantic surged in and gradually submerged the mountain ranges, which segmented the deep, hot depression – a process completed only after the last Ice Age, and probably the basis of the Biblical flood account. Isolated, exposed summits became the Greek islands, Crete being the highest and largest. If the Mediterranean could be re-drained, the coastal ranges of former Yugoslavia, the Albano-Greek Píndos, the Peloponnesian mountains, Crete and the Turkish Toros would form one unbroken system: the so-called Dinaric Arc. The arc has a core of karstic limestone, extremely porous and peppered with caves, sinkholes and subterranean rivers. Glaciers of the last Ice Age also had a role in shaping the mountains as far south as the present-day Gulf of Corinth.

Earthquake zone

Greece remains an active subduction zone, where the African tectonic plate burrows under the European plate. This means numerous faults, frequent – often destructive – earthquakes and a significant level of geothermal activity. Over 100 thermal spas are scattered across both the mainland and the islands. The geothermalism is predictably accompanied by vulcanism: you can trace the boundary of the plate collision zone by "joining up" the extinct

or dormant volcanic islands of Méthana (now a peninsula), Póros, the submerged calderas of Mílos and Thíra, and Nísyros, which has erupted within historical memory. In the northeast Aegean, Lésvos, Límnos and Aï Strátis islands are also of volcanic origin.

Only about one quarter of Greece's surface

area is cultivable, the greater part of this in Thessaly and Macedonia. Much of the farmland occupies low-lying plains or upland plateaux, often the beds of former lakes long since drained to reclaim the land for agriculture or eliminate malarial mosquitoes. Only a few perennial freshwater lakes survive on the mainland north of the Gulf of Corinth: they tend to be shallow and murky, more suited to irrigation, fishing and wildlife conservation than recreation. The largest and most scenic is Lake Trihonída in Étolo-Akarnanía; runners-up include Vegoritída, Mikrá Préspa and Kastoriá in western Macedonia, plus Pamvótida in Epirus. The Epirote Píndos

LEFT: dramatic arches at Cape Skinári, Zákynthos.
RIGHT: the west coast cliffs, Zákynthos.

Mountains have a few glacial tarns, but lakes are almost entirely absent from the large islands owing to overly porous rock strata. Koúrnas, near Haniá on Crete, is the largest and most famous.

Stony or partly forested mountains make up three-quarters of the country – and as Henry Miller put it, nowhere has God been so lavish with rocks as in Greece. The hills are often bonily naked; the country's forests have been under steady attack since ancient times, and the rate of deforestation has

precipitation is highest in the Ionian Islands (particularly Corfu and Zákynthos) and the western mainland, where the Píndos mountain range forces moisture-laden air from the Ionian Sea to disgorge its load as rain or snow.

The rest of the country lies effectively in a "rain shadow", although the directional pattern is reversed at Mt Olympos near Thessaloníki, rising nearly 3,000 metres (9,850 ft) in the space of a few kilometres inland from the moist Thermaic Gulf, which duly sends wet air masses west to be

accelerated alarmingly since World War I. Fires, usually deliberately started, are the main cause: under current climatic conditions, it takes a Greek pine wood more than 50 years to recover completely from a blaze.

Hot summers, cold winters

Greece's stereotypical "Mediterranean" climate and vegetation is in fact limited to the coastal areas; "modified continental" is a more accurate tag for the weather elsewhere, with hot, muggy summers and cold winters. Although there are numerous microclimates – such as the northeast coast of the Pílio peninsula with its temperate rainforest – in general

trapped on the summit of the ancient gods. Olympos is the highest of a score of peaks over 2,300 metres (7,550 ft), home to about a dozen ski resorts. While nobody is likely to fly in from northern Europe specially to ski – snowfall patterns are too unreliable – the resorts are increasingly popular with the Greeks themselves.

Greece's fabled, convoluted coast is claimed to cover a distance equal to that of France, a country four times larger. But, despite figuring prominently on tourist posters, beaches are the exception rather than the rule. Much of the shoreline is inhospitable cliff, providing neither satisfaction for sand-seekers, nor anchorage for mariners. In fact, the most likely visitors are birds, as Greece lies under major migratory paths linking north-central Europe and Africa. When it is not cliff or beach, the Greek littoral is peppered with lagoons, estuaries and salt marshes that serve as important wildlife refuges. Some of the most important of these are at Kalógria near Pátra, Kallóni on Lésvos, the delta of the Évros river in Thrace, the Korissíon lagoon on Corfu, the Alykí marsh on Kós and the vast lagoon complex at Mesolóngi.

Controversial dams

No point in Greece is more than 100 km (60 miles) from the sea, so the numerous rivers

for irrigation and flood control rather than for hydroelectric power. Such projects, evidence of a nonaccountable, central-planning mentality which has waned almost everywhere else in Europe, remain highly controversial – none more so than the Mesohára dam on the Ahelóös, which has been declared illegal by the Greek Council of State, and had its funding revoked by the European Union. If ever filled, this massive reservoir – intended to water the thirsty Thessalian plain – would finish off already threatened fisheries and wetlands at the Ahelóös delta.

Greece's rugged terrain, and its high pro-

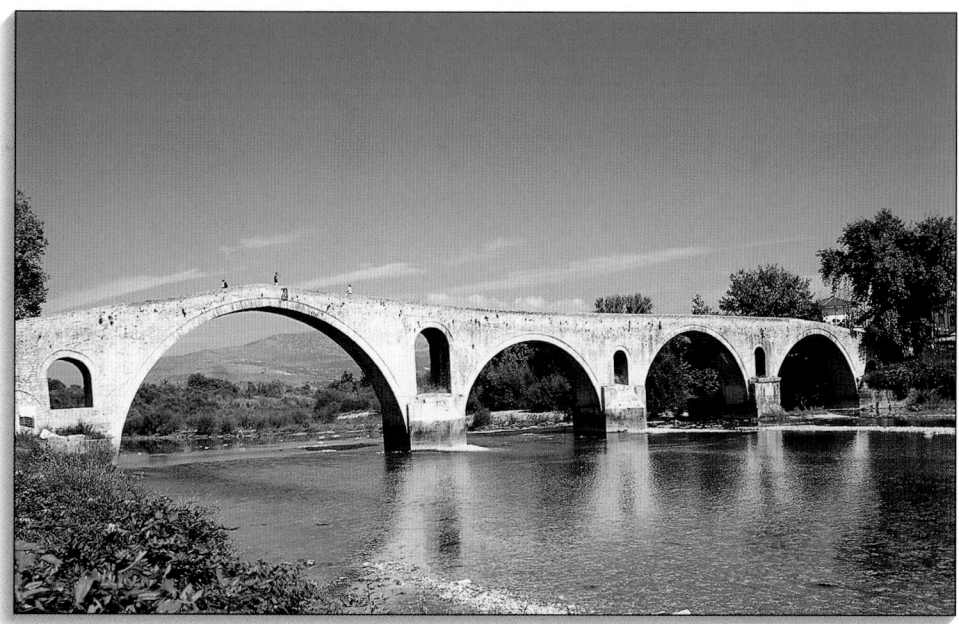

are not only short but swift as they lose altitude quickly, to the delight of the local kayaking and rafting fraternity. The only major rivers to flow lazily along as in northern Europe, in their lower reaches anyway, are the Aliákmonas, the Pínios, the Ahelóös and the Árahthos; the Áxios and Strymónas and Évros in Macedonia and Thrace also conform to most people's idea of a continental river, but have their sources in other Balkan states. Since World War II most rivers north of the Gulf of Corinth have been dammed, usually

portion of territory in island groups, have since the time of the ancient city-states encouraged separate regional development. For such a small country there are numerous dialects, in contrast to, say, far vaster Russia, which has little variation in its speech. Land communications were late in coming; well into the 20th century, it was easier to sail from Athens to the eastern Peloponnesian coast, or from Haniá to Crete's southern shore, than to go overland. Geographical determinism is an easy trap to fall into, but the mutual isolation of the provinces has undoubtedly been a dominant factor in shaping Greek identity, for better or worse. ❏

LEFT: Aráhova, a mountain town near Delphi.
ABOVE: the bridge at Árta, on coastal Epirus.

LA GRECIA
VNIVERSALE ANTICA
Paragonata con la Moderna da
Giacomo Cantelli da Vignola
Con le direttioni delle Carte Migliori e de piu accre:
ditati Scrittori di Geografia : data in luce da Gio:
Giacomo Rossi in Roma alla Pace l' anno 1689...
con Priu. del S. Pont.

Decisive Dates

CYCLADIC AND EARLY BRONZE AGE: *c.* **3000–1400 BC**
3000–2100 BC Cyclades settled from Asia Minor; new colonists introduce metal-working to these islands and to the mainland.
2100–1500 BC Minoan culture, noted for its great cities and palaces, and sophisticated art, reaches its zenith on Crete.
c. **1400 BC** The settlement at Akrotíri on Santoríni is annihilated by a volcanic eruption. Most other centres of Minoan power are destroyed by fire and tidal wave and abandoned.

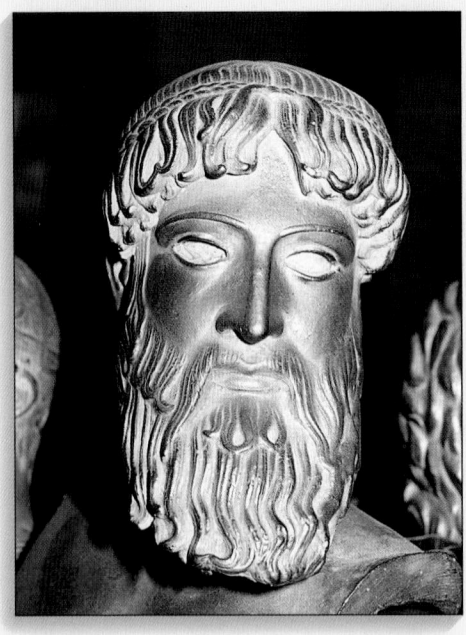

THE BIRTH OF EUROPE

Greece – or to be more precise, Crete – was present at the birth of Europe. A myth, now thousands of years old, recounts how Zeus, the father of the gods, abducted a beautiful, shy princess from her palace in Phoenicia. He fell in love with her and gained her trust by posing as a white bull.

However, as soon as the princess sat on the bull's back she was carried away against her will to the shores of a distant continent, which from then on bore her name: Europa. The rest, as they say, is history…

MYCENAEAN AND DORIAN PERIOD: 1400–750 BC
1400 BC A Peloponnesian tribe, the Myceneans, rise to prominence, building grand fortifications to defend their citadels at Mycenae and Tiryns.
c. **1150 BC** Dorians from the north conquer large areas of the Peloponnese.
776 BC The Dorians hold the first Olympic games, in honour of Zeus and Hera.

ARCHAIC PERIOD: 750–500 BC
750 BC onwards City-states, including Athens, Sparta, Thebes and Corinth, compete for supremacy.
550 BC Sparta forms Peloponnesian League with neighbouring states. Rivalry with Athens increases.
500 BC The Greek city-states control large parts of the Mediterranean coast.

CLASSICAL PERIOD: 500–338 BC
490 BC The Persian king, Darius, attempts to invade and conquer Greece but is convincingly defeated by the Athenian army at Marathon.
481–479 BC Xerxes, Darius's son, invades. The Spartan king, Leonidas, fails to hold back the Persian army at the Battle of Thermopylae. Athens is captured, but then in a surprise attack, Greek boats sink the Persian fleet off Salamis.
431–404 BC The Peloponnesian Wars, with Sparta and Athens the main protagonists. Athens capitulates; Sparta takes control of much of Greece.
338 BC Philip II of Macedonia defeats Athens and Thebes at the Battle of Chaironeia and unites all Greek cities except Sparta.

HELLENISTIC AND ROMAN PERIOD: 338 BC–AD 395
336 BC Philip II assassinated. His son, Alexander the Great, develops Greece into an imperial power with Macedonia at the centre of government.
323 BC Alexander's huge empire is divided on his death amongst his successors, the Diadochi; centres of political power consequently shift from Greece to the Middle East and Egypt.
320–275 BC The Diadochi war among themselves; Macedonia struggles to maintain its position. Rome emerges as a major power.
146 BC Rome annexes Greece as a province of the Roman Empire.

BYZANTINE PERIOD: AD 395–1453
395 The Roman Empire is divided into East and West, with the Greeks dominant in the East.
1204 The Crusaders, assisted by the Venetians, attack and plunder Constantinople. The Franks and Venetians divide Greek territory among themselves.

Fortified harbours and fortresses are built in the Peloponnese and on Rhodes, the east Aegean islands and Crete against the Turkish threat.

1453 Defeat of Byzantine Empire by the Ottomans.

OTTOMAN PERIOD: 1453–1821

1453 Sultan Mehmet the Conqueror leaves civil administration of the Greek Orthodox population to its own clergy.

1500–1600s Life in rural Greek territories is not congenial, with arbitrary taxation and venal governors.

Late 1700s Living conditions improve throughout the Ottoman Empire; a wealthy, often educated Greek Orthodox gentry emerges in places like Mount Pílio, Zagóri, Lésvos, Híos and Pátmos.

1821 The Greek War of Independence breaks out almost simultaneously on the mainland and the Peloponnese, where Archbishop Germanos raises the revolutionary standard at Agía Lávra monastery.

MODERN TIMES: FROM 1821

1827–31 The major European powers intervene in the Greek War of Independence. Their military assistance helps expel the Turks from southern and central Greece.

1832 Russia, France and Great Britain install Prince Otto of Bavaria as the new king of Greece.

1863 King George I succeeds the ousted Otto. Ionian Islands ceded to Greece.

1909 The Liberal Party under Elevtherios Venizelos comes to power and governs until 1920.

1912 The Balkan Wars erupt. Greece wrests southern Macedonia, Epirus, Crete and the east Aegean Islands from the Turks.

1917 Greece enters World War I on the Allied side after bitter wrangles between republicans and monarchists.

1919–22 Encouraged by the Allies, Greek troops attempt to annex Smyrna from Turkey but fail. King Constantine goes into exile; a republic is established, with parliamentary and military rule alternating.

1923 The borders between Greece and Turkey are finally settled and in a traumatic population transfer, 1.4 million Orthodox Greeks leave Asia Minor and 380,000 Muslims leave Greece for Turkey.

1928–32 Venizelos is restored to power.

1933 The royalist Populist Party is voted in.

1935 The monarchy is restored.

PRECEDING PAGES: a 17th-century map of Greece.
LEFT: ancient myth revived in a bust of Poseidon.
RIGHT: Count Ioannis Kapodistrias, Greek president from 1827 until his assassination in 1831.

1936–41 Military (and quasi-fascist) dictatorship under General Metaxas. When World War II is declared, Greece is initially neutral.

1940 Mussolini's invasion repulsed.

1941–4 Hitler's forces occupy Greece. Resistance groups base themselves in the mountains.

1944–9 The Germans retreat, and the Allies attempt to reintroduce civilian rule. Rebel forces defy the right-wing government the Allies install.

1950s The conservatives rule and an uneasy peace reigns. The Communist Party is outlawed.

1967 A group of army colonels under Georgios Papadopoulos seize control of the country.

1974–5 The junta attempts to take over Cyprus

but fails and is forced to resign. The monarchy is abolished and Greece declares itself a republic.

1981–9 The Greek Socialist Party, PASOK, gains power with Andreas Papandreou as prime minister.

1993 A breakaway republic of the former Yugoslavia calling itself (to Greece's anger) Macedonia gains recognition from the European Union and the UN as the Former Yugoslav Republic of Macedonia.

1996 Kostas Simitis succeeds Andreas Papandreou.

2002 Greece adopts the euro as its currency.

2004 Conservative Néa Dimokratía wins the general election under Kostas Karamanlis. Athens plays host to the Olympic Games while Greece wins Euro 2004.

2007 Criticised over its handling of devastating forest fires, Néa Dimokratía still wins snap elections. ❑

ANCIENT GREECE

The rich civilisations that rose and fell in the Aegean
have left a precious inheritance that is still relevant today

The basis for the modern way of life in Greece was laid around 3000 BC, when settlers moved down from the northeast plains on to rockier land in the Peloponnese (Pelopónnisos) and the islands, and began to cultivate olives and vines, as well as the cereals they had originally grown. Some seven centuries later, a prosperous Bronze Age civilisation arose on Crete (Kríti), and spread its influence throughout the Aegean.

The Minoans, whose rituals have filtered down to us through the legend of Theseus and his labyrinthine struggle with the Minotaur, left proof of their architectural genius in the ruined palaces of Knossos and Phaestos (Festós). Adventurous sailors, they appear to have preferred commerce to agriculture. The 5th-century BC historian Thucydides reports that King Minos of Crete established his sons as governors in the Cyclades and cleared the Aegean of pirates. The Minoans also established a number of outposts in the Peloponnese and made contact with the Egyptians.

By 1500 BC their civilisation had reached its zenith. Yet barely a century later, for reasons that remain unexplained, most centres of their power were destroyed by fire and abandoned. The settlement on Santoríni (Thíra), at Akrotiri, was annihilated by a volcanic eruption. But the causes of the wider disintegration of Minoan control remain a mystery. Only Knossos continued to be inhabited as Cretan dominance in the Aegean came to an end.

The Minoans' place was taken by Mycenaeans, inhabitants of Mycenae (Mykínes), the bleak citadel in the Peloponnese. We do not know whether the rulers of Mycenae exerted direct power over the remainder of the mainland. But in the *Iliad* Homer portrays their king, Agamemnon, as the most powerful figure in the Greek forces, which suggests that Mycenae had achieved some sort of overall authority.

LEFT: a Bronze Age Cycladic figure.
RIGHT: an ancient inscription at Olympia.

In its heyday the Mycenean world contained men rich enough to commission massive stone tombs and delicate gold work. Rulers were served by a complex array of palace scribes and administrators who controlled the economic life of the state, exacting tribute, collecting taxes and allocating rations of scarce metals.

The Geometric Period

In the 13th century BC this society, like the Cretan one before it, came to an end. Classical myth connects the decline of the Mycenaean age with the arrival of Dorian tribes. In fact, there was no clear connection between the two events. Mycenaean power had broken down irreversibly by the time the Dorians entered Greece. These invaders, like later ones, entered Greece from the northwest, down over the Píndos Mountains into the Peloponnese. They were probably nomads, which would explain their willingness to travel and account for their lower level of culture.

They also brought their own form of the Greek language. In areas where they settled heavily we find West Greek dialects, while Attica, the Aegean Islands and the Ionian colonies continued to use East Greek forms. The hostility, at a later date, between Athens and Sparta (Spárti) was based in part on this division between Ionian and Dorian peoples.

The Dorian invasion coincided with the onset of the Geometric period (named after its pottery). Historical evidence for the period between the 11th and 8th centuries BC is patchy, but it is clear that civilised life suffered. Trade

A CULTURAL DECLINE

By the 13th century BC the Myceneans had adapted Minoan script into the first written Greek, however, the art of writing was all but forgotten until around 800 BC.

the east was increasingly evident in metalwork and pottery. With the adoption of the Phoenician alphabet, writing revived among a much larger circle than before.

Another, equally important Greek concept was borrowed from the Phoenicians; the notion of the *polis* (city-state). In the Geometric small, isolated settlements were loosely grouped into large kingdoms. This system survived in both western and northern Greece into classical times when Thucydides described how "the Aetolian nation, although

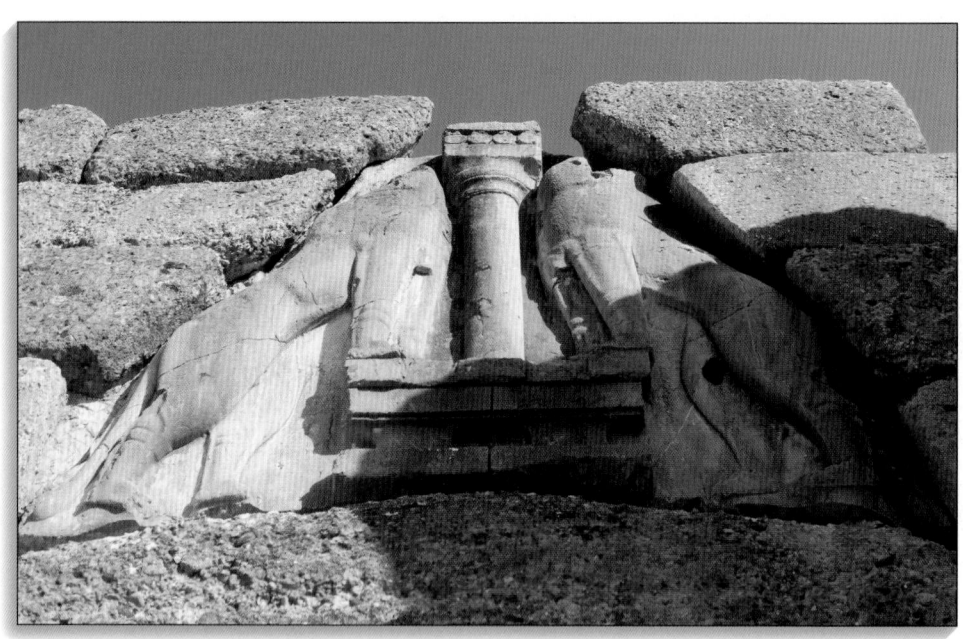

dwindled and communities became isolated from one another. Building in stone seems to have been too great an effort for the small pastoral settlements that had replaced the centres of Mycenean power. Homer's *Odyssey* is set in a simple society where even the rulers busy themselves with menial tasks, and where wealth is measured in flocks and herds.

Writing revives

In the 8th century BC there were signs of revival: trade spread further afield. There were contacts with civilised peoples such as the Etruscans in the west, and the Phoenicians and Egyptians in the east. Artistic influence from

numerous and warlike, yet dwell in unwalled villages scattered far apart".

Elsewhere, however, a network of small independent states grew up. At first, these were based around clusters of villages rather than one large urban centre. But with the population explosion of the 8th century, large conurbations evolved and expanded as surplus population moved from the country to the town. Land became more intensively cultivated and highly priced. In the Geometric the slump in population had caused arable land to fall into disuse. Farmers turned from sowing cereals to stock-breeding; now the process was thrown into reverse. The available land could not support such a rapidly growing population. (There is a clear parallel with the Peloponnese in the 19th century, and in both cases the outcome was the same: emigration on a massive scale.)

Together with the division between the new *polis* and the older *ethnos* (kingdom), there was now a further distinction. Some states, mostly in the Dorian-speaking parts of the country, were reliant on a population of slaves who were excluded from power, such as Sparta, a major *polis*, and Thessaly, an *ethnos*. Other states, such as Athens, although not unfamiliar with slaves, had a more broadly based citizen body that included Greeks from outside the city.

states began to increase in size, and infantry forces acquired a greater degree of strength, more persons were admitted to the enjoyment of political rights". Just as the shift from monarchy to aristocracy had been reflected in the move from chariots to horseback fighting, the emphasis now switched from cavalry to infantry; aristocracy lost ground to democratic pressure. Men would only fight in the new larger armies if the aristocrats granted them political rights.

Military power swung away from the traditional horse-breeding aristocracies of Chalkis, Eretria and Thessaly to new powers: Corinth, Argos and, above all, Sparta, where the state

From kings to aristocrats

In general, Homer's kings must have surrendered power towards the end of the Geometric, giving way to an aristocratic form of rule. But they too became entrenched in power and increasingly resistant to change. As commoners settled on land and amassed wealth, pressure grew for constitutional reform. Aristotle seems to have been right in identifying the connection between the demand for reform and changes in military technique. He said "when

LEFT: 13th-century Lion Gate, Mycenae.
ABOVE: Theseus and Procrustes portrayed on a vase painting from around 470 BC.

was protected by an army of heavily armed foot-soldiers known as hoplites, whose core was a body of citizens who were trained as infantrymen from birth.

Often the demand for radical reform met with resistance from the upper classes, but some individuals, more far-sighted, recognised the need for change. One such was Solon, nicknamed "the Law-Giver", who was elected in early 6th-century Athens to introduce sweeping constitutional changes. Realising that the city's strength would depend upon the organisation of the citizen body, he opened up the Assembly to the poorest citizens and in other ways loosened the grip of the aristocracy.

Inevitably these changes were attacked from both sides, as Solon himself complains in a number of his poems. But they did lay the foundations for the tremendous expansion of Athenian power throughout the next century.

Another result of these political tensions was tyranny. To the ancient Greeks the word "tyrant" was not pejorative; it simply referred to a ruler who had usurped power instead of inheriting it. In the 6th century, tyrants seized power in a number of states. Usually they were dissident aristocrats, who gained the support of the lower classes with promises of radical change – promises which were often kept, as it was in

factor. While the popular religious festivals and games earned revenues – enormous in some cases – for the city that staged them, temples, sacrifices and other rituals were very costly. Apart from waging wars, temple-building was probably the greatest drain on a city-state's resources. Thus it was the scale of its religious activities that provided some measure of the wealth of a community.

Greeks and outsiders

Now, alongside the rise of an artistic culture shared across state boundaries, a process of political unification began to grow. People in

the new ruler's interest to weaken the power of his peers. In the mid-7th century, for example, Kipselis of Corinth was supposed to have redistributed land belonging to his fellow-aristocrats.

But it would be wrong to regard the tyrants as great innovators. They were symptoms of social change rather than causes of it. Conscious of their own vulnerability, they resorted to various propaganda expedients to stay in power. The most potent of these was the religious cult, and it is from the time of the tyrants that religion came directly to serve the purposes of the state.

Religion was not only important to the state as propaganda; it was also a major economic

different cities started to become aware of a common Hellenic culture. The historian Herodotus was a keen promoter of the idea of one Greece, and asserted that the Greeks were "a single race because of common blood, common customs, common language and common religion". This common cultural identity was reinforced by increasing numbers of religious festivals and athletic competitions that attracted participants from numerous Greek states.

But the sharpest spur to unity was a threat from outside: the rise of the Persian Empire. Midway through the 6th century, King Cyrus had conquered the Greek cities on the Asia Minor coast, and Persian aspirations were further encouraged by his son Darius (521–486 BC) who conquered Thrace, subdued Macedonia and, after quashing an Ionian revolt in Asia Minor, sent a massive expeditionary force westwards into Greece. Athens appealed for help from Sparta, militarily the strongest Greek city, but succeeded in defeating the Persians at Marathon before the Spartan forces managed to arrive.

This victory did more than save Attica; it also confirmed Athens as the standard-bearer for the Greek military effort against the Persians. This explains why a frieze displaying the warriors killed at Marathon (situated just

Athens and Sparta

Ten years after the battle of Marathon, when Darius's son Xerxes organised a second attack on Greece, the city-states rallied around Sparta. For while Athens had the largest navy, the Spartans controlled the Peloponnesian League, with its considerable combined land forces. Both the crucial naval victory at Salamis in 480 BC and the military victory at Plataea the following year, were won under Spartan leadership.

But no sooner had the Persian menace been banished than the Greek alliance broke up. There was intense suspicion among the rival city-states, especially between Sparta and

over 23 km/15 miles from Athens) was placed in a prominent and highly unusual position around the Parthenon in the 440s BC. Only then was Athens becoming a power to be reckoned with. The silver mines at Laurion (modern Lávrion) in Attica began producing enough ore to finance a major shipbuilding programme from early in the 5th century. Even so, for two generations after that, Aegina (Égina) remained superior to Athens as a Saronic Gulf trading force.

LEFT: the theatre at Epidauros.
ABOVE: the Caryatids of the Erechtheion, built on the Acropolis at the peak of Athens' glory.

THE RISE OF ATHENS

The Athenian Empire owed much to the Confederation of Delos, a naval alliance formed in 478 BC to liberate the Asia Minor Greeks and continue the struggle against the Persians. It was also underlaid by much anti-Spartan sentiment. Sparta's own version of the alliance, the Peloponnesian League, consisted of land forces, requiring minimum financing. But the creation of a navy called for long-term planning and central coordination – a crucial difference. Athens' smaller allies found it increasingly difficult to equip their own ships, and instead sent money to the Athenians. Thus Athens grew in strength as its allies became impoverished.

Athens. Thucydides described how, as soon as the Persians withdrew, the Athenians rebuilt their city walls for fear that the Spartans would try to stop them.

The development of a Classical "cold war" became obvious as Athens extended its control over the Aegean with the help of the Confederation of Delos. Significantly, the Persian threat had receded long before peace was officially declared in 449 BC. Next, between 460 and 446 BC, Athens fought a series of wars with its neighbours in an effort to assert

HOW TO BUILD EMPIRES

One reason the Greek city-states failed as imperial powers, the Roman Emperor Claudius observed, was because they "treated their subjects as foreigners".

a Spartan ally, Thebes, attacked an Athenian ally, Plataea, and open war broke out between the two superpowers.

The Second Peloponnesian War dragged on for years since neither side was able to deal the deathblow to the other. The Peace of Nikias in 421 BC gave both sides a breathing space, but lasted just six years.

The uncertain peace was finally shattered when the Athenians launched a massive assault against Sicily. Aided by a force of Spartans, Syracuse was able to break

its supremacy. Naval rivals such as Aegina were singled out for attack. There was even small-scale fighting between Athens and Sparta (the First Peloponnesian War), until the so-called "Thirty Years' Treaty" brought an uneasy truce in 445.

In 433 BC Athens allied itself with Corcyra, a strategically important colony of Corinth. Fighting ensued, and the Athenians took steps that explicitly violated the Thirty Years' Treaty. Sparta and its allies accused Athens of aggression and threatened war. On the advice of Pericles, its most influential leader, Athens refused to back down. Diplomatic efforts to resolve the dispute failed. Finally, in the spring of 431 BC,

an Athenian blockade. Even after gaining reinforcements in 413 BC, the Athenian army was defeated again. Soon afterward the navy was also beaten, and the Athenians were utterly destroyed as they tried to retreat.

But even the Sicilian disaster did not put a stop to hostilities – although it had a huge impact on Athenian domestic politics. By 411 BC Athens was in political turmoil: democracy was overthrown by the oligarchical party, which was in turn replaced by the more moderate regime of the Five Thousand. At the end of 411 the rebuilt Athenian navy, fresh from several victories, acted to restore democratic rule. But the democratic leaders refused Spartan peace offerings, and the war continued at sea, with the Spartan and Athenian fleets exchanging costly victories. The end came in 405 when the Athenian navy was destroyed at Aegospotami by the Spartan fleet under Lysander, who had received much aid from the Persians. The next year, starved by an impenetrable blockade, Athens capitulated. Athens' defeat was perhaps the worst casualty in a war that crippled Greek military strength. The most culturally advanced Greek state had been brought into final eclipse.

Civic breakdown

Literature and art both flourished even during these incessant periods of fighting, but economic activity did not. A world where each tiny *polis* was determined to safeguard its independence at any cost carried within it the seeds of its own destruction.

The paradox was that city-states with imperial pretensions chose not to take the steps that might have brought success. Unlike Rome, Greek city-states did not extend citizenship to their subject territories. Nor could the military strength of Athens keep pace with its imperial commitments, which explains the permanent cycle of conquest and revolt. The Spartans had the additional headache of a large slave population, the helots, often prone to revolt in their own province.

The first half of the 4th century continued the pattern. On the one hand, there were long wars between cities; on the other, evidence of prolonged economic difficulties as Corinth fell into irreversible decline, and Athens struggled in vain to recapture its previous prominence. Spartan power remained supreme until 371 BC when Thebes defeated the Spartan army at Leuctra.

The city-state system was gradually starting to fall apart. The old form of citizen army was superseded by a more professional force, which relied upon trained mercenaries. Aristotle noted that "when the Spartans were alone in their strenuous military discipline they were superior to everybody, but now they are beaten by everybody; the reason is that in former times they trained and others did not". Things had certainly changed.

The spread of mercenaries, in fact, reflects the economic problems of the 4th century. Mercenary service, like emigration or piracy, was a demographic safety valve, and whereas in Archaic Greece mercenaries had come from just a few backward areas, in the 4th century they were increasingly drawn from the major cities as well. This points to economic difficulties over an increasingly wide area.

As in earlier times, military changes were connected with political ones. The decline of the citizen armies coincided with a trend away from democracy in favour of more autocratic government. Power shifted from the city-states

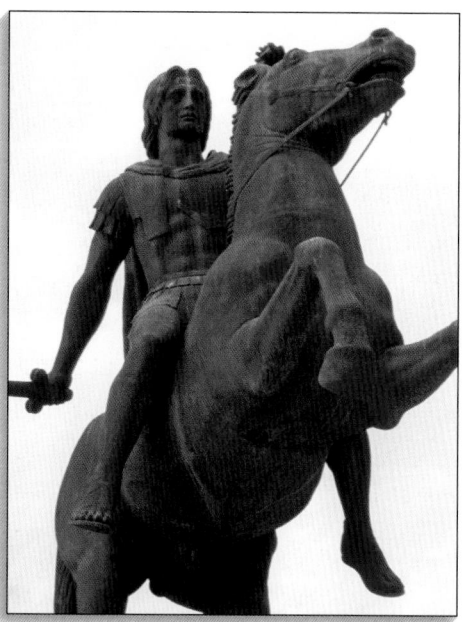

towards Thessaly, an *ethnos* regime, and later still, towards Macedonia, which had been another old-fashioned kingdom.

Both regions had the advantage over Attica in that they were fertile and not short of land. More rural than the city-states to their south, they managed to avoid the domestic political turmoil that periodically erupted in the latter. The military successes of the Thessalian tyrant, Jason of Pherae, in the early 4th century, indicated the confidence of these newcomers.

A little later King Philip II of Macedonia moved southwards, secured the vital Thermopylae (Thermopýles) Pass and, after gaining control of Thessaly, defeated an alliance of

LEFT: a Corinthian column at ancient Corinth.
RIGHT: Alexander the Great's campaigns dramatically extended the boundaries of the Greek world.

Thebes and Athens at Chaeroneia in 338 BC. Banded together in the League of Corinth, the Greek city-states were compelled to recognise a new centre of power, Macedonia.

Alexander's Empire

In the *Republic*, Plato writes: "We shall speak of war when Greeks fight with barbarians, whom we may call their natural enemies. But Greeks are by nature friends of Greeks, and when they fight, it means that Hellas is afflicted by dissension which ought to be called civil strife."

This passage reflects three sentiments that were becoming widespread in the 4th century:

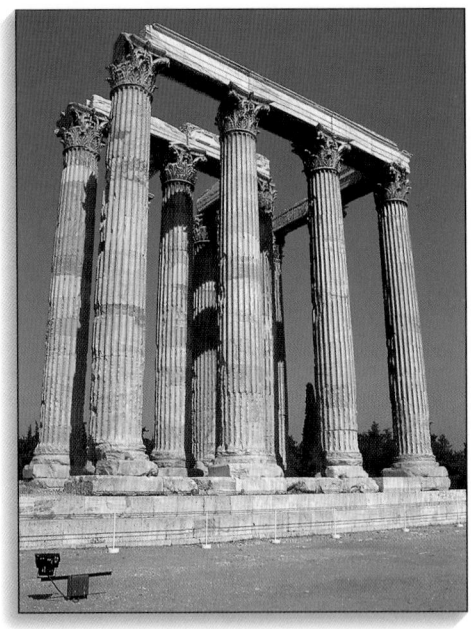

first, that the Greeks were all of one race; second, that warfare between city-states was undesirable; third, that it was natural for the Greeks to fight their enemies in the east. It is ironic in this regard that a successful concerted effort against the Persians was made only under the leadership of Macedonia, traditionally a border power in the Greek world.

Philip's son Alexander mopped up any remaining resistance in Greece, then led a Greek-Macedonian army on a brilliant rampaging campaign to the east and south. In a little over 10 years, he systematically swallowed up the ancient Persian Empire, reaching as far as the Indus Valley (in modern Pakistan). He

even found time to conquer Egypt, where he founded Alexandria.

Alexander the Great's overseas empire drastically altered the boundaries of the Greek world. The city-states of mainland Greece no longer occupied centre stage. The mainland was drained of manpower as soldiers, settlers and administrators moved eastwards to consolidate Greek rule. At the same time, the intellectual and religious world of the Greeks was opened up to new influences.

The Greek-speaking world was not only expanding, it was also coming together: "common" Greek replaced local dialects in most areas. In 3rd-century Macedonia, for example, local culture was "Hellenised", and the native gods were replaced by Olympian deities. For the first time coinage became widely used in trade – something which had been impossible so long as each city had its own currency. Now the Attic drachma became acceptable in an area ranging from Athens to the Black Sea, from Cappadocia to Italy.

But there were limits to this process, for although the city-states gave up their political freedom, they clung to self-determination in other spheres such as local taxation and customs duties. Likewise the calendar: in Athens the year began in July, in Sparta in October, on the island of Delos, January.

Philosophers were debating ideas of communal loyalties that transcended the old civic boundaries. Perhaps this reflected the way in which these were being absorbed within larger units, such as the Hellenistic kingdoms, the Greek federal leagues and, eventually, the Roman Empire. Whatever the cause, the most influential philosophical school, Stoicism, emphasised the concept of universal brotherhood and talked of a world state ruled by one supreme power.

Roman expansion

Gradually but inexorably, the expansion of Macedonia curtailed the political autonomy of the city-states. In the 3rd century they formed federations, and tried to exploit disputes between the generals who had inherited Alexander's empire. The policy had only limited success, mainly because of the paltry military resources available to the Greek leagues.

Early in the 2nd century, disputes among the city-states brought about Roman intervention for the first time in Greek history. Within 20 years Rome had defeated first Macedonia, and then the Achaean League which had organised a desperate Greek resistance to Roman rule. The Roman consul Memmius marked his victory over the League by devastating Corinth, killing the entire male population, and selling its women and children into slavery. As a deterrent to further resistance this was brutal but effective. Conservative factions were confirmed in power in the cities and Greece became a Roman protectorate. In 27 BC, when the Roman Empire was proclaimed, the protectorate became the province of Achaea.

permitted a degree of political self-rule. Philhellenic emperors such as Hadrian even encouraged groups of cities to federate in an effort to encourage a panhellenic spirit.

But the *polis* was no longer a political force. Hellenistic rulers had feared the Greek cities' power; the Roman and later the Byzantine emperors feared their weakness and did what they could to keep them alive. After all, they were vital administrative cogs in the imperial machine. If they failed, the machine would not function.

Two centuries of relative tranquillity were shattered by the invasions of the Goths in the

Greece – a Roman backwater?

By the 1st century AD, Greece was no longer the centre of the civilised world. Athens and Corinth could not rival Alexandria or Antioch, let alone Rome. The main routes to the east went overland through Macedonia; to the south, by sea to Egypt. But while Greece was certainly a commercial backwater, its decline was only relative: along the coast, cities flourished. The *polis* remained much as it had been in Hellenistic times, and the Roman authorities

LEFT: the temple of Olympian Zeus in Athens was completed by the Roman emperor Hadrian.
ABOVE: the Arch of Galerius, Thessaloníki, built in AD 305.

3rd century AD. The invasions were successfully repelled, but the shock led to a loss of confidence and economic deterioration. Civic building programmes continued on a much reduced scale. The wealthy classes became increasingly reluctant benefactors, and two centuries passed before imperial authorities and the church revived the demand for architectural skills.

By that time much had changed. In AD 330, Emperor Constantine had moved his capital from Rome to Constantinople. By the late 4th century, Christianity had been made the official religion of the empire. The transition from Rome to Byzantium had begun. ❑

BYZANTINE GREECE

The legendary wealth of Rome's eastern empire attracted many potential invaders, from the Franks and Venetians to the Ottomans

The Byzantine Empire was established with the foundation of Constantinople, but the final separation of the eastern and western empires was not complete until the late 5th century. With its political structure anchored in Greek tradition and a new religion stimulated by Greek philosophy, the Byzantine Empire survived a millennium of triumphs and declines until Constantinople fell to the Ottoman Turks in 1453.

A revealing incident occurred in the capital Constantinople in AD 968. Legates from the Holy Roman Empire in the west brought a letter for Nikephoros Phokas, the Byzantine Emperor, in which Nikephoros Phokas was simply styled "Emperor of the Greeks" while the Holy Roman Emperor, Otto, was termed "august Emperor of the Romans". The Byzantine courtiers were scandalised. The audacity of it – to call the universal emperor of the Romans, the one and only Nikephoros Phokas, the great, the august, "Emperor of the Greeks" and to style a poor barbaric creature "Emperor of the Romans"!

Cultural mixture

Behind this reaction lies the curious fusion of cultures which made up the Byzantine tradition. From the Hellenistic world came the belief in the superiority of the Greek world, and the summary dismissal of outsiders as barbarians. From Rome came a strong sense of loyalty to empire and emperor. And in the fervour that marked their belief in the moral superiority of *their* empire – which they regarded not as the "Eastern Roman Empire" but as the only true empire – is the stamp of evangelical Christianity.

The inhabitants of this empire did not call themselves Greeks or Byzantines: they were Romans, "Roméï". But the mark of a *Roméos* was that he spoke Greek and followed the rite of the Orthodox Church. Thus three elements of identity – Greek culture and language, Roman

laws and regulations, and Christian morality – became intermingled.

Two crises between AD 330 and 518 helped shape the Greek part of the empire. The first was the invasion by barbarian Huns, Visigoths and Ostrogoths in the 5th century. Constantinople avoided the fate of Rome, which fell to

similar onslaughts, by a combination of skilful bribery and a strong army. So it was that, as the West was carved into minor kingdoms, the East remained largely intact, and the balance of power in the former Roman Empire moved conclusively to the East.

The Emperor Justinian (AD 527–65) laid the foundation on which the Byzantine Empire would rest for nearly a century. An ambitious and dynamic leader, he greatly expanded the empire's territory by conquering the southern Levant, northern Africa and Italy, in an effort to re-create the domain of the old Roman Empire. Justinian's administrative reforms created a centralised bureaucracy, a new fiscal

LEFT: a Byzantine icon depicting the baptism of Christ.
RIGHT: the 14th-century Anafonítria monastery on Zákynthos.

system, and a provincial administration. The codes of Roman law were revised and unified in the Justinianic Code, which remains to this day a cornerstone of European jurisprudence. These reforms greatly advanced the unification of the diverse peoples of the empire in a Hellenic context. In the end, Justinian's institutional reforms proved far more lasting than his military conquests.

The end of antiquity

Justinian's wars brought the empire to the verge of bankruptcy and left it in a vulnerable military position. Threats from both East and West

The real break with Greek antiquity came late in the 6th century when Greece was first attacked and then settled by Slavic-speaking tribes from the north. Major cities such as Athens, Thebes and Thessaloníki were safe behind defensible walls. But much of the indigenous population of the Balkans, Greeks included, fled, especially to Calabria on the southern tip of Italy, or relocated their settlements to higher, more secure regions of the Balkans. The invasions marked the end of the Classical tradition in Greece, destroying the urban civilisation of the *polis*, and with it Roman and Greek culture.

plunged the empire into a spiral of decline that lasted for nearly 300 years. The first menace to the Empire from the East came from the Persian Sassanid Empire. Sassanid forces took control of Palestine, Syria and Egypt, and even threatened the capital, Constantinople, at one point. A more serious threat soon developed with the advent of Islamic expansionism. Exploding out of the Arabian Peninsula, Muslim forces swept northward and westward, taking Egypt, Syria, Iraq, Iran and Afghanistan. Portions of Asia Minor were wrested from the Byzantine Empire, and twice between AD 668 and 725 Constantinople was nearly overrun by Muslim forces.

But the Slavic arrivals were unable to preserve their own distinct cultural identities; very soon their Hellenisation process began. Greek remained the mother tongue of the region, and Christianity remained the dominant faith. Although the Slavic invasions and Islamic conquests of the 7th and 8th centuries reduced the extent of the Byzantine state, it survived as a recognisable entity grounded more firmly than ever in the Balkans and Asia Minor.

The Greek language may have survived, but the old urban culture did not. The disappearance of the city-states is shown by the way in which the word *"pólis"* came to refer exclusively to Constantinople as though there were no other cities. A small urban elite studied and wrote in Ancient Greek but had little impact on the mass of the population; their books were probably read by less than 300 people at any one time. Ancient monuments were left untouched because peasants thought that they were inhabited by demons.

Byzantine revival

When a new dynasty, which came to be called Macedonian, took the throne of the Byzantine Empire in 867, its forces began to roll back the tide of Islamic expansion. Antioch, Syria, Geor-

TEMPLE TO CHURCH

In AD 841 Greece's most famous ancient temple, the Parthenon, became the Orthodox cathedral church of Our Lady of Athens.

reward military service, the area under cultivation expanded. The prosperity of improved agricultural conditions and the export of woven silk and other craft articles allowed the population to grow. Expanding commercial opportunities increased the influence of the nearby Italian maritime republics of Venice, Genoa and Amalfi, which eventually gained control of the Mediterranean trade routes into Greece.

But Byzantium's period of glory was short-lived, lasting from the mid-9th to mid-11th

gia and Armenia were reconquered. The Byzantine fleet regained Crete and drove Muslim pirates from the Aegean Sea, reopening it to commercial traffic. Consolidation of the Balkans was completed with the defeat of the Bulgarian Empire by Basil II in 1018.

The military conquests of the Macedonian dynasty initiated a period of economic growth and prosperity and a cultural renaissance. Agriculture flourished as conditions stabilised and, as emperors increasingly used land grants to

centuries. The empire lacked the resources to maintain tight control over its territories. It was beset on all sides – by the Italian city-states to the west, the Slav kingdoms to the north, the Persians and Turks in the east. The Greek provinces, being less vital than Anatolia, which supplied Constantinople with corn, were ceded more readily to other powers.

The prosperity of the Macedonian dynasty was followed by a period of decline. In 1071 a new enemy, Seljuk Turks from central Asia, cut the Byzantine army to pieces at Manzikert in Anatolia. The threat from the west was soon felt, too. In the late 11th century, a Norman army, allied with the Pope and commanded by

LEFT: the spectacular location of Agíou Ioánnou Prodrómou on the Peloponnese.
ABOVE: mosaic from the Kapnikaréa church, Athens.

Robert Guiscard, ravaged parts of Greece, including Thebes and Corinth. Civil war among rival military factions impaired the empire's ability to respond to such incursions, so Byzantium gave Venice trading rights in Greece in return for protection against the Normans. But before long the Byzantines needed to counter Venetian power by encouraging the Genoese.

Crusaders and Venetians

When the Muslims seized Jerusalem, some European kings, claiming Christian ideology as their motive, but in fact seeing political and commercial advantages too, sailed east to

la Roche, the west coast and various islands by Italians – particularly the Venetians.

Venice was a powerful naval power, with boundless ambition for trade and territory. As a pay-off for the assistance given to the Crusaders, after the sack of Constantinople Venetians were allowed to take control of many of the Greek islands that had been part of the Byzantine Empire. The Ionian Islands were divided into fiefdoms among noble Venetian families (and remained under Venetian control for nearly 600 years); other Venetian aristocrats helped themselves to islands in the Aegean – notably Marco Sanudo, a nephew of the Doge,

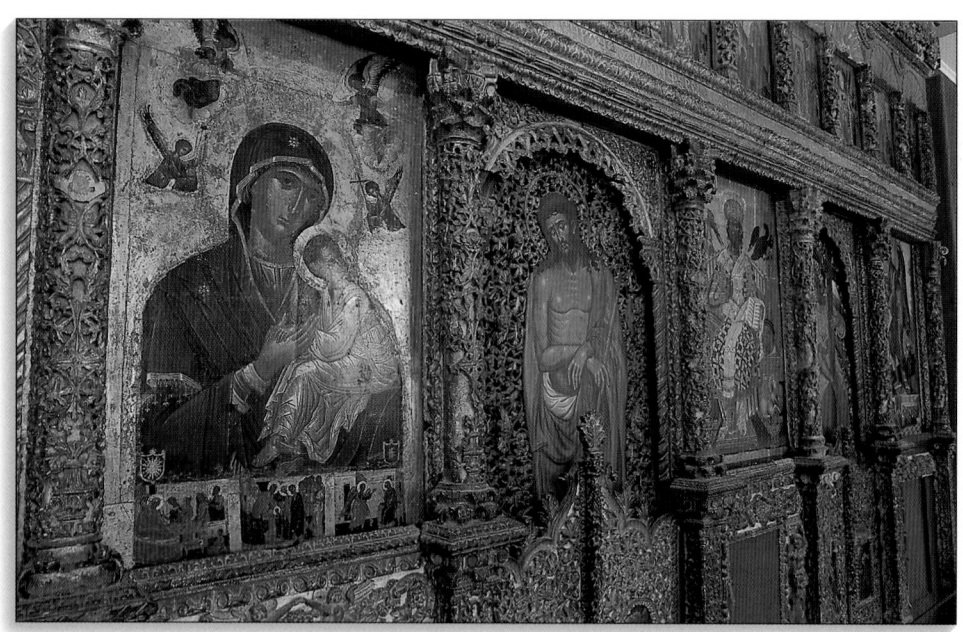

recover the Christian holy places from Muslim control. In the process, they established power bases in territories that had been part of the Byzantine Empire – Cyprus, for example, taken by Richard I of England during the Third Crusade.

This was only a foretaste of still worse misfortune. In 1204 Constantinople itself was sacked by the Crusader forces en route to the Holy Land for the Fourth Crusade – and transported there by the Venetians. The empire was fragmented. Successor states arose in Epirus, Nicaea and Trebizond. Greece itself was divided into small kingdoms ruled by Western princes – the Duchy of Athens under the Burgundian de

who claimed Náxos, founded a duchy and effectively ruled the whole of the Cyclades from there. Even Crete, "the Great Island", became a Venetian territory, sold to Venice for a nominal sum by Prince Boniface of Montferrat, the leader of the Fourth Crusade, in return for its assistance in the conquest of Constantinople. Thus by the mid-13th century, Venice had control of the shipping routes to the Black Sea and Asian Minor, Egypt and North Africa.

Byzantium fights back

Only the resolute resistance of the Palaeologos Dynasty (1261–1453) prevented the Byzantine Empire from collapsing completely. The

Palaeologi fought back into mainland Greece, recaptured Constantinople and most of the southern Balkans. But there was considerable confusion in western Greece, which briefly came under Serbian control, and in Thessaly, where the Vlachs established a separate principality.

Southern Greece and the islands remained under the control of the Venetians, the Genoese, various other Italian adventurers and, in the case of Rhodes and Cyprus, the Knights of St John, a military order which had arisen during the

A FIERCE RESISTANCE

The Aegean Islands held out longest against the Turks. Tínos resisted until 1715 – over 250 years after the mainland fell.

at Bursa, Nicomedia (Izmit) and Nicea. Leadership subsequently passed to his son, Osman I, the eponymous founder of a dynasty – the Osmanli, better known in the West as the Ottomans – that was to endure for 600 years.

Towards the end of the 14th century, Asia Minor and the Balkans had fallen to the Ottoman Turks, and by 1400 the Byzantine Empire had shrunk to just Constantinople, Thessaloníki, Trebizond and the Peloponnese. In April 1453 Mehmet II ("the Conqueror") besieged Constantinople and took

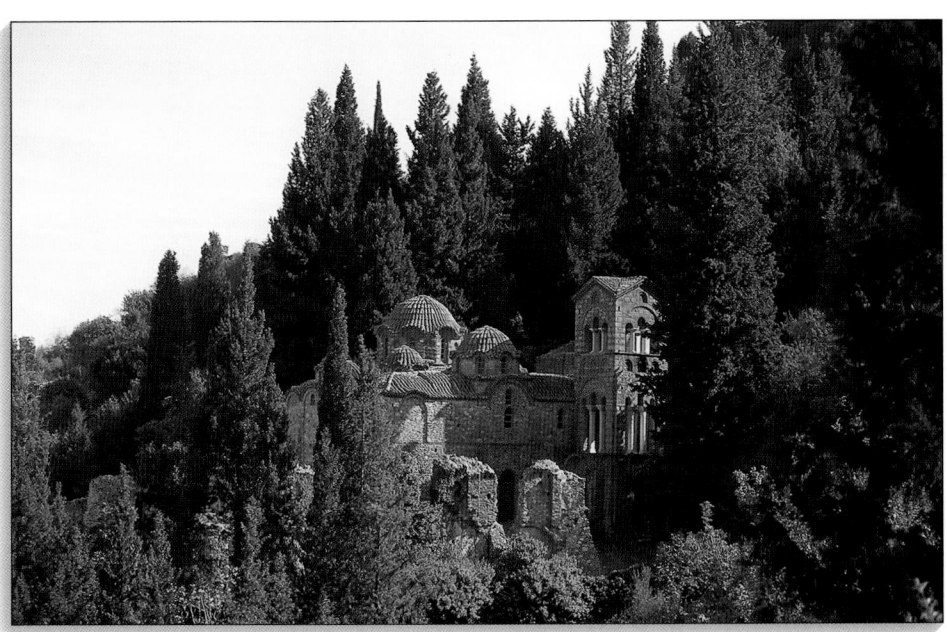

Crusades – although in the 14th century the Palaeologi re-established a Byzantine presence at Mystrás. One of the results of this political confusion was ethnically mixed populations.

A threat from the east

According to semi-legendary accounts, Estugrul, khan of the Kayi tribe of the Öğüz Turks, fled from Persia in the mid-13th century to escape Genghis Khan's Mongol hordes. He was granted territory – if he could seize and hold it – in Bithynia, facing the Byzantine strongholds

it within two months. Eight years later, Trebizond and Mystrás had succumbed, too.

The fall of "The City" reverberated throughout Europe: with it had fallen the last descendants of the Roman Empire itself. Before long, Constantinople would again be the centre of a Mediterranean empire stretching from Budapest to the Caspian Sea and from the Persian Gulf to Algeria – but now it would be as a Muslim city in the empire of the Ottomans. The great Greek Byzantine Empire had come to an end. Although in the West this seemed the inevitable result of Byzantine decline, to the Greeks it was a much more traumatic moment. They had passed from freedom into slavery. ❏

LEFT: 17th-century iconostasis, Zákynthos Museum.
ABOVE: Mystrás on the Peloponnese.

OTTOMAN GREECE

*Greek nationalism grew slowly as the Turkish Empire declined – until
in the 19th century a bloody struggle for independence was launched*

The Ottoman Turks who now controlled the Balkans were the latest in a stream of nomadic tribes who had moved westwards from central Asia. They were highly mobile, and their determination to pursue military conquests made up for their lack of numbers.

News of the fall of Constantinople was heard with horror in Europe, but as an isolated military action it did not have a critical effect on European security. To the Ottoman Empire, however, the capture of the imperial capital was of supreme symbolic importance. The sultan Mehmet II, a man of culture and learning as well as a superb warrior, regarded himself as the successor of the Byzantine emperors without a break in continuity. He made Constantinople the capital of the Ottoman Empire as it had been of the Byzantine Empire, and he set about rebuilding the city. The cathedral of Agía Sófia was converted to a mosque, and Constantinople – which the Turks called Istanbul (from the Greek phrase *eis tin pólin*, "to the city") – replaced Baghdad as the centre of Sunni Islam.

But Constantinople also remained the ecclesiastical centre of the Greek church. The Ottomans' religious tolerance was reflected in the *millet* system of imperial government. The sultan recognised minority religions, and permitted each *millet*, or religious community, a measure of self-government. Thus Mehmet II proclaimed himself the protector of the Greek Orthodox Church, and appointed a new patriarch after the custom of the Byzantine emperors. Patriarch Gennadios II Scholarios guaranteed loyalty and taxes to the Turks, in return for a degree of self-government for the Greeks. The church came to exert both religious and civil powers over Ottoman Greeks.

Under their new masters the Greeks lived in much the same way as they had done earlier. Their houses, like those of the Turks, tended to

be miniature fortresses, built on two floors around a central courtyard. The restored merchant's houses in Kastoriá give a good idea of the effect. Most elements of contemporary Greek cuisine were common then – from the *resináto* wine so distasteful to foreign travellers to the strong coffee which Ali Pasha, the "Lion

of Ioánnina", found helpful in poisoning his rival, the Pasha of Vallona.

Restricted rights

Although the Orthodox Greeks were allowed to conduct their religious affairs without too much interference from the Ottoman hierarchy, they nevertheless had to bear several impositions that did not apply to Muslims. Christians were not allowed to bear arms and were exempt from military service. But in return they had to pay a special tax, the *haratch*.

In a court of law, a Muslim's word was always taken over that of a Christian, although disputes between Greeks were usually settled in

LEFT: Ali Pasha, tyrant of Ioánnina.
RIGHT: Ottoman inscription on a Muslim tomb in Ioánnina.

Greek-run courts. A Christian could not marry a Muslim without converting, and Christians who adopted Islam then reverted to Christianity were invariably punished by death. These "neomartyrs", however, helped to sustain the faith of the Orthodox populations under the Ottoman rule.

The most feared and loathed imposition on the Greeks was the janissary levy or *devshirme*: Christian families were required, at irregular intervals, to surrender a quota of their fittest and most intelligent male children to the

(indeed, except for Lefkáda, the Ionian Islands, with the Venetians well entrenched, never succumbed to the Ottomans).

Lésvos, for example, fell to the Turks in 1462, but it was not until the conquest of Híos in 1566 that all the islands of the northeast Aegean were under Ottoman control. Similarly, the Dodecanese, with its motley population of Greeks, pirates and Italian adventurers, held out until 1521, when the Knights of St John on Rhodes finally yielded to a Turkish force numbering

Ottomans. These were forcibly converted to Islam and trained to serve as imperial troops (janissaries) or civil servants. Some of those conscripted rose to high office and were sometimes able to help their relatives or home villages, but the levy was deeply resented by Greeks. It was all but abandoned by the 17th century – largely because families deprived of their young men found it difficult to pay taxes.

A long-drawn-out conquest

Although the Turks had an undisputed hold on Constantinople/Istanbul after 1453, it took more than two centuries for them to establish control over all of Greece and its islands

over 100,000, after a siege lasting six months. With the fall of Rhodes, the security of the neighbouring islands was undermined, and by 1537 they had all been incorporated into the Ottoman Empire.

Crete took even longer to subdue. Since the early 13th century, the "Great Island" had been Venice's stronghold in the eastern Mediterranean, and its strategic value encouraged the Venetians to reinforce the major cities – Iráklio, Haniá and Réthymno – with solid fortresses that can still be seen today. An attack on an Ottoman convoy in 1645 provided the excuse for a Turkish assault on Crete. The Turks took Haniá after a bloody battle, then Réthymno, and soon had control over the whole island except the capital, Iráklio. It was not until 1669, after a gruelling 22-year siege, that the Turks took the city and finally ruled all of Crete.

Attempts at revolt

Powerful enemies continually threatened the Ottoman grip on Greece. The Venetians (and later the French) were thorns in the Ottoman flesh. Within the empire the Albanians, backbone of the Ottoman armies, often threatened to break loose. The resulting conflicts left Greece much weaker. In 1537, for instance, an Ottoman fleet carried off half the population of

were promptly crushed by the Ottomans. A similar fate befell the short-lived revolt launched by Dionysios Skylosofos in Epirus in 1611.

The Peloponnese was also caught in a bloody tug-of-war between Turks and their enemies. During the Russo-Turkish war of 1768–74, Greeks in the Máni region attempted to revolt against the Ottomans, with devastating results. Their uprising was initially supported by Alexis and Theodor Grigorievitch, members of the aristocratic Russian Orlof family, who brought their fleet to Greece in 1770 and raided the Peloponnese with little permanent result other than exposing the Greeks to Ottoman reprisals.

Corfu after an attack on the Venetian colony there, leaving the island with barely one-sixth of the numbers it had had in antiquity.

The expansionist ambitions of the Ottomans brought them into conflict with other European powers – which provided opportunities for Greeks to stage optimistic but vain uprisings against the empire. In the aftermath of the defeat inflicted on the Ottoman navy by Don John of Austria in 1571, at Lepanto, revolts broke out on the Greek mainland and the Aegean Islands, but

ABOVE: a water colour of Thessaloníki by the great traveller and artist Edward Lear, clearly showing the city's minarets.

They were more successful in the Aegean, destroying the Turkish fleet at Çeşme and occupying many islands until 1774.

Unruly bands

In truth, the Ottomans had never established total control over the Peloponnese. In the mountains, where the Ottoman grip had never been as firm as elsewhere, groups of brigands known as *kléftes* (klephts) had formed. They were bandits, equally likely to plunder a Greek village as a Muslim estate but, thanks to their attacks on Ottoman officials such as tax collectors, in folklore they came to symbolise the spirit of Greek resistance to the Ottoman authorities. They are certainly viewed in this light in the klephtic ballads that emerged, extolling the bravery and military prowess of the *kléftes* and their heroic resistance to the Turkish oppressors.

In an effort to counter the depredations of the *kléftes* and to control the mountain passes, the Ottomans established a militia of *armatolí*. Like the *kléftes*, these were Christians – and the distinction between *kléftes* and *armatolí* was sometimes hard to define. However, the existence of these armed forces meant that, when the struggle for Greek independence broke out in the early 19th century, there was a reserve of military experience on hand.

trines that emanated from the French Revolution – and also discovered the reverence in which the language and culture of ancient Greece were held throughout Europe. By the end of the 18th century, two ideas in particular, philhellenism and nationalism, had found a fertile ground among young educated Greeks.

The struggle for independence

In 1814 three Greek merchants in Odessa formed a secret organisation called "The Friendly Society" (*Filikí Etería*) devoted to "the betterment of the nation", which rapidly acquired a network of sympathisers throughout

Perhaps more important for the development of Greek nationalism was the growth of a Greek merchant community. Commercial links with Europe introduced wealthy Greeks to European lifestyles, and also to European cultural and political ideas. It was this mercantile middle class that supplied the material resources for the intellectual revival which characterised the late 18th century in Greece. They endowed schools and libraries, and sponsored higher education. Large numbers of schoolteachers, with the backing of merchant benefactors, studied in the universities of Europe, notably in Italy and Germany. There they encountered the heady nationalist doc-

the Ottoman lands. A number of vain attempts to secure themselves powerful backing were finally rewarded when their members organised an uprising against Ottoman rule in 1821.

Scattered violent incidents merged into a major revolt in the Peloponnese. With atrocities committed on both sides, the Ottomans found themselves outnumbered and were forced to retreat to their coastal fortresses. Further destruction came in the wake of the uprising. Greeks slaughtered Turks in Trípoli; Turks slaughtered the Greek inhabitants of Híos. Finally Egyptian troops, under Ibrahim Ali, laid waste most of the area.

The struggle for Greek independence, which lasted from 1821 to 1832, was not a straightforward affair. Opposing the Ottomans was a motley crew of *kléftes*, *armatolí*, merchants, landowners and aristocratic families known as Phanariots – all as keen to further their own interests as to advance the cause of Greek nationalism. When they were not fighting the Turks they turned on each other.

Soon after the 1821 uprising, no fewer than three provisional Greek governments proclaimed themselves, each poised to take control of the liberated territories. A democratic constitution was drawn up in 1822, then revised in 1823, by which time the three local governments were unified in a central authority. But the

Russia, all initially unsympathetic to the Hellenic dream, came to put military and diplomatic pressure on the Ottomans to acknowledge Greek independence – a policy of "peaceful interference", as the British Prime Minister Lord Canning described it. The turning point came with the almost accidental destruction of the Ottoman fleet by an allied force at Navarino in 1827.

This intervention by the Great Powers ensured that some form of independent Greece came into being, although its precise borders took some years to negotiate.

Count Ioannis Kapodistrias, a Greek diplomat formerly in the service of the Russian tsar, was

following year feuding between rival groups culminated in outright civil war (prompting one chieftain, Makrygiannis, to protest that he had not taken up arms against the Turks to end up fighting Greeks).

Ironically, the belief that this was a national struggle was held with greatest conviction by the foreign philhellenes – Lord Byron among them – who came to help the Greeks. These men were influential in getting Western public opinion behind Greece. Thus Britain, France and

elected the first president of independent Greece by a National Assembly in 1827. He encouraged Greek forces to push north of the Peloponnese, and his efforts were rewarded when the 1829 Conference of London fixed the new state's northern boundary to run roughly from Árta to Vólos, including the Sporades. But numerous Greeks were dissatisfied with his administration and suspected him of aiming at one-man rule.

On 9 October 1831 he was shot by two chieftains of the Máni as he went into a church at Návplio. While Britain, France and Russia tried to find another suitable candidate to lead the new country, Greece tumbled into a period of bloody anarchy and civil war. ❑

LEFT: Ermoúpoli on Sýros.
ABOVE: Ioannis Kapodistrias, who some feared was aiming for dictatorship, was assassinated.

INDEPENDENT GREECE

Independence did not guarantee peace and stability: civil war, enemy occupation and a military junta have all marked the path to today's democracy

The new state was desperately poor, overrun by armed bands of brigands and beset by quarrelling political factions. In 1834 a rebellion in the Máni resulted in government troops being defeated and sent home without their equipment. There were few good harbours or roads. Athens remained a poor, dusty, provincial town. Internally, conditions were worse than they had been under Ottoman rule.

Bavarian absolutism was partly to blame. On Kapodistrias's death Greece was declared a kingdom and the crown given to Otto, the son of Ludwig I of Bavaria, who arrived at Návplio in 1833 on a British man-of-war. Since he was underage, a regency was established.

Widespread calls for a constitution were ignored until, in 1843, a bloodless coup in Athens forced Otto to dismiss the last of his Bavarian advisers and accept the idea of constitutional rule and parliamentary government for Greece. Despite a poor economy, the 1844 and later the 1864 constitutions endowed the country with the trappings of a democratic state.

The "Great Idea"

The new kingdom contained less than one-third of the Greeks around the Aegean. The prospect of "liberating" the Greeks still under Ottoman rule, of creating a new Byzantium by recapturing Constantinople and avenging the humiliation of 1453 was known as the "Great Idea" and aroused enormous enthusiasm. This had roots embedded in the soil of a fervent nationalism. When King George I succeeded the ousted King Otto in 1863 he characteristically assumed the title of "King of the Hellenes" rather than simply "King of Greece". But the Great Idea was never a realistic policy since, without allies, the Greek army was no match for the Ottomans; yet it survived repeated humiliations such as the debacle of 1897. Only after the catastrophic defeat of 1922 at the

LEFT: a former partisan with a photograph of himself when he was 18.
RIGHT: a naive depiction of Eleftherios Venizelos.

hands of the Turkish nationalists did the vision of the "Great Idea" collapse.

The most prominent populist of the late 19th century, Theodoros Deligiannis, encouraged foolhardy irredentist expeditions to Thessaly and Crete. His more far-sighted rival, Harilaos Trikoupis, realised that such a policy was

unwise so long as Greece was dependent on foreign loans, which gave its creditors the whip hand over any foreign policy initiatives. Trikoupis set out to reduce this dependency by boosting economic activity. Roads were improved, railways constructed and the Corinth Canal dug. Piraeus expanded to become one of the Mediterranean's busiest ports.

But despite the appearance of a few textile and food-processing factories, industrial activity remained minimal right up to World War I. Greece was a rural nation, a country of peasant smallholders. The lack of large estates may have ironed out social inequalities but it also meant that most farmers remained too miserably poor to adopt modern farming methods. The export of currants brought prosperity for a while, but a world slump in 1893 hit the entire economy. Greece became bankrupt, and hunger drove many peasants to emigrate.

A new government

Such domestic problems only increased Greek enthusiasm for the Great Idea. Thessaly and southeastern Epirus had been acquired in 1881, without any fighting, as a by-product of the Congress of Berlin. When troubles on Ottoman

Crete in 1897 provoked a wave of sympathy on the mainland, Greek naval forces were sent to the island while the army marched northwards – only to be checked by Ottoman forces in what turned into a humiliating defeat.

On Crete and in Macedonia, Ottoman rule was crumbling. But the emergence of the new Balkan nations – Bulgaria and Serbia – added a new complication for Greek foreign policy, for both countries shared Greece's aspiration for territory in Macedonia.

A precedent for military intervention in politics had been set with the army's support for the adoption of a constitution in 1843. In 1909 junior army officers staged a revolt

against the political establishment and invited a new politician with a radical reputation, Eleftherios Venizelos, to come over to the mainland from Crete and form a government. A consummate diplomat, Venizelos channelled the untapped energies of the Greek middle class into his own Liberal Party, which was to remain a dominant force in politics for the next 25 years.

A decade of wars

When the Balkan Wars erupted in 1912, Greece was strong enough to wrest southern Macedonia from the Ottoman forces and then to defend its gains, in alliance with Serbia, from a hostile Bulgaria. The full gains from the fighting included – in addition to Macedonia – Epirus, Crete and the east Aegean Islands. Greece's area and population were nearly doubled at a stroke.

There was barely time to consider what burdens the new territories would impose before the country was embroiled in World War I. Venizelos and the new king, Constantine, quarrelled over whether to bring Greece into the conflict. The prime minister wanted Greece to give the Entente active support, while Constantine insisted on keeping the country neutral. The quarrel raised a number of vital issues: who had the final say over foreign policy – the king or parliament? The dispute reached the point of open civil war, ending only in 1917 with Constantine being forced to leave the country and Greece entering the war on the side of the Entente.

Venizelos had hoped that the Entente powers would reward Greece for its support with new territories. The annexation by Greece of Smyrna (Izmir), with its rich hinterland and large ethnic Greek population, had long been a basic tenet of the Great Idea. When in May 1919 the British, French and Americans sanctioned the landing of Greek troops in Smyrna, it began to look as though the dream might at last be realised. It was not to be.

The Asia Minor Disaster

In 1920 the pendulum of Greek political sentiment swung back, removing Venizelos from office and returning King Constantine from exile. Army morale was damaged by politically motivated changes in command, but the revival of Turkish national fervour sparked by the Greek advance and galvanised by the emerging Turkish leader, Mustafa Kemal (subsequently Atatürk), was even more dangerous to Greek interests. The Greek military forces advanced to within 80 km (50 miles) of Ankara in June 1921, but were hampered by their former European allies changing to a "neutralist" position and refusing to sell the Greeks arms – and even selling some to the Turks. Kemal stopped the Greek advance and gradually forced the Greek army back behind long defensive lines ever closer to the coast. After a year-long stalemate, Kemal broke through the Greek

tion, a massive population transfer was agreed upon: 390,000 Muslim inhabitants of Greece moved to Turkey in exchange for 1.4 million Orthodox Greeks. But for a dwindling population in Istanbul and in the islands of Imbros and Tenedos, this exchange ended a 2,500-year Greek presence in Asia Minor. The Greeks refer to these events as "the Asia Minor Disaster", and they remain a defining factor in the Greek perception of both themselves and of the Turks.

The interwar years

Buffeted and impoverished by 10 years of war, the Greek nation now faced the huge problem

lines in late August 1922; the Greek army abandoned Smyrna a few days later. The Turkish army entered the city on 9 September and ran amok, burning both the Armenian and Greek quarters and killing an estimated 30,000 of the Christian inhabitants in the process.

The 1923 treaty of Lausanne, which finally ended the war between the two countries, fixed the boundaries which hold today (with the exception of the Dodecanese islands, held by the Italians until after World War II). In addi-

of absorbing these indigent newcomers into a country that had difficulty in sustaining its existing population. The economy benefited from the cheap labour, and it was in the interwar period that Greece began to become industrialised. But the refugees also increased social tensions. Almost a million of them settled in urban areas – often in squalid shanty towns outside the large cities – to search for jobs.

After the disaster of 1922, King Constantine was forced to leave Greece a second time, and a parliamentary republic was established. It lasted only 12 years and was characterised by political instability and military intervention, including two attempted coups d'état. Governments

LEFT: the notorious Dillesi gang who terrorised northern Greece.
ABOVE: victorious troops returning from Bulgaria.

routinely altered the electoral system in an attempt to keep themselves in power. The only period of stability – Venizelos's years in power from 1928 to 1932 – was terminated by the shock of international economic depression. In 1933 the Liberals were succeeded by the royalist People's Party, whose leaders only half-heartedly supported the republic. Apart from the constitutional issue, little separated the parties.

Return of the monarchy

The feuding of the politicians rendered parliamentary government vulnerable to military pressure. In 1935 this led to the restoration of the king, now George II, Constantine's son. In 1936 the king offered the premiership to an extreme right-wing politician, Ioannis Metaxas, a former senior army officer and a fervent royalist. Soon afterwards, Metaxas responded to a wave of strikes by declaring martial law and abolishing parliament. But the "First Peasant" (as Metaxas styled himself) never managed to establish firm foundations for his so-called "Third Hellenic Civilisation". Despite imitating some of the characteristics of fascist regimes, he remained attached to Britain as Greece's traditional patron in foreign affairs. Germany's increasing dominance in the Balkans

IMPERIALISM IN ACTION

Italy occupied Rhodes and the Dodecanese from 1912 to 1943. During the years of Mussolini's rule, the islanders lived under the farcical prohibitions of a totalitarian regime intent on "Italianising" the islands. An extensive secret police network guarded against nationalist activity; the practice of Orthodox religion was outlawed; the blue and white colours of the Greek flag were prohibited in public; all shop signs had to be painted in Italian, and slogans such as *"Viva il Duce, viva la nuova Italia imperiale!"* were daubed on the walls of recalcitrant shopkeepers. In the 1930s many islanders emigrated to the Greek mainland, Africa, America and Australia.

had to be balanced against Britain's naval strength in the Mediterranean.

But Germany was not the only power with designs on the Balkans. In April 1939 Mussolini invaded Albania and in 1940 he tried to emulate Hitler's record of conquest by crossing the Albanian border into Greece. Metaxas could no longer hope to keep Greece neutral. Receiving the Italian ambassador in his dressing gown in the early hours of 28 October, he listened to a recital of trumped-up charges and responded to the ultimatum with a curt "This means war". *Óhi* or "No" Day is now a national holiday.

Fighting on their own in the mountains of Epirus, the Greek forces were remarkably successful and pushed the Makaronádes ("Spaghetti Eaters", as the Italians became known in later folk songs) back deep into Albania. But in the spring of 1941 Hitler sent German troops south to pacify the Balkans in preparation for his invasion of the Soviet Union.

Victory was swift: the German troops' invasion of Greece began on 6 April, and by the end of the month they had appointed General Tsolakoglou as a quisling prime minister.

Greece was occupied by German, Italian and Bulgarian forces. While the occupiers' hold over the countryside was often tenuous, it was firm in the towns, which suffered most from

Party but commanding a broad base of support. Other groups, drawing on the klephtic tradition of mountain resistance, were also established, making forays down into the plains. Clashes between rival resistance groups were common.

The dominance of EAM and its militia, ELAS, meant that when the British first began to establish contact with resistance groups in 1942, they found that military considerations collided with political ones. EAM, with over 1 million supporters, was well placed to pin down the German troops. The British, suspecting that EAM intended to set up a communist state in Greece after the war, armed other groups to act as a counter-

the shortage of food, notably in the terrible famine of the winter of 1941–2. It was also from the towns that the Germans deported and exterminated Greece's long-established Jewish communities in 1944. King George and the legal government had left the country in 1941 and passed the war under British protection.

Yet in the hills, organised resistance began to emerge. One of the earliest, and certainly much the largest, of these groups was known as the National Liberation Front (the Greek initials of which are EAM), organised by the Communist

weight. EAM/ELAS, for its part, was concerned that Churchill wished to restore the monarchy without consulting the Greek people. In fact, Churchill had little sympathy for the ELAS guerrillas, whom he described as "miserable banditti".

In the autumn of 1944, the German forces retreated, to be replaced by Greek and British troops. In December 1944 bitter fighting erupted in Athens between communist-led resistance fighters and British troops. Inflation continued to soar, the black market flourished and violence spread through the country as old wartime scores were settled.

The fighting in December 1944 marked a decisive turning point in the slide towards the

LEFT: German officers on top of the Acropolis, Athens.
ABOVE: British troops liberate Athens in 1944.

civil war that subsequently broke out between the national government and communist insurgents and that raged from the autumn of 1946 into the summer of 1949. It was in these troubled circumstances that King George returned to Greece in September 1946 following a bitterly disputed plebiscite on the monarchy.

Into the Cold War

Greece in the late 1940s was a key battleground in the developing Cold War. In March 1947 the United States took over from Britain the role of Greece's principal external patron. American propaganda in the form of military

Greece looks West

Democracy had weathered the civil war – but only just. In the following decade a certain stability seemed to have been achieved, with only two prime ministers, both conservatives, in power between 1952 and 1963. Yet this stability was precarious, relying as it did on the restriction of civil liberties.

Greece had joined NATO in 1951, and the pro-Western orientation of its foreign policy secured financial support from the United States. However, the relationship was not straightforward: when the Cyprus dispute flared up in 1954 Greece refused to take part in NATO

and economic aid flooded in, and this was instrumental in enabling the national government, which at times had been very hard-pressed, to defeat the rebel communist army in the mountains of northwest Greece in October 1949. But the victory involved considerable human rights abuses, the rounding up of suspected left-wing sympathisers and the forcible evacuation of entire villages.

The violation of civil rights and the emergence of a powerful security apparatus did not come to an end in 1950. Politics continued to be polarised, although the old pre-war split between royalists and republicans had given way to one between the far Left and the royalist Right.

manoeuvres. This foreshadowed the problems later governments would have in defining Greece's role in Europe. Nonetheless, the Cyprus issue was resolved – for a time – when the island was established as an independent republic in 1960.

A troublesome "miracle"

In the 1950s and 1960s, Greece, like Italy and Spain, experienced an "economic miracle" which transformed the country. Electric power became widespread and communications improved. Athens mushroomed, becoming a chaotic concrete sprawl, until it contained more than one-third of the country's entire population.

Old forms of political control, which had operated best in the small rural communities, began to erode. A new urban middle class arose which regarded the conservative political elite as rooted in the rhetoric of the Cold War and lacking a vision of Greece as a modern state.

The 1961 elections saw the resurgence of the political centre under the leadership of a former Liberal, Georgios Papandreou. It was a bitter contest. When the results were announced in Konstantinos Karamanlis's favour, Papandreou alleged that they were fraudulent.

Public disquiet at possible links between the ruling party and extreme right-wing violence increased in May 1963 when a left-wing deputy, Georgios Lambrakis, was assassinated at a peace rally in Thessaloníki. Shortly afterwards Karamanlis resigned and in the elections that followed Papandreou's Centre Union Party won power, the first centrist ruling party in Greece for over a decade. However, with conservative politicians prepared to surrender power, an extended period of centrist rule now seemed possible, although extreme right-wingers in the military saw the new government as a threat.

Royal interference

When Papandreou demanded a reshuffle of senior army officers he found himself opposed by his defence minister and the young king, Constantine II. The king tried clumsily to bring down the Centre Union Government, but when Papandreou agreed with the main conservative opposition to hold elections in May 1967, Constantine was faced with the prospect of a second Centre Union victory.

However, schemes hatched between the king and senior army officers for military intervention were dramatically pre-empted when a group of junior army officers, working according to a NATO contingency plan, executed a swift coup d'état early on the morning of 21 April 1967. Martial law was proclaimed; all political parties were dissolved. The Colonels were in power.

The rule of the Colonels

The junta was motivated by a mixture of self-interest, anti-communism and ultra-nationalism. This combination was certainly not new: on a

number of occasions in the inter-war period army officers had used the rhetoric of national salvation to head off a possible purge in which they feared they might lose their jobs. In their policies and attitudes, too, the Colonels drew on earlier traditions. They claimed that they wanted the country to "radiate civilisation in all directions" by establishing a "Greece of the Christian Greeks" which would make it once again "a pole of ideological and spiritual attraction". This was the old dream: an escape from the modern world into a fantastic fusion of classical Athens and Byzantium.

The first signs of widespread discontent coincided with the economic downturn of 1973. The

MADE IN GREECE

1967–74

LEFT: women fought with the Resistance during the civil war.
RIGHT: an anti-dictatorship poster.

leaders of the protest were students, whose occupations of university buildings in March and November were brutally broken up. Increasingly the regime was proving incapable of dealing with the ordinary problems of government. In the bloody aftermath of the November student occupation of the Athens Polytechnic, Colonel Papadopoulos, the regime's figurehead, was replaced by an even more sinister figure, Dimitrios Ioannides, who had previously been the commander of the military police.

In the end, it was the Cyprus problem that toppled the junta. A foolhardy Greek nationalist coup, prompted by Athens, against the Cypriot

president Archbishop Makarios, led the Turks to invade northern Cyprus. Ioannides ordered Greek forces to retaliate, but the mobilisation had been so chaotic that local commanders refused to obey his orders. On 24 July 1974 the former premier, Karamanlis, made a triumphant return from exile in Paris to Athens to supervise the restoration of parliamentary democracy.

Karamanlis's "New Democracy"

The transition to democracy proceeded remarkably smoothly considering the enormous problems that Karamanlis faced. Aware of his own vulnerability, he moved slowly in dismissing collaborators of the regime. At the elections

held in November 1974, Karamanlis's New Democracy (Néa Dimokratía or ND) party won an overwhelming victory, though many people seemed to have voted for Karamanlis simply as a guarantor of stability.

Karamanlis himself was well placed to make any necessary political reforms, since a referendum the month after the elections produced a decisive vote for the abolition of the monarchy, compromised by the king's actions before and during the junta. In its place Karamanlis created a presidency with sweeping powers. It was widely believed that in the event of a swing to the Left, Karamanlis would resign his parliamentary seat and become president.

A move to the Left

Signs of such a swing were evident after the 1977 elections in which Andreas Papandreou's Panhellenic Socialist Movement (PASOK) made large gains. The younger Papandreou, Georgios's son, represented a new post-war generation – at home with the "miracle" and its fruits. With his background as a professor of economics in the US, he was well placed to lead a party of technocrats. At this time he still had a reputation as a radical and he vehemently attacked Karamanlis's policies, taking a more belligerent stand over relations with Turkey, and threatening that a PASOK government would take Greece out of both NATO and the EEC, subject to a referendum. Support for PASOK grew, until in 1980 Karamanlis resigned as prime minister and was voted in as president by parliament.

Papandreou and PASOK

After PASOK's victory in the October 1981 elections, based on a simple campaign slogan of *Allagí* ("Change"), Papandreou formed Greece's first socialist government. His significance lies not in his socialism, which was mainly at the level of rhetoric, but in his remarkable success in articulating populist leftist views.

PASOK rhetoric carried the party until the multiple, farcical elections of 1989 and 1990, when accumulated financial and domestic scandals returned the New Democracy party to power. This proved to be only a short interruption, for PASOK won the early elections of October 1993, returning Andreas Papandreou to power until ill health forced him to leave office two years later. PASOK chose as his successor an uncharismatic pragmatist, Kostas Simitis.

There was a marked contrast with the flamboyant style of his predecessor. As prime minister, his task was been to oblige a population long accustomed to government largesse to accept economic reality. Particularly after Andreas Papandreou's death in June 1996, the government followed a tight economic policy to keep inflation down so as to allow Greece to meet the conditions for joining the European Monetary Union (EMU). This was not easy, since many PASOK deputies, not to mention labour unions, were unhappy with the apparent abandonment of their avowed socialist ideals.

Republic of Macedonia and Turkey

In foreign affairs, by the end of the 1990s Greece was reconciled to the existence of an independent Macedonian state on her northern border, although agreement has yet to be reached on the name of the new state. Traditionally poor relations with Turkey took a marked turn for the better in 1999 when there was an upsurge of public sympathy in each country for the other when both were afflicted by earthquakes. Helped by good personal rapport between the Greek and Turkish foreign ministers, the main result was Greece dropping opposition to Turkish EU candidacy.

On the domestic front, Simitis secured a very narrow victory over Kostas Karamanlis's ND party in the election of 2000. Simitis continued with the austerity measures aimed at controlling public expenditure and curbing inflation. These enabled Greece to join the euro-zone in 2001 and it adopted the euro on 1 January 2002 – abandoning Europe's oldest currency, the drachma.

The visit of Pope John Paul II to Athens in May 2002 demonstrated how long historical memories were in Greece when the Pope formally apologised for the wrongdoings of Western Christendom and notably for the sack of Constantinople following the diversion of the Fourth Crusade in 1204.

Just two months later, *Dekaeftá Noemvríou* ("17 November"), Europe's longest lived far-left terrorist group, which had operated with seeming impunity (and 23 fatalities) since 1974, was abruptly liquidated. By the end of 2003, trials had seen most of the principals convicted.

PASOK in eclipse

Simitis resigned before the scheduled elections of March 2004, leaving his polished foreign minister, George Papandreou (son of Andreas), as the PASOK prime ministerial candidate. Despite 17 November having been wound up on PASOK's time, a decisive victory was won by ND under Kostas Karamanlis (nephew of Konstaninos). He appointed himself minister of culture as well as premier to help push forward the well-behind-schedule construction of the Olympic Games 2004 venues. Basic urban infrastructure, such as the new international airport at Spáta and the Athens metro, had been in place since 2001. In

the event, Greece staged memorable games that confounded their most cynical critics – but left a huge hangover of cost overruns and crumbling facilities with no compelling future role.

In 2007, despite a major scandal concerning crooked investments and missing contributions for the national pension scheme, and widespread criticism of ND's handling of August's forest fires – the worst in living memory – Karamanlis called early elections for September and won almost as handily as in 2004. What with

doing poorly (though Papandreou survived a leadership challenge) and parties of the far left and right benefitting from protest votes, Greece's most splintered parliament ever was returned. ❑

LEFT: Andreas Papandreou in 1994 in Washington, DC, during an official visit to the US. **RIGHT:** George Papandreou addresses the ruling Socialist PASOK party in 2004.

MODERN GREECE

In many ways, Greece has become a modern European country. But there are other facets of the national character that have not changed in centuries

Is the phrase "modern Greece" an oxymoron? A Greek might well pose this question to Western visitors, given the history of the past 200 years: to claim a place among the Western European family of nations, Greeks have been obliged to prove themselves more like their 2,500-year-old forebears than their peasant to anxious young women. Gyms have multiplied too, especially after the 2004 Olympics, surfing a wave of shame provoked by the sight of sleek, fit athletes – Greeks of both genders had long been the most obese in the EU, until recently overtaken by the Maltese. And Westernisation has crept into everyday practices, such as the

grandparents. Which is perhaps to say that notions of "modernity" are always in the eye of the beholder, and that contemporary Greece, more so than many parts of the world, is shot through with contradictions.

The spread of Westernisation

Anyone who has been a regular visitor to Greece over the past 30 years cannot help but be aware of the rampant Westernisation of consumption patterns – not just in Athens but also in the small villages. In a country that until recently associated thinness with meanness, one can now find ubiquitous slimming centres and beauty salons hawking the latest dietary and depilation secrets

replacement of traditional Orthodox name-day celebrations with birthdays (on name-days you don't receive gifts, you feed your guests).

Striking changes are also manifest in national politics, as political campaigns – the subject of tremendous passion throughout the 1970s and 1980s – have taken on a much more ho-hum tenor. As Greeks say, politics have moved from the "balconies" of the political rallies and rousing speeches of charismatic leaders such as Andreas Papandreou and his father George, to the "couches" of people's living rooms, where politics now take place on television.

This is reflected in the leadership shift of the socialist party PASOK (which ruled from 1981 through to 2004, discounting the short hiatus of 1990–93): from the populist and familiar Papandreou, known to all simply as "Andreas", to the technocratic Kostas Simitis, referred to by his surname, to Andreas' son George, referred to disparagingly by many as "Georgaki" (Georgie). Simitis's claim to fame was not any great socialist vision, but rather his successful navigation of the Greek economy into the European Monetary Union and the consumers' paradise that it initially promised.

HOME AND AWAY

The population of Greece is currently around 11 million, of whom almost 4 million live in Athens. Thanks to a century of emigration, there are also around 6 million Greeks living overseas.

Greece's working day, with its ostensibly inefficient split into morning and early-evening hours (producing two sets of daily commutes in towns every Tuesday, Thursday and Friday), has also come under heavy attack from "modernisers" and euro-crats. The compromise solution, for many in Athens at least, is north-European style *synéhies óres* (a single shift) from October to April. But come summer, the *mikrós ýpnos* or siesta again reigns supreme as shops revert to the only rhythm sensible in the Mediterranean heat.

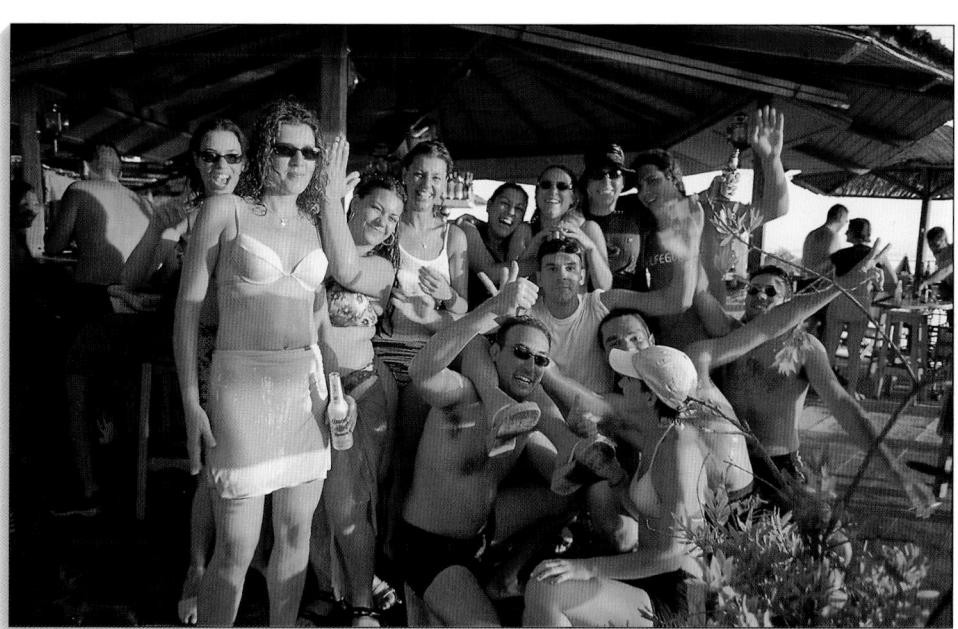

A strong national identity

Yet there is another side to contemporary Greece that stands firm against the tide of Westernisation and homogenisation. It is reflected in such events as the public protest over a proposed law in the mid-1990s which would have forced tavernas and bars to close at 2am rather than 4am. This was supposedly to increase worker efficiency. The widespread and continued outcry over this proposal eventually led to it being shelved, or at worst applied week nights only.

LEFT: priests attending the Óhi Day celebrations (28 October) on Skópelos.
ABOVE: a bar at Vromólimnos on Skiáthos.

Localism and homeland

Another facet of contemporary Greece that stresses the local can also be found in the unusual relationship that exists between villages and the large urban centres of Athens and Thessaloníki. While certainly not free of the snobbery that urban dwellers commonly express for the "backwardness" of their rural cousins, most of Greece is somewhat unusual in having a comparatively short urban memory. There are few Athenians whose grandparents were born in the city. Thus, a Greek who answers the question "Where are you from?" with "Athens" will invariably be asked "Yes, but where is your village?"

What seems an unusual query for anyone from a city such as London, Paris or New York makes perfect sense to the Athenian. These rural loyalties are manifested in the enormous flows of people out of the cities for Easter, the Feast of the Assumption (August 15) and at election time, when many who have grown up in Athens still retain voting privileges in their family's ancestral village. Many city-dwellers – a rapidly increasing proportion of the population – will wax lyrical about the virtues of the food, the air and the water in their village "homeland"; about an uncle's freshly-pressed olive oil, a grandmother's cheese, an aunt's fig or pomegranate tree.

should not be surprising given that in Greek the word "homeland" *(patrída)* is used to refer as equally to one's country and to one's village of birth. Hence the condition of *xenitiá*, or "longing for homeland", experienced by many in the far-flung Greek diaspora is inherently equivocal: is one primarily nostalgic for the sight of the Parthenon or for the view across the valley to the mountains?

The women's sphere

Perhaps nowhere are the paradoxes of contemporary Greece more evident than in shifting gender relations. Gender in Greece has always

And what Greece may have, until recently, lacked in ethnic diversity, it certainly made up for in the multitude of claims to regional diversity. Residents of villages, towns and cities are eager to discuss the myriad differences in manners and customs of their nearby neighbours. Often this may lead to hyperbole: "The Kalymniots are all crazy!" insisted a taxi driver on the neighbouring island of Kós. "The Koans are all lazy", a Kalymniot shoots back. But often it is more a matter of friendly rivalries, with differences in traditional costumes and wedding rituals, or whether Easter lamb (or goat) is prepared on a spit or in a clay oven, becoming topics of lengthy discussion. Such localism

been more complicated than the stereotype of Mediterranean male dominance. Men have certainly dominated the public sphere of politics, but women have always dominated in their own public sphere of the church and religious life (this in spite of the all-male church leadership).

In many parts of Greece, particularly the Aegean Islands, dowry and house ownership have given women a source of control not available to their husbands. With the tourist boom, many of these houses have been turned into lodgings, providing women with a source of economic control as well. This meant that despite a rhetoric of male power, women have often been able to control things from behind the scenes.

As one woman from the island of Kálymnos put it: "Women would make the pretence of consulting their husbands, but more often they would simply make decisions for the family in their husbands' absence. My mother sold the family house while my father was away fishing and then found ways to sugar-coat the news to him when he returned." This notion of female power is perhaps best captured by Lainie Kazan in the Hollywood film *My Big, Fat Greek Wedding* (2002): "Yes the man is the head of the family, but the woman is the neck – she can turn him in any direction she wants."

Thus the many recent changes in Greek society have been nothing if not ambiguous in terms of gender relations. The early 1980s and the coming to power of the PASOK government brought legal changes to improve women's position in relation to property ownership and pensions. And women have moved into national politics in increasing numbers. The two Greek communist parties have been led by women in recent years (Aleka Papariga and, briefly, Maria Damanaki) and the two largest parties include women who are likely to contend for the leadership in the near future – Vaso Papandreou (no relation to Andreas), a leading PASOK politician, and the ND's Dora Bakogianni (daughter of Kostas Mitsotakis), who was elected Athens' first woman mayor in 2002 and is now foreign minister. Women, however, remain under-represented in the Greek Parliament as a whole.

Loosened family bonds

While these changes in the public sphere have been substantial, in everyday life it might be more accurate to think of the most striking changes less in terms of a shift in power from men to women than as a shift from the older to the younger generation. As Greece has moved away from agriculture and other "traditional" occupations into a fully consumer-driven society, parents and other relatives no longer have the crucial technical knowledge that will determine their children's future work lives. Thus the control over the lives and future marriages of the younger generation has largely withered away. No longer can parents "keep their daughters locked up in their houses", as many claimed to do in the old days.

LEFT: a café on Mýkonos.
ABOVE: young Athenian women.

Women in the men's world

Indeed, the traditional Greek coffee shop, the *kafeníon*, serving Greek coffee and ouzo to an all-male clientele, must now compete for space with the growing numbers of café-bars, serving cappuccino, *frappé* and other exotic drinks to a young, mixed-sex crowd. Ironically, recent times have seen the simultaneous growth of "traditional coffee shops", establishments that pride themselves on making Greek coffee the old-fashioned way, heated ever-so-slowly over a bed of ember-heated sand.

In late-night bars it is no longer uncommon to see women engaged in dances that were once

the sole preserve of the man, like *zeïbékiko*, the swaying, eagle-like solo dance which had long been a particular expression of Greek male passion and pain. And the dowry, a source of economic security to an older generation of women, is shunned by the daughters of these women – who indeed do have increased economic opportunities – as an insult to ideas about romantic love.

While older Greeks tend to see a struggle for power between the sexes, many younger people embrace at least a notion of "equality". Fathers now take a large share of the childcare and that extends to pushing the pram – something unthinkable four decades ago. ❑

PEOPLES AND IDENTITIES

*The population of Greece is more diverse today than it has been for
centuries, but Greek character is still defined by ancient traditions*

Until the early 1990s Greece could be considered unusual in the remarkable homogeneity of the ethnic and religious identifications of its population. This apparent homogeneity was itself a historically recent development – the preceeding Byzantine and Ottoman empires were remarkably multicultural by today's standards – and was due in large part to events such as the exchange of populations between Greece and Turkey in 1922 and the extermination of Greek Jews by the Nazis during World War II. This relative homogeneity has meant that Greek citizenship and "Greek" ethnicity have been seen as almost synonymous.

Post-war populations

In the post-war period, then, upwards of 97 percent of the population identified themselves by ethnicity as Greek and by religion as members of the Greek Orthodox Church. This still left room for some different identifications, including a sizeable Muslim minority in Thrace; a Slav/Macedonian identified minority in Greek Macedonia; small Vlach villages throughout mainland Greece; the Pomaks, a separate Muslim group which claims ancestry from the aboriginal Thracians; the remaining Jewish population in Thessaloníki, Lárissa, Ioánnina, Vólos and Rhodes; Greek Catholics largely on the islands of Tínos and Sýros; Roma and Jehovah's Witnesses throughout the country.

There are also ethnically identified Greeks who distinguish themselves in terms of language or origins, including the Greeks from the Pontic region around the Black Sea, Asia Minor Greeks who were expelled in 1922, and Arvanites, those Greeks whose ancestors migrated to Greece in the Middle Ages and who speak a dialect of Albanian.

PRECEDING PAGES: a priest hawks his wares, Skýros.
LEFT: donkey peddling, as with this quiet transaction on a Skyriot backstreet, is now a rare sight.
RIGHT: boys during holy week in Rhodes old town.

Asia Minor Greeks

An interesting case of borderline "ethnic" difference is the Greek refugees from Asia Minor who came to Greece in the Greek-Turkish population exchange of 1922. Although relatively indistinguishable from mainland Greeks in physical features, language and religion,

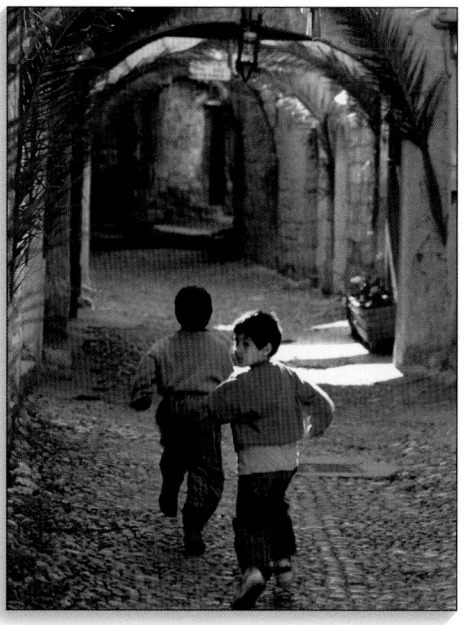

the refugees, most of whom settled around Piraeus, Athens and Thessaloníki, held on to a separate identity several generations after their uprooting.

So what set this group apart from mainland Greeks? They brought with them a shared heritage and historical experience distinct from that of the rest of Greece, a cosmopolitan outlook, a sense of grievance and dispossession (many of the refugees joined the Greek Communist Party in the 1930s), and a distinctive tradition in food and music – indeed, the once underground, now popular musical form called *rebétika* traces its roots to the Asia Minor refugees.

Being under the Ottoman Empire for a cen-

New Immigrants

A few years ago an Athens newspaper ran a cartoon which, without much exaggeration, encapsulated Greece's current demographics. An elderly man stops a little boy on the street and asks, "Can you tell me where is the *Kafenio Ellas* [Café Greece]?". The boy replies, "Sure! Go straight past the Kurdish Culture Club, turn right at the Bengali halal butcher, and it's between the African cheap-call shop and the bar with the Russian floozies, you can't miss it!". Since 1990, over 1.2 million people have migrated to Greece, mostly from Albania and other ex-

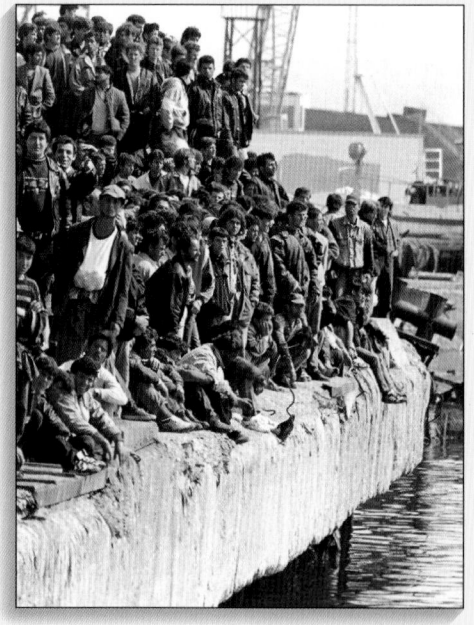

Communist countries of central Europe. But arrivals have also included Afghans, Iraqis, Somalis, Syrians, Egyptians, Filipinos, Kurds, Pakistanis, Bengalis and West Africans. This – over one tenth of the population – is a huge ratio of foreign-born to native in what had previously been a homogeneous, parochial culture, and unsurprisingly has become a major social issue. While there have not been the violent responses seen in other European countries, racist attitudes are common. As one pro-immigrant NGO's leaflet ironically put it, "Our grandfathers refugees, our parents emigrants, and we – xenophobes and racists?".

Yet sociologists predict such reactions, despite (or because of) one's own prior emigrant experience. There is in fact a refugee pecking order: those who can demonstrate Greek ancestry – *Vórii Ipirótes* ("Northern Epirots", Albanians of Greek ethnicity) and *Roussopóndi* (Greeks from the Caucausus who fled there from the Anatolian Pontus after 1922) – are treated marginally better, and some feign such an identity based on perhaps one Greek Orthodox grandparent. Albanians were initially universally detested, blamed for crime and all manner of social ills.

On an official level, Greece has responded to its refugee crisis in substandard fashion, in breach of various UN and EU regulations; though as a member of the Schengen Group the country sees itself, as in past ages, as first line of defence against barbarian hordes from the east. All the east Aegean islands are favourite landing spots for Third World immigrants, packed into overloaded boats by unscrupulous Turkish captains who often scuttle the craft once in Greek waters, requiring rescue operations by the coastguard. After brief detention, most refugees are served with deportation orders – then released to disappear into the immigrant underground.

Accordingly, up to half the Greek immigrant population is illegal. In June 2001, legal residency was offered to the (then) half a million illegals who could demonstrate two years' presence in Greece and make backdated IKA (social insurance) contributions. But fewer than 350,000 applied to be "legalised", and arduous red tape meant that subsequent amnesties netted hardly any more applicants.

Despite any resentment they provoke, "illegals" are unlikely to be expelled en masse: as elsewhere, they do the hard, tedious, dirty and/or dangerous work Greeks now disdain. Albanians in particular are notable stonemasons, a skill nearly extinct among native Greeks; hotel cleaners or night-duty staff are often Russian or Ukrainian. For employers, they are cheap, up to 40 percent less costly than "legals". Greece needs them to support its social insurance system – like Spain and Italy, the country is experiencing a shrinking and ageing native-born population.

And Greek misgivings aside, Albanians are now assimilating successfully, with a second generation (often Greek-born) well integrated in the educational system. Their capacity for saving and wiring large sums "home" is prodigious, driving banks to provide ATM instructions in Albanian. These *ftiná héria* ("cheap hands") are no longer so cheap and newfound prosperity has prompted a hitherto unknown sight – posters advertising expensive Albanian music clubs with imported guest artists. ❑

LEFT: recent refugees.

tury longer than the rest of Greece, they felt a particular tie to Byzantium and the legacy of Constantinople. Their experience of major cosmopolitan cities, particularly Smyrna and Istanbul (or Constantinople as they refer to it), gave a sense of multiculturalism and high culture which didn't exist on the Greek mainland. Indeed, most Asia Minor refugees have positive memories of Greek-Turkish relations, claiming that it was the machinations of politicians and the "Great Powers" which caused problems between them.

They also brought with them a sense of class superiority: many of the refugees from

Food for thought

What does it mean to be Greek? A Greek saying is: "Eat, in order to remember!" In this straightforward, Proustian injunction lies a whole social and moral philosophy. Indeed, if there is something that unites all the diverse regions, classes, rural and urban dwellers, ethnic groups and both genders that make up modern Greece, it is perhaps best found in an attitude towards food as an embodiment of the good life, in which friends, family and community are all mixed in. It is striking to the outsider that Greek food, which has a certain simplicity of ingredients and combinations

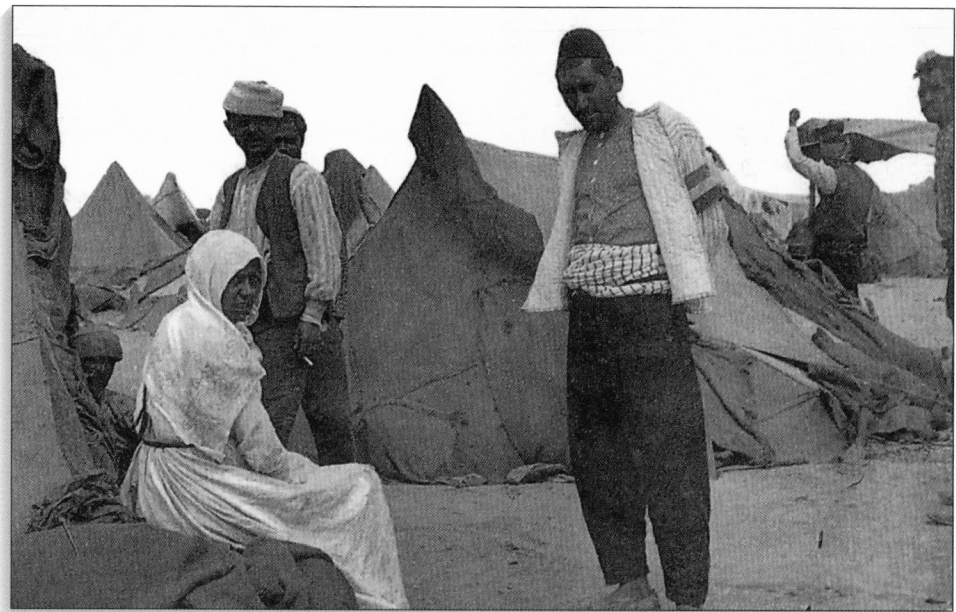

Asia Minor had been educated or were merchants (or both) and felt themselves superior to what they saw as the "peasants" of mainland Greece, even if they no longer enjoyed the financial advantages they once had. As refugees, the only possessions most were able to bring with them as reminders of what they were leaving behind were the skulls of ancestors, a handful of earth from home and religious icons sewn into clothing. These icons were closely guarded, and passed down to children and grandchildren.

ABOVE: refugees in Thessaloníki after the exchange of populations in 1923.

HOME FROM HOME

The refugees were not able to bring many possessions to Greece, but they did carry their memories with them, and often preserved their spatial maps of life in Asia Minor by renaming parts of their new Greek neighbourhoods or even whole towns after the places that they had known (invariably prefixed by "Néu/Néos" (new), for example Néos Marmarás). One man in his twenties whose grandparents were refugees notes: "It's hard to forget about Asia Minor, they are always reminding us. My grandmother has made me promise to go back to her home village just to see it, and to bring back some water and some soil. Even if she is no longer alive she wants me to pour it onto her grave."

that does not rank it among the haute cuisines of the world, can be such a focus of everyday life, conversation and memory.

So what makes Greek food Greek? No doubt a cookbook writer will speak of ingredients and preparations. But equally key is the context of eating, that food be shared among friends, neighbours, even strangers and fortunate tourists, that people dip their forks into collective bowls, with one man spearing a particularly juicy tomato or nicely done bit of fish and force-feeding it to his friend; that there be music and boisterous conversation. That one should always have a

full plate: there is no clearer symbol of the good life in Greece.

A cheese called *Féta*

Féta as a national symbol? The word *féta* means "slice", and it is certainly true that this pungent, delicately textured cheese has been embraced by tourists ever since they discovered slices of it sprinkled with olive oil complementing the motley flavours and colours of a Greek salad. *Féta's* origins are in goat's and ewe's milk, advertised through its distinct odour. But in the mid-1990s, in the wake of challenges by Denmark to the EU calling for the right to produce a cheese called "Feta", this

humble staple took on new national significance in Greece. In this case it was the whiteness of *féta* produced from ewe's milk, compared to what Greeks claimed was the yellower Danish Feta produced predominantly from cow's milk, which seemed to stand for the purity of Greek *féta* – a tasty reflection of the whiteness of those eternal symbols of Greekness themselves, the Parthenon Marbles.

But if *féta* seems simple from the outside, that is not the experience of the Greeks themselves who will discuss the fine distinctions of taste, smell, texture and provenance between different types of tomato, olive oil, fig, even salt. In talking about food Greeks are not wallowing in the mundane, but rather recognising the key role that it plays in creating social/family relations.

Eating with the dead

Kóllyva, made from boiled, sugared winter wheat kernels, is the food that the living offer in memory of the dead, or that the dead symbolically consume as part of their ongoing participation in the community of the Greek Orthodox faithful.

It features as the food prepared for All Souls' Day, when the dead are collectively remembered. Women prepare wheat berries with a variety of other ingredients, which may include pomegranate seeds, sesame seeds, almonds, sugared almonds, walnuts, parsley, breadcrumbs, currants and raisins.

Angeliki (the Greek form of Angela), a woman in her sixties from the island of Kálymnos, prefers almonds, currants and pistachios, formed into the shape of a carnation. She covers the dish with powdered sugar and silver-coloured decorative sweets, laid out in the form of a cross, or sometimes in the shape of flowers.

When preparing the wheat, the entire family must gather and sprinkle a handful of wheat into a plate in the shape of a cross, asking God to forgive the deceased. Once the *kóllyva* is prepared, the female head-of-house takes it to the church to be blessed. After the service, the priest reads each family's list of the names of dead relatives who they wish to be remembered. "It does good for our souls to remember them," says Angeliki. With the church service finished, Angeliki and her neighbours and friends retrieve their lists and decorated plates and, on the steps of the church, feed spoonfuls of *kóllyva* to each other, in a true moment of reciprocity and shared memory.

Any *kóllyva* left over from this communal, commensal act is offered by Angeliki to passers-by, perhaps even to tourists, as she makes her way home. But the obligation to share the food extends even beyond the community of family, neighbours and other visitors to Kálymnos, as Angeliki leaves out a plate of *kóllyva* in the house that evening, with the door open, in order that the dead can also come and partake. In this way, *Kóllyva* is community.

people's homes. Coffee and a variety of baked goods are served, but *kóllyva* is the centrepiece of these memorials. A photograph of the deceased is often placed near the plate of *kóllyva*, as if he or she were offering it to the assembled mourners. This reflects the fact that the living are not only offering *kóllyva* to the dead, but on behalf of the dead; in other words, the soul of the dead person will be lightened of its sins by these acts of generosity on their behalf.

The custom of preparing *kóllyva* is no recently invented tradition, but has a long history, resembling practices carried out in ancient Athens of *panspermia* – offerings of boiled

Honouring the departed

Kóllyva plays a key role not just in these collective rituals of eating with/remembering the dead, but in the regular memorial ceremonies that must be held for each dead person three, nine and 40 days after death, and then three, six and nine months after, and finally every year on the anniversary of the person's death. These memorials begin in church with a liturgy in honour of the dead, and are followed by a reception, sometimes in the church courtyard, sometimes in a nearby reception hall, or, more intimately, in

LEFT: ancient faces evoke the timelessness of Greece.
ABOVE: Christmas family dinner, Athens.

grains to the dead or to Hermes, the god who guided the dead down to the underworld. The use of pomegranate is another link to the ancient Greek symbolism of death.

In the Christian tradition (the practice was proclaimed canonical by the patriarch of Alexandria in the 7th century) the symbolism is clearly one of death and rebirth, as the grain or seed which falls to the ground must rot before it gives forth new life.

Food and faith

Food plays an important role in another key aspect of Greek identity, the Orthodox religion, most notably in the cycle of fasting and feasting throughout the year that sets the daily and sea-sonal rhythms of life for many a Greek rural and urban dweller. As in many aspects of Greek religion, women are the caretakers of the obser-vance, coaxing husbands, children and other family members to stick with the fast. If they prove unable to keep it up, the women will at least fast in their place during the 40 days of Lent that culminate in the Easter feast and other fasts throughout the year, including "Little Lent" before Christmas.

If you attend a Greek liturgy you will notice the predominance of women and children inside the church. Men, when they come to

her and move back to his village for some peace and quiet, "If you leave, you won't have anyone to light a candle for you in church. If you leave, who will tend to your soul then?"

Name days

The great majority of Greeks are named after Orthodox saints, according to a system in which parents name children typically after the children's grandparents. A special bond tends to exist between a child and their eponymous grandparent, and in some cases that child will be favoured in property inheritance from that grandparent. Exceptions to this pattern include

church, tend to sit outside and talk with their friends. It is not that Greek men are not reli-gious, but they do tend to have a long-standing distrust of priests and of women's spaces – some even refer to the church as the woman's coffee shop. Absence from church is further mitigated for men by the fact that women bring blessed bread, incense, basil and other items associated with the church home with them.

Women also prepare the appropriate foods for the different saints' days celebrations, which function like birthdays in Greece. This religious devotion gives women a particular power within the family. As one woman noted when her husband half-jokingly threatened to leave

naming a child after a recently deceased rela-tive, after a protector saint (especially if the pregnancy or birth is difficult) or after an ancient Greek name. But this basic pattern ensures that there are relatively few names cir-culating through the system at any one time.

Traditionally, Greeks did not celebrate on their birthdays (birthdays for children is a recent Western importation), but rather on a day associated with the saint after whom they are named. Thus everyone named Katerina will celebrate on the name day of Agía Ekateríni, a day associated with her life or martyrdom (25 November). Name-day cele-brations do not involve receiving presents or throwing a party, but rather opening one's house to family and neighbours who wish to come by and give you their good wishes, while you provide them with sweets and coffee. Name days thus have a collective aspect absent in birthdays, tying individual Greeks to their community, to grandparents and ancestors who have shared that name, and to the history of Greek Orthodoxy.

A relatively common act of religious devotion in Greece is to build a chapel for one's saint (or for a miracle-working saint) and to hold liturgies in the saint's honour. Saints are protectors and intercessors between humans

the reverberating nasal pitch of the liturgy being sung by the cantors (often projected via loudspeaker throughout the town or village). And of course there is the multicoloured sight of the icons, illustrating key stories from the Bible, and the taste of communion bread and wine mixed to the consistency of gruel and presented by the priest on a spoon. This sensory aspect of Greek Orthodoxy is part of official doctrine as well, an expression of the notion of the "deification of matter", the idea that humans manifest the spiritual not in opposition to the material but in and through the material world.

and God and are seen as responding to people's prayers if they show proper devotion.

Ritual as sensory experience

Orthodox ritual stimulates the senses. Entering a church or chapel in Greece can often be an overpowering sensory experience. From the scents of myrrh and frankincense which are spread by priests, swinging censers rhythmically back and forth, to the flicker of candles which each person lights and places in front of the icon when entering the church, or again to

LEFT: a clerical gathering on the holy island of Pátmos.
ABOVE: priests at an Easter ceremony, Pátmos.

Explosive Easter

Local differences come in many hues, from the typical colours used for housepainting, to the different dialects – such as Cretan, where the sound "k" is replaced by a more ancient hard "ch" found also in Cyprus – to the matrilineal inheritance patterns that characterise many of the Aegean Islands. On the island of Kálymnos difference takes the form of a sonic assault every Easter.

In most of Greece, Easter is celebrated with the setting off of fireworks, an index and an icon of the heavenly activity that Easter commemorates. On Kálymnos fireworks are replaced by dynamite – several thousand euros' worth, formed into projectiles and hurled from the courtyards of churches, from the two mountains that surround the harbour town, or in a "friendly" exchange across neighbouring back yards. No mere firecracker display can quite compare to the sound of dynamite going off around you, and Kálymnos's Easter celebrations have been known to both attract some stouthearted tourists and to send others scurrying for the next boat out.

The practice of dynamite-throwing from the island's mountains can be traced back to the Italian occupation of the Dodecanese in the early 20th century. Legend has it that one Easter, Kalymniots set off dynamite from one moun-

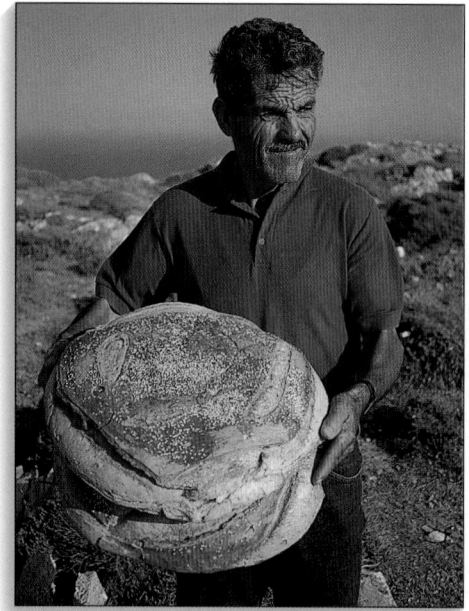

tain and, while the Italian authorities were hurrying to investigate, then set off charges on the opposite mountain. As one man put it, it was a way of saying "We're alive" to the colonisers. Why has this "tradition" persisted, with the Italian occupation now a distant memory? Perhaps as a reminder, not only to neighbouring Turks but to Athenians and other Greeks, that Kálymnos is not to be trifled with.

Hospitality and "the Gift"

Local loyalties run high in Greece. One aspect of localism that tourists may find themselves on the receiving end of is local claims to being more "hospitable" *(filóxeni)* than their neighbours. "Neighbours" is a relative term: people will claim that Southern Europeans are more *filóxeni* than Northern Europeans, Greeks more than Italians, their town or village more than Athenians, and they themselves more than the person across the street. Greeks often buy in bulk – 2 kg of cheese, a couple of watermelons – in order to always have food on hand to offer guests, invited and uninvited alike.

Generosity and honour

If you think you detect a competitive nature to hospitality in Greece you are not far off the mark, as generosity is closely tied to Greek notions of honour. Acts of generosity are part of building one's reputation. They also, in typical fashion noted by anthropologists, make claims to the higher status of the giver than the receiver.

This often has a faint feel of role reversal in cases where the receiver of hospitality comes from a Northern European country or the United States: Greeks are well aware that their country's voice is in danger of being ignored in international contexts, and so by being generous they are in a sense also subtly communicating the message: "You may be from a powerful country, but for the moment you are dependent on me."

All this is in no way to deny the genuineness of generous offers, nor the curiosity they may express about life in other countries over a proffered cup of coffee. A generous appreciation of your host's hospitality and, in some cases, a postcard from abroad is all that is usually expected in return.   ❑

A SONG OF THE MOUNTAINS

Throughout the centuries the Greeks have used their landscape – rugged mountains, rolling plains – as a metaphor to describe the different natures of the people living there, a device this old Cretan folk song (composed by hill-dwellers, one presumes) cunningly exploits:

Fie on the young men down on the plains
Who taste the good things in life,
The choicest foods,
And are base to look at, like creeping lizards.
Joy to the young men up in the hills
Who eat the snow and the dew-fresh air
And are fine to look at, like the orange-tree.

LEFT: bread for the festival of Agía Marína (17 July).
RIGHT: a monk at the Evangelístria monastery on Skiáthos.

LITERATURE

Greece was the cradle of European poetry and drama; modern writers
keep the tradition alive with outstanding novels, drama and especially poetry

When someone asked Greece's most famous composer, Mikis Theodorakis, where he got his inspiration for the hundreds of songs he had written in his lifetime, he said: "It's perfectly simple. I never thought of my music as anything but a way of clothing Greek poetry".

Perhaps only a Greek would have given such an answer. Relative to the size of its population, more poetry is published in Greece than in any other country in Europe, and it is still common for Greeks to present their friends with slim volumes of verse they have written and published at their own expense. Poetry is something people still revere and read for pleasure, and the marriage of poetry and music, familiar from the folksong tradition, still endures.

Folk songs and the oral tradition

Both Greeks and non-Greeks have sought traces of continuity between ancient and modern Greece, and found it – if only in their imagination – in the folk songs and dances of the Greek countryside. In the 19th century, philhellenes and early Greek nationalists looked to the folk tradition as a way of establishing Greece's legitimate claim to liberation from the Turks. Certainly the country's folk songs are remarkable in their rich variety of imagery and metaphor, and it is not surprising that the first poets of modern Greece turned to them as a source of inspiration.

Although the tradition is dying fast, it is still possible, in a village in the mountains of Epirus or the Peloponnese, to come upon a festival or a wedding where the night is filled with songs like this:

Now the birds, now the swallows,
now, now the partridges,
now the partridges chatter and speak:

LEFT: Constantine Cavafy (1863–1933).
RIGHT: Dionysios Solomos, writer of the lyrics to the Greek national anthem.

– Wake, my lord, wake my good lord
wake, embrace a body like a cypress,
a white throat, breasts like lemons…

Some of the most memorable folk lyrics of Greece are the laments for the dead. In these powerful songs, usually performed by women,

Death is addressed in the person of Charos, a sinister figure on a black horse:

Why are the mountains black, why so heavy
with clouds
is the wind fighting them, is rain lashing them?
The wind doesn't fight, nor the rain lash.
Only Death crosses them, carrying off the dead.
He drags the young in front of him, the old
behind
and the tender children are lined up on his
saddle.

You will have to search hard to find the texts of these songs if your Greek neighbour does not translate for you. This is particularly true of the tourist-laden landscape of the Aegean Islands, once the source of an astonishing variety of music, song and dance. The island of Crete is exceptional in preserving a lively traditional music scene where song lyrics are still improvised by local performers, but do not expect to hear the old island songs of Mýkonos, Santoríni or Rhodes when you visit. Fortunately there is an exceptionally active recording industry in Greece, and among the best sources of folk-song texts are the booklets accompanying these recordings, some with translations supplied. Recording notes will also provide the serious

to the 17th centuries that mark the beginning of modern Greek literature. The most famous of these works is the *Erotókritos*, a long romance in verse by Vitsentzos Kornaros. Remarkably, this written text became part of the oral tradition of the island, all 10,000 lines of it being sung as if it were a folk song until the 20th century. It is rare to hear more than a small section of the poem sung today, but it is an exhilarating experience to listen to even a handful of these verses, preserved since the Renaissance in the folk memory, performed in a Cretan nightclub.

Another contender for the source of modern Greek poetry is the Ionian island of Zákynthos.

Greek music fan with lyrics to the popular urban songs of Greece, the *rebétika*. Risqué and laced with slang referring to hashish smoking, they open an interesting window onto the shady life of Piraeus in the early to mid-20th century.

What is modern Greek literature?

The question of where Ancient Greek literature ends and modern Greek literature begins has no clear answer. Most of Greece was untouched by the Renaissance, but a notable exception was the island of Crete, which had been under Venetian rule until its conquest by the Ottomans in the mid-17th century. Some argue that it is the plays and poems produced on that island from the 15th

Like Crete, the Ionian Islands had been part of the Venetian Empire from the 13th century. The aristocracy were Italians, often married to local women, and the poet who is often referred to as Greece's "national" poet was the child of just such a union. Born on the island of Zákynthos in 1798, Dionysios Solomos was educated in Italian but, fired by the spirit of the Greek revolution, he began to write in Greek. His most famous poem is the *Hymn to Liberty*, which became the text of the new nation's anthem. Solomos's compatriot Andreas Kalvos, who spent most of his life in Italy, also achieved national recognition as a poet. Between them, the two poets inspired the national school of Romantic poets.

The 19th century

Emmanuel Roidis's wickedly satiric novel *Pope Joan* has achieved a deservedly wide readership in several languages, but with this exception, it is difficult for the non-Greek reader to discover the prose of 19th-century Greece. This is a pity, especially because of two remarkable prose writers whose complete works are only now appearing in English: Alexandros Papadiamandis and Georgios Vizyinos. Papadiamandis (1851–1911) was the son of a village priest from the island of Skiáthos and most of his fiction is set on that small Aegean island. The 200 stories he

guilt punished by divine rather than human justice; but Papadiamandis's sympathetic treatment of her character brings many assumptions of traditional Greek behaviour into question.

Translations of the half-dozen stories of Georgios Vizyinos (1849–96) have only recently become available in English. Enigmatic and sophisticated, his short stories are, like Papadiamandis's, preoccupied with questions of guilt and traditional Greek mores.

The early 20th century

Poetry flourished during the 20th century in Greece, a period dominated by three tragedies:

produced in his lifetime, including the novella *The Murderess*, offer a vivid, unsentimental portrait of Greek island life. They are written in a combination of high style and village dialect reminiscent of Dickens or Hardy.

The Murderess may well be one of the most daring stories of its day in any language. It tells the story of an old woman who, having witnessed the misery of the local women's lives, begins to murder infant girls rather than let them grow up. At the end of the story she drowns while being pursued by the police, her

LEFT: a plaque commemorating Nikos Kazantzakis.
ABOVE: a statue of early writer Adamantios Korais.

the Greco-Turkish War of 1919–22 that resulted in the loss of Greece's presence in Asia Minor; World War II, when Italian, Bulgarian and German troops occupied the country; and the military dictatorship of 1967–74, which put a temporary end to the Greeks' struggle for democracy and freedom of expression. Poetry, often sung poetry, gave a voice to the suffering of the population during these periods. The banning of poetry and song during these crises was a reflection of how powerful such expression was.

With the restoration of democracy in 1974, Greece's entrance into the European Community and the galloping urbanisation of the post-dictatorship era, tastes in literature changed. Songs and poems no longer talked about the heroism of the people or the beauty of Greek nature, but about the disillusionment of urban life or the private concerns of individuals. Prose, which had occupied a secondary position to poetry, proliferated in the last quarter of the 20th century. With few exceptions, the best of modern Greek prose writers had favoured the short story over the novel; but in the aftermath of the Asia Minor defeat, a group of novelists emerged who chronicled the events of the period and became known as the Aeolian School. Two were

Prizewinning poets

It is the poets who matured in the early to mid-20th century who are best known outside of Greece. In 1963 and 1979 two Greek poets, George Seferis (pseudonym of Georgios Seferiadis) and Odysseus Elytis (Odysseas Alepoudelis), won the Nobel Prize for Literature, drawing attention to the extraordinary flourishing of poetry in a country that was considered a cultural backwater by many western Europeans. A third poet, Constantine Cavafy (Konstantinos Kavafis), was admired by E.M. Forster and W.H. Auden and became one of the most influential poets of the 20th century.

refugees from Asia Minor (Stratos Doukas and Ilias Venezis), and the third (Stratis Myrivilis) from the island of Lésvos, a few miles off the Turkish coast. All three began their literary careers on Lésvos; their prose was realistic and the Greece they depicted was rural.

Meanwhile, in Athens and Thessaloníki, a number of young writers began writing about the new urban reality of a country whose population had increased by almost a quarter as a result of the Asia Minor war. More daring than their rural contemporaries, they experimented with Modernist techniques. The most original of these writers were Nikos Pentzikis, Giannis Skaribas and Giannis Beratis.

Living and writing during his whole life outside the borders of modern Greece, in Alexandria, Cavafy removed himself still further from his contemporaries by setting most of his poems in the past. Like Cavafy, the characters that inhabit his elegant, ironic poems are Greeks of the eastern Mediterranean whose Hellenism is based on language and a common respect for Greek culture. His poem *Ithaka* may be the most often quoted modern Greek poem of all:

Ithaka has given you your lovely voyage
Without Ithaka you would not have set out.
Ithaka has no more to give you now.

Two other poets who received international attention and whose works were translated into many languages were Nikos Kazantzakis and Giannis Ritsos. Kazantzakis's modern sequel to *The Odyssey* (1938), in Kimon Friar's fine translation, was probably read by more English-speakers than Greeks, despite the fact that it is twice as long as Homer's original. These figures tower over modern Greek literature like a formidable Dead Poets' Society, their works overshadowing those of their contemporaries and followers. Kazantzakis, of course, was also a novelist, and if English-speakers have read any modern Greek

they saw as the enduring virtues of the Greek spirit as a way to confront the evils and privations of the war years. For Seferis, Ritsos, Kazantzakis, Embirikos, Elytis, Gatsos, Kavadias and many others, the war was a devastating experience that initially united Greeks against a common enemy and then tore them into two bitterly opposed camps who fought one another in a civil war lasting until 1949. During this period many writers and intellectuals were persecuted by right-wing forces and imprisoned on Aegean Islands. Giannis Ritsos was among those who spent years in prison and exile. Others, like Seferis, spent the war years outside Greece. But

novels, they are probably his *Alexis Zorba*, *Christ Recrucified* or *Freedom or Death*.

Poetry out of conflict

Scarcely known outside Greece are the Greek poets who were Cavafy's contemporaries – Kostas Karyotakis, Kostis Palamas, Angelos Sikelianos and Kostas Varnalis. It was left to the somewhat younger poets who came of age in the 1930s to bring modern Greek poetry into the mainstream of European writing. Despite their political differences, these poets drew on what

LEFT: Odysseus Elytis, Nobel Prize winner in 1979.
ABOVE: George Seferis, Nobel Prize winner in 1963.

A NON-CONFORMIST LIFE

Thanks to his unorthodox views and writings, Nikos Kazantzakis was to court controversy not only throughout his life, but even after his death in 1957. When his book *The Last Temptation of Christ* was first published, the Orthodox Church sought to prosecute him, then excommunicated him. When it was made into a film in 1988, Athenian priests marched on the cinemas, and projection screens were slashed in anger. Today, admirers can make for the Kazantzakis Museum in the village of Myrtiá, 24 km/15 miles due south of Iráklio, where well-arranged displays illustrate what can be regarded as an extraordinary literary and political life.

no Greek writer was left unscathed, and it was these dark years that inspired some of the greatest works of modern Greek poetry.

Elytis, whose long poem *To Áxion Estí* (*Worthy it is*), memorably set to music by Mikis Theodorakis, earned him the Nobel Prize, drew on all the traditional resources of the Greek language – ancient, Byzantine, folk song – to create a modern secular liturgy. Beginning with the poet's childhood in Crete, *To Áxion Estí* spares the reader none of the horrors of the war but ends in a redeeming Gloria, praising the beauty of the Greek landscape and its lovely women:

Sífnos, Amorgós, Alónissos
Thásos, Itháki, Santoríni
Kós, Íos, Síkinos.

Praised be Myrto standing
on the stone wall facing the sea
like a beautiful eight or a jug
with a straw hat in her hand.

The post-war writers

The problem of Greek literature is that so few people read Greek. To become known outside the borders of Greece you have to be translated; and even then the chances of being recognised are small unless you are discovered, like Cavafy, by an E.M. Forster, or recognised by a Nobel Prize. Tourism, which began to grow in the 1950s and continues to expand, has helped create a market for Greek literature, especially if it fits the traveller's ideas of what Greece is all about. Writers who ignore the Hellenic past, and concentrate on the less attractive themes of modern urban life, are less likely to appeal to non-Greek readers.

Greek writers who began publishing in the 1950s and 1960s were mostly born in Athens or Thessaloníki. These writers, many of whom were women, matured in a period of tentative democracy that was rudely interrupted by seven years of stultifying dictatorship (1967–74). Reluctant to adopt the themes of an earlier generation, they wrote about personal relationships, disillusionment and Athenian life. Among the contemporary women Greek poets whose works are available in English translation are Katerina Angelaki-Rooke, Kiki Dimoula, Dzeni Mastoraki, Maria Laina and Rea Galanaki (now better known as a novelist). This is necessarily a shortlist, and not intended to diminish the brilliance of their male contemporaries, among whom Manolis Anagnostakis, Titos Patrikios, Nasos Vagenas, Tassos Denegris, Yiannis Kondos and Mihalis Ganas stand out.

Katerina Angelaki-Rooke

Of her generation, Katerina Angelaki-Rooke is probably the poet who has been most widely translated. She has also had a broad influence on the reception of Greek poetry abroad. Angelaki-Rooke is brilliantly articulate in French, English and Russian and has translated the works of many of the most "untranslatable" writers from those languages into Greek – including Dylan Thomas and Pushkin. Her old red house on Égina has long been a mecca for foreign writers and scholars of Greek literature, many of whom have relied on Angelaki's sharp insights into her country's literature as their guide to reading and translation. Her own poems are characterised by a combination of frank, lyrical sexuality and ironic self-criticism. As she writes in *Penelope Says*:

The body keeps remaking itself
getting up and falling into bed
as if it had been chopped down,
sometimes sick and sometimes in love hoping
that what it loses in touch it gains in essence.

In prose as in poetry, women writers have emerged, in the post-war period, to rival their male counterparts. Novels about Greek society may be the traveller's best guide to the changing mores and manners of Greek life. And since many Greek writers have chosen their own recent history as a subject for their fiction, novels and short stories may also be a good introduction to the vicissitudes of the period. Alki Zei's *Achilles' Fiancée*, for example, is a gripping *roman-à-clef* about the period of the civil war and its aftermath, when guerrilla fighters on the side of the Left took refuge in the Soviet Union. Among the other

promisingly in the 19th century and continues to satisfy the tastes of a large local audience, only a handful of Greek plays have been translated. Surprisingly, women dramatists were among the first to compose original plays, notably Evanthia Kairi, whose *Nikiratos* was produced in 1826.

Many writers better known in other fields turned their hand to writing plays, among them Kazantzakis, Palamas and Sikelianos; but in the post-war period, the theatre has been dominated by a group of writers whose primary concern is the theatre. The most outstanding of these is the prolific Iakovos Kambanellis.

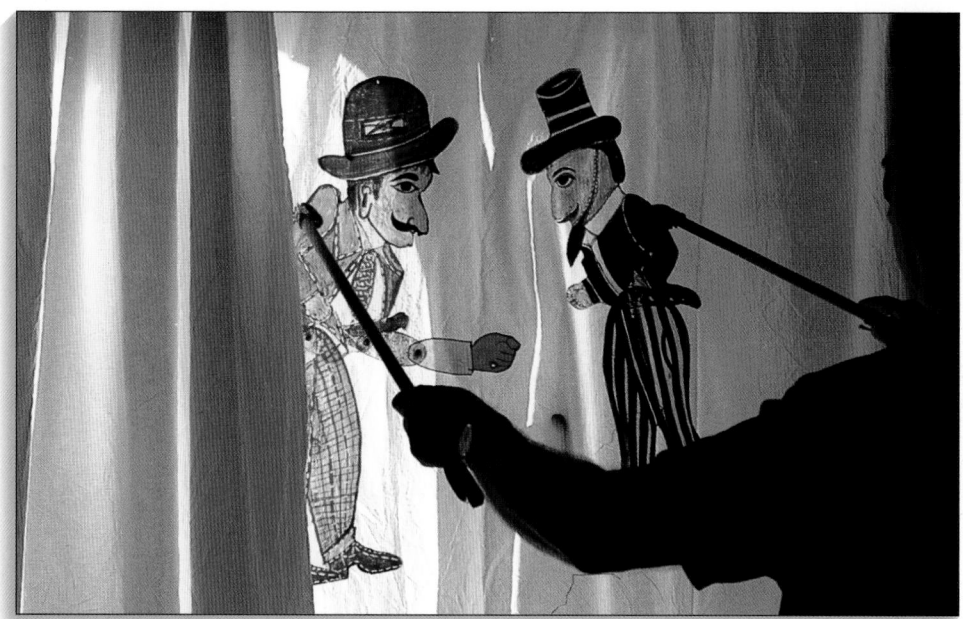

outstanding contemporary Greek novelists whose works have been translated into English are Kostas Tahtsis, Thanasis Valtinos, Margarita Liberaki, Maro Douka, Eugenia Fakinou, Menis Koumandereas, Apostolos Doxiadis and Vangelis Hatziyannidis.

Drama

Modern Greek dramatists have not, as yet, achieved the international recognition of their poetry- and fiction-writing colleagues. Despite a lively national theatrical scene that began

Another delight for those who have some knowledge of Greek is the shadow puppet theatre. The hero of these charming, ribald, satiric performances, Karagiózis, is an anti-hero with whom Greeks have always identified. Set in the Ottoman period, the comic puppet plays, once watched by open-mouthed children and their guffawing parents in the village square, have always been tailored to fit each new political crisis and allowed Greeks to laugh at themselves, even in the harshest periods of their history. As the song-writer, Dionysios Savvopoulos, puts it:

LEFT: Rea Galanaki.
ABOVE: A Karagiózis shadow puppet show.

What consumes me, what saves me
Is that I dream like Karagiózis... ❑

MUSIC AND DANCE

Music in Greece goes far beyond Zorba's Dance played on a bouzoúki
and reflects the country's complex political and cultural history

The sounds of Greece: the whine of motor-bikes; the deep roar of hydrofoils; men, women and taxi-drivers shouting at one another; the clang of church bells; sheep and goats bleating and tinkling, donkeys braying, and music – loud music blaring from radios, nightclubs, cars, cafés. The Greeks do not seem to need or desire quiet; they fill any silence with noise. They also love music, and even if it has to compete with the deafening roar of Athens' traffic or the engine of a ferry boat, they listen to it constantly.

What is surprising to the visitor is that nearly all of the music they play is distinctively Greek music. It may be influenced by American, Spanish or Brazilian music, but more often than not it is Greek in instrumentation or rhythm. Anyone who came to Greece 30 years ago must lament the steady erosion of Greece's trad-itional folk music; however, despite globalisa-tion and modernisation, Greek music is still flourishing and full of surprises.

A continuous tradition?

Anyone who has attended the famous Dora Stratou folk-dance performances in Athens, or any other performance of Greek music for tourists, will have been told that modern Greek music and dance preserve some of the features of their Ancient Greek origin. These claims are hard to substantiate, since we have almost no idea what Ancient Greek music sounded like. We know its instruments and its famous system of modes (such as Dorian, Lydian, Aeolian) but only a few tantalising fragments of notation have survived. Greek vases show dancing fig-ures, accompanied by lyre, flute and tam-bourine, who might be dancing at a modern Greek wedding, but neither these line-dancers nor their instruments are unique to Greece.

What was unique about Greece was the desire of 19th-century western philhellenes and

early Greek nationalists to see, in modern Greece, traces of continuity with the mythical world of antiquity. The claims that early folk-lorists made for a continuous tradition were not only slim, but they were based almost entirely on the poetry of Greek songs, ignoring both the astonishing variety and richness of the music,

and also the ritual context in which it was per-formed. Like all folk music, Greek songs and dances were not originally performed for enter-tainment but were associated with religious festivals, weddings, funerals or seasonal work.

Music of the mainland

While there is some overlap between these cat-egories, Greeks usually make a distinction between regional folk music (*dimotikí mousikí*) and popular or city music (*laïkí*). In the case of regional folk music, they also distinguish bet-ween music from the mainland (*steriní*) and music from the islands and coastline (*nisiótika, paraliakí*). Mainland Greece is further divided

---

LEFT: Mikis Theodorakis, who won international fame.
RIGHT: a busker in Athens plays a Pontian *lýra* from the Black Sea coast of Turkey.

into regions that have their own musical traditions: Epirus, in the northwest, Macedonia, Roúmeli, Thrace and the Peloponnese.

The most common rhythms of the mainland are the threes of the *tsamikós*, the sevens of the *kalamatianós* (named after the town of Kalamáta in the Peloponnese but common throughout central and southern Greece) and the slow duple and triple time of the *syrtós* and *sta tría*. Once, it was common to hear music performed outdoors by the classic pairs of instruments, either the large drum *(daoúli)* and folk oboe *(zourná)*, or the bagpipe *(gáïda)* and tambourine *(daïrés, défi)*; nowadays it is more common at festivals or wed-

Greece where the traveller may still be lucky enough to find live music at a summer *panigýri* (religious festival) are Thrace and Macedonia, both of which have a wide variety of local songs and dances. In central Greece and the Peloponnese you are these days more likely to find recorded music at such events.

The islands and Asia Minor

The islands of Greece once boasted an amazing variety of musical traditions. To the west of the Greek mainland in the Ionian Islands, which had for centuries been under Venetian control, people sang songs in four-part harmony. Called

dings to hear an ensemble that includes the clarinet, violin, drum and perhaps an accordion or a hammered dulcimer *(sandoúri)*.

A well-known Greek singer from the Aegean once said to me, "When I die I want to be born again as a Epirot." The music of Epirus is certainly among the most beautiful of any region in Greece. Epirus is famed for the skill of its clarinet players, who improvise like jazz masters on the folk clarinet (actually a B-flat Albert clarinet, still played by many musicians in Central Europe). It is also one of the regions of Greece where you are still likely to encounter live music at a festival or wedding, especially in the mountain villages. Other areas of mainland

kantádes, these songs, usually accompanied by a guitar, were clearly influenced by Neapolitan folk song. Partly because of their western European character and partly because they were songs that could be sung in a restaurant or tavern, *kantádes* became very popular in Athens where they continued to be sung by groups of men and women until the 1960s. The island of Zákynthos is still famous for its *kantádes* and, although the genre is slowly dying out, it is not uncommon to hear the islanders perform these light and charming songs. The Ionian Islands were also, in the 19th century, a regional centre for Italian opera, which was performed in small opera houses on both Corfu and Kefalloniá.

In the Aegean, music is usually somewhat arbitrarily divided into groups conforming to the grouping of islands. Here, the dance rhythms are mostly double, with the most common dance being some variety of *syrtós*. The exceptions are the nine-beat rhythms of the *zeïbekikó* and *karsilámas* found in the islands of the eastern Aegean, off the coast of Asia Minor, particularly Lésvos, the Dodecanese and Cyprus. The traditional instruments of these islands were the *lýra* (not to be confused with the ancient Greek lyre) or bowed viol, and the *tsaboúna*, or island bagpipe. As with the mainland instruments, there has been a shift in

ing to discover more about Greek folk music might well begin his or her journey in Crete. Still performed on the classic combination of the Cretan *lýra* and *laoúto*, Cretan music continues to flourish and is being performed by young as well as older players. Not only is the tradition of improvised poetic couplets still preserved, but sections of the long poem *Erotókritos*, a 17th-century verse play, are still performed as part of many singers' repertoires. Cretan dancing is spectacular, and the combination of music and dance, whether it is performed in a noisy nightclub or on a mountainside, at a wedding, is still awe-inspiring.

instrumentation, with the violin replacing the *lýra* on most islands, accompanied by the *laoúto*, or folk lute, often with the addition of accordion, hand-drum or clarinet. Improvised rhymed couplets in 15-syllable metre *(mandinádes)* are a common feature of Aegean island music and persist to this day, especially on the island of Crete.

Whereas live music has all but disappeared from many of the Aegean Islands, Crete is something of an exception. Any traveller want-

LEFT: the closest most tourists get to traditional dance is in mediated displays.
ABOVE: a traditional wedding on Kárpathos.

The islands of the central Aegean, including the Cyclades, have become so overwhelmed by tourists that these days it is difficult, on most of them, to hear live music. Those who are lucky enough to encounter it at some special occasion like a wedding will discover the vanishing beauty of the *nisiótika*, songs and dances performed by an ensemble that nearly always includes a violin. The islands near the Turkish mainland, especially the large island of Lésvos, once had a very different musical tradition, one strongly influenced by the cosmopolitan cities of Smyrna (modern Izmir) and Aïvali (Ayvaluk), both of which had large Greek populations until the 1920s. On Lésvos, there were many local varieties of the Asia Minor songs and dances, some only found in a particular village, and it was through its principal town, Mytilíni, that many of the features of Asia Minor music found their way into the popular music of Greece.

One type of music that the tourist is not likely to encounter, but which is rich in its lyrics and striking in its emotional style of performance, is the music of funeral laments. It is becoming increasingly rare for women to perform these songs at funerals in urban centres, but in the countryside, especially in more remote areas, no funeral is complete without

women have been permitted to continue improvising these laments as part of the funeral service, with priest and female chorus taking turns to articulate conflicting messages about the afterlife.

Religious music

Greeks often refer to the music of the Orthodox Church simply as Byzantine music. This is only partly true. While some of the music heard in the Orthodox services dates to the Byzantine period, much of it was composed later. Early Byzantine music was influenced by the chant of Syria and Palestine rather than

its chorus of women lament-singers. In most regions of Greece laments are distinguished from songs. They are a genre apart, and yet they have melodies that may be performed as separate instrumental pieces in other contexts – even at weddings, strangely enough. It is through these songs that women communicate with the other world, addressing the dead directly and often berating them for leaving the living behind.

While these laments are performed in the context of a Christian ritual, they are remarkable in their lack of Christian references and in their striking pagan imagery. Despite repeated clashes with the Orthodox Church, village

Greece or Rome, and was probably based on melodies already familiar to the congregation from the local folk tradition. The *okotéhos* which forms the basis of all Byzantine chant was not a system of modes like those of ancient Greece, but based on such a collection of songs. What was important was the association of a set of melodic formulas with their liturgical function: certain tunes came to have a symbolic function in the Church and were incorporated into the hymns.

By far the greatest composer of Byzantine hymns was Romanos the Melodist, born in Syria in the late 5th century and probably active at the height of the Emperor Justinian's reign.

His combination of dramatic poetry with melody has never been surpassed in the Eastern Christian tradition and his hymns are still performed as part of the Orthodox liturgy.

There is now a considerable variety of music performed in Greek churches, some of it accompanied by an organ, and some including polyphonic arrangements, although many churches still retain the earlier style of monophonic singing (without harmonies) with a chorus supplying a drone. The richest music of the Church calendar can be heard at the Easter-festival, particularly at the Epitáfios, or Easter Friday service.

most famous modern composer, Mikis Theodorakis. It is music and dancing derived from a particular style of Greek music called the *rebétika*, a style that still forms the basis of much of modern Greece's popular music and is played by revival groups all over Greece.

Rebétika is a music associated with certain ports of Asia Minor and Greece from the beginning of the 20th century onwards, though it probably existed around the east Aegean coast and the Black Sea for decades before that. On one occasion, an expatriate Soviet novelist, on exposure to the music, delightedly exclaimed that a nearly identical style, played on the bal-

The sound of the city

For many visitors to Greece, one of the attractions is the "Zorba factor". It is that dance of Anthony Quinn and Alan Bates on a Greek beach in the 1964 movie *Zorba the Greek*, accompanied by the rapid twanging of the *bouzoúki* that spells a particular exuberance and excitement regarded as quintessentially Greek. Granted, the two men are dancing on a Cretan beach, but they are not dancing a Cretan dance. They are dancing city music to a city instrument, music composed by Greece's

alaika, had flourished in the harbour dives of Odessa before the 1917 Revolution.

Rebétika is often, but not always, divided into two types: the Piraeus-style *rebétika*, and the Asia Minor music brought into Greece through the islands and by the flood of refugees who arrived in the mainland following the Turko-Greek War of 1920–22.

The Asia Minor style was generally performed in cafés known as *cafés-aman*, where the ensembles were made up of a violin, guitar, *oud*, *sandoúri* or *kanun* (zither) and perhaps an accordion. Women and men both performed in these venues and their repertoire of songs often included rather daring and humorous songs of

LEFT: a *tsaboúna*, the island bagpipe. **ABOVE:** musicians on guitar and mandolin, Pláka, Athens.

the underworld, songs about hashish, drinking, prison and prostitutes.

With the arrival of the refugees, many more cafés-aman sprang up in Piraeus and Athens, and the taste for this music in the Greek communities of the US led to a burgeoning recording industry. Refugees, many of them poor and unemployed, also joined local musicians in the back streets of Piraeus, where a new sort of music began to grow in popularity, This was performed not by the traditional instruments of the café ensemble, but on the *bouzoúki*, a long-necked, lute-like instrument that was common on some islands.

The heyday of the *rebétika* lasted from the 1930s to the 1950s, but the songs were revived in the 1970s, beginning in the years of the dictatorship (1967–74) when the music of Theodorakis was banned by the colonels and other composers either refused to compose or found their lyrics censored. References to smoking hashish also appealed to a generation of young Greeks who identified with the streetwise, social outcasts of the *rebétika*.

Popular music of the 1960s–1970s

Mikis Theodorakis and his fellow-composer Manos Hazidakis were the leaders of an extra-

By the 1930s the *bouzoúki* and the songs it accompanied were all the rage in Greece. Rather like the urban blues of the US, or the tango of Argentina, the songs of the pre-war *rebétika* were daring in their lyrics and appealed to an audience that revelled in hearing about the shady milieu they depicted.

Markos Vamvakaris, the central member of the "Piraeus Quartet", is often regarded as the "father" of the *rebétika*. Other outstanding figures were Stratos Pagioumtzis, Giannis Papaioannou, the prolific songwriter Vassilis Tsitsanis, and the singer Sotiria Bellou,whose recordings are as fine an introduction as one could wish to the *rebétika*.

ordinary experiment in Greek popular music. After the terrible years of World War II, the German occupation and civil war, Greeks were demoralised and emotionally exhausted. The two composers deliberately set out to provide the public with a new sort of popular music that would elevate and inspire the population at large. They both recognised the *rebétika* as the only musical form that could reach a broad public, but as classically trained musicians, they wanted to extend the boundaries of popular song and combine it with the poetry of the country's leading poets. Beginning in the late 1950s the two composers transformed Greek music and produced some of the most exciting popular music in Europe by joining the rhythms of the *rebétika* (particularly the dramatic 9/8 of the solo male dance, the *zeïbekikó*) with the poetry of Seferis, Ritsos, Gatsos and Elytis. In the case of Mikis Theodorakis, this music acquired a strong political dimension because of his commitment to the freedom of the persecuted Greek Left. During the dictatorship his music was banned and he was imprisoned for years, making his music still more popular among the population at large.

Theodorakis and Hadzidakis's music has had a lasting effect on Greek music. Not only are their songs still popular, but they inspired a

Dalaras), Mariza Koch, Haris Alexiou, Nena Venetsanou, Glykeria, Eleftheria Arvanitaki, Dimitra Galani and most recently Savina Giannatou have all become internationally popular. The phenomenon of World Music has created a demand for certain types of Greek music, both folk and urban, and these singers have represented Greek music to a broad audience.

Composers who came of age in the 1980s, like Stamatis Kraounakis, Nikos Papazoglou and Nikos Xydakis, are less widely known. There is still a very lively musical scene in Athens, with an increasingly divergent instrumentation. The hottest music these days has a

younger group of composers to follow in their footsteps. Among the best known of these composers, who belong to what is loosely termed the New Wave, are Dionysios Savvopoulos, Giannis Markopoulos, Manos Loizos and Stavros Xarhakos.

The contemporary music scene

Some of the best-known figures of the Greek musical scene are singers rather than composers: Maria Farandouri, George Dalaras (Giorgos

---

LEFT: a *bouzoúki* and guitar orchestra in a Pláka club around 1960.
ABOVE: *rebétes* in Piraeus in 1928.

distinctly oriental flavour, and is often performed by a mixture of Greeks and musicians from Asia Minor or North Africa. The *boîtes* or musical clubs of the Pláka are not the place most Athenians now go to hear music, but there are many alternatives spread around the centre of Athens and the outer suburbs. Athens by night is still full of music that lifts the spirits and lasts till morning. And for those fortunate enough to catch a concert of Theodorakis, discover a good *rebétika* group performing in a small club, or stumble on a wedding in the mountains of Epirus, the splendid, haunting music that once filled the air of Greece may still set the night on fire. ❏

MIXING PIETY WITH PLEASURE

Greek religious festivals – and there are many – celebrate saints' days and other events in the religious calendar with devotion and high spirits

Greek island life is punctuated throughout the year by saints' days and religious festivals or *panigýria*. As there are around 300 saints in the Orthodox calendar, there is an excuse for a party most days of the year.

Easter is the most important festival (*preceded by pre-Lenten carnival over the week before Clean Monday). It's a great time to visit, with traditional services marking the Resurrection everywhere from humble chapels to mighty monasteries. Colourful, noisy and potentially dangerous – on Kálymnos they throw dynamite to ensure Christ has truly risen *(see page 67)* – it's like Firework Night and Christmas rolled into one.

During Holy Week, or *Megáli Evdomáda*, churches are festooned in black. On Maundy Thursday monks on Pátmos re-enact the washing of Christ's feet at the Last Supper. On Good Friday the *Epitáfios*, or bier of Christ, is decorated by the women and paraded through the streets *(see above and right)* as hymns are chanted.

On Easter Saturday the churches are decked in white. At midnight everything is plunged in darkness as the priest lights the first candle from the holy flame, to represent the light of the world, and intones: *"Hristós anésti"* (Christ has risen). This is the signal for the congregation to light their candles. Families then break the Lenten fast with Easter soup made from the lamb's viscera and later play conkers with red-dyed eggs.

On Easter Sunday there is great rejoicing as a lamb or kid is barbecued outdoors over charcoal, with the usual music and dancing. There are often parties on Easter Monday, and on some islands an effigy of Judas is filled with fireworks and burned.

▽ **PARADING THE BIER**
Here the symbolic coffin of Christ *(Epitáfios)* is seen parading though the streets of the town, attended to by the priest. The parade is accompanied by the singing of religious songs.

▷ **SCARLET SHELLS**
Hard-boiled eggs, dyed red to symbolise the blood of Christ, are cracked in a game like conkers on Easter Day.

◁ **EASTER TWISTS**
Golden biscuits, *koulourákia*, are made for Easter in various shapes and often sprinkled with sesame seeds.

◁ **MONDAY MAYHEM**
"Clean Monday" is the end of the pre-Lenten carnival, with exuberant celebrations on some islands, including kite-flying and flour fights.

▽ **STEPS TO SALVATION**
Devout women crawl in penance to the church of the Panagía Evangelístria on Tínos on 25 March and 15 August.

◁ **MOUNTAINTOP MASS**
Saints' days are celebrated by *panigýria* (festivals) at hundreds of small chapels throughout the islands. Here Cycladic islanders honour Agía Marína, the protector of crops, on 17 July.

△ **ALL DRESSED UP**
In Ólympos, the remote mountain village on Kárpathos, the eldest daughter or *kanakará* wears her traditional costume and dowry of gold coins for major festivals.

◁ **EASTER PARADE**
Priest and villagers join in traditional chants in an Easter procession on Páros.

CELEBRATING ALL YEAR ROUND

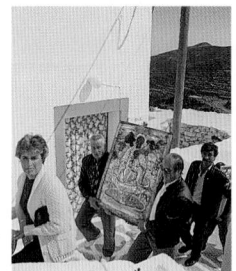

Greeks mix piety and pleasure with gusto for all their festivals, from the most important to the smallest fair. The biggest religious festival after Easter, the Assumption of the Virgin *(Kímisis tis Panagías)* on 15 August, draws Greeks home from all over the world.

Following a liturgy on the evening of the 14th, the icon of the deceased Virgin is solemnly processed through the streets, possibly while brass bands play dirges. There are communal celebrations afterwards, particularly spectacular in Kárpathos, with dazzling costumes, special dances and traditional songs.

Every month there are festivals on the islands for everything from sponges to snakes, and national holidays like *Óhi* or "No Day" (28 October), with patriotic parades to mark the Greeks' emphatic refusal of Mussolini's surrender ultimatum.

Celebrations begin the night before feast days and everyone in the community takes part, from babies to grannies. Patron saints are honoured with services followed by barbecues, music and dance. The picture above shows the feast of Ágios Dimítrios on Síkinos in October, which is conveniently when the first wine is ready to drink.

FOOD AND DRINK

Simple cooking using seasonal, local ingredients is the key to Greek
cuisine – but food for the Greeks is about more than just cooking and eating

The cook sets before you a large tray on which are five small plates. One of these holds garlic, another a pair of sea-urchins, another a sweet wine sop, another ten cockles, the last a small piece of sturgeon. While I'm eating this, another is eating that; and while he is eating that, I have made away with this. What I want, good sir, is both the one and the other, but my wish is impossible. For I have neither five mouths nor five hands...

– Athenaeus: The Deipnosophists

This scene describes the frustration Greeks, as well as tourists, often feel when they fail to taste all the dishes that are part of a meze spread. It is obviously an age-old problem, as the passage comes from a semi-ficitious Greek work of the 3rd century BC. Although pizza, hamburgers, *gýros* and the ubiquitous Greek salad tend to render modern Greek food banal, the age-old tradition of sharing many small dishes – the prelude to a meal or the meal itself – lives on.

Greeks were essentially vegetarian until about the mid-20th century, not by choice but because in their mountainous country it was not possible to pasture large herds and provide meat for everybody. The traditional Greek diet, frugal yet delicious, was mainly based on the agricultural produce of each region: vegetables, weeds and leafy greens – foraged from the hills and fields, or cultivated – and grains, mainly in the form of home-made bread. Fruity olive oil was the principal fat used, while olives, beans and other legumes, local cheeses and yogurt were everyday staples.

Only occasionally was the everyday diet enriched with some fresh or cured fish, or with meat. Meat was a rare, festive dish, consumed on Sundays, at the major festivals of Easter and Christmas, as well as on important family feasts. But after the mid-1960s, as the country became more affluent, imported meat gradually took a significant role at the Greek table. It was around that time that the Greek demographic structure changed.

At least four out of 10 middle-aged Greeks now living in big cities originally came from agricultural areas. They relocated in the last 50 years, bringing with them the cooking and culinary habits of their mothers and grandmothers. Although well settled in the urban environment, most of them have kept their ancestors' village

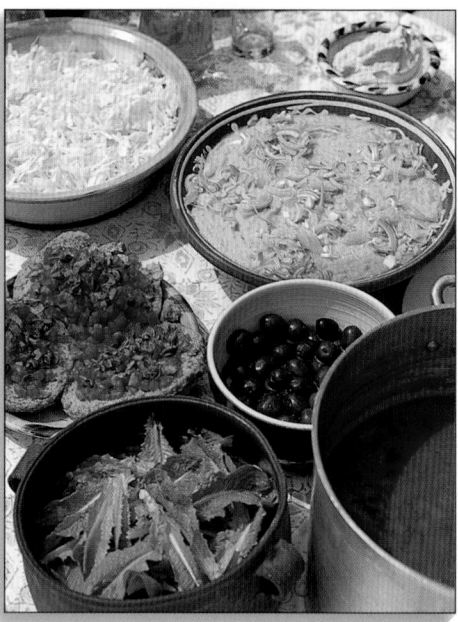

homes and visit them on long weekends, during the summer holidays, as well as at Christmas and Easter. Many have also kept much of their land, so it is common for Greek families to produce the olive oil they consume; about 18 kg (40 lb) per person each year. Olive oil is the core of the Greek diet, its most important element. People who do not produce it themselves buy it from friends who have a surplus.

Along with olive oil, *psomí* (bread) was the basic staple food untii the mid-1960s, as it used to be in ancient and Byzantine times. Although Greeks can now afford a great variety of foods, they still consume enormous quantities of bread. Traditional breads are often made with a combination of wheat, barley and sometimes maize flour, using sour old-dough starter as leavening. Barley grows easily in dry and mountainous southern Greece and on the islands, so it has been a staple for many centuries. Today in Crete and other islands *paximádia* (rusks) – slices of twice-baked and completely dry barley bread which need to be briefly soaked in water to soften – are still very popular. *Paximádia* are perfectly suited to traditional lifestyles: they keep well for many months, they are easy to carry in

Greek cooking. But by far the most important element that has shaped people's eating habits was the rules of the Greek Orthodox Church. Even non-religious Greeks sometimes abstain from foods deriving from animals – meat, dairy products and eggs – during the Lenten days that precede Easter, Christmas and other religious occasions. This is the reason why many traditional dishes such as *gemistá* (stuffed vegetables), *dolmádes* (stuffed grape or cabbage leaves), *píttes* (filo-wrapped pies) come in two

the field and are the ideal food for sailors. Moreover, baked every two or three months, they made good use of the oven heat, as wood is scarce on most islands.

Outside influences

In its long history Greece has been subjected to many culinary influences. The Venetians and Genoans, who ruled much of the country during the Middle Ages, and later the Ottoman Turks, who ruled northern Greece and Crete up until the early 1900s, have all left their marks on

LEFT: a diet of greens, beans and olives.
ABOVE: a wide range of olives for sale.

versions: one with meat and/or cheese, and one without, often called *laderá* (with just olive oil) for the days of fast.

Festival food

Numerous religious holidays are scattered throughout the year. Many of them have evolved from ancient celebrations and are often closely related to the seasons and the lunar calendar. Easter, Greece's most important feast, seems to have its roots in the agricultural spring festivals of antiquity. Celebrated in the open country, amid fragrant herbs and multicoloured flowers, the Easter table features succulent spit-roasted baby lamb or kid – at the right age for slaughter at that time of the year – and salads of wild greens, tender raw artichokes and fresh fava beans. *Magirítsa*, a delicious soup made with chopped lamb's innards, spring onions and dill, with a tart egg-and-lemon sauce, is eaten on Easter Saturday, after the midnight Resurrection Mass. The traditional Easter sweets are made with *myzíthra*, a generic name for the various regional creamy fresh cheeses of the season, usually made with a combination of goat's and sheep's milk.

Pork is associated with Christmas and New Year, as pig slaughtering and curing is done in the heart of the winter. Fish is consumed on 25 March, and always at the meals that follow funerals. Despite its many islands, fish and seafood has never been plentiful enough to become an everyday food in Greece, not even for those who live by the sea. The fish and seafood of the Aegean is delicious but scarce, and the best fish islanders manage to catch is sold to the big cities for much-needed cash.

Dining out

Despite its rich culinary heritage, Greece has no great restaurant tradition and the finest *magirevtá* (cooked dishes) are best savoured in the home. People eat lunch at around 3pm and dinner at around 9pm – in the summer at around 10pm or even later. Breakfast is usually just a cup of coffee and a biscuit. Wine accompanies the meals, especially dinner, and a salad of fresh, raw or blanched seasonal vegetables or greens is always part of the everyday menu. Seasonal fruits are the most common dessert. Sweets were originally part of the festive table but now tend to be eaten at all times of the day, while meat has become an almost everyday staple.

Traditionally there are two kinds of restaurants that attract the Greeks when they want to entertain their families and friends: a *psistariá* (grill house) offers charcoal-grilled meat (baby lamb, kid, pork, veal and occasionally chicken) by weight. Here meat-lovers have a feast at reasonable prices. Tourists are probably more familiar with the other Greek favourite restaurant, *psarotavérna* (fish tavern), as these are scattered all over the shoreline, on the islands and the mainland. Fresh fish and seafood, the catch of the day, is grilled or fried according to the customer's choice. Both meat and fish taverns offer a few appetisers and seasonal salads.

The frugal Greek cooks have learned to combine a few simple items of produce to create an incredible variety of foods. With remarkable ingenuity, they compliment them with rice, potatoes, some cheese and a few pieces of meat to create dishes that dieticians now hold up as models of the famously healthy Mediterranean diet. The irony is that modern Greeks, in their quest to distance themselves from their poverty-stricken past, have enthusiastically left behind this traditional fare and adopted the unhealthy eating habits of the wealthy Europeans and Americans.

Local foods

The traditional foods of Greece's past had nearly disappeared when, in the 1990s, a trend towards grandmother's cooking began to emerge in Athens and gradually all over the country. Visitors need to ask for regional specialities – for example, *píttes* (pies wrapped in fylo) in Epirus; *trahanás* soup (the Greek pasta made with yogurt and sourdough) on the mainland; *dolmádes* (meat-stuffed vine leaves) almost everywhere; *loukánika* (sausages) and *loúza* or *lóza* (pork loin macerated in wine and air-dried or smoked) in the Cyclades. Look out, too, for thyme honey on small, unforested islands and *pastéli* (a sesame seed and honey sweet), home-cured caper greens, and wonderful local shepherd's cheeses, often just called *tyráki* (small cheese). In the Cyclades and the Dodecanese goat's and sheep's milk cheeses are a real treat, but they seldom travel further than their village of origin. Greece is finally beginning to capitalise on its delicious artisan foods, with fancy delis in the largest cities and speciality boutiques on many tourist islands.

The Byzantines continued to add resin to some wines. A more refined legacy of this is the modern *retsína*, a white wine mildly scented with pine resin. *Retsína* was widely consumed up until the mid-1970s. But as the new generation of quality Greek wines gradually spread, its consumption declined sharply. Today many medium-sized and small wineries, employing modern techniques and talented oenologists, experiment combining indigenous and imported grape varieties and produce wines of excellent quality.

The Greek vineyards are diverse, following the contours of the country's morphology.

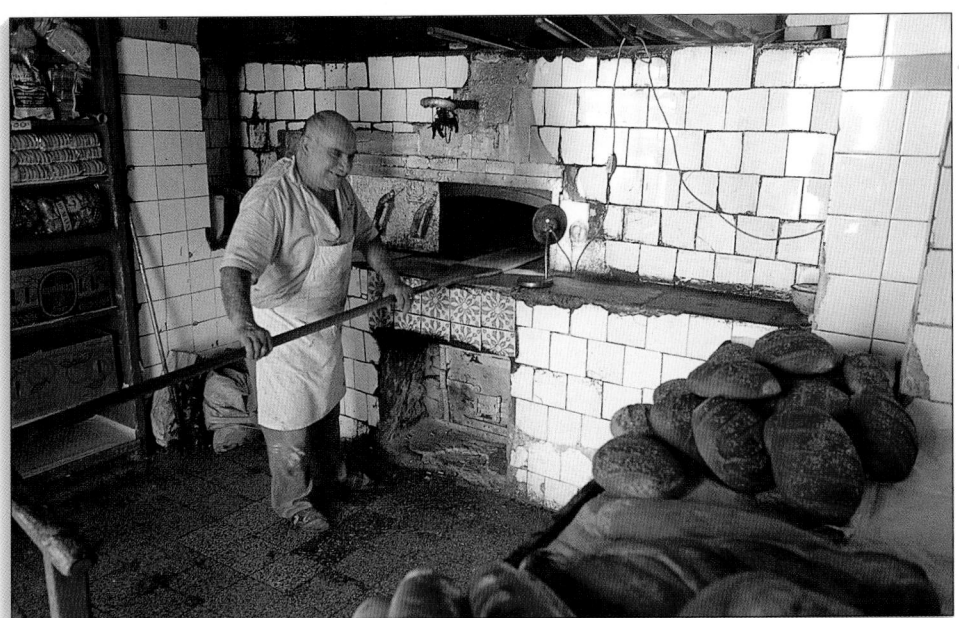

Greek wines

Some of the most admired wines in antiquity were produced in Greece. Manpowered cargo ships carried clay amphoras filled with the precious liquid to ports and markets all over the Mediterranean. Yet if we were to try these wines today, we would probably find them undrinkable. They were mainly sweet, and contained flavourings and herbs such as thyme, mint and even cinnamon. Seawater and pieces of pine bark were also added as preservatives, to keep the wine from turning sour.

Omnipresent hills and mountains divide the land into small regions, each with its own microclimate. Several indigenous grape varieties – many of which existed also in antiquity – are grown, which acquire different characteristics in each region. According to EU regulations and the Greek law, the system of appellations of origin (AOC) matches the Greek varieties to the areas where the best of their kind is traditionally produced. Note, however, that you will also find exceptional regional wines outside of these AOC classifications. A description of the most important wines and grape varieties of each of the country's regions follows.

LEFT: stuffed tomatoes and potatoes.
ABOVE: bread being baked in a traditional oven.

Northern Greece

Starting with Macedonia, the land of the *xinó-mavro* grape which produces the most well-loved Greek *brusco* wine (a robust red). Naoússa is the best-known example, while Amýndeon, made from the same grape, is a light red and can also be a pleasant still or sparkling rosé. *Xinómavro* combined with the *negóska* variety – another Macedonian native – makes Goumenissa, a meaty red. By itself, *negóska* produces a soft red. Extended, relatively new vineyards on the central peninsula of Halkidikí produce the Côtes de Meliton wines, both white and red, from a combination

Thessaly, where most of the Greek grain is cultivated, produces two distinguished wines: Rapsani makes a red with a fine bouquet, from *xinómavro*, *stavrotó* and *krasáto* varieties which grow on the southeastern slopes of Mount Olympos. Anhialos, on the shores of Pagasitikos, produces a fresh white wine, made mostly from *rodítis* grapes.

Central Greece and Peloponnese

Attica, the region around Athens (not an AOC region), produces very interesting wines. The main variety here is *savatianó*, traditionally used for the production of *retsína*, the resinated wine.

of French (Cabernet Sauvignon and Franc) and Greek varieties. On the eastern peninsula, in the secluded monastic community of Mount Athos, the monks, who have been producing wines since Byzantine times, still cultivate both white and red wine-producing grapes. Macedonia is a wonderful and lesser-known area for wine (for maps and details of its Wine Roads, visit www.wineroads.gr).

In Epirus, the most isolated, mountainous region of northwestern Greece, Zitsa, a fresh, fruity, often sparkling white is produced from the *debena* variety. In the valley below Métsovo, Katóï, a fine, rich red, is made from imported Cabernet Sauvignon vines.

Château Matsa in Kántza is one of the finest Greek whites, produced from grapes of an old family vineyard. Additionally, various Greek and foreign varieties produce a new range of wines, such as Villitsa and Attica.

In the Peloponnese, Nemea, made from *aigiorgítiko* grapes grown in the northeastern part of the region, is one of the most versatile Greek reds. Mandinia, a delicate aromatic white wine, is produced on the vineyards north of Trípoli, from *mavrodáfni* and *asproúdes* grapes. The Pátra area yields dry and sweet white and red wines. Muscat of Patras and Muscat of Rio as well as Mavrodafni are three well-loved sweet rich, *vins de liqueur*.

Some scholars believe that the medieval city of Monemvasiá used to be the place where malmsey wine was made (called also malvesian or malvoisie, from the old name of the city). Others claim that the wine mentioned by Shakespeare was produced in Crete, and the boats that transported it stopped at Monemvasiá on their way to Europe. That magnificent sweet white is no longer made in Greece but in Madeira.

The Islands

On the island of Límnos a lovely white wine is produced from Alexandrian Muscat grapes, while the *limnió* variety, mentioned by Aristotle, produces light, fragrant red wines. Vineyards on Sámos, a mountainous island, are planted on terraced hills, rising to 800 metres (2,625 ft). The Sámos sweet and muscat wines are well known and much praised by the French. Rhodes produces dry white wines mainly from *athíri* grapes, as well as sparkling wines of good quality. The red dry wines of the region are made chiefly from *mandilariá* grapes.

Crete produces 20 percent of Greek wines. Although far to the south, the cool etesian winds never let the temperature rise much, and the tall mountain of Mt Psilorítis keeps the hot winds of Africa from reaching the northern part where most of the grapes are cultivated. Arhánes is a dry red made from *kotsifáli* and *mandilariá* grapes. Another red, Dafnés, is made from *liátiko*, probably an ancient variety. From this variety, a sweet red *vin de liqueur* is also produced. Sitía produces a dry and a sweet red. A dry red made from *kotsifáli* and *mandilariá*, and a very popular fruity white from *vilána* grapes, are the Sitía AOC.

Santoríni, the spectacular volcanic island, produces a lovely white wine made from *asýrtiko* grapes. To guard their vines from the strong etesian winds, local growers shape their branches like baskets in which the grapes grow. *Visánto* is a marvellous fortified sweet wine made from partly sun-dried grapes. Similar sweet wines, often called *liastó*, are produced throughout the Cyclades. In the very picturesque island of Páros, the low-pruned vines produce a red with dark colour and a characteristic bouquet, made from *mandilariá* and *monemvasiá* grapes.

Corfu, Zákynthos and Levkáda produce interesting wines, but only Robóla from Kefalloniá, a dry white from the eponymous grapes, is an AOC, together with the local variety of Mavrodáfni, the *vin de liqueur.*

Oúzo and other spirits

The most popular Greek drink, traditionally served with *mezédes*, is undoubtedly *oúzo*, which is produced in many parts of the country. Only *oúzo* made in Greece can bear that name according to EU regulations. *Oúzo* is made from distilled alcohol, and takes its flavour from anise, fennel seeds and other aromatics.

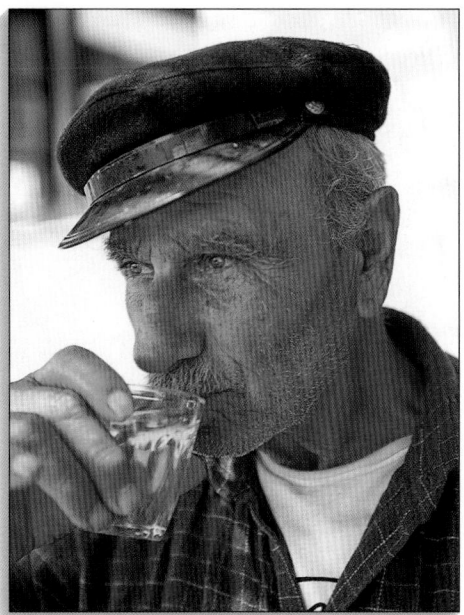

In the north of Greece, *oúzo* is dry, while in the south and the islands it is somewhat sweeter.

Some people say the best *oúzo* is from Lésvos. Others will insist that the *oúzo* of Tyrnávos, Thessaly, or that of Híos is superior. It's a matter of taste, often affected by a person's place of origin. In Híos, there is also *mastíha*, a sweeter version of *oúzo* flavoured exclusively with mastic, the aromatic sap of the mastic bushes that grow on the island. Another popular strong alcoholic drink, akin to the Italian *grappa*, is made from the distillation of grapeskins and stems. It is called *tsípouro* in central and northern Greece and *rakí* or *tsikoudiá* in Crete, where it is recommended as a universal panacea. ❑

LEFT: wine-tasting at Boutari winery, Santoríni.
RIGHT: a glass of *retsína*.

ART AND ARCHITECTURE

The Classical, Hellenistic, Roman and Byzantine eras left Greece
with an artistic heritage that has inspired later artists and architects

Few countries have influenced Western art more than ancient Greece. But because of its geographical position, Greece itself has been subjected to many influences, from Europe, Asia and, through Crete, Africa. The origins of Greek art lay in Neolithic Anatolia, the Middle East and Egypt. Greece in turn influenced Rome, and thus Western Europe and the Byzantine world. Absorbed into the Turkish Ottoman Empire for 500 years, on liberation Greece was on the receiving end of Western influences, often mixed with its Byzantine heritage. The region's fine marbles, good clays and early exploitation of Cypriot copper ensured an enduring artistic gift.

The Bronze Age

The earliest art is that of the Cyclades. Neolithic and Bronze Age cultures developed complex housing schemes, but the most characteristic artefacts are the Cycladic dolls, placed as protective amulets with early burials. Here the Greek love of idealised, perfect forms is already apparent. The facial details may have been added in paint.

By 2000 BC the Minoan civilisation had emerged in Crete and on neighbouring Santoríni, characterised by palace complexes such as Knossos and Phaestos. The architecture was labyrinthine, of stone with plastered and frescoed walls, and looked inwards on to courtyards which were the scene of elaborate games, including bull-leaping as represented in paint and ivory figures.

The sacred bull – suggested by the twin horn symbol – was represented in terracotta, and as rhytons (drinking vessels) of gold or soapstone. The frescoed composite plants and chariots pulled by winged beasts, and the sculpted flounced dress of the snake goddess, a protective deity, demonstrated Mesopotamian influence. Sea and land creatures – shells, octopuses, bees – inspired vase decoration and jewellery.

The double-headed axe, used as a motif, was a sacred symbol.

The peaceable, sophisticated Minoan culture declined around 1400 BC. The Myceneans of the mainland were now a major power. Warlike and great sea traders, they adopted Minoan motifs such as wasp-waisted costumes and the

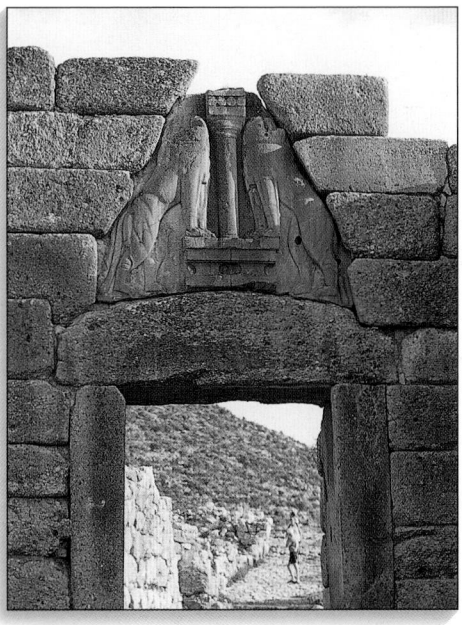

downward tapering column seen on the Lion Gate at Mycenae (*circa* 1600 BC). This entry to the citadel/palace is the first large-scale European sculpture. Set within a corbelled arch, this constructive technique was used for the Cyclopean-scale vaulted chambers at Tiryns, and more adventurously for the tholos ("beehive") tombs, the most impressive of which is the Treasury of Atreus (*circa* 1375 BC) at Mycenae, a 15-metre (49-ft) span dome with side chamber. Earlier shaft graves have revealed elaborate niello-inlaid bronze daggers, lion and bull head rhytons, and the remarkable, haunting and somewhat heraldic gold masks placed over the faces of the dead.

LEFT: *The Artist's Family*, by Nikolaos Kounelakis, 1864.
RIGHT: The Lion Gate, Mycenae.

The Geometric era

Iron Age peoples entered Greece *circa* 1100 BC: Mycenean society collapsed and the so-called Dark Ages, more properly the Geometric period, began. Few artefacts except pottery vessels survive. Decorated with geometric horizontal banding, including spirals and diapers akin to Minoan and Mycenean work, and also the Greek key, these were often associated with burials: some depict funerary processions with geometrised figures. Others assumed anthropomorphic shapes. From *circa* 750 BC small figurines of seated goddesses, charioteers, animals and warriors appeared in bronze, ivory and ceramic.

came closer to reality, but the sense of idealisation was never lost.

Central to this concept was harmonic proportion. In the evolution of the temple a perfectly balanced system of horizontals and verticals developed. Archaic temples followed the Doric form: it was sturdy (it was likened to a man), with sharply fluted columns that had simple capitals and no base. These carried an entablature featuring square metope panels between vertical triglyph mouldings. The form of a colonnaded, box-like structure as a "home" for the deity, often sited on a hilltop, created a perfect backdrop for the open-air ceremonies.

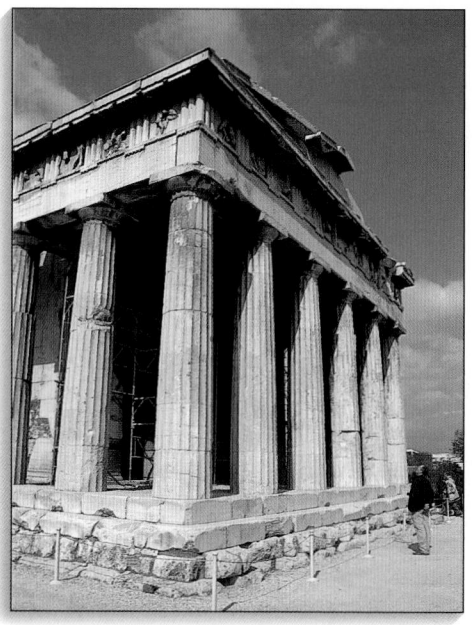

Archaic art

The Archaic period, *circa* 650–490 BC, was one of rapid development. In sculpture, large *kouros* (male youth) and *korai* (clothed female) standing figures were carved, perhaps as personifications of gods, as grave markers, or as worshipper figures. Early *kouroi* demonstrated Egyptian influence in their stance and braided hair. Over time the males become less anatomically stylised and the girls' draperies become more flowing; smiles were depicted, and the feel was for naturalism.

Herein lies a clue to ancient Greek art. These statues represented ideal figures shown in the prime of life: in time the concept of the ideal

Classical art

The subsequent Classical period, 490–336 BC, saw further rapid developments. Although known by report, scarcely any early Greek painting survives: ceramic decoration gives some clues to its qualities. Archaic vase-painting had been dominated initially by a Corinthian "orientalising" style of fabulous beasts, and then by a vigorous Athenian style of figurative ware in which black figures were placed against the red of the pot (black figure ware). Around 500 BC, this gave way to a reversal of the process giving red figure ware, in which a finer linearism captured greater detail and movement, enhanced by the development of foreshortening and eventually a rudimentary perspective. Early writers tell of panel paintings of exact mimicry of nature by the masters Zeuxis and Apelles. In sculpture, too, much has been lost, and many works are now known only through Roman marble copies of lost bronzes. The greater structural strength of bronze when cast hollow led to more adventurous poses of movement, as with the *Poseidon* (Zeus?) recovered from the sea in 1928. The sculptor Polykleitos's *Doryphoros* (Javelin thrower) was originally in bronze. In this he realised *controposto* – the establishment of convincing weight distribution in a figure.

ing her sandal (Temple of Nike Apteros, Athens Acropolis). The narrative interest was paralled in dramas and the creation of semicircular theatres moulded from the contours of the land.

Late Classical sculpture saw the emergence of a more private attitude to the figure, particularly in portraiture and the self-involved statues of Praxiteles; notably his *Cnidian Aphrodite* and the *Hermes with the infant Dionysos*. The former introduced the nude figure, previously rare. A feminine architectural theme was provided by the more slender and elegant Ionic style of temple where the spiral volutes of the capitals were equated to a girl's curling hair. In

From 447 to 432 BC his contemporary, Pheidias, mastered the depiction of narrative schemes and vigorous action in his reliefs and statues for the Temple of Zeus at Olympia and the Parthenon in Athens. The Parthenon reliefs, like much ancient Greek sculpture and architecture, were brightly painted, probably making them less "pure" to modern eyes. For both temples Pheidias created gigantic deities of ivory and gold, now lost. A perfect blend of naturalism with idealism had been achieved, well seen in the *Nike adjust-*

these temples the entablature rejects the Doric metopes and triglyphs, but might include a continuously sculpted frieze section. After 350 BC a more forceful sculptural manner emerged with Skopas. His active military reliefs foreshadowed the dynamic work of Alexander the Great's favoured sculptor Lykippos, whose *Apoxyomenos* (Sweat scraper) was given a tight muscularity and the smaller proportioned head of an aggressive figure.

Hellenistic art

Alexander's accession in 336 BC, marking the beginning of the Hellenistic phase, was followed by the rapid expansion of the Greek

FAR LEFT: the Cretan *Lady of Auxerre*, 640–630 BC.
LEFT: the Doric Hephaeiston, Athens' Agora.
ABOVE: a red figure vase, 5th century BC.

Empire: his capital was established at Babylon, and the centre of artistic production tended to move eastwards, particularly to Anatolia. Pergamon was especially important sculpturally during 250–160 BC. The adoption of the Babylonian cult of Tyche (Fortune), with its associated astrology, led to a breakdown of free thought. In sculpture emphasis was put on movement, as in the *Nike of Samothrace* (now in the Louvre in Paris), realism, the display of emotion and more complex poses. From this period survive many mass-produced ceramic figures of gods, dancing figures and satyrs, often known as Tanagra figures after the town

The absorption of Greece into the Roman Empire by 146 BC reaffirmed Roman admiration and development of Greek forms of art and architecture. Indeed, apart from sculptures a few larger paintings such as the mosaic *Battle of Issus* (Pompeii, *circa* 50 BC) are known by their Roman copies. Roman pillaging of sanctuaries and cities was matched by the employment of Greek artists. The practical bent of the Romans emphasised physically truthful portraiture and its use as propaganda (see the *Augustus* from Athens's Roman agora), and hero worship as with the bust of *Antinoös* from Pátra. Roman forms of arched architecture were

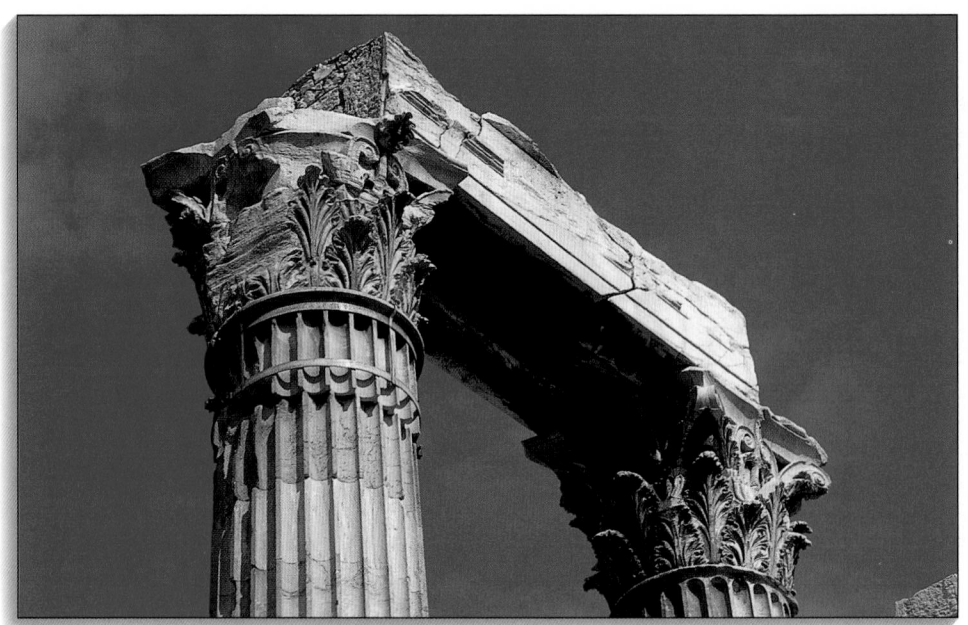

in Boeotia. During this luxury-loving age the continuance of refined goldwork for jewellery, and filigree and leaf diadems was matched by the remarkable Derveni krater, a copper alloy *repoussée* wine vase used as a cinerary urn despite its Dionysiac scenes.

In architecture a new, complex quality was introduced with the foliate Corinthian column capital, first used at the Choragic monument to Lysikrates, Athens, in 336 BC. It was often used on a gigantic scale as for the Olympeion, Athens, *circa* 170 BC. Houses appear to have been simple structures to judge from the painted Thracian tomb chests preserved in Thessaloníki museum.

adopted and also the preference for sumptuous palaces. The surviving Galerius Gateway, AD 298–303, at Thessaloníki conveys something of their splendour: its reliefs reflect the Roman-Hellenic interest in illusionism and narrative.

Christianity and Byzantium

That Christian communities were quickly established in Greece is demonstrated by St Paul's letters to the Corinthians and Thessalonians. Constantine the Great's making Byzantium (modern Istanbul) his capital in 330, coupled with his advocacy of Christianity (though he himself did not convert until on his deathbed), determined the future direction of Greek religion and what is known as Byzantine art. Christianity led to an art of symbolism, and because of a fear of idolatry, sculpture in the round became rare, as did the mainstay of antiquity, the nude; figures thus became described by their drapery. Many artefacts of this mystic art were produced in Byzantium and exported to the Balkans. Levantine motifs, particularly from silks, were mixed with Roman ones in an art that emphasised richness and sophistication, religiously and secularly, although little survives of the latter.

Architecturally, two forms of church emerged alongside the Roman basilica form of nave, aisle and apse: one, the central domed space, some-

was challenged. However, Néa Móni on Híos has good mosaics from *circa* 1050, and Mystrás has fine 14th-century paintings. Other devotional works were relief-carved ivory codex (book) covers, boxes and *pyxes*; but most characteristic were icons (tempera- or occasionally encaustic-painted panels of saints). These were initially domestic and often for women at home, but were later placed on pillars flanking the space to the altar. In turn more icons were added to the *témplon* or barrier before the altar, and in time they multiplied to create an iconostasis or screen separating nave from chancel and congregation from clergy (as with the fine example found in the

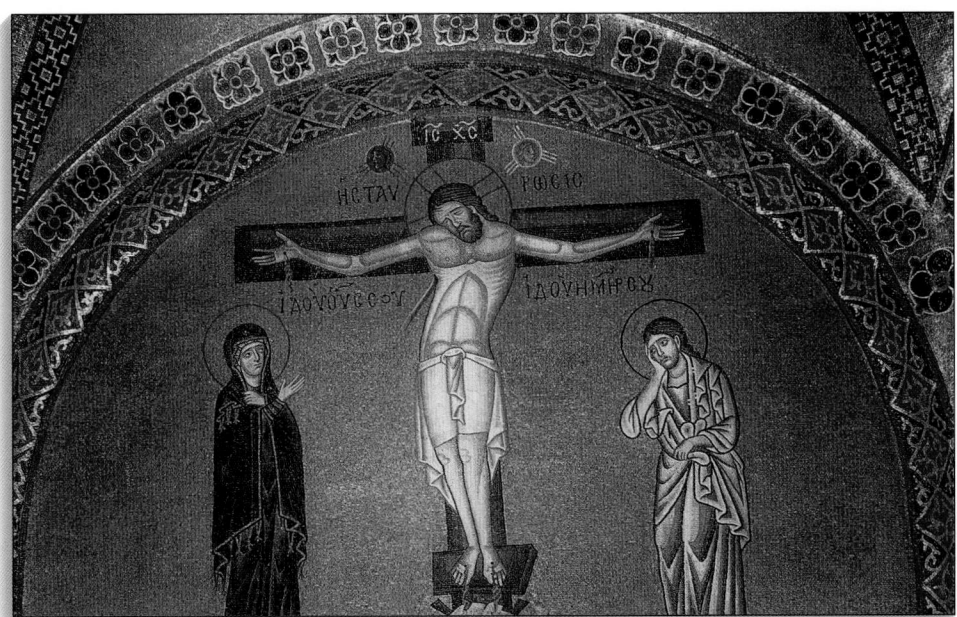

times over an octagon (as at Ósios Loukás), and the other a cruciform domed space (such as Holy Apostles, Athens). In these the dome was often emphasised by the image of Christ giving his blessing (the Pandokrátor), a fitting symbol as one took communion below. Surviving paintings are often mosaics of glass, sometimes gilded, that were set at slight angles so that in the flickering candlelight the images shimmered. Many paintings were destroyed during the Iconoclastic crisis of 726–843 when the whole validity of imagery was challenged.

Left: Corinthian columns on the Temple of the Olympian Zeus, Athens.
Above: Byzantine mosaics, Ósios Loukás.

Megálou Meteórou monastery). An arrangement of a central Christ flanked by Mary and St John the Baptist, Saints Peter and Paul and other apostles and saints in order of importance became known as the Great Deesis. Such screens greatly enhanced the mysticism of the Orthodox religion, which formally dates from the Great Schism of 1054.

Byzantine culture was increasingly under threat, first from Islam but also from the West, particularly its former allies Venice and Genoa. However, it did experience an artistic revival in manuscripts and the paintings at Mystrás, which show a greater interest in plasticity, under the Palaeologue dynasty (1261–1453).

The capture of Byzantium by the Ottoman Turks in 1453 meant Greece became nominally part of the Islamic world, although from as early as 1204 the Ionian and some of the Aegean Islands, the Dodecanese, Crete and several mainland cities were ruled by Venice and other Western powers *(see page 40)*. In consequence, Venetian and Frankish influence was felt in architecture, notably at Haniá, Crete, and other fortresses. After 1453 many refugee painters emigrated to the Venetian-held Ionian Islands and Crete, where Venetian influence tempered icon painting of the 15th to 17th centuries, as in the work of Ioannis Permeniatis and Mihaïl Damaskinos.

> ### "THE GREEK"
>
> Crete's most famous painter is Domenikos Theotokopoulos, whose *Adoration of the Magi* (Benáki Museum, Athens) shows his work as an icon painter before his move to Venice and later to Spain – where he was known as El Greco.

other domestic utensils). Often distinct, lively regional and island vernacular styles are apparent, particularly in embroidery.

Domestic architecture favoured timber-panelled rooms which stylistically linked traditions from İstanbul with European precedents. The emigration of many Greeks, both east and west and known as the diaspora, helped fuse many influences into the Greek arts. One notable example is that of Greek craftsmen working at İznik on ceramic ware with Grecian subject

matter. Many domed Ottoman civic buildings have been destroyed, but numerous others survive, especially in regions united with Greece after 1881. These include the *bezesténi* (covered bazaar), two baths and several mosques in Thessaloníki, a functioning hamam and three mosques in Rhodes, plus scattered mosques, baths and ornate fountains in Ioánnina, Tríkala, Lárissa, Návplio, Halkída, Véria, Kós, Crete, Lésvos and Híos. In the last two locales, hamams have been restored for use as event venues.

Art under the Ottomans

Ottoman rule in Greece allowed religious tolerance, but the Islamic scepticism of figurative imagery was nevertheless felt, particularly in larger public works. Although icon painting persisted – often small-scale and domestic – more emphasis was put on the decorative arts in which Eastern and Western influences are found, especially in textiles, including kilims, jewellery and metalwork (lamps, platters and

Neoclassicism

Roman Pompeii, discovered in 1763, provoked a renewed interest in antiquity, and the writings of the German scholar Winckelmann suggested that Greek art was superior to Roman. Consequently, a pro-Hellenic movement arose in western Europe which, allied to growing nationalist aspirations, led to a resurgence of interest in Classical Greece (often known as neoclassicism) which dominated the arts during and after the Wars of Independence of 1821–8 and full independence in 1830. A German, Otto of Wittelsbach, was appointed king and it is therefore Germanic influence, particularly from Schinkel, that dominates neoclassical architecture – especially in Athens, the capital from 1834. Monumental, largely Ionic structures that reflect

with the vernacular in his own house. This eclectic attitude gained pace and unsurprisingly the Byzantine style found favour, as with Kaftantzoglou's Athens Eye Clinic, and as late as 1933 with the church of Ágios Konstandínos, by Aristotelis Zahos, at Vólos. Scores of houses composed as assemblages of geometric forms with classical detailing and an overall symmetry show the popularity of the neoclassical style.

Just as architecture paralleled the mainstream European patterns, so too did painting and sculpture. Sculpture which had been marginalised during the Byzantine and Ottoman years revived, initially in the Classical taste, especially

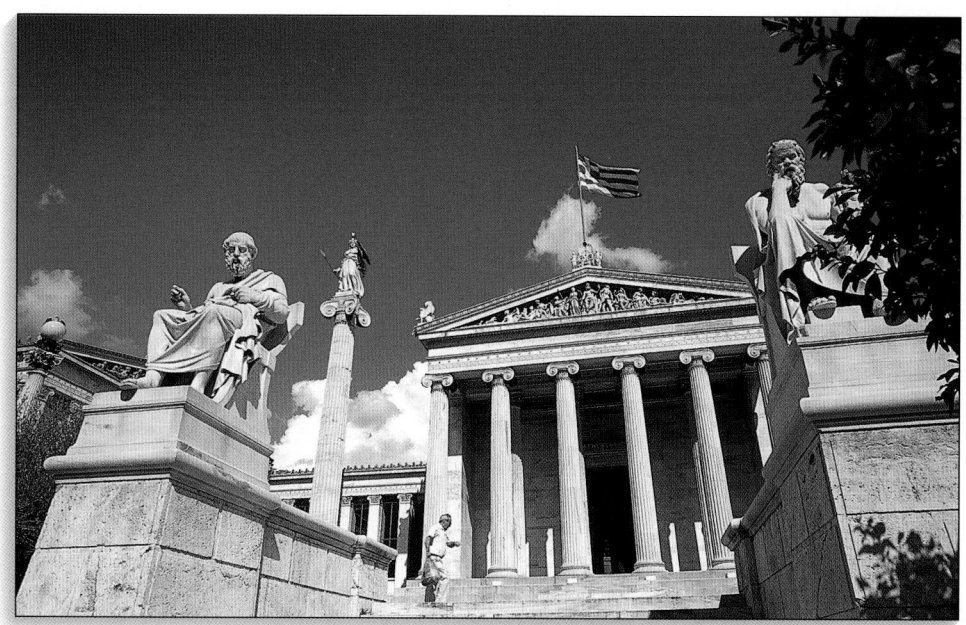

mainstream European neoclassicism are Von Gartner's Royal Palace (1835–41), and the work of two Danish architects, Christian Hansen's National Capodistrian University (1837) and Theophilus Hansen's National Library (1859–91) and Academy (1859–87). Native architects adopted the style, notably Lysandros Kaftantzoglou (Athens Technical University) and Stamatis Kleanthis, Schinkel's student. The latter built the neoclassical Wortheim house (Athens, 1843) and also the revived Renaissance-style Byzantine Museum (Athens, 1840–8), as well as toying

at Tínos where a school of decorative carving had flourished. Examples are Prosalentis's *Plato*, 1815, or Drosis's *Penelope*, 1873 (both in the National Gallery in Athens). Given the dominance of German tutors at the Royal School of Fine Arts, Teutonic concepts affected students like Fytalis whose *Shepherd* (1856, National Gallery) owes something to Schadow. Vitsaris's Pavlopoulos Tomb (1890, Athens Próto Nekrotafío) demonstrated interest in western Baroque, while Demetriades's *Male Figure* (1910, National Gallery) or Philippolis's *Reaper* (1870, Athens Záppio) picked up contemporary naturalist tendencies. In painting, portraiture – at first somewhat naïve – and subject painting took

LEFT: The Yali Tsamisi, Haniá, Crete.
ABOVE: Hansen's neoclassical Academy, Athens.

off following independence, thus supplementing the Venetian-influenced religious works that had been popular in the Ionian Islands in the 18th century, such as Doraxas's *Birth of the Virgin* (Zákynthos Museum).

The 1821–8 wars provoked many dramatic paintings with a romantic flavour and occasional religious overtones, such as Vryzakis's *Exodus from Mesolóngi* (1853, National Gallery). Greek life was also celebrated, as in the German-influenced Nikolaos Gyzis's *Children's Betrothal* (1877, National Gallery) or Nikiforos Lytras's *The Dirge on the Isle of Psara* (pre-1888). Both artists, perhaps surprisingly, were also attracted

appears derivative. Elements of Cubism appear in the paintings of Parthenis, and of Nikos Hatzikyriakos-Gikas, whose *Athenian Houses* is of 1927–8; in *Sky* of 1966 Gikas touches on futurism (both pictures are in the National Gallery). Surrealist imagery akin to de Chirico surfaced with Nikos Engonopoulos (*Poet and Muse*, 1938, National Gallery), and persisted in later artists such as Caras (*Three Graces*, 1974, National Gallery). Perhaps more successful was Ioannis Tsarouhis's interpretation of Matisse's linearism, such as in *Youth in an Overcoat* (1937, National Gallery), which has a strong design also seen in Yiannis Moralis's figurative work of the 1940s

to Orientalist subjects. By the late 19th century other artists were picking up on new subjects, landscape (Lambesis) and still life (Pantazis), while others became attracted to Impressionism and its offshoots – for example, Savvides's *Lady in an Evening Dress* (1889, National Gallery).

The 20th century

Greek artists of the 20th century broadly followed the major European trends and readily accepted modernism, not least because many studied in Paris. However, where most progressive Western developments occurred before 1930, Greek modernist artists were latecomers of the 1920s; consequently, in international terms much

and 1950s (as in *Figure*, 1951, National Gallery). Moralis's classicist realism was typical of much painting produced during the dictatorship; sometimes painterly as with Tetsis, or linear with Mavroïdis, or reflective of Byzantine patterning as with Nikolaou. Such work can feel more truly Greek than the experiments with abstraction and recent conceptual and post-modernist art.

Sculptors of the early 20th century were likewise often trained in Paris. Consequently the impact of Maillol is felt in Tombros's *Fat Woman* (1926, National Gallery), and Despiau in Raftopoulou's *Sculpture* (1932, National Gallery). These matched an interwar concern for the figure while embracing some abstraction, a trend that lingered into the 1950s and 1960s with Kastriotes's enchanting *Dance* (1953, National Gallery), and Pappas's *Male Figure* (1965, artist's collection). But generally, from 1949 abstraction and the international style tended to prevail. Koulentianos's *Tree* (1988, Athens, Portalakes collection) reflected the spirit of Chadwick; Takis's *Light Signals* (1985, Paris, private collection) revealed a dull post-modernist wit; and Hrysa's *New York Landscape* (1971–4, Athens, Mihalarias collection) used light intriguingly but in a formally predicable presentation.

In architecture the eclecticism that persisted into the 1930s extended to vernacular forms. Not

worked in Perret's studio. The latter worked on the ambitious ministry-led programme of new school building in the 1930s. Many Athenian blocks of flats were in the modernist manner, examples being those by Panagiotakos on Themistokléous Street, or those by Mihaïlidis and Valentis on Zémi and Stounára streets.

Post-civil war (1944–9) rebuilding of the rapidly expanding cities saw, as in most countries, much shoddy and uninspired concrete building of official and private offices, apartment blocks, and vast numbers of "industrial vernacular" houses. Nevertheless, certain structures, essentially to internationalist patterns, are partic-

just with Zahos, who drew inspiration from Macedonian and Aegean traditional building, but also Pikionis who, with a greater eye for functionalism, came closer to modernism in his Pefkákia School (1933, Athens). Zahos was also in part responsible for the rebuilding of Thessaloníki following the fire of 1917, giving Byzantine overtones to the manner of Hausman in Paris. True modernism was introduced by the Bauhaus-trained Despotopoulos; Mihaïlidis, who worked with Le Corbusier; and Karantinos who

LEFT: War Scene, Theodoros Vryzakis, 1849.
ABOVE: Kamoni, Santoríni, Konstantinos Maleas, 1918–28.

ularly distinguished, especially around Athens: the Mégaro Mousikís (1975); the Athens School of Music (1976); the Museum of Cycladic Art by J. Vikelas (1985) with its serene interior; the solar-powered Mytaras house by Sauvatzidis (1985); the Agios Dimitrios School by Zenetos (1976); and the sculptural E. Benaki Street apartments by Atelier 66 (1972). These and others parallel the best architecture in any modern city. But perhaps one of the most satisfying and relatively modest structures to combine modernist with vernacular elements is Konstantinidis's Hotel Xenia at Mýkonos, 1960. The confidence of the best recent architecture bodes well for the future cultural progression of Greek art as a whole. ❑

FLORA AND FAUNA

As befits its wide variety of habitat, Greece contains a great diversity
of wildlife – including some of Europe's last bears, wolves and jackals

Greece is a land of tremendous ecological diversity, second in Europe, in this respect, only to the Iberian Peninsula. From the temperate forests of the Píndos and Rodópi mountains in the north to the arid semi-desert of eastern Crete; and from the rocky alpine vegetation on the bald upper slopes of mountains like Smólikas and Ólympos to the delta marshlands of Évros or again the dunes of islands such as Rhodes and Límnos. The current mosaic of landscapes and habitats is due to a combination of geography and the hand of man. Sited in the region where Europe butts up against Asia Minor, and only a short hop from Africa, Greece lies at a kind of ecological crossroads.

Since Neolithic times (12,000 to 3,000 BC) man has wrought enormous changes on the landscape, clearing the primeval forests that once covered much of the country for fuel, ship-building, pasture and agriculture.

Typical trees

Somewhat less than a quarter of Greece is now forested, with the largest tracts being in the north of the country, in the Rodópi Mountains and the Píndos ranges. Here you have a range of oak, chestnut, beech and other broadleaf woodlands, with tracts of fir and pine forest that are more related to the Scandinavian north than to the Mediterranean south of Europe. Drive inland, north from Amfípolis in Central Macedonia, and you will pass through three of Europe's major vegetation zones in the space of 150 km (90 miles): Mediterranean, Central European and Northern conifer, typified by trees like birch, Scots pine and Norway spruce.

Pastureland covers some 40 percent of the country, while some 30 percent is cultivated land. Areas where traditional agriculture is still practised are often rich in wildlife but, as elsewhere in Europe, labour-intensive traditional practices are declining. Lands that are unsuited

to modern agriculture are being abandoned to scrub, which means a decline in the diversity of habitat; and where intensive modern agriculture is practised, the use of herbicides, insecticides and fertilisers degrades the land from a wildlife perspective. There are, however, still plenty of mature olive groves which

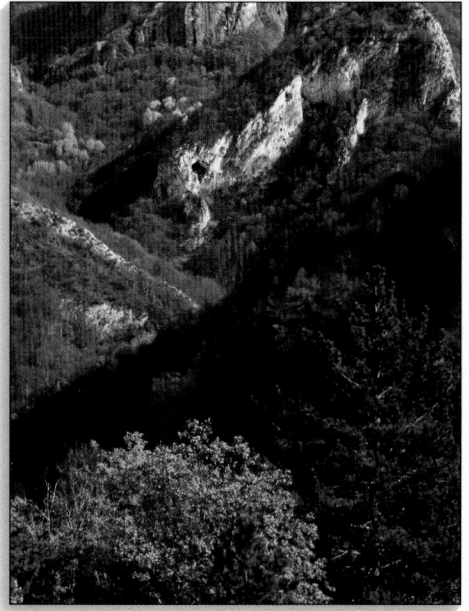

provide a good habitat for birds and insects.

One of Greece's most emblematic habitats is Mediterranean *maquis* – the scrubby, drought-resistant vegetation that covers much of the mainland and islands. This consists of low trees like the glossy-leaved kermes oak (*Quercus coccifera*) and the holm oak (*Quercus suber*), with its thinner, tapering leaves; hardy shrubs like myrtles, arbutus, strawberry tree and bay; and the fragrant underlayer of phrygana – plants like wild rosemary, oregano, lavender and thyme.

On the banks of rivers, you will notice trees like willows, plane trees and poplars; species such as Australian eucalyptus have also been widely introduced. Eucalyptus thrives in the

LEFT: wolves roam the mountains of northern Greece.
RIGHT: Rodópi Mountains, East Macedonia and Thrace, Greece.

dry climate, but ecologists view the species with circumspection or downright hostility due to the amount of water these trees suck out from the soil and the damaging effects that has on the soil's pH value.

Wetlands are one of the most threatened habitats in Greece – three-quarters of the country's original wetlands have been lost, and many others are under extreme pressure, what with the heavy demands for water for agriculture and tourist usage as well as targeted drainage for construction. Nevertheless, Greece still possesses several wetlands of great international importance, including 10 that are

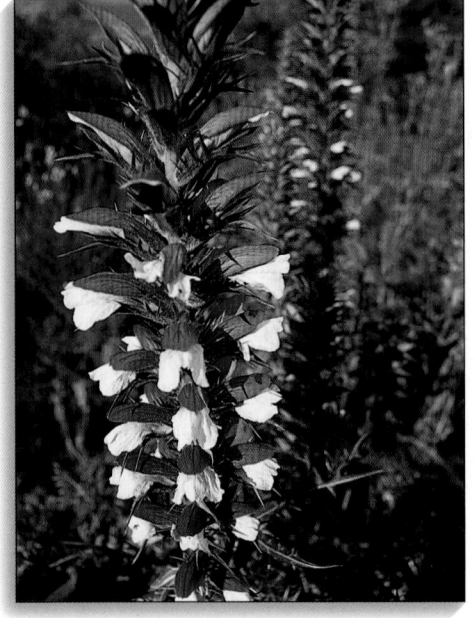

listed as being of international importance under the Ramsar Convention: Pórto Lágos and lakes Vistonís and Ismáris; Néstos Delta; Lake Mikrí Préspa; Mesolóngi lagoons; Amvrakikós Gulf; Vólvi and Korónia lakes; Lake Kerkíni; Aliákmon Delta, Axiós and Loudías; Évros Delta; and the Kotýhi lagoons. These encompass a variety of habitats from river deltas, shallow lagoons, salt-marsh, swamps, reedbeds and lakes.

Elusive mammals

Man's impact on the wildlife of Greece has been as significant as his impact on the land's habitats. The Barbary lions and Anatolian

leopards known to the ancient Greeks are long since gone, hunted to extinction. And many of the most famous species that have survived are scarce and elusive – only the luckiest or most patient visitors will glimpse them in the wild.

In the mountains of northern Greece you can still find areas of real wilderness, and it is here that some of the country's rarest land mammals are to be found. First among these are the continent's most southerly population of European brown bears *(Ursos arctos)*, found in the North Píndos range along the border with Albania and FYROM, and also in the Rodópi Mountains of Eastern Macedonia and Thrace, close to the border with Bulgaria.

The conservation body Arcturos (www. arcturos.gr) – which has an information centre in Actós, near Flórina – sets out to protect both the 150-odd animals that survive and the habitat they live in. Bears have been protected by law since 1969, but still suffer from illegal hunting and habitat destruction.

Arcturos also works to protect Greece's population of wolves *(Canis lupus)* and has a sanctuary at Agrapídia, Flórina prefecture. It is only fairly recently that the wolf has enjoyed protected status – official bounties were paid until 1980 and, until 1991, it was still considered "vermin", which allowed hunting to protect livestock. Although wolves do take sheep from time to time, other ungulates form the preferred diet: mainly red deer *(Cervus elaphus)*, fallow deer *(Dama dama)* and roe deer *(Capreolus capreolus)*.

The wolf is officially listed as "vulnerable": population estimates range from a few hundred to low thousands, mainly in the Rodópi Mountains along the border with Bulgaria, but also along the borders with FYROM and Turkey, the high mountains of central Greece, Kerkíni, Falakró and the Évros region. Wolves died out in the Peloponnese some time between 1940 and 1970, and their survival elsewhere is by no means secure: they are threatened principally by habitat loss through logging, illegal hunting, road kills, hybridisation with dogs, and habitat disturbance through recreational tourism.

Other woodland mammals include the wild boar *(Sus scrofa)* and the common Eurasian badger *(Meles meles)*. Driving at night in northern Greece you may spot a crested porcupine *(Hystrix cristata)*, an animal that may well have been introduced from Africa in ancient times as a food source. However, the most common nocturnal mammals you are likely to see are the country's numerous species of bat. In conifer forests, look out for the red squirrel *(Sciurus vulgaris)* with its bushy tail, white underbelly and ear tufts; and the pine marten *(Martes martes)*, distinguished from its cousin, the beech or stone marten *(Martes foina)*, by its creamy, yellowish throat patch, as compared with the latter's which is pure white. In addition to these two types of martens, you

PYGMY PONY

A type of very small wild horse has lived on the island of Skýros since ancient times. There are fewer than 150 surviving pure-bred members of this unique breed.

sylvestris) – resembling a large grey domestic cat, with black stripes and a bushy tail – which are found in a variety of habitats on the mainland and as part of a small, threatened population on Crete, only confirmed to exist in the late 1990s.

The red fox *(Vulpes vulpes)* is common and widespread, unlike a similar-looking animal more commonly associated with Africa: the golden jackal *(Canis aureus)*. Greece is the northernmost limit of the jackal's range, but populations have col-

might see other members of the mustelid family, including the weasel *(Mustela nivalis)* and the polecat *(Mustela putorius)*.

Otters *(Lutra lutra)* can still be found but are scarce, and your best chance of seeing them is in national parks like Préspa or Víkos-Aóös in Epirus. Similarly elusive are members of the cat family – the endangered lynx *(Lynx lynx)*, with its characteristic ear tufts, which survives in the southern Víkos-Aóös Park; and the much smaller wild cat *(Felix*

lapsed even in the last 20 years. Now only a few hundred remain, mainly in wetlands and *maquis* regions of Fokída, the Peloponnese, Halkidikí and the island of Sámos. The WWF has recently instigated a project to study the country's golden jackal population and draw up an action plan to protect them. Hunting jackals was forbidden in 1990, but they are still persecuted for stealing sheep and chickens, frequently taking the blame for kills by stray dogs. In fact, 50 percent of their diet is vegetarian, and the rest comes from carrion and hunting small animals such as reptiles, frogs, insects, small rodents and the ubiquitous rabbits.

LEFT: a native plant known as "bear's breeches", or acanthus.
ABOVE: brown bears in the Rodópi Mountains.

Other notable mountain mammals include three species of wild sheep: the nimble chamois (*Rupicapra rupicapra*), the European mouflon (*Ovis musimon*) and the Cretan wild goat/ibex (also known as the *agrími* or *krí-krí*; *Capra aegagrus cretica*), with its bearded chin and curved horns, most dramatic on the large males. This latter species, worshipped in antiquity, is now endangered, largely due to hunting. It is mainly found in the Gorge of Samariá national park in Western Crete, but in the 1960s breeding colonies were established on nearby islands like Día and Ágii Pándes in an effort to save it from extinction.

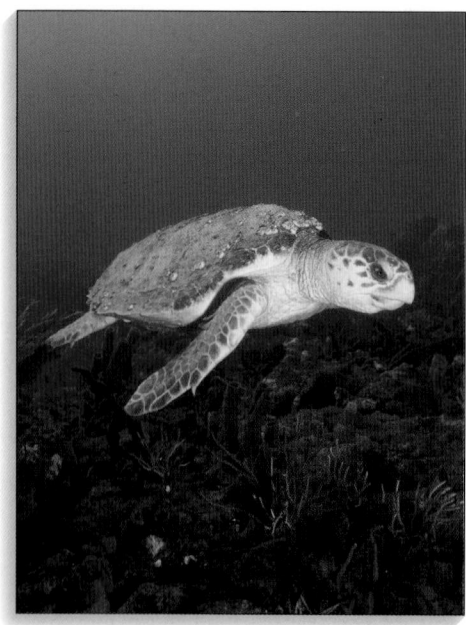

Cold-blooded creatures

Not all of Greece's wildlife is elusive, and nor does tracking it down always demand hours of strenuous exercise. Some species actually visit you, in what you might call the wildlife equivalent of room service. Perhaps the most enchanting of these are the country's many species of geckos – the most keen-sighted of all lizards, whose large eyes are perfect for hunting insects at night or in darkened rooms. Most astonishing is their ability to run up and down vertical surfaces due to the adhesive pads on their feet – an inspiration in the scientific development of adhesives.

Other curious lizards of Greece to look out for include the Mediterranean chameleon (*Chamaeleo chamaeleo*), growing up to 30 cm (1 ft) long, and unmistakeable with its prehensile tail and bulbous eyes; and the large, rough-scaled agama lizard (*Laudakia* or *Agama stellio*), found on Salamína, the Cyclades and islands of the eastern Aegean. The Aegean Islands have a high number of reptilian endemics: six species of lizards and three types of snake are not found anywhere else in Europe.

Greece's snake species include Europe's most venomous, the nose-horned viper (*Vipera ammodytes*), with distinctive zigzags on its back; but most – like the grass snake (*Natrix natrix*) or the fast-moving Dahl's whip snake (*Columber najadum*) – are harmless.

One of Greece's most famous reptiles is the yellowish Hermann's tortoise (*Testudo hermanni*), once heavily exploited for the pet trade, but now protected. It is found in scrubby land in coastal regions of the country; keep an eye out for it when looking around ruins. A more localised cousin found in northern Greece is the spur-thighed tortoise (*Testudo graeca*).

Marine life

Many visitors to Greece will have more opportunity to familiarise themselves with the country's marine wildlife than that which is to be found inland. Greece has more coastline than any other Mediterranean country – some 15,000 km (9,300 miles) of it. The benign temperature of the Aegean and its relatively small tides make it good snorkelling territory. Look out for octopuses, of which there are two types – the common (*Octopus vulgaris*), with double rows of suckers, and the curled (*Eledone cirrosa*), with single rows of suckers – and cuttlefish, sea urchins, starfish, sea cucumbers and anemones. You may also see pipefish (*Sygnathus spp.*) and seahorses (*Hippocampus ramulosus*).

Visit the local harbour and you might see conger eels, ocean fish, parrot fish, dolphin fish and even sharks – both blue (*Prionace glauca*) and mako (*Isurus oxyrinchus*) – among the fishermen's catch. The Mediterranean is heavily overfished, with industrial fleets being particularly to blame; one of the species that bears the brunt of this is the tuna (*Thunnus thynnus*).

Resist the temptation to buy or collect other sea products, such as threatened red coral (*Coralium rubrum*) or bath sponges (*Spongia officinalis*), though the latter are now imported.

Loggerhead turtles

Another vulnerable marine species is the loggerhead turtle *(Caretta caretta)*. Many die each year, entangled and drowned by fishing nets, but the real threat to their continued survival is the status of their ancestral nesting sites. Many of the beaches turtles once chose to nest on in areas such as the Peloponnese and Crete have lost out over the years to tourism developments (the only large nesting sites are on Zákynthos). Natural hazards have always meant that only a tiny proportion of eggs laid make it to full turtlehood: animals like foxes predate on the eggs (which are laid between the end of May

If you are keen on turtle protection, stay away from nesting beaches and think of joining Archelon, the Sea Turtle Protection Society of Greece (Solomoú 57, GR-104 32 Athens, Greece, tel: 00 30-210-523-1342; www.archelon.gr). They have set up protected zones and rescue stations on Crete, the Peloponnese, Kefalloniá, and Zákynthos, though on the latter mismanagement of the National Marine Park and hostility from tourist concerns at Laganás have led to limited success.

Marine mammals

On boat trips, keep your eyes peeled for one of the cetaceans that can be found in Greek waters:

and August), and birds eat hatchlings (which emerge from July to the end of October) as they make their way to the sea. But human disturbance can have an even more devastating effect. Noise and curious tourists can cause adult turtles to abandon nests, and light pollution can disorientate hatchlings, causing them to head inland, where they die, rather than out to sea. Similar problems afflict the green turtle *(Chelonia mydas)*, which can also be found in Greek waters and still breeds in Cyprus too.

LEFT: the endangered loggerhead turtle is a protected species.
ABOVE: Mediterranean monk seals are also protected.

the common dolphin *(Delphinus delphis)*, which is frequently to be seen playing in schools in the bow wave of boats; its larger, darker cousin, the bottlenose dolphin *(Tursiops truncatus)*, which is the type of dolphin most commonly seen in aquariums; the striped dolphin *(Stenella coeruleoalba)*; a long-finned pilot whale *(Globicephala caretta)*; a sperm whale *(Physeter catadon)*; or a fin whale *(Balaenoptera physalus)*.

The monk seal

Perhaps Greece's most important marine mammal, however, is the Mediterranean monk seal *(Monachus monachus)*. This animal, predominantly brown or grey in colour, is unusual among seals because it lives in warm waters. It eats mainly fish, squid and octopus, and can grow to over two metres (6 ft) in length and weigh more than 300 kg (660 lb). In ancient times, monk seals were common – they figured on Greek coins from as far back as 500 BC and featured in the writings of Homer, Plutarch and Aristotle. Now, however, they are one of the most endangered mammals in the world. Only 300 to 500 individuals survive, with Greece, Dalmatia and Morocco having the only significant populations, and it is a battle to save them.

Whereas in ancient Greek times they were trusting, they are now shy of man and are

confined to the most isolated coasts. In Roman times and in the Middle Ages they were hunted heavily for their pelts, meat and oil, but they have also been hard hit in the last hundred years by pollution and a steep decline in fish stocks. Until very recently, they were persecuted by fishermen who viewed them as competition for fish stocks and who resented them for damaging fishing nets. Now one of the reasons for their continued vulnerability is disturbance through tourism – often unwittingly, such as when yachts seek out the type of deserted coves where the caves in which the seals live and breed are located.

One of their last remaining strongholds is the Alónisos National Marine Park in the Northern Sporades, created in 1992, which has a population of about 55 seals. The main society fighting for their protection is the Hellenic Society for the Study and Protection of the Monk Seal (www.mom.gr). It is based in Alónisos, where it runs an exhibition centre in Patitíri and the Seal Treatment and Rehabilitation Centre for sick and orphaned seal pups at Stení Vála. Its work has helped bring about some small encouraging signs: local attitudes towards the animals have shifted, so that they are no longer intentionally killed; and scientists believe that seal birth rates – about eight annually – have stabilised. More information on this fascinating creature and the world's other monk seal species can be found at www.monachus-guardian.org

Birds

Sited on important avian migration routes, Greece is an excellent destination for bird-watchers, especially in spring and autumn, but also in winter, when many northern European birds come to avoid the cold. Enthusiasts should contact the Hellenic Ornithological Society (www.ornithologiki.gr/en/enmain.htm).

One of the best wetland sites in the country is Lake Mikrí Préspa National Park, on a mountainous plateau in western Macedonia, on the borders of Albania and FYROM. Here you can find breeding colonies of both white pelican *(Pelecanus onocrotalus)* and Dalmatian pelicans *(Pelecanus crispus)*, as well as the threatened pygmy cormorant *(Phalacrocorax pygmaeus)*, which also breeds on lakes Kerkíni and Petrón.

Another majorly important site is the Évros Delta, where you can see wetland and pastureland birds like the lesser white-fronted goose *(Anser erythropus)*, the crane *(Grus grus)*, the spoonbill *(Platalea leucorodia)*, the glossy ibis *(Plegadis falcinellus)*, the purple heron *(Ardea purpurea)* and the white stork *(Ciconia ciconia)*. Greater flamingos *(Phoenicopterus ruber)* overwinter on the islands of Kós, Sámos, Lésvos and Límnos. As for seabirds, one of the most important is the Audouin's gull *(Larus audouinii)*, which is endangered and pretty much endemic to the Mediterranean, while great cormorants *(Phalacrocorax carbo)* are widespread in the Sporades and east Aegean.

Short-toed larks *(Calandrella brachydactyla)* and calandra larks *(Melanocorypha calandra)*

are common on open agricultural land. Your eye might also be caught by the vivid hues of the turquoise-coloured roller *(Coracias garrulus)*, not to mention the smaller bee-eater *(Merops apiaster)*, both of which you may see perched on fence or telegraph wires.

The most glamorously coloured birds of all are the golden oriole *(Oriolus oriolus)*, which is frequently found in woodland and orchards; and the kingfisher *(Alcedo atthis)*, found near streams and waterways. In olive groves and open country, watch out for the ground-feeding hoopoe *(Upupa epops)*, with its unmistakeable pinkish head and crest and its

mountainous regions of the country, but, like most birds of prey, they are vulnerable to hunting and bait laced with strychnine, often put down to kill foxes or – illegally – wolves. In Crete you can still find a few lammergeiers *(Gypaetus barbatus)*, a type of vulture that is famous for its habit of dropping bones from a great height to smash them so that it can extract the bone marrow from within. Three other types of vulture are also to be found in Greece – the griffon vulture *(Gyps fulvus)*, the black vulture *(Aegypius monachus)* and the white-and-black Egyptian vulture *(Neophron percnopterus)*. Other major birds of prey include the fish-eating

long curved bill. The *maquis* scrub is excellent territory to find songbirds such as warblers, linnets and buntings.

Birds of prey

The Dadiá Forest in Évros is one of the best places in Europe to see birds of prey, including two highly endangered birds: the imperial eagle *(Aquila heliaca)* and the white-tailed or sea eagle *(Haliaetus albicilla)*. Perhaps as many as 200 pairs of golden eagles exist in remote

---

LEFT: the dramatically-marked hoopoe is often found in olive groves.
ABOVE: a white-tailed sea eagle.

osprey *(Pandion haliaetus)* and numerous types of kites, harriers, hawks, buzzards and falcons.

Perhaps the most famous of Greece's falcons is the Eleonora's falcon *(Falco eleonorae)*. Similar to a peregrine but with a longer tail and more slender wings, it is often seen in groups hunting off coastal cliffs in the Aegean. Over two-thirds of the entire world population of this threatened bird spend their summer months in Greece, hunting insects during spring and early summer, and delaying their breeding season so that they can raise their fledglings on migrant birds heading to Africa in the autumn, before they too head off on their long annual migration to overwinter in Madagascar. ❏

PLACES

*A detailed guide to the entire country, with principal sites
clearly cross-referenced by number to the maps*

As Henry Miller wrote in *The Colossus of Maroussi*, "marvellous things happen to one in Greece – marvellous *good* things which can happen to one nowhere else on earth. Somehow, almost as if He were nodding, Greece still remains under the protection of the Creator. Men may go about their puny, ineffectual bedevilment, even in Greece, but God's magic is still at work and, no matter what the race of men may do or try to do, Greece is still a sacred precinct – and my belief is it will remain so until the end of time."

Another quotation, this time from a dictionary, defines the Greek word "chaos" as "disordered, formless matter said to have existed before the ordered universe." Chaotic is certainly one way of describing the physical geography of a country characterised by heaps of rocks, furrowed mountain ranges and a jagged coastline. Green, fertile areas such as the Thessalian plain are the exception.

The extensive Pindos mountain range in the west forms the country's backbone, while in the east the peaks of Mount Olympos, at nearly 3,000 metres (10,000 ft), are the highest in Greece. The coast is a series of so many coves and inlets that it runs to a length of 15,000 km (9,300 miles). The hundreds of islands that spill out into the seas surrounding Greece are divided into distinct groups: the Ionian islands to the west, the Sporádes to the east, and the Cyclades and Dodecanese trailing out southeast from Athens. The three largest islands are Crete, Lésvos and Évvia, the latter little known outside of Greece.

In this section, our expert writers will take you on 15 individual journeys. Starting with the capital, Athens, we travel from south to northeast through the mainland and then set sail for the many islands, finishing in the "Great Island" of Crete. En route, you will find the history, geography and local culture of each area covered in detail. The opening hours given for sites and museums are for summer only (May–September), unless otherwise stated; different hours usually apply from October to April. Tourist facilities on the islands in particular tend to close abruptly once the summer season has finished – which varies from early September when school starts, to late October.

The chapters have been loosely designed as two-week itineraries, but of course the longer you stay, the better. Perhaps, like Lord Byron, you will one day be able to declare: "It is the only place I ever was contented in." ❏

PRECEDING PAGES: Metéora; Ía on Santoríni; the view over Athens from the Acropolis.
LEFT: Fiskárdo harbour, Kefalloniá.

Greece

0 — 50 km
0 — 50 miles

ITALY

Brindisi

Lecce

Durrës
Tiranë
Cermenica
Elbasan
Ohridsko Izero
Partizanit 2417
Berat
Vlorë
ALBANIA
Prespansko Izero
Bitola
Florina
Kastoria
Vernon Óros
Vóira Pindos
Zagori
Tymfi 2204
Kérkyra (Corfu)
Kérkyra
Igoúmenítsa
Páramos
Ioánnina
Árachthos
Notía Pindos
Aóos
Kozáni
Grevená
Elasóna
Kalabáka
P1niós
Lárisa
Tríkala
Kardítsa
Fársala

MACEDONIA

Mavrovoůń 1179
Nidze
Édessa
Langa
Véria
Aliákmonas
Katerini
Óros 2917▲
Ólympos
Thermeïkós Kólpos
Kassán
GREECE
Vólos
Pílio Óros
Skí
Sí

Páxí (Paxos)
Antípaxi

Párga
Árta
Prevéza
Tehnítí Límni Kremastón
Tymfristós ▲2315

IONIAN

SEA

Levkáda
Levkáda (Lévkas)
Eláti 1158
Meganísi
Astakós
Itháki
Argostóli
Kefalloniá (Cephallonia)
Póros
Zákynthos (Zante)
Zákynthos
Kerí
Kylini
Pýrgos

Agrínio
Návpaktos

Lamía
Ág. Konstandíno
Óri Vardoúsia
Ámfissa
Livadiá
Palovoúna 1748
Pátra
Korinthiakós Kólpos
2224
Peloponnisos
(Peloponnese)
Tripoli
Taýgetos
Kalamáta

Kórinthos
Pire
Salam
Argos
Návplio
Argolikós Kólpos
Leonídion
Spárti
Spêtses
Argo-Sa
Gýthio
Lakonikós Kólpos
Neápoli
Kýthira
Andíký

Ka
Kissá

MACEDONIA   **BULGARIA**   **TURKEY**
Dhrama
Xanthi Rodhopi
Kilkis Serres Kavala
Pela
ALBANIA Florina
Kastoria Imathia Thessaloniki
Kozani Pieria Halkidhiki Óros
Grevena Ágio
Ioannina Larisa
Kérkyra Thes-protia Trikala Magnisía Lésvos
Preveza Arta Kardhitsa Évri
tania Fthiotida
Etolia
Lefkáda Akarnania Fokidha Évia
Kefallonía Viotia
Ahaïa Korinthia Atiki
Ilia Pireas Híos
Zákynthos Arkadía Sámos
Argolida
Messinía Kykládes
Lakonía
Dodekánisa
Haniá
Réthymno Iráklio
Lasithi
GREECE   **TURKEY**

BULGARIA
Kărdžàli
Edirne
BLACK SEA

ràma
Xánthi
Komotiní
TURKEY
İstanbul

avála
Keşan
Marmara Denizi

onikós
pos
Alexandroúpoli
Liménas
Thásos

Áthos
Kavakköy

Sithonía
Samothráki
Fengári
1611
Thermá
(Loutrá)
Bandırma
Bursa

Thrakikón Pélagos
Çanakkale

Gökçeada

Gioúra
Mýrina
Límnos
Balıkesir

Pipéri
Ágios
Evstrátios
Ayvaçık
Edremit

Sporádes
Skýros
Skyros
Lésvos
Mytilíni
TURKEY

ea)
Paralía Kýmis
Psará
Akhisar

a)
ns)
Ándros
Ándros
Híos
Híos
Pyrgí
Úrla
İzmir

AEGEAN SEA

Kéa
Tínos
Ikaría
Sámos
Vathý
(Sámos)
Aydın
Denizli

Giáros
Tínos
Karlóvassi
Foúrni
Ág.
Kírykos
Agathónísi

Kýthnos
Ermoúpoli
Sýros
Mýkonos
Arkí
Lipsí
Milâs
Muğla

Cyclades
Páros
Náxos
Náxos
Pátmos
Léros
Bodrum

Sérifos
Kálymnos

Sífnos
Andíparos
Amorgós
Kós
Kós
Fethiye

Kímolos
Síkinos
Íos
Kéfalos

Mílos
Folégandros
Astypálea
Nísyros
Symi
Ródos
Kaş

Thíra
(Santoríni)
Anáfi
Sýrna
Tílos
Mt Atávyros
1215
Megísti
(Kastellórizo)

Hálki
Dodecanese

Kritikó Pélagos
Ródos
(Rhodes)

Kárpathos

Réthymno
(Rethimno)
Kríti (Crete)
Kásos

Ida
(Psiloritis)
2456
Iráklio
(Heráklion)
Ágios
Nikólaos
Sitía

Gávdos

THE MAINLAND

The mainland of Greece contains a wealth of historical monuments, in landscapes that are often breathtaking

Many visitors to Greece head straight for the islands – of which there are of course dozens to choose from, offering everything from sybaritic nightlife to serene tranquillity, from historical marvels to stunning natural beauty. Naturally, this book explores Greece's offshore assets in great detail later on (*see page 215*). But to bypass the Greek mainland is to overlook the heart of the country, to miss its range of dramatic scenery, and to neglect some spectacular ruins recalling the grandeur of ancient civilisations.

The six chapters that follow explore this rich and varied land, starting in Athens, birthplace of democracy and home to the most impressive remains from the Classical period to be found anywhere. Relics of ancient civilisations can in fact be seen throughout the mainland – the ancient strongholds of Mycenae and Tiryns, predating the Trojan War; the holy site of Delphi, regarded by the ancients as the centre of the world; the stadium and temples of Olympia, where the Olympic Games began; and wonderfully preserved theatres at Epidauros, Argos, Dodona and elsewhere.

Monuments from the Byzantine period include elegant churches and monasteries decorated with glorious mosaics. Thessaloníki, the second city of the Byzantine Empire, has a rich heritage of these stylish churches, and the monasteries of Dafní and Ósios Loukás are world famous for their art treasures. Venetian and Frankish occupation enriched Greece's coastline with picturesque castles and walled cities such as Monemvasía and Koróni. Throughout the country, archeological museums are treasure-houses of beautiful and intriguing relics of Greece's complex past.

But the Greek mainland is not just about history: its timeless landscapes are often breathtaking. The rugged mountain ranges of central and southern Greece descend through craggy ridges to sea-girt peninsulas and promontories. Deep gulfs and inlets penetrate the land, bounded by mountains cradling tiny harbours and fishing villages, or bordered by pine slopes. While elsewhere, the narrow coastal plain meets the sea in a fretwork of bays, some of them inaccessible overland. ❑

LEFT: the roofs of Monemvasía, Peloponnese.

Athens

0 ____ 200 m
0 ____ 200 yds

Lykavitós

Theatre of Lykavitós

Lykavitós

Ág. Geórgios (St George's Church)

HOIDA

DORAS DISTRIA

Gennadios Library

Kolonáki

PL. MEGALISTOU GENOUS SCHOLIS

Hymettus (Ymettós), Moni Kaisariani; Megaro Moustikis

Numismatic Museum

Benáki Museum

Goulandris Museum of Cycladic Art

PL. PAVLOU (VASILISIS SOFIAS)

Agios Geórgios

Nat'l Gallery & Alexandros Soutzos Mus.

PL. MADRITIS

LEOF. EL. VENIZELOU (VASILISIS SOFIAS)

SYNTAGMA

Parliament (Old Palace)

PL. P. MELA (RIGILLIS)

War Museum

EVANGELISMOS

LEOF. MIHALAKOPOULOU

Byzantine & Christian Museum

NATIONAL GARDENS

Presidential Palace

Záppio (Exhibition Hall)

PL. SKOUZE

VASIL. GEORGIOU II.

Ethnikós (Athletics Field)

1896 Olympic Stadium

ERATOSTHENOUS

EFTYHIDOU

PL. MESOLOGHIOU

EFTYHIDHOU

Sounion ↓

ATHENS

*Both East and West converge in this vibrant metropolis, lively
and brimming over, just like its inhabitants. The city is also home
to some of the country's most important historical sites*

I f there is one quality for which Athens (Athína in Greek) should be credited,
it is elasticity. Throughout its long history the city has been obscure, triumphant, forgotten and, now, the capital of the modern Greek state. Athens
is barely mentioned in Homer. It emerged as a growing power in the 6th century
BC. Then came the Periclean "golden age", when Athens became a great centre
of art and literature, commerce and industry. With Macedonian expansion came
the first shrinkage, though Athens remained a prestigious intellectual centre
with particular emphasis on philosophy and oratory.

In the Hellenistic age, Athens was overshadowed by the great monarchies
founded by Alexander's successors – but not obliterated. The rulers of Egypt,
Syria and Pergamum courted the old city with gifts of buildings and works of
art. Yet it was already beginning to rest on its laurels, to turn into a museum-city,
a "cultural commodity" rather than an active, living organism. Besieged and
sacked by Sulla in 86 BC, restored and pampered under two philathenian Roman
emperors, Augustus and Hadrian, sacked again by the Herulians in AD 267 and
Alaric the Goth in AD 395, Athens entered the Byzantine era shorn of all its
glory – a small provincial town, a mere backwater. The edict of the Byzantine
emperor Justinian forbidding the study of philosophy there (AD 529) dealt a
death-blow to the ancient city.

LEFT: *Évzone*
guards outside the
Parliament.
BELOW: a café in
Syndagma Square.

A sudden elevation

Under Latin rule (1204–1456), invaded, occupied and
fought over by the French, Catalans, Florentines and
Venetians, Athens shrank even further. It was only
after the Ottoman conquest in the 15th century that it
began to expand again, but still falling far short of its
ancient limits. There were more setbacks, including a
devastating Venetian incursion in 1687. Athens finally rose from its ruins after the War of Independence,
an "exhausted city", as Christopher Wordsworth noted
in 1832, and was suddenly raised, unprepared, to the
status of capital of the new Greek state.

Athens is thus a city that has grown haphazardly,
and too fast. It never had a chance to mellow into venerable old age. Old and new have not blended too
well; you can still sense the small prewar city pushing
through the huge sprawl of today's modern capital,
like the proverbial thin man struggling to get out of
every fat man. Occasionally, you come across what
must have been a country villa, ensconced between
tall office buildings, its owner still fighting against
the tide, its windows hermetically closed against dust,
pollution, the roar of the traffic.

Traffic in Athens can be unbelievable, particularly
when there is some protest demonstration going on
and traffic is forced off the main streets. The section

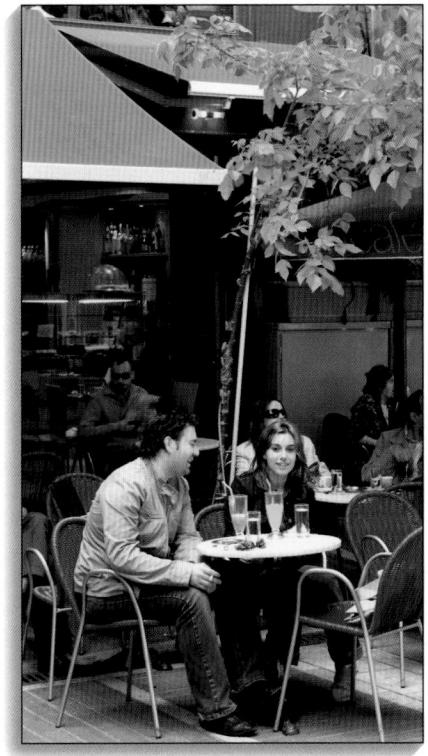

of the metro inaugurated in 2000, however, has worked wonders. From the day it opened, huge numbers of Athenians have been using it, making journeys of just a few minutes through the heart of the city that once took well over an hour by car. Suddenly, central Athens has become accessible.

In addition, branching off from the frenzied central arteries are the minor veins of the city, relatively free from congestion. Most apartment blocks have balconies and verandas, and there you can see the Athenians in summer emerging from their afternoon siesta in underpants and nighties, reading the paper, watching the neighbours, watering their plants, eating their evening meal.

The previously traffic-clogged road of Dionysíou Areopagítou around the base of the Acropolis has been pedestrianised, part of a plan to link the ancient sites with a car-free promenade. It quickly established itself as a popular place for the evening vólta, or stroll.

Ancient Athens

Seen from the right angle driving east on the **Ierá Odós** (the Sacred Way) or looking up at its rocky bulk from high in Pláka, the **Acropolis** Ⓐ still has a presence that makes the grimy concrete of modern Athens fade into insignificance. Climb up in early morning in summer or early afternoon in winter, when the crowds are thinnest, and a strip of blue sea edged with grey hills marks the horizon. On a wet or windy day, walking across its uneven limestone surface feels like being on a ship's deck in a gale (daily Apr–Sept 8am–7pm, Oct–Mar 8am–4.30pm; the ticket for the Acropolis is also valid for the Ancient Greek Agora, *page 131*, the Theatre of Dionysos, *page 131*, the Roman Agora, *page 133*, the Keramikós Cemetery, *page 131–2*, and the Temple of Olympian Zeus, *page 133*).

The Acropolis nowadays looks like a stonemason's workshop, much as it must have done in the 440s BC when the **Parthenon** was under construction as the crowning glory of Pericles' giant public works programme. Some of his

Acropolis

0   100 m
0   100 yds

Erechtheion

Propylaia

Beule Gate

Temple of Athena Nike

Sanctuary of Artemis

Halkotheke

Temple of Rome and Augustus

Parthenon

N

Theatre of Herod Atticus

Asklepieion

Stoa of Eumenes

Odeon of Pericles

Theatre of Dionysos

DION. AREOPAGITOU

PROPYLEON

ERECHTHEIOU

Roman Bath

DION. AREOPAGITOU

New Acropolis Museum

contemporaries thought it extravagant: Pericles was accused of dressing his city up like a harlot. In fact, the Parthenon celebrates Athena as a virgin goddess and the city's protector. Her statue, 11 metres (37 ft) tall and constructed of ivory and gold plate to Pheidias's design, once gleamed in its dim interior; in late antiquity it was taken to Constantinople, where it disappeared.

Conservators have taken down hundreds of blocks of marble masonry from the Parthenon to replace the rusting iron clamps inserted in the 1920s with noncorrosive titanium (rust made the clamps expand, cracking the stone, while acid rain turned carved marble surfaces into soft plaster). The restorers also succeeded in identifying and collecting about 1,600 chunks of Parthenon marble scattered over the hilltop, many blown off in the 1687 explosion caused by a Venetian mortar igniting Ottoman munitions stored inside the temple. When they are replaced, about 15 percent more building will be on view. New blocks cut from near the ancient quarries on Mount Pendéli (14 km/9 miles north of Athens), which supplied the 5th-century BC constructors, will fill the gaps.

The **Erechtheion**, an elegant architecturally complex repository of ancient cults going back to the Bronze Age, is already restored. The Caryatids now supporting a porch over the tomb of King Kekrops, a mythical founder of the ancient Athenian royal family, are modern copies. The surviving originals were moved to the Acropolis Museum to prevent further damage from the *néfos*, the ochre blanket of pollution, now thankfully less frequent, that hangs over Athens.

Completed in 395 BC, a generation later than the Parthenon, the Erechtheion also housed an early wooden statue of Athena, along with the legendary olive tree that she conjured out of the rock to defeat Poseidon the sea god in their contest for sovereignty over Attica.

Map, pages 124–5

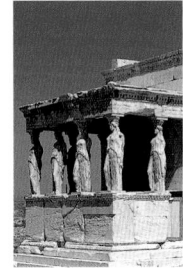

In Ottoman times the Turkish military commander housed his harem in the Erechtheion.

BELOW:
recording the Parthenon remains.

THE PARTHENON FRIEZE

The Parthenon Marbles are a 76-sq-m (500-sq-ft) stretch of sculpted figures – mostly from the frieze – carved under the direction of the master-sculptor and architect Pheidias. By 1799, when Lord Elgin was appointed British ambassador to Turkish-occupied Greece, the Parthenon was in a sorry state, having been practically destroyed and then plundered by the invading Venetians in 1687. Elgin negotiated a permit from the sultan to remove "some blocks of stone with inscriptions and figures", shipped the marbles back to Britain, and in 1816 sold them to the British Museum, where they remain today.

The marbles are an integral part of one of the most beautiful buildings that still survives from antiquity, say the Greeks, and can be better appreciated in the city that made them. Key to the building of the **New Acropolis Museum** *(see page 130)* has been the aim to reunite the surviving sculptures that once adorned the Parthenon: with its controlled environment, there were hopes that the museum would overcome what had ostensibly been the main objection to the return of the marbles, namely Athens' lack of a suitable location in which to display them. So far however, the world's major museums claim that to return the marbles would set a disastrous precedent.

Sculpture in the Stoa of Attilus, in the Ancient Greek Agora.

BELOW: the impressive New Acropolis museum.

The **Propylaia**, the battered official entrance to the Acropolis built by Mnesikles in the 430s BC, was cleverly designed with imposing outside columns to awe people coming up the hill. Parts of its coffered stone ceiling, once painted and gilded, are still visible as you walk through. Currently dismantled, the exquisite square temple of **Athena Nike** (finished in 421 BC) stood on what was once the citadel's southern bastion. It supposedly occupied one of the spots – the other is at Cape Sounion – where Theseus's father, King Aegeus, is said to have thrown himself to his death on seeing a black-sailed ship approaching the harbour. Theseus had promised to hoist a white sail for the return voyage if he had succeeded in killing the Minotaur on Crete, but carelessly forgot.

The sculptures that Lord Elgin left behind are in the **New Acropolis Museum** Ⓑ, below the Parthenon and close by Akrópoli metro station (until the museum's full opening, the ground floor can be visited daily 10am–noon; www.newacropolismuseum.gr). In construction from 2004 to 2007 but only fully open to the public from late 2008/early 2009, the New Acropolis Museum is the result of a competition (the fourth such, others proving abortive) won by New York-based Swiss architect Bernard Tschumi. From outside, the concrete-and-glass building, with its retro, mid-20th-century feel, is starkly antipathetic. It doesn't help that because of it, two neighbouring buildings, on Dionysíou Areopagítou, were formerly listed but are now threatened with demolition (no. 17, of 1930s vintage, has been hailed as Athens' best surviving example of Art Deco).

Once inside however, the building works much better, its main concern revealed as the harnessing of natural light for the optimum presentation of sculptural objects (a different proposition from the kind of light called into play when displaying paintings or drawings). From the entry on Dionysíou Arepagítou, a glass walkway leads over recently excavated sections of ancient Athens, including dwellings, wells, water and sewage works, an olive press, and even a classical symposium hall with mosaic flooring. The excavations extend well under the museum which hovers above, supported by 100 massive anti-seismic columns, and muted natural light filters through the glass panels that make up much of the flooring.

The lowest gallery houses finds from the Acropolis slopes. Leading to the upper levels is a ramp, simulating the approach to the Acropolis and watched over by the six scarred but still impressively female Caryatids (one of them a copy, as the sixth is kept by the British Museum in London). On the first floor, the Archaic exhibition features the famous "Calf-bearer" or Moschophoros, and various coquettish *korai* revealing a pre-classical ideal of beauty – look closely and you can make out their make-up, earrings and the patterns of their crinkled, close-fitting dresses. Then up to the top floor and the pièce de résistance: a glass gallery holding a reconstruction of the Parthenon pediments, of the same size and compass orientation as the real Parthenon looming just outside the wrap-around windows. The friezes, including the triangular western aetoma, are mounted at eye level – unlike the originals which sat overshadowed by the eaves so that the ancient Athenians couldn't really appreciate them. The authentic fragments which Greece retains have been mounted; everything else is a plaster cast, pointedly awaiting the return of the prototypes, the so-called Elgin Marbles, from the British Museum.

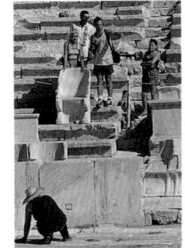

The Theatre of Dionysos had 64 tiers of seats and held 17,000.

Just to the north of the Acropolis is the **Ancient Greek Agora** (open daily summer 8am–7.15pm, winter 8.30am–3pm; entrance fee included in Acropolis entrance fee). The main entrance to this site is on Adrianoú Street, but there is an alternative way in behind the Church of the Holy Apostles. While the Acropolis was mainly a religious site, the Agora was used for all public purposes: commercial, religious, political, civic, educational, theatrical, athletic. Today it looks like a cluttered field of ruins. The reconstructed **Stoa of Attalos**, a 2nd-century BC line of shops, contains a wonderful, small archeological museum (open Tues–Sun 8am–7pm, Mon 11am–7pm, upper floor Mon–Fri 9am–2.30pm; entrance fee included in site fee). The **Hephaesteion** (also known as the "Theseion"), the temple opposite, is the most complete surviving Doric order temple and gives some idea of what the Parthenon looked like.

BELOW: monument to Lysicrates.

Across from the Agora, on the far side of the Piraeus metro line, one corner of the **Painted Stoa** has been exposed in Adrianoú Street. This building gave its name to Stoicism, the stiff-upper-lip brand of philosophy that Zeno the Cypriot taught there in the 3rd century BC.

On the south side of the Acropolis lies the **Theatre of Dionysos **. The marble seating tiers date from around 320 BC and later, but scholars generally agree that plays by playwrights such as Aeschylus, Sophocles, Euripides and Aristophanes were first staged here at religious festivals during the 5th century BC. A state subsidy for theatre-goers meant that every Athenian citizen could take time off to attend (entrance on Leofóros Dionysíou Areopagítou; open daily summer 8am–7.30pm, winter 8.30am–3pm; entrance fee included in Acropolis entrance fee).

Past Monastiráki, the **Keramikós Cemetery** in the potters' district of the city was a burial place for prominent ancient Athenians. An extraordinary variety of sculptured monuments – tall stone urns, a prancing bull, winged sphinxes and melancholy scenes of farewell – overlooked the paved Sacred Way leading to the Dipylon Gate from Eleusis, where the mysteries were held. The site museum's collection of grave goods is an excellent guide to Greek vase-painting, from a squat geometric urn with a rusting iron sword twisted around its neck to the white *lekythoi* of classical Athens and self-consciously sophisticated Hellenistic pottery (open daily summer 8am–7.30pm, winter 8.30am–3pm; entrance fee included in Acropolis entrance fee). Also in the area, on the corner of Agíon Asomáton and Dipýlou Streets, the Benaki Museum's **Islamic Art Collection** ranks among the best in the world. More than 8,000 works of art chart the evolution of Islamic art and civilization up to the 19th century. The superb displays include a 16th-century velvet saddle from Bursa and the marble-faced interior of a 17th-century Cairo reception room (open Thur–Sun & Tues 9am–3pm, Wed 9am–9pm; entrance free every Thur or daily for concessions).

At the southern end of Pláka, on Platía Lysikrátous, is the **Choregic Monument to Lysikratos**. This is important as it is the earliest example of the use of external Corinthian columns (the latest and most ornate order of ancient Greek architecture). The inscription commemorates the victory of Lysikratos in 334 BC in a drama contest; the elegant monument was originally crowned by a tripod.

Roman Athens

A few Roman monuments recall a time when Athens was a city to be revered, but stripped of its movable artworks. The 2nd-century **Emperor Hadrian**, a fervent admirer of classical Greek culture, erected an ornate **arch ❸** marking the spot

The komboli – a small chain of stone or wooden "worry-beads" – is good for relieving tension.

BELOW: preparing for the festival in the Herod Atticus Theatre.

where the classical city ended and the provincial Roman university town began. On the side facing the Acropolis is the inscription "This is Athens, the ancient city of Theseus", on the side facing the Olympieion it reads "This is the city of Hadrian and not of Theseus". Little of this Roman city can be seen beneath the green of the **Záppio Park** and the archeological area behind the towering columns of the **Temple of Olympian Zeus** (Stilés Olympíou Diós), but recent excavations in the corner of the Záppio indicate that Roman buildings in this area, including public baths, extended at least to the stadium built by Herod Atticus. Work on the Temple of Olympian Zeus had been abandoned in around 520 BC when funds ran out, but Hadrian finished the construction and dedicated the temple to himself (open daily summer 8am–7.30pm, winter 8.30am–3pm; entrance fee).

Later in the century, Herod Atticus, a wealthy Greek landowner who served in the Roman senate, built the steeply raked theatre on the south slope of the Acropolis (the **Herod Atticus Theatre** ❻, now used for Athens Festival performances) as a memorial to his wife. And a 1st-century BC Syrian was responsible for the picturesque **Tower of the Winds** ❼, in the **Roman Agora**, a well-preserved marble octagon overlooking the scanty remains of the Roman Agora. It is decorated with eight relief figures, each depicting a different wind direction, and once contained a water-clock (open daily 8am–7pm; entrance fee). Later it served as a *tekke* (ceremonial hall) for the Ottoman dervishes.

Pláka

Pláka ❽, the old quarter clustering at the foot of the Acropolis, has been refurbished and restored to its former condition (or rather to a fairly good reproduction of it), the more garish establishments have been closed down, cars

Map, pages 124–5

Pláka is full of tourist souvenirs.

BELOW: the Tower of the Winds.

prohibited (for the most part), houses repainted and streets tidied up. It has become a delightful, sheltered place to meander in; you might almost imagine yourself in a village, particularly in the winding narrow streets of the Anafiótika district that nestles below the Acropolis.

Pláka is also the best place to track down Athens' Ottoman past. The 15th-century **Fethiye Mosque** in the Roman Agora is one of the finest, and oldest, examples of Muslim architecture in the city; it is unfortunately closed to visitors. However, nearby on Platía Monastiráki is the Tsizdaráki Mosque (1759), now home to the **Kyriazopoulos Collection of Pottery** (open Wed–Mon 9am–2.30pm; entrance fee). The mosque's interior has been sensitively conserved and is well worth a look, especially the brightly painted *mihrab*. Perhaps the most fascinating remnant of Turkish life, however, is the 16th-century **Abdi Efendi Hamam** on Kyrrístou (Wed–Mon 9am–2.30pm; entrance fee). This *hamam* (Turkish bath) has been beautifully restored and its warren of rooms is very atmospheric to explore. A well-produced guide gives background on the building and the place of bathing in Greek and Turkish culture.

As well as those mentioned above, Pláka has a number of other excellent museums. Chief among these is the **Museum of Greek Folk Art** on Kydathinéon (open Tues–Sun 10am–2pm; entrance fee). Among the many exhibits is a superlative collection of regional Greek costume, including carnival costumes from the *dodekámero* (12 days of Christmas) and the faintly disturbing *géros* disguise from Skýros. Among the silverwork look for the *támata* (votive offerings) still seen attached to icons in Orthodox churches.

Opposite is the **Children's Museum** (open Tues–Fri 10am–2pm, Sat–Sun 10am–3pm; entrance fee). Geared towards play, this is a good place to visit for people with young children. There is plenty to build, paint and deconstruct; in an inspired piece of foresight, overalls are provided. At the end of Kydathinéon, on Níkis (No. 39), is the **Jewish Museum of Greece** (open Mon–Fri 9am–2.30pm, Sun 10am–2pm; entrance fee; www.jewishmuseum.gr). After you have rung the doorbell to be admitted you find yourself in a cool, modern interior (based on a spiral) full of exemplary displays. The museum is particularly effective in demonstrating the long history of Jewish settlement, and tolerance towards it, in this part of the world.

The **Paul and Alexandra Kanellopoulos Archeological and Byzantine Museum** (open Tues–Sun 8.30am–3pm, Wed until 11pm; closed for works) is housed in a 19th-century mansion in Anafiótika. It is a smaller treasure-trove of objects from many periods of Greek art, acquired by erudite, obsessive collectors. Also in Pláka and housed in a neoclassical mansion, is the excellent **Museum of Popular Instruments– Research Centre for Ethnomusicology** (open Tues, Thur–Sun 10am–2pm, Wed noon–6pm; free), based around the collection of Fivos Anoyanakis. The museum divides the exhibits into aerophones (blown instruments, such as the *flogéra* or reed flute), chordophones (stringed instruments, like the *bouzoúki*), idiophones (instruments where the sound is produced by its body, like cymbals) and membranophones

The history of Greek Jewry, celebrated in the Jewish Museum of Greece (right), stretches back unbroken to before the 3rd century BC, but 87 percent of local Jews were wiped out in World War II. Today only about 5,000 Jews live in the country.

BELOW: busy Pláka.

("drums"); each can be heard at the adjacent listening posts. There is also a good shop where you can find rare recordings of Greek traditional music.

Monastiráki

This entire area, essentially Athens' bazaar, is a huge sprawl of shops, which get more upmarket towards Platía Syndágmatos. **Monastiráki ❶** brings to mind the market described in a 4th-century BC comedy by Euboulos: "Everything will be for sale together in the same place at Athens, figs, summoners, bunches of grapes, turnips, pears, apples, witnesses, roses, medlars, honeycombs, chickpeas, lawsuits, beestings-puddings, myrtle-berries, allotment machines, irises, lambs, waterclocks, laws, indictments." Kitsch-collectors will find much to interest them: Greek kitsch is debatedly the most orgiastically hideous in the world. Monastiráki Square, by the metro station, is now in the throes of a thorough overhaul to make it less tatty and more inviting.

Retaining a traditional pattern, the whole area still falls into rough zones, as can be seen from the shops around the **Mitrópolis** (Athens' cathedral), specialising in ecclesiastical articles. The cathedral itself dates from the mid-19th century and is large if undistinguished. However, next door is the small **"old cathedral"** (formally known as Panagía Gorgoepikoös or Ágios Eleftheríos). This church dates from the 12th century but is a hotchpotch of materials reused from earlier churches of the 6th to 7th centuries. Above the door arch is a 2nd-century relief showing the calendar of Attic festivals.

Away from the robust vulgarity of **Pandrósou Street** to the narrow side streets off the **Flea Market**, you step back in time into an almost pre-industrial era. This is the district of traditional crafts (crafts minus "arts"), wholesale

Map, pages 124–5

Guarding the Mitrópolis

BELOW: Abdi Efendi Baths, Pláka.

shops selling refreshingly nondecorative, down-to-earth stuff like screws, chains of varying thickness, nails, boxes and crates, brushes and brooms, mousetraps and herbs (the mountains of Greece are a botanist's paradise), resin in big amber-coloured chunks alongside incense and bright blue chunks of copper sulphate used for plants (and catching octopus) – truly a serendipitous accumulation.

As are the goods in the old **Varvákio ❶**, a 19th-century gem roughly halfway between Monastiráki and Omónia squares on the east side of Athinás Street (you can also enter far more dramatically from the passageway at 80 Eólou Street). This is the city's main covered meat and fish market, where shoppers mill between open stands displaying fish, seafood and any type and part of animal you can imagine. Fruit and vegetables are available in the far less successful open area directly across Athinás Street to the west, but the milling scene there is just as vibrant.

Omónia to Sýndagma

The city's heart lies within an almost equilateral triangle defined by **Platía Omónias ❷** in the north, Monastiráki in the south and **Platía Syndágmatos ❸** to the southeast. Except for three small cross streets, no cars are permitted in this area, which means it has taken on a new lease of life.

North of Omónia (close to Viktória metro station) and crammed with treasures from every period of antiquity is the **National Archeological Museum ❹**. Some years ago, its redesigned Egyptian galleries were unveiled – modern, light and displayed in an exemplary manner – boding well for the integral renovation of one of the city's most important sights. Work was recently completed and the restructured museum has reopened its doors (open Mon 12.30–5pm,

Relief in the National Archeological Museum.

RIGHT: the neoclassical front of the National Library.
BELOW: the National Archeological Museum.

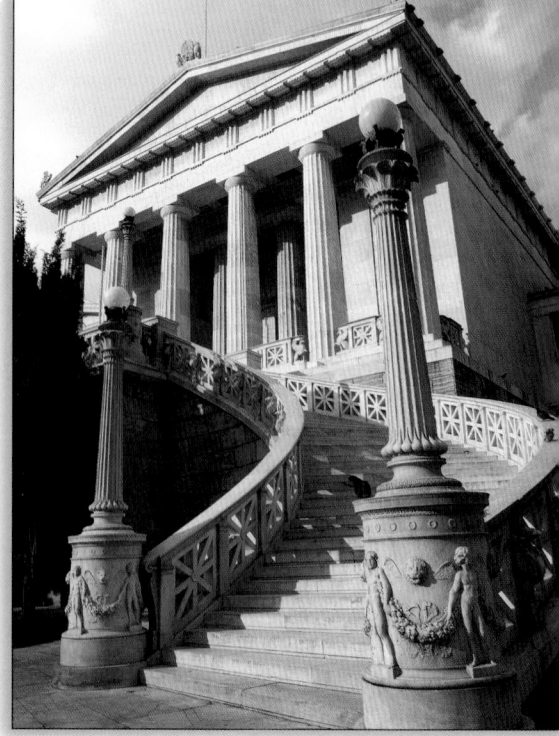

Tues–Fri 8am–5pm, Sat–Sun 8.30am–3pm; entrance fee; *see also pages 144–5.*)

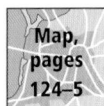
Map, pages 124–5

Omónia itself went in for a facelift at the millennium. However, it is still traffic-plagued and the rather bleak concrete piazza that now covers the centre of the busy square has been widely criticised; at best it can be said to be unimaginative. The parallel streets of Stadíou and E. Venizélou (also known as Panepistimíou) run southeast from Omónia to Platía Syndágmatos. Halfway down Venizélou is Christian and Theophilus Hansen's neoclassical trilogy of the **National Library**, **University** and **Academy**. Erected between 1839 and 1891, they are built of Pentelic marble and draw heavily on Ancient Greek architectural forms. The startlingly bright painting and gilding gives some idea of how the now-stark marble of ancient monuments may have first appeared. Behind the university is the small **Hellenic Theatre Museum** (open Mon–Fri 9am–2pm), which has a charming series of re-created changing rooms of famous Greek actors, including Maria Callas.

Further on is the house of Heinrich Schliemann, designed in an Italianate style by Ziller (1878). It now houses the **Numismatic Museum** (open Tues–Sun 8.30am–3pm; entrance fee). Of greater interest is the **National Historical Museum** which occupies the prominent Old Parliament Building on Stadíou (open Tues–Sun 9am–2pm; entrance fee). This recounts the history of Greece from the fall of Constantinople (İstanbul) in 1453 to World War II.

Sýndagma Square (Platía Syndágmatos, or Constitution Square) is the centre of the city. Dominated by the **Parliament Building**, it has been pleasantly landscaped following the metro works. The Parliament meets in what was the old Royal Palace, built in 1836–42 for King Otto. The changing of the *Évzone* Guard, a favourite tourist spectacle, takes place in front of the Parliament.

Ermoú, running west from the square, was once a traffic-clogged mess, but is now a long pedestrian walkway with reinvigorated shops, enlivened by pavement buskers and pushcarts. Many buildings have been refurbished, while improved lighting makes this an attractive area to wander in the evening in search of a bar or café. Also on Ermoú is the attractive Byzantine church of **Kapnikaréa**, thought to date from the 11th century.

The **National Gardens** Ⓝ (open sunrise to sunset; free) are just behind the parliament building. Full of tangled bowers, romantic arbours and quiet fishponds, there are thin but constant trickles of water running along secret leafy troughs, ducks and a large population of cats. It was laid out by Queen Amalia as the palace gardens in the 19th century. She used the new Greek navy to bring back botanical specimens from their voyages around the world. Here you can observe the Athenians at rest; lovers meet, old men meditate and businessmen hastily wolf down sandwiches or sip drinks at the two cafés.

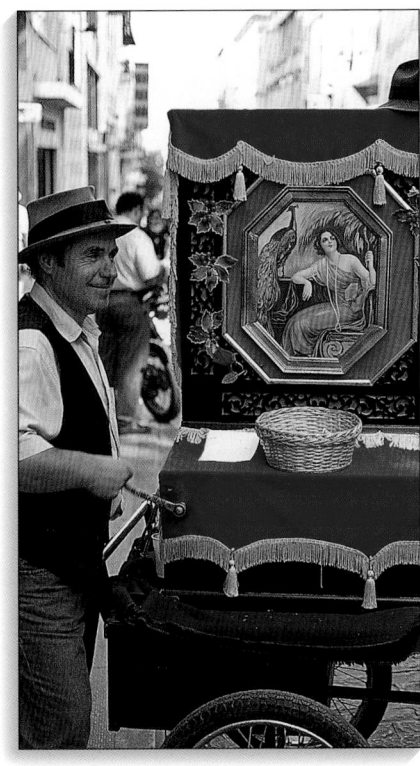

BELOW: an organ-grinder on Ermoú.

Kolonáki

Chic and expensive, Kolonáki is the city's upmarket shopping district, as well as being the location of many diplomatic missions and some highly desirable apartments. The haunt of Athenian ladies who lunch and shop, if you are looking for designer clothes,

The Benáki Museum contains treasures from all periods of Athens' history.

BELOW: the Museum of Cycladic Art.

shoes and accessories Kolonáki is where you should head for. It is not, however, devoid of culture; Kolonáki has some of the finest museums in the city.

Going back to 3000 BC, the **Goulandris Museum of Cycladic Art** (open Mon, Wed, Fri 10am–4pm, Thur 10am–8pm, Sat 10am–3pm; entrance fee; www.cycladic-m.gr) displays a unique collection of slim, stylised Cycladic statuettes in white marble, beautifully mounted. These figures were scorned by 19th-century art critics as hopelessly primitive, but their smooth, simple lines attracted both Picasso and Modigliani. Mostly female and pregnant, the figures derive from robbed graves scattered throughout the Cyclades islands; to this day, scholars are still uncertain of their true purpose.

The **Benáki Museum** can lay claim to being the best museum in Athens. Its wonderfully eclectic collection of treasures from all periods of Greek history, including jewellery, costumes and two icons attributed to El Greco. Among the most impressive displays are the collection of traditional costume, mostly bridal and festival dresses, and the reconstructed reception rooms of a mid-18th-century Kozáni mansion. Also of great interest are the displays of gold on the ground floor, and the collections relating to the Greek struggle for independence. The museum has an excellent gift shop and a pleasant terrace restaurant (open Mon, Wed, Fri, Sat 9am–5pm, Thur 9am–midnight, Sun 9am–3pm; entrance fee; www.benaki.gr). (A complex of neoclassical buildings located in the Keramikós district now houses the museum's separate Islamic art collections, *see page 131*.)

Mount Lycabettus (Lykavitós; 215 metres/704 ft) rises above Kolonáki, crowned by the tiny chapel of Ágios Geórgios. The easiest way to get to the summit is by the funicular railway that starts from Ploutárhou Street, near Platía Kolonáki (runs every 30 minutes, in summer 8am–10pm, in winter 9.30am– 4.40pm). From the top, the views over the city are spectacular. While not strictly in Kolonáki (they are on the wrong side of Vassilísis Sofías), there are two other museums close by that are worth a visit. The **Byzantine and Christian Museum ®** (open Tues–Sun 7.30am–7.30pm; free every Sun Nov–Mar and on select days) is housed in a mock-Tuscan villa, commissioned by the French 19th-century Duchesse de Plaisance. It contains a brilliant array of icons and church relics from the 13th to the 18th centuries. A long-running project to construct multi-level, semi-underground galleries, state-of-the-art restoration workshops and educational facilities, the whole surrounded by an outdoor archeological park, was finished in 2004, allowing much more of the museum's huge collection to be on permanent display.

Near the Hilton hotel is the **National Gallery and Alexandros Soutzos Museum** (open Mon, Wed 9am–3pm, 6–9pm, Thur–Sat 9am–3pm, Sun 10am–2pm; entrance fee). This, the national collection of painting and sculpture, is housed in a cool, modern building. It is the Greek paintings here that are best. Particularly interesting are the works from the Ionian School, the late-19th-century realist works, and those which move towards the more Greek sensibility of the early 20th century (see those by Parthenis, Gyzis and Lytras).

Further along Vasilísis Sofías, beside the wonderful **Mégaro Mousikís** concert hall (www.megaron.gr), is **Eleftherías Park**. During the military dictatorship (1967–74) this was the location of the HQ of the military police, where dissidents were detained and tortured. After the fall of the junta the site was turned into a park and cultural centre. It was extended and replanted with more than 200 trees and shrubs in 2001–2002.

Athens is a treasury of Byzantine art.

BELOW: evening in Athens by Iakovos Ritsos, 1897.

Byzantine Athens

Of the city's Byzantine past little remains, but a dozen or so churches, many dating from the 11th century, can be tracked down in Pláka. One of the best is **Ágii Theodóri** , just off Platía Klavthmónos. It was built in the 11th century in characteristic cruciform shape with a tiled dome. The masonry is picked out with slabs of brick and decorated with a terracotta frieze of animals and plants. The church of **Sotíra Lykodímou** on Filellínon Street dates from the same era but was bought by the Tsar of Russia in 1845 and redecorated. It now serves the city's small Russian Orthodox community; the singing is renowned.

Christ Pandokrátor is surrounded by gold on the dome of Dafní monastery.

On Athens's eastern and western limits lie two famous monasteries: Kaisarianí and Dafní. **Kaisarianí** on Mount Hymettus, surrounded by high stone walls, is named after a spring which fed an aqueduct constructed on Hadrian's orders. Its waters, once sacred to Aphrodite, the goddess of love, were long credited with healing powers (and encouraging child-bearing), though sadly no longer potable. The monastery church goes back to AD 1000 but the frescoed figures who gaze out of a blue-black ground date from the 17th century. The monks' wealth came from olive groves, beehives, vineyards and various medicines made from mountain herbs (open Tues–Sun 8.30am–3pm; entrance fee).

Dafní is 11 km (7 miles) out of town on the road to Eleusis (take a bus from Platía Eleftherías, close to Omónia). This small monastery is a curious architectural combination of Gothic and Byzantine, decorated inside with magnificent 11th-century mosaics, and occupies the site of an ancient sanctuary of Apollo. A fierce-looking Christ Pandokrátor, set in gold and surrounded by Old Testament prophets, stares down from the vault of the dome. The building dates from 1080 and the Gothic porch was added in the 13th century when Dafní belonged to Cistercian monks from Burgundy and was used as the burial place of the Frankish Dukes of Athens (closed until further notice for restoration).

BELOW: serving in a Piraeus bar.

Piraeus

Athens' port is a city in its own right and is where most people pass through on their way to the islands. It is most easily reached by metro (line 1; allow around 40 minutes for the journey from the centre of town); alternatively, a bus leaves from Sýndagma, but this can be very slow. An express bus runs direct to Piraeus (Pireás) from Athens' airport (the X96), with stops near the hydrofoil quay, Platía Karaïskáki, the metro station and the northeast quay.

Finding your boat can be daunting, but the ticket agent will tell you which quay/gate (numbered E1–E10 going clockwise around the port) your ferry departs from. As a general guide, most boats to the Cyclades depart from E5–E7 opposite the metro station; slow boats to the Argo-Saronic from E8 on the far side of Platía Karaïskáki, southwest of the metro; direct boats to Crete leave from E2–E4 along Aktí Kondýli, on the north side of the port; hydrofoils to Argo-Saronic islands leave from E9 on Aktí Miaoúli; while Dodecanese-bound boats leave from E10 a bit further down Miaoúli, or all the way around the port at E1, also a departure point for the northeast Aegean.

Piraeus Archeological Museum (open Tues–Sun 8.30am–3pm; entrance fee) has a number of wonderful bronzes. On the first floor is the graceful, Archaic Apollo *kouros*, pulled from the sea in 1959, which was made in 530–20 BC and is the earliest life-sized bronze statue. Two other bronze statues, of Athena and Artemis and both dating to the 5th century BC, were found at about the same time in Piraeus when new sewers were being dug. There is a further superb bronze of Artemis, this one dating from the mid-4th century BC. Also impressive, on the ground floor, is the restored mausoleum of an Istrian merchant.

The **Hellenic Maritime Museum**, full of models of ships from all ages, is close by on Zéa Marina (Aktí Themistokléous; open Tues–Sat 9am–2pm, Sun 9.30am–2pm; entrance fee). **Zéa Marina** is crowded with medium-sized yachts – a floating campsite in summer – and you may see huge, old-fashioned two- and three-masters as well as sleek motor-yachts moored. Further round the headland are cafés and fish restaurants overlooking the Saronic Gulf.

The hills

Athens is said to have eight hills. As well as Lykavitós and the equally conspicuous rock of the Acropolis, flanked by the **Pnyx** on one side, and the hill of **Philopappus** (Filopápposu) ❼ on the other, where Athenians fly kites on the first day of Lent, there are: the hill of **Ardittós** ❶, next to the marble horseshoe **stadium**, built by Herod Atticus in AD 143 and totally reconstructed in 1896 (the first modern Olympic Games were held there); the **Hill of the Nymphs**, capped by the grey dome of the **Observatory**; the barren, windblown **Tourkovoúnia**; and the hill of **Lófos Stréfi**, far less touristy than Lykavitós, and more built up.

Map, pages 124–5

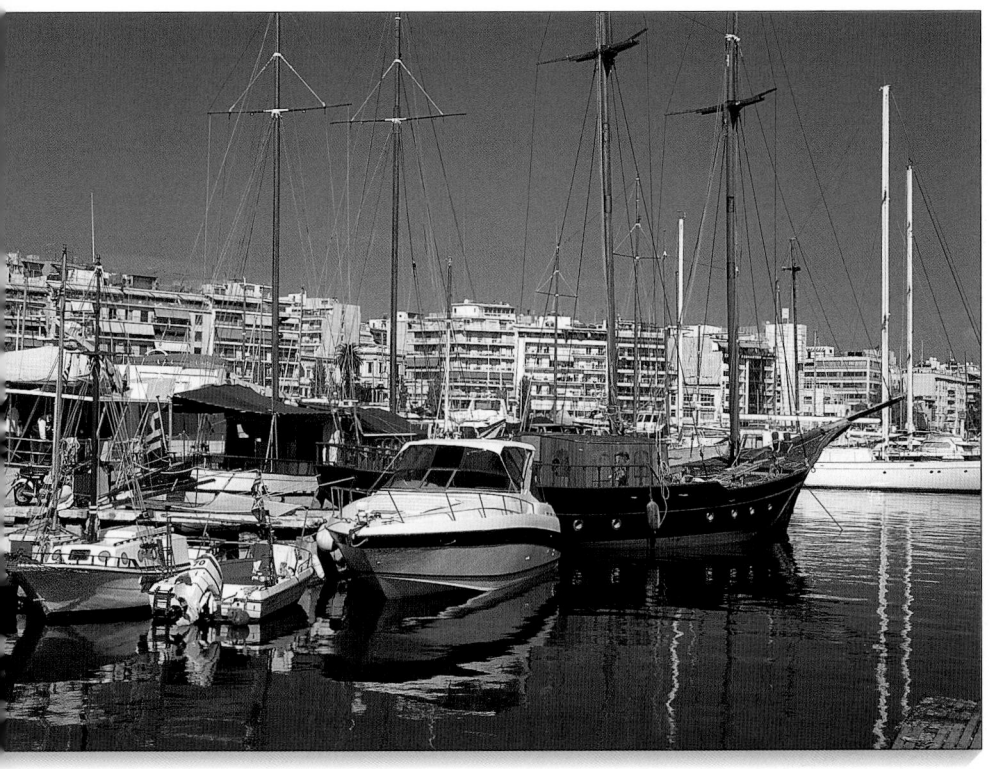

BELOW: Zéa Marina.

Along with small hidden cafés there is more than a measure of coolness on some of these hills. For a real escape, however, you have to go further afield, up one of the three mountains that encircle Athens. **Mount Hymettus** (Ymettós), 5 km (3 miles) east of Athens, beloved of honey-bees, glowing violet at sunset, is perhaps the most beautiful. Driving up the winding road past the monastery of **Kesarianí** you reach a tranquil vantage point from which to contemplate the whole of Attica. The city is panoramically visible, yet totally, eerily inaudible. **Mount Párnitha** (Párnis), just over an hour northwest, was sadly burnt to a crisp in August 2007, losing all of its fir forest. **Mount Pendéli**, to the north, is crowded, lively and popular.

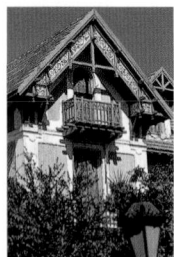

A villa in leafy Kifisiá, Athens' most exclusive suburb.

Below Mount Pendéli is Athens' most exclusive suburb, **Kifisiá**. Populated, like Kolonáki, with the city's great and sometimes not so good, who reside in its neoclassical villas, Kifisiá is a pleasant place to hang out in one of its expensive cafés. Also here is the **Goulandris Museum of Natural History and Gaia Centre** (open Tues–Sun 9am–2.30pm; entrance fee) which has very informative collections devoted to the flora, fauna and geology of Greece.

Attica

Outside Athens, a 69-km (43-mile) drive to **Cape Sounion** on the windy tip of the Attica peninsula takes you to the Doric **Temple of Poseidon** (open daily 9.30am–sunset; entrance fee). Completed in 440 BC, its slender, salt-white columns are still a landmark for ships headed toward Piraeus. Lord Byron carved his name on a column on the north side. The marble came from nearby Agríleza. Down the hillside, you can see the remains of ancient ship sheds in the bay below: the Athenians once organised warship races off Sounion and it later became a pirates' lair.

BELOW: the Temple of Poseidon.

The battle of **Marathon** in 490 BC was fought on a plain by the sea 42 km (26 miles) northeast of Athens, between the villages of Néa Mákri and Marathónas. What can be seen today associated with the battle are the burial mound of the Athenians, the burial mound identified by the excavator as that of the Plataeans, and the Archeological Museum (open Tues–Sun 8.30am–3pm; entrance fee).

The burial mound of the Athenians, simply a circular mound of earth 9 metres (30 ft) high, 50 metres (164 ft) in diameter, and 185 metres (600 ft) in circumference, has a modern copy of the ancient stele on the top (the original is in the National Archeological Museum). The mound is impressive, but nothing compared to the victory it symbolises. The mighty Persian Empire, the largest on earth, had sent its army against Athens, and approximately 9,000 Athenian soldiers were joined before the battle by 1,000 soldiers from Plataea, a town in Boeotia. A runner was sent to ask the Spartans for help, but the Spartans did not arrive until after the battle. The Athenians won against overwhelming odds, with the Persians losing 6,400 men and the Athenians 192. The Athenians were cremated and buried together in the mound. The mound of the Plataeans is near the archeological museum, about 3 km (2 miles) to the west. There is nothing to mark the Persian graves, but they seem to have been buried to the northeast, in the area around the small church of the Panagía Mesosporítisa.

Ramnous (open daily summer 8am–5pm, winter 8.30am–3pm; entrance fee), the site of an ancient fortress town on the northern borders of Attica with a sanctuary of Nemesis, is 53 km (33 miles) from Athens. The sanctuary contains two temples. The older, built right after 490 BC, was dedicated to Nemesis and also to Themis, the god of justice. The slightly larger Doric temple of Nemesis, built in 436–32 BC, almost touches the older temple. The garrison town, roughly 800 metres (½ mile) down from the sanctuary on the shore, flourished in the 5th and 4th centuries BC.

The city-state that built the **Sanctuary of Amphiareion** (Tues–Sun 8.30am–3pm; entrance fee) late in the 5th century BC was ancient Oropos, now buried beneath the modern town of Skála Oropós, where a ferry leaves for Évia. The sanctuary was particularly well known in the Hellenistic period, visited by people from all over the Greek world in search of advice or medical help. The supplicant sacrificed a ram to Amphiaraos, after which a dream would either cure the illness or answer a question.

More out of the way is the **Sanctuary of Artemis** at **Brauron** (now called Vravróna) on the east coast of Attica, 35 km (22 miles) from Athens. A 5th-century BC colonnade visited by owls at twilight is flanked by a 16th-century Byzantine chapel, built on the site of an altar to Artemis. In classical times, well-born female children aged from five to ten ("little bears") performed a ritual dance at a festival honouring Artemis as the goddess of childbirth. Their statues – plump, with solemn expressions, and dressed like miniature adults – are now in the site museum (both site and museum open Tues–Sun 8.30am–3pm; entrance fee). ❑

Map, pages 124–5

BELOW: an ancient exhibit.

A NATIONAL TREASURE TROVE

The National Archeological Museum in Athens houses a fabulous collection of ancient art and artefacts

The National Archeological Museum provides a survey of the various artistic styles of Greek antiquity available nowhere else in the world. Don't be intimidated by the apparent size of the collection but, at first, concentrate on certain key rooms.

The 2002 refurbishment to some extent scrambled the old gallery layout, so get hold of an up-to-date catalogue in order to locate the most interesting works; for example, the best of the free-standing bronze statues, a 5th-century BC Poseidon in the act of hurling a now-vanished trident.

The museum has retained rooms dedicated to its prehistoric artefacts, and finds from the Cycladic period, most of them dating between 3000 and 2000 BC. The Mycenaean Collection (1600–1100 BC) has been kept together, with its focus the so-called Mask of Agamemnon which Heinrich Schliemann found in Mycenae.

Also contained in the museum are examples of ancient Greek sculpture, in marble and bronze, from the Archaic period (700–480 BC) to the Classical (480–338 BC) and Hellenistic (338–146 BC) periods, and up to the Roman Period (146 BC–AD 330).

There is also a vast array of ancient Greek pottery from 900 BC to 300 BC; the Egyptian and Stathatos collections; along with the famous Thera frescoes.

The picture at the top of this column is of the bronze Horse and Jockey of Artemisium (2nd century BC).

▷ **ARCHAIC YOUTH**
This *kouros* (statue of a young man) was found in the Sanctuary of Poseidon at Sounion, the tip of Attica. In the Archaic style, it was carved in the 7th century BC.

▷ **AGAMEMNON**
This gold death mask found by Heinrich Schliemann at Mycenae and dating to the 16th century BC has become famous as the "Mask of Agamemnon". In fact, the Trojan Wars occurred much later.

▽ **GRAVE STELAE**
The range of exhibits in the museum is huge; it has one of the world's largest collections of carved reliefs.

▷ ANCIENT HARPIST

This seated figure in marble playing the harp dates from the 3rd millennium BC and was found on the Cycladic island of Kéros, near Náxos.

▽ MOVEMENT IN STONE

The museum gives an excellent overview of the development of Greek statuary, from early works to the classical ideal.

▽ TAKING AIM

This bronze statue of Poseidon poised to throw his trident, a rare survivor from antiquity, dates from around 450 BC. It was found in the sea off Évia.

△ IMPERIAL LIKENESS

This wonderfully lifelike equestrian bronze statue of the Roman emperor Augustus dates from the late 1st century BC.

FABULOUS FRESCOES

In the middle of the 2nd millennium BC the Cycladic island of Thera (today Santoríni), was much influenced, perhaps even ruled, by the Minoan civilisation of Crete. A Minoan settlement at Akrotíri on Santoríni, dating to approximately 1600 BC, was excavated by Spyridon Marinatos between 1967 and 1974. The most beautiful finds from Akrotíri are the frescoes. Most of these are kept in the National Archeological Museum but a few can be seen in Santoríni. Sometime around 1500 BC Thera's volcano erupted in a tremendous explosion. The entire settlement of Akrotíri, including buildings up to three storeys high, was beautifully preserved beneath volcanic ash. The frescoes decorated the interior walls of houses in the ancient city. Most of them show everyday scenes, such as a naked fisherman carrying home a bountiful catch, the elegant ladies, the graceful antelopes, and the two boxing boys shown at the top of this column, but there is also a 5.5-metre- (18½-ft-) long detailed fresco of a naval campaign.

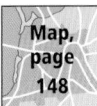

THE PELOPONNESE

Steeped in ancient history – from Agamemnon's Mycenae to the first Olympic stadium – the southern provinces also offer fine beaches, turquoise-coloured bays, and the wild and unspoilt Máni

The Peloponnese (Pelopónnisos) takes its name from the legendary hero Pelops, plus the Greek for island, *nísos*, although it is seldom thought of as an island. Driving over from Attica (Attikí), it's easy to miss the little isthmus – riven by the Corinth Canal, lending some credence to the "island" tag – that joins the Peloponnese to the mainland. The area's medieval name was the Moreás, now rarely used; it derives either from an abundance of mulberry trees (*mouriá*) or more probably from the mulberry-leaf shape of the peninsula.

Korinthía: key to the Moreás

By an administrative quirk, Korinthía province in the northeast includes a bit of the geographical mainland northeast of the canal; 13 km (8 miles) beyond the spa resort of Loutráki lies the **Perahora Heraion**, with an archaic **Hera temple** and a *stoa*. Another important ancient sanctuary, the venue for the quadrennial Isthmian games, can be found at **Isthmía** on the southwest side of the canal; the Roman baths here retain extensive floor mosaics of sea creatures real and imaginary, while the site **museum** (open Tues–Sun 8.30am–3pm; entrance fee) features vivid *opus sectile* panels portraying harbour scenes, Nile bird life and revered ancient personalities. The canal itself, dug between 1882 and 1893, is obsolete in our era of mega-container ships, but a few freighters and tour ships still squeeze through its 23-metre (75-ft) channel, to the delight of spectators up on the bridge gangway.

Ancient **Corinth**, 4 km (2½ miles) southwest of modern **Kórinthos** ❶, could not help but prosper through domination of trans-Isthmian haulage in pre-canal days. The Hellenistic city was razed by the Romans in 146 BC in reprisal for resistance, but refounded a century later as capital of Greece. What remains, despite devastating earthquakes in AD 375 and 521, is the most complete imperial Roman town plan in Greece. Corinth's well-deserved reputation for vice and luxury predictably exercised Saint Paul when he arrived in AD 52 for an 18-month sojourn.

A typically Roman obsession with plumbing is evident: there are the graphically obvious latrines off the marble-paved **Lehaion Way**, the still-functioning **Lower Peirene Fountain** at its end, and the ingenious **Glauke Fountain**, its four cisterns hewn from a monolith and filled by an aqueduct (site open summer 8am–7.30pm, winter 8am–5pm; entrance fee).

Of the earlier Greek city, only seven columns from a Doric **Apollo Temple** still stand, though the site **museum** – despite a selective 1990 burglary – retains a generous collection of late archaic pottery and some intricate Roman-villa mosaics from Corinth's glory years (open Tues–Fri 8am–7pm, Sat–Sun 8.30am–

LEFT: parts of columns at Olympia. **BELOW:** the rocky Máni peninsula.

Peloponnese

0   30 km

0   30 miles

pm). Rather more evocative, however, is the nearly impregnable hilltop fortress f **Acrocorinth** (open summer daily 8am–7pm, winter Tues–Sun 8.30am–3pm; ree), long the military key to the peninsula and necessarily held by every occupying ower. Enter via the gentler west slope through a set of **triple fortifications** to ind yourself amid weedy desolation; little is left of the Ottoman town here, evacated after Greek rebels took it in 1822. Most sieges, however, were successfully esisted thanks to the **Upper Peirene Fountain**, a subterranean structure near the outheast corner of the ramparts. At the very summit stand foundations of an **Aphrodite Temple**, reputedly once attended by 1,000 sacred prostitutes; the view ll around is quite marvellous, stretching up to 60 km (40 miles) in every direction.

The wide tollway to Trípoli forges southwest from modern Kórinthos. Near **Dervenákia**, exits lead west 8 km (5 miles) to ancient **Nemea**, yet another shrine with its own biennial games. You can see the **stadium** where these events – supposedly inaugurated by Hercules, slayer of the Nemean lion – were held, but the most striking landmarks are three surviving Doric columns of a 4th-century BC **Zeus Temple**; its fellows, toppled by Byzantine vandals, lie all about like many sausage slices. The site (open summer daily 8am–7.30pm, winter Mon noon–7pm, Tues–Sun 8.30am–3pm; entrance fee) occupies the floor of a bucolic valley; surrounding vineyards produce the grapes for the full-bodied Nemea red wines, some of Greece's best.

The word "currant" derives from the word "Corinth" – a reference to the city's long-established trade in dried grapes, still one of Greece's most successful exports.

Argolída: Mycenaean cradle

The old highway enters the Argolid plain at modern **Mykínes**, a village devoted to citrus and tourism; nearby stands ancient **Mycenae ❷**, a fortified palace complex covering an easily defendable, ravine-flanked ridge. Mycenae gave

BELOW: the Corinth Canal was completed in 1893.

Mycenae's treasures were uncovered by the archeologist Heinrich Schliemann.

its name to an entire late Bronze-Age era – and made the reputation of a German self-taught classical scholar (and self-made millionaire), Heinrich Schliemann. From 1874 to 1876 he excavated here, relying on little other than intuition and a belief in the literal accuracy of Homer's epics. Greek archeologists had already revealed the imposing **Lion Gate** of the citadel, but the rich tomb finds Schliemann made, now in the National Museum of Athens, amply corroborate Mycenae's Homeric epithet "rich in gold". These days, revisionists point to Schliemann's sloppy excavating techniques and economy with the truth – the gold death mask which prompted his boast "I have gazed upon the face of Agamemnon" is now dated to 300 years before Troy – but the dedicated amateur did beat the experts to the greatest archeological trove of that century.

At the site itself, little remains above waist height inside the perimeter walls of the palace, though a rather alarming secret stairway descends to a siege-proof cistern in the northeast corner. Outside, however, are two burial chambers of unsurpassed ingenuity: the *tholos* tombs dubbed, very speculatively, the **Treasury of Atreus** and the **Tomb of Clytemnestra**, also known as "beehives" after the manner of their construction (open summer Tues–Sun 8am–7.30pm, Mon 12.30–7pm; winter daily 8.30am–5pm; entrance fee).

Ancient Argos

The road across the Argolid plain divides at **Árgos** ❸, capital of Argolída province and a major agricultural centre. Tomatoes and citrus – the latter introduced by American advisers after World War II – are grown extensively; the modern town itself is of little interest apart from its **Archeological Museum** (open Tues–Sun 8.30am–3pm; entrance fee). But just south, beside the Trípoli-bound road, sprawl the ruins of **ancient Argos** (same hours as museum), one of the oldest Greek settlements; most notable is the huge, steeply raked theatre. From here, walk up to the Frankish castle atop Lárissa hill, site of the ancient **acropolis**, for a view nearly on a par with Acrocorinth's. To the northwest is **Mount Kyllíni**, snow-capped in season. Ahead, beyond a foreground of orchards and the occasional cannery, you can make out Mycenae and the low hillock of ancient Tiryns en route to the town of Návplio (Nauplion), stacked up against the promontory on the far side of the Argolid Gulf.

BELOW: inside the Treasury of Atreus at Mycenae.

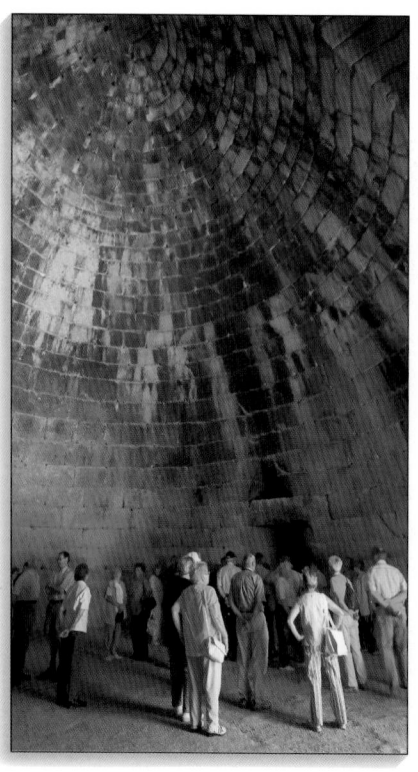

Just over halfway to Návplio from Árgos loom the 13th-century BC ruins of Homer's "wall-girt" **Tiryns** (open daily 8.30am–3pm; entrance fee), another royal palace complex. The site, an 18-metre (60-ft) bluff rising from an ancient marsh, was not as naturally defensible as its neighbour, Mycenae, so the man-made fortifications – originally twice their present height – were necessarily more involved. Massive masonry blocks reaching 3 cubic metres (100 cu. ft) each were joined in mortarless walls termed "Cyclopean", after the only beings thought capable of manoeuvring them. No heraldic lions over the entry-gate here, and no beehive tombs; but Tiryns satisfies enough with a **secret stairway** to the westerly postern gate and, near the southeast corner, a corbel-ceilinged **gallery**, its walls polished smooth by the millennial rubbings of sheltering sheep.

Návplio ④, rising in tiers at the southeast corner of the valley, is more than a little mirage-like, for the well-preserved old town retains an elegance a world away from scruffy, utilitarian Árgos just 12 km (7 miles) to the northwest. The neoclassical architecture, pedestrian-friendly marble streets and interlocking fortresses date mostly from the second Venetian occupation of 1686–1715, and subsequent Ottoman reconquest; the fortified rock here had been a pivotal point in their struggles for control of the Aegean from the 15th century onward. Between 1829 and 1834 Návplio served as the country's first capital, but today it's a laid-back place, despite playing a role as an upmarket resort; it even stays busy in winter, thanks to Athenian weekenders. Visit the excellent **Peloponnesian Folklore Foundation** at Vassilis Alexandrou, 1 (open daily 9am–3pm and 6–9pm, closed Tues morning and Sun evening; entrance fee).

Návplio is overawed by **Akronavpliá**, four separate fortresses of various ages just overhead, plus, on an easterly hill, the sprawling, early 18th-century castle of **Palamídi**, whose meandering curtain wall encloses seven self-contained bastions designed to withstand the strongest artillery of the era. Yet its Venetian garrison capitulated with barely a fight in 1715 to the Ottomans, who in turn surrendered to the Greek rebels after a more protracted siege in 1822. Just under 900 steps lead up from the Old Town to the summit – and to more eyefuls of the Argolid (open daily 8am–7pm, 6pm in winter; entrance fee).

Some 27 km (17 miles) east of Návplio, **Epidauros (Epídavros) ⑤** is visited for the sake of its magnificent 4th-century BC **theatre**, whose perfect acoustics tour guides perpetually demonstrate with coins dropped on the orchestra floor. Because it lay buried until the late 19th century, the theatre masonry survived the ages relatively unscathed, and restoration has been minimal.

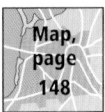

Map, page 148

BELOW:
Návplio waterfront and the fortress-island of Boúrtzi.

The shady grottoes of Arcadia were where Pan played his pipes and frolicked with nymphs.

bits are the classical **stadium**, its stone benches and starting line still visible; the monumental gateway and stretch of buckled pavement, part of the sacred way to the port (today's beach resort of **Paleá Epídavros**), and the *tholos*, a circular originally domed structure with a concentric maze in the foundations thought to contain serpents (sacred to Asklepios) or to be the venue for a priestly initiation rite (open daily 8am–7.30pm, until 5pm in winter; entrance fee).

The closest village to the site is **Lygourió**, which formerly lived mainly from its extensive olive groves but which now hosts most of the tourist traffic which comes for the summer festival of ancient drama. Performances by both Greek and international theatre companies take place by night in the ancient theatre, with special buses from Athens laid on for ticket-holders.

Heading west from Návplio, you can avoid re-entering Árgos by using the beachfront road along the gulf, joining the highway to Trípoli at **Lerna** (modern **Mýli**), where Hercules slew the many-headed Hydra.

Arkadía: Arcadian idylls

The modern 1970s highway – though not the 1990s toll expressway – leaves the flatlands of fragrant citrus at Mýli to enter gorges culminating in the high, pear- and apple-planted upland plateaux around **Trípoli ⑥**, capital of Arkadía province. The name Trípoli recalls the three ancient towns of **Tegea**, **Mantineia** and **Palladium**, the latter an undistinguished Roman-imperial foundation. Mantineia, north of modern Trípoli, retains much of its ancient walls, and a reputation for excellent modern wine, while Tegea to the south offers the tumbled ruins of the **Temple to Athena Alea** in the middle of modern Aléa village. Trípoli (then Tripolítza) was the Morean capital in Ottoman times, but was burned during the

BELOW: the classical theatre at Epidauros.

War of Independence. Aside from a good **archeological museum** (Tues–Sun 8.30am–3pm; entrance fee), there's little here to interest casual tourists.

The northbound, toll-free road skirts the base of forested, blade-like **Mount Ménalo** via the handsome villages of **Levídi** and **Vytína ❼**, the latter a popular "hill station" and ski resort for Greeks. Beyond Vytína, towards Ilía province, the most logical and compelling halt is **Langádia ❽**, its famous masons responsible for sturdy stone houses teetering on a slope above the gorge of the same name. But the main attraction of montane Arkadía lies due west of Trípoli, accessible either from the Megalópoli road or a turning south between Vytína and Langádia. **Megalópoli ❾** itself, saddled with steam-belching power plants, is a shabby modern successor to **ancient Megalopolis**, a vast artificial classical township abandoned within two centuries of inauguration, leaving only the largest amphitheatre (Tues–Sun 8.30am–3pm; free) in Greece to mark its passing.

Hyperbolically dubbed the "Toledo of Greece", thanks to its evocative castle and houses overlooking a kink in the **Alfiós River**, the sleepy demeanour of **Karýtena ❿** belies a tumultuous history. Established as the seat of a Frankish barony during the 13th century, it was later retaken by the Byzantines, who endowed Karýtena with three churches and an arched bridge over the Alfiós. Both bridge and town figured on one side of the old 5,000-drachma note; the beturbanned Independence War chieftain Kolokotrónis glared out from the other, for he successfully resisted a long Ottoman siege here in 1826.

Heading north along the paved road towards Dimitsána, you'll travel roughly parallel to the east flank of the **Loúsios Gorge**: a short route, but in terms of concentrated interest one equalled by few other parts of the Peloponnese. At **Ellinikó** village, a narrow road descends into the canyon, emerg-

Map, page 148

Shepherds' crooks in Langádia village.

BELOW: three generations of Arcadian women.

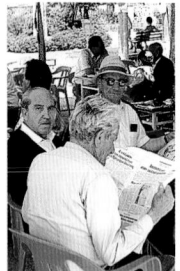

Taking it easy in the mountain village of Vytína, a popular "hill station" for Greek tourists.

BELOW: Ioánnou Prodrómou is one of Greece's most spectacular monateries.

ing at the medieval Kokkorás bridge and the Byzantine chapel of **Ágios Andréas**. Nearby are the excavations of ancient **Gortys**, an *asklipeion* or therapeutic centre; the architectural highlight here is a peculiar round structure, thought to be a bath-house.

Stemnítsa ⓫, further along the paved road, has been officially renamed **Ypsoúnda** but the Slavic name remains more popular; it's an atmospheric, introverted place in a hidden cirque, with imposing mansions looking only at each other. A single jewellery shop recalls the former silver-smithing industry. Near the head of the Loúsios valley, **Dimitsána** sprawls engagingly over a saddle demarcated by the river, its skyline graced by four belfries. The mansions here, like Stemnítsa's, date from its mercantile golden age, the 1700s.

Dimitsána also marks one end of the hiking route threading the gorge; the path proper begins in **Paleohóri** hamlet, following red-and-white blazes and diamonds with the legend "32". The first significant stop is the **Néa Filosófou monastery** on the west bank, with late 17th-century frescoes including Jesus walking on the Sea of Galilee; a little beyond, the 10th-century **Paleá Filosófou** monastery is largely ruined and almost indistinguishable from its cliff-side surroundings. Finally, where the path divides (the west-bank option leads to Gortys), you should recross the river for the most spectacular monastery of all: 11th-century **Agíou Ioánnou Prodrómou** (St John the Baptist) is one of those swallow's-nest-type monasteries which the Orthodox Church loves to tuck into cliff faces. It has limited accommodation (for male pilgrims only), so try to budget enough daylight time to hike onwards by trail to Stemnítsa.

From Karýtena a westerly road follows the Alfiós, past its co-mingling with the Loúsios, to **Andrítsena** ⓬, roughly halfway between Megalópoli and the sea.

Resolutely traditional shops and a morning produce market in the central square recall the village's historical status as a major entrepôt. Today, however, it seems scarcely touched by the steady trickle of tourist traffic passing through to the 5th-century temple of **Apollo Epikourios** at **Bassae** (Vásses), 14 km (9 miles) south. Although the most intact ancient shrine in Greece and a UNESCO World Heritage site, it's unlikely to enchant in its present condition – concealed by a colossal, guy-wired tent to protect it from winter frosts, it is off-limits for major renovation. More rewarding for many is the **gorge of the River Nédas** a few kilometres south, just below the modern village and ancient ruins of **Figalia**, whose citizens originally built the temple in gratitude for Apollo having lifted a plague.

Map, page 148

In 1821 Germanos, the local Archbishop of Dimitsána, called for an uprising against the Turks, which led to the liberation of all Arkadía.

Lakonía: ancient Spartan heartland

As you descend the 60-km (37-mile) road from Trípoli to modern Spárti, the long ridge of **Mount Taÿgetos** with its striated limestone bands looms into sight on the right. Ahead stretches the olive-and-citrus-rich floodplain of the Evrótas River, belying the stereotypical image of ancient Sparta as a harsh, "spartan" place (the province's name, Lakonía, also lives on abroad as "laconic" – supposedly the distinguishing characteristic of the classical natives).

Spárti ⓭, the modern successor to ancient Sparta, is an unexciting place redeemed only by some attractive squares and neoclassical facades, vestiges of a bout of Bavarian town planning in 1834. Stop, if you do at all, for the excellent **museum** and traces of an **ancient acropolis**. The museum (open Mon–Sat 8.30am–3pm, Sun 9.30am–2.30pm; entrance fee) is particularly rich in late Roman floor-mosaics from local villas, and eerie votive offerings from the **sanctuaries of Apollo** at Amýkles and **Artemis Orthia** on the acropolis – where youths were

BELOW: café life on the Peloponnese.

The Mitrópolis cathedral in Mystrás stands in a courtyard.

BELOW: Mystrás's Perívleptos church has some superb frescoes.

flogged until bloody to honour the goddess. At the acropolis itself, however, 700 metres (½ mile) northwest of town, not much remains aside from a badly eroded theatre and the sparse remains of the Byzantine church of **Ágios Níkon**.

What little the Spartans built was appropriated for the construction of Byzantine **Mystrás** , 6 km (4 miles) west (open daily summer 8am–8pm; winter 8am–2pm; entrance fee). A romantically ruined walled town, clinging to a conical crag and topped by a castle, Mystrás's name is a corruption of *mezythrás*, the Greek for "cream-cheese maker" – thought to be a reference to this cheese's traditional conical shape.

Originally founded by the Franks in 1249, Mystrás grew to a city of 20,000 souls under the Byzantines, becoming the capital of the Morean despots after 1348. Until the Ottomans took over in 1460, it flourished as a major cultural centre, attracting scholars and artists from Serbia, Constantinople and Italy to its court. The latter's influence is evident in the brilliantly coloured (and remarkably well-preserved) frescoes which adorn Mystrás's churches – uniquely in Greece, these are as crammed with extraneous figures, buildings and landscapes as any Italian painting of the time. Architecturally, the churches are a composite of three-aisled-basilica ground plan and domed cross-in-square gallery, making them airily well lit by Byzantine standards. Proto-Renaissance sensibilities (and the Frankish wives of most of the despots) inspired belfries and colonnaded porticoes. It is easy to see why Mystrás is regarded as the last great Byzantine architectural outpouring before the onset of the Ottoman era.

The church of **Perívleptos monastery** contains a complete cycle of frescoes depicting the *Dodekaeorton* or 12 major feasts of the year, with such light touches as children playing in the Entry to Jerusalem. Nearby **Pandánassa**, the

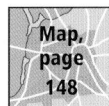

Map, page 148

newest church built in 1428, has a typically Gothic exterior as well as vivid frescoes within, the best of these neck-craningly high. By contrast, the oldest of the churches, the **Mitrópolis** or cathedral of Ágios Dimítrios, is resolutely conservative in structure, notwithstanding awkward domes added later; here frescoes include a complete cycle of Christ's Miracles. The **Vrondóhion** monastic complex harbours yet another 14th-century church, the more daring **Afendikó**, the weight of its six domes borne by a system of piers below and colonnaded gallery above. Sea monsters bob in the Baptism fresco, while above the altar, apostles marvel at Christ ascending in a mandorla.

Mystrás has a miniature "echo" in **Geráki** (25 km/16 miles east of Spárti), of which few have heard and fewer still bother to visit. Although an ancient town (Geronthrai) existed here, its masonry has been liberally recycled into the half-dozen churches scattered about. Geráki's fortified **acropolis** is less spectacular than that at Mystrás, and closes earlier (open Tues–Sun 8.30am–3pm; entrance fee); if time is limited, find the key-keeper by the post office (8am–2pm) who will open up four frescoed churches in and around the modern village.

Completing the trio of Lakonian Byzantine towns is **Monemvasía** ⓫, 94 km (58 miles) southeast of Spárti. Like Mystrás, it's a fortified double town, clinging to a limestone plug rising 350 metres (1,150 ft) from the sea and inevitably nicknamed the "Gibraltar of Greece" – although the "Dubrovnik of Greece" would be an equally apt term for the tile-roofed, wall-encased lower town on the south slope. Supporting 50,000 souls in its heyday as a semi-autonomous city-state, Monemvasía prospered by virtue of its fleets and handy location, halfway between Italy and the Black Sea. Never taken by force, it did surrender, if necessary, to prolonged siege – no food could grow on the rock,

Monemvasía's fortifications cling to a crag by the sea.

BELOW: a view over Monemvasía.

though enormous cisterns provided water. Nearby vineyards produced the famous Malvasia sweet wine – similar to Madeira, and known as Malmsey or Malvoisie in the west – but local production ceased by the 15th century. Following the opening of the Corinth Canal, Monemvasía lost all commercial and military significance.

The lower town, within its 900-metre (½-mile) circuit of Venetian walls on three sides, is invisible as you cross the causeway until the massive west gate (closed to vehicles) suddenly appears. Immediately above the gate perches the house in which prominent poet Giannis Ritsos was born in 1909; one wonders what the conservative locals made of his forthright Marxism and bisexuality. On his death in 1990 he was buried in the nearby cemetery, with one of his poems chiselled on the gravestone in lieu of religious sentiment.

Linked by a maze of tunnels, arcades and cul-de-sacs at the end of steep, cobbled lanes, many of the lower-town houses have been bought up and restored by wealthy Athenians and foreigners. Masoned steps zigzag up the cliff face overhead to the older, upper town, first settled and fortified in the 6th century AD but abandoned since the early 1900s and now utterly ruined. The sole exception to the desolation is the 14th-century **Agía Sofía** church with its 16-sided dome, poised at the edge of the northerly cliff and the first point in Monemvasía to catch the sunrise.

Gýthio , 47 km (29 miles) southeast of Spárti, is a port town on the ferry routes to Kýthira and Crete, a holiday resort in its own right, and a deceptively congenial gateway to the austere Máni. The quay is lined by tiled vernacular houses and pricey fish tavernas; across the Lakonian Gulf the sun rises over **Cape Maléa**, and Mount Taýgetos is glimpsed one last time on the north. In

Cherries for sale, in Monemvasía lower town. In medieval times, food supplies were the rock-city's weak point; everything had to be imported from the mainland.

BELOW: Gýthio waterfront.

ancient times Gýthio served as Sparta's port, and until recently it exported acorns used in leather tanning. There are few sights, apart from a Roman theatre and the historical museum (open Tues–Sun 9.30am–3pm, but often closed; entrance fee) on **Marathonísi** islet (ancient Kranae) tied to the mainland by a causeway. It was here that Paris and Helen legendarily spent their first night together, and so launched a thousand ships.

The Máni – home of Greece's hard men

An arid, isolated region protected by Taýgetos' southern spur, the **Máni** was the last part of Greece to espouse Christianity (in the 9th century), but made up for lost time by erecting dozens of small country chapels. Little grows except stunted olive trees, though in late summer an extra dash of colour is lent by hedges of fruiting prickly pears. "Outer" or **Éxo Máni** (Ítylo northwest to Kalamáta) is more tourist-friendly, fertile and better watered; "Inner" or **Mésa Máni**, south of a line connecting Ítylo with Gýthio, has the more noteworthy churches on the west shore, and tower-studded villages sprouting from the east-coast settlements. But extreme conditions have prompted wholesale depopulation, and the villages here only fill during the autumn hunting season.

From Gýthio, the main road into the Máni passes by the castles of **Passavá** and **Kelefá**. These were the sole Ottoman attempts at imposing order locally. The road takes you to **Areópoli** ⓱, main market town and tourist base of the Inner Máni. Formerly Tsímova, stronghold of the Mavromihális clan, it was renamed after Ares the god of war after independence, in recognition of its contribution to the independence struggle. Two churches, both 18th-century, distinguish it: **Taxiárhis** with its campanile and zodiacal apse reliefs, and frescoed **Ágios Ioánnis**.

Map, page 148

In Roman times Gýthio supplied the nobility with murex, a purple dye extracted from a species of mollusc, which was used to give togas their aristocratic colour.

BELOW: Pýrgos Diroú beach.

TIP

To see the best examples of the distinctive Maniot tower-houses, head for the villages of Váthia, Kítta, Nómia and Flomohóri.

Some 8 km (5 miles) south, just off the west-coast road towards **Cape Mátapan** (Ténaro), the caverns at **Pýrgos Diroú** are the sole organised tourist attraction in the Máni; visits are partly by boat along a subterranean river, and queues can be long. Between here and Geroliménas lie over half-a-dozen frescoed Byzantine churches; sadly, most are permanently locked, and hunting for the warden can be time-consuming. Two of the best, at Áno Boularí, are also the easiest to access. Apply in the Geroliménas post office for the keys to **Ágios Stratigós**, with extensive frescoes from the 12th to the 18th centuries; and to nearby **Ágios Pandelímon** which has the earliest (10th-century) frescoes around, with figures of saints Pandelímon and Nikítas in the apse. **Geroliménas** ⓫ itself, 20 km (12 miles) from Areópoli, can offer tavernas and accommodation, but not much else – it dates only from 1870. The 35 ridgetop tower-houses of dramatic **Váthia** ⓯, 10 km (6 miles) further east, have become photogenic synonyms for the Máni.

The main tarred road out of Geroliménas loops along the eastern shore via **Lágia** (famed for its broad-based, tapering towers and purple-marble quarries) and **Flomohóri** ⓴ (with the highest towers and pebbly **Kótronas** beach below) before re-emerging at Areópoli. Just across the ravine dividing Inner Máni and Areópoli from Outer is bluff-top **Ítylo** ㉑, lushly set and – unlike so many of its neighbours – relatively prosperous; below the village lie the frescoed monastery of **Dekoúlou** and the beach resort of **Néa Ítylo**.

The pride of **Langáda** village ㉒, 14 km (9 miles) north, is the central 11th-century church of **Ágios Sótiros**, whose frescoes still await uncovering and restoration; contiguous **Plátsa** and **Nomitsís** between them have four more Byzantine chapels. Tourism takes over at the picturesque fishing port of **Ágios Nikólaos** (Selenítsa); nearby **Stoúpa** ㉓ has two sandy bays and plenty of

BELOW:
Váthia in the Máni.

FEUDS IN THE MÁNI

While there may be some truth to Maniot claims that they are descended from the ancient Spartans, more crucial to the region's medieval history was the arrival, during the 13th to the 15th centuries, of refugee Byzantine nobility. These established a local aristocracy, the Nyklians, which formed competing clans as in Scotland; only they had the right to erect tower-mansions.

Poor farmland and a fast-growing population spurred not just piracy and banditry, but complex vendettas between clans. Blood feuds could last for years, with sporadic truces to tend crops; women, who delivered supplies, were inviolate, as were doctors, who treated the wounded impartially. Combatants fired at each other from neighbouring towers, raising them as high as five storeys so as to lob rocks onto their opponents' flat roofs. The vendettas generally ended either with the annihilation or utter submission of the losing clan. Rather than rule the Máni directly, the Ottomans encouraged the feuding in the hopes of weakening any concerted rebellions, appointing a Nyklian chieftain as *bey* to represent the sultan.

The office passed between rival clans, but under the last *bey*, Petros Mavromihalis, the clans united, instigating the Greek independence uprising on 17 March 1821.

facilities as well. **Kardamýli ㉔** ranks as the premier resort before Kalamáta, offering among its charms a long pebble beach, a late-medieval citadel and some good walking just inland.

Messinía: the Peloponnesian banana belt

Kalamáta can also be approached directly from Spárti via the spectacular 60-km (37-mile) road which crosses Mount Taýgetos. On the Lakonian side, near **Trýpi** village, is the **Keádas**, an abyss where the ancient Spartans supposedly hurled their sickly or malformed babies. **Kalamáta ㉕** itself suffered a devastating 1986 earthquake which left half the population homeless; despite subsequent emigration it's still the biggest town hereabouts (40,000 people), with an attractive seafront, some lively untouristy tavernas and its famous shiny purplish-grey olives to recommend it.

Most visitors to Messinía province have their sights set on the low south-westerly promontory ending in **Cape Akrítas**, with its fine beaches and balmy climate. Prime target is **Koróni ㉖**, founded by Venice in 1206 to guard the sea lanes between the Adriatic and Crete. The castle here still shelters a few houses, orchards and pine groves, but a convent occupies most of it. The town outside the walls (built since 1830) has weathered tourism well, its vernacular houses with their wooden balconies still lining the steep stair-streets. **Zánga beach**, one of the best in the Peloponnese, extends for 3 km (2 miles) west.

Methóni ㉗, another "eye of Venice" lying 35 km (22 miles) west, grew wealthy after 1209 from the pilgrim trade to Palestine. Its sprawling castle, lapped on three sides by the sea, combines military architecture of various eras: beyond the Venetian sea-gate, a Turkish octagonal tower – the Baírtzi – over-

Map, page 148

The caves at Pýrgos Diroú get very busy in high season; to preserve the magic, try to get there early.

BELOW: a ruined church in Kardamýli.

Kalamáta is best known for its prosperous export trade in large, shiny purplish-grey olives. They are excellent eaten with oúzo.

looks two islets, while a French arched bridge of 1828 spans the Venetian moat. Little remains of the medieval town inside, however, and the modern village outside the walls is not nearly as attractive as Koróni's, nor is the beach.

Pýlos 28, 12 km (7 miles) north, is another somewhat lacklustre town; despite its pleasant setting on huge, landlocked **Navaríno Bay**, what life there is seems confined to the immediate environs of **Platía Tríon Navárhon**, the main square. The bay has seen two momentous naval battles: in 425 BC, when the Athenians bested the Spartans off **Sfaktiría island**, and in October 1827, when a combined French, Russian and English armada sank Ibrahim Pasha's Ottoman fleet, thus guaranteeing Greek independence. The three allied admirals are honoured by an obelisk in their namesake square. For beaches you'll have to head for the north end of the bay, to Giálova just off the main road to the Bronze Age **Palace of Nestor** (summer Tues–Fri 8am–7.30pm, Sat–Sun 8.30am–3pm; winter daily 8.30am–3pm; entrance fee), discovered in 1939 and now protected by a synthetic roof.

Ilía: Olympia and the Cape

From pretty **Kyparissía**, north of Nestor's Palace, it's a pleasant coastal drive to the site of ancient **Olympia 29**, where the Kládeos River meets the Alfiós. The sanctuary here was in use for two millennia as a religious and athletic centre; of all the Hellenic competitions associated with shrines, the Olympic Games, held every four years at the late-summer full moon, were the most prestigious, and the Panhellenic truce declared for their duration was honoured by the various city-states on pain of stiff fines. Although the first verified games were held in 776 BC, the **Áltis**, a sacred forest at the base of Krónio hill, was consecrated to pre-Olympian deities as early as the second millennium BC.

BELOW: the bay of Voïdokiliá near Pýlos.

The most salient monuments are the **Palaestra** training centre, whose courtyard colonnade has been re-erected; the **workshop of Pheidias**, the celebrated sculptor (identified by a cup found with his name inscribed); the Archaic **Hera temple** with its dissimilar columns; the enormous **Zeus temple**, now reduced to column sections; and the **stadium** with its 192-metre (630-ft) running course and surviving vaulted entrance (open summer daily 8am–7pm; winter Mon–Fri 8am–5pm, Sat 8.30–3pm; entrance fee).

In the **site museum**, pride of place goes to the relief pediments recovered from the Zeus temple debris, now on display in the central hall (open summer daily 8am–7.30pm; winter Mon 10.30am–5pm, Tues–Fri 8.00am–5pm, Sat–Sun 8.30am–3pm; entrance fee).

Aháïa: Pátra and its hinterland

Entering Aháïa province along the coast north of **Kyllíni**, sample the enormous, 7-km (4-mile) beach of **Kalógria** and the swamps (plus umbrella-pine dune forest) just behind. This, one of the largest wetlands in the Balkans, has yet to gain significant protection as a wildlife reserve; go now before the developers scare off the incredibly rich birdlife.

Pátra ㉚, 38 km (24 miles) further, is Greece's third-largest city, and the principal port for ferries to Italy and some of the Ionian Islands. With its fearsome traffic, anonymous post-war architecture and lack of beaches, it's hardly the ideal spot for a quiet holiday retreat; only the ancient **acropolis** (with an originally Byzantine castle) seems peaceful. But linger at Carnival time to witness Greece's best observance, with parades, floats and conspicuous attendance by students and the gay community. ❑

Map, page 148

Greece was the setting for the first Olympic Games, held in 776 BC, and more lately in 2004.

BELOW: Pýlos harbour.

CENTRAL GREECE

A region rich in temples and monasteries, from Delphi – mythical centre of the ancient world – to the Monastery of Ósios Loukás and the dramatic Metéora peaks

Map, page 166

Roúmeli, the poetic medieval term for south-central Greece, encompasses the present-day provinces of Étolo-Akarnanía, Evrytanía, Fokída, Viotía and Fthiótida – even more ancient place-names revived by the modern Greek state. Few contemporary visitors concern themselves much with these tongue-twisting toponyms as they rush headlong towards the main attraction of the region, the Classical site at Delphi. Their single-mindedness is forgiveable, since Delphi uniquely combines a wealth of monuments with a breathtaking setting.

The drive from Athens takes anywhere from 2½ to 3½ hours depending on your route; the most historic, scenic one follows a steep but well-paved road over the pine-covered mountains from dreary **Elefsína** – perhaps detouring for a fish lunch at **Pórto Germenó ❶** on the Gulf of Corinth – to **Thíva (Thebes) ❷**. The modern city has been built on top of the ancient one, so little is visible of the ancient Thebes so prominent in Greek myth and history. A small ancient palace has, however, been excavated and the excellent archeological museum (closed for complete reconstruction until 2010; entrance fee) contains tomb and sanctuary finds from Bronze Age to Classical Boeotia, especially the painted sarcophagi from Tanagra. The next main town, **Livadiá ❸**, was a major power base for the Frankish Crusader fiefdoms during the 13th and 14th centuries. In the gorge of the River Érkyna yawns the entrance to the ancient Oracle of Trophonios, near a graceful Ottoman bridge and below the Catalan-built castle. The river's springs nurture a dense colony of plane trees, a pleasing backdrop to the handful of tavernas on the pedestrianised banks.

Beyond **Livadiá**, the road west begins to climb into the foothills of **Mt Parnassós**. The left turn for Dístomo village and the **Monastery of Ósios Loukás ❹**, dedicated to a local 10th-century ascetic named Luke, is clearly marked. The monastery (open May–mid-Sept 8am–2pm, 4–7pm; otherwise 8am–5pm; entrance fee) commands a wonderful view over a secluded valley in the shadow of Mt Elikónas. The smaller chapel of the Virgin (on the left) dates from the 10th century; the 11th-century *katholikón* or main church contains superb mosaics, survivors of a 1659 earthquake. The best and easiest to view, including a *Resurrection* and *Washing of the Apostles' Feet*, are in the narthex.

The village of **Aráhova ❺** clings to the toes of Parnassós; formerly a bastion of pastoral culture, it has now woken up to a new life as a ski resort, with Athenian-weekender chalets sprouting rapidly on the outskirts. Tourist souvenirs, including various types of pasta and the almost-purple wine particular to the area, are pitched more at Greeks than foreigners.

LEFT: Agías Triádos monastery, Metéora.
BELOW: Ósios Loukás monastery.

Central Greece

Delphi

The ancient site of **Delphi** ➏ is 11 km (7 miles) further along, built on terraces at the base of sheer cliffs, the whole poised to topple over into the Plístos Gorge. Since its excavation by the French towards the end of the 19th century, Delphi has ranked as the most popular, memorable ruin on the mainland, attended as well by gliding birds of prey launching themselves from the palisades. A visit involves steep climbs rewarded by ever-changing viewpoints and new monumental treasures.

The first locale, on the south side of the road, is the so-called **Marmaria** (open daily same hours as main site; free), comprising a gymnasium (complete with a straight track and a round bath) and the sanctuary of Athena Pronaia. Pronaia means "guardian of the temple" and ancient visitors passed first through this shrine. The original 7th-century BC temple was destroyed by the Persians, and replaced by the present complex; the most interesting structure here is the circular, 4th-century *tholos*, whose purpose remains unknown.

On the north side of the road gushes the Castalian Spring (fenced off). Parts of the older, rectangular fountain right next to the road date to the 6th century BC, although thin marble slabs on the floor are Hellenistic or early Roman. All pilgrims had to perform ritual ablutions here.

The main sacred precinct at Delphi is the **Sanctuary of Apollo**, above the road past the Castalian Spring (open daily summer 7.30am–7pm, winter 8am–5pm; entrance fee). Many of the ruins exposed today date from Roman times, but just as many monuments, including the stadium and main temple, are earlier. For the casual visitor, highlights include the Athenian Treasury, the Athenian stoa and the Temple of Apollo.

The top sights

The Doric-order **Athenian Treasury** (late 6th- or early 5th-century) was pieced together by French archaeologists in 1904–06, using the inscriptions covering its surface as a guide. The late-6th-century **Athenian stoa**, today retaining three complete Ionic columns before a polygonal wall, was a roofed area protecting souvenirs from various Athenian naval victories, including the defeat of the Persians at Salamis in 480 BC. An inscription reads: "The Athenians have dedicated this portico with the arms and bow ornaments taken from their enemies at sea."

The **Temple of Apollo** just above the Athenian stoa is the third confirmed temple to have stood here, and there are literary rumours of three even earlier ones; two 7th- and 6th-century predecessors were done for by fire and earthquake respectively. What you see dates from 369–329 BC, and is impressive enough, measuring 66 by 26 metres (215 by 85 ft): six columns were re-erected by the French. The god Apollo was associated, among other things, with prophecy, his main function here. His oracle resided under the temple flooring in the *adyton* chamber, where a chasm in the earth belched forth noxious and possibly mind-altering vapours. Consulting the oracle of Delphi consisted of several stages. The petitioner's question would be relayed to the god Apollo by a priestess known as the Pythia, who could

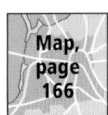

Map, page 166

BELOW: the Sanctuary of Athena Pronaia, Delphi.

Plays were performed at Dephi's theatre during the Pythian Festival, held every four years.

hear the answer only when she was in a trance – induced, conveniently enough, by residing in the vapour-filled adyton. Her ravings, in turn, could be understood only by the sanctuary's priests, who interpreted them for the supplicant – often ambiguously – for a suitable fee. One of the oracle's more memorable pronouncements was that Oedipus would kill his father and marry his mother – thereby giving the world its most tragic hero and Freud his Oedipus complex.

The small **theatre** above the temple, originally 4th-century but thoroughly restored during the Roman era, seats 5,000 people and has marvellous acoustics. The **stadium**, a long narrow oval, is well worth the somewhat steep walk beyond the theatre. It retains 12 rows of seats on the north side and six rows of seats, now mostly tumbled, on the south (sadly, off-limits). You will easily find the starting and finishing lines, the limestone blocks complete with grooves for the runners' toes.

The Delphi **museum** (summer Mon 12.30–6.30pm, Tues–Sun 7.30am–7.30pm; winter daily 8.30am–2.45pm; entrance included in site ticket) underwent a comprehensive refit in the run-up to the 2004 Athens Olympics, further highlighting its magnificent collection. The bronze charioteer of 470 BC with his onyx eyes is the most famous denizen, but look out also for two huge 6th-century *kouroi*, the votive, life-sized bull made from hammered silver sheets, the Ionic Sphinx of the Naxians, dating from 565 BC, and the Siphian frieze with scenes from the Trojan War and a battle between the gods and the titans.

The coast of Fokída

BELOW: Delphi's Temple of Apollo.

Below Delphi and its namesake modern, touristic village, a vast plain of olive trees stretches south towards the Gulf of Corinth. Literally gritty **Itéa** was once the ancient port of Delphi and still ships out the odd cargo of purple-red bauxite, strip-mined from the flanks of Mt Gióna to the west. But the real star of this often bleak coast is little **Galaxídi** ❼. With its Venetian-influenced mansions, the place seems closer in style to Koróni or Návpaktos than the rough-hewn village houses of Fokída. Local shipowners prospered during the 18th and 19th centuries when Galaxídi was, amazingly, the fourth-busiest harbour in Greece – thus the elaborate mansions. But captains refused to convert to steam after the 1890s, and the place sank into obscurity until being rediscovered by wealthy Athenians looking for a pleasant weekend bolthole. Foreign tourists are thus few, but there are plenty of comfortable lodgings and decent restaurants along the south harbour quay, where yachts congregate.

The coastal road of Fokída heads west, passing **Ágios Nikólaos** (regular ferries to Égio on the Peloponnese) and **Trizónia**, the only inhabited island in the Gulf of Corinth, before arriving at **Návpaktos** ❽, just inside Étolo-Akarnanía. The Ottomans used it as a base before sailing out to defeat in the naval battle of Lepanto (the Venetians name for Návpaktos), crushed by an allied Christian armada commanded by John of Austria in 1571. An Ottoman chronicler lamented, "The Imperial fleet encountered the fleet of the wretched infidels and the will of Allah turned another way." For all its resonance in the West, however, the battle – gleefully celebrated as the first major bloodying of the "Terrible Turk" – had little local effect, since the Ottomans had already taken Cyprus that summer, quickly rebuilt their navies and went on to conquer Crete within a century. In cool weather, climb up from the little egg-shaped Venetian harbour to the sprawling, pine-tufted castle above. Much the largest place on the gulf's north shore, today Návpaktos gracefully combines the functions of low-key resort and market town. The better hotels and most restaurants stand behind

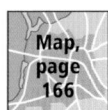

Map, page 166

Cervantes, then a crewman on a Spanish ship, lost his left arm to a cannonball at the battle of Lepanto, fought off Návpaktos in 1571.

BELOW: the Rio Andirrio bridge in the Gulf of Corinth.

plane-tree-shaded Grímbovo beach, although bathing there is dubious; retire instead to the westerly beach of Psáni.

Étolo-Akarnanía

Continuing further west into Étolo-Akarnanía from Návpaktos, the landscape becomes flatter and less dramatic; the main sight en route is the earthquake-proof **suspension bridge** inaugurated in 2004 at the **Río-Andírrio straits**, the longest in the world and clearly visible from jets 10,500 metres (35,000 ft) up. The road veers inland briefly before arriving at **Mesolóngi** , where Lord Byron died on 19 April 1824. The Ottomans had been trying to take the town since 1822; in April 1825 the final attack was mounted by 30,000 troops against 5,000 active insurgents. After a year of close siege, about half the population of 20,000 – combatants and civilians alike – broke out but were ambushed, with only about 1,600 surviving. Those remaining in town fired their own powder magazines, killing themselves, several thousand children and the elderly, and many Turkish attackers.

The northeast entrance to the town through the Venetian wall is known as the **Gate of the Sortie**, built by King Otho where the inhabitants defied the siege. To the west lies the **Garden of Heroes** (signposted "Heroes' Tombs"), with a tumulus covering the bodies of the anonymous defenders; the tomb of the Greek commander, Markos Botsaris; and a statue of Byron. Today Mesolóngi is, more on sentimental than practical grounds, the capital of Étolo-Akarnanía, and lives mostly from the products of the vast and sometimes whiffy lagoons which surround the town on three sides: salt, *avgotáraho* or compressed grey-mullet roe, and smoked eels. The latter two items can be sampled at several tavernas on and around Athanasíou Razikótsika, at the heart of the old quarter.

The Venetian castle at Návpaktos extends to ramparts guarding the harbour.

BELOW: Návpaktos harbour.

Beyond Mesolóngi, and the enormous walls of ancient **Pleuron** on the mountainside, the road splits near **Etolikó** ❿, a strange place built as a medieval refuge on an island in a lagoon. The more popular highway goes through the **Klisoúra Gorge** past unsightly **Agrínio**, commercial capital of the province, and on through tobacco fields to **Amfilohía** at the southernmost tip of the Amvrakikós Gulf.

A more interesting route to western Epirus veers off at Etolikó and mostly follows the coast all the way. Once across the mighty Ahelóös River and over the hills of the **Lesíni ash forest**, you emerge at **Ástakos**, a minor ferry port with services to Itháki but also a major yacht anchorage. The onward road offers spectacular views over small and large members of the Ionian archipelago before cruising through **Mýtikas** and **Páleros**, two little resorts in the lee of Levkáda which make excellent meal stops or overnight halts. At the end of the journey is **Vónitsa** with its little castle, gulf-front tavernas and, as ever hereabouts, a merely functional beach; from here you are poised to head either southwest to Lefkáda or northwest through a tunnel under the mouth of the Amvrakikós Gulf to Préveza.

North into Evrytanía

From Návpaktos, a little-used but highly scenic road goes northeast into the valley of the Évinos River, beloved of rafters, and then climbs again to the basin of Lake Trihonída, the largest natural body of fresh water in Greece. On a plateau out of sight to the northeast lies the lively town of **Thérmo** and its predecessor, ancient **Thermon** ⓫ (open Tues–Sun 8.30am–3pm; free), the main religious centre of the ancient Aetolians. Beyond Thérmo, the gradient steepens as you head north through the forest to Evrytanía province. First up are **Prousós** ⓬ village and monastery, poised on the precipitous, landslide-prone north slopes of

Map, page 166

Jason, who set out in his ship Argo to find the Golden Fleece, began his journey in Iolkos, an ancient site on the outskirts of Vólos.

BELOW: Welcoming Lord Byron at Mesolóngi by Theodoros Vryzakis, 1861.

Mt Panetolikó; its isolation made the area a haunt of revolutionary hero Karaískakis. Some spectacular gorges bring you to the main **Karpenisiótis valley**, heart of Evrytanía and nicknamed the "Greek Switzerland". Helvetic indeed are the green slopes and fir trees, matched by Swiss-style stratospheric accommodation prices. The ski centre on Mt Veloúhi, north of the provincial capital of **Karpenísi** ⑬, is a popular target, as are day-walks up Mounts Kaliakoúda and Helidóna, the valley's 2,000-metre (6,200-ft) flanking peaks. The main villages just outside of war-ravaged Karpenísi, more appealing for a stay or a meal, are Megálo Horió, Mikró Horió, Voutýro, Gávros and Koryshádes.

North from Fokída to Thessaly

From the Delphi area, it is also possible to head straight north between mounts Parnassus and Gióna towards **Lamía** ⑭, capital of its own province and a pleasant lunch stop. On the way you pass near to a hallowed site of Ancient Greek heroism. In antiquity, **Thermopylae** ⑮ was a narrow passage between the cliffs and the sea, although today silt from a nearby river has displaced the coastline by almost 5 km (3 miles). In 480 BC the Spartan general Leonidas held the pass for three days against a vastly larger Persian army, until the Persians, tipped off by the traitor Ephialtes, outflanked the defenders by using a higher pass. Leonidas ordered most of the Greek army to retreat, but fought to the end with his hand-picked guard of 2,300 men. A monumental statue of Leonidas now marks the spot, across the road from the grave mound for the Greek dead. Just beyond are the still-popular hot sulphur springs (Thermopylae means "hot gates") after which the pass is named.

Less than one hour's drive along the motorway from Lamía, **Vólos** ⑯ – capital of the Thessalian province of Magnisía – is certainly not the most photogenic of

BELOW: Vólos seen from Makrynítsa.

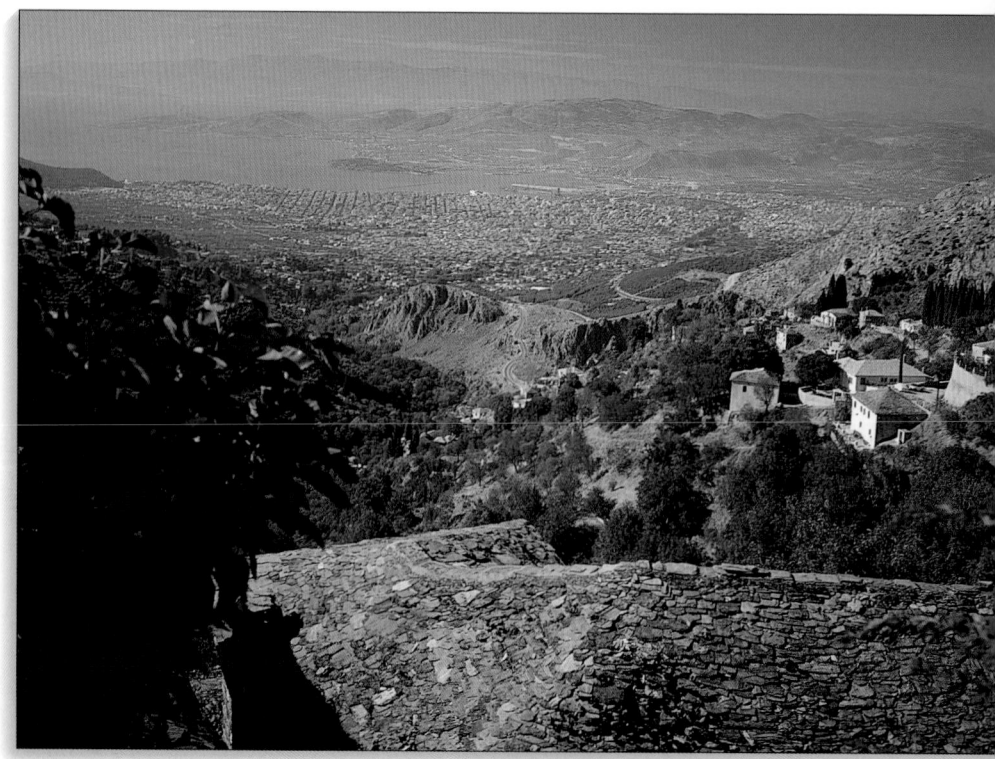

Map, page 166

owns. Destroyed by several earthquakes between 1947 and 1957, it is a busy, modern port, a sort of compressed version of Thessaloníki and Piraeus. That said, it is also a spirited town, with (like most of Thessaly) a tradition of Communist politics, a university, and arguably the largest Greek concentration of *ouzerís* along its waterfront. This gets leafier and more Aegean as you head east towards the excellent **archeological museum** (open Tues–Sun 8.30am–3pm; entrance fee), which houses finds dating back to Neolithic times and Vólos' early days as ancient Iolkos.

Mount Pílio

The great Thessalian plain, once the bed of an inland sea, is ringed by mountains; the only natural outlet is where the Piniós River exits through the fabled **Vale of Témbi**, a 10-km (6-mile) gorge between **Mount Olympos** (Ólympos) and **Mount Óssa**. Looming above Vólos is **Mount Pílio**, legendary home of the centaurs. These fantastic beings had the legs and bodies of horses, the arms and heads of men, and – well-versed in magic and herbology – served as the wise tutors of several ancient heroes, including Achilles. Probably the centaurs were a mythologisation of an aboriginal tribe who, hiding in the dense Pílio forests, preserved the lore of pre-Hellenic ages.

Intriguingly, the entire region was a prominent centre of learning in Greece during the 17th and 18th centuries. Many important officials of the Austro-Hungarian Empire, of the sultan's inner circle and even of the Russian court were educated on Mount Pílio. The peninsula probably became such a nursery of Greek erudition owing to its timber-based wealth and distance from grasping Ottoman officials.

The Pílio Peninsula has two faces: the damp, shaggy northeast flank dropping to the Aegean, with excellent sand beaches of near-Caribbean hue; and the

The Megálou Meteórou monastery contains 16th-century frescoes by Franco Catellano.

BELOW: Pílio specialities.

Willows, planes and laurels border the Piniós River which cuts through the Vale of Témbi, making it a delightful place to hike. You can also take a canoe or kayak trip through the gorge.

BELOW: Labinoú beach on Pílio.

balmy, olive-covered slopes fringed with pebble shores lapped by the Pagasitic Gulf. Even if you go by charter flight to Vólos airport (a military base recently opened to civilian flights) and have use of a hire car, a week is realistically needed to tour it. The obvious, over-subscribed target is **Makrynítsa** ⑰, 17 km (11 miles) north of Vólos, with its large concentration of 18th-century mansions and a fountain-and-church-flanked square. But **Vyzítsa** ⑱ to the east is quieter, with nearly as many grand houses.

Zagorá ⑲ and **Tsangaráda** in the northeast each comprise four villages in one, their several parishes strung out along kilometres of road: because of abundant water, few Pílio communities form dense clusters as on the islands. The main developed resorts are **Ágios Ioánnis** ⑳ near Zagorá, **Plataniá** in the far south and **Áfyssos** closer to Vólos. For contrast, try to stop at relatively unfrequented villages like **Láfkos**, **Sykí** and **Promýri** in the south. **Tríkeri** ㉑ and its port Agía Kyriakí, at the crab-claw southwest tip, lead a largely separate existence, with a strong maritime tradition. Beaches are too numerous to list although the postcard stars tend to be of **Mylopótamos** with its natural arch, and **Damoúhari** port with its tiny Venetian castle, both below Tsangaráda.

The Metéora

Heading up to the Metéora, you may want to detour to **Ambelákia**, some 30 km (20 miles) north of Lárisa, where the world's first cooperative was founded in 1778 around the production of scarlet yarns. The village's outstanding architectural heritage includes the mansion of George Schwartz, whose rooms provide a rich archive of domestic interiors from times past.

As you approach **Kalabáka** from Tríkala, towering rock formations – the Metéora ㉒ – rise before you in one of the great spectacles of mainland Greece. Some of the most extraordinary monasteries in the world cling to these massive pinnacles, whose name derives from the verb *meteorízo*, "to suspend in the air". These cones, cylinders and rounded buttresses, flecked with vegetation and caves like so many unbrushed, carious molars, are remnants of river sediment deposited at the margins of the prehistoric sea covering the plain of Thessaly some 25 million years ago. Tectonic-plate pressure and erosion by the young Piniós River are jointly responsible for their present shape.

Religious hermits were already colonising the caves here by the 10th century, but legend attributes the first rock-top monastery (Megálou Meteórou) to the Athonite monk Athanasios, midway through the 14th century. Progress was slow as materials were transported first by rope ladder, then by winches and baskets, and it took nearly three centuries to finish Megálou Meteórou, by which time it was just one of 24 religious communities that were flourishing on the summits. After the 17th century the monastic impetus slowed, and the more flimsily erected structures began to crumble on their exposed perches; the vicissitudes of modern Greek history since the Revolution further hastened decline, and today only eight survive, of which just six are inhabited and open to pilgrims.

Heading north out of Kalabáka through the village

Map, page 166

of **Kastráki**, set unimprovably in the shadow of the rocks, you encounter monasteries in the following order. **Agíou Nikoláou Anápavsa** (open Sat–Thur 9am–3.30pm; winter until 3pm), built around 1388, has well-cleaned frescoes by the monk Theofanes of the Cretan School (*circa* 1527), including a stylite (column-dwelling) hermit being supplied by winch-hoist, as would have been done locally. **Megálou Meteórou** (open summer Wed–Mon 9am–5pm; winter Thur–Mon 9am–4pm) is the largest and highest monastery, although its church is overshadowed by a collection of rare icons and manuscripts in the refectory. **Varlaám** (open summer daily 9am–4pm; winter Sat–Wed 9am–3pm), founded in 1517, offers 16th-century frescoes by Franco Catellano (partly retouched in 1870), including an Ascension and a *Pandokrátor* in the two domes respectively. It is also the last monastery to preserve in situ its old windlass mechanism, formerly used for elevating monks and supplies; a new electric pulley lifts the latter now.

Beautiful little **Roussánou** (open summer daily 9am–6pm, winter Thur–Tues 9am–2pm), completely occupying a knife-edge summit, was built in 1545 for monks, later abandoned, and re-occupied by nuns in the 1970s. It too has vividly gory 17th-century frescoes dwelling on martyrdom by various unpleasant means. **Agías Triádos** (open Fri–Wed, summer 9am–5pm; winter 9am–12.30pm, 3–5pm), with a final approach of 130 steps tunnelled through a rock, has frescoes in its *katholikón* which were thoroughly cleaned during the 1990s. Like other monastic churches here, this was built in two phases, resulting in two domes, two *Pandokrátors* and two complete sets of Evangelists. **Agíou Stefánou** (open Tues–Sun, summer 9am–2pm, 3.30–6pm; winter 9am–1pm, 3–5pm), like Roussánou, is run as a convent but, heavily damaged by bombs during World War II, is the one to skip if time is running short. ❑

BELOW: the Varlaám monastery as seen from the Holy Monastery of the Transfiguration of Jesus.

EPIRUS

A spectacular mountain region of limestone peaks, wooded valleys and traditional stone villages, the northwest also offers a pristine national park where bears and wolves still roam

Map, page 178

nland Epirus (Ípiros in Greek) is a world apart from the azure, sun-bleached Greece of the coasts. Its character is determined by the limestone peaks and deep river gorges of the Píndos range, which attains its greatest height just efore the Albanian border in mounts Smólikas (2,635 metres/8,645 ft) and Grámos (2,520 metres/8,270 ft). The winter precipitation, the highest in mainland reece, ensures that forests are shaggy and the rivers foaming. An isolation nforced by both mountains and climate fostered the growth of medieval semiutonomous villages built by traders and craftsmen returning from abroad. ocal stone and wood has been transformed into imposing houses, with street obbles, walls and roof slates blending in a uniform grey which, far from being epressing, is a classic example of harmonious adaptation to environment.

In antiquity, this was considered the limit of the civilised world; few ruins ave been unearthed besides shadowy oracles at Dodona (Dodóni) and Acheron. he Romans and Byzantines had scarcely more time for this rugged terrain outh of the Via Egnatia, even though during the 13th and 14th centuries the Despotate of Epirus extended from the Ionian Sea to Thessaloníki. This ministate sheltered members of the Byzantine nobility who had fled the imperial apital when it was sacked by the Fourth Crusade in 1204. They left behind ntriguing churches around Árta, joining earlier masterpieces at Kastoriá in western Macedonia.

Like the rest of northern Greece, Epirus was not ncorporated into the modern state until March 1913, uring the First Balkan War and some 80 years after he end of the initial Greek War of Independence.

clipse – and Renaissance?

During the 20th century, the remoteness that once protected the area undermined its continued vigour. The avages of World War II and the subsequent civil war, long with poor communications, the unviability of raditional livelihoods and apparently punitive government neglect, spurred massive emigration, particularly to North America, Germany and Australia. By he 1970s, many Epirot villages were in an advanced tate of physical and social decline. Numerous houses vere left to decay (or shoddily repaired), while others heltered an ever-dwindling population of the economically inactive elderly.

But since the early 1980s, matters have slowly hanged. The government has acted to integrate the egion into the national economy, most obviously with requent flights to Ioánnina and good roads, including he Via Egnatia expressway and its ambitious tunnels hrough the Píndos, plus the pending Ionian Highway up rom Mesolóngi. Emigration has slowed down and just occasionally – thanks to tourism, subsidies for logging

LEFT: shepherd in the Píndos mountains, near Zagória.
BELOW: the coast at Préveza.

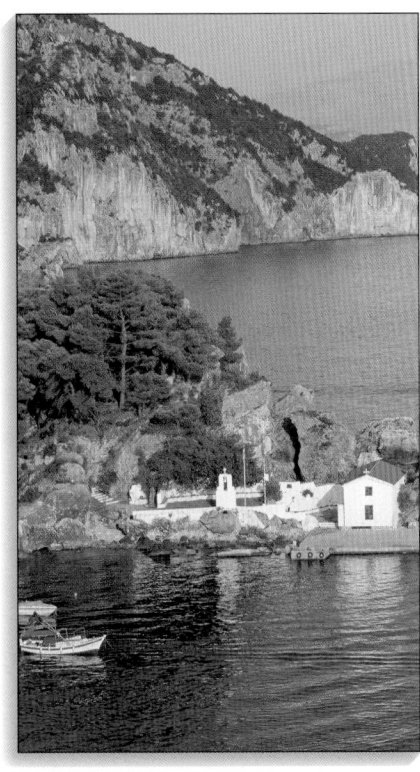

or grazing, and better infrastructure – even halted. Attitudes towards village li
have softened, with traditional architecture and methods now viewed less as stun
bling blocks to economic prosperity and more as cultural heritage to be preserve

The core issues of this new era are most visible in the Zagóri district of Epiru
Archeological initiatives and financial incentives have led to the restoration of
many buildings, so that entire villages are now preserved as homogeneous trad
itional settlements. Simultaneously, old roads have been widened and paved, an
new ones bulldozed, giving access to the tiniest hamlets. Because of the natu
of tourism here, Zagóri is one of the few places in Greece where more than li
service is paid to the idea of quality trekking routes – although trails off the mo
popular itineraries can be haphazardly marked and maintained at best, and faci
ities in the villages where you finish a day's hike can be rudimentary.

As in the whole of Greece, a touristic plum as lucrative as Zagóri ha
inevitably become the focus of ongoing battles between conservationists, deve
opers and entrepreneurs. Dirt roads serving timber tracts and the high pasture

Epirus and Northwest Macedonia

scar the landscape, as does the national power corporation's reservoir at the sources of the Aóös River. Cuttings and tunnellings for the partly opened Via Egnatia have a significant visual impact, especially near Métsovo. Yet during the late 1980s and early 1990s, not a few shepherds and villagers allied themselves with urban mountaineers, local tourism personnel, international ecologists and even the European Kayaking Federation to halt a scheme promoted by Ioánnina-based interests for a second dam on the lower Aóös, plus various ski lifts and roads which would have ruined the national park at the heart of Zagóri. Low-impact, high-quality tourism – specifically accommodation in some of the many restored houses – has been successfully promoted, particularly in the gateway villages for the park where the inhabitants sided with the conservationists.

Coastal Epirus

The modern port of **Igoumenítsa** ❶, at the very northwestern corner of mainland Greece, is the third busiest in the country after Pátra and Piraeus (Pireás), a turnstile sort of a place where an enforced halt should be avoided at all costs. Far more rewarding is the coastal road south, which after 33 km (20 miles) reaches the side road for **Karavostássi**, indisputably the finest beach in Thesprotía province. Two rivers at each end of the long strand are responsible for the ample sand, and since it is a protected area development is still limited. Just up the hill from the side-turning sits the village of **Pérdika**, whose pedestrianised centre offers a range of tavernas and a surprisingly lively night scene, courtesy of Athenian Greeks and Greeks returned from overseas.

From the Karavostássi-Pérdika junction, a few more kilometres – via the well-preserved castle of **Agiá** (open daily all day; free) – suffice to bring you to

Map, page 178

BELOW:
the Víkos Gorge.

Local goat's cheese makes a tasty snack.

BELOW: boats moored in the bay of Párga.

Párga ❷, Epirus's main coastal resort and deservedly so for its fine beaches, tiered houses and dominant Norman-Venetian castle. From the 14th to the late 18th centuries this was the Serene Republic's lone stronghold in Epirus, peopled by Souliot Orthodox Christians in constant conflict with their Muslim neighbours, as well as a small community of Jews who lived from the export of citrons to Europe for Jewish liturgical use. The British acquired it in 1814 and soon ceded it to the rapacious Ali Pasha of Ioánnina; the townspeople collected their holy relics and moved to Corfu and Paxí. Párga now enjoys 100 percent hotel occupancy (mostly from package tours) from late June through to early September, although out of season it still makes an atmospheric stop.

Some 22 km (14 miles) southeast, beside **Mesopótamos** village, lies the **Necromanteion** ❸ (Nekromándio) of Acheron (open daily 8.30am–3pm), the venerable oracle of the dead described by Circe in *The Odyssey*. Today the Ahérondas River (one of the legendary rivers swirling around Hades) has silted up the surrounding agricultural plain, but in Homeric times the oracle was a suitably mysterious, tree-fringed island in a lagoon. Supplicants entered the sanctuary via a maze of corridors and were then lowered by a pulley into a vaulted underground chamber to experience whatever spectral hoax the resident priests had concocted.

The Ahérondas enters the sea at **Ammoudiá** ❹ just 5 km (3 miles) to the west. The river makes bathing at the beach here cold, and should you choose to stay the night, the mosquitoes are out in force after dark. But lunching at the row of tavernas on the pedestrianised quay, where tour boats for hire to the Necromanteion bob at anchor, is exceedingly pleasant; and a small but excellent "visitor information centre" at the town entrance (open Mon–Sat erratic hours; free) covers the natural history and ethnology of the area.

Inland from the Necromanteion, closer to its source, the Ahérondas squeezes through a spectacular gorge. From the village of **Glykí** ❺, a side track signposted for the "Skála Dzavélenas" dead-ends at the start of the *skála*: a spectacular 90-minute path down to the river bed and up into the realm of the Souliots, a Christian tribe never completely subdued by the Ottomans. From Glykí, continue south another 30 km (19 miles) to the combined side turning for **Zalóngo** and ancient Kassope. The former, a mountaintop monastery of little intrinsic interest, was witness to a dramatic incident in 1806 which has since become a staple of Greek nationalist legend known by every schoolchild: trapped by Ali Pasha's forces, several dozen Souliot women fled to a nearby pinnacle, where – rather than submit to the enemy – they danced off the edge into thin air clutching their children. An incongruous modern sculpture celebrates their defiance.

Nearby **Kassope** ❻ (open daily 8.30am–3pm, may be open other times; entrance fee) is less visited and eminently rewarding: a minor Hellenistic city whose jumbled ruins are matched by a fine view over the Ionian Sea and Lefkáda island. No such paeans apply to the artificial Roman city of **Nikopolis**, some 15 km (9 miles) south and 600 metres (2,000 ft) below, which promises much from the sheer extent of its ruins but offers little close up. **Áktio**, the promontory dovetailing with Préveza at the mouth of the Amvrakikós Gulf, was Roman Actium, also the name of the naval battle in which Octavian defeated Anthony and Cleopatra's forces in 31 BC. Octavian then named himself Emperor Augustus and established Nikopolis, "Victory City", nearby.

Préveza ❼, once a sleepy, shabby provincial capital, has been spruced up, partly to cater for package tourists in transit between Áktio airport and the fine

Map, page 178

TIP

The hill-top ruins of ancient Kassope make a glorious vantage-point from which to watch the sunrise. If you're tempted, a daily bus from Préveza makes the trip at 6am.

BELOW: Nikopolis, "City of Victory", was founded by the emperor Augustus.

beaches to the north, or on Lefkáda. In its old bazaar, with rather more charac-ter than Párga's, a clutch of restaurants still offer the gulf's famous sardines, and summer nightlife is loud and varied. In 2003, a tunnel under the mouth of the gulf finally replaced the old RO-RO ferry ride across to Áktio.

Some 50 km (31 miles) over on the far side of the gulf lies **Árta** ❽, the ancient Ambracia and capital of King Pyrrhus (of the original pyrrhic victory). It later became the seat of the Despotate of Epirus, and retains a legacy of churches from that era. Most notable is the enormous, cubic **Panagía Parig-orítissa** (open Tues–Sun 8.30am–3pm; entrance fee), which dates from the late 13th century and betrays Italian influences in its palazzo-like exterior. High in the dome, supported by a gravity-defying cantilever system, floats a magnificent mosaic of the Pandokrátor (Christ in Majesty), the finest on the mainland after Dafní near Athens, despite damage from World War II bombing by the Italians.

In the citrus groves around the town lie other late Byzantine churches and monasteries, the most beautiful of which is **Panagía Vlahernón** in the village of **Vlahérna** ❾, 6 km (4 miles) to the north. Despot Michael II added the domes in the 13th century, and is thought to be entombed inside. A magnificent floor mosaic is on view under glass near the altar.

Ioánnina

Lining the shores of **Lake Pamvótis** (Pamvótida), spread below the stark face of Mount Mitsikéli, **Ioánnina** ❿ has been one of Greece's great cities for over 1,000 years: a beacon of Hellenic culture, a traders' *entrepôt* and, in the 19th cen-tury (its last glorious epoch), the capital of the infamous Ali Pasha. Nicknamed "the Lion of Ioánnina", this maverick Albanian Muslim tyrant paid only minimal

TIP

During the summer, Préveza makes a good base for visiting the Ionian Islands, with frequent hydrofoil connections – although schedules often change at random.

BELOW:
church of Panagía Parigorítissa.

allegiance to the ruling Ottoman Empire while establishing an autonomous fiefdom. Today the town remains one of Greece's liveliest provincial centres.

Unlike most large Greek centres, Ioánnina's history does not predate early Christian times, when an earthquake blocked the natural drainages of the surrounding plain and thus created the lake. Its name derives from an early church of St John the Baptist, long since vanished. After the Latin conquest of Constantinople in 1204 and the establishment of the Despotate of Epirus, Ioánnina grew in size and importance as refugees from "The City" swelled its population. It surrendered to the Ottomans in the 15th century; in 1788 Ali Pasha designated this town of 35,000 inhabitants (large for that time) his headquarters.

Ioánnina's layout is testimony to Ali's dubious legacy. While he left behind the city's most distinctive monuments (its mosques, and the redoubtable Kástro in its present form), he also had much of the city burned to deny it to a besieging Ottoman army, sent by the sultan to put down his unruly vassal in 1820. This, along with a 1960s penchant for large apartment blocks, has resulted in the relentlessly modern Ioánnina which lies outside the old town.

The wide expanse of central **Platía Pýrrou**, joined to the plazas of Akadimías and Dimokratías and lined by various public buildings, makes an obvious starting-point for a city tour. Just east of Dimokratías stands the Archeological Museum (closed temporarily), home to a fine collection of bronzes and tablets inscribed with questions for the Dodona oracle.

Except for a couple of cinemas with good first-run fare, this area is no longer the main nocturnal hub of Ioánnina. That has shifted downhill along Avérof towards the Kástro, past two shopfronts selling the famous local *bougátsa* (custard or cheese pie) at Dimokratías 2 and Avérof 3 respectively, to take better advantage of the town's setting. State-of-the-art late-night bars cluster at the far end of Ethnikís Andístasis, in a former tradesmen's bazaar by the lake, and around Platía Mavíli, on the opposite side of the citadel. On summer nights, the latter – better known as Mólos – throbs with townspeople strolling past vendors selling roast corn, *halvás* and bootleg tapes of local clarinet music from gas-lit pushcarts.

Kástro, the five-gated, walled precinct of various Epirot rulers including Ali Pasha himself, best conjures up Ioánnina's colourful past. A tangle of alleyways rises to a fortified promontory jutting out into the lake; at the lower corner looms the **Aslan Pasha Mosque**, now home to the Municipal Ethnographic Museum (open daily summer 8am–8pm, winter 9am–4pm; entrance fee) with its diverse collection of Epirot costumes, jewellery and relics from the city's once-large Jewish community.

One of Ali Pasha's most infamous exploits – involving Kyra Frosini, the beautiful Greek mistress of Ali's eldest son – is supposed to have taken place near the mosque-museum. In the most common variant of the tale, Ali punished the girl for resisting his advances by having her and 17 female companions tied up in weighted sacks and drowned in the lake. Islamophobic-kitsch oleograph postcards of the incident are still sold, depicting wild-eyed "barbarians" and swooning Greek maidens in the clutches of their tormentors.

Map, page 178

The Aslan Pasha Mosque, now the Municipal Museum, has fascinating relics of Ioánnina's colourful past.

BELOW: across Lake Pamvótis to the city of Ioánnina.

The monastery of Agíou Nikoláou Filanthropinón, near the island-village of Nissí, is worth a visit for its vivid frescoes.

At the summit of the citadel looms the **Fethiye Tzami** (Victory Mosque) and one of Ali's heavily restored palaces – today an indifferent Byzantine Museum (open summer Mon 12.30–7pm, Tues–Sun 8am–7pm; winter Tues–Sun 8am–5pm; entrance fee). The former treasury nearby makes an appropriate showcase for displays on the city's traditional silver industry.

After defying the sultan for three decades, Ali finally met his end on the isle of **Nisí**, on the far side of the visibly polluted lake (bus-boats make the trip from Mólos all day until 11pm). A small house in the grounds of Ágios Pandelímon monastery was his last hide-out; here, trapped on the upper storey by a Turkish assassin, Ali was shot through the floorboards then decapitated. His head was sent to Istanbul as a trophy, after having toured the provinces which it had lately so terrorised.

Monasteries with more peaceful histories, and a fine island loop walk, lie in the opposite direction. The nearest Nisí village, **Agíou Nikoláou Filanthropinón**, contains vivid late-Byzantine frescoes; some depict unusually gruesome martyrdoms, while others, by the entrance, depict ancient sages such as Plutarch, Aristotle and Thucydides. Alas, the island's tavernas are touristy and poor in quality; if Ioanninans want a lakeside meal, they patronise the half-dozen restaurants which line **Pamvotídas**, the shoreline street heading northwest from Mólos.

Diversions around Ioánnina

BELOW: Ioánnina's lake and Aslan Pasha Mosque.

Some 20 km (12 miles) south of Ioánnina lies **Dodona** (Dodóni), Epirus's main archeological site (open daily June–Aug 8.30am–6pm, Sept–May 8.30am–3pm; entrance fee), nestling in a valley at the foot of Mount Tómaros. According to Herodotus, its oracle (the oldest in Greece and, until the 4th century BC, the most important) was established by a priestess abducted from a similar one in Egyptian Thebes. Zeus – considered resident in the trunk of a holy oak tree – was worshipped here, priests and priestesses deciphering the rustlings of the leaves which were the god's sacred pronouncements. The carefully restored **theatre**, dating from the 3rd-century reign of King Pyrrhus, has a capacity of 17,000 spectators – always far too large for the needs of the little town that existed here from 1000 BC until early Byzantine times. It is now, sadly, roped off; foundations of the Zeus sanctuary lie beyond it.

Until the Via Egnatia expressway south of town opens for business (estimated for 2010), the only highway east into Thessaly is the old one curling clockwise around the lake. On this route you will pass **Pérama** (open daily summer 8am–8pm; winter 8am–sunset; entrance fee), one of Greece's most spectacular cave systems, on the outskirts of Ioánnina. Then, after a long, twisting ascent, the village of **Métsovo** ⓬, 58 km (36 miles) from Ioánnina, appears in a ravine below. It ranks as the Vlach "capital", famous for its imposing houses, handicrafts, cheeses and the traditional costumes still worn by some of the older inhabitants.

Apart from the wonderful frescoes covering the interior of the medieval monastery of Ágios Nikólaos, a short walk below town, the only other recognised sight is the **Arhondikó Tosítsa Museum** (open Fri–Wed 8.30am–1pm, 4–6pm; winter 3–5pm; guided tours only; entrance fee), its reconstructed interior displaying fine woodwork and textiles.

Unlike so many Greek mountain villages, Métsovo is thriving: local worthies who made their fortunes abroad have set up endowments to encourage

Map,
page
178

Exhibits in the
Arhondikó Tosítsa
Museum, Métsovo.

BELOW:
Dodona's theatre.

local industry, such as the nearby ski resort whose clients periodically fill the dozen or so hotels – of a better standard than most in Ioánnina. And while many of the souvenirs pitched at coach tours are bogus – notably imported Albanian rugs – locally sold food is not: the red *katoï* wine, cheese, salami and *trahanás* (sourdough "pasta" for soup) all make excellent purchases.

Continuing east towards the Metéora in Thessalía (Thessaly), soon after Métsovo you negotiate the Katára Pass ("Curse Pass") – at 1,694 metres (5,557 ft) the highest paved road in the country and the main route across the central Píndos Mountains, at least until the Via Egnatia tunnels open.

The Zagorohória

The road northwest out of Ioánnina leads to **Zagória,** which forms a culturally and geographically distinct region of Epirus. Its 46 villages – the Zagorohória – lie in an area bounded by the Métsovo–Ioánnina–Kónitsa highway and the Aóös River. Because of the region's infertile soil, local men emigrated to major commercial centres in Eastern Europe during the Ottoman era, subsequently returning to their homeland with considerable wealth. This allowed locals to hire a representative to send taxes to the sultan directly rather than suffer from tax-farmers, securing a large measure of autonomy.

Zagória's villages differ markedly: the east is populated largely by Vlachs (more properly, Arouman), a people rooted in Greece since antiquity, speaking a Romance language and living as caravan-drovers and shepherds driving their flocks from summer to winter pastures. Early in 1944, the occupying Germans retaliated for local resistance by burning most of the eastern villages, later rebuilt haphazardly. The western and central Zagorohória show more of a

BELOW: inside the caves at Pérama.

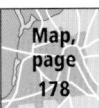
Map, page 178

Slav/Albanian influence in place names and architecture; happily, most survived the war unscathed and today constitute one of Greece's showpieces.

The Zagorian landscape is dramatically varied, embracing sheer rock faces, limestone dells, dense forests, upland pasture and deep canyons. The national park at its core, comprising the Víkos Gorge and lower reaches of the Aóös, was established partly to protect a threatened population of bears, lynx, wolves and birds of prey. Yet even in the remotest corners there are signs of man: a post-Byzantine monastery with belfry, or a graceful, slender-arched bridge from the Ottoman period. Unfortunately, the pastoral culture that used to feature prominently is in sharp decline; EU subsidy policy means that few shepherds now occupy the high pastures, and unattended cattle herds are rapidly replacing the tenanted sheepfolds of yesteryear.

Central Zagória is best reached by the side road some 14 km (9 miles) out of Ioánnina, prominently marked for the **Víkos Gorge**. **Vítsa** village has fine traditional houses, a shaded central square, one of the oldest churches in the region (Ágios Nikólaos), and the easiest trail access to the floor of the gorge, the intricately engineered Skála Vítsas. Just up the road, more frequented **Monodéndri** **⑬** supports a taverna offering hearty local cuisine on its lower plaza, near the photogenic basilica of Ágios Athanásios flanking the classic path descending to the gorge. For the less committed, either the 1990s-vintage, rather gaudy *kalderími* (cobbled path) to the eyrie of Agía Paraskeví monastery, or the 7-km (4-mile) drive up to the Oxiá overlook, will afford breathtaking views.

From the junction below Vítsa, the easterly main road passes the turning for exquisite **Dílofo** on its way to the major villages of Kípi, Kapésovo and Tsepélovo. **Kípi** **⑭** stands nearest to a much-photographed cluster of 18th- and 19th-century packhorse bridges, the most famous of which is the three-arched Plakída span. East of Kípi, **Negádes** has a frescoed basilica, one of the best examples of the Zagorian style, while above and to the north perches Kapésovo, with a rural museum in its enormous old school.

Kapésovo also marks the start of a one-hour path incorporating the most amazingly sinuous of all Zagorian *kalderímia*, ending at **Vradéto**, the highest – and formerly most desolate – village in the area, now enjoying a mild renaissance (although the winter population is still only seven). Continue on foot for about 40 minutes and you will reach Belói viewpoint, more or less opposite Oxiá. Twelve kilometres (7 miles) further, the paved road arrives at **Tsepélovo** **⑮**, flanked by rural monasteries and crammed with more mansions. Rangóvou monastery is just below.

Back on the Ioánnina-Kónitsa highway, you pass through **Kalpáki**, where in the early winter of 1940–41 the Greeks halted the Italian invasion, rolling Fascist troops back into the snowy Albanian Mountains for a season of hell; a small roadside museum tells the tale in full. Just beyond, a 19-km (12-mile) side road heads east to the focus of most Zagorian tourism, the paired villages of **Pápingo** **⑯**, **Megálo** and **Mikró**. Since the early 1990s they have become quite fashionable, especially during peak holiday seasons, but there is no denying their superlative setting

BELOW: the mansion of the Tositsa family in Métsovo is now a folk museum.

at the foot of the 600-metre (1,970-ft) Pýrgi, the vertical outriders of Mount Gamíla. This massif (the heart of the national park) offers fine hiking, most notably to newt-filled **Drakólimni** (Dragon Lake).

The icy **Voïdomátis River**, popular with kayakers, drains out of the lower Víkos canyon at Klidoniá, where a lovely old bridge marks the edge of the national park a few hundred metres in from the busy highway. An even bigger one spans the Aóös River some 10 km (6 miles) north, where it exits some narrows to a vast floodplain. A 90-minute walk along the southern bank of the Aóös Gorge leads below steep, forested slopes to the **Stomíou monastery**, magnificently perched on a cliff.

Kónitsa ⓲ itself offers a fine view of the floodplain; an earthquake in 1996 and massive shelling during the civil war put paid to any real architectural distinction here. For that, head 23 km (14 miles) west to the monastery and namesake village of **Molyvdosképastos**, just where the Aóös enters Albania. The monastery's early 14th-century church betrays a Serbian influence with its high, stovepipe dome and barrel-roof nave. Early in the 1990s it was reinhabited by rather zealous monks, who encourage your conversion on the spot.

Due east of Kónitsa looms 2,635-metre (8,650-ft) **Mount Smólikas**, roof of the Píndos and second summit of Greece after Mount Olympos. From several of the Vlach villages along the Aóös, trails lead up towards the peak and yet another "Dragon Lake".

The 105-km (65-mile) road from Kónitsa to **Neápolis** is the single paved connection between Epirus and western Macedonia. It follows the valley of the Sarandáporos River upstream, between Smólikas and Mount Grámmos, site of the final battles of the civil war, passing the occasional blue-painted graffiti

BELOW: Kónitsa bridge, Zagória.

:leuthería Gia Vória Ípiros!" ("Freedom for Northern Epirus!") – an expression
lingering irredentist sentiment for the Albanian portion of Epirus, home to
ughly 100,000 remaining Greek Orthodox.

Map,
page
178

king in the Píndos

he North Píndos offer many rewarding hiking routes, from strenuous, multi-
y, high-level treks to various interconnected day hikes. Landscapes vary from
e limestone dells of the Gamíla uplands to the forested Víkos Gorge floor. In
ese days of global warming, the best seasons are no longer high summer but
om mid-May to mid-June, and September to early October. Although the local
ail system is extensive on paper, it is unevenly maintained and often badly
aymarked; the usual method is multicoloured paint splodges or, for the long-
stance O3 route, metal diamond-shaped symbols nailed to trees.

The 1:50,000 *Pindus Zagori* topographic map issued by Anavasi cartogra-
ers (available in Greece and the UK) is essential if not infallible, as is a keen
nse of direction, an ability to double-check trail information from villagers,
d a good sense of humour. In any month the Píndos weather can change
pidly with little warning, so rain gear and a light tent are essential – the lat-
r also because indoor accommodation can fill up suddenly. Overnight trekkers
ould purchase three to four days' worth of foodstuffs in Ioánnina, as stocks in
llage shops remain quite limited.

The four-to-five-day hiking loop outlined below begins and ends in the
ápingo villages where there is plentiful (if slightly pricey) accommodation, as
ell as reliable tavernas and a twice-weekly bus service to Ioánnina. You should
erefore be prepared to hike into and out of Pápingo, along the trail linking it

BELOW: Drakólimni,
the 'Dragon Lake'.

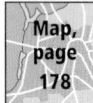

Map,
page
178

to Klidoniá village on the Ioánnina–Kónitsa highway, if you happen not to coin cide with the bus service.

The alpine refuge on Astráka col, just visible from Megálo Pápingo, is oper from May to October (to reserve bunks tel: 697 3223 100). It is a 900-metr (2,950-ft) ascent of at least three hours, with water available at regular interval If the refuge is full, camp near the spring at the north end of the season **Xiróloutsa pond** (15-minute path descent east from the col). Spend the baland of the day with a short walk (1 hr each way) up to **Drakólimni**, an alpine tar at 2,050 metres (6,725 ft) altitude, ideal for views and picnics, just northwest the 2,500-metre (8,200-ft) Gamíla peak.

A five-to-seven-hour hike the next day takes you between mounts Astráka ar Gamíla, through alpine meadows grazed by cattle, and past the head of th Mégas Lákkos Gorge to Tsepélovo (steep final descent; net altitude loss 850 metres/2,800 ft). Water is scarce, so plan accordingly. You should have comfortable overnight stay in one of Tsepélovo's dozen hotels and smaller inns although reservations are advisable during July and August.

From the ravine flanking Tsepélovo to the west, a crumbled but discernib *kalderími* climbs the cliff to the uplands towards Vradéto; after about 90 min utes you are forced onto a paved road for the final 45 minutes. From Vradé (café serving drinks only) descend the amazing *skála* to Kapésovo (45 mir utes), then use the old dirt track (not the asphalt highway) to arrive in **Koukoú** within the next 45 minutes and in time for lunch. You can stay overnight her at one of two inns, or carry on eastwards to Kípi (another 45 minutes), which h another taverna as well as several inns.

From either Koukoúli or Kípi there are marked routes into the upper end the Víkos Gorge, crossing it by the Misíou bridge ar ascending the stair-*kalderími* to Vítsa (2 hrs), wit abundant accommodation and a taverna open in th evenings. A three-hour track partly shortcuts the roa up to Monodéndri, 300 metres (985 ft) above Kíp with several more inns and tavernas.

A signposted, well-renovated *kalderími* takes yc down to the usually dry bed of the Víkos Gorg (45 minutes). A fairly strenuous path marked as th O3 route negotiates the length of the canyon, on true left bank after the first few minutes. At the inte section of the gorge and the Mégas Lákkos sic canyon (2½ hrs), a potable spring flows (unreliab after July). Continue through thick forest, then op pasture, before reaching the movable sources of th Voïdomátis River (4½ hrs from Monodéndri), whic well out of the base of the Pýrgi formations.

Bearing left on an obvious cobbled path leads **Vitsikó** (Víkos) village, 45 minutes away, where yc will find two inns; the O3 route crosses the rive heading up and right, reaching either of the Pápinge within two hours, for a day's total of 6½ hour About 90 minutes along, there is a divide in the pat where you cross a stream on the left to head up Megálo Pápingo, rather than continue straight t Mikró Pápingo. The net elevation drop amounts only 100 metres (330 ft), but there are plenty sharp gradients.

Below:
stone houses and cobbled streets in Zagorohória.
Right: Mikró Pápingo village in the Zagorohória.

THESSALONÍKI

Greece's second city does not live in the shadow of Athens.
It has its own distinctive character, with many Turkish
influences and a host of splendid Byzantine churches

Map, pages 202–3

To a visitor approaching by sea, contemporary **Thessaloníki ❶** presents the uniform facade of modern apartment blocks characteristic of so many Mediterranean seaside cities. At the beginning of this century, the same view was marked by minarets rising elegantly from a tile-roofed town picturesquely climbing between medieval ramparts to an upper quarter, with vast cemeteries outside the walls. When more than half the town was destroyed by the Great Fire of August 1917, British and French architects (who were accompanying Allied expeditionary forces at the time) were promptly commissioned to produce a new town plan.

Surviving Art Deco buildings enhance the wide, sea-facing boulevards they designed, although their advice to ban high-rises was disregarded. But the fire spared much, including the old hillside quarter of **Kástra**. Roman ruins, Byzantine churches, Ottoman public and domestic buildings, and displaced Jewish tombstones lie encircled by Roman and Byzantine walls, or scattered alongside asphalt boulevards and pedestrian lanes. And after years of neglect, this great architectural heritage has been signposted and selectively renovated.

One of Greece's liveliest and most interesting cities, Thessaloníki was founded in 316–315 BC by the Macedonian king Kassander, who named it after his wife, and it rose into prominence under the Romans, boosted by their **Via Egnatia** "trunk road" which stretched from the Adriatic to the Hellespont (Dardanelles). Saint Paul visited twice, and wrote two Epistles to the Thessalonians; Christianity (and the city) got further boosts from the Byzantine emperors, especially Theodosius (who issued his edict here, banning paganism) and Justinian, who began new churches to supplement those adapted from Roman structures. Despite Slavic and Arab raids, frequent earthquakes, fires, adjacent malarial swamps and a spotty water supply, resilient Thessaloníki prospered. Even in temporary decline it made a rich prize for the Ottomans in 1430.

LEFT: the Arch of Galerius, Thessaloníki.
BELOW: a café-bar on the waterfront.

Sephardic settlers

After 1500, large numbers of Sephardic Jewish refugees from Spain and Portugal settled here, giving Salonica – as they called it – its most distinctive trait for the next four centuries. On the eve of the Balkan Wars they accounted for just over half the population of 140,000, making it the largest Jewish city of that era. In 1943, 70,000 remained to be deported to the Nazi death camps, and fewer than 1,000 remain today.

Following the three wars leading up to 1923, the city came to epitomise a Greek refugee town: in absolute numbers Athens may have had more, but by proportion of population, Thessaloníki contains more citizens with Turkish ancestry than anywhere else in

During Ottoman rule, most Byzantine churches were converted into mosques, and their interiors coated in whitewash. This fresco, from Ágios Dimítrios in Thessaloníki, is one that survived.

Greece. There are abundant Turkish surnames (such as Dereli and Mumtzis) and spicy cuisine rarely found elsewhere in Greece; indeed the city has some of the best places to eat in the country. Its own self-deprecating nicknames have long been *I Protévousa tón Prosfigón* (The Refugee Capital), after the ring of 1920s settlements, all prefixed "Néa" (New), across eastern Macedonia, and *Ftohomána* (Mother of the Poor).

But 21st-century Thessaloníki is not all changing demographics. After years in Athens' shadow, it is coming into its own. The International Fair held every October in permanent grounds by the university promotes the city as a Balkan trade centre and the natural gateway to the upper Balkans. Thessaloníki is confidently on the move, with innovative restaurants and clubs occupying historic buildings, its native musicians (such as Sokratis Malamas and Nikos Papazoglou) frequently at the forefront of Greek song.

They say you can always tell a Thessalonian in the rest of the mainland; with a spring in their step, they seem a head taller than the characteristically hunched-over, downtrodden Athenians. The Thessalonians are also perhaps recognisable from their clothes, as it is said to be the best-dressed city in Greece – and so it should be, given its variety of boutiques and department stores. **Platía Aristotélous** is the hub of the downtown city, stretching up from the waterfront towards the Roman Agora and the dominant church of Ágios Dimítrios. The sunny cafés and bars are popular here, especially in the early evening, while morning shoppers enjoy the daily market to the west, and lunchtime and evening diners fill the pavement tables of market restaurants to the east. Leofóros Níkis follows the seafront and is a good place for a stroll or a fashionable bar-hop from the port to the White Tower, with views across the wide blue bay to Mount Ólympos.

Thessaloníki

0   500 m
0   500 yds

The city's current prosperity has an inevitable downside, with heavy rush-hour traffic and increasing levels of pollution. To ameliorate this, an underground metro system, following the line of Egnatía, is due to be completed by 2012, and there are ambitious plans to sink the seafront road below ground to leave the zone free for pedestrians and the bar clientele to enjoy.

Map, page 194

A city tour

Begin behind the White Tower at the **Archeological Museum Ⓐ**, which displays Macedonian, Hellenistic and Roman finds from the entire region, including the notable **Síndos** collections. Sumptuous jewellery and household effects in gold, silver and bronze vie for your attention (open summer Mon 12.30–7pm, Tues–Sun 8.30am–7pm; winter Mon 10.30am–5pm, Tues–Sun 8.30am–3pm; entrance fee). Just beyond the Archeological Museum is the **Museum of Byzantine Culture** (open Tues–Sun 8am–7pm, Mon 12.30–7pm; entrance fee; combined tickets recommended) with artefacts from the Early Christian period (4th–7th century) through to the Middle Byzantine period (8th–12th century). The exhibits in this modern building are beautifully displayed and clearly explained; among the most impressive pieces are a 5th-century mosaic floor, wall paintings from a local house, and some extraordinary early textiles.

Roman Thessaloníki can be seen in **Platía Navarínou Ⓑ** in the shape of the excavated remains of the Hippodrome and the **Palace of Galerius Caesar**, the Christian-hating Emperor who martyred the city's patron saint, Demetrius, in AD 305. And on the inland side of Via Egnatia survives the western part of **Galerius's** triumphal **Arch**, erected over this highway in AD 297 to celebrate a victory over the Persians. The reliefs on the arch repay close inspection showing, as well as Galerius himself, Diocletian and Julius Caesar.

BELOW: the White Tower was added to the Roman-Byzantine walls by the Venetians.

The other remaining building in this Roman complex is the **Rotunda of Ágios Geórgios Ⓒ** (open Tues–Sun 8.30am–3pm; free), just northwest of the arch. Perhaps intended as Galerius's mausoleum, this is one of the few remaining examples of circular Roman architecture, enduring largely through conversion into a church, then a mosque. Glorious 4th-century wall mosaics partially survive, high up inside the dome and recesses; the truncated minaret is the city's last surviving one.

The largest Greco-Roman site is the **Agora Ⓓ** or forum (AD 32–138) on Platía Dikastiríon, uncovered in 1966, which was the social and religious centre of ancient Thessaloníki. Its theatre provides a summer concert space.

Byzantine Thessaloníki

More fine and important Byzantine churches survive in Thessaloníki than in any other Greek city. The earliest examples are clear adaptations of the colonnaded Roman basilica, in turn descended from Greek temples, with the outermost columns replaced by walls. The most significant are near the Agora: 5th-century **Ahiropíetos Ⓔ** (hunt for fine mosaic patches under the arches, between ornate columns) and its heavily restored contemporary, **Ágios Dimítrios Ⓕ**, the largest church in Greece. Both are double-aisled basilicas with a central nave.

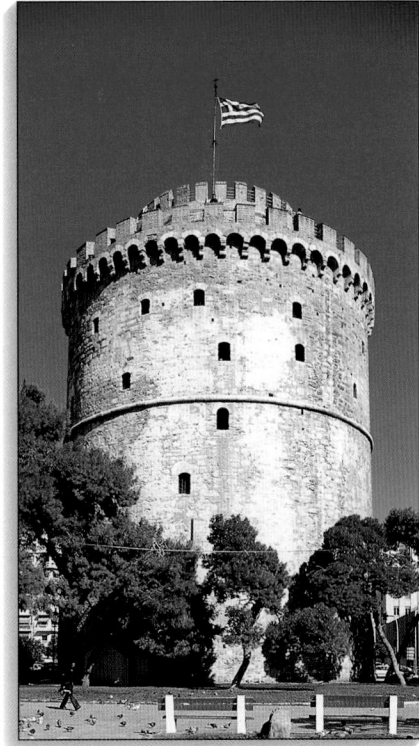

Ágios Dimítrios is the city's main church. It was founded shortly after the saint's demise, on the site of his martyrdom and was almost entirely rebuilt after the 1917 fire which spared only the apse and the colonnades. Six small mosaics of the 5th to 7th century, featuring the saint, survive mostly above the columns standing on either side of the altar. The fire was responsible for the rediscovery of the crypt (Sun 11am–3pm, Mon 12.30–7pm, Tues, Thur 3–7pm, Fri 8am–2pm), which is thought to be partly constructed from the Roman baths where the saint was imprisoned; a reliquary found on the site supports this. Also here are the attractive remains of a fountain that previously fed a fishpond.

Below the Agora to the west of Ahiropíetos is **Panagía Halkéon**, founded in 1028. The brick-built church is in the shape of a cross and contains a cycle of frescoes dating back to the 11th century. During the Ottoman occupation it served as the mosque of the local coppersmiths.

South of Ahiropíetos is the 8th-century **Agía Sofía ⑥** (Holy Wisdom; open daily 8.30am–1pm, 5.30–8pm; entrance fee), built in conscious imitation of its namesake in Constantinople. This one, 10 metres (33 ft) wide, has a vivid Ascension, with the Apostles watching Christ borne heavenward by angels, rather than the *Pandokrátor* (Christ Enthroned) that became the rule later. In the apse and the *ikonostásis*, you can detect traces of an earlier mosaic of the Cross behind the Virgin Enthroned. It was one of a pair, and the other figural cross survives in the adjacent vault.

The steep alleys of **Kástra** are about a 20-minute walk from the seafront. Since the late 1980s this neighbourhood of dilapidated half-timbered houses below the acropolis (citadel) has been transformed from poor, despised and "Turkish" to renovated and trendy, with scattered tavernas and cafés.

BELOW: Panagía Halkéon, one of the city's many Byzantine churches.

Tiny 5th- or 6th-century **Ósios Davíd** Ⓗ, all that's left of the **Látomos Monastery**, is tucked away in this district (all these Byzantine churches open according to demand and have much shorter hours, or are closed, off season). The west end of this church has vanished, but visit for the sake of an outstanding early mosaic in the apse, revealed in 1921 when Ottoman whitewash was removed. It depicts the vision of the Prophet Ezekiel of Christ Emmanuel, shown as a beardless youth seated on the arc of heaven, surrounded by the symbols of the Evangelists. Together, the mosaics of Ósios Davíd and Ágios Dimítrios rank as the best pre-Iconoclastic sacred art in Greece, and predate the more famous work at Ravenna in Italy.

Another batch of churches all well uphill from the Via Egnatia date from the 13th and 14th centuries – examples of a cultural "golden age" at odds with the Byzantine Empire's political decline and the numerous disasters visited on Thessaloníki from the 10th to the 12th century. Financial constraints meant that frescoes, rather than mosaics, were the preferred ornamentation in these churches, most of them attached to now-extinct monasteries. By far the best of these is **Ágios Nikólaos Orfanós** ⒤, at the northeast edge of Kástra (open Tues–Sun 8.30am–2.30pm; free). Among the better-preserved and more unusual frescoes are *Christ Mounting the Cross* and *Pilate Sitting in Judgment*, the very image of a Byzantine scribe; in *Washing of the Feet*, it seems the talented painter inserted an image of himself on horseback, wearing a turban.

At the neaby monastery of **Vlatadon**, the only one among the city's 20-odd to still be occupied by monks, you may hear peacocks cry. The monastery was founded in around 1360 by the Empress Anna Paleologina, but 11th-century wall paintings survive in the small church, which is open during services.

The city walls

Thessaloníki's seafront **Lefkós Pýrgos** ⒥ (White Tower; open daily; free), effectively the city's logo, was built during the brief Venetian occupation as an addition to the Roman-Byzantine walls. The Ottomans used it as a prison; that, and the massacre of unruly Janissaries here in 1826, earned it the epithet "Bloody Tower". The Greeks whitewashed it post-1912 – thus the new alias – and then removed the pigment in 1985. A spiral staircase, with small windows, emerges at a lovely café and then the crenellated roof terrace, affording fine views over the seafront and bay, and up to Kástra.

The vanished curtain wall leading inland from here past the university linked the White Tower with the **Chain Tower**, the northeastern corner of the fortifications; beyond it lies the **Eptapyrgío** (Yedi Küle in Turkish), the Seven Towers Fortress, on the northeastern corner of the old walled **acropolis**. The seven towers on the northern side of the Eptapyrgío incorporate part of the Early Christian acropolis walls, and the six towers on the southern side were built during the Middle Byzantine period. The Ottomans made considerable additions, transforming it into a jail in the late 19th century, and it continued to function as a jail until the 1980s. It is now sometimes used as an exhibition space.

Map, page 194

BELOW: fish in Modiáno market.

Exhibit in the Archeological Museum, Thessaloníki.

BELOW: the Roman Rotunda, built in the 4th century AD, is now the church of Ágios Geórgios.

Ottoman and Jewish Thessaloníki

Thessaloníki was taken by the Ottomans in 1430, 23 years before the fall of Constantinople. The new overlords converted most churches into mosques during the first century of their rule, tacking on minarets and whitewashing over mosaics and frescoes. As a result, there are few purpose-built Ottoman mosques, though there are other interesting civic buildings. Worthy 15th-century specimens include the graceful Ishak Pasha or **Alatza Imaret Mosque** at the base of Kástra – around the corner from the **Yeni Hamam**, or bath-house, engagingly restored as a bistro, concert hall and summer outdoor cinema – and the dilapidated **Hamza Bey Mosque** on the Via Egnatia, last used as the Alcazar cinema. Perhaps it may soon get the same treatment as the nearby **Bezesténi**, a refurbished six-domed covered market now tenanted by luxury shops. The nearby **Bey Hamam** ❾ (Mon–Fri 11am–8pm, Sat noon–5pm; entrance fee) dating from 1444 has intact stalactite vaulting over the entrance and inside.

At the rear of the Turkish consulate, at 7 Apostolou Pavlou, stands the wooden house where Mustafa Kemal (Atatürk), founder of the Turkish republic, was born in 1881. And a few hundred metres east of the Archeological Museum, at the edge of the 19th-century "New Town", is the **Yeni Cami** or "New Mosque" – an Art Nouveau folly erected by the influential Ma'min (Dönme). This so-called crypto-Jewish sect followed the 17th-century self-proclaimed Messiah, Shabbetai Zvi, into Islam. In the mass exchange of populations between Greece and Turkey in 1923, most of the Ma'min were among the 100,000 Muslims who left the city.

By contrast, there are few tangible traces of Thessaloníki's Jewish past, owing to the 1917 fire and the Nazi desecration of cemeteries and synagogues in 1943.

Only the Art Deco **Monastiriótou synagogue** ❶, near the Ministry of Northern Greece, survived the war. Centrepiece of the vast central market – which extends to either side of Aristotélous, selling everything from wooden furniture to live poultry – is the covered **Modiáno** ❶, a fish, meat and produce-hall named after the Jewish family that established it. (Their former mansion, out beyond the Yeni Cami, now houses the Folklife Museum). Though only half-occupied today, the Modiáno still supports several authentic, atmospheric *ouzerí* in the west arcade. Close by, the Louloudádika Hamam or Flower-Market Bath was also known as the **Yahouda Hamam** or Jewish Bath ❶; the Jewish clientele is gone, but the flowers are still outside. In the same area, on Agíou Miná, is the **Jewish Museum of Thessaloníki** (open Tues, Fri, Sun 11am–2pm, Wed, Thur 11am–2pm, 5pm–8pm; free). This two-storey museum presents the history of the Jewish community in Thessaloníki and contains interesting material from the ancient, destroyed, Jewish cemetery.

Maps:
City 194,
Area 202

For atmospheric bars, restaurants and clubs, head for Ladádika, the former red-light district and port quarter behind the passenger ferry terminal.

Outside the city

For an escape from the city, try a half-day excursion to **Panórama**, an affluent village 11 km (7 miles) to the east whose views justify its name; several *zaharoplastía* sell such Anatolian specialities as *salépi* (orchid-root drink), *dódurma* (Turkish ice cream) and *trígona*, triangular cream pastries. **Hortiátis**, 10 km (6 miles) north of here, has since ancient times supplied Thessaloníki with water, and retains some pines spared by arsonists, plus good tavernas. From either point, you can on a clear day look southwest across the Thermaïc Gulf to glimpse the bulk of **Mount Olympos** (Ólymbos) to the southwest, the traditional separation point between Macedonia and Thessaly. ❑

BELOW: flamingoes along Thessaloníki's waterfront.

MACEDONIA AND THRACE

*Along with a landscape of fertile plains and forbidding
mountains, you'll find a wondrous mix of peoples
here – as well as the major holiday playground of Halkidikí*

Map, pages 202–3

hessaloníki, first city of northern Greece and "capital" of Macedonia and Thrace, stands halfway between Albania to the west and Turkey to the east, and scarcely 100 km (60 miles) south of FYROM (the Former Yugoslav Republic of Macedonia) and Bulgaria – a boundary settled after World War I. Bordering so many Balkan states, into which ancient Macedonia and ancient Thrace spread, has given the region great ethnic variety and cultural richness. Northern Greece does not possess the magnificent archeology and stunning temples of the centre and the south and its latitude spells a short summer season. But it does have some key sites, a large number of Byzantine churches and some handsome Ottoman-era domestic architecture; as well as varied and dramatic landscapes and exceptional areas of wildlife, from snowcapped mountains to broad, fertile plains.

Northwest Macedonia

Coming from Epirus, you officially enter Macedonia just before **Pendálofos ❷**, the only place of any importance or appeal en route. Its fine stone houses – still in the Epirot style – straggle across the ravines which give the town its name ("Five-hills"). At **Neápolis ❸**, the road divides: north to Kastoriá, southeast to **Siátista ❹**. Perched on a bleak ridge some 20 km (12 miles) from the fork, this small town is noted for its fine 18th-century mansions or *arhondiká* – the residences of the *árhons*, or leading citizens – offering a glimpse into the self-contained society that flourished here during late Ottoman times. Then a wealthy centre for fur-trading, tanning, wine-making and a stopping point for caravans on the trade route to Vienna, Siátista declined when commercial networks changed after Greek independence.

Start with the **Nerandzópoulos mansion** on Platía Horí, whose warden has the keys to other interesting structures such as the **Manoúsi, Kanatsoúli** and **Poulikídou residences**. Visiting these will give you a good background for nearby Kastoriá, another town which prospered from the fur trade.

Returning north, the road follows the upper valley of the **Aliákmonas River**, the longest in Greece, whose 300-km (185-mile) course arcs from the Albanian border to the Thermaic Gulf. Soon you reach the **lake of Orestiáda**, or Kastoriá, almost divided in half by the eponymous town built on a peninsula. On the town's southern outskirts lies a significant military cemetery, the last resting place of government troops who were killed during the battle for Grámmos-Vítsi, which brought an end to the civil war. In the town itself, a lakeside plaza named after General James Van Fleet serves as a reminder that American equipment and advisers guaranteed a royalist victory over communist insurgency.

LEFT:
a fresco from Agíou Dionysíou, Áthos.
BELOW:
waterfall at Édessa.

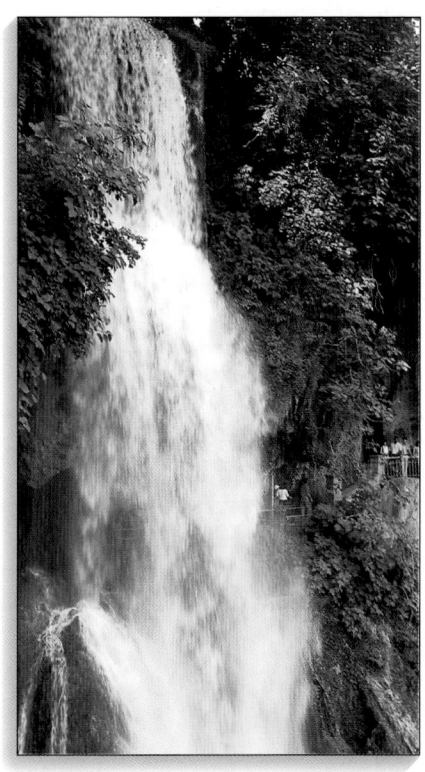

A Byzantine county town

Panagíaki Koumpelidíki is one of 54 medieval churches in Kastoriá.

Kastoriá ❺ is one of northern Greece's more appealing spots, a peaceful mountain town on a peninsula jutting into a large tranquil lake, with a popular promenade of restaurants and bars. Its 54 surviving medieval churches indicate its importance in Byzantine times. Many were erected as private chapels by rich furrier families, and shops still sell myriad furry items, mostly made from mink. (*Kastóri* is the Greek for beaver, now extinct.)

The Byzantine art and architecture here is among Greece's finest, showing strong folk and Slav influences. You can see the best in a single morning, starting with the fine icon collection at the **Byzantine Museum** (open Tues–Sun 8.30am–3pm; entrance fee; the warden here also has control of the keys to most of the churches), and working your way south to the **Karyádis quarter**, with its fine old mansions.

Triple-aisled **Ágii Anárgyri** – built in 1018 by Emperor Basil II – sits at the northeast edge of town, overlooking the lake. Nearby **Ágios Stéfanos** is the second-oldest church in town (10th-century), again with intricately geometric masonry and an unusual women's gallery inside. South of the museum, tiny **Panagía Koumbelidíki** is unmistakeable with its disproportionately tall, drum-shaped dome, the only one in town, painstakingly rebuilt after Italian bombing in 1940. There are some fine frescoes inside and a highly unusual Holy Trinity, complete with bearded God, in the barrel vault.

Continuing south and downhill, the extensive frescoes of the single-aisled basilica **Ágios Nikólaos Kasnítsi** are the best-preserved in Kastoriá; female saints predominate in the narthex, which long served as the women's section, while the image of the Virgin in the Assumption on the west wall is curiously reversed right-to-left. Finally, the **Taxiárhis tis Mitropóleos** is the oldest surviving church (9th-century), with a later (14th-century) fresco of the Virgin Platýtera adored by archangels in the apse.

In the low-lying Karyádis (Dóltso) district, inland from the southern lakefront, stand the restored **Natzís** and **Immanouíl** *arhondiká*, of the same style and era as those in Siátista. The **Folklore Museum** (open Mon–Sat 10am–1pm, 4–7pm, Sun 11am–1pm, 4–7pm, entrance fee) is lodged in the Mansion of Nerantziz Aïvazís on nearby Kapetán Lázou. The refurbished mansion dates from the late 17th century when it stood on the lake shore, and it shows how the wealthy Christian and merchant Aïvazís family lived. From here, a narrow lakeshore lane heads 2.5 km (1½ miles) east to **Panagía Mavriótissa** monastery, now in ruins apart from two Siamese-twin churches – one 11th-century, the other 14th, both with fine frescoes. Peacocks strut, providing a fine view for the diners who patronise the adjacent lake-view restaurant.

To the Préspa Lakes and east

Some 36 km (22 miles) north of Kastoriá, following a branch of the Aliákmonas, is the side road to the Préspa Lakes basin. This atmospheric backwater where the northwestern borders of Greece meet those of FYROM and Albania was designated a Balkan Park by the governments of the three countries in 2000. There are two lakes: **Mikrá Préspa**, shallow and reedy, lying mostly in Greece, and deeper, reed-free **Megáli Préspa**, shared by Albania, FYROM and Greece. Mikrá Préspa is the nesting ground for an extraordinary bird life, notably two endangered species of pelicans and pygmy cormorants, but also for a unique trout and a hardy breed of small cattle. The society for the protection of Préspa operates

Northern Greece has not that many cheap flights from abroad, and not such a wide choice of accommodation, except perhaps on the Halkidikí peninsula.

> **Map, pages 202–3**

Macedonia and Thrace

two information centres, one in Ágios Germanós, the other on the shore of Megáli Préspa lake in Psarádes. The extraordinary bird life is most active in the spring. There is a hardy breed of small cattle in the surrounding hills, also a haven for bears and wolves, although you will be lucky to spot any of them.

The best single target in the region is **Ágios Germanós ❻**, which has a visitor centre, good lodging and two frescoed Byzantine churches. **Psarádes**, the only Greek village on **Megáli Préspa**, also has an information centre and more tourist facilities and offers the opportunity to take a highly worthwhile boat excursion to the painted cave-church of **Panagía Eleoússa**. Mikrá's islet of **Ágios Ahíllios** has an evocatively ruined 10th-century basilica and is connected to the mainland by a 1-km (½-mile) long pontoon. The main road leading east passes through nondescript **Flórina**, then on towards Thessaloníki.

On the northern horizon you will notice snowy **Mount Vóras** (Kaïmaktsalán). This area saw little peace during the first half of the 20th century, with the Macedonian Struggles (1903–08), the Balkan Wars (1912–13), and a two-year battle in World War I between Serbs and Greeks on one side, Germans and Bulgarians on the other. World War II and subsequent civil war strife adde to a narrative equalled in few parts of the globe.

Macedonian sites

Traces of Phillip II of Macedonia (382–336 BC) who united the Greek people, and of his son Alexander the Great (356–323 BC), whose empire stretched as far as India, are scattered in a broad arc west to southwest of Thessaloníki, at the edges of the current flood plains of the Axiós and Aliákmonas rivers. In ancient times the Thermaïc Gulf covered this plain, but the silt-bearing rivers have

It is possible to drive all the way round Lake Prespa through Albania and FYROM, where there are many more ancient churches.

BELOW: Mikrá Préspa.

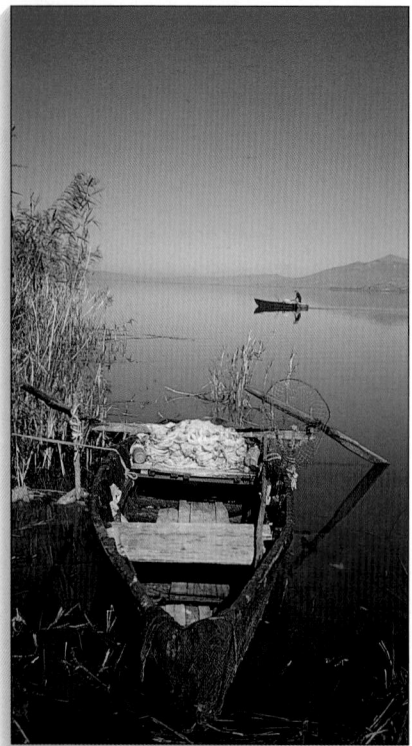

MOUNT OLYMPOS

The imposing bulk of Mt Olympos (Ólympos) – Greece's highest mountain at 2,917 metres (9,568 ft) – dominates the horizon southwest of Thessaloníki. The ancient Greeks believed the mountain was the home of the gods, presided over by Zeus. Its summit defied climbers for years, not least because of the numerous bandits who lurked in the surrounding region. Sultan Mehmet IV is supposed to have attempted the mountain in 1669, but it was not until 1913 that two Swiss mountaineers with their Greek guide managed to scale the highest peak, Mýtikas ("the needle").

The climb is usually tackled from the village of Litóhoro, south of Kateríni, with an overnight stay in either the Giósos Apostolídis or Spílios Agápitos mountain refuge (book in advance during the summer through the SEO or EOS mountaineering clubs respectively, both of which have an office in Litóhoro). The climb itself is not technically difficult: the initial part is just a walk in, but the last section is steep and very exposed. You will need a good sense of balance and a head for heights, particularly when taking what is known as the Kakí Skála ("evil stairway") for the final few hundred metres. This overlooks the Kazánia chasm, a sheer drop of 500 metres (1,650 ft).

pushed the shoreline east. All of these sites can be toured with your own transport in a full day out of Thessaloníki.

Dion, northeast of Mount Olympus (Ólympos), was founded by Macedonian kings both as a military mobilisation ground and a precinct holy to the Olympian gods; its ruins, dating largely from the Roman and Byzantine eras, were buried by an earthquake-triggered mudslide in the 5th century AD (site open Mon–Sun 8am–7pm, museum open Mon 12.30–7pm, Tues–Sun 8am–7pm; entrance fee). Since 1990, well-preserved mosaics have been found here, the best – of Medusa – transferred to safekeeping in the village museum (same hours). However pride of place in the museum goes to a 1st-century BC hydraulis or water organ, a type of pipe organ and the oldest to be found in the world.

Vergína ❼, on the south bank of the Aliákmonas, was formerly **Aigai**, the first Macedonian capital, and remained the royal necropolis. It got its modern name after the exchange of populations in 1923, when incoming Greeks called it after a fairytale queen. Now a UNESCO World Heritage Site, the subterranean chamber tombs of Philip II and three others lay undiscovered until Manolis Andronikos of the Aristotle University of Thessaloníki broke through to the tombs on 8 November 1977. It was one of the most important archaeological discoveries of the 20th century. The dazzling treasures, including gold artefacts, ivory carvings and vivid paintings, are impressively displayed as Andronikos found them (open Mon noon–7pm, Tues–Sun 8am–7pm; entrance fee). Lesser tombs and a summer palace, the **Palatítsa**, lie just up the hill (sites are open daily 8am–7pm; entrance fee).

Some 18 km (11 miles) northwest, **Véria** sits at one end of an escarpment running north to Édessa. Extensive Ottoman neighbourhoods of vernacular houses have been preserved, and more than 35 Byzantine churches are open to the public. Begin at the Véria Byzantine Museum (open Tues–Sun 8.30am–3pm; entrance fee), wonderfully housed in a restored 19th-century flour mill at Thomedoú 1, but don't miss the 14th-century wall paintings in the Hristós Monastery (open Tues–Sun 8.30am– 2pm; entrance free).

North of Véria, Aristotle's School can be seen in the Mieza section of **Náousa**, and imposing Macedonian tombs can be visited at **Lefkádia** (open Tues–Sun 8:30am-3pm; entrance fee).

Some 43 km (27 miles) from Véria, **Édessa ❽** is unlike any other Greek town because of the numerous rivulets that wind through it heading for its famous waterfalls. A path leads down the ravine, through cascade mist, past a cave in the cliffside; upstream, on top of the bluff, is a medieval bridge serving the Via Egnatia. Offering further reasons to linger, the attractive 19th-century Vársi quarter at the precipitous edge of town has a Folklore Museum, an open-air Water Museum and a Hemp Museum.

Pella, a third of the way back to Thessaloníki, was the Macedonian capital after the mid-4th century BC. From here, Philip II ruled a united Greece after 338 BC, and here also his son Alexander studied under Aristotle – and trained for his fabled campaigns in the Orient. Most of the imperial capital is yet to be unearthed, but the superb mosaics of a lion hunt, Dionysos riding

A gold casket found at Vergína. Its lid bears the star which was the emblem of Philip II's Macedonian dynasty.

BELOW:
Mount Ólympos.

a panther, and other mythological scenes, more than justify a visit to the site and the museum (both open Tues–Sun 8am–7pm, Mon noon–7pm; entrance fee).

East to Halkidikí

Many roads lead east out of Thessaloníki. One heads initially north to the town of **Kilkís** and the Greek shore of **Lake Doïránis**, then into the Strimónas river valley towards the only paved road crossing into Bulgaria at **Promahónas**. This route is also followed by the railway, which in this part of Macedonia traces incredible inland loops connecting relatively contiguous coastal points.

A more direct, northeasterly road leads to **Sérres** ❾, important since Byzantine times and still a prosperous town. It was burned down by the retreating Bulgarians in 1913 and has been largely rebuilt, but two Byzantine churches remain, much altered by war and restoration: 11th-century **Ágii Theodóri** and 14th-century **Ágios Nikólaos**. A domed Ottoman building in the central square serves as a museum.

In a wooded mountain valley 19 km (12 miles) north is another, more venerable foundation: the monastery of **Tímiou Prodrómou**, where Gennadius Scholarios, first patriarch of Constantinople after the city was captured by the Ottomans in 1453, elected to retire and is entombed.

The busiest road east of Thessaloníki skirts the lakes of **Korónia** and **Vólvi** en route to Thrace, but a slightly less travelled one veers southeast towards **Halkidikí**, a hand-like peninsula dangling three fingers out into the Aegean. Long a favoured weekend playground of Thessalonians, since the 1980s it has also seen ever-increasing foreign patronage, especially Hungarians, Czechs, and Bulgarians in search of sun, sand and sea on a cheap sunny package or on a few tanks of fuel. Little is left to suggest the area's important role in classical times, when local colonies of various southern Greek cities served as battlefields during the first decade of the Peloponnesian War between Athens and Sparta. However, fossils and a half-million-year-old skull have been discovered in the **Petrálona Cave**, 50 km (31 miles) southeast of Thessaloníki, revealing the existence of prehistoric settlement (open daily 9am–7pm in summer; closes 5pm in winter; entrance fee).

The tips of Halkidikí

At **Stágira** on the way to Áthos, a modern statue of Aristotle overlooks the Ierissós Gulf and the philosopher's birthplace, ancient Stageira. **Xerxes's Canal**, now silted up, was built around 482 BC across the neck of Áthos peninsula to help the Persians avoid the fate suffered in their previous campaign, when their fleet was wrecked sailing round Áthos cape. This and Xerxes's floating bridge over the Hellespont were considered by the Greeks to be products of Persian megalomania – "marching over the sea and sailing ships through the land." The medieval **Potídea Canal** still separates the **Kassándra** peninsula from the rest of the mainland and serves as a mooring ground for fishing boats.

The beautifully forested slopes of Mount Holomóndas cover the "palm's" centre of rolling hills; **Polýgyros**,

BELOW: Pella's Lion Hunt mosaic.

with a dull Archeological Museum, is the provincial capital, but **Arnéa** ⑩ sees more tourists for the sake of its woven goods and well-preserved old houses. Kassándra, the westernmost "finger", had little life before tourism – most inhabitants were slaughtered in 1821 for participating in the independence rebellion, and the land lay deserted until resettlement by post-1923 refugees from the Sea of Marmara. **Néa Potídea** ⑪ by the canal and **Haniótis** near the tip are probably your best bets for human-scale development on a generally oversubscribed bit of real estate.

Sithonía, the middle finger, is greener, less flat and less developed; the **Mount Áthos** monasteries owned much of it before 1923, so again there are few old villages, apart from rustic **Parthenónas**, just under Mount Ítamos. The adjacent clutter of **Néos Marmarás** ⑫ and the mega-resort of **Pórto Karrás** are exceptions to the rule of ex-fishing villages converted slowly for tourism, with ample campsites, low-rise accommodation and beautiful sandy beaches. **Toróni** on the west coast is still relatively unspoiled, while nearby **Pórto Koufós**, landlocked inside bare promontories, is a yachter's haven. **Kalamítsi beach** on the east coast has an idyllic double bay, although **Sárti** further north is the main package venue.

Following the coast north past **Pyrgadíkia** fishing hamlet brings you to the base of Áthos, the easterly finger, whose pyramidal summit rises in solitary magnificence across the gulf to the east. Several resorts, including the beach-ringed islet of **Ammoulianí** and cosmopolitan **Ouranoúpoli** ⑬, grace Áthos, but most people come here for the Holy Mountain because Ouranópoli is the entrance to Mount Áthos. For people not entering Mount Áthos, tour boats from Ouranópoli go around the peninsula, making it possible for these impressive monasteries to be seen from a respectful distance.

Mount Áthos

The fame of **Áthos** ⑭ derives from its large monastic community, today nearly 2,000 strong. In past ages these monks earned it the epithet "holy", now an intrinsic part of the Greek name: **Ágion Óros**, the Holy Mountain. Its Christian history begins with the arrival of hermits in the mid-9th century, roughly 100 years before the foundation of the first monastery. Peter the Athonite, the most famous of the early saints, is said to have lived in a cave here for 50 years.

The first monastery, **Megístis Lávras**, was founded in AD 963 by St Athanasios, a friend of the Byzantine emperor, Nikiforos Fokas. Thereafter, foundations multiplied under the patronage of Byzantine emperors who supported them with money, land and treasures; in return, these donors are prayed for, and imperial charters zealously guarded in the monastery libraries.

The 20 surviving monasteries are all coenobitic, a rule in which monks keep to strict regulations under the direction of an abbot, or *igoúmenos*. Property is communal; meals are eaten together in the *trapezaría* or refectory. All monasteries observe a Greek liturgy except for the Russian **Pandelímonos**, the Serbian **Hilandaríou** and the Bulgarian **Zográfou**; all adhere to the Julian calendar, 13 days behind the Gregorian, and all (except for **Vatopedíou**) keep Byzantine time,

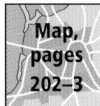

Porto Karrás is a gated community created by Greek ship-owner Yiannis Karrás in 1973. The Grand Resort has two massive 5-star hotels and the biggest private marina in northern Greece.

BELOW: Ouranoúpoli on Halkidikí.

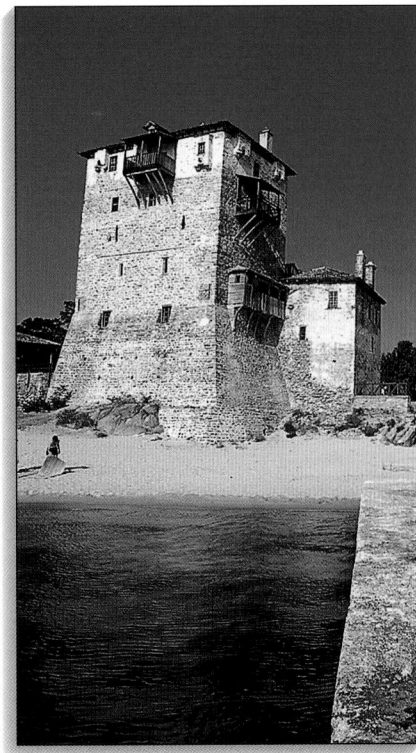

reckoned from the hour of sunrise or sunset. Many monks prefer to live in smaller, less regimented monastic communities, the *skítes* and *kelliá* which are dotted around the peninsula but still dependent on the main monasteries. A few choose to live like hermits in an *isyhastírion*, a rough, unadorned hut or a cave, perched precipitously on a cliff edge.

In the 1970s, Áthos was perhaps at its nadir, with barely a thousand monks – many of limited educational and moral attainment – dwelling in dilapidated monasteries. Since then, a renaissance has been effected. The Holy Mountain's claims to be a commonwealth pursuing the highest form of spiritual life known in the Orthodox Christian tradition appear to have struck a chord, and the quality and quantity of novices from every corner of the globe (especially Russia, following the collapse of communism) is on the rise.

The number of pilgrims to Áthos has grown, too, even though the appropriately Byzantine process of obtaining an entry permit is expressly designed to discourage the frivolous and the gawkers. Only genuine religious pilgrims need apply; or at least that is the ideal. Political if not doctrinal strife is never far from the Holy Mountain. Most monks are born Greek, and prefer Greek predominance. Slavic novices and pilgrims have complained, since 1990, that they are discriminated against vis-à-vis Greeks. But divisions among Greek monks are well known, involving entire bodies of monks moving from one monastery to another in stormy disputes with abbots or civil authorities. Traditionalists decry, as elsewhere in Greece, the bulldozing of paths and the selling of timber to finance renovations – much of it in highly brutalist style.

You must phone or fax most monasteries to reserve space in guest quarters often bursting with as many as 100 visitors a night in full season and, once there,

BELOW: Dionysíou monastery, built on a rock high above the sea.

FORBIDDEN FRUITS

Áthos is probably most famous for the *ávaton* edict, promulgated in 1060 by Emperor Constantine Monomahos, which forbids access to the Holy Mountain to all females more evolved than a chicken (although an exception seems to have been made for female cats, which are kept to control the rodent population).

How did this come about? Revisionists point to prior chronic hanky-panky between monks and shepherdesses, while the religious claim that the Virgin, in numerous visions, has consecrated lush Áthos as Her private garden – and women would simply be an unnecessary temptation. Over the years, many women have tried to gatecrash in disguise, only to be ignominiously ejected; a variety of women's groups in Greece and abroad have now taken up the issue.

A more serious challenge was posed in 1998 when the (female) foreign ministers of Sweden and Finland threatened to refuse to sign a decree upholding the Mount's "special status", since it contravenes one of the European Union's most cherished laws: freedom of movement (Greece is one of 11 EU states that signed the Schengen Accord abolishing border controls among member states in 2000). The Athonite authorities have, nonetheless, vowed to resist all attempts to change the Holy Mountain's single-gender character.

ut up with the squealing of other guests' mobile phones. Accommodation and
ood are free, but taxi rides from one monastery to another can be costly. Walk-
ng is the best way to visit the monasteries but the distances can be great and you
vill only get to visit a handful of monasteries anyway in your limited allotted
ime. Only time will tell if the Mountain can defend itself against the world.

Eastern Macedonia

North of Áthos, the coast road threads through several resorts on the Strymonic
Gulf, popular with Thessalonians and Serrans, before crossing the Strimónas
tself at ancient **Amphipolis**. Scant ruins remain of this city, a Thracian settle-
nent colonised by Athens in 438 BC, atop a bluff protected on three sides by the
river. Most passers-by content themselves with a glimpse from the river bridge
of the **Lion of Amphipolis**, a colossal statue reassembled from fragments from
the 4th and 3rd century BC. On the east bank, the road forks: a faster but less
scenic coastal highway, or the inland road along the base of Mount Pangéo via
Elevtheroúpoli, threading through picturesque, slate-roofed villages.

Both routes converge on the port of **Kavála** ⓲, Macedonia's second city; as
Neapolis, it was an important stop on the Via Egnatia, and a port for ancient
Philippi. Well into the 1920s Kavála was a major tobacco-curing and export
centre, though today the harbour sees more passenger ferries en route to Thásos and the north Aegean than it does commercial traffic. A mansion from the
tobacco boom days houses the Folk and Modern Art Museum, featuring the
Thásos-born sculptor, Polygnotos Vagis (open Mon–Fri 8am–2pm, Sat
9am–2.30pm; entrance fee). The treasures in the modern Archeological Museum
(open Tues–Fri 8am–7pm, Sat–Sun 8am–2.30pm, entrance fee) include tomb
finds from both Avdira and Amphipolis.

The medieval walled **Panagía** quarter, southeast of
the harbour, merits a leisurely stroll up to the hilltop
citadel, tethered to the modern town by a 16th-century
aqueduct. Start along **Poulídou**, passing a clutch of
restaurants favoured by locals, arriving soon at the
gate of the **Imaret** – a sprawling domed compound,
allegedly the largest Islamic public building in the
Balkans. Originally an almshouse and hostel, it is now
an atmospheric hotel.

Philippi

Some 14 km (8½ miles) northwest, ancient **Philippi** ⓳
– although named after Philip II – contains little that
is Macedonian. From the acropolis, where three
medieval towers rise on the ruins of Macedonian
walls, you have extensive views of the battlefield
which made Philippi famous. Here in 42 BC, the fate
of the Romans hung in the balance as the republican
forces of Brutus and Cassius, participants in the assassination of Julius Caesar in 44 BC, confronted the
armies of Caesar's avengers, Antony and Octavius.
Upon their defeat, both Cassius and Brutus committed suicide; the Battle of Actium in 32 BC ended the
struggle between the two victors.

The **Roman ruins**, mainly to the south of the
highway, include foundations of both the forum and
palaestra, plus a well-preserved public latrine in the

Map,
pages
202–3

TIP

The northeast has
hotter summers and
cooler winters than
the rest of Greece. The
best time to visit
Halkidikí is in June or
early July, when the
land is still green and
the hills still covered
in flowers.

BELOW: the Lion
of Amphipolis.

southwest corner of the grounds (open Tues–Sun 7am–3pm; entrance fee). Philippi is reputedly the first place in Europe where St Paul preached the gospel. He arrived in AD 49, but offended the local pagans and was thrown into prison (a frescoed Roman crypt now marks the site). In AD 55, however, he got a better reception from the congregation later addressed in his *Epistle to the Philippians*. By the 6th century, Christianity was thriving here, as the remains of several early basilica-churches testify.

Driving east from Kavála, you soon cross the Néstos River, the boundary between Macedonia and Thrace, at the apex of its alluvial plain, a vast expanse of corn and tobacco fields. Some beautiful scenery along the Néstos Gorge can best be seen by train, or from the old highway, between Dráma and Xánthi.

Thrace and its Muslims

Ancient Thrace covered much of present-day Bulgaria and European Turkey, as well as the Greek coastal strip between the Néstos and Évros rivers. Greek colonisation of the coast from 800 BC onwards often led to conflict with the native Thracian tribes. The Via Egnatia spanned the area, leaving scattered Roman and later, Byzantine fortifications. Later, Thrace was overrun and settled by both Slavs and Ottomans. It was eventually and messily divided between Bulgaria, Turkey and Greece, between 1913 and 1923, following various wars. Although a traumatic population exchange between Turkey and Greece occurred in 1923, the Muslim inhabitants of the Greek part of Thrace were allowed to remain in return for protection granted to 125,000 Greek Orthodox living in Istanbul. (Today the Greeks in Istanbul have been reduced to a few thousand, whereas the population of Muslims of Thrace has increased slightly to about 130,000.)

BELOW:
Xánthi old town.

An ethnic Turkish minority dwells principally in Xánthi, Komotiní and the plains southeast of the two cities; gypsies who adopted Islam and the Turkish language are also settled here. Another Muslim minority, the Pomaks, live in the Rodópi range above Xánthi and Komotiní; descended from medieval Bogomil heretics, they speak a Slavic language and traditionally cultivate tobacco on mountain terraces.

The open-air Saturday market at **Xánthi** ⓱, just 53 km (33 miles) from Kavála, makes a good introduction to the region's Muslim demographics. The call to prayer rings out over the town five times a day. Turkish and Pomak women favour long, dark overcoats and plain-coloured yashmaks (head-scarves) now gradually being replaced by more stylish grey or brown coats and printed scarves. The gypsy women stand out in their colourful *shalvar* bloomers, their scarves tied behind the ears. Many men still wear burgundy-coloured velvet or felt fezzes, or white skullcaps. By night, the numerous, modern bars and cafés along nearby **Vasilisís Sofías** do a roaring trade thanks to students from the University of Thrace which has a campus here.

Xánthi became a prosperous commercial and administrative centre in the 19th century, thanks to tobacco. Renowned masons were brought from Epirus to build merchants' mansions, tobacco warehouses and *hans* (inns). The *hans*, large square buildings around a central courtyard, were resting spots and trade centres near the marketplace. One of the handsome 19th-century mansions at the base of the old town has become a Folk Museum. Further uphill lie the minarets and houses of the Turkish quarter, with numerous satellite dishes for tuning into Turkish-language TV.

At **Komotiní** , 56 km (35 miles) east of Xánthi via the bird-stalked lagoon of **Vistonída** and the water-girt monastery of **Ágios Nikólaos**, Muslims constitute nearly half the population. The Democritus University of Thrace is based here and though it is less immediately attractive than Xánthi, there is an old bazaar of cobbled lanes (Tuesday is the busiest day), with tiny shops, 14 functioning mosques and many old-fashioned coffee houses. A **Folk Museum** just off the central park displays local embroidery, costumes and metalwork (open Mon–Fri 10.30am–1pm; entrance fee); the **Archeological Museum** keeps finds from such Thracian sites as **Avdira**, south of Xánthi, and **Maroneia**, south of Komotiní (open daily 8.30am–6pm; free).

Avdira itself does not repay a visit in its bedraggled state, although it nurtured two major philosophers: Democritus (*c*.460–370 BC), who first expounded atomic theory and whose name the university has taken, and the sophist Protagoras to whom is attributed the maxim "Man is the measure of all things." Odysseus legendarily called at Maroneia after leaving Troy on his return to Ithaca, procuring a sweet red wine which later saved him and his companions from the cyclops Polyphemus. Trapped in his cave, they plied Polyphemus with the wine, and then as he slept poked his single eye out with a red-hot brand and escaped by hiding under his sheep's bellies. A cave north of the sparse clifftop site retains the name of **Polyphemus's Cave**; more rewarding, perhaps, is the medieval village of **Marónia**, preserving a few wooden mansions, and tiny Platanítis beach, with a good fish taverna.

Alexandroúpoli to the border

The old road from Komotiní zigzags 65 km (40 miles) through barren hills before coming down to the rather drab port of **Alexandroúpoli** , gateway to Samothráki island.

It's wisest to press on into the valley of the Évros River, especially if you're a bird-watcher. The delta, east of the Roman spa of Traianopolis, is excellent for waterfowl, while the **Dadiá Forest Reserve**, a successful World Wide Fund for Nature (WWF) venture, shelters black and griffin vultures. In between you can pause at **Féres** for the sake of its 12th-century church, **Panagía Kosmosótira**, whose lofty, five-domed interior is generally open to visitors.

North of the turning for Dadiá, the first town of any size is **Souflí** , once famous for silk production. Corn fields have now replaced the mulberry trees whose leaves once nourished the silkworms, and only a small museum commemorates the vanished industry. **Didymótiho**, 30 km (18½ miles) further upstream, has a Byzantine fortress at the old town's summit, and an abandoned mosque on the square whose features speak of Seljuk (and earlier) prototypes.

From here, most traffic is bound for Turkish **Edirne**, whose graceful minarets are just visible from the Greek border town of Kastaniés. ❏

Map, pages 202–3

During work on the 680-km (423-mile), $7.9 billion Egnatia highway, due for completion in 2008, Roman road-building techniques were revealed at a site near Komotiní. Much of the road has lasted 2,000 years, but it was here that archeologists fully discovered the genius of Roman technology.

BELOW: Pomak women in Xánthi market.

THE ISLANDS

Greece has more inhabited islands than any other European country – but it's anyone's guess how many there are

The poet Odysseus Elytis once said: "Greece rests on the sea." It's an observation that few countries could claim with such authority. Some 25,000 sq. km (10,000 sq. miles) of the Aegean and Ionian seas are covered by islands. And, in characteristic Greek fashion, the exact number of them has been the topic of discussion and dispute. There may be 3,000 islands and islets, of which 167 are inhabited. Or, according to someone else's calculations, there may be only 1,000, of which fewer than 70 are populated.

The criterion that defines a populated place is open to interpretation. Does a tiny outcrop, bare save for one goatherd and six goats, constitute an inhabited island? Can an island that is totally deserted except for annual pilgrimages to a small chapel at its summit claim to be inhabited?

The arithmetic matters far more to foreigners than to the Greeks, who are interested in sea and sky, in food and festivals, rather than in facts and figures. What is indisputable, however, is the sheer variety of landscape and experience to be found lurking behind the familiar images.

This is what we attempt to show in this section – islands with an ancient past and a modern outlook, the complex choice and the pure, simple pleasures. In order to accommodate everything that is encompassed in the phrase "a Greek island", we have devoted space to tiny islands such as Kímolos and Lipsí, as well as the well-known giants like Crete and Rhodes and the holiday favourites such as Mýkonos and Corfu. We do not ignore the familiar, popular islands, of course, but we explore them to seek out the true heart of the place behind the tourist clichés.

The best way to enjoy the islands is to arrive with a certain attitude of mind. By all means, begin by uncritically enjoying the cluster of blisteringly white buildings against a shimmering sea, donkeys set against a backdrop of olive groves, and so on – the vista seared into the senses by holiday brochures. But, when the novelty wears off, or perhaps earlier, examine each island as if it were an onion and start stripping off the skins. How to strip the onion is a large part of what this book is about.

So, welcome aboard the ferry and prepare for a cruise around Europe's most fascinating and welcoming islands – however many of them there might be. ❑

PRECEDING PAGES: the harbour at Sitía on Crete.
LEFT: Horzoviótissa monastery, Amorgós Island, Cyclades.

ISLANDS OF THE SARONIC GULF

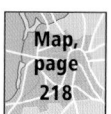

Map, page 218

Salamína, Aegina, Póros, Hydra and Spétses are all within easy reach of the mainland and popular with Greek day-trippers. But they are distinctive, rich in history and remarkably attractive

A thens and the islands of the Saronic Gulf are often lumped together in guidebooks. There is sense in this since many Athenians frequent these islands at weekends, while during the summer the islands become veritable extensions of the more fashionable Athenian neighbourhoods. Yet this view of the Argo-Saronic islands doesn't take into account their separate identities. They are islands, not suburbs. Each has its own character and deserves more of a potential visitor's attention.

Salamína (Salamis)

Salamína is best known for an ancient naval battle (480 BC) in which outnumbered Athenian ships routed the enormous Persian fleet – the ships being the "wooden walls" that the Delphic oracle had predicted would save Athens. Pride of the island is the 17th-century **Faneroméni Monastery** on the Voudóro peninsula, just 6 km (4 miles) from the capital, **Salamína Town ❶**.

The island is decidedly not posh but it is relatively undeveloped and can be reached so quickly, just a few minutes' ride across from Pérama to the port town of **Paloúkia ❷**. Most of the inhabitants live in Salamína (also called **Kouloúri**), which has an archeological and a folk museum. Cyclists may find Salamína an ideal escape from the urban jungle of Athens and Piraeus, as the island's back roads are uncrowded and untaxing on the stamina. The pleasant village of **Eándio** on the west coast has a good hotel.

Aegina (Égina)

Aegina is close enough to be within easy reach from the mainland and far enough to retain its island identity. About an hour and a half by ferry from Piraeus – or 45 minutes by Flying Dolphin hydrofoil – it has had little trouble attracting visitors. The island remains more popular with Athenians seeking a retreat from the city than with foreign tourists or Greeks from elsewhere. The main produce is pistachio nuts, sold all along the harbour street.

Shaped on the map like an upside-down triangle, the island's southern point is marked by the magnificent cone of **Mount Óros**, the highest peak in the Argo-Saronic islands, visible on a clear day from Athens's Acropolis. The island's centre and eastern side is mountainous; a gently sloping fertile plain runs down to the northwestern corner where **Aegina Town ❸** overlays in part the ancient capital of the island.

The town has numerous 19th-century mansions constructed when the first Greek president, Ioannis

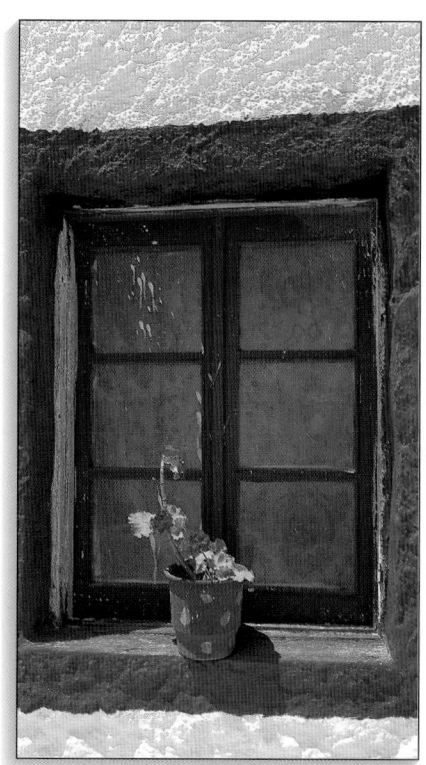

LEFT: Ýdra harbour and old town.
BELOW: bright colours on Aegina.

Aphaea.

Kapodistrias (1776–1831), lived and worked here. Some 3 km (2 miles) north of town is the **Christos Kapralos Museum** (open June–Oct Tues–Sun 10am–2pm, 6–8pm; Nov–May Fri–Sun 10am–2pm; entrance fee), dedicated to this prominent Greek sculptor and painter, occupying his former studios. The modern harbour, crowded with yachts and caïques, is next to the ancient harbour, now the shallow town beach north of the main quay, towards the ancient site of **Kolóna**.

Kolóna, meaning "column", is named after the one conspicuously standing column of the **Temple of Apollo**. The temple (Doric, six columns by 12, built in 520–500 BC) was superseded by a late Roman fortress, fragments of which survive on the seaward side. Although from the sea the position of the temple looks unimpressive, the view from its promontory is very pleasant. There is a small **museum** on the site, and the reconstructed mosaic floor of an ancient synagogue (open daily 8.30am–3pm; single entrance fee for both site and museum).

The island's most famous ancient site is the **Temple of Aphaea ❹**, in the northeast, above the often packed summer resort town of **Agía Marína**. The temple stands at the top of a hill in a pine grove commanding a splendid view of the Aegean. Built in 490 BC in the years after the victory at Salamis, it has been called "the most perfectly developed of the late Archaic temples in European Hellas". It is the only surviving Greek temple with a second row of small superimposed columns in the interior of the sanctuary (open Tues–Sun 8am–7.15pm, winter until 5pm; entrance fee).

On the way to the temple you will pass by the modern **Monastery of Ágios Nektários**, the most recent Orthodox saint, canonised in 1961. Across the ravine from the monastery is the ghostly site known as **Paleohóra** ("old town"), built

Argo-Saronic Islands

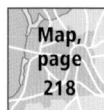

in the 9th century as protection against piracy. Abandoned in 1830 after Greek independence, most of the 38 churches left standing are in utter disrepair, but you can still see the fragments of brilliant post-Byzantine frescoes in several unlocked chapels.

The west coast of the island is quite gentle, with a good sandy beach at **Marathóna**, but better reasons to head out here are to enjoy a meal in one of the many fish tavernas along the harbour at **Pérdika ❺**, or to go by hired boat to swim at the clean and sheltered bay on the tiny uninhabited island of **Moní**.

Angístri

Angístri is the small island facing Aegina Town. All boats stop at **Skála**, the main hotel-resort with the only sandy beach, though **Mýlos** to the west has more character. The most attractive beach is gravelly Halikiáda south of Skála, reached by steep path. **Metóhi** and **Limenári** are the inland hamlets, with tavernas.

Póros

The island of Póros is separated from the Peloponnese by a small passage of water – the word *póros* in Greek means "passage" or "ford". As your boat turns into the ford from the northern entrance, the channel opens ahead and lovely **Póros Town ❻** comes into view. Almost landlocked, it is one of the most protected anchorages in the Aegean: your first glimpse will be of white houses and bright orange rooftops, with the clock tower on top of the hill. Póros can be reached not only by ship and Flying Dolphin but also (with considerably more effort) by driving via the **Isthmus of Corinth** to **Epídavros** (Epidauros) and then down to the coast at little **Galatás**, just across the channel.

In the 7th century BC, Aegina became a leading maritime power, thanks to its strategic position; its silver coins – known as "tortoises" – became common currency in most of the Dorian states.

BELOW: Aegina's waterfront.

Although a number of hotels have been built on the island, and prominent Athenians have owned vacation houses here for decades, it has never been as fashionable as Ýdra or Spétses (chiefly because the beaches are fewer and not as good); but during summer it gets every bit as crowded as Aegina.

In 1846 a Greek naval station was established on the northwest side of Póros, on the peninsula just before the narrow stream separating Póros Town from the larger part of the island, known as Kalávria. When the station moved to Salamína in 1878, the site was used as a school; it is now used for training naval cadets. This area contains several fine family mansions with well tended gardens and can be a refreshing place to stroll on a hot summer afternoon.

Weathered fruiterer's sign, Ýdra Town.

The main sight on Póros is the **Monastery of Zoödóhou Pigís** (Virgin of the Life-Giving Spring), beautifully situated on a wooded hillside (20 minutes from town by bus). Only a few monks still live there today. Noteworthy is a wooden, gold-painted iconostasis dating from the 19th century.

In front of the monastery a road encircling the heights to the east climbs through the pine woods to the ruins of the **Sanctuary of Poseidon** in a saddle between the highest hills of the island. The temple was excavated by the Swedish School in the 19th century, and they are digging again, so much is roped off, but its setting is rewarding. The sanctuary was the headquarters of the Kalavrian League, an association of several towns that included Athens. The Athenian orator Demosthenes, who had opposed the imposition of Macedonian rule over Athens, sought refuge in the sanctuary after an Athenian revolt following the death of Alexander the Great was quelled by Antipater, Alexander's successor in Macedonia. When Demosthenes was found, he took poison but stepped outside the sanctuary before dying so he would not defile holy ground.

BELOW: Póros Town.

Ancient **Troezen** is about 8 km (5 miles) from Galatás across the straits on the Peloponnese. The mythological Greek hero Theseus is supposed to have grown up here before he went off to Athens to become king. The rock he is said to have raised to prove his strength is still here, next to the Sanctuary of the Muses. Theseus is also meant to have returned to Troezen in his old age, providing Euripides with the plot for his famous play, *Hippolytus*, about the young queen Phaedra who unjustly accused Theseus's son of having violated her. Nearby, contemporary drama is provided by a gorge spanned by a natural rock "bridge", the **Diavologéfyro** (Devil's Bridge). For peace, go to the **Lemonódasos**, a beautiful grove consisting of some 2,000 lemon trees, about half an hour's walk on the other side of Galatás.

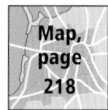

Map, page 218

Ýdra (Hydra)

The island of Ýdra – in antiquity Ydrea, "the well watered" – now appears as a long, barren rock. But the harbour and the white and grey stone buildings which make up the town are still lovely; they have drawn the artistic and the fashionable since the 1950s and many, many more ever since. It is one of the few places in the country that has reined in the uncontrolled growth of concrete construction, thus keeping its beauty.

A splash of Greek colour in Ýdra.

The heart of the island is its harbour-town, also called **Ýdra** ❼. All around the picturesque bay white tile-roofed houses climb the slope, accented by massive grey *arhondiká* (mansions built by the shipping families who made fortunes in the 18th and 19th centuries), many of them designed by architects from Venice and Genoa. Along the quay are the colourful shops of the marketplace, with the clock tower of the 18th-century **Monastery of the Panagía** in the centre;

BELOW: boarding the ferry at Ýdra.

much of the stone used to build it was taken from the ancient Sanctuary of Poseidon on the island of Póros. The harbour itself, girded by a little thread of a breakwater, forms a crescent, its two ends flanked by 19th-century cannons.

The town has many good tavernas and restaurants, as well as extremely popular bars and clubs. Yet the higher reaches and the hills beyond remain surprisingly untouched, charming and full of Greek colour. Narrow alleys and steep staircases lead from one quarter to the next. The uniformity of white walls is broken again and again by a century-old doorway, a bright blue window frame, a flight of striking scarlet steps, or a green garden fence.

Mandráki , northeast of town, has the only sand beach, but the southwest is more interesting. A wide path goes along the coast to **Kamíni** and to **Vlyhós**, with its early 19th-century arched stone bridge. There are some good tavernas in both places, and seasonal water-taxis available if you've had too much good fish and wine. Water taxis are the only way to reach **Ágios Nikólaos** and **Bísti** beaches, the island's best, at the southwest tip, unless you undertake an arduous cross-country hike, equipped with a good map. An easier walk by path leads southeast and within 80 minutes to the equally good, pine-shaded pebble beach at **Limnióniza**.

Privately owned Villa Giasemía, near Agía Paraskeví on Spétses, is the original of magical Bourani in John Fowles's 1966 novel The Magus.

Spétses

Spétses is the southwesternmost of the Argo-Saronic Gulf islands, with occasional hydrofoil links to the Peloponnese (Návplio and Monemvasía). In antiquity it was known as Pityousa, "pine tree" island, and, despite huge fires in 1990 and 2001, it is still (only just) the most wooded of the group. Tourist development here is more extensive than on Ýdra but less than on either Póros or Aegina, and in recent years responsible planning has helped keep the island's charm.

BELOW: Spétses' Old Harbour.

Although **Spétses Town** 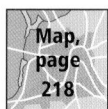 has its share of bars and fast-food places, the Paleó Limáni (Old Harbour) still radiates a gentle grace. The 18th-century *arhondiká* you see in this part of the town are now the property of wealthy Athenian families who return to the island every summer.

Like Ýdra, Spétses' heyday was the late 18th century, when mercantile trade made it wealthy. Also like Ýdra, it became a centre of activity during the Greek War of Independence, offering its merchant fleet of over 50 ships for the Greek cause. The island is distinguished for being the first in the archipelago to revolt against Ottoman rule in 1821, and the fortified main harbour, still bristling with cannons, now forms one of the town's focal points, the **Dápia**.

Bouboulina, Greece's national heroine of the Greek War of Independence, was a Spetsiot woman who took command of her husband's ships after he was killed by pirates off the North African coast. She contributed eight of the 22 Spetsiot ships that blockaded the Turks in Návplio (Nauplion) for more than a year until the garrison surrendered in December 1822.

In the September before Návplio surrendered, an Ottoman fleet attempted to lift the blockade by threatening Spétses. The fighting was indecisive but the Ottoman fleet eventually withdrew. They were encouraged to leave by fezes being placed on the asphodel plants that grew in masses along the shore (from a distance the fezes swaying in the wind looked like men, presumably armed).

Spétses has been synonymous with shipping for centuries.

This great victory is celebrated annually, every 22 September, by a *panigýri* focused on the church of the **Panagía Armáta** on the lighthouse headland close to the Old Harbour. A mock battle is staged, a Turkish flagship made out of cardboard is burned in the middle of the harbour and there follows a display of fireworks.

BELOW: in Ýdra's Byzantine Museum.

Although after the War of Independence Spétses' fleet declined with the emergence of Piraeus as the main seaport, the traditions of shipbuilding continue unabated. The small **museum** (open Tues–Sun 8.30am–3pm; entrance fee) in the imposing 18th-century *arhondikó* of Hatzigianni Mexi, a major shipowner, contains coins, costumes, polychrome prows of ships from the revolutionary fleet, weapons and other memorabilia from the island's past, including the bones of the famous Bouboulína. The house in which she lived is behind the Dápia.

Outside of town to the northwest is **Anargýrios and Korgialénios College**, a Greek impression of an English public school. John Fowles taught here and memorialised both the institution and the island in his 1966 novel *The Magus*. The school no longer operates, and the buildings are used only occasionally as a conference centre or for special programmes. This section of town, called Kounoupítsa, has some fine small tavernas and luxurious places to stay.

The town beach by the church of **Ágios Mámas** and the one with amenities east of town at **Ligonéri** are not as nice as the beautiful beaches of **Ágii Anárgyri**, **Agía Paraskeví**, **Zogeriá** and **Xylokériza**, (going around the wooden southern coast of the island from east to west). In addition, there are various beaches opposite Spétses on the Peloponnesian coast, of which the most accessible is at **Kósta**. For those who enjoy water-skiing, **Pórto Héli** with its protected bay provides the perfect setting. ❏

THE CYCLADES

From the hectic nightlife of Mýkonos and Íos to the rugged beauty of Mílos and Sérifos, and the unspoilt seclusion of Síkinos and Kímolos, there is something for all tastes among these islands

Map, pages 226–7

For many people the Cyclades *are* Greece; other island chains are mere distractions from this blue Aegean essence. They were inhabited by 5000 BC; by the third millennium a fascinating island culture flourished here, with fine arts and crafts and lively commerce – as anyone who visits the excellent Goulandris Museum of Cycladic Art in Athens will appreciate (*see page 138*).

Of the 56 islands, 24 are inhabited. There are two basic ferry routes: the first, eastern and central, takes in bucolic Ándros and religious Tínos, includes Sýros, Mýkonos, Páros, Náxos and Íos – traditionally the backpackers' (and now everyone else's) beat – and concludes in spectacular Santoríni or remote Amorgós. The second, western, arches by Kýthnos, Sérifos, Sífnos and Mílos; somewhat less popular islands, with different cultural attributes. Off both ferry routes, Kéa attracts Athenian weekenders.

Ándros

Ándros was settled centuries ago by Orthodox Albanians; their stone dwellings of the north contrast with the whitewash and red tile of the other villages. The port town, **Gávrio**, is only that. **Batsí ❶**, 6 km (4 miles) south, is a pleasant Cycladic "fishing" town: cafés, a long beach, package tours, and development at the outskirts. On the east coast, **Ándros Town (Hóra) ❷** remains remarkably unspoiled. This is because so many rich Athenians have weekend houses here (less than three boat hours from Athens) that tourism has not been assiduously pursued. The prize exhibit in the **Archeological Museum** (open Tues– Sun 8.30am–3pm; entrance fee) is the famous Hermes of Ándros, a 4th-century AD copy of Praxiteles' statue. South of the Paleópolis/Hóra road is the most spectacular of Ándros's 13 monasteries, **Panahrándou ❸**; 1,000 years old, it still retains ties with Constantinople (Istanbul).

Ándros has many beaches – the easiest to get to are **Nimbório** just south of the port, the string of lovely strands between Gávrio and Batsí, and **Gialiá** (near Steniés, north of Ándros Town) – plus a number of beautiful and remote coves such as **Ágios Pétros**.

Kéa

Kéa-bound boats leave from the mainland port of Lávrio, some 50 km (30 miles) from Athens, and land at **Korissía**, locally called **Livádi**. The main town, **Ioulída (Hóra) ❹**, huddles below a rounded ridge overlooking the island's northern reach, a site chosen for its inaccessibility from foreign marauders. The famous **Lion of Kéa**, a smiling, maneless beast almost 6 metres (20 ft) long, is a 15-minute walk northeast of Hóra. Carved from grey granite, it is probably early Archaic.

LEFT: classic architecture on Íos.
BELOW: Church of Panagía Evangelístria, Tínos.

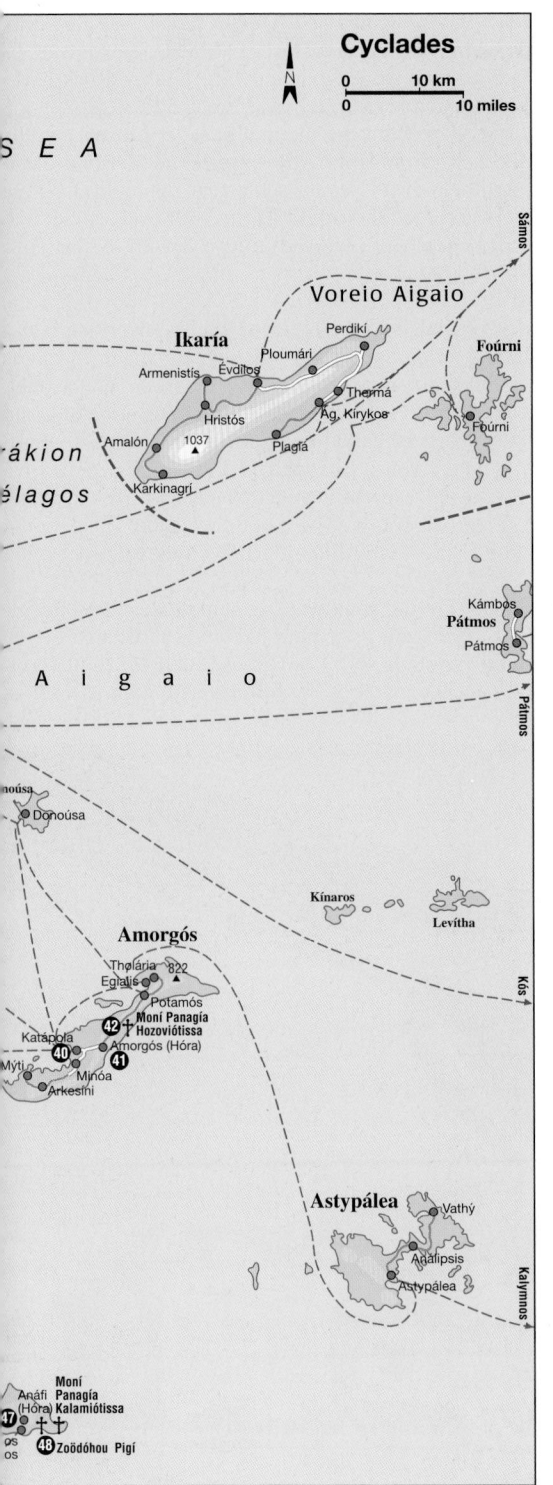

Cyclades

In the 19th century there were a million oak trees on well-watered Kéa, and many still provide shade. Olive trees, however, are absent; since ancient times, the island has been noted for its almonds. The jagged west coast has many sandy coves, some accessible by boat only. **Písses** and **Koúndouros** are two of the more developed beaches. Close to Korissía is **Vourkári ❺**, with **Agía Iríni**, a Minoan excavation, and a square, Hellenistic watchtower at **Agía Marína**, near Písses.

Tínos

Tínos receives many thousands of tourists – but they are mostly Greeks here for the church, the **Panagía Evangelístria** "Annunciated Virgin". In 1823, the nun Pelagía dreamt of an icon; it was duly unearthed and the church was built to house it. The icon's healing powers have made **Tínos Town (Hóra) ❻** the Lourdes of Greece. Women fall to their knees upon arrival, and crawl painfully to the church (less painfully so since a carpeted lane for that purpose was instated on the main approach). Healing miracles often occur.

For a reminder of the Ottoman conquest, visit the peak of **Exóbourgo ❼**, 643 metres (2,110 ft), with its ruined fortress (Tínos was the last island to fall to the Turks, in 1723). A bus ride to Exóbourgo and beyond will also reveal some weird, mushroom-shaped, wind-sculpted rocks, especially above **Vólax** village, known for its basket-weaving.

Kolybíthra in the north is Tínos's best beach. **Ágios Sóstis**, near Pórto on the south coast, is also a decent stretch of beach. Of the monasteries to see, the abandoned **Katapolianí**, near **Istérnia ❽**, is exceptional. **Kardianí**, the village southeast of Istérnia, is Tínos's most spectacularly set – though arcaded **Arnádos** and adjacent **Dýo Horiá** give it competition.

Kýthnos

After iron-mining operations ceased, Kýthnos lost its prime source of income. Foreign tourism has not supplemented it, but Athenian tourism has helped. **Mérihas** on the west coast has the biggest choice of accommodation. In summer, a "taxi-boat"

Freshly-caught octopus is served in most of the Cycladic islands.

BELOW:
Ermoúpoli on Sýros.

runs from Mérihas to **Episkopí**, **Apókrousi** and **Kolóna** beaches to the north. **Kýthnos Town (Hóra)** ❾, 6 km (4 miles) northeast of Mérihas, is exquisite. Its streets are spanned by wood-beamed arches joining facing houses. Rock pavements are decorated with white-painted fish, stylised ships and flowers.

Elderly residents and visitors frequent the thermal baths at **Loutrá**, on the northeast coast 5 km (3 miles) east from Hóra. Above Loutrá, at Maroúla, excavations have revealed the earliest known Cycladic settlement, dating from before 4500 BC. A stream bed splits tile-roofed **Dryopída** ❿ (the medieval capital) into two; the chambered **Katafíki cave** here is linked in legend with the Nereids.

Sýros

Sýros remains the Cyclades' capital, but when Piraeus (Pireás) overtook it as a trade centre in the late 1800s, its port went into decline. However, it retains excellent inter-island ferry links and useful, if low-key, facilities. The capital, **Ermoúpoli** ⓫, has been "discovered" since the 1980s, with renovation of grand buildings public and private. The area called **ta Vapória** ("the ships"), uphill from the shopping streets, is where you'll find many 19th-century neoclassical mansions (a few doubling as hotels), especially around the marble-paved, plane-tree-shaded main square, Platía Miaoúlis. The Apollon Theatre, next to the Town Hall, was modelled on La Scala in Milan. Its 1980s renovation is still a point of pride.

Fínikas ⓬, a beachside town in the southwest, is named after the Phoenicians, probably Sýros's first inhabitants – or more likely after just a palm tree (*fínikas* in Greek). The island's south is softer and greener than the thinly populated north and has good beaches, namely **Possidónia** and **Vári** as well as

Fínikas. Up the west coast, **Galissás** and **Kíni** are popular resorts. During the civil war and the 1967–74 junta, political prisoners were interned on **Giáros**, the empty island to the north.

Map, pages 226–7

Mýkonos

Mýkonos has made itself glamorous. Otherwise unprosperous, it has turned its rocky, treeless ruggedness into a tourist-pleasing package that works – incidentally making it more expensive than most other Greek islands. Summer draws thousands of tourists to **Mýkonos Town ⑬** to sample the celebrated bars, September gay scene, restaurants serving Lobster Thermidor, and the clothes and jewellery shops. Despite the glitz, the town is among the most solicitously preserved in the Cyclades, with its wooden balconies loaded with flowers, multi-coloured domed chapels and billows of whitewash. The odd-shaped **Paraportianí** (Our Lady of the Postern Gate) is probably Greece's most photographed church.

Little Venice (aka Alefkándra), a row of buildings hanging over the sea at the north, is the least frenetic part of town. The **Folklore Museum** (open Mon–Sat 5.30–8.30pm, Sun 6.30–8.30pm; free) and the **Archeological Museum** (open Tues–Sun 8.30am–3pm; entrance fee), at different ends of Mýkonos's quay, are full of interesting objects. Caïques also depart from here for **Delos ⑭**, the sacred island that is the centre of the Cyclades (in myth Mýkonos was Delian Apollo's grandson – *see also page 241*). Or one can strike inland to **Áno Merá ⑮** 7 km (4 miles) east, the only real village, and visit the red-domed Tourlianí monastery, which houses some fine 16th-century icons and embroideries.

Mýkonos is famous, indeed notorious, for its all-night bars and all-day beaches. For bars, you must enquire – the scene changes all the time. For

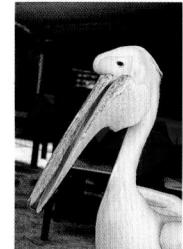

Pétros the pelican, mascot of Mýkonos Town.

BELOW: Little Venice on Mýkonos.

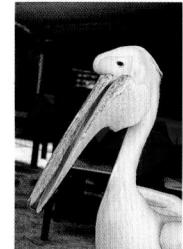

The Cycladic Bronze Age

B ronze Age Cycladic peoples left behind beautiful artefacts that provide evidence of an organised and flourishing culture, most famously in their stylised marble sculptures, all of which have been found in tombs. The settlements and cemeteries excavated on a number of islands are generally considered to be the first complex, organised, settled communities in Europe.

The Early Cycladic Bronze Age began about 3200 BC and is thought to have lasted until around 2000 BC. The later Bronze Age is divided by scholars into Middle and Late Cycladic. These latter periods increasingly display the influence of the Minoan culture of Crete, and show a move towards urban settlement. In general, the term Cycladic Culture refers to the Early Cycladic, and it is during this period that the individuality of the culture of the Cycladic islands is most evident.

The settlements of the Early Cycladic were small, of around 50 people, comprising densely packed stone-built housing, usually only of one storey. Accompanying the settlements, outside the residential area, were cemeteries of small cist graves (rectangular graves lined with stone) and chamber tombs, clustered in family groups. The dead were inhumed in a contracted (foetal) position along with everyday objects. Much of the evidence we have of how Early Cycladic society functioned comes from these cemeteries.

The often stark differences in grave goods between tombs provides evidence of a stratified society. While some graves contain a very rich variety of artefacts, including gold and silver jewellery, others have very little, often only a single marble figure. How these differences between rich and poor played out is a matter of conjecture, but many artefacts display a high degree of skill in their manufacture, indicating a class of skilled craft workers. Hunting, fishing, animal husbandry and agriculture provided food. The islanders were practised traders, pointing to the existence of a merchant class, presumably, among the wealthier members of society. Skilled sailors, they had contact with the Greek mainland, Crete, Turkey and even the distant Danube Basin.

Of all the items left by these peoples, the marble figurines are perhaps both the most beautiful and intriguing. Their importance is such that they are used as a diagnostic tool by scholars to delineate the Cycladic Culture. The predominately female figures are generally around 20 cm (8 ins) in length (a few near life-sized sculptures have been discovered) and are made of white marble. Almost two-dimensional in their execution, they have flattened oval heads and folded arms; many features would have been painted on the marble (on the face, only the nose is rendered in stone). It is conjectured from the position of the feet that they were intended to lie horizontally, but there is no conclusive evidence for this, just as there is no evidence for their function. Explanations from scholars range from their being apotropaic (warding off evil), to divinities, symbolic companions or ancestors. ❑

LEFT: a Cycladic marble figurine.

beaches, **Paradise** is half straight nude, **Super Paradise** half gay nude, and both are beautiful; **Kalafáti** is popular with windsurfers, and Eliá exclusively gay, both reached from Áno Merá; **Platýs Gialós** and **Psárrou** in the west are popular with families. And the reservoir lake in the island's centre attracts thousands of migrating birds.

Sérifos

A long easterly promontory encloses **Livádi** ⑯, Sérifos's harbour. With a half-dozen each of tavernas, hotels and café-bars, this is a pleasant place to stay, with good beaches on either side. **Sérifos Town (Hóra)** ⑰ clings to the mountain above, which gives it a precipitous beauty. Regular buses ascend to Hóra, but the flights of old stone steps (a 40-minute climb) make for a more authentic approach.

Hóra has two parts: Káto (Lower) and Áno (Upper). The upper is the more interesting; its ridge leads in the west to the old ruined **Kástro**. The view from here of the gleaming bay and the other islands is spectacular. The beach to the east that looks so inviting, **Psilí Ámmos**, really is.

The road is paved as far as the fortified Byzantine **Taxiárhon Monastery** ⑱ to the island's extreme north. The scenic path-walk there from Áno Hóra's main square takes about one hour and a half, via the village of **Kállitsos**. The rustic villages of **Galáni**, **Pýrgos** and **Panagía** focus on the magnificent valley southwest of the Taxiárhon. You can cross this valley by one of two footpaths around the hill that bisects it, or stick to the road.

Sérifos abounds in little bays, many accessible only on foot and therefore unspoiled. In the far southwest, **Megálo Livádi** and **Koutalás** once lived from mining; today they have two of the quietest Serifan beaches.

Map, pages 226–7

BELOW:
Mýkonos nightlife.

Sífnos

Sífnos was and is a potter's isle. In the narrow, pretty harbour, **Kamáres** ⓳, and in Vathý, Platýs Gialós, and especially isolated Hersónisos, potters still set out long racks of earthenware to dry in the sun. Weaving and jewellery-making are the other crafts; there are fine examples of local weaving in the folklore museum of the capital, **Apollonía** ⓴ (open daily 9.30am–2pm and 6–10pm). Connected to Apollonía, **Artemónas** is Sífnos's richest town, with mansions and old churches.

The oldest community, however, is **Kástro** ㉑, the medieval capital, perched 100 metres (330 ft) above the sea and 3 km (2 miles) to the east of Apollonía. Catalans and Venetians once ruled the island; the walls they built are still in evidence, as are some remains of an ancient acropolis. Most of the buildings are from the 14th century. The big Venetian building in the centre of Kástro is the **Archeological Museum** (open Tues–Sun 8am–2.30pm; free).

Sífnos's south shore settlements make tranquil beach-side bases. A paint-blazed footpath leads from **Kataváti** just south of Apollonía to **Vathý** ㉒, a potter's coastal hamlet provided with a road only in 1993. Vathý's most visually stunning feature is the **Taxiárhis** (Archangel) **Monastery**, poised as though ready to set sail onto the sands. But Sífnos's most beautiful spot may well be **Hryssopigís** (Golden Wellspring) **Monastery**, built in 1653 on an islet reached by a small footbridge.

Andíparos

Once, a few thousand years ago, this small, pretty island was joined to Páros. A narrow channel now separates the two, plied by fishing boats and excursion boats bringing visitors to its famous cave, **Spílio Stalaktitón** ㉓ (the Cave of the

One of Sífnos's delightful sugar-cube churches.

BELOW:
boats in the harbour on Sífnos.

Stalactites; open summer daily 10.45am–3.45pm; entrance fee). At the entrance to the cavern stands the church of Ágios Ioánnis Spiliótis (St John of the Cave). Though cement steps lessen the adventure, the cave's primordial beauty still stuns. Buses run from Andíparos Town to the cave; if you choose to walk, it will take about one hour.

Andíparos Town itself is engaging, its inhabited kástro, complete with central plaza, is of a type seen elsewhere only at Síkinos and Kímolos. The island is only 11 km by 5 km (7 miles by 3 miles), so there are no impossible distances. Good beaches and bars have lured to Andíparos some of Páros's former business. **Ágios Geórgios**, on the southwest coast, has a beach and two tavernas, and faces the goat island of **Despotikó**, where excavations are in progress.

Páros

If you arrive at this heavily trafficked island in August, expect to sleep either under the stars or expensively. The cheap rooms go fast. **Parikía (Páros) ㉔** resembles Mýkonos in appearance and in nightlife, but it is gentler in spirit. The four main things to see here are the beautiful 4th–6th-century **Ekatondapylianí church** (Our Lady of a Hundred Doors), the **Archeological Museum** (open Tues–Sun 8am–2.30pm; entrance fee), the ancient **cemetery** (next to the post office), and the Venetian **Kástro** in the centre of town, built wholly of classical marbles. Páros is famous for the world's most translucent marble; you can still visit the ancient tunnel-quarries in **Maráthi** and pick up a chip.

Lévkes ㉕, the medieval capital, is the largest inland village. There are several 17th-century churches, the two most prominent edged with an opaline-blue wash. In beautiful **Náousa ㉖**, on the north coast, the little harbour's colourful

Map, pages 226–7

A detail from Ekatondapylianí church, Parikía.

BELOW: Náousa old town and harbour.

boats seem to nudge up right against the fishermen's houses. Though the village has become fashionable, with upmarket boutiques and restaurants, the harbour is still sacrosanct. Caïques leave here for several fine beaches; the world windsurfing championship has been held at **Hrýsi Aktí** (Golden Beach).

In the west is the much-visited **Valley of the Butterflies**, or **Petaloúdes**, a big well-watered garden with huge trees (open daily June–Sept 9am–8pm; entrance fee). The black and yellow butterflies – Jersey Tiger moths actually – are colourful and countless in early summer. A big road goes there, but no bus. The bus does, however, go to **Poúnda**, from where the small ferry to Andíparos leaves.

Náxos

Náxos is the largest and most magnificent of the Cyclades. High mountains, long beaches, inaccessible villages, ruins, medieval monasteries and fascinating history make any visit here too short. **Hóra** (**Náxos Town**) is a labyrinthine chaos of Venetian homes and castle walls, post-Byzantine churches, Cycladic to medieval ruins and garden restaurants. Hóra is divided into sections whose place names reflect the port's long Venetian occupation. Higher up, within the **Kástro**, live a few elderly descendants (still Catholic) of the Venetian overlords: look for their coats of arms over doorways. The former French School, built into the ramparts, now houses the **Archeological Museum** (open Tues–Sun 8.30am–3pm; entrance fee). On an islet to the north of Hóra's ferry dock, a colossal free-standing marble doorframe marks the entrance to the never-completed **Temple of Delian Apollo** of 530 BC.

On the northern shore of Náxos is the resort town of **Apóllonas**, a one-time hippie enclave that's now a family resort. A huge 6th-century BC *kouros* – probably bearded Dionysos – lies on the hillside above the settlement, abandoned when the marble cracked.

Olive and fruit trees grow densely around the many rural villages of Náxos, concealing Byzantine churches and crumbling Venetian manors. Four villages on the road from Hóra to Apóllonas are particularly worthy of attention: Komiakí, Apíranthos, Filóti and Halkí.

Komiáki, the highest village on the island, is extremely attractive, has wonderful views over the surrounding vineyards, and is the original home of the local *kitrón* liqueur. **Apíranthos** (aka Apérathou) was originally settled by Cretan refugees in the 17th and 18th centuries. The town, whose streets are marble, even looks Cretan. There are three small museums in the maze of lanes, one highlighting the local emery-mining industry.

Filóti, on the slopes of Mount Zás, is Náxos's second-largest town. If you are there for the three-day festival (from 14 August), don't bother even trying to stay sober. **Halkí**, the Tragéa's main town, has several fine churches, the best being **Panagía Protóthronis** (First-Enthroned Virgin), actually 500 years older than its official foundation date, 1052. The Annunciation fresco over the sanctuary is a masterpiece.

Goats and migrating birds are southern Náxos's chief inhabitants. From **Sangrí**, a paved road descends 5 km (3 miles) through a beautiful valley to the recently reconstructed Temple of Demeter (*circa* 530 BC).

Flowering shrubs adorn the old houses climbing up the hillsides in Náxos Town. Náxos is the most fertile island of the Cyclades chain.

BELOW: the Temple of Delian Apollo.

Náxos has been known for its beaches since the 1980s. Some of the best in the Cyclades are on the west coast, facing Páros. **Ágios Geórgios** south of the port is convenient; **Agíos Prokópios** and **Agía Ánna** are the most popular; **Pláka and Kastráki** ❸⓪ are less developed, with naturist areas.

Mílos

Mílos is a geologist's paradise. Snaking streams of lava formed much of the island's coastline, thrusting up weirdly shaped rock formations. The island has always been extensively mined, once for obsidian, now for bentonite, perlite and china clay, among others. Gaping quarries disfigure the landscape.

Mílos has graciously adapted to its growing stream of tourism, concentrated in **Adámas** ❸①, the port, and Pollónia, a fishing village in the northeast. Inside the **Agía Triáda** church in Adamás, Cretan-style icons dominate; Cretan refugees founded the town in 1853. The island's capital, **Pláka** (also called **Mílos**) ❸②, has both an **Archeological Museum** (open Tues–Sun 8.30am–3pm; entrance fee) and a **Folklore Museum** (open Tues–Sat 10am–2pm, 6–9pm, Sun 10am–1pm; entrance fee). A sunset hike to the **Panagía Thalassítra** (Mariner Virgin), the chapel above Pláka, and the old **Kástro** walls gives splendid views of Mílos and, on a clear day, as far as Páros.

Southwest of Pláka lies the **Vale of Klíma,** on whose seaside slope the ancient Milians built their city. Excavations undertaken in the late 19th century uncovered a Dionysian altar here, and remains of an ancient gymnasium. The **theatre** is very well preserved, probably because of its Roman renovation. Nearby, a marble plaque marks the spot where a farmer unearthed the Aphrodite of Mílos (Venus de Milo) in 1820. Below the theatre lies one of the island's prettiest vil-

Map, pages 226–7

When the original Venus de Milo was unearthed on the island in 1820, both arms were still intact. They were "amputated" during her clumsy removal from the island by the French.

BELOW: fishing off the island of Mílos.

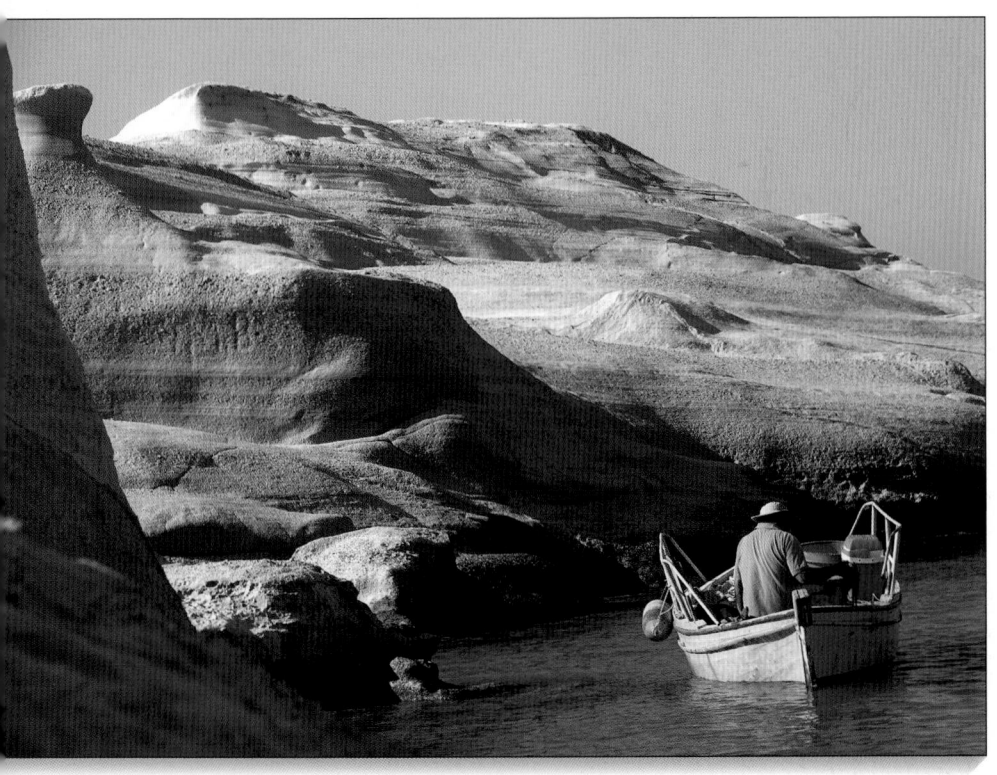

lages, **Klíma**, with brightly painted boathouses lining the shore, as well as the only **Christian catacombs** in Greece. Carved into the hillside, they are the earliest evidence of Christian worship in the country. A 200-metre/yd corridor is lined by tombs (all looted) which held around 5,000 bodies.

Ten km (6 miles) northeast from Adamás lies the rubble of the ancient city of **Phylakopi**, whose script and art resemble the Minoan. It flourished for a thousand years after 2600 BC. **Pollónia** ㉝, a restful base in the northeast, is a popular resort with a tree-fringed if windy beach – making it a major windsurfing centre.

The tiny island of **Kímolos** – 35 sq. km (14 sq. miles), with a population of 800 – is an alluring presence for anyone who is staying in Pollónia. The small ferry takes just 20 minutes to cross the narrow channel to Kímolos's only landing, **Psáthi**. Kímolos, once a pirates' hide-out, today provides refuge from the more crowded islands. Although it is blessedly undeveloped, it has several beaches, all within easy walking distance. **Hóra**, the one town, is a 20-minute walk up from Psáthi port, flanked by beaches at Rémma and Skála. Core of Hóra is the gated, 16th-century Venetian **Kástro**, its perimeter houses still inhabited.

Folégandros

Despite its tiny size – 32 sq. km (12 sq. miles) populated by barely 500 people – Folégandros's role in very recent history has not been insignificant: many Greeks were exiled here during both the 1930s' dictatorship and then the colonels' junta.

Folégandros (Hóra) ㉞ is a magnificently sited medieval town with an inner **kástro** high above the sea. **Hrysospiliá** (Golden Cave) near Hóra, gapes over the sea. It is rich with stalagmites and stalactites. Excavations show this was a place of refuge in the Middle Ages. The island's "trunk road" continues beyond Hóra to the scattered ridge-line houses of **Áno Meriá**; paths and tracks lead southwest down to sheltered sandy beaches.

Síkinos

Although connected by ferry to Piraeus and other Cyclades two or three times a week, and by caïque to Folégandros in summer, rocky Síkinos so far seems to have shrugged off tourism. It also escapes mention in the history books for long periods of time, but there are antiquities and churches to be seen.

The three beaches, **Aloprónia** (also the port), **Ágios Nikólaos** and **Ágios Geórgios** to the northeast face Íos. From Aloprónia harbour it is an hour's hike (or regular bus ride) to **Síkinos Town** ㉟, which consists of the simple village (**Hóra**) and the medieval **Kástro**, with its wonderful village square arranged for defence. The abandoned convent of **Zoödóhos Pigí** sits above.

Síkinos is a sparse island with few obvious diversions. One site of note, the **Iroön** ㊱, stands on what was once thought to have been a temple to Apollo; this is now reckoned to be an elaborate Roman tomb, incorporated into a church during medieval times.

Íos

A tiny island with few historic attractions, Íos is not devoid of natural beauty or charm. The harbour is one of the Aegean's prettiest. The hilltop Hóra,

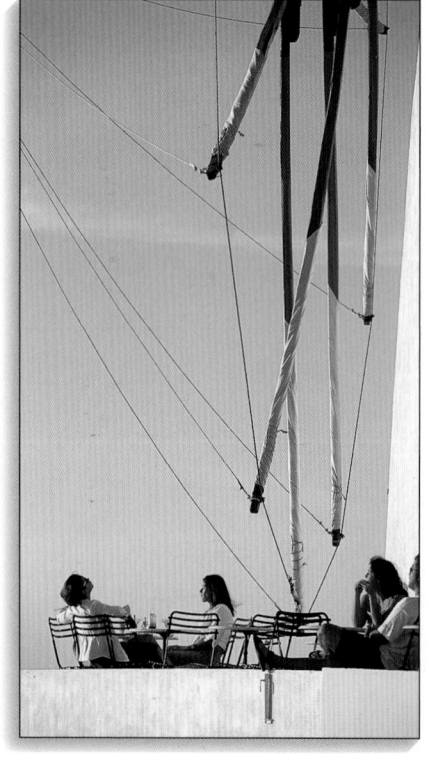

BELOW: sitting out by Ía's windmill, Santoríni.

capped by a windmill, blazes with the blue domes of two medieval churches. Its layout and the palm trees that flank it look almost Levantine. But ever since the 1960s, Íos has drawn the young and footloose, and this is its defining characteristic. Most nightlife shifts constantly about the little capital town, **Hóra** (also called **Íos**) ❸❼. Indeed, after the sun sets, Íos resembles a downmarket, younger Mýkonos. At around 11pm, beach stragglers break the quiet ready for night-time revels (a bus runs regularly between beach and harbour via Hóra). Once ensconced inside a bar, they could be anywhere in the Western world, with few older Greeks in sight.

However, Íos also has many good swimming beaches, especially on the southwest coast, where the main developed resort is **Mylopótas** ❸❽ (aka Mylopótamos). There are summer caïques to **Manganári bay** in the south and **Psathí** in the east.

On the way to Psathí are the remains of **Paleokástro** ❸❾, an elevated fortress containing the marble ruins of what was the medieval capital. At a lonely spot toward the northern tip, behind the cove at **Plakotós**, is a series of prehistoric graves, one of which the islanders fiercely believe belongs to Homer, who is said to have died en route from Sámos to Athens.

Amorgós

A spine of mountains – the tallest is Krikelas in the northeast, at 820 metres (2,696 ft) – precludes expansive views here unless you're on top of them. The southwesterly harbour town of **Katápola** ❹❶ occupies a small coastal plain, while the elevated **Hóra** (or **Amorgós Town**) ❹❶, accessible by a regular bus service, centres on a 13th-century Venetian castle. Hóra has no fewer than 40

Alternative transport in Amorgós.

BELOW: Tholária, traditional taverna, Amorgós.

Urn from the site at Akrotiri on Santoríni. The largest Minoan city outside Crete, it was destroyed in a volcanic eruption in 1500 BC – at first, archeologists thought they'd found Atlantis.

BELOW:
Firá, Santoríni.

churches and chapels – including one that holds only two people, the smallest church in Greece – as well as stepped plazas.

The island's two most famous churches are outside Hóra. **Ágios Geórgios Valsamítis**, 4 km (2 miles) southwest, is built over a sacred spring; this church's pagan oracle was only cemented over after World War II. Half an hour east of Hóra, clinging limpet-like to tawny cliffs, the 11th-century Byzantine monastery of the **Hozoviótissa** ⊕ – one of the most beautiful in Greece – is home to a revered icon of the Virgin from Palestine.

Beaches in the northeast of Amorgós, around the second port-resort of **Egiáli**, are most alluring, especially the trio reached by the trail that runs west from the main beach. **Langáda** and **Tholária** are exquisite villages up the hillside, reached by well-marked paths, with tavernas and lodging.

Santoríni

Entering the bay of Santoríni on a boat is one of Greece's great experiences. Broken pieces of a volcano's rim – Santoríni and its attendant islets – form a multicoloured circle around a bottomless lagoon that, before the volcano's eruption (c.1635 BC), was the island's high centre. Thíra, or Thera, are the island's official and ancient name respectively. Greeks, however, prefer its medieval name, Santoríni, after St Irene of Salonica, who died here in 304. **Firá** ⊕, the capital, sits high on the rim, its white houses (many barrel-vaulted against earthquakes) blooming like asphodels. To the east of Firá, the land smoothes out into fertile fields. A few bare cliffs push up again in the southeast. On one of them sits **Ancient Thera** ⊕ (9th century BC), where naked boys danced in a famous ritual. **Akrotiri** ⊕ in the south, a Minoan town preserved in volcanic ash like Pompeii,

Map, pages 226–7

continues to be excavated. Many of the finds – pots and frescoes – are in Firá's **Museum of Prehistoric Thera** (open Tues–Sun 8.30am–7.30pm; entrance fee).

Though Firá is most developed, many other places offer plentiful accommodation. **Ía (Oia) ⓠ**, on the island's northernmost peninsula, is perhaps Greece's most photographed village. Nearby, beautiful *skaftá* ("dug-out") houses, converted into highly sought-after accommodation, are a local speciality. There are also more places available to stay and eat in **Kamári** and **Périssa**, busy resorts on the east coast. Périssa has the main campsite. Both have roasting hot black pebble beaches. They make a good starting point from which to climb up to Ancient Thera.

Small ferries and excursion boats put in below Firá at **Skála Firá**, from where you ascend by donkey, by funicular or by foot up the stone stairway. Big ferries anchor at **Athiniós**, 10 km (6 miles) further south. The most popular boat excursions offered are to **Thirassía**, Santoríni's sleepy and beachless satellite islet opposite Ía; and to the volcanic islets of **Paleá** and **Néa Kaméni** in the middle of the submerged caldera, where passengers have the opportunity to bathe in hot mud springs or clamber over a still-steaming cinder cone.

Anáfi

Fewer than 300 people live on Anáfi in winter, surviving mainly by fishing and subsistence farming. Summer tourism, mostly Greek, has boosted the economy, but development is slow. It is served by a twice-weekly caïque from Santoríni and several ferries from Piraeus.

The south-facing harbour, **Ágios Nikólaos**, has rooms available in summer. A short bus ride or half-hour walk up, the main town, **Anáfi** (Hóra) ⓥ offers

BELOW:
colourful Cycladic architecture.

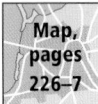

Map, pages 226–7

a wider choice, and life in the streets is still fairly untouristy. **Zoödóhou Pigís Monastery** ⓽ was erected over the ancient shrine to Apollo at the island's eastern extreme. Extensive courses of marble masonry in its walls are believed to be remnants of the old temple. Above the monastery soars the smaller monastery of **Panagía Kalamiótissa**, high on a pinnacle that is Anáfi's most distinctive feature. Between this and Ágios Nikólaos are four outstanding beaches.

The Back Islands

The so-called "Back Islands" near Náxos were once thickly populated. Now **Donoúsa**, **Iráklia**, **Skinoúsa** and **Koufonísi** have permanent populations of 100 to 200 each, while **Kéros** is completely uninhabited. For all the "Back Islands" there are now main-line summer ferry services from Piraeus twice or thrice weekly, plus a regular small caïque (the *Express Skopelitis*) that calls from Amorgós and Náxos. These islets, especially Koufonísi, also support ample tourist facilities – though no bank ATMs so far.

Hilly Donoúsa is covered with vineyards; views from the harbour take in the barren Makáres islands and the grand profile of Náxos. Iráklia has two settlements: the harbour, Ágios Geórgios, and Hóra, just over an hour's hike above, plus a visitable cave. Skinoúsa's hilltop Hóra has a medieval fortress at its back; Almyrós and Tsigoúri beaches have facilities. Koufonísi has an east coast beach with a seasonal taverna and a lively 15 August *panigýri*. Kéros was a third-millennium BC burial site. Much of the Cycladic material in great museums comes from here; it is unvisitable unless you've lots of money to privately charter a caïque. ❑

BELOW: small fishing boats still play their part in the economy of the Cyclades.

Ancient Delos

Minuscule Delos (Dílos), to the southwest of Mýkonos, is heaven for archeologists. Extensive Greco-Roman ruins occupying much of the island's 4 sq. km (1.5 sq. miles) make Delos the near-equal of Delphi and Olympia.

If you suffer from seasickness be forewarned: the island is a "windy wasteland battered by the sea". The caïque trip takes about 40 minutes; if it is windy (it often is), it is wise to forego breakfast. In summer there are also daily trips to Delos from Tínos, Náxos and Páros.

Delos became a shrine because Leto, a nymph pregnant by Zeus, gave birth there to Artemis (actually on adjacent Rheneia), then, clutching a palm tree, to Apollo. A floating rock, Delos was rewarded for braving Hera's jealous wrath by four diamond pillars that anchored it in the heart of the Cyclades.

Most of the ruins occupy two arms of a right angle. To the right (southern arm) are the theatre and various domestic buildings. To the left are the sanctuaries to which pilgrims from all over the Mediterranean came with votive offerings and sacrificial animals.

For nearly a thousand years, Delos was the political and religious centre of the Aegean, and host to the Delian Festival, held every four years and, until the 4th century BC, Greece's greatest religious gathering. The Romans turned it into a grand trade fair, and made Delos a free port. It also became Greece's slave market, where as many as 10,000 slaves were said to be sold daily. In 88 BC, Mithridates, king of Pontus, sacked Delos; it never recovered, and fell into disuse.

Follow the pilgrim route to a ruined, monumental gateway leading into the Sanctuary of Apollo. Within are three temples dedicated to Apollo and one to Artemis, and the remains of a colossal marble statue of the god. Close by is the Sanctuary of Dionysus, with several Dionysic friezes and phalli standing on pedestals – including a marble phallic bird, symbolising the body's immortality.

Continue to the stunning Lion Terrace, where five Archaic lions squat. (These are copies; the weathered originals are in the museum.) Below this is the Sacred Lake, and a palm tree which marks the spot of Apollo's birth.

Most visitors delight in that part of Delos which was occupied by artesans rather than gods. Their houses, close to the port, are a regular warren, separated by narrow lanes lined by 2,000-year-old drains, with niches for oil-burning streetlamps. The main road leads to the theatre, which seated 5,500. It is unimpressive, but there are superb views from the uppermost of its 43 rows. On the way to the theatre are grander houses surrounded by columns and with exquisite mosaics.

From here, a gentle stroll leads to the summit of Mount Kýnthos (110 metres/360 ft), from which the views of the ruins and the Cyclades are memorable. Finish off your tour by descending first past the grotto of Hercules, and then stopping at the Sanctuaries to the Foreign Gods. In classical times practically the entire Levant traded here, under the tutelage of shrines erected to their divinities. ❑

RIGHT: one of the lean Lions, carved in the 7th century BC, which guard Delos' Sacred Lake.

THE ISLANDS IN BLOOM

The Greek islands are at their most bountiful in spring and early summer, when every hillside and valley is decorated with glorious colour

Greece in spring is a botanist's dream and a gardener's despair. Some 6,000 species of wild plant grow in Greece and the islands, and in the spring (March to May) visitors may enjoy a magnificent cornucopia of flowers and fragrances.

Hillsides resemble giant rock gardens, while brilliant patches of untended wasteground outdo Northern Europe's carefully tended herbaceous borders with ease. Winter rains, followed by a bright, hot, frost-free spring, produce a season's flowers compressed into a few, spectacular weeks before the summer's heat and drought become too much. By late May or early June the flowers are over, the seeds for next year's show are ripening, and greens are fading to brown to match the tourists on the beaches.

SUMMER SURVIVAL

Except in the cooler, higher mountains, most plants go into semi-dormancy to survive the arid summer. The first rains of autumn, which could come as early as October or as late as November, tempt a few autumn bulbs into flower but also initiate the germination of seeds – plants that will grow and build up strength during the winter in preparation for the following spring, when their flowers will again colour in the waiting canvas of the hills and valleys.

The richness and diversity of the flora are due in part to the islands' location between three continents – Europe, Asia and Africa – partly to the Ice Age survival in temperate Greece of pre-glacial species, and partly to the wonderful variety of habitats. Limestone, the foundation of much of Greece, is a favoured home for plants, providing the stability, minerals, water supply and protection they need.

▷ **THE HILLS ARE ALIVE**
Sunshine, colour and quantity mark the spring flowering of the islands, as here in the mountains of Crete in mid-April.

△ **A GOOD REED**
Not bamboo – but it has similar uses. The giant reed (*Arundo donax*) can even be made into pan pipes.

▽ **CUP OF MANY COLOURS**
Ranunculus asiaticus is an unlikely buttercup, with poppy-sized flowers in shades of white, pink, orange, red – and occasionally yellow.

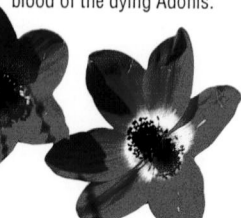

▽ **SCARLET MEMORIAL**
The startling reds of *Anemone coronaria* mark the arrival of spring in February and in myth represent the spilt blood of the dying Adonis.

▽ **HANDY BUSH**
The long flowering period of the native oleander makes it popular in gardens and as an ornamental roadside crash barrier.

BEETLES, BEES AND BUTTERFLIES

The profusion of flowers and plants provides food for an equal profusion of insects. Butterflies are conspicuous from spring to autumn, including the lovely swallowtail (*above*) whose colourful caterpillars feed on the leaves of common fennel. Its larger, paler and more angular relative, the scarce swallowtail, despite its name, is even more abundant.

Look for clouded yellows and paler cleopatras, reddish-brown painted ladies and southern commas, white admirals, and a myriad of smaller blue butterflies.

Butterflies, bees and day-flying hawk moths tend to go for flowers with nectar, while beetles and flies go for the pollen. Some insects even use the heat accumulated in the solar cup of many flowers in order to warm up their sex lives.

The leaves of plants feed armies of insect herbivores, which themselves are eaten by more aggressive insects. Some of the omnivorous Greek grasshoppers and crickets are as happy munching through a caterpillar, or even another grasshopper, as the grass it was sitting on.

◁ **FIRE FENNEL**
According to legend, fire was brought to earth by Prometheus hidden in the smouldering stem of a giant fennel *(Ferula communis)*.

▽ **NATURAL FOOD**
Wild artichokes are painfully spiny to prepare for the pot; but their flavour is prized by Greek country folk over the spineless cultivated variety, and their market price increases accordingly.

RHODES

According to the ancient Greeks, Rhodes is "more beautiful than the sun". Even today's brash resorts cannot dim the appeal of its benign climate, entrancing countryside and unique history

Maps:
City 247
Island 248

he largest and best-known of the Dodecanese islands, Rhodes (Ródos) is endowed with a balmy climate and a wealth of monuments from many eras. Ancient Rhodes originally consisted of three city-states: Kameiros, Ialyssos and Lindos. Following Athenian attacks they decided to unite, founding the city of Rodos at the island's northeast tip, separated from Asia Minor by only a 13-km (8-mile) strait. Fortifications were completed by 408 BC, and the town laid out in the popular grid plan of that era, championed by a certain Hippodamus.

Well-defended by its fleet and strategically positioned, Rhodes prospered as a trading-station and led a charmed life despite fickle alliances, as the moment suited, with Athens, Sparta, Alexander the Great, or the Persians. Under Alexander, Rhodes forged links with the Ptolemies; consequently, the Rhodians refused to fight the Egyptians alongside King Antigonos. After Alexander's death, Antigonos sent his son, Demetrios Polyorketes, along with 40,000 men to attack the city in 305 BC; he failed after a year-long siege. The leftover bronze military hardware was melted down to make the island's most famous landmark, the Colossus of Rhodes, a representation of Apollo. A beacon to passing ships, it stood over 30 metres (100 ft) tall, somewhere near the harbour entrance, for nearly 70 years before it collapsed during an earthquake in 226 BC.

The city emerged from the siege with prestige and prosperity enhanced, eclipsing Athens as the cultural beacon of the east Mediterranean. However, it got ideas above its station when it unwisely tried to reconcile the warring Romans and Macedonians. Rome retaliated in 168 BC by effectively making Rhodes a Roman vassal; involvement in Rome's civil wars a century later saw Rhodes sacked by Cassius and its fleet destroyed. After Octavius's victory in 42 BC and the establishment of imperial Rome, Rhodes regained some autonomy, and again served as a finishing school and sybaritic posting for officialdom. But its glory days were over. In late Roman and Byzantine times the island endured second-rate status, prone to barbarian raids.

Early in the 14th century, the Knights of St John – expelled from Palestine and Cyprus – settled on Rhodes, ejecting the Genoese who had been holding the island on sufferance of the Byzantines. They proceeded to occupy and fortify virtually all of the Dodecanese, rebuilding Rhodes Town's rickety Byzantine city walls and acting as a major irritant to the sultan with their depredations of Ottoman shipping. Finally, in the spring of 1522, Süleyman the Magnificent landed an army of 200,000 on Rhodes to end the problem; Rhodes's second siege was shorter and more conclusive than the first, but only just. The Knights resisted valiantly, but finally were forced to surrender.

LEFT: Agathí beach, on the east coast.
BELOW: Ágios Nikólaos fort guards Mandráki harbour.

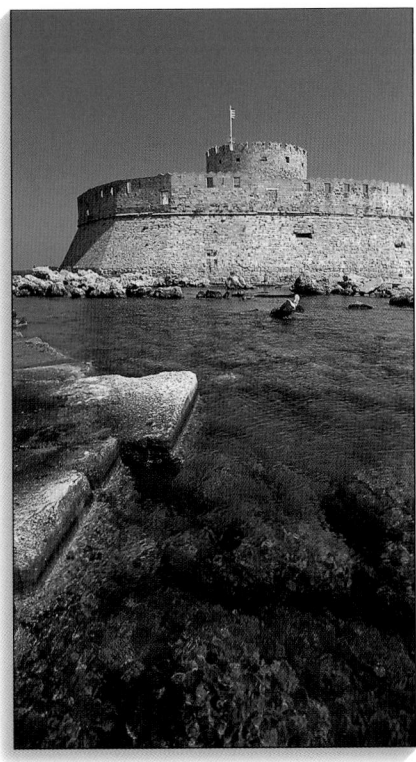

On New Year's Day 1523, 180 survivors concluded honourable terms of surrender and sailed off to exile on Malta.

The Ottomans suitably appreciated their hard-won possession, at least initially, and instituted the regime common to fortified cities in their empire: Christians were forbidden from staying overnight within the walled old town, although Jews were tolerated in their small quarter to the east. This exclusionary edict gave rise to the *marásia* or Orthodox suburb villages which hem Rhodes Town on three sides, often bearing the names of their main parish churches. The Ottomans built a few grand mosques from scratch within the walls, but more usually appropriated small Byzantine and Crusader churches as *mescids* (the Muslim equivalent of a chapel). Even at the zenith of Ottoman power, the Muslim population of the entire island never much exceeded 15 per cent. Ottoman rule became increasingly desultory and inefficient until the Italians effectively annexed Rhodes in spring 1912 (*see page 48*).

The Old City

Despite still-visible damage from Allied bombing in early 1945, the Old City of **Rhodes 1** is one of the architectural treasures of the Mediterranean, a remarkably complete walled medieval town. The ramparts themselves (one-hour tours only; currently suspended; entrance from gate beside Palace of the Grand Masters; entrance fee) give a good perspective over the palm-and-minaret-studded lanes. At the northwest summit stands the **Palace of the Grand Masters** (open summer Mon 12.30–9pm, Tues–Sun 8am–7.30pm; winter Mon 12.30–3pm, Tues–Sun 8.30am–3pm; entrance fee), destroyed in 1856 by an ammunition explosion and hastily reconstructed by the Italians during the 1930s. On the

Legend has it that the Colossus stood with one foot on either side of Mandráki harbour entrance. But to do so it would have had to have been over 10 times its probable size – an impossible feat of engineering.

BELOW: a mosaic floor in the Palace of the Grand Masters.

round floor are two excellent galleries detailing medieval and ancient Rhodes, with exemplary layout and labelling.

From outside, the better-restored **Street of the Knights (Odós Ippotón)** ❸, where the chivalric order once housed its members according to their native language, leads downhill to the badly labelled **Archeological Museum** ❸ (open Tues–Sun 8.30am–2.45pm; entrance fee) with its "Marine Venus" beloved of Lawrence Durrell; the **Byzantine Museum** ❸, opposite in the former cathedral of the Knights (open Tues–Sun 8.30am–2.45pm; entrance fee), with its exhibits of local icons and frescoes; and the ethnographic **Decorative Arts Collection** Tues–Sun 8am–2.45pm; entrance fee), with doors and chests salvaged from Dodecanesian village dwellings.

Despite an enduring resident Turkish minority, Ottoman monuments are not much highlighted except for the **Ottoman Library** (open Mon–Sat 9.30am–4pm; ip custodian) and a wonderful, still-functioning **Turkish Bath** ❸ (open Mon–Fri 10am–5pm, Sat 8am–5pm) on Platía Aríonos. The arcaded synagogue of **Kal Kadosh Shalom** ❸ (open Sun–Fri 10am–3pm; donation), in the former Jewish quarter, can also be visited. It serves largely as a memorial to the more than 1,800 Jews of Rhodes and Kós who were deported to Nazi death camps in June 1944.

Maps:
City 247
Island 248

Aphrodite Louomene
*(Aphrodite Bathing),
referred to by
Lawrence Durrell as
the Marine Venus.*

The New Town

Established by the Orthodox Greeks who were banished from the Old City by the Ottomans, and developed by the Italians when they took control in the early 20th century, the New Town (**Neohóri**) is the commercial centre of Rhodes and the administrative capital of the Dodecanese. Here, smart shops abound, peddling Lacoste, Benetton and Trussardi. Watch the world go by and the yachts

BELOW:
Líndos beach
and acropolis.

Ancient Kameiros.

bobbing from one of the pricey, touristy pavement cafés at **Mandráki** port. Marginally cheaper are the cafés inside the **covered market (Néa Agorá)** G, though it's largely a tourist-trap of bad restaurants redeemed in part by the Art Deco fish market gazebo at the centre.

Mandráki's quay buzzes night and day with caricature artists, popcorn vendors, sponge-sellers and touts hawking boat trips. Excursion boats leave by 9am for the island of Sými, calling first at Panormítis Monastery, or down the east coast to Líndos. Hydrofoils depart from the base of the jetty, while full-size ferries leave from Kolóna harbour, a 15-minute walk east.

Mandráki, guarded by the round bastion-lighthouse of **Ágios Nikólaos (St Nicholas' Fort)** H, is also an established port of call for the international yachting circuit, with local charters, too. By the harbour entrance stands a cluster of Italian monuments: the Governor's House with its Gothic arches, the **church of St Joseph the Evangelist (Evangelismós)** I next door and, across the way, the post office, Town Hall and Municipal Theatre. Opposite the theatre, the **Mosque of**

Rhodes

0 — 10 km
0 — 10 miles

AEGEAN   SEA

Kós, Piréas

Ákra Koumboúrno
Kritiká
Ródos (Rhodes) 1

Triánda   Ixiá
Kremastí
Filérimos · Ialyssós 4
Paradísi   Asgoúrou
Pastida   Ákra Vóos
Koskinoú
Theológos Damatriá   Kallithéa
Soroni   Thermes Kallithéas
Fánes   Maritsá
Kalavárda   Petaloúdes 13   Kalythiés   Faliráki 9
Kameiros 3   Psínthos   Ákra Ladikó
Mandrikó   Sálakos   95   Traganoú
Kápi   Dimiliá   Afandoú
Alímia   Kámiros   Profítis Ilías   Eleoúsa   Afándou
Skála   Náni   798
Krítinia 5   Apóllona   Arhipolis   Kolýmbia
Kritinía   Ágios Nikólaos Foundoúkli †   Platánia   Eptá Pigés 12   Moní Tsambíka
Hálki   Embonás   Tsambíka 10
Emborió (Hálki)   Mt Atávyros 7 1215   Arhángelos
Ródos (Rhodes)   Profítis Ilías 512   Ákra Arhangélos
Glyfáda   Steliés   Malóna   Másari   Agathí
Ákra Armenistís   Ágios Isídoros   Haráki   Feraklós
Siánna   Láerma
Ákra Monólithos   Monólithos 6   Moní Thárri † 8   Kálathos   Kaláthou 11
Istríos   Vlyhá   Acropolis
Profília   Lárdos   Líndos 2
Apolakkiá   Arnítha   Váti   Asklipió 14   Péfki (Pefkos)
Kiotári
Gennádi
Mesanagrós

MEDITERRANEAN SEA

Laháni 15
Kattaviá   Ákra Laháni
Ag. Pávlos   Hóhlakas
Plimýri
Ág. Geórgios
Prasonísi
Ákra Prasonísi 16

Kárpathos Kásos, Sitía

Murad Reis ❿ stands beside one of the island's larger Muslim graveyards. Beyond this is the **Villa Cleobolus**, where Lawrence Durrell lived from 1945 to 1947.

Away from the harbour, Neohóri throbs with nightlife, revellers spilling out of the bars on to the pavements in high season, though the area's heyday is long over, with perhaps half of its one-time 200 bars still functioning. Orfaní-dou in particular is informally dubbed "Skandi Street" after the new Vikings.

Maps:
City 247
Island 248

Three ancient city-states

One of the original Dorian city-states, **Líndos ❷**, 44 km (27 miles) south along the east coast, is the island's other big tourist magnet. Settled early thanks to its fine natural harbour – the island's only one aside from Mandráki at Rhodes Town – its strong acropolis supports a scaffolded Hellenistic Athena temple and another Knights' castle (open summer Mon 12.30–6.45pm, Tues–Sun 8am–6.45pm, closes 5.45pm in spring and autumn; winter Tues–Sun 8.30am–2.45pm; entrance fee). Clustered below is the late-Medieval village of imposing mansions built by local sea-captains; with its barren surroundings, the place has always lived from the sea. Italian, German and British bohemians first rediscovered Líndos in the 1960s, attracted by the pellucid light. But its role as an artists' colony has long since been replaced by one as a package-tour dormitory: midsummer visits, when you can hardly move down the narrow, cobbled streets, are not recommended.

Tsambíka monastery is a magnet for childless women.

The second of the original city-states, **Kameiros ❸**, 33 km (20 miles) down the windswept west coast from Rhodes Town, merits a visit for displaying a perfectly preserved classical townscape, without the usual later accretions (open summer Tues–Sun 8am–6.45pm; winter Tues–Sun 8.30am–3pm; entrance fee). Unlike old Lindos, it was abandoned shortly after 408 BC. Not so ancient **Ialyssos ❹** (open

BELOW: the castle at Monólithos, built by the Knights of St John.

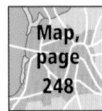

Map, page 248

Tues–Sun 8.30am–2.45pm; entrance fee), 12 km (7½ miles) southwest of Rhodes Town. Only a Doric fountain and some Hellenistic temple foundations are evident from the ancient city-state. Today the town is best known for its appealing medieval monastery of **Filérimos**, now well restored after World War II damage.

Island sights

Although bus frequencies have actually improved in recent years, Rhodes is most easily explored by hire car. Superbly sited Knights' castles at **Kritinía ❺** and **Monólithos ❻**, both beyond Kámiros, make suitable targets, along with the village of **Siána** in between, well equipped for visitors, with numerous tavernas. All lie under the shadow of 1,215-metre (3,985-ft) **Mount Atávyros ❼**, the highest point on Rhodes; from just north of Ágios Isídoros a marked path goes to the summit with its foundations of a Zeus temple. The best Byzantine monuments in the interior are the late Byzantine church of **Ágios Nikólaos Foundouklí** with smudged frescoes, just below 798-metre (2,600-ft) Profítis Ilías, and the monastery of **Thárri ❽**, with its glorious, cleaned 14th-century frescoes, hidden amid unburned pine forest between Líndos and Monólithos.

The southern tip of Rhodes is popular with windsurfers.

The best beaches cluster on the more sheltered east coast. The first resort travelling south from Rhodes Town is **Kallithéa**, which sprang up around the spa established there by the Italians. Round the headland is Kallithéa Bay, one of the best beaches on the island and the most energetically exploited for tourism. On the south side of the bay is **Faliráki ❾**, one of Greece's more notorious resorts and very popular with young package tourists though much subdued after a 2003 crime spree. By day, every form of watersport is available; by night, when the neon lights are switched on, bars compete with loud music and improbably alcoholic cocktails.

BELOW: a local in Rhodes Town.

Pebbly **Traganoú**, at the north end of Afándou bay, has caves and overhangs, and is mostly patronised by Rhodians. **Tsambíka ❿** huddles beneath a giant promontory on which stands a tiny monastery of the Virgin in her avatar of fertility goddess – hundreds of *ex-votos* testify to her successful intervention for childless couples. **Paralía Kaláthou ⓫** is the best undeveloped beach on this coast.

Inland from Tsambíka, **Eptá Pigés ⓬** is an enduringly popular oasis, its reservoir an Italian legacy. Northwest of there, the **Petaloúdes (Butterfly Valley) ⓭** is the home of millions of Jersey Tiger moths, attracted by the *Liquidambar orientalis* trees in this secluded stream canyon.

Beyond the Líndos promontory, there are few specific sights aside from the wonderfully frescoed 11th-century church at **Asklipío** village ⓮, just inland from the mushrooming resort of Kiotári. There are more, usually empty beaches at Gennádi; and further south, the ravine-hidden, well-watered village of **Lahaniá ⓯** has attracted a second generation of drop-outs after the original Líndos scene, who renovate traditional houses here under long-lease agreements. Land's End for Rhodes is the sandspit-tethered islet of **Prasonísi ⓰**, reached from Kattaviá village. Topography and winds combine to make the broad, flat beach here one of the premier venues for windsurfing in Greece, with two schools operating every season. ❏

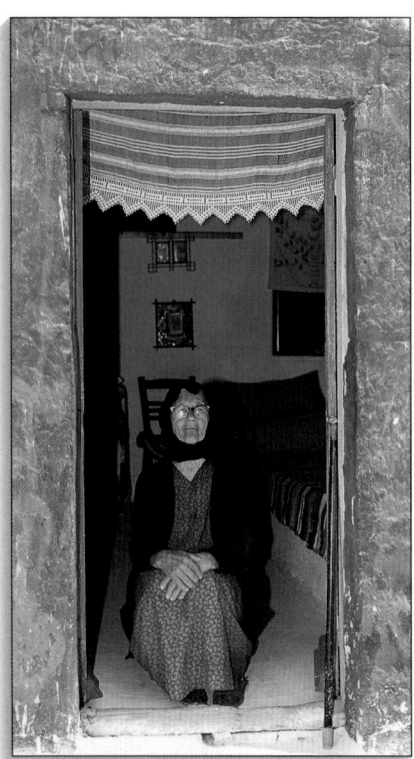

Italian Architecture in the Dodecanese

The Italians, who occupied the Dodecanese from 1912 until 1943, adorned the historic centres of Rhodes and Kós towns with grandiose public buildings, constructed a huge naval base and the planned town of Porto Lago (Lakkí) on Léros, and did much to reconstruct Kós after the 1933 earthquake. Because of its associations with Fascism, anything linked to this period, whatever its quality, was until recently disparaged if not neglected.

In Rhodes, a new administrative centre – the Foro Italica – was created, comprising all public services, and centred on the all-important Fascist Party Headquarters with its tower and speaker's balcony. Beyond lay the new city's tourist area, which included La Ronda Sea Baths (today Élli), the Albergo delle Rose (now the casino) and the aquarium at the far cape.

Art Deco style featured in the Fascist Youth Building and the football stadium; other buildings, such as the nautical club, the aquarium and the Customs House mixed elements of Art Deco with abstract Ottoman motifs. Out in the countryside, the Kallithéa Baths (*shown below*) are the best example of orientalised Art Deco, stylishly blending with their surroundings.

The later phase of Fascist rule, from 1936, coinciding with the harsh tenure of Governor Cesare Maria de Vecchi, stressed the perceived continuity between the Knights Hospitallers and the Italians. Many monuments of the Knights were restored, and new buildings in a "neo-Crusader" style, such as the Bank of Rome, were erected. At the same time, buildings such as the Albergo delle Rose and the Courthouse were "purified" by removing the allegedly superfluous, orientalising features of Art Deco, and replacing these with a cladding of poros stone. In this final stage, Italian architecture in the Dodecanese conformed to Rationalist-Internationalist canons of the decade, with more monumental and rigidly symmetrical structures. The Puccini Theatre (now the Municipal Theatre) on the Piazza del'Impero was the best example of many such around this square. ❏

THE DODECANESE

*Closer to Turkey than Greece, the archipelago has enormous
variety, from holy Pátmos to busy Kós, from wild Kárpathos to
tranquil Tínos, from fertile Tílos to the volcano that is Nísyros*

Map,
page
254

Greek place names often reveal history, and "Dodecanese" (Dodekánisos), a new name by Greek standards, is no exception. Through four centuries of Ottoman rule these islands were known as the Southern Sporades, a name still appearing on older maps. During this period, smaller, more barren islands here were granted considerable privileges – in effect, being invited to look after themselves – while larger, more fertile Rhodes and Kós were more strictly governed and colonised by Muslims. After the establishment of an independent Greece in 1830, and periodic armed hostilities between it and the Ottoman Empire, such privileges were gradually withdrawn. The 12 larger islands (*dódeka nisiá* in Greek) submitted a joint objection against these infringements in 1908; it failed but the new name stuck, despite there being – depending on how one counts – 14 or even 18 inhabited isles in this chain, extending northwest to southeast in an arc along the Turkish coast.

In 1912 the Italians, as part of a larger war against the Turks, took this group to cut the Ottoman supply lines to Libya. Despite initial promises to relinquish the archipelago once the Turks left Tripoli, the Italian annexation was consolidated by World War I and the subsequent rise of the Fascist regime after 1923, when the group was officially renamed the "Italian Islands of the Aegean". The Fascists were busy colonialists, erecting numerous distinctive edifices *(see page 251)*, planting eucalyptus to drain swamps, building roads and imposing their language, religion and political culture on public life. Repression was stepped up considerably in 1936 when governor Mario Lago was replaced by Cesare de Vecchi, a zealous Fascist who helped depose Mussolini and was condemned by the Salo Republic (though he escaped). In a series of bloody actions against now pro-Allied Italian forces, the Germans assumed control of the Dodecanese in late 1943, but in turn surrendered the islands to the British two years later.

Finally, in early 1948, after a 10-month interlude of Greek military rule imposed to weed out local collaborators with the Italians, the Dodecanese were united with Greece to become the country's southeasternmost, and most recent, territorial acquisition. Massive emigration to Australia, South Africa and North America ensued, as in chaotic post-war Greece union with the "mother" country initially brought little other than freedom of movement. Today the islanders live – as they always have – largely off the sea, which has brought them a catch of vital importance to the local economy: tourists.

LEFT: windmill on Kárpathos.
BELOW: evening light on Léros.

Kárpathos, Kásos and Hálki

The most dramatic way to arrive at **Kárpathos** is by ship from Rhodes, invariably departing before dawn. After several hours' journey, the island appears with

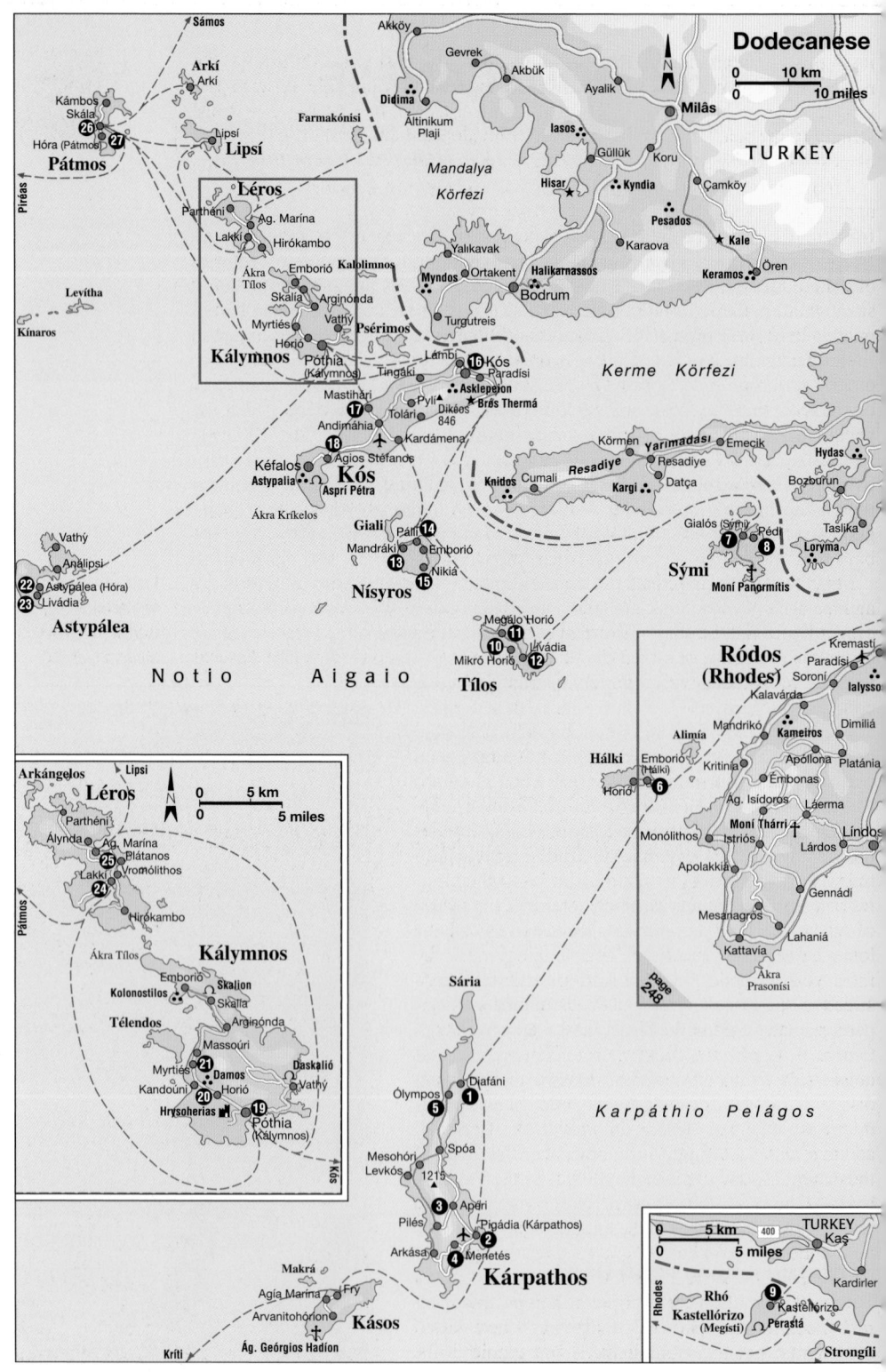

Dodecanese

0   10 km
0   10 miles

Sámos

Arkí
Arkí

Kámbos
Skála
26
27
Hóra (Pátmos)
Pátmos

Lipsí
Lipsí

Farmakónisi

Akköy

Gevrek
Akbük
Ayalik

Didima
Altinikum
Plaji

Milâs

Iasos
Güllük   Koru

TURKEY

Piréas

Levítha

Kínaros

Léros
Parthéni
Ag. Marina
Lakkí   Hirókambo

Ákra   Emborió   Kalolimnos
Tílos
Skália   Arginónda
Myrtiés   Vathý
Horió   Psérimos
Kálymnos   Póthia
(Kálymnos)   Tingáki

Mandalya
Körfezi

Hisar
Kyndia
Çamköy

Pesados

Yalıkavak
Ortakent   Karaova   Kale
Myndos   Halikarnassos   Keramos   Ören
Bodrum

Turgutreis

Lámbi
16   Kós
Paradísi

Kerme   Körfezi

Mastihári
17
Andimáhia
18   Kardámena
Ágios Stéfanos
Astypalia   Kós
Aspri Pétra

Ákra Kríkelos

Pyli
Tolári   Dikéos
846
Asklepeíon
Brós Thermá

Körmen
Cumali   Resadiye   Resadiye
Knidos   Kargi   Datça
Emecik

Yarimadasi

Hydas

Bozburun

Gialós (Symi)   Pédi
7   8
Loryma

Taslika

Kéfalos

Vathý
Análipsi
22   Astypálea (Hóra)
23   Livádia
Astypálea

Giali   Páli   14
Mandráki   Emborió
13   Nikiá
15
Nísyros

Sými
Moní Panormítis

Notio   Aigaio

Megálo Horió
11
Mikró Horió   10   Livádia
12
Tílos

Hálki
Emborió
(Hálki)
Horió   6

Ródos
(Rhodes)
Kalavárda
Alimía   Mandrikó   Kameiros
Kritiniá   Apóllona
Émbonas
Ág. Isídoros   Láerma
Monólithos   Moní Thárri
Istriós   Lárdos
Apolakkiá
Mesanagrós
Kattaviá   Lahaniá
Ákra
Prasonísi

Kremastí
Paradísi
Soroní   Ialyssos
Dimiliá
Platánia
Líndos
Gennádi

page
248

Arkángelos   Lipsí
Léros
0   5 km
Partheni   0   5 miles
Álynda   Ag. Marina
25   Plátanos
Lakkí   Vromólithos
24
Hirókambo

Ákra Tílos
Emborió
Kolonostilos   Skálion
Skálla
Télendos
Massoúri
Myrtiés   21   Arginónda
Kandoúni   Damos
20   Horió
Hrysoherias   19
Póthia
(Kálymnos)

Kálymnos

Makrá
Agía Marina   Fry
Arvanitohórion
Kásos
Ág. Geórgios Hadíon
Kríti

Sária

Ólympos   Diafáni
5   1

Karpáthio   Pelágos

Mesohóri   Spóa
Levkós   1215
Apéri
3
Pilés   Pigádia (Kárpathos)
2
Arkása
4   Menetés

Kárpathos

TURKEY
Kaş
0   5 km
0   5 miles   400

Rhodes

Rhó
Kastellórizo
(Megísti)   Perastá
9   Kastellórizo

Kardirler

Strongíli

its imposing, often cloud-flecked summit-ridge. Boats stop at **Diafáni** ❶, the northerly port given a jetty only in 1996. By the mid-morning light, onward passengers have an hour to get acquainted with Kárpathos. Its eastern shore drops steeply to the sea, baby pines sprouting from slopes denuded during the fierce blazes of the 1980s; occasionally, the cliffs relent at large, white, empty beaches.

After these first impressions, the main port of **Pigádia** ❷ is inevitably a disappointment, with little to recommend it other than its fine setting; it dates only from the 19th century, but the islanders themselves – not invading forces – effectively wrecked it with concrete constructions from the 1960s onwards. This lack of distinction also has something to do with Kárpathos's status as a backwater since ancient times; neither the Knights of St John nor the Ottomans bothered much with it, leaving it to the Genoese and Venetians, who called it Scarpanto.

Getting to a beach is apt to be a top priority. An excellent one stretches immediately north for 3 km (1¾ miles) along Vróndi Bay. More secluded ones, visible on the ferry ride in, prove close-up to have aquamarine water and white-sand or pebble shores, guarded by half-submerged rock formations. The best of these are Ápella, Aháta and Kyrá Panagiá, accessible either on small-boat excursions or overland – although some Kárpathiot roads are appalling (even if the east-coast road is now mostly paved) and hire cars expensive. The west coast is served by good roads but far more exposed, though at remote Levkós, a series of three bays tucked in between headlands, there are excellent beaches and a busy resort.

Most villages are well inland and high up, the standard medieval strategy against pirates, of whom Kárpathos had more than its fair share. The wealthiest settlements are a trio – **Apéri** ❸, Óthos and Voláda – just south of cloud-capped Mount Kalilímni, 1,215 metres (3,985 ft) high, plus **Menetés** ❹ near Pigádia, all studded with a variety of traditional and contemporary villas.

The source of the wealth seems mysterious at first, since there is little fertile lowland, no industry, and mass tourism began only in the late 1980s. In fact, Kárpathos lives largely off remittances from seamen and emigrants (mostly in the US); this economy has profoundly affected local culture, architecture and attitudes. It has deliberately slowed the development of tourism and, paradoxically, also enhanced the position of women who stayed behind. Overseas values have left their mark on house-building, although even the most vulgar modern pile may sport a date of construction, the owner's initials and a traditional emblem, perhaps a mermaid or double-headed Byzantine eagle.

In its original form, the vernacular Karpathiot house consists of a single, mud-floored space appropriately divided; to one side a raised wooden platform or *dórva*, where the bride's dowry linen, festival clothing and mattresses are kept, the latter rolled out at night. In the centre, a wooden pole – the "pillar of the house" – upholds the ceiling, and to complete the symbolism a painting or photograph of the couple is pinned to the pole under their wedding-wreath – a custom perhaps developed to acquaint children with chronically absent fathers. The walls are decked with shelves and plate-racks, containing hundreds of kitsch and near-kitsch ornaments: not local handicrafts, but ethnic dolls,

Map, page 254

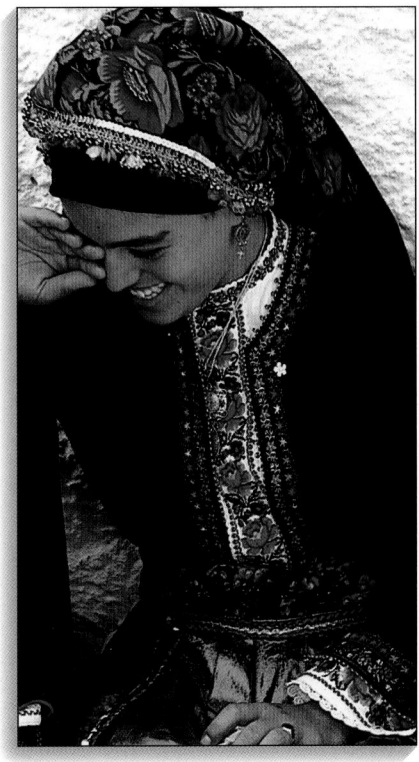

BELOW: a young woman in traditional dress, Ólympos.

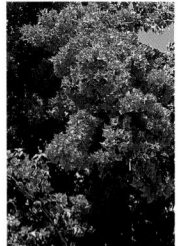

Bougainvillea brightens Ólympos village.

gaudy pottery and other baubles collected by wandering Karpathiot sailors. Even modern, multi-room villas still model their *salóni* (sitting room) on this pattern.

Many Dodecanese islands are matrilineal (as opposed to matriarchal). On Kárpathos it's merely more evident, at least in the northernmost villages of **Ólympos ⑤** and **Diafáni**, where some women still wear traditional dress; the well-travelled men have worn approximations of Western garb for as long as anyone can remember. The women's waistcoats, aprons, headscarves and boots are still locally made, but this everyday costume is completed by Irish wool scarves and imported sequins and embroidery, much of it Chinese and Bulgarian. Festival dress is rather more colourful and includes a gold-coin collar, the number of coins signalling a girl's wealth to prospective suitors.

Two of the most renowned festivals – Easter and Assumption Day – are still celebrated with special verve at Ólympos, which is draped over a windswept ridge. It has long been something of a honeypot for anthropologists, academic and amateur, owing to its relict Dorian dialect, the aforesaid costumes, music and communal ovens. But conventional tourism here has been as distorting – and rescuing – as subsidies from abroad have been elsewhere on Kárpathos; the last of several windmills stopped working as a real accessory to life late in the 1970s, but one was restored as a functioning museum-piece a few years later.

If you stay in either Diafáni or Ólympos, much the best way to spend time is to go for walks on the path network across the north of the island; Avlóna farm hamlet, the beach and ruins at Vrykoúnda, more ambitiously to Trístomo inlet, or simply down the canyons to Diafáni are popular targets.

Just southwest of Kárpathos, **Kásos** is its bleak satellite, devastated by an Ottoman massacre in 1824 and totally dependent ever since on seafaring.

BELOW: Ólympos village, Kárpathos.

Effectively protected from conventional tourism by its lack of beaches, it consequently has limited tourist facilities – especially off-season – and is thus frequented mostly by overseas-based Kassiots during the summer festival period.

Hálki, just off Rhodes, is another bare speck of limestone enlivened by the colourful port of **Emborió ❻**. Formerly home to sponge-divers, most of it was restored in the late 1980s and it is now packed from April to October with upmarket package tourists.

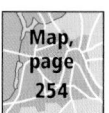
Map, page 254

Sými

Sými lies northeast of Rhodes, between the outstretched "claws" of Turkey's Datcá Peninsula. Although still retaining some forest, it is waterless and dependent on cisterns or tanker-boats, which has limited tourism. Most visitors come for the day to the photogenic harbour, which at the end of the 19th century supported a greater population (25,000) than Rhodes Town. Prosperity rested on sponge-diving, for which the island long held the Ottoman monopoly, and the related caïque-building industry. Although the Italian takeover of both the Dodecanese and the Libyan coast (where the sponges were harvested) failed to break the Greek hold on the sponge industry, World War II and the rise of synthetic sponges brought down the curtain on an era. War-related privations scattered the population to Rhodes, Athens and overseas, and today fewer than 3,000 call **Gialós ❼** (the quayside settlement) and Horió (the hillside village) home. Some caïques are still fashioned in the Haráni boatyards, but the sponges sold from Gialós's souvenir-stalls are mostly imported from Florida and the Philippines.

Gialós hospitality featuring traditional dress.

Sými's self-government during the Ottoman period was typical of "infidel" communities providing a desirable commodity, generally left to themselves as

BELOW:
Sými harbour.

long as they paid a yearly tribute-tax (in Sými's case, a boatload of sponges for the sultan's harem). Two *dimogérondes*, or municipal elders, were elected for one-year terms each January: one presided over the local council and outstanding judicial matters, and managed relations with the Ottoman bureaucracy, while the other oversaw community revenues. The number of (male) voters was unlimited, although they had to be over 21 and under 80, literate, of sound mind, with their taxes paid up and no penal sentence pending. The local council was elected initially by acclamation, but by secret ballot after 1902.

Pédi ❽, the valley south of Horió ridge, is the only arable patch of land on the island. There is a small waterside hamlet, too, and some scraps of sand beach, set now to succumb to a new, ill-advised yacht marina. Emborió bay, north of Gialós, offers an artificial sand beach, a Byzantine mosaic floor and a small catacomb complex. However, most of the island's beaches are pebbly, and accessible only by arduous hikes or boat excursions; the favourites are Ágios Vassílios, Marathoúnda and Nanoú (the latter two have tavernas). Among rural monasteries, the most artistically distinguished are **Mihaïl Roukouniótis**, due west of town, with its vivid 18th-century frescoes, and (even better) **Sotíras Megálos Nerás**, south along the paved road to the gargantuan monastery of **Mihaïl Panormítis**. Being on the sea-lane in from Rhodes, this gets the most visitors, irrespective of merit – a small museum, a large pebble courtyard and a sombre memorial to resistance fighters executed here in 1944 are the main sights.

Kastellórizo (Megísti)

Kastellórizo, some 70 nautical miles east of Rhodes in the shadow of Anatolia, has similarly come down in the world. At the turn of the 19th century, this limestone dot on the map had a population of over 10,000 thanks to the best natural harbour between Piraeus and Beirut, and the schooner fleet based here. But the fleet was sold rather than motorised; the island was heavily shelled during World War I while occupied by the French, then rocked by a 1926 earthquake and a 1944 munitions blast, which together destroyed three-quarters of the houses.

Most "Kassies" emigrated after the war to Rhodes and Western Australia, leaving a virtual ghost town barely clinging to life. The US Government even tried to convince Greece to cede the island to Turkey in 1964, in return for limited hegemony in Cyprus. Geopolitical realities still prevail: the islanders are obliged to get everything, from haircuts to fresh vegetables, across the way in Turkish Kaş, where a number of Turks are of part-Kassie ancestry.

In the end, it was pleasure-yachting and a film (*Mediterraneo*, filmed here in 1989–90) that probably saved Kastellórizo from desolation. A steady stream of (initially Italian) tourists has revived its fortunes, along with an airport and other government subsidies. There are no beaches and little to see other than rural monasteries, an ancient acropolis, a sea-cave entered only by boat and a tiny red-stone Crusader castle that gives the island its Italianate name. But the social scale of **Kastellórizo Town** ❾ is cosy, and the nightlife surprisingly lively.

TIP

If you decide to buy a natural sponge as a souvenir of Sými, make sure to ask for one that has not been bleached. Bleach is used to make the sponge look more inviting, but it also weakens the fibres.

BELOW: the huge monastery of Mihaïl Panormítis, Sými.

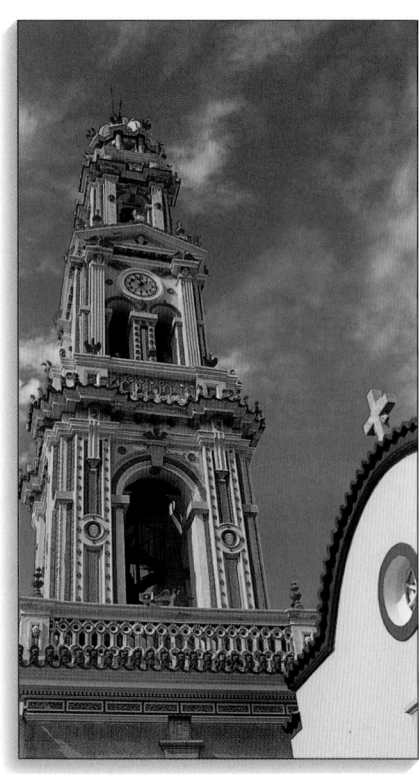

Tílos and Nísyros

Seahorse-shaped **Tílos**, north of Hálki and west of Rhodes, is the least maritime of these islands. With fertile volcanic soil and sufficient ground water, the islanders instead made Tílos the granary of the Dodecanese. Since the late 1980s, discerning tourists have been attracted by tranquillity, some fine beaches and good hiking opportunities. Historically there were just two villages, imaginatively named **Mikró Horió** 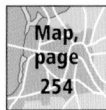 (Little Village, in the east) and **Megálo Horió** ⑪ (Big Village, in the west), continually at odds with each other. Mikró was abandoned after World War II in favour of **Livádia** ⑫, the port and main tourist resort. The rivalry supposedly ended with the election in 1998 of a single municipal council – the only sensible solution for a registered population of 500.

The crags above the plains hide seven small castles of the Knights of St John, as well as several medieval chapels. Éristos in the west is the largest and (arguably) best beach; inland extends a great *kámbos* planted with citrus, the whole surveyed by Megálo Horió. In the far west, **Agíou Pandelímona** is the main monastery, and venue for the principal festival (25–7 July, annually).

Circular **Nísyros**, between Tílos and Kós, is not merely "volcanic", as it is often described, but is actually a volcano – a dormant one that last erupted in 1933. Accordingly, what water exists here is sulphur-tainted, but the island is paradoxically green with oak, almond and other plants that thrive on volcanic soil. Once you're away from the harbour, **Mandráki** ⑬, the port and capital, is attractive with its close-packed houses overawed by Panagí Spilianí, installed in the inevitable Knights' castle, and the even more imposing remains of the 7th-century BC Doric citadel of **Paleókastro** just south. **Pálli** ⑭ is the alternative port for fishermen and yachties, just east of the mineral-water spa. You don't

Map, page 254

Nísyros is nicknamed the "Polo Mint island", thanks to its clusters of white cube houses and its hole in the middle – the hissing crater of Polyvótis volcano.

BELOW: Kastellórizo.

come to Nísyros for beach life, but on the east coast **Liés** and **Pahiá Ámmos** are more than decent.

There are two inland villages: **Emborió**, essentially abandoned and bought up by outsiders, and the more thriving **Nikiá** 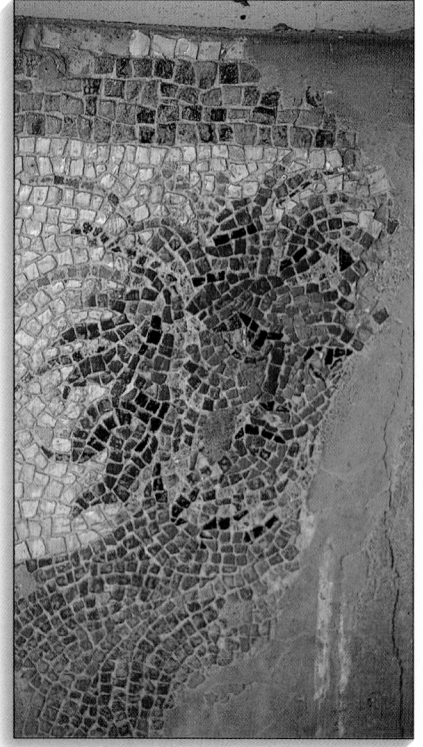 in the southwest, at the edge of the volcanic caldera created in 1422 when the (originally much taller) island blew its top. Coach tours of tourists based in Kós descend periodically, but otherwise the lifeless crater-floor, with its hissing steam-vents and sulphurous smell, is deserted.

Kós

The second-largest Dodecanese island in population, **Kós** is also tied for second in size with Kárpathos. It follows the lead of Rhodes in most things: a shared history, give or take a few years; a similar Knights' castle guarding the harbour, plus a skyline of palms and minarets; and an agricultural economy displaced by tourism. However, Kós is much smaller than Rhodes, and much flatter – amazingly so – with only one mountain, Díkeos. The margin of the island is fringed by excellent beaches, most easily reached by motorbike or even pushbike.

An earthquake in 1933 devastated most of **Kós Town** 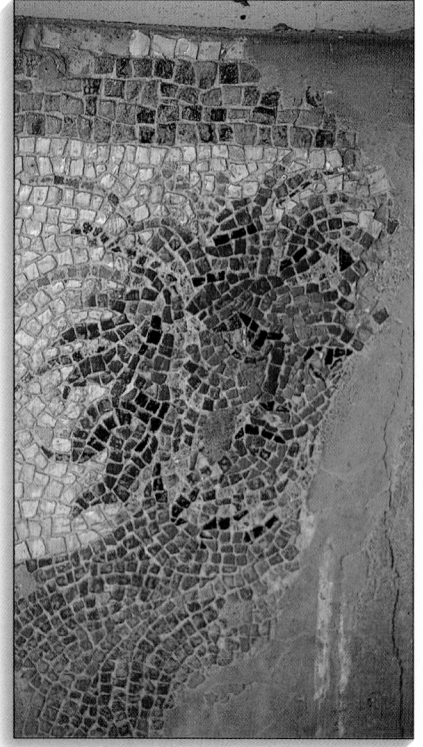, but gave Italian archeologists a perfect excuse to comprehensively excavate the ancient city. Hence much of the town centre is an archeological park, with the ruins of the **Roman agora** (the eastern excavation) lapping up to the 18th-century **Loggia Mosque** and the millennial **Plane Tree of Hippocrates**, not really quite old enough to be contemporary with the great ancient healer. The western digs offer covered mosaics and the colonnade of an indoor running-track; just south stand an odeion and the **Casa Romana**, a restored Roman villa with more mosaics and murals (closed for restoration until 2010).

*(captions left margin)*
BELOW: mosaic in the Hellenistic Asklepeion, Kós.

The Italian-founded **Archeological Museum** (open Tues–Sun 8.30am–2.30pm; entrance fee) has a predictable Latin bias in exhibits, although the highlighted statue, purportedly of Hippocrates the father of medicine, is in fact Hellenistic. Hippocrates himself (*circa* 460–370 BC) was born and practised here, but probably died just before the **Asklepeion**, the ancient medical school 4 km (2½ miles) southwest of town, was established. The site (open Tues–Sun 8am–6pm, until 2.30pm in winter; entrance fee) impresses more for its position overlooking the straits with Turkey than any structures, for the masonry was thoroughly pilfered by the Knights to build their enormous castle, which – unlike the one at Rhodes – was strictly military.

Between the Asklepeion and Kós Town, pause at **Platáni**, roughly halfway, to dine at one of three excellent Turkish-run tavernas – although as on Rhodes most local Muslims have chosen to emigrate to Turkey since the 1960s. There was a small Jewish community here too, wiped out with the Rhodian one in 1944, leaving behind only the marvellous Art Deco **synagogue** by the town agora.

The road east of town dead-ends at **Brós Thermá** enjoyable hot springs which run directly into the sea. West of town are the package resorts of **Tingáki** and **Marmári** with long white beaches, and the less frantic **Mastihári** 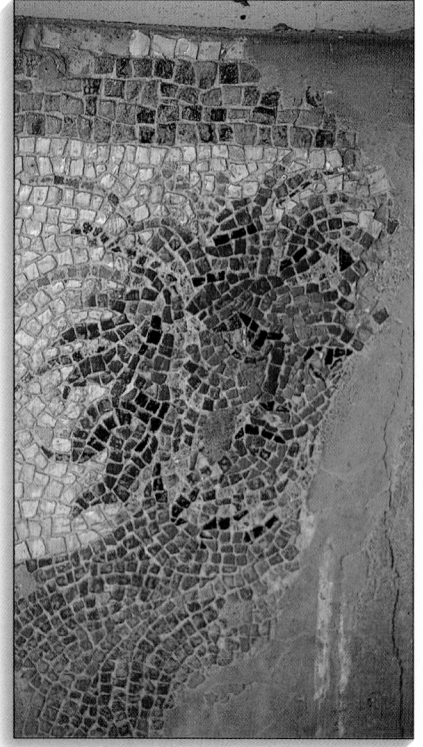, with a broader beach and a commuter boat to Kálymnos. In the far southwest, facing

Nísyros, are the most scenic and sheltered beaches, with names like "Sunny" and "Magic"; at nearby **Ágios Stéfanos** , twin 6th-century basilicas are the best of several early Christian monuments on the island. The Kéfalos headland beyond saw the earliest habitation of Kós: Asprí Pétra cave, home to Neolithic man, and Classical Astypalia, birthplace of Hippocrates, with its remaining little theatre.

On the western flank of Mount Díkeos, the Byzantines had their island capital at old Pýli, today a jumble of ruins below a castle at the head of a spring-fed canyon. Closer to the 846-metre (2,776-ft) peak cluster the appealing villages collectively known as **Asfendioú**, on the forested north-facing slopes looking to Anatolia. At Ziá, tavernas seem more numerous than permanent inhabitants. Asómati's vernacular houses are slowly being bought up and restored by foreigners.

Kálymnos

First impressions of **Kálymnos**, north of Kós, are of an arid, mountainous landmass, and a decidedly masculine energy to the main port town of **Póthia** ⑲. The now almost-vanished sponge industry has left many reminders: Kálymniot *salónia* crowded with huge sponges and shell-encrusted amphoras, souvenir shops overflowing with smaller sponges, and, more ominously, various crippled old men.

In the old days, divers used to submerge themselves by tying heavy stones to their waists. Holding their breath, they retrieved the rock-bound sponges spied from the surface; they could usually get two or three before they had to resurface. Better divers could reach a depth of 10 fathoms before the "machine" was introduced late in the 19th century. The "machine" is the local term for the first diving apparatus, a rubber suit with a bronze helmet connected to a long

Map, page 254

Brightly coloured embroidered cushions in Kós Town's Old Bazaar.

BELOW: the Plane Tree of Hippocrates and the minaret of the Loggia Mosque.

rubber hose and a hand-powered air pump. The diver was given enough air-hose for his final depth, where he could stay a long time owing to the constant air supply.

Too long, as it soon turned out – compressed air delivered to divers at the new, greater depths bubbled out of solution in their bloodstream as they rose, invariably too rapidly. The results of this nitrogen embolism – informally known as "the bends" – included deafness, incontinence, paralysis and often death. By the 1950s this had been understood and the carnage halted, but it was too late for hundreds of Kalymniot crewmen.

To the northwest loom two castles: Hrysoherías, the Knight's stronghold, and the originally Byzantine fort of Péra Kástro, above the medieval capital of **Horió ❷⓪**, still the island's second town. Most visitors stay at the beach resorts on the gentler west coast between Kandoúni and Massoúri, with **Myrtiés ❷①** the most developed of these, and also the port for the idyllic, car-free islet of **Télendos**. The east coast is harsh and uninhabited except for the green, citrus-planted valley extending inland from the fjord of Vathýs.

Astypálea

Lonely, butterfly-shaped **Astypálea**, stuck out on a subsidised ferry line between the Dodecanese and the Cyclades, would be probably more at home among the latter archipelago. The Knights did not make it this far; a Venetian clan is responsible for the fine castle at the summit of **Astypálea Town (Hóra) ❷②**, the most dazzling Dodecanese hill-village aside from the Hóra on Pátmos. Houses with colourful wooden *poúndia* (balconies with privies) adorn the steep streets and until the 1950s there was also a separate hamlet inside the upper castle. Hóra

BELOW: preparing sponges on Kálymnos.

aside, however, Astypálea is rather bleak, with only a few good beaches to the southwest (Tzanáki, Ágios Konstandínos and Vátses) plus a few more like those at Marmári and Stenó along the island's narrow middle. Most travellers stay at the uninspiring port of Skála, at more congenial **Livádi ㉓** west of Hóra, or at Análipsi (Maltezána) by the airport.

Map, page 254

Léros

Léros, with its half-dozen deeply indented bays, looks like a jigsaw-puzzle piece gone astray. The deepest inlet, Lakkí, sheltered an important Italian naval base from 1935 onward, and from here was launched the submarine that torpedoed the Greek battleship *Elli* in Tínos harbour on 15 August 1940.

Today the main ferry port, **Lakkí ㉔** seems incongruous, an Internationalist-Rationalist-style planned town far too grand for the present token population. Its institutional buildings, long neglected as reminders of colonial subjugation, finally began to be restored in 2001. The local atmosphere is not cheered by the presence of three hospitals for handicapped children and mentally ill adults. Substandard conditions in all of these prompted an uproar when exposed by the international press in 1988, and the institutions are now being wound up.

The rest of Léros is more inviting, particularly **Pandéli** with its waterfront tavernas, just downhill from the capital of **Plátanos ㉕**, draped over a saddle culminating in a well-preserved Knights' castle. South of both, **Vromólithos** has the best, easily accessible car-free beach on an island not known for soft sand. **Ágia Marína**, beyond Plátanos, is the hydrofoil harbour; like Pandéli, it offers good tavernas. **Álynda**, to the north around the same bay, is the oldest established resort and has a long coarse-sand and gravel beach.

Mailboxes are highly visible.

BELOW: windmill on Léros.

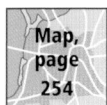

Lipsí and baby islets

Lipsí, the small island just north of Léros, has like Tílos awakened to tourism since the 1980s. It has also awakened to unwanted notoriety as the "Island of Terrorism" since alleged November 17 supremo Alexandros Giotopoulos was arrested here in 2002 prior to conviction on terrorism charges. The island's fertile appearance is deceptive – there is only one spring, and up to four times the current impoverished local community have emigrated (mostly to Tasmania) since the 1950s. All facilities are in the single port town, built around the best natural harbour; smaller bays, with beaches, are at Katsadiá in the south and Platýs Gialós in the northwest.

Beyond Lipsí are other tiny islets, which see few visitors outside of high summer. **Arkí** (pop. 35) clings gamely to life, its scattered houses dependent on solar panels and visits from yachts to the sheltered Port Augusta, with all tourist facilities. Across the way sprawls **Maráthi**, with a long sandy beach and three taverna-rooms. **Agathonísi**, halfway to Sámos, is a metropolis in comparison, with 140 year-round inhabitants scattered in three hamlets. Goats graze the mastic-and-carob-covered hills sloping down to pebble beaches.

Pátmos

Pátmos has been indelibly linked to the Bible's Book of Revelations (Apocalypse) ever since tradition placed its authorship here, in AD 95, by John the Evangelist. The volcanic landscape, with its eerie rock formations and sweeping views, seems suitably apocalyptic. **Skála 26** is the port and largest village, best appreciated late at night when crickets serenade and yacht-masts glimmer against a dark sky. By day Skála sacrifices any charm to stampeding cruise-ship patrons; all island commerce, whether shops, banks or travel agencies, is here. Buses

BELOW:
monks in the
monastery of Agíou
Ioánni Theológou.

leave regularly from the quay for the hilltop **Hóra ㉗**, but a 40-minute walk along a cobbled path – a short-cut avoiding the road – is preferable.

Just over halfway stands the **Monastery of the Apocalypse** (open daily 8am– 1.30pm, Tues, Thur, Sun 4–6pm; free), built on the grotto where John had his Revelation. A silver band on the wall marks the spot where John laid his head to sleep; in the ceiling yawns a great cleft through which the divine voice spoke.

Hóra's core, protected by a huge, pirate-proof fortress and visible from a great distance, is the **Monastery of Agíou Ioánnou Theológou** (same hours), founded in 1088 by the monk Hristodoulos. A photogenic maze of interlinked courtyards, stairways, chapels and passageways, it occupies the site of an ancient temple to Artemis. The Treasury (entrance fee) houses Greece's most impressive monastic collection outside of Mount Áthos: priceless icons and jewellery are on display, although the prize exhibit is the edict of Emperor Alexios Komnenos granting the island to Hristodoulos. The Library, closed to all but ecclesiastical scholars, contains over 4,000 books and manuscripts.

Away from the tourist-beaten track, Hóra is filled with a pregnant silence, its thick-walled mansions with their pebble courtyards and arcades the preserve of wealthy foreigners. From Platía Lótzia on the north side, one of the finest views in the Aegean takes in at least six islands on clear days.

The rest of the island is inevitably anticlimactic, but the beaches are good. The biggest sandy one is **Psilí Ámmos** in the far south, accessible by boat trip or a 20-minute walk from the road's end, and favoured by naturists. Beaches north of Skála include Melóï, with a good taverna; Agriolivádi; Kámbos, popular with Greek families; isolated Livádi Yeranoú, with an islet to swim to; and finally Lámbi, sprinkled with colourful volcanic pebbles, and an excellent taverna. ❑

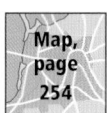

Map, page 254

The Monastery of St John was built as a fortress to protect its treasures from pirates: there are even slits in the walls for pouring boiling oil over attackers.

BELOW: the monastery walls.

THE NORTHEAST AEGEAN

While the cosmopolitan eastern islands of Sámos, Híos and Lésvos once played a leading role on the world's stage, the scattered isles of the northeast are still relatively untouched by tourism

The islands of the northeast Aegean have little in common other than a history of medieval Genoese rule. The northerly group, comprising Thásos, Samothráki and Límnos, has few connections with the south Aegean; indeed Thásos belongs to the Macedonian province of Kavála, and Samothráki to Thracian Évros. These islands, so conveniently close to the mainland, with a short summer season, inevitably attract Greek (and Bulgarian) vacationers far more than tourists from further overseas.

Lésvos, Híos and Sámos to the southeast once played leading roles in antiquity, establishing colonies across the Mediterranean and promoting the arts and sciences, though little tangible evidence of ancient glory remains. All three islands served as bridges between Asia Minor and the rest of the Hellenic world and were, in fact, once joined to the coast of Asia Minor until Ice Age cataclysms isolated them. Turkey is still omnipresent on the horizon, a mere 2 km (1 mile) across the Mykale straits at Sámos. Politically and legally, however, the two countries have often been light years apart, something reflected in the frequent unreliability of the absurdly overpriced short boat trips across.

LEFT: gold-leaf mosaic in Néa Moní monastery, Híos.
BELOW: a helicopter drops water on a forest fire on Thásos.

Thásos

Just seven nautical miles from mainland Macedonia, mountainous and almost circular **Thásos** is essentially a giant lump of marble, mixed with granite and schist, crumbling into white beach sand at the island's margins. Along with numerous illegal ones scarring the landscape, Greece's largest legal marble quarry provides employment; the cut slabs, lying stacked or being trucked about, are a common sight. In antiquity, gold, silver and precious stones were also mined here.

Ferries and hydrofoils for Thásos leave regularly from Kavála; there are also ro-ro services for drivers from Keramotí further east. Bus services around the coastal ring road are adequate, though most visitors hire motorbikes – Thásos is small enough for a long-day tour – or cars. The east and south coasts have the better beaches; the west coast has access to most inland villages. Honey, preserved walnuts and *tsípouro*, the northern Greek firewater, are favourite souvenirs.

Thásos's past glory as a wealthy mining island and regional seafaring power is most evident at the harbour capital of **Liménas** (or **Thásos Town**) ❶, where substantial remnants of the ancient town have been excavated by the French School; choice bits of the ancient acropolis overhead are nocturnally illuminated. The biggest area, behind the picturesque fishing harbour, is the agora; the nearby **Archeological Museum** (open Tues–Sun 9am–3pm; entrance fee) displays a 4-metre (13-ft) *kouros* carrying a ram.

Beginning at the **Temple of Dionysos**, a path permits a rewarding walking tour of the ancient **acropolis**. First stop is the Hellenistic **theatre** (only open for summer festival performances); continue to the medieval **fortress**, built by a succession of occupiers from the masonry of an Apollo temple. Tracing the course of massive 5th-century BC walls brings you next to the foundations of an **Athena temple**, beyond which a rock outcrop bears a shrine of Pan, visible in badly-eroded relief. From here a vertiginous "secret" stairway plunges to the **Gate of Parmenon** – the only ancient entry still intact – at the southern extreme of town.

The first village south from Liménas, slate-roofed **Panagía ❷** is a busy place whose life revolves around the plane-tree-filled square with its four-spouted fountain. **Potamiá ❸**, further down the valley, is less architecturally distinguished. Visitors come mainly for the **Polygnotos Vagis Museum** (open Tues–Sat 9.30am–12.30pm, summer also 6–9pm, Sun 10am–1pm; entrance fee), featuring the work of this locally born sculptor. Beyond, the road plunges to the coast at

Due to frequent forest fires during the 1980s and early 1990s, Thásos is now three-quarters denuded of its original pine forest, which survives only in the northeast.

'otamiá Bay. **Skála Potamiás**, at its south end, is purely lodging and tavernas, with more of that just north at Hryssí Ammoudiá; in between stretches a fine, blonde-sand beach. There are even better strands at **Kínyra**, 24 km (15 miles) from Liménas, but most one-day tourists schedule a lunch stop at the several beachfront tavernas in the hamlet of **Alykí ❹**, architecturally preserved thanks to adjacent ruins: an ancient temple and two atmospheric Byzantine basilicas.

Rounding the southern tip of Thásos, you pass three beach resorts at Astrída, Potós and Pefkári. Only **Astrída** remains attractive, Potós in particular being an overbuilt package dormitory. At **Limenária ❺**, now the island's second town, mansions of the departed German mining executives survive. More intriguingly perhaps, it's the starting point for a safari up to hilltop Kástro, the most naturally pirate-proof of the inland villages. Beyond Limenária, there's little to compel a stop on the coast.

Theológos ❻, actually reached from Potós, was the island's Ottoman capital, a linear place where most houses have walled gardens. **Mariés** sits piled up at the top of a wooded valley, just glimpsing the sea. By contrast **Sotíros** enjoys phenomenal sunsets, best enjoyed from its central taverna shaded by enormous plane trees. Of all the inland settlements, **Megálo Kazazvíti ❼** (officially Megálo Prínos) has the grandest *platía* and the most numerous traditional houses, snapped up and restored in variable taste by outsiders.

Samothráki (Samothrace)

Samothráki raises forbidding granite heights above stony shores and storm-lashed waters, both offering poor natural anchorage. Homer had Poseidon perched on top of 1,611-metre (5,285-ft) **Mount Fengári**, the Aegean's highest summit,

Map, page 268

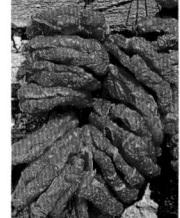

Tomatoes drying in the sun – growing them is a cottage industry here.

BELOW: a stunning bay on Thásos.

to watch the action of the Trojan War to the east. Over time, the forest cover ha receded from the now-barren peak, where modern climbers – on rare occasion – still have the same view, extending from northwestern Turkey to Mount Áthos

Fengári (Mount Moon) and its foothills occupy much of the island, with littl level terrain except in the far west. Tourism is barely developed, and the remain ing islanders prefer it that way; in its absence the permanent population has dippe below 3,000, as farming can support only so many. Certainly an overpriced car ferry from Alexandroúpoli on the Thracian mainland does not help matters. Boat and occasional hydrofoils dock at **Kamariótissa**, the functional port where hir vehicles are in short supply, and although most roads are now paved, only the wes of the island has a rudimentary bus service. **Samothráki (Hóra) ❽**, 5 km (3 miles) east, is more rewarding, nestled almost invisibly in a circular hollow. cobbled commercial street serpentines past sturdy, basalt-built houses. From out door tables at the two tavernas on Hóra's large *platía*, you glimpse the sea beyon a crumbled Byzantine-Genoese fort at the edge of town.

Samothráki's other great sight is the **Sanctuary of the Great Gods**, tucke into a ravine some 6 km (4 miles) from Kamariótissa along the north-coas road. From the late Bronze Age until the coming of Christianity, this was th major religious centre of the Aegean. Local deities of the original Thracian set tlers were easily syncretised with the Olympian gods of the later Aeolia colonists, in particular the *Kabiri*, or divine twins Castor and Pollux, patrons c seafarers – who needed all the help they could get in the rough seas hereabouts

The sanctuary ruins (open daily 8am–7.30pm; until 3pm in winter; entranc fee) visible today are mostly late Hellenistic, and still eerily impressive if ove grown. Obvious monuments include a partly re-erected temple of the second in

A May Day wreath hangs on a door in Samothráki.

BELOW: looking back from the ferry leaving Thásos.

tiation; the odd, round **Arsinoeion**, used for sacrifices; a round theatral area for performances during the summer festival; and the fountain niche where the celebrated Winged Victory of Samothrace (now in the Louvre) was discovered.

Some 6 km (4 miles) further east, hot springs, cool cascades and a dense canopy of plane trees make the spa hamlet of **Thermá** ❾ the most popular base on the island, patronised by an unlikely mix of the elderly infirm and young bohemian types from several nations. Hot baths come in three temperatures and styles – including outdoor pools under a wooden shelter – while cold-plunge fanatics make for **Krýa Váthra** canyon to the east. Thermá is also the base camp for the climb of Mount Fengári, a six-hour round trip.

Villages south of Hóra see few visitors, though they lie astride the route to **Pahiá Ámmos**, the island's only sandy beach. From **Lákoma** village ❿, it's about 8 km (5 miles) by unpaved road to the beach, where a single seasonal taverna operates. Beyond Pahiá Ámmos, you can walk to smaller **Vátos** nudist beach, but you'll need a boat – or to drive clockwise completely around Samothráki – to reach the gravel beach of **Kípi** in the far southeast.

Límnos

Nowhere in the Aegean does legend match landscape so closely as here. In mythology, Zeus cast hapless Hephaestos from Mount Olympos (Ólymbos) onto Límnos with such force that the fall lamed him permanently. The islanders rescued the god, revering him as a fire deity and patron of metallurgy, an understandable allegiance given the overtly volcanic terrain of Límnos. Hephaestos re-established his forge here; now-solidified lava crags in the west oozed forth as late as the Classical period, reassuring Limnians that Hephaestos was at work.

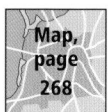

Map, page 268

The 4th-century BC statue of Victory (Athena Nike) was discovered on Samothráki in 1863 by a French diplomat, Charles Champoiseau, who immediately sent it to Paris. The Greek government has long demanded its return, but so far has had to settle for a plaster copy.

BELOW: goat herding on Thásos.

Garden urn in Plomári, Lésvos's second town.

BELOW: the poet Sappho looks over the waterfront in Mytilíni.

Dominating the sea approaches to the Dardanelles, Límnos has been occupied since Neolithic times, and has always prospered as a trading station and military outpost, rather than a major political power. The Greek military still controls much of the island's extent, including half of the huge airport, belying an otherwise peaceful atmosphere. The volcanic soil crumbles to form excellent sandy beaches, or produces excellent wine and a variety of other farm products; the surrounding seas yield plenty of fish, thanks to periodic migrations through the Dardanelles.

Most things of interest are found in the port-capital, **Mýrina** ⓫, or a short distance to either side – luckily, since the bus service is appalling. Volcanic stone has been put to good use in the older houses and street cobbles of Mýrina, while elaborate Ottoman mansions face the northerly town beach of Romeïkós Gialós with its cafés; the southerly beach of Toúrkikos Gialós abuts the fishing port with its seafood tavernas. Public evidence of the Ottoman period is limited to an inscribed fountain and a dilapidated octagonal structure – probably a dervish *tekke* (lodge) – behind a supermarket, both near the harbour end of the long market street. Festooned engagingly over the headland above town, the ruined **kástro** (always open) is worth the climb for sunset views. Mýrina's admirably presented **Archeological Museum** (open Tues–Sun 8.30am–3pm; entrance fee) holds finds from the island's major archeological sites: Kabeirio (Kavírio), Hephaestia (Ifestía) and Polyochni (Polyóhni). These are all a long trip away in the far east of Límnos, and of essentially specialist interest.

Sadder relics of more recent history flank the drab port town of **Moúdros** ⓬ – two Allied cemeteries maintained by the Commonwealth War Graves Commission. During World War I, Moúdros was the principal base for the disastrous Gallipoli campaign; of about 36,000 casualties, 887 are interred outside of Moúdros on the way to Roussopoúli, while 348 more lie behind the village church at **Portianoú** ⓭, across the bay.

The road north from Mýrina passes the Italian-dominated Aktí Mýrina resort en route to good beaches at **Avlónas** and **Ágios Ioánnis**. In the opposite direction lie even better ones at **Platý** and **Thános**, with tiered namesake villages on the hillsides just above; continuing southeast from Thános brings you to **Nevgátis**, justifiably acclaimed as the island's best beach.

Ágios Efstrátios (Aï Strátis)

A tiny wedge of land south of Límnos, **Ágios Efstrátios** (Aï Strátis) is doubtless the most desolate spot in the northeast Aegean – all the more so since a 1968 earthquake devastated the single village. Thanks to junta-era corruption, reparable dwellings were bulldozed and the surviving inhabitants (22 were killed) provided with ugly, pre-fab replacement housing laid out on a grid plan. This, plus two dozen surviving older buildings, is all you see as you disembark the regular ferries stopping here on the Lávrio–Límnos–Kavála route, or (in summer) the small Límnos-based ferry. Despite all this, the island has grown in popularity as a summer retreat, and you may just have company at the several beaches; the remotest are a tough 90 minutes' walk north or south of "town".

.ésvos (Mytilíni)

Maps, pages 268, 274

Greece's third-largest island, measuring 70 by 40 km (44 by 24 miles) at its extremities, distant, fertile **Lésvos** is the antithesis of the *nisáki*, or quaint little islet. Between its far-flung villages lie 11 million olive trees producing 45,000 liquid tonnes of oil a year. Shipbuilding, carpentry, *oúzo*-distilling and pottery remain important, but none rivals the olive, especially since it complements the second industry, tourism. Nets to catch the "black gold" are spread in autumn, after the last charter flight has left.

Early inhabitants were related to the Trojans; in *The Iliad* the Achaeans punished Lesbos for siding with Troy. Natives were later supplemented by Aeolian colonists, who – in a convoluted topography created by two penetrating gulfs – founded six city-states, the most important being Eressos, Mithymna, Antissa and Mytilene. Although they vied for political supremacy, Lesbos developed a uniform culture, nurturing such bards as Terpander and Arion well before Alkeos and Sappho in the 6th century pushed lyric poetry to new heights, while their contemporary Pittakos (no friend of aristocrats like Alkeos or Sappho) initiated democratic reforms.

With its thick southern forests and idyllic orchards, Lésvos was a preferred Roman holiday spot; the Byzantines considered it a humane exile for deposed nobility, while the Genoese Gattilusi clan kept a thriving court here for a century. To the Ottomans it was "The Garden of the Aegean", their most productive, strictly governed and heavily colonised Aegean island. Following 18th-century reforms within the empire, a Christian land-owning aristocracy developed, served by a large population of labouring peasants. This quasi-feudal system made Lésvos fertile ground for post-1912 Leftist movements, and its

The ancient city-state of Eressos in western Lésvos is thought to be the birthplace of the poetess Sappho; it has subsequently become something of a place of pilgrimage for gay women from all over the world.

BELOW: the harbour at Mytilíni.

AEGEAN SEA

Kavála

Límnos
Mólyvos (Mithymna) **5**
Sykaminiá **4**
Pétra **6**
Kápi
Mandamádos **3**
Antissa
Skalohóri
Stypsi
M. Perivolís
M. Límonos
Ag. Parasketi
M. Ypsiloú **7**
Sigrí
Ántissa
Vatoúsa
Kalloní
Paleokastro
Eressós
Parakilá
Ágra
Kólpos Kallonís
Eressós
Skála Eressoú **8**
Vasiliká
Skála
Polyhnítos
Ambelikó
Ólympos 968
Vaterá **10**
Skópelos
Plomári **9**

Lésvos

Alibey Adesi
Armutova
Ayvalik
Karayit
Kozak
Trarium
TURKEY
Seytan Sofrasi
Mystegna
Thermi
Pýrgí Thermís
Thermi
Altinova
Melene
Melene
Pamfyllá
Mytilíni **1**
Variá **2**
Dikili
Loútra
Peráma
Ákra Agríla
Bademlı
Çandarlı
Agiásos **11**

Atanneus

Gryneion
Çandarlı Körfezi
Aliaga
Yenifoça
Tatilköyü
Foça
Buruncu
Gediz
Menemen
Seyrek
Tuzçullu
Çamalti
Uzun Ada
İzmi

Psará
Psará

Agiásmata
Ágion Gála
Melaniós
Kambiá
Ákra Vanvákas
Mármaron
Fytá
Kardámyla
Voliss̄ós **15**
Pityoús
Langáda
Sidiroúnda
Anavatos **17** 796
Avgónyma
Néa **18**
Híos
Moní **16**
Híos (Hóra) **12**
Ág. Geórghios
Sikoúsis
Kámbos
Çeşme
Efáta
Véssa
Kalimasiá
Mestá
Kalamotí
Ákra Mestón **14**
Pyrgí
Nénita
Emborios **13**
Kómi

Inoússes
Haseki
Salman
Karaburun
Küçükbahçe
Kaynarpınar Isk
Ak Dağ 1212
848
Bölmeç Dağı 505
Kara Adasi
Vrontádos
Köste
Ildır
Çeşme
Sifne
Barbaros
Çiftlikköy
Uzunköyü
Tursite
Zeytineli
Balıklıova
Çesmealtı
Urla
Camli
Bademler
Düzce
Menderes
Kale
Siğacik
Teos
Seferihisar
Efençukuru
Doğanbey
Kusadasi Körfezi

Sámos
Karlóvassi **26**
Vourliótes
Kosmadéi
Petaloúda **25**
Kókkári **24**
Vathý (Sámc **23**
Pandrosón
1150
Samos
Psilí
Pythagório **22**
Moní **28**
Hóra **27**
Marathókambos
Votsalákia
Megális Panagías
Pagóndas
Íreon

Ikaría
Perdíki
Ploumári
Armenistís
Évdilos **20**
Thermá
Nás **21**
Ag. Kírykos
Hristós
19
Amalón
Plagiá
Thýmena
Foúrni
Karkinágri
Ág. Mínas

Cycládes
Piréas
Pátmos

Lésvos, Híos, Ikaría and Sámos

0   10 km
0   10 miles

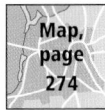

Map, page 274

abit of returning Communist MPs since the junta fell has earned it the epithet of "Red Island" among fellow Greeks.

The years after 1912 also saw a vital local intelligentsia emerge, among them novelists Stratis Myribilis and Argyris Eftaliotis, but since World War II Lésvos's socioeconomic fabric has shrunk considerably with emigration to Athens, Australia and America. However, the founding here in 1987 of the University of the Aegean brought hope for a cultural revival.

Mytilíni ❶, the capital (its name is a popular alias for the entire island), has a revved-up, slightly gritty atmosphere, as befits a port town of 30,000 – interesting to stroll around, though few outsiders stay. Behind the waterfront, assorted church domes and spires enliven the skyline, while **Odós Ermoú**, one street inland, threads the entire bazaar, from the fish market to the now-disused north harbour of Epáno Skála, passing a mosque (ruined) and Turkish baths (well restored) en route. Behind the ferry dock stands the **Archeological Museum** (open Tues–Sun 8.30am–3pm; entrance fee), spread over two premises; the new, uphill annexe features superb mosaics rescued from local Roman villas.

Also noteworthy are a pair of museums in **Variá ❷**, 5 km (3 miles) south of town. The **Theophilos Museum** (open daily 10am–4pm; entrance fee) contains over 60 paintings by locally born Theophilos Hazimihaïl, Greece's most celebrated naive painter. The nearby **Theriade Museum** (open Tues–Sun 9am–2pm, 5–8pm; entrance fee) was founded by another native son who, while an avant-garde art publisher in Paris, assembled this collection, with work by Chagall, Picasso, Rouault, Giacometti, Matisse and Léger.

The road running northwest from Mytilíni follows the coast facing Turkey. **Mandamádos ❸**, 37 km (23 miles) from Mytilíni, has on its outskirts the

Mytilíni's castle, one of the largest in the eastern Mediterranean, has been used and rebuilt by the Romans, Byzantines, Venetians and Ottomans.

BELOW: the Roman aqueduct that supplied Mytilíni.

A painting in the Theophilos Museum, Variá. A wandering tramp, Theophilos painted murals to earn a crust. After he died in 1934, his naive paintings became internationally known.

BELOW: the fishing harbour at Mólyvos.

enormous **Taxiárhis Monastery** with its much-revered black icon. At Kápi the road divides; the northerly fork is wider, better paved and more scenic as it curls across the flanks of Mount Lepétymnos, passing by the handsome village of **Sykaminiá** ❹ and its photogenic, taverna-studded fishing port. You descend to sea level at **Mólyvos** ❺, linchpin of Lésvos tourism and understandably so: the ranks of sturdy tiled houses climbing to the medieval castle are an appealing sight, as is the stone-paved fishing harbour. Its days as a bohemian artists' and alternative activities colony are over, however, with package tourism dominant since the late 1980s. **Pétra** ❻, 5 km (3 miles) south, accommodates the overflow on its long beach, while inland at the village centre looms a rock plug crowned with the Panagía Glykofiloússa church. At its foot the 18th-century **Vareltzídena Mansion** (open Tues–Sun 8am–2.30pm; free) is worth a look, as is the 16th-century frescoed church of **Ágios Nikólaos**.

From Pétra, head 17 km (10 miles) south to the turning for **Límonos Monastery**, home to an ecclesiastical museum, before continuing west towards the more rugged half of the island, with its lunar volcanic terrain. Stream valleys foster little oases such as the one around **Perivolís Monastery**, 30 km (19 miles) from Limónos (open daily 10am–1pm, 5–6pm; donation welcome), decorated with wonderful frescoes. Some 10 km (6 miles) beyond, atop an extinct volcano, the **Monastery of Ypsiloú** contemplates the abomination of desolation – complete with scattered trunks of the "Petrified Forest", prehistoric sequoias mineralised by volcanic ash.

Sígri ❼ (90 km/56 miles from Mytilíni), a sleepy place flanked by good beaches, is very much the end of the line, guarded by a Turkish-built fort. Most prefer **Skála Eressoú** ❽, 14 km (9 miles) south of Ypsiloú, for its beach; in particular numerous lesbians come to honour Sappho, who was born here.

Southern Lésvos, between the two gulfs, is home to olive groves rolling up to 968-metre (3,175-ft) Mount Ólympos. **Plomári ⑨** on the coast is Lésvos's second town, famous for its *oúzo* industry; most tourists stay at pebble-beach **Ágios Isídoros** 3 km (2 miles) east, though **Melínda** 6 km (4 miles) west is more scenic. **Vaterá ⑩**, whose 7-km (4-mile) sand beach is reckoned the best on the island, lies still further west; en route, you can stop for a soak at restored medieval spas outside Lisvóri and Polyhnítos, 45 km (28 miles) from Mytilíni.

Inland from Plomári, the remarkable hill village of **Agiásos ⑪** nestles in a wooded valley under Ólympos. Its heart is the major pilgrimage church of Panagía Vrefokratoússa, which comes alive for the 15 August festival, Lésvos's biggest.

Map, page 274

Psará

Scarcely 350 inhabitants remain on melancholy **Psará**, its bleakness relieved only by occasional fig trees and the odd cultivated field. Besides the lone port village, there's just one deserted monastery in the far north. Six beaches lie northeast of the port, each better than the preceding, though all catch tide-wrack on this exposed coast. A few tourists trickle over from Híos, on regular local ferries from Híos Town; big ferries call weekly from Lávrio or Kavála.

Híos (Chíos)

Although the island had been important and prosperous since antiquity, the Middle Ages made the **Híos** of today. The Genoese seized control here in 1346; the Giustiniani clan established a cartel, the *maona*, which controlled the highly profitable trade in gum mastic. During their rule, which also saw the introduction

BELOW: harvesting resin from the mastic trees, Híos.

A STICKY BUSINESS

The mastic bushes of southern Híos are the unique source of gum mastic, the basis for many products before petroleum was refined. It was popular in Constantinople as chewing-gum, and allegedly freshened the breath of the sultan's concubines. The Romans made mastic toothpicks to keep their teeth white and prevent cavities; Hippocrates praised its therapeutic value for coughs and colds; and lately practitioners of alternative medicine make even more ambitious claims on its behalf.

In the 14th and 15th centuries, the Genoese set up a monopoly in the substance. At its peak, the trade generated enough wealth to support a score of *mastihohoriá* (mastic villages). However, the coming of the Industrial Revolution and the demise of the Ottoman Empire was the end of large-scale mastic production.

Today, smaller amounts are generated in a process which has not really changed since ancient times. In late summer, incisions made in the bark weep resin "tears", which are scraped off and cleaned. Finally, the raw gum is sent to a central processing-plant where it is washed, baked and formed into "chiclets" of gum. Some 150 tons are produced annually, most of it exported to France, Bulgaria and Saudi Arabia for prices of up to $35 a kilo.

Tomatoes are strung out for drying in September.

of mandarin fruit, Híos became one of the wealthiest and most cultured islands in the Mediterranean. Local prowess in navigation was exploited by 150 ships calling here annually and Christopher Columbus apocryphally came to study with Hiot captains prior to his voyages.

In 1566 the Ottomans expelled the Genoese, but granted the islanders numerous privileges, so that Híos continued to flourish until March 1822, when poorly armed agitators from Sámos convinced the reluctant Hiots to participate in the independence uprising. Sultan Mahmut II, enraged at this ingratitude, exacted a terrible revenge: a two-month rampage commanded by Admiral Kara Ali killed 30,000 islanders, enslaved 45,000 more, and saw all settlements except the mastic-producing villages razed. Híos had only partly recovered when a strong earthquake in March 1881 destroyed much of what remained and killed 4,000. Today Híos and its satellite islet Inoússes are home to some of Greece's wealthiest shipping families.

Its catastrophic 19th-century history ensures that **Híos Town** or **Hóra ⑫** (pop 25,000) seems at first off-puttingly modern. Scratch the ferroconcrete surface however, and you'll find traces of the Genoese and Ottoman years. The most obvious medieval feature is the **Kástro**. Moated on the landward side, it lacks a seaward rampart, destroyed after the 1881 quake. Just inside the imposing Porta Maggiora stands the **Giustiniani Museum** (open Tues–Sun 8.30am–2pm; entrance fee), a good collection of religious art rescued from rural churches. Off a small nearby square is a Muslim cemetery with the tomb of Kara Ali – he of the massacres, blown up along with his flagship by one of Admiral Kanarís's fireboats in June 1822. Further in lies the old Muslim and Jewish quarter with its derelict mosque and overhanging houses; Christians had to settle outside the walls.

BELOW: a typical example of *xystá* decorations on a house in Mestá.

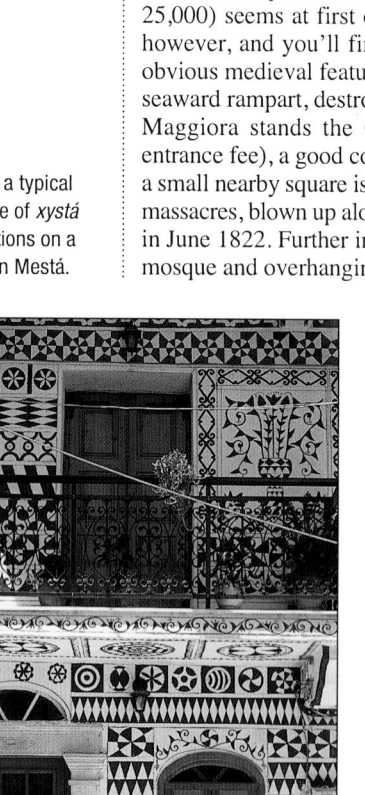

South of Hóra you pass through **Kámbos**, a broad plain of high-walled citrus groves dotted with the imposing sandstone mansions of the medieval aristocracy, standing along narrow, unmarked lanes. Many were destroyed by the earthquake, while a few have been restored as accommodation or restaurants. Irrigation water was originally drawn up by *manganós* or waterwheel; a few survive in ornately paved courtyards.

The onward road heads southwest towards southern Híos, with its 20 **mastihohoriá**, built as pirate-proof strongholds by the Genoese during the 14th and 15th centuries. Laid out on a dense, rectangular plan, their narrow passages are overarched by earthquake buttresses, with the backs of the outer houses doubling as the perimeter wall.

Pyrgí ⑬, 21 km (13 miles) from Hóra, is one of the best-preserved *mastihohoriá*, most of its façades adorned with black-and-white geometric patterns called *xystá*. A passageway off the central square leads to the Byzantine Ágii Apóstoli church, decorated with later frescoes. In the back alleys, tomatoes are laboriously strung for drying in September by teams of local women.

Some 11 km (7 miles) west, **Mestá ⑭** seems a more sombre, monochrome labyrinth, which retains defensive towers at its corners – several three-storeyed houses have been restored as accommodation. Such quarters are typically claustrophobic, so guests will appreciate the nearby beach resorts of **Kómi** (sand) and **Emboriós** (volcanic pebbles).

With your own car, the beautiful, deserted west coast with its many coves is accessible via attractive **Véssa**, the paved road eventually taking you to castle-crowned **Volissós** ⓯ in the far northwest. Around this half-empty village are the island's finest beaches – and scars from a series of 1980s (and more recent) fires which burnt two-thirds of Híos's forests. Between Kastélla and Elínda bays, a good road snakes east uphill to **Avgónyma** ⓰, a clustered village well restored by returned Greek-Americans. Just 4 km (2½ miles) north perches almost-deserted, crumbling **Anávatos** ⓱, well camouflaged against its cliff; from this in 1822, 400 Hiots leapt to their deaths rather than be captured.

Some 5 km (3 miles) east, the monastery of **Néa Moní** ⓲ (open daily 8am–1pm, 4–8pm) forms one of the finest surviving examples of mid-Byzantine architecture, founded in 1049 by Emperor Constantine Monomachus IX on a spot where a miraculous icon of the Virgin had appeared. It suffered heavily in 1822 and 1881, first with the murder of its monks and the pillage of its treasures, and then with the collapse of its dome. Despite the damage, its mosaics of scenes from the life of Christ are outstanding, though not viewable until 2011 owing to repair works.

Ikaría and Foúrni

The narrow, wing-shaped island of **Ikaría** is named after mythical Icarus, who supposedly fell into the sea nearby when his wax wings melted (the Greek Air Force has adopted him as patron, apparently impervious to the irony). One of the least developed large islands in the Aegean, Ikaría has little to offer anyone intent on ticking off four-star sights, but appeals to those disposed to a decidedly eccentric environment. For three brief months after 17 July 1912, when a certain

Map, page 274

Detail from the Byzantine monastery of Néa Moní, Híos.

BELOW:
local fishermen.

Composer and former communist Mikis Theodorakis, best known for his 1964 film score for Zorba the Greek, was held in a concentration camp on Ikaría during the Greek civil war.

Dr Malahias declared the island liberated, it was an independent republic, with its own money and stamps. In later decades, Ikaría served as a place of exile for hundreds of communists; the locals thought they were the most noble, humanitarian folk they'd ever met and still vote Communist in droves – not quite what Athens intended.

Ágios Kírykos ⓳ is the capital and main southerly port, its tourist facilities geared to the clientele at the neighbouring spa of Thermá. Taxis are more reliable than the bus for the 41-km (25-mile) drive over the 1,000-metre (3,300-ft) Atherás ridge to **Évdilos ⓴**, the north-facing second port. Another 16 km (10 miles) takes you past **Kámbos**, with its sandy beach and ruined Byzantine palace, to the tiny port-resort of **Armenistís ㉑**. Here only do foreigners congregate, for the sake of excellent beaches – Livádi and Mesahtí – just east though the surf can be deadly. **Nás**, 4 km (2½ miles) west, is named for the *naos* or temple of Artemis Tavropolio on the banks of the river draining to a popular pebble cove. **Gialiskári**, a fishing port 4 km (2½ miles) east, is distinguished by its photogenic jetty chapel.

There are few bona fide inland villages, as the proud Ikarians hate to live on top of each other, keeping plenty of room for orchards between their houses. Above Armenistís are four hamlets lost in pine forest, collectively known as **Ráhes**; at Hristós, the largest, people cram the café-bars all night, sleep until noon and carry belongings (or store potent wine) in hairy goatskin bags. The surrounding countryside completes the hobbit-like image, with vertical natural monoliths and troglodytic cottages for livestock made entirely of gigantic granite slabs.

Foúrni, one of several islets southeast of Ikaría, lives from its thriving fishing fleet and boatyards; seafood dinners figure high in the ambitions of arriving

BELOW: the castle and harbour of Pythagório, Sámos.

tourists, who mostly stay in the surprisingly large port town. A road links this with Ágios Ioánnis Hrysóstomos in the south and remote Hrysomiliá in the far north, the only other villages, but path-walking (where possible) and boat-riding are more relaxing ways of getting around. Best of many beaches are at **Kámbi**, one ridge south of port, or at naturist **Áspa**, a tough trail walk beyond.

Map, page 274

Sámos

Almost subtropical **Sámos**, with vine terraces, cypress and olive groves, surviving stands of black and Calabrian pine, hillside villages and beaches of every size and consistency, appeals to numerous package tourists. Forest fires – the worst of these in July 2000 – and development have blighted much of the island, but impassable gorges, the Aegean's second-highest mountain and beaches accessible only on foot hold sway in the far west.

From the immense harbour mole at heavily commercialised **Pythagório ㉒**, constructed by Classical slaves and scarcely changed, you can watch majestic Mount Mykale in Turkey change colour at dusk. The port's shape suggested a frying-pan, hence Tigáni, the town's former name – perhaps too prophetic of what it's become: a casserole of lobster-red Scandinavians fried in suntan-oil. The authorities changed the name in 1955 in honour of native son Pythagoras.

The 1,040-metre (3,410-ft) **Evpalínio Órygma** (Eupalinos's Tunnel; open Tues–Sun 8.30am–2.30pm; entrance fee), an aqueduct built during the rule of the brilliant but unscrupulous tyrant Polykrates (538–522 BC), cuts through the hillside northwest of town. It is one of the technological marvels of the ancient world: surveying was so good that two work crews beginning from each end met with no vertical error, and a horizontal one of less than 1 percent. You can visit

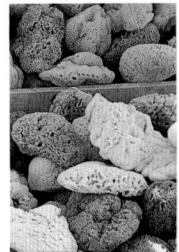

Sponges on sale, Pythagório harbour.

BELOW: the frescoes at Megális Panagías.

The Archeological Museum in Vathý has a rich trove of finds from the ancient Sanctuary of Hera.

much of it, along the catwalk used to remove spoil from the water channel far below. One re-erected column and sundry foundations – the ruins of what was once a vast **Sanctuary of Hera** – lie 8 km (5 miles) to the west of Pythagório, past coastal Roman baths and the airport (open summer daily 8am–7.30pm; winter Tues–Sun 8.30am–3pm; entrance fee).

Vathý or **Sámos Town ㉓**, built along an inlet on the north coast, is the main port, founded in 1832. Tourism is less pervasive here; the main attraction is the excellent, two-wing **Archeological Museum** (open Tues–Sun 8.30am–2.30pm; entrance fee), with a rich trove of finds from the Sanctuary of Hera. Star exhibit is a 5-metre (16-ft) high, nearly intact *kouros* (male votive statue), the largest ever found. The small-objects collection confirms the temple's Middle Eastern slant of worship and clientele: orientalised ivories and locally cast griffin's heads.

Áno Vathý, the large village clinging to the hillside 1.5 km (1 mile) southeast, existed for almost two centuries before the harbour settlement; a stroll will take you through steep cobbled streets separating 200-year-old houses, their over-hanging second stories and plaster-lath construction akin to those of northern Greece and Anatolia, though many are senselessly destroyed annually.

First stop of note on the north-coast road (12 km/7 miles) is **Kokkári ㉔**, a for-mer fishing village now devoted to tourism. The original centre is cradled between twin headlands, while windsurfers launch themselves from the long, westerly pebble beach. Overhead loom the scorched crags of Mount Ámbelos (1,150 metres/3,800 ft), while just past Avlákia a road climbs to the attractive and thriving little village of **Vourliótes ㉕**, named after its first inhabitants (who came from Vourla in Asia Minor), and justly famous for its wine production.

The coastal highway continues west, sometimes as a sea-level corniche route, to

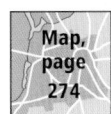

Map,
page
274

Karlóvassi ㉖, 29 km (18 miles) from Vathý. It's a sprawling, somewhat dishevelled place, little touristed and lumped into five neighbourhoods. Néo, the biggest, houses post-1923 refugees and has cavernous, derelict warehouses down by the water in Ríva district, vestiges of a leather-tanning trade which thrived here before 1970. Meséo is more villagey, as is Paleó, lining a green valley behind the sentinel church of Ágia Triáda. Limín, below Áno, has most local tourist facilities, including the ferry port. The shore west of here has some of Sámos's best beaches, including sand-and-pebble **Potámi**, visited by most of Karlóvassi at weekends. Beyond here, you must walk to a pair of remote, scenic beaches at **Seïtáni**.

Karlóvassi lies roughly halfway around an anticlockwise loop of the island; head south, then east through an interior dotted with small villages of tiled, shuttered houses and stripey-domed churches. At **Ágii Theodóri** junction, choose southwest or east.

Going southwest takes you past Marathókambos and its sleepy, atmospheric port, Órmos, to **Votsalákia** ㉗, Sámos's fastest-growing beach resort. Less busy beaches like Psilí Ámmos and Limniónas can be found further west along the road curling around the base of Mount Kérkis (1,437 metres/4,725 ft), which forms the west end of the island. The mountain is usually climbed from the **Evangelístria convent** on the south or Kosmadéï on the north – either way it is a full day's outing. Returning to Pythagório, schedule stops at the roadside stalls before **Pýrgos** for a jar of local honey, and just below Mavratzéï, at the monastery of **Megális Panagías** ㉘, with smudged frescoes dating from after 1586 (there are older, better ones at **Petaloúda** church, near Karlovássi). The vast *platía* of **Pagóndas** village nearby hosts the island's liveliest *panigýri*, on the Sunday night of *Agíou Pnévmatos* (Pentecost). ❑

BELOW: church of Marathókambos.

THE SPORÁDES AND ÉVIA

The four "scattered islands" (Sporádes) are all different –
Skiáthos lively and busy, Skópelos quieter and beautiful, Alónisos
the least developed, and Skýros with its own unique culture

Map
on page
286

The scythe of **Koukounariés ❶** on **Skiáthos** is used as evidence on thousands of postcards that the Aegean can produce the kind of beach normally associated with the Caribbean. Propriety would prevent as many postcards from featuring **Mikrós Krasás** (colloquially "Little Banana Beach") because it caters for gay nudists. The fact that no one cares whether bathers at Banana Beach strip off or not is typical of the easy-going nature of the people of Skiáthos as a whole. The island has beaches for all occasions: some among the supposed 60 will always be sheltered wherever the wind is coming from.

Koukounariés and Banana Big (straight) and Little are near-neighbours at the end of the twisting, busy 18-km (11-mile) road that runs along the south coast of Skiáthos. There are dozens of beaches along it, many with a taverna or at least a kiosk selling drinks and sandwiches, and many even with luxury hotels – Vromólimnos has the best bar scene. North-coast beaches like **Mandráki** and **Eliá** are more pristine. Round-the-island boat trips pass the rocky and otherwise inaccessible northern shoreline where the only human construction is the **Kástro ❷**, the abandoned 16th-century capital once connected to the rest of the island by a single drawbridge. For 300 years the islanders huddled on this wind-buffeted crag, hoping the pirates would pass them by. In World War II, Allied soldiers hid out there, waiting for evacuation. Today it is an obligatory stop for the excursion caïques after they have dipped into technicolour grottoes and dropped anchor at **Lalária**, a cove famous for its smooth, round stones, and before proceeding to a beach taverna (usually at Megálos Aséli-nos) for lunch.

LEFT: Pánormos beach on Skópelos.
BELOW: Óhi Day celebrations, Skópelos.

Skiáthos Town

The bluff above under-used **Xánemos** beach at the end of the very busy airport runway has produced fragments suggesting a prehistoric settlement, but neither it nor the rest of the island have ever been properly excavated. German bombing of an Italian ammunition dump in September 1943 severely damaged much of the pretty prewar town, burned again in August 1944. But **Skiáthos Town ❸** makes up in liveliness what it may lack in architectural merit. In fact, its nightlife is probably the most important consideration after the beaches for the type of visitor that Skiáthos attracts in intimidating numbers during summer.

The preferences of the fast-living set change constantly, but it is not difficult to spot which places are in vogue, whether one's preference is for beer and blues, wine and Vivaldi, or tequila and techno. The lights are brightest but also the tackiest along **Papa-diamántis**, the paved pedestrian street which bisects the two hills on which the town stands, and along the old harbour. The atmosphere is more Greek-oriented at the designer clubs on the water past the yacht marina. Expect restaurants, with international flavours as well as Greek, rather than tavernas, and be prepared to pay accordingly, especially along the seafront.

A scooter or hired car is useful to follow the unpaved roads looping through the mountains. They provide stunning views as well as the chance to pop into monasteries which, with Kástro, are more or less the only buildings of historic interest. Of these, the grandest and closest to town is **Evangelistrías**, with frescoed **Panagías Kehreás** and **Panagías Kounístras** also pilgrimage-worthy if the beaches should pall.

Skópelos

The Church of Christ, a Skópelos landmark.

Skópelos's distinguished past is not so much demonstrated by prominent historical sites as by the exceptionally fine houses in **Skópelos Town ❹**, a handsome amphitheatre around a harbour lined with cafés and tavernas under mulberry trees. The island escaped earthquakes and Nazi vindictiveness and is therefore the most "authentic" and traditional of the three northern Sporádes (Skýros being in a class by itself). Slate roofs, wooden balconies, hand-painted shop signs and flagstone streets give it a serenity and dignity rarely found in Skiáthos in season. On the other hand, beaches are not as sandy or as numerous as on Skiáthos – mostly on the south and west coasts – though nudists are welcomed at **Velanió** just beyond the family beach at **Stáfylos** (where a gold crown and ornate weapons dating from Minoan times were found).

Further along the coast, **Agnóndas** serves as an alternative harbour when Skópelos Town is storm-shut; there are good tavernas but not much of a beach.

Ágios Pétros Palamári
Trahiá Kareflou
Skýros Gyrismata
Atsítsa Melá Mólos
Stereá Ólympos Magaziá
Elláda 403 Skýros
Skyropoúla Ágios Aspoús
Fokás
Pélkos Liniariá Loutró
Valáxa Kalamitsá Kohýlas
772
Kolybáda
Rénnes
Tris Boúkes
Sarakinó

Thessaloníki

AEGEAN SEA

Psathoúra

Gioúra 570

Kyrá Panagiá Prásso Pipéri

293

Alónisos Agios
Dimítrios
Skiáthos Kástro Lalária Thessalía Steni Peristéra
Evangelistrías Vála Kalamákia
Asélinos Kehriás 456 Leftós Gailós
Loutráki Glóssa Kokkinókastro
Krassás Troúllos Skiáthos Paleá Patitíri
Koukounariés Kanapitsá Klíma Alónisos
Kastáni Skópelos Ag. Marpoúnda
Tsougriá Miliá Pródromos Skántzoura
Pánormos Metamórfosis
Limnonári Stáfylos
Cyclades Agnóndas

Sporádes

0   10 km
0   10 miles

Cyclades, Paralía,
Kýmis (summer only)

For more of those, carry on down the island "trunk road" to **Pánormos** ❺, the biggest resort after Hóra and environs, with a long gravel beach and yacht shelter at Bló inlet. Better, pine-backed beaches lie just around the corner at **Miliá** and **Kastáni**. The road passes the quake-damaged village of **Paleó Klíma** – now bought up and renovated by outsiders – before ending in the northwest at **Glóssa** ❻, Skópelos' second village whose architecture (like Paleó Klíma's) betrays the strong Thessalian influence tangible on all the northern Sporades. Far below Glóssa to the south is **Loutráki**, another rather nondescript ferry port; some of the very few north-facing Skópelos beaches lie in the other direction, at **Perivolioú** and **Hondrogiórgis**.

Inland and north from the main road, Skópelos has denser forest than Skiáthos, still mostly unburnt and crisscrossed by a mix of dirt tracks and paved lanes. These pass by a reputed 40 monasteries and hundreds of churches (of these, 123 are scattered around Hóra alone). On the side of the island's summit – Mt Délfi – are three ancient cyst-type tombs: the **Sendoúkia**, with their lids ajar. The 15-minute walk there prominently signposted.

Children on Skópelos at the annual 28 October parade marking Greece's defiance of Italy's invasion in 1940.

Alónisos

On the hill above **Patitíri** ❼, the last port on the Vólos/Ágios Konstandínos-based ferry and hydrofoil routes, is the **Hóra**, the former capital destroyed by an earthquake in 1965. This compounded the blow the islanders had already suffered when all their grapevines withered and died from phylloxera only a decade earlier. Alónisos seems to have been ever thus: the previous capital, Ikos, the name by which the island was known in Classical times, literally disappeared when the ground on which it stood sunk into the sea.

BELOW: Glóssa is Skópelos's second town.

The submerged remains of the capital, off **Kokkinókastro** beach, may be explored with a snorkel but not with scuba tanks (this is a general rule in the Aegean to prevent pilfering and damage). The way the island has adjusted to its unrealised potential and bad luck is something for which many visitors should be grateful. Its people are laid-back and charming, its atmosphere cheerful and unpretentious. It is also the least developed of the Sporádes, a much quieter island surrounded by an interesting collection of islets. Some of them are off-limits to tourists and fishermen alike, protected areas within the 1992-established National Marine Park reserved for the endangered monk seal and other rare fauna. **Gioúra**, for example, is home to a unique breed of wild goat and also has a cave that is full of stalactites and stalagmites. It and **Pipéri** may not be visited but caïques leave Patitíri on calm days for excursions to the closer islets of **Peristéra** and **Kyrá Panagía**, where ancient pot-shards can be seen on the sea bed and the eponymous monastery on the latter island still has one monk. Passenger numbers allowing, trips extend to remote **Psathoúra**, with its huge lighthouse and long sandy beach.

A paved but twisty road links the south and north of the island, including a detour to the little yacht anchorage of **Stení Vála**, with its scuba centre and summer-only information post on the monk seal (the main, all-year information centre is in Patitíri). Otherwise, several high-season caïques at Patitíri take bathers to the beach of their choice – the best east-coast ones are **Leftós Gialós**, with two good tavernas, and **Ágios Dimítrios**, with a naturist zone. Walkers are well catered for with a network of 14 routes, waymarked and maintained with EU funding. One of them leads up pleasantly, in 45 minutes, to the earthquake-shattered Hóra, aka **Paleá Alónisos** ❽ or **Alónisos Town**. Thanks largely to foreigners who, in the 1970s, spied a bargain and bought damaged houses to fix up,

BELOW:
feline fulfilment.

it is now largely reinhabited – though cute and not particularly Greek except for one tiny shop selling local dairy products. Boutiques are everywhere along the former commercial street, while several bars and restaurants serve up stunning views along with the food and drink.

Skýros

Skýros was probably two islands originally, the halves joining near where there is now a road linking **Linariá ⑨**, the main port, with the little village of **Aspoús** on the way to Skýros Town. The southern part of the island is mountainous and largely barren, and visitors are unlikely to venture below **Kolybáda** unless they are heading for **Rénnes** beach or the poet Rupert Brooke's grave in an olive grove at **Trís Boúkes ⑩**. Trís Boúkes is about a 30-minute drive from Kolybáda, and it's another 15 minutes more to the trailhead for Rénnes (final approach by path).

The real appeal of the southern part of the island is from the sea, for cliffs along most of the coast from Rénnes all the way around to **Ahílli Bay** near Aspoús fall straight down into the sea. These cliffs are inhabited by a few wild goats and seemingly innumerable Eleanora's falcons, which can be seen darting around the heights all the way over to Skýros Town. Excursions by boat can be arranged at the port of Linariá, where the island-owned ferry comes in to land.

Skýros Town ⑪ is on the northern half of the island on the east coast, high above the long sand beach that runs between the now contiguous settlements of Magaziá to the south and Mólos at the north end. Life in the town is played out all along the meandering main street, which runs from the main lower square with its nocturnal bars to the elevated plaza at the northern edge of town. Here, the highly romantic statue of Rupert Brooke commands the view over the excel-

Map on page 286

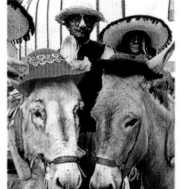

The annual Skýros carnival takes place just before Lent, but in fact has its roots in a pre-Christian pagan festival.

BELOW:
Skýros Town.

A CORNER OF A FOREIGN FIELD...

It was quite by chance that Skýros became the burial place of the poet Rupert Brooke. When war broke out in 1914, Brooke first thought of becoming a war correspondent, but soon changed his mind and decided to join up. He enlisted as a second lieutenant in the newly formed Royal Naval Division, and briefly saw action at the fall of Antwerp. In the spring of 1915, he arrived on the island of Limnos, where ships and men had begun massing in preparation for the ill-fated assault on Gallipoli.

Moúdros Bay became so crowded that Brooke's detachment was ordered to wait instead off the bay of Trís Boúkes, in the far south of Skýros. Between manoeuvres, he and some fellow officers rested on shore in a small olive grove above the bay which, the others remembered, the poet particularly liked. Three days later he died of blood-poisoning on a hospital ship, aged 27; his fellow officers buried him in the olive grove.

Brooke was subsequently beatified in the eyes of a nation mourning its youthful heroes, even though he never lived to see the horrors of trench warfare. Today, the site can be reached by caïque, a long walk from Kolybáda, or by vehicle. There is also a memorial to Brooke in Skýros Town – a highly romanticised bronze statue of "Immortal Poetry".

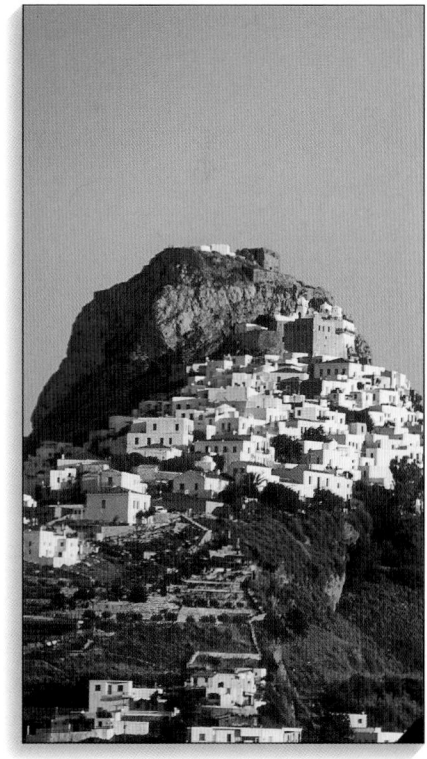

lent, private **Faltaïts Museum** of ethnographic displays (daily 10am–noon and 5.30–8pm or 6–9pm; entrance fee). A series of small side streets wander up to the **kástro** (not open to the public), the old Byzantine/Venetian castle on the heights.

The beach below the Hóra runs from Magaziá over to Mólos, with stretches of better if more exposed beach such as at **Gyrísmata**, **Karefloú** and **Ágios Pétros** further along the north coast. At **Palamári**, an important Bronze Age town (open Mon–Fri 7.30am–2.30pm; free) is being excavated. Beyond Palamári, and the turning to Ágios Pétros, pine forest appears, compensating for the mediocrity of west-coast beaches either side of **Atsítsa** and **Ágios Fokás** (each with tavernas). The paved road loops back all the way to Linariá from Atsítsa.

Évia (Euboea)

Évia, Greece's second-largest island (after Crete) lies just off the coast of mainland Greece, looking on the map like a large jigsaw-puzzle piece just slightly out of position. The island's main town, **Halkída ❶**, is close enough to the mainland for a small drawbridge and a new, far larger suspension bridge to make easy connection. Aristotle is supposed to have been so frustrated in trying to understand the tides here in the narrow Europis channel, which are highly irregular and sometimes quite fast, that he jumped into the waters.

Halkída is a brash industrial town, but the **kástro** with its mosque and church of **Agía Paraskeví** are worth visiting, as is the Archeological Museum in the new town. There is also a synagogue, rebuilt after a fire in 1854 and still used by the very small (60-member) but active Jewish Romaniote community. **Erétria ❷** to the south is a crowded summer resort town where the ferries land from **Skála**

Oropoú on the mainland. As with Halkída, Erétria is a town to pass through, but the small **Archeological Museum** on the west side of town is very good, as are the remains of excavated ancient Eretria.

   In general, the southern part of the island is drier and less green. The coastal road from Erétria is dotted with villages and summer homes until just before **Alivéri** where it turns inland. The turning for the south, notably the prosperous seaside town of **Kárystos ❸**, is at **Lépoura**. From here the main road forges eastwards through the hamlet of **Háni Avlonaríou**, with the large and unusual 14th-century church of **Ágios Dimítrios**, before continuing through often beautiful hilly farmland to drop down on the east coast to **Stómio** where a small river reaches the sea. The wide road then runs along the shore through **Platána** to the harbour at **Paralía Kýmis ❹** and the boat to Skýros. North of Halkída – or east from Kými on a very scenic paved road – the small village of **Stení ❺** on the slopes of **Mount Dírfys** is a favourite goal for Athenians seeking clean air and grill restaurants. **Límni ❻** on the west coast is the most atmospheric and historic port on the island. Just south, in the dense forest of Mt Kandíli, **Galatáki convent** is home to six nuns, one of whom will show you 16th-century frescoes in the narthex.

   Good pebble beaches begin just north of Límni, appearing intermittently en route to **Loutrá Edipsoú**, with its stunningly refurbished spa-hotel. Beyond, the main road curls around Évia's north cape – where the famous bronze of spear-throwing Poseidon was fished from the sea in 1928. The east coast is mountainous, with rocky shoulders dropping sharply down to the sea, but the road does pass a series of beaches: **Ellinikú, Psaropoúli, Paralía Kotsikiás, Angáli**. The first is the smallest and most scenic, the last the most developed.   ❑

Map on page 290

BELOW:
Halkída, Évia.

CORFU

Few places have been as exploited and developed for tourism as Corfu. Yet, away from the package-tour resorts, there is much to savour on this beautiful green island

Maps:
Town 294
Island 296

Strategically poised between the Ionian and Adriatic seas, just off the Greek mainland, Corfu (Kérkyra) has an unsurprisingly turbulent history and a long catalogue of invaders. The Venetians in particular left a rich legacy of olive groves, which still form much of the island's vegetation. Despite a million-plus visitors a year, tourism has not entirely steamrollered the entire island: 10 km (6 miles) from the most brazen fleshpots you can drive along a one-lane potholed road through sleepy villages whose inhabitants stare or wave at you.

Habitation dates back 50,000 years, although Corfu enters history as "Corcyra" in the 8th century BC, when it was colonised by ancient Corinth. By the 5th century BC, Corcyra had become a major, independent naval power, siding with Athens against Sparta (and Corinth) in the Peloponnesian Wars.

Nearly eight centuries of Byzantine tenure from AD 395 brought a measure of stability and prosperity; but latter years saw incursions by "barbarians", the Norman-Angevin Kingdom of the Two Sicilies, the Despotate of Epirus, and the Venetians. Weary of misrule and piracy, in 1386 the Corfiots submitted voluntarily to Venetian rule, in place for 411 years despite four Ottoman sieges. Napoleon dissolved what remained of the Venetian Empire in 1797, and the French held the island until 1814 (except for the brief reign of the Ottoman-Russian-controlled "Septinsular Republic"). The British held sway between 1814 and 1864, when all the Ionian Islands were ceded as a sweetener for George I's ascent of the Greek throne.

During World War I, Corfu was the final destination of a retreating Serbian army, and memorials and cemeteries from that era remain. World War II saw Kérkyra Town suffer extensive damage under a German bombardment to displace the Italian occupiers, who had surrendered to the Allies. During a brief but brutal occupation, the Nazis deported Corfu's significant Jewish community.

A historic capital

Corfu Town, also known as **Kérkyra ❶**, occupies a central east-coast location. "Corfu" is a corruption of *koryfí*, "peak", of which there are two on a Byzantine-fortified outcrop transformed into the **Paleó Froúrio ❹** (**Old Fort**; open daily 8am–7.30pm, until 3pm winter; entrance fee) by the Venetians during the 15th and 16th centuries, when they cut a canal to make the citadel an island. The Old Fort overlooks the **Old Port**, where the ferries from the mainland dock. The more complete **Néo Froúrio (New Fort) ❺** to the west (same hours as Old Fort; entrance fee) is strictly Venetian and offers superb views.

With its tottering, multistoreyed apartments and maze-like lanes ending in quiet plazas, the Old Town

LEFT: clear water off Corfu.
BELOW: Corfu Town's Listón.

constitutes a *flâneur*'s paradise. Vacant bomb sites still yawn near the Néo Froúrio, and many main thoroughfares are brashly commercialised, but the backstreets are surprisingly unspoilt, festooned with washing lines and echoing to pigeon coos. An elegant counterpoint is the **Listón** **Ⓒ**, to the east, built by the French as a replica of the Parisian Rue de Rivoli. The name refers to local aristocrats listed in the Venetian Libro d'Oro, who were the only citizens with sufficient social standing to walk beneath the arcades.

The Listón faces the **Spianáda** (Esplanade) **Ⓓ**, a large and grassy open space cleared by the Venetians to deprive attackers of cover. On the southern half of the Esplanade is the plain **Ionian Monument**, which celebrates the island's union with Greece in 1864. It is surrounded by marble reliefs displaying the symbols of the seven Ionian Islands (the *Eptánisa*). Nearby is the Victorian bandstand, where Sunday concerts are held in summer, and the Maitland Rotunda, dedicated to the first British High Commissioner. At the far end is the statue of Greece's first president (1827–31) and Corfu's greatest son, Ioannis Kapodistrias. Today the Spianáda hosts idiosyncratic cricket matches, an enduring British legacy, as is the enormous Victorian cemetery outside town, and the ginger beer that is still available at some of the Listón's cafés.

The Spianáda is also the focus for Corfu's famous Orthodox Easter celebrations. On Good Friday, each parish parades its *Epitáfios* (Bier of Christ) to the accompaniment of uniformed brass bands, playing dirges that can make grown men weep. On Saturday morning the relics of local patron saint Spyrídon go walkabout, and the tunes gets jollier as people shower crockery from their balconies to banish misfortune. Fireworks top off the Saturday midnight Resurrection Mass.

*The Greeks call these west-coast islands the **Eptánisa** – the seven isles. But as Kýthira, the seventh isle, lies off the southern tip of the Peloponnese, it remains quite isolated from the others.*

BELOW: Paleó Froúrio, one of Kérkyra's two Venetian fortresses.

Corfu Town

Map on page 294

Both music and Saint Spyrídon are integral parts of Corfiot life. Until it was destroyed by Nazi bombs, Kérkyra had the world's largest opera house after Milan's La Scala; there are still regular opera performances and thriving conservatories. A few blocks back in the streets behind the Listón is the 16th-century **Church of Ágios Spyrídon** ❺. Spyrídon, after whom seemingly half the male population is named "Spýros", was a 4th-century Cypriot bishop whose remains were taken to Constantinople in the 7th century and then, in the 15th, smuggled to Corfu, where he is credited with saving the island from several disasters. His casket, prominently displayed in the church, is processed around town four times a year.

Across the north side of the Spianáda stands the imposing **Palace of St Michael and St George** ❻, erected in 1818–23 as the residence for the British High Commissioners. When the British left, Greek royalty used it as a summer residence. The bronze toga-clad figure who stands above a lily pond in front of the palace is Sir Frederick Adam, Britain's second High Commissioner. The pool and its water spouts are there to remind people that Adam was the first to ensure Kérkyra Town a reliable water supply, with an aqueduct system still in use today. The palace's state rooms now house the **Museum of Asiatic Art** (open Tues–Sun summer 8am–7.30pm, until 3pm winter; entrance fee). Its collection of over 10,000 Asian artefacts is one of the most comprehensive collections of its kind in the world.

But the town's one unmissable indoor sight is the **Archeological Museum** ❼ (open Tues–Sun 8.30am–3pm; entrance fee), with superb late Archaic art. The star exhibit is the massive Gorgon pediment from a 6th-century BC temple of Artemis at Paleopolis; but for some the smaller, more detailed pediment of a

There was an old man of Corfu/Who never knew what he should do/So he rushed up and down/ Till the sun turned him brown/That bewildered old man of Corfu.

—EDWARD LEAR

BELOW: Voulgáreos Street at twilight, Corfu Town.

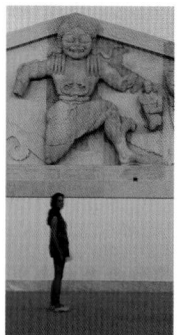

The Gorgon Pediment in the Archeological Museum of Corfu.

BELOW: the 13th-century Angelókastro.

Dionysiac symposium equals it. Both came from excavations in Mon Repos estate, the birthplace of Britain's Prince Philip. Just south of this at Kanóni are the photogenic islets of **Vlahérna**, with a little monastery and causeway to it, and **Pondikonísi**, said to be a local ship petrified by Poseidon in revenge for the ancient Phaecians helping Odysseus.

The north of the island

The coast northwest of town supports busy resorts such as **Kondókali, Komméno, Dasiá** and **Ýpsos**. The best beach along this coast is the farthest, at **Barbáti**. Beyond it, the mountains plunge more sharply to the sea and the landscape becomes more stereotypically Mediterranean, mingling cypress with olive trees. To escape the bustle of the resorts, wander inland on an uphill journey past quiet villas and olive groves to **Káto Korakiána**. Here, set in the grounds of an old Venetian villa, is the **Castello Art Gallery** (open daily 10am–2pm, 6–9pm; free), which exhibits works on loan from the Greek National Art Gallery.

The mini-Riviera between **Nisáki ❷** and **Ágios Stéfanos Sinión ❸** basks in the nickname of "Kensington-on-Sea" after a clientele who stay in villas – there are almost no hotels – and enjoy secluded pebble coves. The adjacent villages of **Kalámi** and **Kouloúra** were beloved of the Durrell family. Lawrence Durrell wrote *Prospero's Cell* while living in the White House in Kalámi (now a taverna), while Kouloúra was the birthplace of his brother Gerald's *My Family and Other Animals*. Mass tourism resumes at **Kassiópi ❹**, once a small fishing village and now a busy resort. The Roman emperor Nero gave a song recital here in AD 67, but only the crumbled Angevin castle recalls past prominence. There are several wonderful pebble beaches.

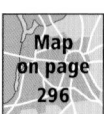

Map on page 296

Alternatively, head up the north slopes of 914-metre (2,950-ft) **Mt Pan-okrátor** to **Paleá Períthia**, a well-preserved Venetian-era village. Back on the coast, **Aharávi**, **Róda** and **Sidári** ❺ are three over-developed resorts. From Sidári ply the most reliable boats to the three small inhabited Diapóndia islets, Mathráki, Erikoússa and Othoní (the westernmost point of Greece), popular with Italians. The town's finest feature is the series of striking rock formations that rise out of the sea at the western end of the resort.

The west-coast beaches beyond Sidári are calmer, beginning below **Peruládes** ❻ with its superlative sunsets, continuing through Ágios Stéfanos Avliotón, Arílas and Ágios Geórgios Págon. Beyond **Kríni** looms the shattered but still impressive Byzantine-Angevin **Angelókastro**, guarding the approach to the beautiful double bay of **Paleokastrítsa** ❼, once idyllic but now swamped. The best view of Paleokastrítsa is from the mountain above it, at the Bella Vista café outside the village of **Lákones**. Beaches resume at **Érmones**, but the small **Myrtiótissa** ❽ – beloved of naturists – or the big sandy beach at **Glyfáda** are better, while **Ágios Górdis** is a backpackers' paradise. Inland, **Pélekas** offers island panoramas from the "Kaiser's Throne".

The south of the island

Inland and south of Kérkyra stands the pretentious **Achilleion Palace** ❾, built in 1890 for Empress Elisabeth of Austria, then acquired after her assassination by Kaiser Wilhelm II. It once housed a casino, has also hosted European Union meetings, and is now a museum (open daily summer 8am–7pm, winter until 5pm; entrance fee). **Benítses** ❿ resort has seen its heyday come and go. The main street in **Moraítika** is one line of restaurants/bars/shops, but the beach is good. The older part of Moraítika is up on a hill just off the main road, and has no tourist development, just an attractive taverna or two providing a pleasant antidote to the hectic resort below. **Mesongí** ⓫ is marginally more pleasant, although an increasing amount of development now spreads back from the long but very narrow beaches. Behind the beach, Mesongí has some of Corfu's oldest olive groves, planted by the Venetians more than 500 years ago.

The main road turns inland here and reaches a crossroads at Áno Mesongí. Continue straight on to Halikoúna beach at the northwest end of the **Korissíon lagoon** ⓬, a protected nature reserve. From the village of **Ágios Matthéos** ⓭, you can access long, sandy **Paramónas** beach.

Turning left at Áno Mesongí, then leaving the main road at **Argyrádes** takes you to the coastal hamlet of **Boúkari**, spared exploitation by an utter lack of beaches. On the opposite shore lies **Ágios Geórgios Argyrádon** ⓮, a frankly unpleasant sprawl with only a splendid beach to its credit. The northernmost part of the beach is **Íssos**, which borders the southwest end of the Korissíon Lagoon. The Corfiots have deliberately quarantined the Club 18–30 element at the far southeast tip of the island, at **Kávos** ⓯. **Levkímmi** ⓰, the underrated second-largest town on Corfu, with a picturesque river, goes about its business just inland, seemingly oblivious to its neighbour. ❑

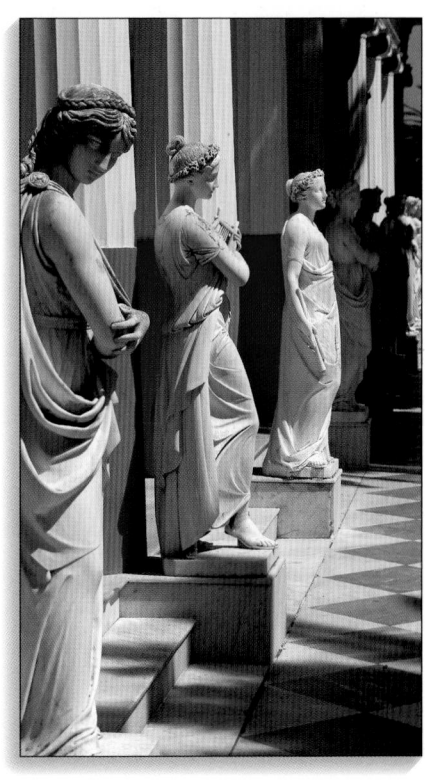

BELOW: inside the Achilleion Palace.

THE IONIAN ISLANDS

*Lushest of all the Greek island chains, the Ionians offer
superb beaches, great natural beauty and a distinct culture –
including a graceful Venetian influence in the local architecture*

Map on
page
300

T hroughout the Ionian archipelago, as on Corfu, the long Venetian domination (1396–1797) left an indelible mark. Culturally, these islands look west to Europe rather than north to the Balkans or east to Anatolia; only Levkáda had a brief period of Ottoman rule.

A heavy rainfall makes the Ionians among the greenest of Greek island chains. Olive groves and vineyards are reminders that agriculture, rather than tourism, still claim a part in the economy. However, this same unsettled weather has dampened many a traveller's holiday: from mid-September until mid-May, rains can wash out any beach visit quite without warning. The rest of the year, the northwest wind or *máïstros* substitutes for the *meltémi* blowing elsewhere in Greece.

Paxí (Paxós)

Small, hilly and green, **Paxí** (or **Paxós**) has a rugged west coast with cliffs and sea caves, and various pebble beaches on the gentler east shore. Paxí figures little in ancient history and mythology, and was systematically populated only during the 15th century. Here too the Venetians left a legacy of olive trees, and Paxiot oil ranks among the best in Greece.

All boats dock at the small capital, **Gáïos ❶**, arrayed around its main square and sheltered by the two islets of **Ágios Nikólaos** (castle) and **Panagía** (small monastery). Gáïos offers narrow streets and a few 19th-century buildings with Venetian-style balconies and shutters, plus most island shops.

Paxí's single main road meanders northwest through olive groves and tiny hamlets consisting of a few houses and perhaps a *kafenío* at lane junctions. Walking is still the best way to explore the maze of old walled paths, dirt tracks and paved lanes crisscrossing the island. **Longós ❷** on the northwest coast is the most exclusive resort, flanked by the popular beaches of Levréhio and Monodéndri. The "motorway" ends at **Lákka ❸**, favoured by yachts and the majority of landbound tourists, with small beaches like Orkós lying nearby.

The satellite islet of **Andípaxi (Andípaxos) ❹** shelters two excellent beaches mobbed by daytrippers in season, when four tavernas operate. Andípaxi's vineyards produce a heavy red wine favoured for local festivals, and a lighter tawny white.

Levkáda (Lévkas)

Levkáda is barely an island, joined to the mainland by a floating drawbridge over a canal dredged in ancient times. Yet Levkáda feels like one of the Ionians, with predictable Venetian influences on speech

LEFT: Navágio
beach, Zákynthos.
BELOW: Vasilikí
harbour, Lefkáda.

Southern Ionian Islands

0   10 km
0   10 miles

and cuisine, plus the imposing fort of Santa Maura by the bridge. Levkáda's rugged landscape has preserved rural lifestyles in the hill villages: older women still wear traditional dress, while local crafts and foodstuffs are avidly promoted.

Levkáda Town ❺ faces the canal and the lagoon enclosed by Gíra sandspit, with safe mooring for numerous yachts on the southeast quay. Much of downtown is off-limits to cars. Part of the main walkway is named for Wilhelm Dorpfeld, the early 20th-century German archeologist whose quixotic life's work attempted to prove that Levkáda was in fact Homeric Ithaca. There are several ornate Italianate churches dating from the late 17th or early 18th century, their Baroque relief work sitting oddly beside antiseismic belfries modelled on oil derricks. Secular architectural responses to the 1953 earthquake could be termed "Caribbean-Tudor"; stone-built ground floors are often preserved, supporting lighter, half-timbered upper stories sheathed in corrugated tin.

Heading down Levkáda's east coast, the little port-resorts of **Lygiá** and **Nikiána**, with pebble coves and fish tavernas, are calmer than **Nydrí** ❻, 20 km (12 miles) south of Levkáda, opposite a mini-archipelago of four islets. Until the 1970s it was a tiny fishing village, where Aristotle Onassis used to pop over for dinner from Skorpiós, his private island. Now, Nydrí is a busy package resort despite poor beaches. Some 3 km (1½ miles) inland, the **Roniés waterfalls** prove suprisingly impressive, revealing abundant water at the heart of Levkáda. Beyond this stretches a fertile upland, studded by churches with Venetian belfries. The main village here is **Karyá** ❼, its vast central *platía* shaded by several giant plane trees.

Beyond Nydrí, Dorpfeld excavated at Stenó and is buried on the far side of sumpy Vlyhó bay. The island ring road curls past **Mikrós Gialós** and **Sývota** bays before descending to **Vasilikí** ❽, 40 km (25 miles) from town, one of Europe's premier windsurfing resorts.

Beyond Cape Levkátas (Ákra Doukáto) – from where Sappho legendarily leaped to her death – lie spectacular west-coast beaches, accessible by roads of varying steepness. **Pórto Kátsiki** ❾ stars on every third postcard of Levkáda; **Egremní** and **Gialós** are less frequented but nearly as good, while panoramic **Atháni** village has the closest tourist facilities. Further on, **Drymónas** has the best rural architecture, while **Kalamítsi** has an eponymous beach and "shares" **Káthisma**, Levkáda's longest, with **Ágios Nikítas (Aï Nikítas)** ❿. The only port actually on the west coast has become its main resort, worth avoiding in peak season.

Itháki (Ithaca)

Most boats dock at the main town, **Vathý** ⓫, at the end of a deeply inset bay. The town was badly damaged by an earthquake in 1953, but much has been restored. The attractive harbour front is known for its huge number of tavernas. To the south of the town are a number of sites supposedly associated with events in Homer's Odyssey. These include the **Arethoúsa Spring**, the **Cave of the Nymphs** and, near the port of **Píso Aetós**, ancient **Alalkomenes**. Above Píso Aetós is the island's deserted medieval capital of **Perahóri**. The route across the isthmus and along the west coast to the villages of **Lévki** and **Stavrós** in the northern half of the island is particularly beautiful.

Stavrós ⓬ is a pleasant but undistinguished town above the west-coast beach and port at **Pólis**. Remains of the island's oldest settlement are on **Pelikáta hill** here. A road winds up past the little hill-village of **Exogí** to a chapel, from where there are spectacular views over the bay of **Afáles**. Another road from Stavrós leads to **Platrithiás**, which also has Mycenean remains. The two lovely port villages of **Fríkes** and **Kióni** are ideal places to stay, but very popular.

In 1939 Itháki had a population of around 15,000; now it is nearer 3,000, thanks to mass emigration – particularly to Australia and South Africa – following the 1953 earthquake.

Map, page 300

BELOW: Itháki's main town, Vathý, by night.

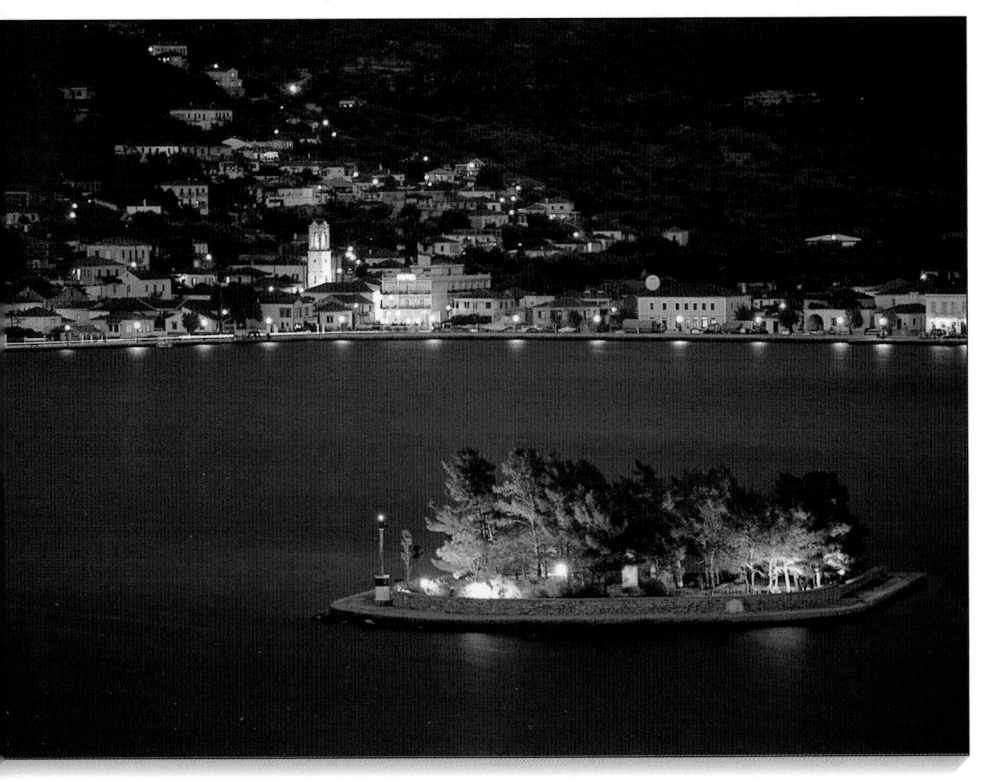

Kefalloniá (Cephalonia)

Kefalloniá is the largest and second most mountainous of the Ionian Islands. It holds the highest peak in the Ionian Islands, **Mount Énos** (1,628 metres/5,340 ft) whose summit is set aside as a national park to preserve the native Cephalonian fir.

Argostóli , the island's capital, is on the west coast on the large Argostóli Gulf. Almost completely destroyed in the huge 1953 earthquake, it has now been rebuilt and is a convenient base from which to explore. The town itself has a few attractions – a small but well-laid-out **archeological museum** (open Tues–Sun 8.30am–3pm; entrance fee), the fascinating **Korgialenios Museum** with its exhibits of bourgeois island life (open Mon–Sat 9am–2pm; entrance fee), and the **Fokas-Kosmetatou Foundation** in a beautifully restored neo-classical mansion (open Mon–Sat 9.30am–1pm, Tues–Sat 7–10pm; entrance fee). Just south of the town is **Votanókypos Kefaloniás**, a botanical garden set in an old olive grove which aims to preserve rare species from the island's flora (open Tues–Sat 10am–2pm, 6–8pm; entrance fee). Further south, across the Livathó plain, are the ruins of the island's Venetian capital, **Ágios Geórgios** (open June–Oct Tues–Sun 8.30am–3pm; entrance fee), perched on a hill above the village of Peratáta. The views from the citadel's ramparts are superb.

To the north of Argostóli are the *katavóthres* ("sea mills"). Here seawater sinks into swallow holes, only to appear in the Melissáni Cave (*see below*) on the other side of the island. Although now just a trickle, before the 1953 earthquake the flow was strong enough to power flour mills. Continuing on along the western coast there are some good beaches beginning with Makrýs and Platýs Gialós at **Lási** , Kefalloniá's largest resort, and continuing all the way down the coast to **Kateliós** and **Skála** (the site of a Roman villa) on the south coast.

Mountain goat, Kefalloniá.

BELOW: in the huge Drongaráti Cave.
RIGHT: Melissáni is an underground lake.

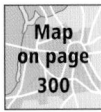

Map on page 300

Lixoúri on the Pallikí Peninsula on the western side of the Argostóli Gulf can be reached by a frequent car ferry from Argostóli. The town itself is rather sleepy, but the **Museum and Library** (open Tues–Sat 9.30am–1pm; entrance fee) is worth a look. South of Lixoúri, across the earthquake-ruptured plain of Katogís, are the wonderful red sand beaches of **Mégas Lákkos** and **Xí**. Beyond Xí is **Kounopétra**, the huge boulder that used to rock on its base until the 1953 earthquake set it still. The beautiful fine-pebble beach at **Petaní** is in the northwest of the peninsula.

Crossing the island, by the spectacular road over the col between Mount Énos and Roúdi, brings you to the port of **Sámi**. The harbour and the wonderful nearby beach of **Andísamis** were the locations for much of the filming of *Captain Corelli's Mandolin*, the book of which was set on the island. Close by Sámi are the caves of **Melissáni** and **Drongaráti**. The **Melissáni Cave** (open May–Oct daily 8am–7pm, Nov–Apr Fri–Sun 10am–4pm; entrance fee) is an underground lake with part of the roof open to the sky; when the sun shines down on the water it becomes a bright translucent blue. The large chamber of **Drongaráti** (open summer only daily 9am–8pm) is decorated with hundreds of stalactites and stalagmites. The main road south from Sámi leads to the pleasant resort of **Póros** and the excavated Mycenean tholos tomb at **Tzanáta**.

The northern part of Kefaloniá comprises sheer mountains whose cliffs fall preciptiously to the sea, as well as pretty villages that largely escaped the 1953 earthquake. The west-coast road is a spectacular, if rather worrying, ride. The famous beach at **Mýrtos** is impressive from above but consists of coarse pebbles and has a dangerous undertow. Further north is the perfect horseshoe harbour of **Ásos**. On the isthmus leading to a large hill that rises sharply out of the sea is a large 16th-century Venetian fort. However, the island's most upmarket resort is

Kefaloniá is noted for its honey (thyme-scented), quince jelly, rabbit stew and a local speciality called riganáta – féta cheese mixed with bread, oil and oregano.

BELOW: the clear waters of Eblísi beach, Fiskárdo.

A good catch in Zákynthos.

the small port of **Fiskárdo ⑮**, slightly too pretty and popular as a yachting harbour for its own good. There are many wonderful small pebble beaches, many of them backed by cypress trees, all around this northern part of the island.

Zákynthos (Zante)

Dubbed "Zante, Fior di Levante" by the Venetians, the central plain and eastern hills of Zákynthos still support luxuriant vegetation. The south and east coasts shelter excellent beaches, some almost undeveloped, others home to rampant and unsavoury tourism. The once-elegant harbour town of **Zákynthos ⑯** was rebuilt after the 1953 earthquake in the same style and though not quite convincingly Venetian, the atmosphere is still pleasant. At the southern end of the harbour is the church of **Ágios Dionýsios**, the island's patron saint, rebuilt after an earthquake in 1893 and again in 1948. At the harbour's northern end is Platía Solomoú, surrounding which are the town's other main attractions: the church of **Ágios Nikólaos tou Mólou**; the **Museum of Post-Byzantine Art** with its superb 17th- and 18th-century paintings (open Tues–Sun 8am–3pm; entrance fee); and, tucked behind on Platía Márkou, the **Museum of Eminent Zakynthians**, chiefly dedicated to the poet Dionysios Solomos (open daily 9am–2pm; entrance fee). Above the town is the Venetian fort at **Bóhali** (open daily summer 8am–7.30pm, until 2pm winter; entrance fee) with a very attractive pine-filled interior and wonderful views.

At the southeastern tip of the island is the beautiful **Vasilikós Peninsula**, location of some of the better beaches on the island. The best of these is **Gérakas** on its western side. However, the beaches on Laganás Bay are some of the last few nesting sites of the Mediterranean loggerhead turtle. As the majority of visitors to the island are flown into the brash and raucous resort of **Laganás ⑰**,

BELOW: the banana-boat ride at Alykés.

here is an agglomeration of hotels, restaurants and bars, fast-food joints and clubs along this coast, severely endangering the survival of the turtles. In response the **National Marine Park of Zákynthos** has been set up, encompassing the whole gulf between capes Gérakas to Kerí. All affected beaches have wardens to protect the nests, dawn-to-dusk curfews, and boating and land access are restricted.

The broad central plain is the most fertile region in the Ionians and is given over to intensive agriculture. One highlight is the **Skaliá Cultural Centre/Théatro Avoúri** near Tragáki, a series of stone-built auditoria where storytelling events are held. The village of **Maherádo** to the west has the pilgrimage church of Agías Mávras with its ornate gilded Baroque interior. Over on the east coast are the popular, and slightly tacky, resorts of **Tsiliví** and **Alykés**.

The mountainous west coast is much wilder, and sees far fewer tourists. From the cliffs at **Kerí** 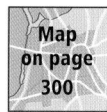, on the southwest peninsula, there are incomparable views of the sea. A string of pretty hill villages runs along the western side of the mountains. The most attractive is **Loúha**, one of the highest settlements on the island, like its neighbours, undamaged by the 1953 tremor. From **Kiloméno** the road runs north past **Kábi** where a huge cross on a headland commemorates a wartime massacre. Before Kábi, down by the sea is a beautifully situated *tavérna* at **Limniónas** where you can swim off the rocks. Further north, past the monasteries of **Anafonítria** and **Ágios Geórgios tón Krimnón**, is perhaps the Ionians' most iconic tourist sight: the shipwreck at **Navágio Bay**, surrounded by towering white cliffs. Further on is the mountain village of **Volímes**, noted for its honey and textiles. At the very northern tip of the island (Cape Skinári) are the **Blue Caves**; sun on the clear water here reflects an iridescent blue on the cave walls (excursions run from the small port of Ágios Nikólaos and Alykés).

The National Marine Park of Zákynthos was set up to protect nesting turtles.

BELOW:
old women in Vólimes, Zákynthos.

Kýthira – bridge to Crete

The island of **Kýthira** sees at least one ferry boat daily from Gýthion and/or Neápoli. Essentially a bleak plateau slashed by well-watered ravines, the island forms part of a sunken land-bridge between the Peloponnese and Crete. It is very much an in-between sort of place, with a history of Venetian and British rule like the other Ionian isles with which it, in theory, belongs, although it is now lumped administratively with the Argo-Saronics under Pireás. Architecturally, it's a hybrid of Cycladic and Venetian styles with an Australian accent, courtesy of remittances from the 60,000-odd locals who headed Down Under in the 1950s.

The island does not put itself out for visitors: accommodation is dear and oversubscribed, the season short, and good tavernas thin on the ground. Yet Kýthira seems increasingly popular thanks to regular flights from Athens. **Kýthira Town** is also one of the finest island capitals of the Aegean, with medieval mansions and Venetian fortifications. Far below, **Kapsáli** is the yacht berth, though there are better beaches on the east coast, as far as the fishing anchorage of **Avlémonas**. More castles are to be found there and at Venetian **Káto Hóra**, just above **Agía Sofía cavern**, the principal west-coast attraction. In the northeast, the ravine-edge ghost village of **Paleohóra** was the capital from 1248 until 1537, when it failed the pirate-proof test. ❑

CRETE

Greece's largest and southernmost island is characterised by soaring mountains, Venetian cities, a proudly independent people and unique remains of Europe's first great civilisation

Maps:
Island 308
City 310

Megalónisos (Great Island) is what Cretans call their home, and "great" refers to far more than size. It can certainly be applied to the Minoan civilisation, the first in Europe and the core of Cretan history. Visitors by the thousand pour into the ruins of Knossos, Phaestos, Malia and Zakros, before heading towards one of the scores of excellent beaches. With three major airports, Crete cannot be classified as undiscovered, but through its size and scale it manages to contain the crowds and to please visitors with widely divergent tastes. While a car is essential for discovering the best of the island, car hire is, unfortunately, comparatively expensive.

For almost half the year, snow lies on the highest peaks which provide a dramatic backdrop to verdant spring meadows ablaze with flowers. This, as botanists and ornithologists know well, is by far the best time to visit. The former arrive to view more than 150 species which are unique to the island, while the latter are thrilled by more than 250 types of bird heading north. It is in spring that the island is redolent with sage, savory, thyme, oregano – and dittany, the endemic Cretan herb. Bathing in an infusion of dittany is rumoured to increase sexual desire.

Crete, much more than other Greek islands, is a place both for sightseeing and for being on the beach. Minoan ruins are the major magnets, but there are also Greek, Roman and Venetian remains, and a score of museums. There are hundreds of Byzantine churches, many with rare and precious frescoes. If the church is locked, enquire at the nearest café. Even if you don't track down the key, you will enjoy the encounter with local people.

Iráklio (Heráklion)

The capital of Crete since 1971, **Iráklio ❶** has nearly a third of the island's population and is Greece's fifth-largest city. Although it vaunts the highest per capita income of any Greek city, this wealth does not show in the civic infrastructure. Indeed, much of Iráklio is a building site, thanks to a tendency to spend money on starting buildings without sufficient capital for completion.

Most tourists head for the Minoan site of **Knossos ❷** (open daily summer 8am–7.30pm; winter 8.30am–3pm; entrance fee; *see also pages 318–19*). To fully comprehend the site and its contents, this should be combined with a visit to the Iráklio's outstanding **Archeological Museum ❹** (currently closed for renovations). The tourist office is almost next door, and both are moments from the cafés and restaurants of **Platía Eleftherías** (Freedom Square) **❸**.

Iráklio's other major attractions are from the Venetian era, testifying that this was Crete's most

LEFT:
the harbour at Sitía.
BELOW:
sunset in Hánia.

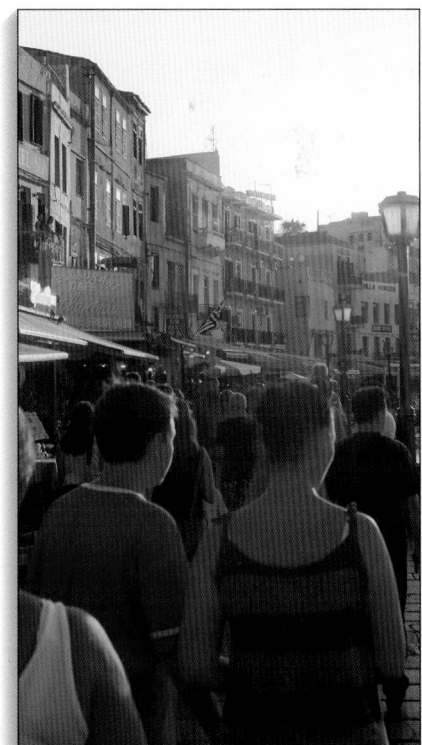

prosperous period in historical times. Head seawards to the old harbour and visit the **Venetian *arsenali*** (covered boat-building yards) **ⓒ** and the restored **Koúles fortress ⓓ** (open Tues–Sun 8.30am–3pm; entrance fee) whose three high-reliefs of the Lion of St Mark confirm its provenance.

A few minutes to the west of the old harbour on S. Venizélou is the **Historical Museum ⓔ** with collections from early Christian times onwards (open Mon–Sat 9am–5pm; entrance fee). Head towards the city centre and the upmarket cafés of **Venizélou** (also Lion or Fountain) Square which takes its popular names from the stylish 17th-century **Morosíni fountain ⓕ** and guardian marble lions. Overlooking the square is the handsome, rebuilt, Venetian *loggia* (city hall) **ⓖ**, flanked by the churches of **Ágios Márkos ⓗ** and **Ágios Títos ⓘ**. Since 1966, when it was returned from St Mark's in Venice, the skull of St Titus, St Paul's apostle to Crete and its first bishop, has been housed in Ágios Títos.

Walk south through Odós 1866, "market street", redolent with tantalising smells, jammed with people and resonant with decibels but now very touristy (the true city markets take place in Iráklio's suburban streets) and then west to the **Icon Museum** (open Mon–Sat 9.30am–7.30pm; entrance fee), housed in the small church of **Agía Ekateríni ⓙ**. The museum contains some exquisite icons, six of them by the 16th-century master, Mihaïl Damaskinos.

Challenging but rewarding is a circumambulation of the 15th-century **city walls**, in their day the most formidable in the Mediterranean, once besieged for 21 years. They stretch for nearly 4 km (2½ miles) and in parts are 29 metres (95 ft) thick. En route, pause a moment at the tomb of the great Cretan author and iconoclast **Níkos Kazantzákis** to enjoy the spectacular views.

Walk Iráklio's Venetian walls and you will reach the tomb of local author Níkos Kazantzákis, of Zorba the Greek fame. His epitaph reads: "I believe in nothing, I hope for nothing, I am free."

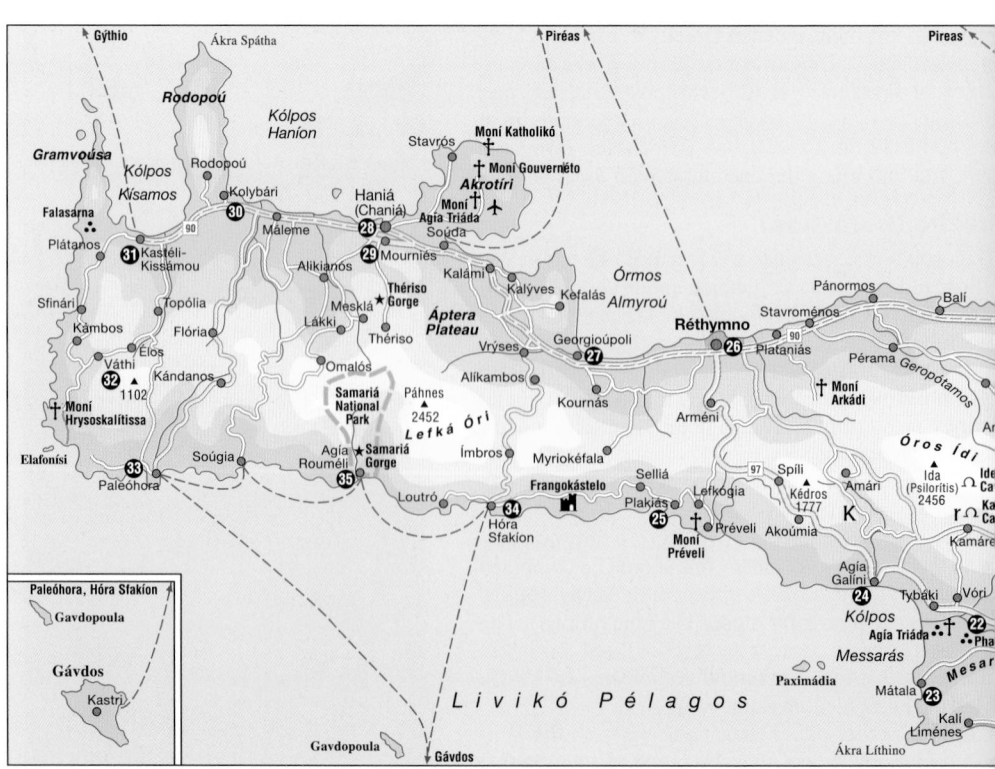

In and around the village of **Arhánes ❸**, 12 km (8 miles) south of Knossos, are three churches with interesting frescoes and icons, and three Minoan sites. Evidence suggests that when the **Anemóspilia** temple was destroyed, by an earthquake, a priest was in the ritual act of sacrificing a youth. This conjecture has outraged some scholars as much as Níkos Kazantzákis's books outraged the established Orthodox Church.

A steep climb from Arhánes (allow one hour) leads to the summit of **Mount Gioúhtas** (811 metres/2,660 ft), from where you can admire the panorama while griffin vultures soar overhead. Resembling a recumbent figure, said to be Zeus, the mountaintop has a Minoan peak sanctuary, a 14th-century chapel, and caves in which Zeus is buried. Perhaps this proves the truth of the aphorism that "all Cretans are liars" because to most Greeks, Zeus is, after all, immortal.

Týlisos ❹, 13 km (8 miles) southwest of Iráklio, possesses three well-preserved Minoan manor houses (open daily 8.30am–3pm; entrance fee) and is one of the few present-day villages to retain its original pre-Hellenic name. Twenty km (13 miles) further west on the same road, the village of **Anógia ❺** is a weaving and embroidery centre. Many locals wear native dress but this is no stage setting: Anógia has a long tradition of resistance and revolt – the village was razed in 1944 – and its men and women are among the fiercest and bravest in Crete.

From Anógia the road climbs to the magnificent **Nída plateau** from where it is a 20-minute uphill stroll to the **Idean Cave** which was the nursery, if not the birthplace, of Zeus. Here the infant god was hidden by the Kouretes, who clashed their weapons to drown the sound of his cries, while the nymph Amaltheë fed him goat's milk. Strong walkers might wish to push on to the summit of **Mount Psilorítis**, at 2,456 metres (8,060 ft) the highest point on Crete.

Maps:
Island 308
City 310

TIP

It's usually possible to arrange for a taxi driver to drop you off somewhere and pick you up a few hours later. Alternatively, you can negotiate a private sightseeing tour.

Crete

0   10 km
0   10 miles

N

Kritikó Pélagos

Thíra · Thíra

Día

Agía Pelagía

Iráklio (Heráklion) ❶
Amnisós

le

∴ **Týlissos** ❹ · ∴ **Knossos** ❷
Myrtiá

Hersónisos ❻ **Mália**
Stalida (Stális) ❼ ❽
Avdoú · **Mália**

Neápoli

Mílatos

Akro Ágios Ioánnis

Spinalónga

Elounda ⓫

Dragonáda

Gianisáda

Ákra Síderos

Kásos

∴ **Ítanos**
Vái

Moní Toploú ✝ ⓯

Palékastro

Ágios Mýronas
Arhánes ❸ ∴

Thrapsanó · Kastélli

Tzermiádo

Psyhró ❾

Agía Varvára

Arkalohóri

Ligórtynos

ri

tyn

ji Déka
ropótamos

Pýrgos

Lebéna

as

Ánapodiáris

Tsoútsouros · Keratókambos · Árvi

Myrtiá

Ω **Diktian Cave**

Lasíthi Plain

Óros Díkti

Áno Viánnos

Kaló Horió

Lato
✝ **Panagía Kerá**
Kritsá

Kolpos Miraméllou

Psíra

Móhlos

Sitía ⓮

Piskokéfalo

Pahiá Ámmos

⓫ **Ágios Nikólaos** ❿

Makrýgialos

Gourniá ⓭ ∴

⓳

Ierápetra ⓱

Myrtos ❽⓲

✝ Moní Kapsás

Zákros ❿

Zíros

Ravine of the Dead ★

Káto Zákros
⓰ ∴ Zakros

Xerókambos

🐚 Koufonísi

The Diktian Cave, supposedly the birthplace of Zeus. His father, the Titan Kronos, had been told he'd be overthrown by a son, so he ate all his offspring. Only Zeus survived, as he was hidden here for protection.

East from Iráklio

Return to Iráklio and continue eastwards along the national highway for 24 km (15 miles). You have reached the Cretan Riviera – a stretch reminiscent of Blackpool or Coney Island – with the resorts of **Hersónisos ❻**, Stalída (Stalís) **❼** and **Mália ❽**. It is neither elegant nor ethnic: bars, heavy rock, pizzerias and fast food abound. However, the beaches are among the best and busiest.

The palace at **ancient Mália** (open daily 8.30am–3pm; entrance fee), traditionally associated with King Sarpedon, brother of Minos, is contemporary with Knossos. The ruins are not as extensive as Knossos or Phaestos, but even without reconstruction, they are more readily understood. The remarkable number of store- and workrooms suggests a wealthy country villa more than a palace. Recent excavations have unearthed the **Hrysólakkos** (Golden Pit) from the proto-Palatial period (2000–1700 BC), an enormous necropolis with numerous gold artefacts.

From either Mália or Hersónisos, twisting mountain roads lead up to the **Lasíthi Plain**, 840 metres (2,750 ft) above sea level and 57 km (36 miles) from Iráklio. This fertile and impeccably cultivated land supports a cornucopia of potatoes and grain crops, apples and pears. For many years the 10,000 windmills here, with their canvas sails, served to pump up water from the limestone below. More recently, however, they have been replaced by diesel pumps. **Psyhró ❾** is the starting point for the giant **Diktian Cave**, another birthplace of Zeus.

Onwards to **Ágios Nikólaos ❿**, 69 km (43 miles) from Iráklio, invariably abbreviated by tourists to "Ag Nik". Magnificently situated on the Gulf of Mirabello and overlooked by the eastern mountains, this was once the St Tropez of Crete. Between here and **Eloúnda ⓫** (10 km/6 miles away) are some of the

Iráklio

0 — 300 m
0 — 300 yds
N

Map,
pages
308–9

island's best and most expensive hotels, although Ag Nik does lack a decent beach, having built a football pitch over its best one. Hotels, discos and cafés cluster around Ag Nik's **Mandráki** harbour and **Lake Voulisméni**, 64 metres (210 ft) deep and once believed to be bottomless. Eloúnda's **Spinalónga** island, an isolated leper colony until 1957 (the last in Europe), with a ruined Venetian fortress and poignant memories, is readily reached from Eloúnda by boat.

Clinging to the hillside 11 km (7 miles) from Ag Nik is **Kritsá** ⑫, said to be the home of the best weavers on the island. Their brilliantly coloured work hangs everywhere – for sale – complementing the flowers and contrasting with the whitewashed homes that line the narrow village alleyways. Immediately below is the church of **Panagía Kerá**, Crete's greatest Byzantine treasure. The entire interior is an illustrated bible of 12th–15th-century frescoes. Until the 1960s Panagía Kerá was a functioning church; with changing times, it is now a museum (open Mon–Sat 9am–3pm, Sun 9am–2pm; entrance fee).

Leave Ag Nik and head southeast. After 19 km (12 miles), **Gournia** ⑬ (open Tues–Sun 8.30am–3pm; entrance fee), the remains of the streets and houses of a Minoan town, is spread over a ridge that overlooks the sea. In spring, when the site is covered with a riot of flowers and filled with their perfume, even those bored with old stones will be delighted to be here.

Sitía ⑭, 70 km (44 miles) from Ag Nik, is a laid-back town which, to the delight of visitors and the chagrin of locals, has not yet hit the big time (though it will once the big new airport opens in 2009). Here are the almost obligatory Venetian fort, **Archeological Museum** (open Tues–Sun 8.30am–3pm; entrance fee) and **Folklore Museum** (open Mon–Sat 10am–1pm; entrance fee), and an unimpressive beach. After a further 24 km (15 miles) is **Váï** ⑮, renowned for its

The remains of the leper colony on Spinalónga island.

BELOW:
Ágios Nikólaos.

The minaret of Ierápetra's Ottoman mosque.

myriad palm trees, large sandy beach and tropical ambience. The palm trees are native, not from a desert island, and the beach is usually crowded.

Kato Zakros ⓰, 43 km (27 miles) from Sitía, is the fourth great Minoan site (open daily 8.30am–5pm, until 3pm winter; entrance fee), situated below the spectacular **Ravine of the Dead**, where caves were used for Minoan burials. The main dig has the customary central courtyard with royal, religious and domestic buildings and workshops radiating outwards; most date from 1900–1600 BC, the apogee of Minoan civilisation. Crete's eastern end is sinking, however, so they are often waterlogged when the sea filters in.

Back at Gournia, a flat road crosses the island to **Ierápetra** ⓱ (35 km/22 miles from Ag Nik), the south coast's only large town and Europe's southernmost. Recently, Ierápetra has enjoyed a boom in both market gardening and in tourism, although it is hardly atmospheric, mainly a promenade behind an average beach and a tiny Venetian fort. Fifteen km (9 miles) to the west lies the pretty village resort of **Mýrtos** ⓲, which takes advantage of mild weather to remain open throughout the winter. Eastwards 24 km (15 miles) from Ierápetra is the summer resort (and reasonable beach) of **Makrýgialos** ⓳, from where a side road leads to the 14th-century **Kapsás Monastery** set snugly into the cliffs at a gorge entrance.

South from Iráklio

Head south from Iráklio over the island's spine and you reach a breathtaking view of the **Plain of Mesará**, whose rich soil and benign climate make it an agricultural cornucopia. At the edge of the plain, 40 km (25 miles) from Iráklio, is the village of **Ágii Déka** (Holy Ten) with its heavily restored medieval church; fragments from nearby Gortys have been incorporated into its walls.

BELOW: palm trees backing Váï.

Gortys (Górtyn) **20** is 1 km (½ mile) further. This was the capital of the Romans, who came to Crete in the 1st century BC to settle feuds but who stayed and conquered the island. Outstanding are the Roman *odeon* and a triple-naved basilica, the latter by far the best-preserved early church in Crete, built to house the tomb of St Titus (open daily 8am–7.30pm; entrance fee). But the most renowned artefacts are some stone blocks incorporated into the *odeon*. About 2,500 years ago a 17,000 character text, the Code of Gortys, was incised on these – rules governing the behaviour of the people. The script is written in ox-plough manner – reading left to right along one line, then right to left along the next.

Church bells at Mátala resort.

Those in search of more classical ruins, of health and of good swimming might wish to turn off and drive south to **Léndas 21** (72 km/45 miles from Iráklio), before continuing to Phaestos. Nearby **ancient Lebena** was the port for Górtyn, and its therapeutic springs made it a renowned sanctuary with a temple to Asklepios, the god of healing. Traces of this, with mosaic floors and large baths, can be seen. **Phaestos** (modern Festós) **22**, Crete's second great Minoan site (open daily 8am–7.30pm; entrance fee), occupies a magnificent location 16 km (10 miles) west of Gortys. State-rooms, religious quarters, workshops, store-rooms and functional plumbing can all be identified; those purists who bristle at Knossos's reconstruction can let their imaginations run riot unhindered here.

Next, on to **Mátala 23**, 70 km (44 miles) from Iráklio. The resort first gained renown when the sandstone caves in the cliffs around the small sandy beach became home to the world's hippies. Joni Mitchell stayed and wrote a song (*Carey*) about it. The scenic 30-minute walk south to Red Beach is highly recommended, though **Kómmos** beach to the north is much larger and has a recently excavated Minoan site. The larger south-coast resort of **Agía Galíni 24**

BELOW: the mountainous interior.

Arkádi Monastery, Crete's most sacred shrine.

also lies on the Gulf of Mesará, though a little further west. The harbour, with a short wide quay and a tiny main street jammed with tavernas and bars, is enclosed within a crescent of steep hills covered with modest hotels. Further into western Crete is **Plakiás** ㉕, with its five large beaches and spectacular mountain backdrop, 112 km (70 miles) from Iráklio.

West from Iráklio

Back in Iráklio, an oleander-lined expressway runs west towards Réthymno. Leave the new road 25 km (16 miles) from the capital to arrive in **Fódele**, a small village rich in orange trees and locally made embroidery. A restored house here is said to be the birthplace in 1545 of Domenikos Theotokopoulos, better known as **El Greco**. Fódele's fame may be fleeting for the latest word is that El Greco was probably born in Iráklio.

At Stavroménos or Plataniás, just before Réthymno, turn southeast for the beautifully situated **Arkádi Monastery** (80 km/50 miles from Iráklio), Crete's most sacred shrine for its resistance to the Turks. The elaborate 16th-century western façade of the church figured on the retired 100-drachma note.

Réthymno (Réthimno) ㉖, which prides itself on being Crete's intellectual capital, has an intact old town with a small, picturesque Venetian harbour; the quayside – choc-a-bloc with colourful fish restaurants – is guarded by an elegant lighthouse. To the west is the immense ruined **Fortétsa**, said to be the largest extant Venetian castle, with excellent views (open daily 8am–8pm; until 6pm winter; entrance fee). The town's other attractions – the **Rimóndi Fountain**, the **Archeological Museum** (open Tues–Sun 8.30am–3pm; entrance fee) and the **Neratzés Mosque** – all lie between the harbour and the fortress. Venetian houses

BELOW: Haniá's Venetian-built waterfront.

ICONS AND EL GRECO

The artist El Greco (1545–1614), a Cretan native who studied under Titian, is best known for his portraits and religious pictures painted in Rome and Toledo. His highly distinctive style anticipated modern impressionism by his use of cold white, blue and grey colour schemes, and by his sacrifice of realism to emotional effect. His work also strikingly fuses Byzantine and Renaissance influences, a legacy of his early training as an icon-painter in Iráklio.

These icons were not objects of idolatrous worship, but this was precisely the indictment of the so-called Iconoclasts in the 7th and 8th centuries. In an effort to purify the religion they proceeded to literally deface thousands of icons throughout Byzantium. Intact pre-9th-century icons are consequently very rare. The church of Agía Ekateríni here has a fine collection of icons, including a group by Mihaïl Damaskinos, a contemporary of El Greco. Both artists are thought to have studied at the church, all that remains of the Mount Sinai Monastery School, founded by exiles from Constantinople after the fall of "the City".

Only one work by El Greco can be viewed on Crete – *View of Mount Sinai and the Monastery of St Catherine* in Iráklio's Historical Museum (*for details, see page 308*).

with unexpected architectural delights line the narrow streets linking these sights, while minarets and wooden oriels give the place a Turkish-style raffishness.

Réthymno and – to the west – Haniá are joined by an expressway and an old road. Leave the highway after 23 km (14 miles) to enter **Georgioúpoli** 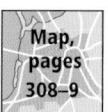 at the mouth of the River Armyrós. This delightful, princely hideaway has a good long beach and a eucalyptus-shaded square.

Haniá (Chaniá) ㉘, 59 km (37 miles) from Réthymno, is Crete's second city and was its capital until 1971. It is a larger version of Réthymno and claims to be one of the oldest continuously inhabited cities in the world. Its jewel is the outer **Venetian harbour**. Here, the quayside is wide and backed by characterful, colourful old buildings whose reflections shimmer in the water. The ambience is of the Levant and this is *the* place for the *vólta* – the evening stroll. The **Archeological Museum** (open Mon 1.30–7pm, Tues–Sun 8am–7.30pm; entrance fee) occupies the church of the Franciscan priory, one of the best-preserved and largest of a score of still-standing Venetian churches. The medieval synagogue has been wonderfully reconstructed.

Those with a sense of history will visit Mourniés and Thériso, villages south of Haniá. The house in which Eleftherios Venizelos, father of the modern Greek nation, was born is now a museum, in **Mourniés** ㉙.

West from Haniá

The road west from Haniá hugs the coast, passing several busy small resorts that merge imperceptibly, before arriving at **Kolybári** ㉚. Proceed westwards, passing memorable views of the plain of Kastéli and the Bay of Kísamos enclosed within the peninsulas of Rodopoú and Gramvoúsa. The road makes a tortuous

Cans of olive oil in Haniá's covered market make colourful souvenirs.

BELOW: fruit and veg for sale in Réthymno old town.

descent to the plain and to pleasant but rather characterless **Kastéli-Kissámou** ③ (42 km/26 miles from Haniá), which does actually have an outstanding museum (open Tues–Sun 8.30am–3pm; free) with fine Roman mosaics.

Turn left at **Plátanos** and a twisting corniche leads after 44 km (28 miles) from Kastéli to **Váthy** ③ and several splendidly frescoed Byzantine churches. From Váthy a poor road through a ravine leads in a dusty 10 km (6 miles) to the **Hrysoskalítissa Convent**. The name, meaning "Golden Stairway", comes from the legend that one of the 90 steps descending from the terrace is made of solid gold, invisible to sinners. From here, a barely negotiable road terminates at the broad sands of **Elafonísi**, bordering a shallow lagoon. Wade across to the island of the same name which has excellent beaches – hence very busy in high season – and you are at westernmost Crete.

Around the corner to the southeast lies **Paleóhora** ③ (76 km/48 miles from Haniá), a relatively unspoiled resort with a choice of accommodation and restaurants and both sand and shingle beaches. **Hóra Sfakíon** (Sfakiá) ③, 75 km (47 miles) from Haniá, is the capital of the Sfakians, who epitomise the independent and unmanageable Cretans. A small, picturesque port with a brave past, its sole *raison d'être* today – but don't tell this to the Sfakians – is a transfer point for exhausted tourists returning by ferry from their Samariá Gorge excursion.

Taking it easy in Hóra Sfakíon.

The Samariá Gorge

Crete offers an exciting and spectacular walk through the **gorge of Samariá**, the longest (18 km/11 miles) in Europe. The walk starts by descending a steep stairway at **Xylóskalo**, 1,200 metres (3936 ft) above the sea, at the southern end of the vast Omalós plain, itself a 45 km (28 miles) tortuous drive from Haniá.

BELOW: the "Iron Gates" in the Samariá Gorge.

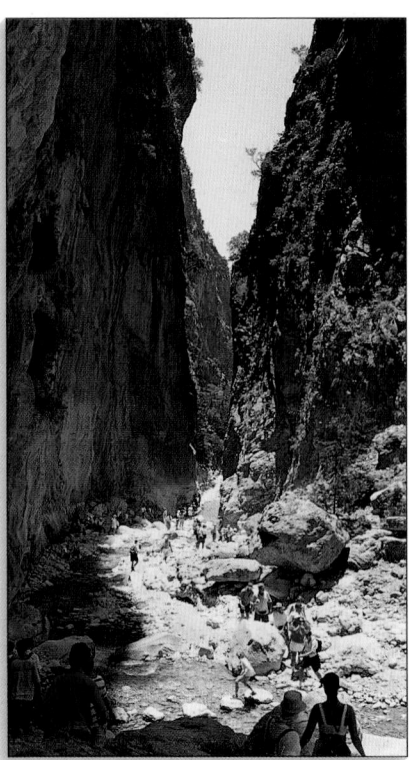

SUPERSTITIONS

The Cretans still observe countless practices that could be summarily dismissed as superstition, but which derive from ancient pagan religions, or early Christian observance, or actual historical events. Some examples:

● After Mass early on Easter Day, believers take home candles lit from the holy flame and use their smoke to mark a cross on the door lintel. This protects the house from bad luck and evil spirits for the rest of the year.

● Hard-boiled eggs are painted red on Holy Thursday to symbolise the blood of Christ. On Easter Day, people strike their eggs against other people's: the owner of the last egg to remain unbroken is considered lucky.

● A knife that was made during Holy Week offers protection against evil spirits.

● In eastern Crete, it is bad luck to give a knife as a present; but in western Crete, giving a knife to the best man at a wedding brings good luck.

● If an unexpected and unwanted guest arrives, someone creeps outside the door and spills salt on the ground. This is supposed to ensure the speedy departure of the visitor.

● Constantinople fell to the Turks on 29 May 1453 – a Tuesday. Many Cretans still believe in Unlucky Tuesday and are reluctant to do important business on that day.

After about 10 km (6 miles), with most of the steeper descent over, the abandoned **village of Samariá** and its church come into view. Stop and admire the church's lovely 14th-century frescoes – an opportunity to regain your breath without loss of face. The going now gets tough and involves criss-crossing the river-bed (be warned: flash floods can occur and wardens' warnings should be heeded). There is a lot of scree on the way, so you should wear sturdy walking shoes and be careful you don't slip. As the gorge narrows, the walls soar straight upwards for 300–600 metres (1,000–2,000 ft). Soon after passing the church of Aféndis Hristós, the **Sideróportes** (Iron Gates) are reached: here the gorge – scarcely penetrated by sunlight – is little more than 3.5 metres (11 ft) wide.

The park is under the strict aegis of the Haniá Forest Service, which specifically forbids certain activities, including singing. While you are walking, the elusive Cretan wild goat, the *agrími*, will probably be nearby, though it is unlikely that you will see many. On the other hand, you may spot bearded vultures overhead.

And so to old Agía Rouméli and the church of the Panagía. However, there is a further 3 km (2 miles) of hot and anticlimactic walking before celebrating with a longed-for swim or cold drink at new, coastal **Agía Rouméli ㉟**, with its tavernas and pensions. In ancient times, this is where Cretan cypress wood, much coveted in the ancient world, was exported to Egypt. Once refreshed, the only practical exit from the gorge – other than more tough hiking east along the coast – is by boat eastwards to Hóra Sfakíon or westwards to Soúgia and Paleóhora. There are no roads.

The gorge is open from about the beginning of May until early October (entrance fee). Allow four to six hours for the walk. ❑

**Map,
pages
308–9**

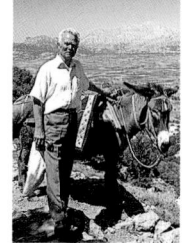

*Cross-country
transport,
Samariá Gorge.*

BELOW:
Agía Rouméli.

CENTRE OF EUROPE'S FIRST CIVILISATION

Until a century ago, Crete's Minoan civilisation was little more than a myth. Now its capital is one of the largest and best restored sites in Greece

Knossos is a place of questions, many unanswered. Many visitors to the site find the concrete reconstructions and repainted frescoes (often from very small existing fragments) aid comprehension. But for many, used to other, more recent ruins that are clearly defensive or overtly religious, the site is mysterious. Can we hope to look back at fragments of a culture from 3,500 years ago and understand its imperatives and subtleties?

In legend, Knossos was the labyrinth of King Minos, where he imprisoned the minotaur, the human-bovine child of his wife Pasiphae. In reality, the role of the Minoan palace was probably not in the modern sense of a palace, but perhaps as an administrative and economic centre, unified by spiritual leaders.

Among the 1,300 rooms of the main palace were both the sacred and the commercial: lustral baths for holy ceremonies; store rooms for agricultural produce; workshops for metallurgy and stone-cutting. Nearby are the Royal Villa and the Little Palace.

Try to visit earlier or later in the day, to avoid the worst of the crowds, and to avoid being swept along by the flow. Look for the subtle architectural delights – light wells to illuminate the larger rooms; hydraulic controls providing water for drinking, bathing and flushing away sewage; drains with parabolic curves at the bends to prevent overflow.

Combine that with a afternoon visit to the archeological museum – to take full advantage of the air-conditioning inside the building.

△ **OVERVIEW**
The scale of the site is most apparent from the air – nearly 2 hectares (4 acres) of palaces ruled a population of perhaps 100,000.

▽ **EMPTY VESSELS**
Huge earthenware jars, *pithoi*, were used to store grain, olive oil, wine or water.
Similar jars are still made in a few Cretan villages today.

△ **CHAIR OF STATE**
The throne room, possibly court or council room, has gypsum throne flanked by benches, and frescoes of griffins. These may have symbolised the heavenly, earthly and underworldly aspects of the rulers.

△ THE PLAY'S THE THING

The theatre was used for plays and processions. An engineered road, one of the oldest in Europe, leads from here to the Little Palace.

▽ ALL AT SEA

The fresco in the Queen's apartments (which included an en suite bathroom) features dolphins, fishes and sea urchins.

◁ BULL AND GATE

A (replica) fresco depicting the capture of a wild bull decorates the ramparts of the north entrance, leading to the road to Knossos' harbour at Amnissos.

▽ DILEMMA OF HORNS

The famous double horns now sitting on the south facade were once regarded as sacred symbols, though perhaps this is an overworking of the bull motif of the site.

◁ COLOUR CODING

The South Propylon (pillared gateway) has near life-size frescoes of processionary youths, including the famous slender-waisted cup-bearer. In Minoan art, male figures were coloured red, female white.

CONTROVERSIAL EXCAVATIONS

In 1878 a local merchant, Minos Kalokairinos, uncovered a fragment of the remains at Knossos, but the Turkish owners of the land prevented further excavation and even the wealthy German Heinrich Schliemann couldn't afford their asking price when he attempted to buy the site.

However, once Crete gained autonomy from the Turks in 1898, the way was open for the English archeologist Arthur Evans (later knighted) to purchase the area and begin excavating. He soon realised that this was a major discovery. He worked at Knossos over a period of 35 years, though by 1903 most of the site had been uncovered.

Evans' methods of using concrete to reconstruct the long-gone timber columns, and to support excavated sections of wall have received much criticism. While these preserved some of the structure *in situ*, it also involved much interpretative conjecture on the part of Evans (pictured above with a 1600 BC steatite bull's head from the Little Palace).

Excavation continues to this day, under subtler management.

INSIGHT GUIDES

TRAVEL TIPS

GREECE

TRAVEL TIPS

TRANSPORT

GETTING THERE AND GETTING AROUND

GETTING THERE

By Air

Greece has good air connections with the rest of the world and is serviced by numerous international airlines. Charter flights generally operate from mid-April to the end of October, even into November to Rhodes and Crete. Nowadays, unless you're on a multi-stop or Opodo round-the-world ticket, e-tickets bought online are the way to go – many airlines no longer issue paper tickets. The airlines' own websites are often a good source of discount tickets, matching (or nearly so) the prices offered by general websites like Expedia.

The majority of scheduled airline passengers travelling to Greece make Athens' Eleftherios Venizelos Airport their point of entry, though a number of services (from the rest of Europe only) arrive at Thessaloníki's Macedonia

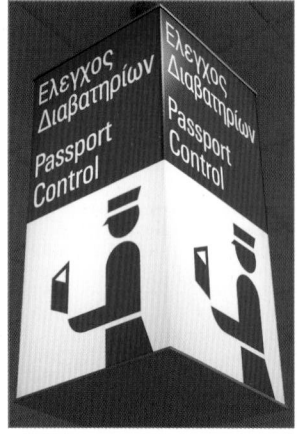

Airport, Rhodes, Corfu and Iráklio, Crete. Macedonia Airport is 15 km (9 miles) southeast of Thessaloníki. Regular buses go to the city centre (50 cents) and take around 35 minutes. Taxis take 15–20 minutes and cost €10–12.

Between Eleftherios Venizelos Airport at Spáta, central Athens and Piraeus there are various connecting services. Line 3 of the metro takes you – surprisingly slowly – into town for €6. Alternatively, take the E95 express bus all the way to central Sýndagma Square (every 25–35 minutes), or the X96 express bus to Pireás port (every 20–40 minutes). The Piraeus terminus for the X96 bus is all the way anticlockwise around the port, at gate E1 (Dodecanese sailings), however it does make stops all along the quay in each direction. Tickets for the E95 and the X96 cost €3.20 for a single journey.

Should you need to use one, a taxi from Venizelos Airport into Athens will cost €28–40 depending on time of day/night and your final destination, but including airport supplement and per-bag fee. Traffic congestion has improved since the opening of the Attikí Odós, or toll ring highway, around northern Athens, but the journey time can still amount to over an hour.

By Sea

Most visitors entering Greece by sea do so from the west, from Italy. You can catch a boat to Greece from Venice, Ancona and Bari, but the most regular service is from Brindisi. Daily ferry lines (less frequent in the low-season) connect Brindisi with the three main western Greek ports: Corfu, Igoumenítsa and Pátras. Corfu is a 6½-hour trip; Igoumenítsa 8 hours;

and Pátras 11–14 hours, depending on whether you take a direct boat or one that makes stops in Corfu and Igoumenítsa. The "Superfast" ferries between Ancona and Pátras offer an efficient 22-hour crossing.

Igoumenítsa is the ideal port of call for those setting off to see central-western Greece. Pátras is best if you want to head directly to Athens or into the Peloponnese. Regular buses and trains connect Pátras and Athens (4 hours by bus, 5 hours by train). If you plan to take your car with you on the boat, you should definitely make reservations well in advance. Otherwise, arriving a few hours before the departure time should suffice, except during peak seasons when booking in advance is essential for seats or berths.

By Land

From Europe The most direct overland route from northwestern Europe to Greece is a long one: 3,000 km (1,900 miles) from London to Athens. It has always been a rather arduous and impractical travel option if you're just trying to get to Greece for a brief holiday; sporadic troubles in former Yugoslavia may mean even longer detours through Hungary, Romania and Bulgaria, with substandard road conditions in the latter two countries. Check with your local Greek tourist office or motoring organisation for the latest information before leaving.

There is also the option of making use of the one or two remaining, reputable **bus** lines that connect Athens and Thessaloníki with many European cities (taking 3½ days from London, for example).

The various **trains** you can take from northwest Europe will take about as long as the bus, and cost considerably more, but fares include the Italy-Greece ferry crossing, and may get you to Greece feeling more intact.

From Asia via Turkey If you are travelling strictly overland to Greece from Asia you will pass through Istanbul and cross into Greece at the Évros River. The best way to do this is by car or bus. The road is good and the journey from Istanbul to Thessaloníki takes approximately 15 hours; several bus companies serve the route.

The train has the appeal of following the route of the old Orient Express, with better scenery than the road. But, unless you're a great rail fan, the travel time can be off-putting: 17 hours by the timetables, up to 19 hours in practice, including long halts at the border.

Another popular option is to take one of the small boats between western Turkish ports and select Greek islands just opposite. Fares are overpriced for the distance involved, but it is undeniably convenient. The most reliable links are from Çesme to Híos, Marmaris to Rhodes and Kusadasi to Sámos.

GETTING AROUND

Public Transport

By air
Flying is considerably more expensive than travelling by boat, bus or train (three times more than a ferry seat, usually just under double the price of a boat berth), though still reasonable when compared to the price of domestic flights in other countries. For example, the 50-minute ATR flight between Athens and Sámos costs anywhere from €45 to €120 – fares are now deregulated, pitched on a demand basis.

Greece's national airline, Olympic Airways is perennially up for sale (no takers as yet) and is famous for flight delays or outright cancellation. So, leave plenty of leeway in your domestic flight arrangements if you have to be back in Athens for an international flight. Island flights are often fully booked over the summer, so book at least a week in advance. Olympic are now largely web-based, with walk-in sales offices only in Athens, Thessaloníki, Iráklio, Rhodes and a few other towns, with heavy surcharges for agency tickets. They can be reached nationwide on low-cost number 801 11 44444, or on the web at: www.olympic-airways.gr.

Currently the only private alternative is Aegean Airlines, which flies from Athens and Thessaloníki to most major domestic destinations. Their nationwide low-cost number is 801 11 20000, or you can book online: www.aegeanair.com.

By bus
A vast network of bus routes spreads across Greece; the KTEL is a syndicate of bus companies whose buses are cheap and generally punctual, though rural depopulation has meant that schedules on many routes have been thinned or axed completely. KTEL buses on the more idiosyncratic rural routes often have a distinct personal touch, their drivers decorating and treating the bus with great care.

In the larger cities there may be different KTEL stations for different destinations. Travelling from Thessaloníki to Halkidikí, for example, you will leave from a remote eastern station, though all other destinations are served by the more modern unitary terminal. Athens has two terminals, while Iráklio in Crete has three.

An additional bus service is provided by OSE, the state railway organisation. Their coaches run only along the major routes, but often dovetail usefully with the KTEL for departure times.

City buses
Many of the regular Athens blue-and-white buses are now modern, air-conditioned vehicles, and using them is much less of an ordeal than it used to be. They are still usually overcrowded, and the routes are a mystery even to residents. But they are eminently reasonable, at 70 cents per ticket, or €3.20 for an all-day pass. Tickets, valid on trolleys as

well, are sold individually or in books of 10, from specific news kiosks and special booths at bus and metro stations, and at various points around the city. Most bus services run until nearly midnight.

Trolley buses, with an overhead pantograph, are marginally faster and more frequent, and serve points of tourist interest. Number 1 links the centre of Athens with the railway stations, number 5 passes the Archaeological Museum, and number 7 does a triangular circuit of the central districts.

The most useful suburban services for tourists are the orange-and-white KTEL Attica buses going from 14 Mavromatéon Street, Pédio toú Áreos Park, to Rafína (an alternative ferry port for the Cyclades and northeast Aegean) and Soúnio (for the famous Poseidon temple there).

Rural buses
In the countryside and on islands buses can be converted school buses or modern coaches, or even pick-up trucks with seats installed in the payload space to transport tourists. Some drivers ricochet through mountain roads at death-defying speeds; bus accidents, however, appear to be rare. Just stow your luggage carefully to be on the safe side.

On islands, a bus of some description will usually meet arriving ferries (even if a boat is delayed) to transport passengers up the hill to the island's *hóra*, or capital. Bus stops are usually in main squares or by the waterfront in harbours and vehicles may or may not run to schedule.

A conductor dispenses tickets on the bus itself; often the fare required and the ticket will not show the same

ACCOMMODATION EATING OUT ACTIVITIES A – Z LANGUAGE

price, with the lower old price over-stamped. This isn't a con, but merely a practice – bus companies use pre-printed tickets until the supply is gone, which may take several years.

By metro

The Athens metro system opened in January 2000, halving travel times around the city and making a visible reduction in surface traffic. The stations themselves are palatial and squeaky-clean, with advertising placards kept to a minimum. The old ISAP electric line, in existence since the 1930s, has been refurbished and designated Line 1 (green on maps); it links Piraeus with Kifisiá via the city centre and runs until 2am. Line 2 (red) links Agios Dimítrios in the south with Agios Andónios in the northwest of town, with extensions planned all the way down to Glyfáda and up to Thivón. Line 3 (blue) joins Egáleo via Monastiráki with the airport at Spáta. The main junction stations are Omónia, Sýndagma and Monastiráki. Lines 2 and 3 run until 12.30am.

The best strategy for visitors is to buy a day pass for €3, which includes bus and tram lines. If you're caught by the ubiquitous plainclothes inspectors with an expired ticket, or no ticket, you get a spot fine of 60 times the standard fare.

Summer 2004 saw the addition of three tram lines: Néos Kósmos metro station to Agios Kosmás, Glyfáda to Néo Fáliro, and Sýndagma to Glyfáda. Day cards are valid on these too.

Thessaloníki has recently begun construction of its own metro/light rail system, but inauguration is several years away.

Ferry/Catamaran/Hydrofoil Timetables

The best schedule resource is the website of the GTP (Greek Travel Pages), www.gtp.gr, which is fairly accurate, with updates at least every few weeks.

Alternatively, major tourist information offices (Rhodes, Iráklio, etc) supply a weekly schedule, and most offices hang a timetable in a conspicuous place so you can look up times even if the branch is closed. This should, however, not be relied on implicitly – you may miss your boat. In general, for the most complete and up-to-date information on each port's sailings the best source is the Port Police (in Piraeus and most other ports), known as the *limenarhío*.

Be aware that when you enquire about ferries at a travel agent, they will sometimes inform you only of the lines with which they are affiliated.

By train

The best thing about rail travel in Greece is the price – it is even cheaper than the bus. Otherwise, the Greek railway service, known as OSE (www.ose.gr), is quite limited, both in the areas it reaches and frequency of departures. Trains are also fairly slow and, unless you are doing the Athens– Thessaloníki run overnight in a couchette, or the quickish run down to Pátras (where the station is virtually opposite the docks), you will probably find the bus more convenient.

However, you can speed things up by taking an Intercity express train if you're willing to pay a considerable surcharge. If you're on a tight budget you can really cut costs by taking the train round-trip, in which case there is a 20 percent reduction.

Students and people under 26 are usually eligible for certain discounts. All the common railpasses are honoured in Greece, though you may still have to pay certain supplements and queue for seat reservations.

By sea

Ferries

Piraeus is the nerve centre of the Greek ferry network, and chances are you will pass through it at least once; in diminishing order of importance, Rafína, Thessaloníki, Lávrio, Vólos, Pátra and Kavála are also used. In high season, routes vary from "milk runs" stopping at five islands en route to your destination, to "express" direct ones, so it is worth shopping around before purchasing your ticket. It is also advisable not to purchase your ticket too far in advance: very rarely do tickets for the boat ride actually sell out, but there are frequent changes to schedules which may leave you trying to get a refund.

Personalised ticketing for all boats has been the rule since 2001, so it is no longer possible to purchase tickets on board as in the past. The only exceptions seem to be a few of the ro-ro short-haul ferries (eg Igoumenítsa-Levkímmi).

When you buy your ticket, get detailed instructions on how to find its berth – the Piraeus quays are long and convoluted. The staff who take your ticket should make sure you are on the right boat.

Above all, be flexible when travelling the Greek seas. Apart from schedule changes, a bad stretch of weather can keep you island-bound for as long as the wind blows. Strikes too are often called during the summer, and usually last for a few days. Out on the islands in particular, the best way to secure accurate, up-to-the-minute information on the erratic ways of ferries is to contact the Port Authority *(limenarhío)*, which monitors the movements of individual boats. Port Authority offices are usually located on the waterfront of each island's principal harbour, away from the cafés.

If you are travelling by car, especially during the high season, you will have to plan much further ahead because during the peak

TRANSPORT ♦ 327

TRANSPORT

ACCOMMODATION

EATING OUT

ACTIVITIES

A – Z

LANGUAGE

season, car space is sometimes booked many weeks in advance. The same applies to booking a cabin for an overnight trip during summer.

Gamma class – also known as deck, tourist or third – is the classic, cheap way to voyage the Greek seas. There is usually a seat of one sort or another – though in the new generation of boats, very limited deck space. And if the weather turns bad you can always go inside to the "low-class" lounge or the snack bar.

Catamarans/"high speeds"

Fleets of sleek new "high speed" ferries or true catamarans, made in France or Scandanavia, are steadily edging out most ordinary craft (as a stroll around the quays at Piraeus will confirm). They have some advantages over hydrofoils *(see below)* – they can be even faster, most of them carry lots of cars, and they're permitted to sail in wind conditions of up to Force 7, whereas "dolphins" are confined to port at 6.

The bad news: there are usually no cabins (because they mostly finish their runs before midnight), food service is even worse than on the old ferries and there are no exterior decks. The aeroplane-seating salons are ruthlessly air-conditioned and subject to a steady, unavoidable barrage of banal Greek TV on overhead monitors (even in *diakikriméni* or "distinguished" class). Cars cost roughly the same to convey as on the old-style boats, but seats are priced at hydrofoil levels.

Catamarans come in all shapes and sizes, from the 300-car-carrying behemoths of NEL Lines in the northeast Aegean, Cyclades and central Dodecanese, to the tiny *Sea Star* in the Dodecanese. The useful Dodekanisos Express serves more of the Dodecanese, and can take five cars.

Hydrofoils

Though catamarans are undoubtedly the wave of the future, there is still a network of scheduled hydrofoil services to many islands. Like catamarans, hydrofoils are more than twice as fast as the ferries and about twice as expensive but, as ex-Polish or ex-Russian river craft, are not really designed for the Aegean, and prone to cancellation in conditions above wind Force 6.

Hydrofoils (nicknamed *delfínia* or "dolphins" in Greek) connect Piraeus with most of the Argo-Saronic region (Égina, Póros, Ýdra, Spétses and Peloponnese mainland ports as far as Monemvasía), as well as Vólos and the three northerly Sporades

(Alónissos, Skiáthos, Skópelos). In the northeast Aegean, there are local, peak-season services between Thásos or Samothráki and the mainland, while in the Dodecanese all the islands between Sámos and Rhodes, inclusive, are well served.

Phone numbers for the few surviving hydrofoil companies are constantly engaged, or spew out only pre-recorded information in rapid-fire Greek, so the best strategy is to approach the embarkation booths in person. In Piraeus these are on Aktí Miaoúli quay, services no longer depart from Zéa marina. At Vólos, apply to the gatehouse for the harbour precinct; elsewhere tickets are best obtained from travel agents in towns.

Private Transport

Taxis

Taxis in Greece, especially in Athens, merit a guidebook to themselves. There are three stages to the experience.

First: getting a taxi. It's almost impossible at certain times of the day in Athens, and probably worst before the early afternoon meal. When you hail a taxi, try to get in before stating your destination. The drivers are very picky and often won't let you in unless you're going in their direction. If you see an empty taxi, run for it, be aggressive – otherwise you'll find that some quick Athenian has beaten you to it.

Second: the ride. Make sure the taxi meter is on "1" when you start out, and not on "2" – that's the double tariff, which is only permitted from midnight to 5am, or outside designated city limits. Once inside, you may find yourself with company. Don't be alarmed. It is traditional practice for drivers to pick up two,

three, even four individual riders, provided they're going roughly in the same direction. In these cases, make a note of the meter count when you get in. In fact, because taxis are relatively affordable, they can end up functioning as minibus services.

Third: paying up. If you've travelled with other passengers, make sure you aren't paying for the part of the trip that happened before you got in. You should pay the difference in meter reading between embarking and alighting, plus the €0.90 minimum. Otherwise, the meter will tell you the straight price, which may be adjusted according to the tariff that should be on a laminated placard clipped to the dashboard. There are extra charges for each piece of luggage in the boot, for leaving or entering an airport or seaport, plus bonuses around Christmas and Easter.

Athens' Rush Hour

Drive at your peril in Athens during its multiple rush hours (7–9.30am, 2–3pm, 4.30–5.30pm, 8–10pm). The twin perils of traffic jams and pollution reached such heights in the capital that a law was introduced during the 1980s: on even days of the month only cars with even-numbered licence plates are allowed in the centre; on odd days only those with odd-numbered plates. This has done little to improve the congestion, noise and smog in Athens, as many families have two cars (one of each type of number plate) and alternate according to the day of the week – and in any case the law seems to be going unenforced. Rental cars are exempt from this rule.

Some drivers will quote you the correct price, but many others will try to rip you off, especially if it seems that you're a novice. If the fare you're charged is clearly above the correct price, don't hesitate to argue your way, in whichever language, back down to a normal price.

These rules apply more to Athens than to the islands, although it's still necessary to be pretty assertive on Crete and Rhodes. On the smaller islands, expect to share your taxi, not only with other passengers, but also with an animal or two.

Various radio taxi services exist in Athens and most other larger towns. They can pick you up within a short time of your call to a central booking number.

Cars

Having a car in rural Greece enables you to reach a lot of otherwise inaccessible corners of the country; however, driving a car in Athens or Thessaloníki is unpleasant and confusing. Tempers run short, while road signs, or warnings of mandatory turning lanes, are practically non-existent.

EU-registered cars are no longer stamped into your passport on entry to the country, can circulate freely for up to six months, and are exempt from road tax as long as this has been paid in the home country – however, you are not allowed to sell the vehicle. Non-EU/EEA nationals will find that a bizarre litany of rules apply to importing cars, chief among them that you must re-export the car when you depart, or have it sealed by Customs in an off-road facility of your choosing.

Driving in Greece

All EU/EEA licences, and licences held by returning diaspora Greeks irrespective of issuing country, are honoured in Greece. Conversely, all other licences – this includes North American and Australian ones – are invalid, as many tourists from those nations attempting to hire cars have discovered to their cost. These motorists must obtain an international driving permit before departure (issued by the AAA or CAA in North America on the spot for a nominal cost); the Greek Automobile and Touring Club (ELPA) no longer issues them to foreign nationals in Greece. Similarly, with the advent of the single European market, insurance Green Cards are no longer required, though you should check with your home insurer about the need for any supplementary premiums – many policies now include pan-European cover anyway.

Greek traffic control and signals are basically the same as in the rest of continental Europe, though round-abouts are handled bizarrely by French or English standards – in many cases the traffic entering from the slip road, not that already in the circle, has the right of way – watch for "stop" or "yield" signs or pavement markings.

Motorways speeds are routinely in excess of the nominal 100–120 kph (62–75 mph) limits, and drivers overtake with abandon. A red light is often considered not so much an obligation as a suggestion, and oncoming drivers flashing lights at you on one-lane roads means the opposite of what it does in the UK. Here, it means: "I'm coming through" (although sometimes it can mean "Beware! Police checkpoint ahead"). Greece has the highest accident rate in Europe after Portugal, so drive defensively.

Greece has a mandatory seatbelt law, and children under 10 are not

Breakdowns

The Greek Automobile Association (ELPA) offers a breakdown service for motorists, which is free to AA/RAC members (on production of their membership cards).

Phone 10400 for assistance nationwide. Some car-hire companies have agreements instead with competitors Hellas Service (tel: 1057), Interamerican (tel: 1168) or Express Service (tel: 1157), but these call centres can be slow to dispatch aid. Always ring a local garage number if this is what the hire company instructs you to do.

allowed to sit in the front seat. It is an offence to drive without your licence on your person (this incurs a stiff fine). Every car must also carry a first-aid kit in the boot (though hire companies tend to skimp on this). Police checkpoints at major (and minor) junctions are frequent, and in addition to the above offences you can be done for not having evidence of insurance, paid road tax or registration papers in/on the vehicle.

Super and normal unleaded petrol, as well as lead-substitute super, are readily available throughout Greece, though filling up after dark can be difficult. Most garages close around 8pm and, although a rota system operates in larger towns, it is often difficult to find out which station is open. International petrol stations operated by companies like BP usually take credit cards, but Greek ones often don't.

Road maps

Gone are the days when visitors had to suffer with mendacious or comical maps which seemed based more on wishful thinking (especially projected but unbuilt roads) than facts on the ground. There are now three commercial Greek companies producing largely accurate maps to the Greek mainland, mountain areas and islands: Road Editions, Emvelia and Anavasis. They can be found country-wide, in tourist-shop racks and better bookshop chains like Newsstand or Papasotiríou.

Motorcycles and bicycles

On most Greek islands and in many mainland tourist areas, you'll find agencies that hire small motorcycles, various types of scooters, 50cc and under, and even mountain bikes. These give you the freedom to wander where you will, and weekly rates are reasonable.

Car Hire (Rental)

Hiring a car in Greece is not cheap owing to high insurance premiums and import duties. Prices vary with the type of car, season and length of rental and should include CDW (collision damage waiver) and VAT at 18 percent. Payment can, and often must, be made with a major credit card. You must be at least 21 years old and have a full driving licence (EU/EEA residents) or an Inter-national driving permit (all others).

In the UK and North America, you can book a car in advance through international chains such as Hertz, Avis, Budget or Sixt – their websites have all-inclusive quotes and booking/payment facilities. But there are many reputable, smaller chains, some particular to Greece, that offer a comparable service at lower rates. In Athens most are near Syngroú Avenue in the Makrigiánni district.

Autorent
Syngroú 11, tel: 210 92 32 514
Kosmos
Syngroú 9, tel: 210 92 34 695
Reliable
Syngroú 3, tel: 210 92 49 000
Avance
Syngroú 40, tel: 210 92 40 107
Bazaar
Syngroú 27, tel: 210 92 28 768

For any bike of over 50cc, helmets and a motorcycle driving licence are both theoretically required, and increasingly these rules are enforced. The ill-fitting helmets offered are a bit of a joke, but if you refuse them you may have to sign a waiver absolving the dealer of criminal/civil liability – and police checkpoints *(see above)* can be zealous, levying stiff fines (nearly €150) on locals and visitors alike.

Before you set off, make sure the bike of whichever sort works by taking it for a test spin down the street. Brakes in particular are sometimes badly set, lights may need new fuses or bulbs, and spark-plugs get fouled – ask for a spare and the small spanner (wrench) to change them. Otherwise, you may get stuck with a lemon, with the added insult of being held responsible for its malfunctioning when you return it.

Reputable agencies now often furnish you with a phone number for a breakdown pick-up service.

Above all, don't take unnecessary chances, like riding two on a bike designed for one. More than one holiday in Greece has been ruined by a serious scooter accident. It is strongly suggested that where possible you stick with the traditional, manual-transmission Honda/Yamaha/Suzuki scooters of 50–100cc, with skinny, large-radius, well-treaded tyres. The new generation of automatic, button-start *mihanákia/papákia* (as they're called in Greek slang), with their sexy fairings and tiny, fat, no-tread tyres, look the business but are unstable and unsafe once off level asphalt. In particular, if you hit a gravel-strewn curve on one of these you will go for a spill, and at the

Cruises

Apparently one in six of all visitors to Greece embarks on an Aegean cruise. These cruises can range from simple one-day trips to the Saronic Gulf islands close to Athens and Piraeus, to luxury four-day journeys taking in part of the Turkish coast, Rhodes and Crete. Many people opt for a seven-day excursion, which offers an opportunity to see a couple of islands in the Cyclades, a few of the Dodecanese islands, and a foray over to Istanbul for good measure.

Accommodation, prices and standards on board ship vary widely and it would be a very good idea to read the small print and shop around for a good price.

Ticket agencies in Athens are the places to visit, with cruise opportunities prominently displayed in windows. (However, if you have ever been at Mýkonos harbour

when the ships arrive and watched the frantic preparations of shop managers adjusting their prices upwards, it may change your mind about a cruise entirely.)

The most comprehensive company is **Royal Olympic Cruises**; it is accustomed to dealing with foreigners, and offers a variety of cruise durations. Details can be found from most Greek travel agents or by contacting Royal Olympic's headquarters at 87 Aktí Miaoúli, 185 38, Piraeus, tel: 210 42 91 000.

UK-based **Swan Hellenic Cruises** offer more upmarket, all-inclusive holidays on large luxury liners, with guest speakers instructing passengers on anything from archaeology to marine biology. Swan Hellenic are at 1 Victoria Way, Burgess Hill, West Sussex RH15 9NF; tel: 01444 462 180; www.swanhellenic.com.

very least lose most of the skin on your hands and knees.

Yacht charter

Chartering a yacht is one of the more glamourous ways of island-hopping in Greece. It is by no means cheap, although hiring a boat with a group of friends may not far exceed the price of renting rooms every night for the same number of people.

Depending on your nautical qualifications and your taste for autonomy, you can either take the helm yourself or let a hired crew do so for you. There are over a thousand yachts available for charter in Greece, all of which are registered and inspected by the Ministry of the

Merchant Marine. For more information about chartering contact:
The Hellenic Professional Yacht Owners' Association
43 Freattýdos Street, Zéa Marina, Piraeus; tel: 210 45 26 335.
The Greek Yacht Brokers and Consultants Association
36 Alkyónis Street, Paleó Fáliron, Athens; tel: 210 98 16 582.

Kaïkia and taxi boats

Apart from conventional ferries, most of which carry cars, there are swarms of small *kaïkia* (caïques) which in season offer inter-island excursions pitched mostly at day-trippers. Since they are chartered by travel agencies, they are exempt from Ministry of Transport fare controls – as well as the rule that vessels over 30 years old should be scrapped, which is enforced in Greece for scheduled ferries – and can be very pricey if used as a one-way ticket from, say, Sámos to Pátmos. The stereotypical emergency transfer by friendly fisherman is, alas, largely a thing of the past; never comfortable at the best of times, it is now highly illegal. Knowing this, skippers quote exorbitant prices if approached, and must undertake the journey when the port policeman's gaze is averted.

On many islands where there are remote beaches with poor overland access – most notably Sými, Itháki, Alónisos, Skiáthos, Halkí – local taxi boats provide a fairly pricey shuttle service.

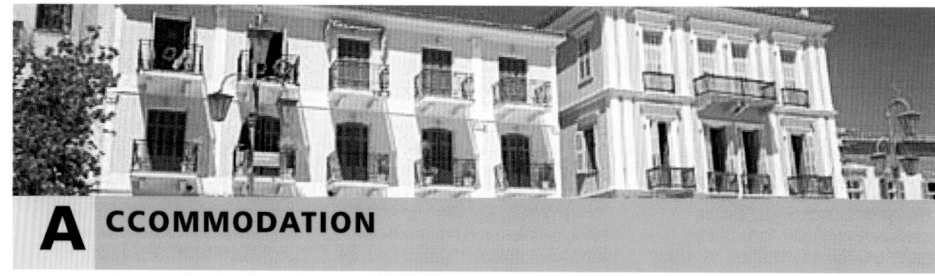

A CCOMMODATION

HOTELS, YOUTH HOSTELS, BED AND BREAKFAST

How to Choose

There is a broad range of accommodation in Greece, from deluxe hotels
to student hostels. Listed are a
sample of different categories across
the country.

On the islands and in many parts
of the mainland, the main type of
affordable lodging is private rented
rooms *(domátia)* and, increasingly
common these days, self-catering
studios or apartments *(diamerís-
mata).* These are classified
separately from hotels, but also
subject to official regulation.

In general, when looking for any
kind of accommodation, local tourist
offices or the Tourist Police can be of
help if you're in a fix – most obviously
if no rooms are on offer when you
disembark at the dock. The best

Rental Agencies

Doufexis Travel
Stoúpa, Peloponnese
Tel: 27210 77833
Fax: 27210 77677
Email: douftvl@hellasnet.gr
Accommodation and car-hire all
year round.
Palmyra Travel
Kalisperidón and Agíou Dimitríou,
Iráklio, Crete
Tel: 28102 44429
Fax: 28102 82229
Email: palmyra@her.forthnet.gr
Accommodation, conferences,
small groups, throughout Crete.
Porfyra Travel
Livádi, Kýthira
Tel: 27360 31888
Fax: 27360 31889
www.kythira.info
Accommodation, car-hire, ferry
agent.

system though, increasingly used by
travellers equipped with mobile
phones, is booking a room yourself a
few days (or weeks) in advance.

Hotel Categories

The Greek authorities have six
categories for hotels; this is
currently expressed as letters but is
due to be replaced by a star system
(no-star = E, five-star = deluxe),
although this is being resisted by
hoteliers. Although the current
letters are supposed to accurately
reflect the hotels' amenities, a
conference hall, swimming pool or
tennis court could place an
establishment in the A or B bracket
even though in every other respect it
has indifferent facilities. Also, the
number of rooms can limit the
maximum rating, so you commonly
encounter 14-room C-class hotels
which are superior in every respect
to a nearby 50-room B-class.

The following general principles
apply though: Luxury, A-, B- and C-
class hotels all have private bathrooms. Most D-class hotels have en-
suite bathrooms, while the dwindling
number of E-class hotels don't.

Luxury and A-class hotels must
have a bar and restaurant and offer a
full choice of breakfasts. B- and C-
class should provide a buffet
breakfast in a separate dining room,
but classes below that will often offer
little better than a bread roll, jam and
coffee, if that.

Luxury and A-class hotels should
have some or all of these auxiliary
facilities: a swimming pool, fitness
centre, "private" beach, conference
hall, internet access from the rooms
and/or Wi-fi signal, 24-hour desk
attendance, reliable taxi service.

Mountain Refuges

Mountain refuges are run by the
various Greek mountaineering clubs
and can range from a small 12-bed ski
hut where you need to bring your own
food and supplies to 100-bed lodges
where all meals are provided. There
are over 40 of them, but very few are
permanently staffed – most conspicuously, two on Mt Olympus, one in
Zagóri and one in Crete's White
Mountains – and getting the key for the
others from the controlling club is
generally more trouble than it's worth.

Monastery Stays

Monasteries and convents can
occasionally provide lodging for
travellers, though their *xenónes*
(guest lodges) are intended primarily
for Orthodox pilgrims. Mt Áthos, of
course, has a long tradition of this
hospitality (for men only). If you have
found a monastery that does accept
overnight guests, you will have to
dress and behave appropriately. The
doors may close as early as sunset
and some kind of donation may be
expected.

Youth Hostels

Greece has a limited (and steadily
dwindling) number of official, YHA-
affiliated youth hostels for which you
theoretically need a youth hostel card.
However, you can often buy a card on
the spot or just pay an additional
charge for the night, so it's not worth
buying a YHA card in advance.

There are surviving hostels in
Athens, Olymbía and Thessaloníki, and
on Santoríni plus Crete at Iráklio, Sitía,
Réthymno, and Plakiás. There is also
private, unaffiliated backpacker
accommodation of varying quality and

repute in Athens and on numbers of islands such as Náxos and Corfu.

Traditional Settlements

Traditional settlements *(paradosiakí ikismí)* are villages that have been recognised by the Greek government as forming an important part of the national heritage and have been protected from modern intrusions and constructions by law. Buildings in these villages were variably restored under NTOG initiative as tourist inns back in the 1970s and 1980s.

Almost all of these inns have been sold off and are now in private hands, although still protected by law. Private renovators have moreover brought other, generally higher-quality inns into service. Such houses and villages are, in their different ways, strikingly beautiful, and highly recommended for a long retreat in rural Greece.

Restoration inns are known to exist in the following villages, and more are appearing all the time:

Areópolis, Inner Máni (tower houses)
Monemvasiá, Peloponnese (several restoration inns)
Ýdra (Hydra) Town (several sponge-captains' mansions, now hotels)
Ía, Santorini (interlinked village houses)
Mestá, Híos (several restored houses, as room-only or entire apartments)
Kámbos region, Híos (several restored mansions, usually with restaurant on-site)

Réthymno, Crete (several old Venetian mansions converted into hotels)
Pediná, Áno (two restoration inns)
Makrynítsa, Pílio (a half-dozen mansions, on a room-only basis)
Vyzítsa, Pílio (a half-dozen mansions, of a higher standard than Makrynítsa)
Pápingo, Megálo/Mikró, Zagória (at least 10 mansions, high standard rooms)
Koukoúli, Zagória (two restoration inns)
Vítsa, Zagória (two restoration inns)
Kípi, Zagória (two restoration inns)
Tsepélovo, Zagória (restoration inns)
Galaxídi, near Delphi (restoration inns)
Nymféo, Macedonia (three deluxe restoration inns)
Rhodes Old Town (several high-quality, and expensive, restoration inns)
Haniá, Crete (many fine restoration inns around the old harbour)
Gialós and **Horió**, Sými (several old houses restored and divided into apartments)
Corfu (three restored olive mills or manor-houses in remote locations)

For a selection of the above, refer to the particular region in the listings on the following pages.

Camping

Large numbers of visitors to Greece rough it in one form or another. This can range from sleeping on the deck of ferries overnight to bringing a tent and setting up camp by a secluded beach.

Those who want to stay at organised campsites will find them

all over Greece; these are all privately owned.

The most beautiful campsites in Greece, however, are usually ones you find on your own. While in most places it is officially illegal just to lay out your sleeping bag or pitch a tent, if you're discreet you will rarely be bothered. That always means asking permission from the owners if you seem to be on private property, avoiding unofficial campsites set up in popular tourist areas (which can get pretty squalid), and leaving the place looking better than it did when you came.

In the mountains camping is the rule as few alpine refuges are staffed *(see page 330)*, but even here you should get the local shepherds' consent if they're around, as you may be turfing down in the middle of a prime grazing site.

ATHENS

Acropolis View
Webster 10 and Robértou Gáli
Tel: 210 921 7303
www.acropolisview.gr
The implied view of the Acropolis is available from only a few of the 32 rooms, but also from the roof terrace. Rooms themselves are small but clean and well cared for, and the hotel had the inevitable pre-Olympic makeover. The location is excellent with nearby metro. **€€**

Airotel Alexandros
Timoléontos Vássou 8
Tel: 210 643 0464
Fax: 210 644 1084
www.airotel.gr
Located on a private crescent behind a chapel

which helps shield it from busy Vassilísis Sofías, this hotel offers comfortable accommodation. The high-ceilinged lounge is flanked by a brick-and-pastel-panelled breakfast room, doubling later in the day as the Don Giovanni restaurant. Most fair-sized rooms have good firm beds, and deep balconies which ensure privacy; bathrooms are small but marble-clad. Free off-street parking, Wi-fi. **€€**

Best Western Museum
Bouboulínas 16
Tel: 210 523 8038
Fax: 210 523 1548
www.hotelsofathens.com
Since acquisition by the Best Western chain, the

Museum has had its original rooms redone and a new wing of larger units added. Standard rooms are on the small side with the feel of an American hotel, but the junior suites are spacious and their bathrooms a notable improvement on the standards. Executive suites have marble-clad bathrooms. No restaurant; breakfast served in the slightly-below-ground-level bar. **€€**

Cecil
Athinás 39
Tel: 210 321 7079
Fax: 210 321 8005
www.cecil.gr
A well-restored 1850s vintage mansion has become a characterful

small hotel, right down to its iron-cage, inter-war lift. The rooms only have ornamental balconies but do offer parquet floors, iron bedsteads, double glazing and tiled bathrooms. Common areas are limited to a breakfast room with its original wooden floor and painted ceiling, and a street-level café. **€**

PRICE CATEGORIES

Price categories are based on the cost of a double room for one night in the high season.
€ = under €60
€€ = €60–110
€€€ = over €110

TRANSPORT

ACCOMMODATION

EATING OUT

ACTIVITIES

A – Z

LANGUAGE

ABOVE: inside the Grande Bretagne

Grande Bretagne
Sýndagma Square
Tel: 210 333 0000
Fax: 210 332 8034
www.grandebretagne.gr
Expensive and plush in its own special way, the Grande Bretagne is the doyen of Athenian hotels. Recently refurbished, this historic building oozes class, from its luxurious rooms, to its beautiful spa, to its highly recommended restaurant. €€€€

Hera
Falírou 9
Tel: 210 923 6682
www.herahotel.gr
Yet another result of the wave of pre-Olympic upgradings, the Hera has perhaps the best roof-garden in this neighbour-hood, with (unusually) a heated bar-restaurant for all-year operation. Rooms are on the small side but have everything you would expect in this (A) class;

fifth-floor suites have bigger balconies; bathrooms are much the same throughout. The dome-lit atrium-breakfast room and friendly staff are further assets. €€

Hermes
Apóllonos 19
Tel: 210 323 5514
Fax: 210 322 2412
www.hermeshotel.gr
The Hermes has all-marble bathrooms, variable in size, and oak-effect-floored rooms – which also vary: front-facing ones are smaller but benefit from a terrace (due to be partitioned into private spaces); rear rooms are larger, some with sofas. The breakfast room is decorated with group manager Dorina Stathopoulou's professional photographs of the 2004 Olympics. If they're full, you'll be offered space in one of their three affiliated hotels

nearby. Closed Christmas–mid-March. €€

Marble House
A. Zínni 35, Koukáki
Tel: 210 922 8294/923 4058
Fax: 210 922 6461
www.marblehouse.gr
This inexpensive, clean and friendly hotel is probably the best deal in Athens. Close to the Syngroú-Fix metro. Some rooms have air conditioning (the others have powerful ceiling fans) and breakfast is available for an extra charge. It has been done up recently and the prices remain low for the city. €

Orion/Dryades
Emmanuíl Benáki 105/Dryádon 4
Tel: 210 330 2387
Fax: 210 380 5193
Email: orion-dryades@mail.com
These co-managed, almost adjacent hotels (joint reception in the Orion) serve a youngish crowd who've outgrown hostels but still take advantage of the self-catering kitchens in each well-maintained building (the Orion's has a particularly stunning city view). Washbasins only in the Orion's rooms; the pricier Dryades is fully en-suite, though its wood-panelled rooms are a little on the gloomy side. Some units have balconies with views. €

Periscope
Háritos 22
Tel: 210 729 7200
Fax: 210 729 7206
www.periscope.gr
Unlike many Athens hotels, the lounge and common areas here are minimal as well as minimalist: the focus is instead on the

black-, white- and grey-toned rooms aimed at a business clientele. Aerial photos of the city comprise the wall and ceiling art, along with real-time projections of the skyline relayed by... a periscope! The higher in the building you go, the better, as it culminates in airy suites with balconies and a rooftop jacuzzi. All units have wood floors, flat-screen TVs, CD/DVD players and a choice of pillows. €€€

St George Lycabettus
Kleoménous 2, Kolonáki
Tel: 210 729 0711
Fax: 210 729 0439
www.sglycabettus.gr
Since its pre-Olympic refit, the St George now styles itself as a "boutique hotel". The cool, comfortable rooms and suites are elegant and subdued, and the rooftop pool is a delight. The external (more expensive) rooms have one of the best views in the city. Two good restaurants, one with a view over the Acropolis. €€€

YHA
Victor Hugo 16
Tel: 210 523 2540
Fax: 210 523 2540
www.hihostels.com
A very cheap and well-maintained place to stay close to Omónia Square, the railway stations and the National Museum. The four- or twin-bedded rooms are clean, and the in-house travel service offers discount tickets. Other facilities include a kitchen and luggage store. €

PELOPONNESE

Areópoli

Pyrgos Kapetanakou
Tel: 27530 51479
This three-storey tower is one of the better executed EOT restoration projects. It is set in a pleasant walled garden, and comprises rooms of various sizes. There are communal balconies, and also a ground-floor refectory. €€

Arhéa Kórinthos

Shadow
Approach road
Tel: 27410 31481
The rear rooms at this simple inn are the best, with good views over the lush plain. There is usually some noise from the restaurant's live music at weekends, so try to get a room some distance away. €

Diakoftó

Chris-Paul Hotel
Tel: 26910 41715
Fax: 26910 42128
www.chrispaul-hotel.gr
Named after the family's two children, this small, friendly and spotlessly clean hotel is conveniently situated for the start of the journey up through the Vouraïkós Gorge. €€

Dimitsána

Xenonas Kazakou
Tel: 27950 31660
www.xenonaskazakou.gr
Externally austere, this stone-and-wood mansion from 1853 is discreetly comfortable inside – with central heating for the chilly mountain winters. Situated near the top of the village, it's very quiet, apart from

church bells on Sunday. A rich traditional breakfast, including *loukoumádes*, is served in the cellar. €€

Giálova

Helonaki
Tel/fax: 27230 23080
Email: helonaki@panafonet.gr
Very hospitable small hotel, with a very popular restaurant underneath (so not for light sleepers). Fabulous sea-views over Navarino Bay. Rooms have a fridge. €

Gýthio

Aktaion
Vassiléos Pávlou 39
Tel: 27330 23500
Fax: 27330 22294
Refurbished neoclassical pile at the north end of the quay; some traffic noise, but all balconied rooms have sea view and air conditioning. €€

Kalamáta

Haïkos Hotel
Navarínou 115
Tel: 27210 88902
www.haikos .gr
Friendly staff and good-sized rooms in this modern hotel on the seafront. €€
Iviskos Hotel
Fáron 196
Tel: 27210 62511
Fax: 27210 82323
Set in one of Kalamáta's neoclassical buildings and lovingly cared for. Just seven rooms. €€

Kalávryta

Filoxenia Hotel
Ethnikís Andistásis 20
Tel: 26920 22422
Fax: 26920 23009
www.hotelfiloxenia.gr
Traditional hospitality and efficient service. One of the main hotels for the ski season on Mt Helmós. €€

Koróni

Auberge de la Plage
Zánga Beach
Tel: 27250 22401
Fax: 27250 22042
www.delaplage.gr
No prizes for its 1970s modernist architecture, but

the setting overlooking sand and sea is incomparable. €€

Kosmás

Xenonas Maleatis Apollo
Tel: 27570 31494
Another place to escape some of the summer's heat, this traditional guesthouse is 1,150 metres (3,775 ft) up in a delightful village on Mt Párnon. A great base for touring this remote part of Arkadía. Simple rooms; some kitchen facilities. €€

Monemvasiá

Lazareto
Tel: 27320 61991
Fax: 27320 61992
Email: lazaretohotel@yahoo.com
At the foot of the Monemvasiá rock, overlooking the causeway, the stone-walled ruins of the old hospital have been converted into a discreetly luxurious hotel with a good restaurant. €€€
Malvasia
Tel: 27320 63007
Fax: 27320 63009
www.malvasia-hotel.gr
The scattered units of this complex are some of the best in town. Each room, well furnished in wood and marble, is unique, with features such as fireplaces and balconies. Unit size varies from simple doubles to an apartment. €€€

Mykínes (Mycenae)

La Belle Hélène
Main road
Tel: 27510 76225
Fax: 27510 76179
Reasonable, with the feel of an English country B&B (conservation rules mean no en-suite bathrooms). The archaeologist Schliemann lived here while excavating Mycenae, and the restaurant has celebrity signatures in its guestbook. €

Návplio

Ilion Hotel and Apartments
Evthimiopoúlou 4/Kapodistríou 6
Tel: 27520 22010
Fax: 27520 24497
www.ilionhotel.gr
Spectacularly decorated rooms and suites, some

self-catering, on the slope below the Acronavplía. €€€
Marianna Pension
Potamaníou 9
Tel: 27520 24256
Fax: 27520 99365
www.pensionmarianna.gr
A beautifully refurbished *pension*, tucked in under the walls of the Akronavplía fortress. Breakfast terrace has wonderful views. €€
Nafplia Palace
Akronavplía
Tel: 27520 70800
Fax: 27520 28783
www.nafplionhotels.gr
Low-key but luxurious, set inside the walls of the Akronávplia fortress, and with fabulous views out across the sea to Boúrtzi island. Standard rooms, villas, plus conference facilities and a spa. €€€

Néos Mystrás

Byzantion
Tel: 27310 83309
Fax: 27310 20019
Email: byzanhtl@otenet.gr
Most rooms at this hotel offer an unbeatable view of the Byzantine ruins. Most bathrooms have full-sized tubs. €€

Olympía (Olympia)

Hercules
Tel: 26240 22696
Fax: 26240 23035
www.hotelhercules.gr
Quiet location near the church for this welcoming place; simple rooms, a pleasant breakfast hall, off-street parking and Wi-fi. €

Pátra

Byzantino
Riga Feréou 106
Tel: 26102 43000
Fax: 26106 22150
www.byzantino-hotel.gr
A beautifully decorated, high-class hotel, near the centre of town in a neoclassical refurbishment. Conference facilities; open all year. €€€
Galaxy
Agíou Nikoláou 9
Tel: 26102 75981
Fax: 26102 78815
www.galaxyhotel.com.gr
A hospitable designer hotel, on a pedestrianised street

at the very heart of the city. Some street noise from Pátra's trendiest street cafés and bars. €€€

Spárti

Cecil
Paleológou 125
Tel: 27310 24980
Fax: 27310 81318
Near the main street, this small hotel is well placed for both Spárti's archaeology and city life. Informative and friendly management. €€

Stoúpa

Lefktron
Tel: 27210 77322
www.lefktron-hotel.gr
Well sited hotel in the centre of the resort, 5 minutes' walk from the beach. Comfortable rooms, friendly management, and pool. €€

Taýgetos

Touristiko Taïgetou
Selibovés, the pass between Kalamáta and Spárti
Tel: 27210 99236
Fax: 27210 98198
A high-altitude refuge (1,375 metres/4,500 ft), at the hub of numerous tracks leading into the mountains. The restaurant provides both views over alpine fir forest and 2,000-metre (6,500-ft) peaks and tasty home-cooking. Open all year. €

Vytína

Art Mainálon
Areos Square
Tel: 27950 22217
www.artmainalon.gr
Elegant hotel, wood-trimmed inside and out, with suitably rustic stone cladding. Busiest during winter (small ski centre nearby), but also lovely in summer as it overlooks what's left of Mt Mainálon's fir forest. €€€

PRICE CATEGORIES

Price categories are based on the cost of a double room for one night in the high season:
€ = under €60
€€ = €60–110
€€€ = over €110

CENTRAL GREECE

Ágios Ioánnis

Anesis
Shore road
Tel: 24260 31123
Fax: 24260 31223
www.hotelanesis.gr
One of the first hotels here,
renovated in the 1990s,
and one of the few still
welcoming walk-in trade;
civilised management
presides over tasteful
rooms in pastel shades. €€

Aráhova

Lykoreia
West edge of town
Tel: 22670 32132
www.lykoria.com.gr
Huge standard balconied
doubles, plus suites, have
emerged from a 2007 refit
with designer bathrooms.
Common amenities include
a terrace garden, pool, gym/
sauna, Wi-fi signal and
buffet breakfast served in a
somewhat dark salon; easy
(for Aráhova) parking. €€€
Xenonas Generali
Eastern outskirts, below the
primary school and clocktower
Tel: 226 703 1529
www.generalis-xenon.com
A restoration inn offering the
best standard in town: nine
rooms, all different (most
with fireplace), the decor of
which can be a bit garish,
but the welcome is warm
and the breakfasts are
calorifically "enhanced"
during ski season, when a
pool, spa, hamam and
sauna also operate. €€€

Argalastí

Agamemnon
Village centre
Tel/fax: 24230 54557
www.agamemnon.gr

Another restored mansion,
with exposed stonework
and fireplaces in the
rooms, antiques in the
common areas and a large
pool outside – a good base
in the south of the
peninsula. €€

Aspropótamos

**Pyrgos Mantania
(Mantania Tower)**
Near Kalliroe village
Tel: 24320 87351
www.mantania-ae.gr
A superb stone-built inn,
poised to take advantage
of river-kayaking and forest-
walking aficionados who
visit this area. Families are
catered for in the upstairs
4-bedded suites with
fireplaces, plus the five
newer units by the pool;
cheaper but still large
standard rooms on the
lower floors. Well-regarded
restaurant-bar in a separate
building. €€

Damoúhari

Damouhari Hotel
Centre bay
Tel: 24260 49840
Fax: 24260 49841
Part of this mock-trad,
stone-built studio complex
can be monopolised by
package companies, but
the bayside annexe, with
five state-of-the-art rooms
over the restaurant, is kept
back for walk-ins. You still
have access to the hillside
pool, and the eclectically
decorated bar. €€

Delfí (Delphi)

Pan
Vassiléon Pávlou and Frederíkis 53
Tel: 22650 82294

Fax: 22650 83244
An excellent mid-range hotel,
with plain doubles but
excellent family suites with
large bathtubs. Their 2002-
built annexe across the
road, Artemis, has a higher
standard – most of the
bathrooms have mini-tubs –
but you sacrifice the view. €
Sun View
Apóllonos 84
Tel: 22650 82349
Fax: 22650 82815
Email: dalentzis@internet.gr
Very quietly located *pension*
on the uppermost street;
rooms are decorated in
pastel shades, with art on
the walls. There's a
breakfast salon downstairs,
and parking outside. €

Galaxídi

Galaxa
Hillside above Hirólakas bay
Tel: 22650 41620
Fax: 22650 42053
Rooms at this restored-
house hotel are somewhat
casually maintained, but the
views are superb and the
welcome friendly. The best
bit is the garden bar, under
the vines across the way,
where breakfast and drinks
are served. €€
Ganimede/Ganymidis
Nikólaou Gourgoúri 20
(southwest market street)
Tel: 22650 41328
Fax: 22650 42160
www.ganimede.gr
Under the energetic
management of Kósta and
Hrysoúla Papaléxis since
2004, this is the clear
winner amongst local
lodging, despite the lack of
sea views. Four refurbished
doubles in the old house
(best is No. 1), with fridges
and satellite TV, and a family
suite with loft and fireplace.
The copious breakfast still
features founder Bruno's
recipes for pâtés and jams,
plus novelty breads from the
bakery. Free Wi-fi signal. €

Kalambáka

Alsos House
Kanári 5
Tel: 24320 24097
www.alsoshouse.gr

This inn at the top of the old
town, near the path up to
Agías Triádos monastery,
has units of doubles, triples
and a quad suite, plus a
well-equipped communal
kitchen. The helpful owner
speaks good English. €

Karpenisiótis Valley

Agrambeli
Gávros
Tel: 22370 41148
www.agrambeli.gr
A riverside *pension* with
cool, cavernous rooms
redone in 2006; there's a
breakfast bar and large
swimming pool in the
middle of the lawn. €
Helidona
Old Mikró Horió
Tel: 22370 41221
www.ihelidona.gr
In a region known for very
pricey lodging, this 2001-
reburbished hotel remains
affordable. Superbly set on
the old *platía* with a ground
floor restaurant; great views
from the rear rooms. €€

Karýtsa

Dóhos Katalymáta
Between Karýtsa and Stómio
Tel: 24950 92001
On the slopes of Mt
Kíssavos, this 2002-built
hotel nestles in the forest
above some of the best and
least visited beaches in
Greece. Huge wood-floored
rooms or suites; all have
sea-facing balconies and full
bathtubs, while some have
cooking facilities. The stone-
floored common areas
include a concert hall,
hosting special events all
summer. Pool. €€

Kastráki

Doupiani House
West edge of village, well-signed
above road to monasteries
Tel: 24320 77555
Fax: 24320 75326
Email: doupiani-house@kmp.forthnet.gr
The in-your-face views of the
rock formations, good air
conditioned rooms, and
Thanássis' and Toúla's
welcome mean you always
have to pre-book here. €

BELOW: Domotel Xenia Volou in Vólos.

Ziogas Rooms
Set well off noisy through road
Tel: 24320 24037
Most of the large balconied
units face onto the rocks.
There is heating for the
winter, and a combination
breakfast salon and taverna
on the ground floor. €

Kastráki Meteóron

Xenonas Sotiriou
Mesohóri Plaza
Tel: 24320 78104
www.guesthouse-sotirou.gr
Stone-built mansion from
1845 – one of the few
buildings that escaped the
Nazis' 1944 reprisal burning
here – restored as a quality
inn. Some rooms have a
fireplace; all have wood
floors and ceilings and
mock-antique furniture. €€

Makrynítsa

Arhondiko Pandora
300 metres/yds below centre
Tel: 24280 99404
www.pandoramansion.gr
Much the best of various
restored mansion-inns here,
redone by an architect/
designer owner of inter-
national repute. Very private,
gated courtyard with a café-
restaurant. €€€

Moúressi

The Old Silk Store
Curve in access road by bakery
Tel/fax: 24260 49086
www.pelionet.gr/oldsilkstore
Nineteenth-century silk-
merchant's mansion lovingly

converted into a B&B by
Cornishwoman Jill Sleeman,
who also leads walks in the
area. Excellent breakfasts
(own-made jams and
wholemeal breads) served
in the idyllic garden. €€

Návpaktos

Akti
Grímbovo, by the fountain-stream
Tel: 26340 28464
Fax: 26340 24171
Email: akti@otenet.gr
This hotel is the town's
clear winner, set behind the
town's easterly beach: it's
the little touches like insect
screens and oblique sea
views from about half the
rooms that make the dif-
ference. Good standard of
breakfast; palatial top-floor
suites. €€
Ilion
Inland at the base of the *kástro*
Tel: 26340 21222
For a stay in the old town,
try this quiet little ten-room
inn – though it's best to be
travelling light, as you're
some way distant from the
nearest parking. €€

Portariá

Kritsa
Central platía
Tel: 24280 99121
Fax: 24280 90006
www.hotel-kritsa.gr
Taste is the keyword here,
transforming an indifferent,
interwar hotel building into
something worth going out
of your way for. It has just
eight rooms (some of them

suites), four with balconies
and views over the square.
The massive breakfast puts
to shame bog-standard
continentals offered at the
same price elsewhere. €€

Potistiká

Elytis
On slope above the beach
Tel/fax: 24230 54482
If you just want a seaside
holiday without cultural
distractions, this is probably
the best place on Pílio to do
it: a pristine, undeveloped
bay, and this welcoming, if
bland-roomed hotel just
inland, with an attached full-
service restaurant. €

Tsangaráda

Konaki
Agía Paraskeví district, below the
through highway
Tel: 24260 49481
All rooms here have fridges
and views of some sort,
some have iron beds and
balconies. NIce basement
breakfast area. €€

Vólos

Domotel Xenia Volou
Plastíra 1
Tel: 24210 92700
www.xeniavolou.gr
A 1960s ugly duckling
transformed into a swan in
2006. Great position in
secluded seafront gardens
(half the rooms do face
inland). Pool, spa, fitness
centre and abundant
breakfasts. €€€

Roussas
Iatroú Tzánou 11
Tel: 24210 21732
Fax: 24210 22987
At the east end of the
seafront, this is the city's
best budget hotel, under-
rated at E-class – a bargain.
Well kept en-suite rooms,
and free parking nearby,
though no breakfast. €

Vyzítsa

Kondou
Up the slope from the car park
Tel: 24230 86793
A good standard of
restored accommodation
(dating from 1792) on two
floors, at an affordable
price; mind your head on
the low doorframes.
€€
Thetis
By the church and central car park
Tel: 24230 86111
Maybe not the grandest
restored *arhondikó* here,
but popular, thanks to its
kafenío (serving breakfast)
and excellent value. A mix
of wood-trimmed rooms,
both en-suite and not. €

Zagorá

Arhondiko Gayani
Tel: 24260 23391
Fax: 24260 22671
www.villagayannis.gr
One of the few surviving
18th-century mansions in
the north of Pílio. Well-
converted rooms, spacious
common areas (including
the courtyard) and a good
buffet breakfast. €€

EPIRUS

Ano Pediná

Porfyron
Tel: 265 307 1579
www.profyron.com
Lovely antique-furnished
rooms in a restored
mansion with painted/
carved ceilings, plus a big
garden with arbour and
parasols. The taverna,
showcasing organic fare, is
open to all. The inn is
frequently booked by walking
groups; your best chance
on-spec is high summer. €€

Elati

Iy Elati
Village centre
Tel: 26530 61492
Fax: 26530 71181
A bit away from the heart of
the national park, but that
means you're more likely to
happen on a vacancy, and
there are stunning views of
Mt Gamíla from the outdoor
terrace. The manager is
returned Greek-Canadian;
the restaurant is
competent. €€

Ioánnina

Kastro
Androníkou Paleológou 57
Tel: 26510 22866
Fax: 26510 22780
www.epirus.com/hotel-kastro
Small, cosy restoration inn
on the way to the inner
citadel, with seven varied
rooms (ground-floor ones,
with fans but no air-con,
are a tad cheaper).
Limited street parking;
open all year.
€€

Orizon/Horizon
Lykiades village, 12km out of town
Tel: 26510 86180
www.hotel-horizon.gr
Stunning views over the
entire lake valley from this

PRICE CATEGORIES

Price categories are based
on the cost of a double
room for one night in the
high season:
€ = under €60
€€ = €60–110
€€€ = over €110

well-designed hotel, refurbished in 2007. Rooms vary but are all huge with wood floors, some with fireplaces. Very popular with Greek weekenders, so mandatory to reserve. €€

Politeia
Anexartisías 109A
Tel: 26510 22235
www.etip.gr
Studio-hotel on the site of an old tradesmen's hall. Though units including big upstairs suites are self-catering, breakfast is offered in the courtyard. Pretty quiet, despite the location; open all year. €€

Karavostási

Karavostasi Beach
Back from the middle of the beach
Tel: 26650 91104
Fax: 26650 91568
www.hotel-karavostasi.gr
Well designed beach hotel with large pool, well-kept gardens and decent breakfasts. The rooms are all-white spartan, but perfectly adequate. Open end May–early Oct. €€

Kónitsa

Grand Hotel Dentro
On town access road from main highway
Tel: 265 502 9366
www.grandhoteldentro.gr
The best facilities offered within town limits; standard

doubles have good bathrooms, and sometimes balconies, while top floor suites offer fireplaces and hydromassage tubs. On-site restaurant. €€–€€€

Métsovo

Bitouni
Main street
Tel: 26560 41217
Fax: 26560 41545
www.hotelbitouni.com
Luxurious digs managed by English-speaking brothers who spent many years in London. Most rooms have balconies, plus there are attic family suites and a sauna for the ski season. €

Filoxenia
Near the central plaza
Tel: 26560 41021
Fax: 26560 42009
An excellent-value inn on the side of the square. Comfortable rooms in two grades; the rear ones have stunning views. €

Pápingo (Megálo)

Nikos Tsoumanis
Village centre
Tel: 26530 42237
www.tsoumanisnikos.gr
Attached to the namesake restaurant, these seven units built in traditional style are comfortable if a bit dark. Beds with down duvets. €€

Papaevangelou
North end of the village
Tel: 26530 41135
Fax: 26530 41988
www.papaevangelou.gr
The best traditional-style inn here, with enormous rooms (some self-catering), and equally spacious bar, where the better-than-average breakfast is served. Friendly, willing management. €€€

Pension Koulis
Behind central *kafenío*
Tel: 26530 41138
The original village inn, converted in 1993 to en-suite rooms; Koulis himself has retired and sons Níkos and Dimítris are now at the helm. €

Pápingo (Mikró)

O Dias
Tel: 26530 41257
Fax: 26530 41892
An excellent renovation inn spread over two traditional buildings, bracketing a terrace restaurant and a bar. The proprietor is particularly trekker-friendly and helpful, as mountaineering is the main enterprise hereabouts. €€

Párga

Golfo Beach
Kryonéri beach
Tel: 26840 32336

Fax: 26840 31347
The diametric opposite of Magda's *(below)*: a slice of 1970s Greece, the oldest inn at Párga. Rooms are basic, about half en-suite. Half of them face the sea, the others a pleasant garden. Good restaurant downstairs. Open May–Oct. €

Magda's Apartments
Below road to Agiá
Tel: 26840 31728
Fax: 26840 31690
www.magdas-hotel.com
The best standard within the town: several ranks of self-catering studios and superior apartments in an olive grove, with a bar, spa and pool terrace. There is some package allotment, so book early; open Greek Easter–late Oct. €€

Tsepélovo

Anthoula Gouri
East side of village
Tel: 26530 81214/81288
Mobile: 694 7561 463 for English
Run by Anthoúla and daughter María, this welcoming en-suite inn has long been popular with walkers in the region, thanks to the late Alékos Goúris' efforts to promote local trekking. If you're offered half board, it is advisable to accept it, as the *platía* tavernas are very average. €

THESSALONIKI

ABC Hotel
Angeláki 41
Tel: 2310 265421
Fax: 2310 276542
www.hotelabc.gr
Very handy for the Thessaloníki Annual Fair, this east side business hotel is smartly functional, sporting renovated rooms with most mod cons for a mid-range hotel. €€

Best Western Vergina
Monastiríou 19
Tel: 2310 516021
Fax: 2310 529308
www.vergina-hotel.gr
Part of the Best Western chain, the Vergina is very

close to the port and the train station. Comfortable, businesslike and similar to other hotels in the chain. €€

Bristol Capsis
Oplopioú and Katoúni 2
Tel: 23105 06500
Fax: 23105 15777
www.capsishotel.gr
Perhaps Thessaloníki's most sumptuous boutique hotel. Sixteen individually named rooms, each immaculately restored, in the shell of the former Bristol Hotel. €€€

Capsis Hotel
Monastiríou 18
Tel: 2310 596800
Fax: 2310 510555

www.capsishotel.gr
This modern city-centre hotel offers all the expected luxury facilities including a roof garden, gym swimming pool and sauna. €€€

Electra Palace
Plateía Aristotélous 9
Tel: 2310 294011
Fax: 2310 294001
www.electrahotels.gr
Another central hotel, overlooking the broad Platía Aristotélous. Neoclassical facade, very imposing and very comfortable. €€€

Hotel Alexandria
Egnatía 18
Tel: 2310 536185

Fax: 2310 536154
A good budget choice from among the many cheapies at the western end of Egnatía. The management is a bit sullen, but the rooms are very decent. €

Kinissi Palace
Egnatías 41 and Syngroú
Tel: 23105 08082
Fax: 23105 23904
www.kinissipalace.gr
A renovated city-centre hotel retaining its original style and atmosphere. Rooms are large and airy with double glazing; there's also a small sauna and massage centre. €€€

ABOVE: the Electra Palace.

Le Palace
Tsimiskí 12
Tel: 2310 257400
Fax: 2310 221270
www.lepalace.gr
Another central hotel in an old (1926) building. Fully renovated in 2002, Le Palace has a style reminiscent of Paris in the 1930s. Has a relaxing in-house cafeteria called the Deli Deli. €€

Luxembourg
Komninón 6
Tel: 2310 252600
Fax: 2310 252605

www.hotelluxembourg.gr
In the heart of the commercial district, this hotel is vaguely Art Deco in style. Rooms are standard but comfortable enough. €€

Makedonia Palace
Megálou Alexándrou 2
Tel: 2310 897197
Fax: 2310 897211
www.classichotels.com
A short way south of the White Tower is another landmark luxury hotel that draws many business travellers and VIPs. Oozes distinguished class. €€€

Mediterranean Palace
Salamínos 3 and Karatásou
Tel: 2310 552554
Fax: 2310 552622
www.mediterranean-palace.gr
You can't get closer to the port or the Ladádika district than with this imposing Belle Epoque hotel. Large, lavishly furnished rooms and airy public areas. €€€

Minerva Premier
Egnatías 44 and Syngroú 12
Tel: 2310 566440
Fax: 2310 566436
www.minervapremier.gr
Built within a 1929 neo-classical building, the hotel's standard rooms are

comfortable, its business rooms mini-offices. Lots of marble, crystal, wood. €€€

Orestias Kastoria
Agnóstou Stratiótou 14
Tel: 2310 276517
Fax: 2310 276572
Of all the budget choices, this one stands out from the others. Away from the noise of Egnatía, this hotel, in a neoclassical building, has light, clean and airy rooms that are very presentable. €

Philippeion Hotel
Dásos Séich-Soú
Tel: 2310 203320
Fax: 2310 218528
www.philippion.gr
Outside the city centre, in the Séih-Soú forest. Good views down to the city, more than comfortable rooms and a free shuttle bus service to/from the centre. €€€

Tourist Hotel
Mitropóleos 21
Tel: 2310 270501
Fax: 2310 226865
www.touristhotel.gr
A comfortable mid-range hotel with standard-sized and reasonably well appointed rooms. Very central. €€

The Tobacco Hotel
25 Agiou Dimitriou
Tel: 2310 515002
Fax: 2310 530711
www.davitel.gr
A fairly central, modern hotel in one of the city's oldest tobacco houses, the 57 rooms are furnished in smoky brown tobacco tones. Modern facilities, including a business centre. €€

Panórama

Hotel Panorama
Analípseos 26
Tel: 2310 344871
Fax: 2310 344872
www.hotelpanorama.gr
A 1970s renovated hotel in the hills above Thessaloníki, the Panorama is good for travellers with transport. Comfortable rooms and panoramic views. €€€

Nefeli
Komninón 1
Tel: 2310 342002
Fax: 2310 342080
Email: nepheli@otenet.gr
Another good, out-of-town choice. Pretty roof garden, splendid views. comfortable rooms and good restaurant. €€€

MACEDONIA AND THRACE

Alexandroúpoli

Thraki Palace
4 km (2½ miles) along Alexandroúpoli-Thessaloníki road
Tel: 25510 89100
Fax: 25510 89119
www.thrakipalace.gr
One of several up-market hotels that have blossomed recently in Alexandroúpoli. A little out of the city centre for travellers without transport, but self-contained and with its own private beach. A nicely designed place with well thought-out public areas, restaurant and bar. €€€

Amoulianí

Agioníssi Resort
1½ km (1 mile) from the port
Tel: 23770 51102
Fax: 23770 51180
www.agionissiresort.com
Top-class accommodation

in this low-key bungalow-style island resort. Built amphitheatrically close to a sandy beach, the individual bungalows are spacious and well-appointed, with local furnishing touches from Halkidikí. There's a pool and manicured garden, and a private ferry service to and from the Athos coastline opposite. €€

Arnéa

Oikia Alexandrou
Platía Patriárhou Vartholoméou 1st
Tel: 23720 23210
Fax: 2310 227767
www.oikia-alexandrou.gr
A family home turned into a boutique *pension*. The immaculately decorated interior features cosy, wood-floored rooms with all modern conveniences. The bar-cum-restaurant

downstairs serves up wholesome Macedonian dishes and in winter there is a welcoming log fire. €€€

Dadiá

Ecotourism Hostel
1 km (½ mile) beyond Dadiá village
Tel: 25540 32263
Fax: 25540 32463
www.ecoclub.com/dadia
Run by the Visitors' Centre for WWF's Dadiá Wildlife Refuge, each of the simply furnished en-suite rooms has been named after birds that frequent the Dadiá Forest. This is the best place to stay if you want to get up early to see the raptors soaring and feeding in the Refuge, an hour's brisk uphill hike deep into the forest. There are a couple of decent tavernas in the village. €

Édessa

Varósi
Arhieréos Meletíou 45-47
Tel: 23810 21865
Fax: 23810 28872
Tucked away in the back streets of the town's Ottoman quarter, this faithfully refurbished old home is now an inexpensive, cosy boutique *pension*. The modern yet traditional-styled rooms are wooden-floored and stone-walled. Enormous optional breakfast in the fireplace-equipped dining/sitting area. €

PRICE CATEGORIES

Price categories are based on the cost of a double room for one night in the high season:
€ = under €60
€€ = €60–110
€€€ = over €110

Kastoriá

Aíolis
Agíou Athanasíou 30
Tel: 24670 21070
Closer to the centre of town than the Arhondikó tou Vérgoula, a delightful restored German-style mansion, once used as a consulate. A neat boutique hotel, with lavishly furnished rooms and all the expected mod cons. There is a welcoming cafeteria and bar. €€
Arhondikó tou Vérgoula
Aidístras 14
Tel: 24670 23415
Fax: 24670 23676
A converted old mansion on the quiet side of town. Ideal for a weekend getaway, the old-fashioned rooms in this mansion simply ooze old-world style. There is a large yet homely breakfast room and wine bar downstairs. €€

Kavála

Hotel Nefeli
Erythroú Stavroú 50
Tel: 2510 227441
Fax: 2510 227440
www.nefeli.com.gr
For a town not noted for its hotel accommodation, this one breaks the rules. Renovated thoroughly in 2002, the Nefeli manages to combine convenience of location (it's very central) with comfort. As a business hotel it provides all the expected amenities. For travellers it's as close as you can get to bus and ferry links onwards. €€

Komotiní

Olympos Hotel
Orféos 37
Tel: 23510 37690
Fax: 25310 37693
www.hotel-olympos.gr

Most of Komotiní's hotels are business-oriented and impersonal. The Olympos is an exception – friendly and welcoming, but modern and up to date after recent renovation. It's very handy for the centre of town and a clutch of good-quality local restaurants. €€

Litóhoro

Villa Pantheon
West end of Litóhoro village
Tel: 23520 83931
Fax: 23520 83932
Claiming possibly the best location in this small base village for Mt Olympus, this is a very pleasant and well-appointed family-style hotel. Rooms are all solidly furnished, with small kitchenettes, minibars, satellite TV and air conditioning. €€

Préspa

Ágios Germanós Hostel
Centre of Ágios Germanós village
Tel: 23850 51357
Fax: 23810 88105
www.prespa.com.gr
In two buildings converted from a stone and wood farmhouse opposite the main church. Ten well equipped and very comfortable rooms, centrally heated, two with working open fireplaces. €€

Xánthi

Hotel Demokritos
28 Oktovríou 41
Tel: 25410 25111
Fax: 25410 25537
In a business-oriented town, the Demokritos has gone to some lengths to make itself appealing to travellers too. All rooms have fridges and TVs (and dedicated ISDN lines). Very central. €€

SARONIC GULF

Aegina

Hotel Brown
Égina Town
Tel: 22970 22271
Fax: 22970 25838
www.hotelbrown.gr
Right on the southern waterfront a five-minute walk from the ferry quay is this converted sponge factory, now a hotel still owned by the original family whose ancestry was partly English (hence the name). Rooms are spacious and tidy and there's a large, leafy garden with bungalow units. €€
To Petrino Spiti
Petrítou 5, Égina Town
Tel: 22970 23837
A three-floored stone house (pétrino spíti) a 10-minute walk from the harbour. Very comfortable and distinctive. There are nine studios all done out in different styles – a couple of them in antique style. €

Angístri

Rosy's Little Village
South end of Skála, at clifftop
Tel: 22970 91610
www.rosyslittlevillage.com

Family-friendly resort with a 1980s feel and basic but adequate pastel-decor rooms, private pebble-strewn lido below, and decent on-site restaurant with a Greek menu despite a largely British clientele. €

Póros

Hotel Manessi
Póros Town
Tel: 22980 22273
Fax: 22980 24345
Email: manessi@otenet.gr
A very pleasant waterfront choice right in the middle of the action. Housed in a neoclassical building, all rooms are well equipped with central heating and air conditioning, TV and fridge, and most have balconies looking over the port. €
Sto Roloi
Hatzopoúlou and Karrá 13,
Póros Town
Tel: 22980 25808
Fax: 210 963 3705
www.storoloi-poros.gr
Sto Roloi ("at the clock") is located near the prominent clock tower on top of the hill behind Póros town, in a 200-year-old house converted

into three apartments, with several more next door at Anemone House and Limeri Residence. All decorated with traditional furnishings. €€€

Salamína

Gabriel
Eándio
Tel: 210 466 2275
Not plush but the best hotel on the island, in the seaside village of Eándio, right by the water. Standard facilities and comfortable enough should you stay on Salamína. €€

Spétses

Armata Boutique Hotel
Inland from Dápia on pedestrian lane
Tel: 22980 72683
Fax: 22980 75403
www.armatahotel.gr
A converted-mansion hotel, opened in 2004, with 20 very plush rooms, copious breakfast and (unusually for the island) a pool. €€€
Economou Mansion
Kounoupítsa shore
Tel: 22980 73400

Fax: 22980 74074
www.spetsesyc.gr/economoumansion.htm
Another restoration inn, occupying part of a vintage (1851) property. The ground floor of the main house has six well converted rooms retaining ample period features; an outbuilding hosts two luxury sea-view suites. Breakfast is served by the fair-sized pool. €€€
Yachting Club Inn
Kounoupítsa
Tel: 22980 73400
Fax: 22980 74074
www.spetsesyc.gr/yachtingclubinn.htm
Under the same management as the Economou, this is a relatively modest lodging in bland modern style which does, however, have good views from the top floor and (unusually) is open all year. €€

Ýdra

Bratsera
200 metres/yds in from centre quay
Tel: 22980 53971
Fax: 22980 53626
www.greekhotel.com/saronic/hydra/bratsera
The island's top choice for

comfort and room size (six grades to choose from here) at this A-class/4-star hotel occupying a former sponge factory. Vast common areas (bar, restaurant, conference room and pool) serve as a de facto museum of the sponge industry with photos and artefacts. €€€

Miranda
Ýdra Town
Tel: 22980 52230
Fax: 22980 53510
www.mirandahotel.gr
Set in a mansion built in 1810, Miranda is a traditional-style hotel with 14 differently decorated rooms, some traditional,

others Art Deco. The classy atmosphere is enhanced by the in-house art gallery. Breakfast is served in the garden. €€

Orloff
Ýdra Town
Tel: 22980 52564
Fax: 22980 53532
www.orloff.gr

A very comfortable mansion turned hotel with all creature comforts. All rooms are individual, in different shapes and sizes. Some look out over the town, others onto the flower-filled courtyard, where a large buffet breakfast is served. €€€

CYCLADES

Amorgós

Aigialis
Órmos Egiális
Tel: 22850 73393
Fax: 22850 73395
www.amorgos-aegialis.com
Modern, comfortable hotel built in tiers on the north hillside beyond the bay, with stunning views. Most rooms (in two grades) have been refurbished since 2006, there's a large outdoor pool and decent restaurant, plus a stunning indoor spa and pool used year-round by the locals – a telling accolade. €€

Pagali Hotel
Langáda
Tel: 22850 73310
Fax: 22850 73368
www.pagalihotel-amorgos.com
Assorted, large, white-decor rooms and studios in one of the more attractive villages on the island, often booked by special-interest groups. A main advantage is an excellent affiliated restaurant next door. €€

Panorama Studios and Pension
Hora
Tel: 22850 74016
http://panorama-studios.amorgos.net
A mix of ordinary doubles and self-catering studios in a commanding position, of a standard one notch up from the normal island decor of Swedish pine furniture and white tiles. €€

Andíparos

Hryssi Akti
Near Kástro
Tel: 222840 61206
Fax: 22840 61170
Elegant hotel with good rooms right on the beach on the east coast. €€

Ándros

Andros Holiday Hotel
Gávrio
Tel: 22820 71384
Fax: 22820 71443
www.androsholidayhotel.com
Overlooking the beach just outside town. Attractive rooms with sea-view terraces, swimming pool, tennis courts and restaurant. €€€

Mare e Vista – Epaminondas
Batsí
Tel: 22820 41682
Fax: 22820 41681
www.mare-vista.com
The island's best hotel, with big rooms and terraces, a large pool, gardens and a garage; 15 minutes' walk from the town, even less to the beach. €€

Niki
Ándros town
Tel/fax: 2282 29155
Opened in 2002, this redone main-street mansion is convenient, elegant and inexpensive. All rooms have balconies, some facing the main street, some the sea. €€

Paradisos
Ándros town
Tel: 22820 22187
www.paradiseandros.gr
An elegant neoclassical mansion near the centre of town, incorporating a walled tennis court and pool. Airy rooms with superb views from the balconies. €€€

Folégandros

Anemomylos
Hóra
Tel: 22860 41309
Fax: 22860 41407
www.anemomilosapartments.com
A fully equipped apartment

complex built in traditional Cycladic style around a courtyard. Stunning views from the balconies over-hanging the cliff edge. €€€

Castro
Hóra
Tel/fax: 22860 41230
www.hotel-castro.com
A 500-year-old traditional house that is actually part of the ancient Kástro walls. Quaint rooms have pebble mosaic floors, barrel ceilings and spectacular views down sheer cliffs to the sea. €

Fani-Vevis
Hóra
Tel: 22860 41282
Comfortable hotel in a neoclassical mansion with antique-furnished rooms overlooking the sea. €€

Íos

Acropolis
Mylopótas
Tel/fax: 22860 91303
Clean, simple rooms with balconies overlooking the beach below. €

Ios Palace
Mylopótas
Tel: 22860 91269
Fax: 22860 91082
Email: iospalas@otenet.gr
Modern hotel near beach designed and decorated in the traditional style. Very comfortable rooms, marble-lined bathrooms, balconies overlooking the sea. €€€

Kéa

Porto Kea Suites
Livádi district, Korissía
Tel: 22880 22870
Fax 22880 22873
www.portokea-suites.com
Well executed bungalow hotel, mimicking local architectural elements with

its stone cladding, arrayed around a pool. The top standard on the island. €€€

Mílos

Kapetan Tassos
Pollónia
Tel: 22870 41287
www.kapetantasos.gr
Designer apartments in traditional blue-and-white island architecture, with good sea views. 11 km (7 miles) from Adamás, so you need transport. €€

Panorama
Klíma
Tel: 22870 21623
Fax: 22870 22112
Small seafront hotel, family-run with friendly service. The owner sometimes takes guests fishing. €

Popi's Windmill
Trypití
Tel: 22870 22286
Fax: 22870 22396
A luxuriously converted windmill with all the amenities of an elegant hotel, plus beautiful views towards Adamás port. Actually two windmills, each with two bedrooms. €€

Mýkonos

Cavo Tagoo
Hóra
Tel: 22890 23692
Fax: 22890 24923
www.cavotagoo.gr
Jet-set luxury on a hillside

PRICE CATEGORIES

Price categories are based on the cost of a double room for one night in the high season:

€ = under €60
€€ = €60–110
€€€ = over €110

500 metres/yds) north of Hóra. Beautiful furnishings, prize-winning Cycladic architecture, impeccable service, friendly atmosphere, good views, pool, and Mykonos' best restaurant. €€€

Deliades
Ornós Beach
Tel: 22890 79430
Fax: 22890 26996
www.hoteldeliadesmykonos.com
Built in 2001 in quiet good taste, a short walk up the hill from Ornós beach. Every room has a big terrace with sea view. Relaxed atmosphere, pool, on-site restaurant. €€€

Myconian Inn
Hóra
Tel: 22890 23420
Fax: 22890 27269
www.myconianinn.com
Right on the upper edge of town, this hotel is convenient, quiet, unpretentious and tasteful. Balconies overlook the port. €€

Villa Konstantin
Ágios Vasílios
Tel: 22890 26204
Fax: 22890 26205
www.villakonstantin.com
700 metres/yds from the town, in authentic island style but with all the luxuries. All units have terraces, most with sea views, some have kitchens and many are suitable for groups or families. €€€

Náxos

Apollon
Hóra
Tel: 22850 22468

Fax: 22850 25200
www.naxostownhotels.com
An efficient, convenient place to stay in town with parking, on the picturesque pedestrian museum square by the cathedral. €€

Chateau Zevgoli
Hóra
Tel: 22850 26123
Fax: 22850 25200
Email: chateau-zevgoli@nax.forthnet.gr
Quiet, plush and exclusive, high up in the old town. A Venetian mansion with only 10 rooms, each lovingly decorated. One has a four-poster bed, most have great views. €€

Páros

Astir of Paros
Náousa, Kolymbíthres beach
Tel: 22840 51986
Fax: 22840 51985
www.astirofparos.com
One of Greece's finest deluxe hotels, right on the beach, across the bay from the town. Spacious rooms with original art and antiques, and bathrooms lined with Parian marble. Large pool, golf course, extensive gardens. €€€

Dina
Parikía
Tel: 22840 21325
Fax: 22840 23525
www.hoteldina.com
Friendly hotel in the heart of the old town. Spotlessly clean rooms around a lovely flowered courtyard. Only eight rooms, book early. €

Pandrossos Hotel
Parikía
Tel: 22840 21394

Fax: 22840 23501
www.pandrossoshotel.gr
On a pretty hill at Parikia's edge, yet in town. Beautiful views of the bay, pool, good restaurant, eclectic pastel rooms. €€

Santoríni

Aigialos Houses
Firá
Tel: 22860 25191
Fax: 22860 22856
www.aigialos.gr
Every house is different in this complex; all are tastefully luxurious, quiet and convenient, and have spectacular views, with balconies or terraces overlooking the caldera. €€€

Atlantis Villas
Ía
Tel: 22860 71214
Fax: 22860 71312
www.atlantisvillas-santorini.com
These traditionally furnished cave-apartments are many white steps down the Ía cliffside. Very friendly, with all services, and caldera views from terrace and pool. €€€

Fanari Villas
Ía
Tel: 22860 71008
www.fanarivillas.com
Traditional *skaftá* cave houses converted into luxury accommodation for up to four people. Pool, breakfast terrace, bar and 240 steps down to Ammoudiá Bay. Attentive, friendly service. €€€

Katikies
Ía
Tel: 22860 71401
www.katikies.com
One of the best on the island. Lovely modern apartments built in traditional style, spectacular views and a wonderful pool. Excellent service. €€€

Theoxenia Hotel
Firá
Tel: 22860 22740
Fax: 22860 22950
www.theoxenia.net
Right on the main cliifside street, this attractive small hotel is friendly and efficient, and has all amenities including a hot tub. Upstairs rooms have caldera views. €€€

Sérifos

Areti
Livádi
Tel: 22810 51479
Fax: 22810 51547
Family-run hotel (and cakeshop) near ferry landing, on a hill with superb views. Peaceful terraced garden overlooking the sea. €€

Sífnos

Apollonia
Apollonía
Tel: 22840 31490
Charming small hotel (only 9 rooms) with traditional island architecture and friendly service. €

Artemon Hotel
Artemónas
Tel: 22840 31303
Fax: 22840 32385
Simple, attractive family hotel. Rooms overlook fields rolling towards the sea. €€

Platis Gialos Hotel
Platýs Gialós
Tel: 22840 71324
Fax: 22840 31325
Large, Cycladic-style hotel at the far end of the beach. Well furnished and tastefully decorated with wood-carvings and wall paintings. The flagstone terrace reaches to the sea. All amenities, including a restaurant with view. €€€

Síkinos

Flora
Aloprónia
Tel: 22860 51214
Simple rooms built around courtyards on the hillside above the port. Great sea views – and most rooms face the sea. 10-minute walk from the beach. €

Kamares
Aloprónia
Tel: 22860 51234
Fax: 22860 51281
Traditional-style, affordable hotel with comfortable rooms. €€

Porto Sikinos
Aloprónia
Tel/fax: 22860 51220
www.portosikinos.gr
The best accommodation on the island: a complex of 18 Cycladic-style buildings right on the beach. Bar and restaurant. €€

BELOW: sea view at the exclusive Cavo Tagoo, Mykonos.

Sýros

Dolphin Bay Hotel
Galissás
Tel: 22810 42924
Fax: 22810 42843
www.dolphin-bay.gr
The largest and most modern resort-hotel on the island, with conference facilities, large swimming pool, restaurant, and beautiful views over the bay.
€€€

Hotel Faros Village
Azólimnos
Tel: 22810 61661
www.faros-hotel.com
Large hotel by the beach, five minutes' drive from the capital, with all the usual facilities including two pools and a restaurant. All rooms have verandas with either sea or garden views. €€€
Omiros
Ermoúpoli
Tel: 22810 24910
Fax: 22810 86266

Email: omirosho@otenet.gr
150-year-old neoclassical mansion restored to a high standard. Rooms furnished in traditional style with views of the lively harbour. €€

Tínos

Alonia
Agía Sofía (3 km/1½ miles towards Pórto)
Tel: 22830 23541
Fax: 22280 23544
www.aloniahotels.gr

Unprepossessing from the outside, this is Tinos' most welcoming hotel. The pool is big and surrounded by greenery, the balconies have beautiful views and the food is good. €€
Tinion
Hóra
Tel: 22830 22261
www.tinionhotel.gr
Charming old-world hotel in the centre of town, with tiled floors, lace curtains and a large verandah cafeteria. €€

RHODES

Andreas
Omírou 28D, Rhodes Old Town
Tel: 22410 34156
Fax: 22410 74285
www.hotelandreas.com
An old favourite under friendly but dynamic new management, this *pension* in an old Turkish mansion was thoroughly refurbished in 2006. En-suite rooms are in a variety of formats (including family-size, and a spectacular tower unit for two). A terrace bar serves evening drinks and excellent breakfasts. Two-night minimum stay. Open all year. €€
Lindian Village
Near Glýstra cove, east coast
Tel: 22440 35900
www.lindianvillage.gr

Formerly indifferent bungalow village thoroughly restored in 2005 to become one of the prime island properties, with a little artificial stream bubbling through it and golf-carts delivering guests and their bags to the units. The better suites have private pool-gardens. Common amenities include two gourmet restaurants, spa/gym and private beach. €€€
Marco Polo Mansion
Agíou Fanouríou 42,
Rhodes Old Town
Tel/fax: 22410 25562
www.marcopolomansion.gr
Superb conversion of an old Turkish mansion; all rooms are en-suite and furnished with antiques

from the nearby eponymous gallery. Large buffet breakfasts included. One-week minimum stay, advance booking required. €€€
Melenos
Líndos, second lane above the north beach, by the school
Tel: 22440 32222
www.melenoslindos.com
No expense has been spared in these 12 exclusive suites with semi-private, *votsalotó* terraces, from the Turkish tiles in the vast bathrooms to the antiques and wooden bed-platforms; there's an equally pricey on-site garden-bar and restaurant. €€€
Miramare Wonderland
Ixiá
Tel: 22410 96251

Fax: 22410 95954
Fake-vernacular bungalows painted in traditional colours, in a landscaped setting just behind the beach. Tasteful mock-antique furnishings and jacuzzis in some tubs. A private mini-railway salvaged from a Welsh mine shuttles guests around the huge grounds. €€€
Niki's
Sofokléous 39, Rhodes Old Town
Tel: 22410 25115
Fax: 22410 36033
www.nikishotel.gr
An excellent budget hotel, most rooms (redone 2006) having balconies and air-con. Helpful management and credit-card acceptance are other bonuses. €

DODECANESE

Astypálea

Restored studios or entire houses up in Hóra are beginning to show their 1980s vintage – despite 2003–5 upgrading – but still make for an atmospheric stay. Prices €–€€ for two people, according to season. Enquire at Kostas Vaïkousis' antique shop on the quay or to reserve tel: 22430 61430 or 69774 77800.

Australia
Skála
Tel: 22430 61067
Rooms and studios in separate blocks, with

phones, fans, air conditioning; good affiliated restaurant. €€
Kilindra Studios
West slope of Hóra
Tel: 22430 61966
Fax: 22430 61131
www.astipalea.com.gr
Mock-traditional units built in 2000 in the shadow of the castle, offering all luxury amenities including a swimming pool; open Apr–Dec. €€€
Venetos Studios
Base of west hillside, Livádia
Tel: 22430 61490
Fax: 22430 61423
Email: venetos@otenet.gr
Units in several buildings scattered across an

orchard; facilities range from basic rooms to four-person apartments. €€

Hálki

Most accommodation is block-booked by package companies from April to October; here are two exceptions.
Captain's House
North of the church and inland
Tel: 22460 45201
Five-room, en-suite *pension* in a converted mansion with garden bar and helpful management. €
Hotel Halki
Emborió
Occupying the old sponge

factory on the south side of the bay, with its own lido, this historic building was gutted and rebuilt in 2007–8 and should offer quality accommodation free of the damp and staffing problems of the past. Contact Vice-Mayor Takis Khrysovergis on tel: 69462 12836 for bookings. €€

PRICE CATEGORIES

Price categories are based on the cost of a double room for one night in the high season:
€ = under €60
€€ = €60–110
€€€ = over €110

Kálymnos

Akroyiali
Massoúri
Tel: 22430 47521 or 69389 13210
Exceptionally tastefully appointed beachside apartments quietly below the road, sleeping two adults and two children. Unsurprisingly they require booking long in advance. €€
Villa Melina
Evangelístria district, Póthia
Tel: 22430 22682
www.villa-melina.com
The town's top choice: en-suite rooms in a 19th-century mansion, plus an annexe of modern studios behind the pool and gardens. Main house refurbished 2006; very good breakfasts served on the patio; open all year. €

Kárpathos

Akrogiali Studios
Potáli bay, Paralía Lefkoú
Tel: 22450 71263
Fax: 22450 71178l
www.lefkos-akrogiali.de
Just eight, spacious units, all with views towards the pebble beach; friendly management, minimarket downstairs for restocking. €
Astro
Ólymbos
Tel: 22450 51421
A good, relatively comfortable en-suite guesthouse in this traditional village, kept by two sisters, who manage the Café Restaurant Zefiros where breakfast is served. €
Atlantis
By the Italian "palace", Pigádia
Tel: 22450 22777
Fax: 22450 22780
www.atlantishotelkarpathos.gr
Helpful, well appointed hotel with quiet setting, easy parking, space held back for non-package travellers and a small pool. €€
Glaros
Diafáni
Tel: 22450 51501
Fax: 22450 51259
www.hotel-glaros.gr
The most comfortable lodgings here, 16 studios on the south hillside, some with four beds. €
Vardes Studios
Amopí beach
Tel: 22450 811111/697 2152901

www.hotelvardes.com
The best standard here among outfits accepting walk-in trade, with huge units overlooking well tended gardens some way inland. Family environment, good breakfasts available. €

Kastellórizo

Karnayo
Platía at west end of the south quay
Tel: 22460 49225
Fax: 22460 49266
Email: karnayo@otenet.gr
The best restoration accommodation on the island, architect-designed. Rooms, studios and a four-bed apartment occupy two separate buildings, with wood-and-stone interiors. €
Kastellorizo Hotel Apartments
West quay
Tel: 22460 49044
www.kastellorizohotel.gr
These air-conditioned, quality-fitted studios or galleried maisonettes, some with sea view, offer the best facilities on the island. Tiny plunge pool, and its own lido in the bay. €€€
Mediterraneo Pension
North end of the west quay
Tel: 22460 49007
www.mediterraneo-kastelorizo.com
Another architect-executed refurbishment, this offers simple but well-appointed rooms with mosquito nets and wall art, half with sea views, plus an arcaded ground-floor suite and optional breakfast with proprietress Marie's homemade marmalade. Unusually, open all year. €€

Kós

Afendoulis
Evrypýlou 1, Kós Town
Tel: 22420 25321
Fax: 22420 25797
www.afendoulishotel.com
Welcoming, family-run C-class hotel: cheerful en-suite rooms with air con and fridges, most with balconies, plus some cooler basement "caves" much sought after in summer. Open Apr–late Oct. Credit cards accepted. €

Alexis
Irodótou 9, Kós Town
Tel: 22420 25594
A backpackers' home-from-home in a villa overlooking the Hellenistic baths. Rooms large, though most not en-suite. Self-catering kitchen and terrace; open late Mar–early Nov. €
Fenareti
Mastihári
Tel: 22420 59028
Fax: 22420 59129
Hillside hotel in the least packaged of Kós's coastal settlements, overlooking the widest part of the beach; rooms and studios in a peaceful garden environment. €
Kos Imperial Thalasso
Psalídi
Tel: 22420 58000
Fax: 22420 25192
www.grecotel.com
One of the premier members of the Grecotel chain, this standard-wing and bungalow hotel with stunning common areas abuts a good beach in landscaped tiers. Individual units are spacious and well-appointed, though not cutting edge. The thalasso-spa is of course the heart of the establishment. Unfortunately when the wind blows in a certain direction there are whiffs from the nearby sewage plant. €€€

Léros

Alinda
Álynda beach
Tel: 22470 23266
Fax: 22470 23383
www.alindahotel.gr
The first hotel established here, this has well-kept 1970s vintage rooms with a mix of sea and mountain views and a respected restaurant with garden seating. €
Archontiko Angelou
Álynda, signposted well inland
Tel: 22470 22749
www.hotel-angelou-leros.com
Marvellously atmospheric converted Belle Époque mansion hiding amidst orchards with the feel of a French country hotel. Victorian taps in the baths, beamed ceilings, old tile or wood floors and antique furnishings. €€

Crithoni's Paradise
Kríthoni
Tel: 22470 25120
Fax: 227470 24680
www.crithonisparadisehotel.com
Léros' top-rated accommodation, a low-rise complex with a smallish pool, disabled access and large, well-appointed rooms redone in 2006. Buffet breakfast; open all year. €€€
Rodon
Between Pandéli and Vromólithos in Spiliá district
Tel: 22470 23524/22075
Small but well kept, mostly balconied rooms better than this hotel's official E-class rating; also ground-floor 3-person studios, with less of a sea view. €

Lipsí

Aphrodite
Behind Liendoú beach
Tel: 22470 4100
A 1997-built, attractive studio bungalow-hotel complex, with large units; top standard on the islet. €€
Galini Apartments
By the ferry jetty
Tel: 22470 41212
Fax: 22470 41012
Well appointed rooms with balconies and fridges, very welcoming family. €

Nísyros

Porfyris
Mandráki centre
Tel: 22420 31376
Fax: 22420 31176
By default, the best conventional hotel on the island, though bathrooms and phone system are desperately antiquated – only partly offset by fridges and air-con in the rooms. These overlook either orchards and the sea, or the large saltwater pool. €€
Ta Liotridia
On the shore lane near the windmill
Tel: 22420 31580
Email: Eliotridia@nisyrosnet.gr
Two comfortable suites in a restored house – one of the few such projects on Nísyros – arguably worth the premium price for the sea views and volcanic-stone-and-wood decor. Lively bar downstairs, but apparently noise not a problem. €€€

Pátmos

Blue Bay
Skála, Konsoláto district
Tel: 22470 31165
Fax: 22470 32303
www.bluebay.50g.com
The last building on the way out of town towards Gríkou, and spared the late-night ferry noise that plagues most hotels here. Friendly Australian-Greek management, on-site internet café. €€

Effie
Skála, Kastélli hillside
Tel: 22470 32500
Fax: 22470 32700
Bland, blonde-pine-and-tile rooms spread over two hotel wings, but with balconies and air conditioning they're good value in a quiet setting. Open all year. €€

Galini
Skála
Tel: 22470 31240
Fax: 22740 31705
In a quiet cul-de-sac near the ferry quay, this C-class hotel offers B-class standards in furnishings and bathrooms, and excellent value. €€

Porto Scoutari Romantic
Hillside above Melói beach
Tel: 22470 33123
Fax: 22470 33175
www.portoscoutari.com
The island's top digs, renovated in 2007 with a spa added. Enormous self-catering suites, arrayed around the pool area, have sea views and air-con/heating, as well as mock-antique furnishings and original wall art. Elina the proprietress is a font of island knowledge. €€€

Studios Mathios
Sápsila cove
Tel/fax: 22470 32583
www.mathiosapartments.gr
If you've a car or bike, these rural, superior self-catering units make an idyllic base thanks to their creative furnishing, extensive gardens and a welcoming managing family. The coarse-pebble cove, however, is not great for swimming. €€

Sými

Albatros
Gialós marketplace
Tel: 22460 71707
www.albatrossymi.gr
Partial sea views from this exquisite, small hotel with French co-management; pleasant second-floor breakfast salon, air-con. Families should ask also about their more expensive Villa Symeria. €

Fiona
Top of the Kalí Stráta, Horió
Tel: 22460 72088
Mock-traditional hotel building, large airy rooms with double beds and stunning views; breakfast in mid-air on the communal terrace. €€

Iapetos Village
Gialós
Tel: 22460 72777
Fax: 22460 71477
www.iapetos-village.gr
The best of several fair-sized

bungalow complexes in Gialós, inaugurated in 2007. It comprises maisonettes fitting up to six and self-catering studios, arrayed (rather extravagantly for dry Sými) around a pool. Actual room decor is simple – exposed roofbeams, pale tiles – but adequate. €€€

Les Catherinettes
North quay, Gialós
Tel: 22460 72698
Email: marina-epe@rho.forthnet.gr
Creaky but spotless en-suite *pension* above the restaurant of the same name, in a historic building with painted ceilings and sea-view balconies for most rooms. €€

Symi Visitor in Gialós square is an agency run by affable Greek-Australian Nikos Halkitis and his partner Wendy Wilcox, offering a variety of accommodation in all price ranges, from double studios to entire houses, mostly in Horió; tel: 22460 72755; www.symivisitor.com.

Télendos

On the Rocks
Tel: 2243 48260
www.otr.telendos.com
Just four smartly appointed rooms with double glazing, mosquito nets etc, above amiable Greek-Australian-run bar of the same name. €€

Porto Potha
Tel: 22430 47321
www.telendoshotel.gr

At the very edge of things, but this hotel, a mix of standard doubles and studios, has a large pool and a friendly managing family. €

Tílos

Blue Sky Apartments
Ferry dock, above Blue Sky taverna
Tel: 22460 44294
Fax: 22460 44184
www.tilostravel.co.uk
Well-appointed, galleried two-person units with sea views, built in 2002. €€

Eleni Beach
About halfway around the bay
Tel: 22460 44062
Fax: 22460 44063
www.elenihoteltilos.gr
Willing management for large, airy, white-decor hotel rooms with bug screens and Wi-fi, requiring advance booking. New rear wing added in 2007. €€

Irini
200m/yds inland from mid-beach
Tel: 22460 44293
Fax: 22460 44238
www.tilosholidays.gr
Long the top hotel on Tilos, Irini still wins points for its beautiful grounds and common areas, including large pool. The same management keeps the hillside **Ilidi Rock Aparthotel** (revamped 2007), which has outstripped its stable-mate with a conference hall, gym (but no spa), private beach and one wing with disabled access.
Ilidi Rock €€€, Irina €€

NORTHEASTERN AEGEAN

Híos

Chios Rooms
Egéou 110, Híos Town
Tel: 22710 20198
www.chios rooms.gr
Upstairs rooms with high ceilings and tile-and-wood floors, some en-suite, in lovingly restored building managed by a New Zealand/Greek couple. Best is the "penthouse", with a private terrace. €

Kyma
East end of Evgenías Handrí
Tel: 22710 44500

Fax: 22710 44600
Email: kyma@ehi.forthnet.gr
B-class hotel inside a converted neoclassical mansion (plus less attractive modern extension). Very helpful management, good breakfasts in the original salon with painted ceiling. €€

Markos' Place
South hillside, Karfás beach
Tel: 22710 31990/697 32 39 706
www.marcos-place.gr
Inside a disused monastery, Markos Kostalas has

created a uniquely peaceful, leafy environment. Guests are lodged in the former pilgrims' cells; individuals are welcome (several single "cells"), as are families (two "tower" rooms sleep four). Minimum stay 4 days, open Apr–Nov. €

Spitakia
Avgónyma
Tel: 22710 20513 or 81200
Fax: 22710 43052
www.spitakia.gr
A cluster of small but well-restored houses taking up to five people, near the

edge of this stunningly set west-coast village. €€

Volissos Travel in Volissós is a little booking office that handles 16 old village houses restored in the late 1990s. Units, all with

PRICE CATEGORIES

Price categories are based on the cost of a double room for one night in the high season:
€ = under €60
€€ = €60–110
€€€ = over €110

period features, usually accommodate two people, prices €–€€. Tel: 22740 21413; fax: 22740 21521; www.volissostravel.gr.

Ikaría

Akti
On a knoll east of the hydrofoil and *kaíki* quay, Ágios Kírykos
Tel: 22750 22694
www.pensionakti.gr
Not a place for a long stay, but ideal if waiting for an early ferry. Friendly and spotless; some rooms en-suite. Refurbished in 2006–7. Wi-fi signal. €

Daidalos
Aremenistís
Tel: 22750 71390
www.daidaloshotel.gr
One of the less "packaged"-feeling hotels in this resort, with decent breakfasts on a shady terrace, rooms appointed with quirky artistic touches, and, like the Erofili, an eyrie-pool above the sea. €€

Erofili Beach
Right at the entrance to Armenistís
Tel: 22750 71058
Fax: 22750 71483
www.erofili.gr
Considered the best hotel on the island, though the ample common areas are more impressive than the sea-view rooms. A small saltwater pool perches dramatically over Livádi beach. €€€

Lésvos

Clara
Avláki, 2km/1½ miles south of Pétra
Tel: 22530 41532
Fax: 22530 41535
www.clarahotel.gr
The large, designer-furnished rooms (in grades up to 1- and 2-bedroom suites) of this bungalow complex look north to Pétra and Mólyvos. Particularly renowned for its ample buffet breakfasts relying on local products. Tennis courts and pool. €€–€€€

Molyvos I
Mólyvos beach lane
Tel: 22530 71496
Fax: 22530 71460
Nominally B-class outfit on the pebble shore, behind

the tamarisks and a stone-paved terrace where breakfast is served. Large, tile-floored, 1980s rooms; reasonable buffet breakfast. You get the use of (and shuttle to) the pool and sports facilities at sister hotel Molyvos II at Eftaloú, though there is a "private" beach area here. €€

Pyrgos
Eleftheríou Venizélou 49, Mytilíni
Tel: 22510 25 069
www.pyrgoshotel.gr
The town's premier restoration accommodation, a 1916 mansion with over-the-top kitsch decor in the common areas. Rooms, most with balcony, are perfectly acceptable, and there are three round units in the tower. €€€

Vatera Beach
Vaterá
Tel: 22520 61212
Fax: 22520 61164
www.vaterabeach.gr
Rambling, Greek/American-run hotel behind the best beach on the island. Rooms with air-con and minibar fridges, free sunbeds, in-house restaurant relying on own-grown produce and free advice from Barbara the proprietress. €€

Límnos

Evgatis Hotel
Opposite (N)evgátis beach
Tel: 22540 51700
Small, modern hotel expanded in 2008, overlooking the best beach on the island (100 metres/yds across the road) and with a decent attached taverna. You'll need a car though, as the Límnos bus service is almost non-existent. €€

Ifestos
Andróni district, Mýrina
Tel: 22540 24960
Fax: 22540 23623
Attractive small hotel whose rooms have a mix of seaward and hillside views. Balconies, fridges, air conditioning. €€

Porto Myrina Palace
Ávlonas beach, 2km/1½ miles north of Mýrina
Tel: 22540 24805
Fax: 22540 24858

Considered the best, and most easily bookable, luxury hotel on the island, with grounds incorporating a small Artemis temple. €€€

Villa Afrodite
Platý beach
Tel: 22540 23141
Fax: 22540 25031
Run by returned South African Greeks, this comfortable small hotel has a poolside bar and sumptuous buffet breakfasts. €€

Sámos

Amfilisos
Bállos beach, near Órmos Marathókambos
Tel: 22730 31669
Fax: 22730 31668
The hotel itself is nothing extraordinary, but Bállos is a deliciously sleepy place, perfect for doing very little except exploring the coast to the southeast and sampling the local food. €€

Arion
1km (½ mile) west of Kokkári
Tel: 22730 92020
Fax: 22730 92006
www.arion-hotel.gr
The best accommodation on Sámos' north coast, a family-friendly, well-designed hotel-wing and bungalow complex on a hillside. Famously good breakfasts. €€€

Doryssa Seaside Resort
Potokáki, near airport
Tel: 22730 88300
Fax: 22730 61463
www.doryssa-bay.gr
One of the few actual beachfront resorts on Sámos, with a saltwater pool just in from the sand if the sea's too cold. Choose between the designer-refitted hotel wing or the meticulously constructed fake "village", no two houses alike and incorporating all the vernacular styles of Greece. €€€

Kerveli Village
Approach to Kérveli beach
Tel: 22730 23631
Fax: 22730 23006
www.kerveli-village.gr
This is a well-executed, smallish bungalow hotel set among olive trees and cypresses, with superb

views across to Turkey and over Kérveli Bay. A good selection of beaches and tavernas are within walking distance or take advantage of in-house car rental. €€€

Samothráki

Eolos
Kamariótissa
Tel: 25510 41595
Fax: 25510 41810
Samothráki's port and capital is home to a few hotels including this decent mid-range choice. Rooms are simple but clean and welcoming. Some have views overlooking the hills, others towards the sea. Continental breakfast is included. Cash only. €€

Mariva Bungalows
Loutrá Thermá
Tel: 25510 98230
Fax: 25510 98374
www.mariva.gr
Situated in the island's resort centre, these lovely flower-shrouded bungalows are built on a gentle hillside. All units are self-contained, comfortable, with colourful or mock-antique furniture, and reasonably spacious. Ideal for a longer stay. €€

Thásos

Alkyon
Liménas
Tel: 25930 22148
Fax: 25930 23662
Spacious rooms, with harbour or garden view, plus gregarious Anglo-Greek management and afternoon tea, make this a firm favourite with English-speaking travellers. €

Myrioni
Liménas
Tel: 25930 23256
Fax: 25930 22132
Very well priced and comfortable spot with a large breakfast salon; also with a cheaper annexe. €€

Thassos Inn
Panagía village
Tel: 25930 61612
Fax: 25930 61027
Quiet except for the sound of water in runnels all around, this modern building in traditional style has most rooms facing the sea. €€

SPORADES AND EVIA

Alónisos

Konstantina's Studios
Hóra (Old Alónisos)
Tel: 24240 66165
Fax: 24240 66165
High up in the old renovated village this small, traditional building houses eight studios and one apartment. All have exceptional sea views and wooden balconies with canvas deckchairs. €€

Liadromia
Patitíri
Tel: 24240 65160
Fax: 24240 65096
Email: liadromia@alonnisos.com
One of the first hotels to open in Alónisos, it has an old-world charm with a dash of modernity. Rooms have stucco walls, stone floors and tasteful decor. Over-looking the harbour at the north side of Patitíri Bay, handy for island facilities. €€

Milia Bay
Miliá
Tel: 24240 66032
Fax: 24240 66037
www.maesylla.gr
Tucked away overlooking tiny Miliá Bay, this quiet retreat consists of 12 ecologically constructed self-catering apartments, all very spacious and taste-fully decorated. If you don't fancy the short walk to the part-sand beach there's a pool, as well as the in-house restaurant. €€€

Évia

Hotel Karystion
Kriezótou 2, Kárystos
Tel: 22240 22391
Fax: 22240 22727
www.karystion.gr
A busy foreigner-friendly hotel in the far south of Évia, close to the fortress on the south side of town. Neat, air-conditioned rooms, redone in 2005. The town's best bathing spots are a few minutes' walk way. €€

Island of Dreams
Erétria
Tel: 22290 61224
Fax: 22290 61268
www.dreamisland.com.gr
An unusual resort hotel on an island connected to the

mainland by a short causeway. Accommodation is individual bungalows set among olive trees and all within minutes' walk of a sandy beach. €€€

Thermai Sylla Spa Wellness Hotel
Loutrá Edipsoú
Tel: 22260 60100
Fax: 22260 22055
www.thermaesylla.gr
Perhaps Greece's only official anti-stress hotel, this magnificent edifice at the northern end of the promenade is an old-world experience brought up to date with beauty and therapy treatments based on the waters of the ancient spa. Non-guests can use spa on a day basis. €€€

Skiáthos

Aegean Suites
Megáli Ámmos, 1.5 km (1 mile) west of town
Tel: 24270 24069
Fax: 24270 24070
www.santikoshotels.com
A suite hotel redone in 2007, the adults-only sister to its chain-mate the Skiathos Princess. Not a beachfront position, but high enough to avoid road noise. There are only 21 units – which adds to the exclusive feeling – all of them big (55–60 sq. metres), with bug screens, Wi-fi and sound systems, "de luxe" ones only having an unobstructed sea view. Large pool, small but pleasant gym, parking and a "live cooking" poolside restaurant. €€€

Atrium
Plataniás
Tel: 24270 49345
Fax: 24270 49444
www.atriumhotel.gr
The Atrium Hotel combines casual elegance with traditional architecture, somewhat like a monastery. It's chic, beautiful and enjoys a splendid view. Rooms and suites are more than comfortable and some have private balconies or patios. There's a pool and a poolside restaurant. €€€

Nostos Village
Tzanéria

Tel: 24270 22520
Fax: 24270 22525
www.center.gr/nostos
A large complex on the Kanapítsa peninsula midway between Skiáthos Town and Koukounariés. Built into a verdant hillside, one of the better and more popular resort choices for visitors to the island. Choose from simpler rooms or self-catering bungalows among pine trees. €€€

Skópelos

Adrina Beach
Pánormos
Tel: 24240 23373
Fax: 24240 23372
www.adrina.gr
This expansive hotel complex (42 standard rooms and 10 bungalows) occupies a large tract of hillside just to the north of Pánormos Bay, looking out onto a virtually private beach. If you want to get married while on holiday, there is even a small on-site chapel. €€€

Kyr Sotos
Hóra, just in from mid-quay
Tel: 24240 22549
Fax: 24240 23668
www.skopelos.net/sotos/
Rambling, old-house *pension* with wood-floored, en-suite rooms that's justifiably a favourite budget option. Rear units (all en-suite with air-con) facing the courtyard are quieter; best is No. 4, with a fireplace. Open all year. €

Skopelos Village
Hóra, far east side bay.
Tel: 24240 22517
Fax: 24240 22958
www.skopelosvillage.gr
The top digs here, redone in 2007 – when some of the *Mamma Mia!* film parties took place here. Units range from studios up to large family apartments; all with touches like Victorian taps. Two outdoor pools, Wi-fi, superior restaurant terrace, lovely breakfast salon. €€€

Skýros

Nefeli – Skyriana Spitia
Hóra
Tel: 22220 91964
Fax: 22220 92061

www.skyros-nefeli .gr
Combining standard hotel rooms and a stand-alone group of Skyrian houses (in practice 2–3 person studios) this is a tidy complex at the entrance to Hóra. The studios are very cosy. Good low-season deals. €€€

Perigiali
Magaziá
Tel: 22220 92075
www.perigiali.com
Very welcoming, secluded mix of studios and well furnished rooms with phone, overlooking a large garden where breakfast is offered. Open all year; heated. €€

Skyros Palace
Gyrísmata, Péra Kámbou
Tel: 22220 91994
Fax: 22220 92070
www.skiros-palace.gr
Tucked away at the northeastern end of the Magaziá-Mólos strip, down on the beach, the Skyros Palace is a fairly sumptuous place to stay though its location may be a little inconvenient for some. Free bus shuttles ply between the hotel and Hóra. Open summer only. €€€

BELOW: Adrina Beach hotel, Skópelos.

CORFU

The official Greek Hotel guide lists over 400 licensed hotels on the island. Many of these remain in the firm grip of tour operators from May to October, closing in winter. The following are open off-season and/or to independent travellers. Additionally, if you have a car, you can usually find *domátia* or apartments on a walk-in basis at the less packaged resorts of Astrakerí, Kalamáki, Afiónas and Aríllas in the north, plus Paramónas and Boúkari in the southwest.

Kérkyra Town and around

Bella Venezia
Napoleóntos Zambéli 4
Tel: 26610 46500/20708
www.bellaveneziahotel.com
Neoclassical mansion renovated in 2006, well adapted as a B-class hotel in a central yet quiet location at the south edge of the old town. No pool or extra amenities other than a large patio garden with bar. €€€

Corfu Palace
Dimokratías 2, north end of Garítsa Bay
Tel: 26610 39485
www.corfupalace.com
The town's only deluxe-class establishment, which enjoys a high level of repeat clientele, including VIPs and foreign dignitaries, especially in May and September. They come for the huge rooms with marble bathtubs, the spa, big breakfasts and the assiduous level of service. Open all year. €€€

Grecotel Corfu Imperial
Komméno
Tel: 26610 88400
Fax: 26610 91881
Email: gman_ci@ci.grecotel.gr
Perhaps the best and most contemporarily decorated hotel on the island, and stratospherically expensive. Three grades of accommodation: standard rooms, bungalows, and a few super-deluxe villas with their own pool. All the

facilities you'd expect for the price. €€€

Kavalieri
Kapodistriou 4, Kérkyra
Tel: 26610 39041
Fax: 26610 39283
www.cavalieri-hotel.com
A-class hotel in a 17th-century building overlooking the Spianáda. Frankly overpriced, with smallish rooms, but all have sea views and the roof garden makes the place. €€

Konstantinoupolis
Zavitsiánou 11, Old Port
Tel: 26610 48716
Fax: 26610 80716
Email: polis@ker.forthnet.gr
1862 building, once a backpackers' dosshouse, now lovingly restored as a well-priced C-class hotel with sea and mountain views. Comfortable rooms and common areas, lift; open all year. €€

Kontokali Bay
Tel: 26610 90000
Fax: 26610 91901
www.kontokalibay.com
Slightly more affordable and larger than the Corfu Palace, consisting of a hotel wing and bungalows in a leafy environment with two "private" beaches and a new spa. Lots of facilities for kids. €€€

Nefeli
Komméno
Tel: 26610 91033
Fax: 26610 90290
This small inland hotel in mock neoclassical style, spread over three buildings among olive groves, has a loyal clientele, good service and air conditioning in most units. Open May–Oct. €€

Palace Mon Repos
Anemómylos district, Garítsa Bay
Tel: 26610 32783
Fax: 26610 23459
Renovated in the late 1990s, this hotel is the closest thing Kérkyra Town has to a beach resort. The lido opposite is of indifferent quality, but there are views to the sea, Old Fort and Mon Repos woods, and a small swimming pool. Open May–Oct. €€

Centre-west of Corfu

Casa Lucia
Sgómbou hamlet, at Km 12 of Kérkyra–Paleokastrítsa road
Tel: 26610 91419
Fax: 26610 91732
www.casa-lucia-corfu.com
Peaceful setting at the very centre of the island. A restored olive-mill complex set among lovingly tended gardens comprises 11 units ranging from studios to family cottages. Most have kitchens and all share a large pool, though furnishings are resolutely 1980s. Open Apr–Nov. Often hosts special-interest groups. €€–€€€

Fundana Villas
Accessed by side road from Km 17 of Kérkyra–Paleokastrítsa highway
Tel: 26630 22532
Fax: 26630 22453
www.fundanavillas.com
Another 1980s restoration inn, this time converted from a 17th-century manor, with a commanding ridge-top position in the middle of a gorgeous nowhere. Their old olive press is on display, too. Units from double studios to family apartments; most have brick-and-flagstone floors; several adjoin the pool. Open Apr–Oct. €€

Levant Hotel
Above Pélekas, right beside "Kaiser's Throne"
Tel: 26610 94230
Fax: 26610 94115
www.levanthotel.com
1990s-built hotel in mock-traditional style, with superb views both east and west over the island. Rooms are wood-floored, baths marble-trimmed, ground-floor common areas faux-rustic. There's a small pool, and some of the island's best beaches a few kilometres away. Open Apr–Oct. €€€

Liapades Beach Hotel
Liapádes
Tel: 06630 41294
Two smallish wings make up this amiable C-class at one of the quieter beach resorts on this coast. Open Apr–Oct. €€

Pelecas Country Club
Km 8 of Kérkyra–Pélekas road
Tel: 26610 52239
Fax: 26610 52919
www.country-club.gr
Corfu's most exclusive rural hotel, just 26 units in an 18th-century mansion set in over 25 hectares (60 acres) of grounds. Outbuildings are now self-catering studios and suites, all antique-furnished. Stylish breakfasts in the central refectory, pool, tennis, helipad. Open Jan–Nov. €€€

The north of the island

Nisaki Beach
Krouzéri Bay, between Nissáki and Kalámi
Tel: 22630 91232
Fax: 22630 22079
www.nissakibeach.gr
A-class hotel with brutal 1970s architecture but popular for its open buffet restaurant, varied water-sports and children's beach activities. Rooms, mostly with sea views, are large and recently redone. €€€

Villa de Loulia
Perouládes, 500m from beach
Tel: 26630 95394
Fax: 26630 95145
www.villadeloulia.gr
The third of Corfu's rural restoration inns, this 1803 mansion has been refurbished to a high-standard. The bar, lounge and breakfast area are in a purpose-built structure flanking the large pool. Heating but only fans, no air-con. You're paying for the exclusivity – better value out of peak season. Open Mar–Oct. €€€

The south of the island

Boukari Beach
Boúkari, 4km/2½ miles beyond Messongí
Tel: 26620 51791
Fax: 26620 51792
www.boukaribeach.gr
Sea-view A-class apartments for up to four. All amenities including coffee machines; excellent restaurant. Open Apr–Oct. €€

THE IONIANS

Ith[á]ki

Captain Yiannis
On east quay, Vath[ý]
Tel: 26740 33311
Fax: 26740 32849
The closest thing to an exclusive "resort" on the island, with just 11 self-catering units set in ample walled grounds with a pool and tennis court. €€–€€€

Captain's Apartments
Ki[ó]ni
Tel: 26740 31481
Fax: 26740 31090
www.captains-apartments.gr
Set up on the hill towards Rah[í], with commanding views of Ki[ó]ni's bay, each spacious air-conditioned studio has cooking facilities, cable TV and a veranda. There is also a communal garden to relax in. €€

Nostos
About 200 metres (220 yds) inland from the quay, Fr[í]kes
Tel: 26740 31644
Fax: 26740 31716
www.hotelnostos-ithaki.gr
Smallish but upmarket C-class hotel where all rooms look over a field towards the sunrise. €€

Perantzatha 1811 Art Hotel
Odyssea Androutsou, Vath[ý]
Tel: 26740 33496
Fax: 26740 33493

www.arthotel.gr
Chic and fairly pricey but by far the loveliest hotel in Vath[ý]. The 12 understated and tasteful rooms have been individually designed and are very comfortable. Not on the harbourfront itself (and so quieter than some other places), the rooms look out over Vath[ý]'s pretty rooftops to the sea. The breakfasts are excellent. €€€

For rooms or villas across the island, contact one of these two travel agencies:
Delas
Tel: 26740 32104
www.ithaca.com.gr
Polyctor
Tel: 26740 33120
www.ithakiholidays.com

Kefalloni[á]

The Architect's House
[Á]sos
Book through: Simply Ionian
Tel: (00 44) 020 8541 2202
www.simplytravel.co.uk
This lovely traditional building, one of the few places to stay in [Á]sos itself, has three double bedrooms (sleeps 6) and is down by the harbour. There is plenty of space – a separate living room and kitchen – and the

beach and good places to eat are close by. €€–€€€
Emelisse Art Hotel
[É]mblisi, near Fisk[á]rdo
Tel: 2610 624900
www.arthotel.gr
Expensive (A class) but chic, this "boutique" hotel (one of the small local Tsimaras Hotels chain) is set in a traditional building. The well designed rooms have luxurious bathrooms and, inevitably, the hotel's infinity pool has a lovely view. For this sort of money you should expect to be pampered and the service lives up to expectations. €€€

Hotel Ionian Plaza
Plat[í]a Vallian[o]ú, Argost[ó]li
Tel: 26710 25581–4
Fax: 26710 25585
www.ionianplaza.gr
Excellent value C-class designer hotel, with modern bathrooms and balconies overlooking the palm-studded square; the rooms are on the small side, but the staff are friendly. Open all year. €€

Kastro Hotel
S[á]mi
Tel: 26740 22656/22282
Fax: 26740 23004
www.kastrohotel.com
A little way out of town, but close to the sea is this medium-sized, good value B class hotel. The good, if smallish, rooms either look out over the pool and sea or to the mountains. Breakfast is provided and there is also a restaurant. €€

La Cit[é]
Lixo[ú]ri
Tel: 26710 92701
Fax: 26710 92702
This compact hotel four blocks up from the seafront has been completely reno-vated with air conditioning and stylish furnishings to add a touch of the French ambience its name suggests. Competitively priced and by far the best option in town. €€

Moustakis Hotel
Agia Evfim[í]a
Tel: 26740 61060/61030
Mobile: 693 419 7495
www.moustakishotel.com
Smallish and tucked away

behind the harbour front, this is one of the most pleasant hotels in town. All the rooms have air-con and balconies. Breakfast is available for an extra charge. Discounts are available for long stays. €€

Odysseus Palace
P[ó]ros
Tel: 26740 72036
Fax: 26740 72148
www.odysseuspalace.com
This modern hotel is a comfortable place to stay in town. Good discounts may be available for the large and airy rooms (studios and apartments). Being away from the seafront, the hotel is quieter than most. Open all year. €€

Regina's
Fiskardo
Tel/fax: 26740 41125
Most of the smallish but well-maintained rooms in this lovely family guest house at the back of the village have balconies that look towards the harbour or across the pleasant court-yard. Better value and less cliquey than many Fiskardo establishments. €–€€

Tara Beach
Sk[á]la
Tel: 26710 83341/83250
Fax: 26710 83344
www.tarabeach.gr
A large but unobtrusive hotel right on the excellent beach. The rooms are decent and, if you can't be bothered to waddle the few metres to the sea, there is a good pool in the pleasant gardens, beside which is a handy bar. €€–€€€

Trapezaki Bay Hotel
Trapezaki
Tel: 26710 31501-2
www.trapezakibayhotel.gr
Perched on the hillside just over five minutes' walk from delightful Trapezaki beach, this large modern hotel

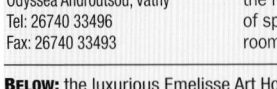
BELOW: the luxurious Emelisse Art Hotel.

PRICE CATEGORIES

Price categories are based on the cost of a double room for one night in the high season:
€ = under €60
€€ = €60–110
€€€ = over €110

offers all amenities in its rooms, each of which has a private parking slot. There is also a large pool, restaurant and bar complex. Better value in high summer because prices are fixed for the whole season. €€€

Kýthira

Kýthira has a short season, with most accommodation only open May–Oct; advance booking is recommended.

Porto Delfino
Kapsáli
Tel: 27360 31940
Fax: 27360 31939
A pleasant bungalow complex with views over the bay and Hóra. €€–€€€

Xenonas Keiti
Hóra
Tel: 27360 31318
Lovely accommodation in – for a change – non-smoking rooms, set in a rambling 18th-century mansion. The hotel has a remarkably distinguished guest-list. €€

Xenonas Porfyra
Pótamos
Tel: 27360 33329
Fax: 27360 33924
Nicely furnished studios, arranged around a pretty, walled courtyard in characterful Pótamos. €€

Lefkáda

Nefeli
Póndi Beach
Tel: 26450 31515
Email: clubnefeli@hotmail.com
This beachfront hotel makes a good alternative to staying in nearby, congested Vasilikí; its popular outdoor bar and windsurf facilities on site are pluses. €€

Olive Tree/Liodendro
North approach road, Ágios Nikítas
Tel: 26450 97453
www.olivetreelefkada.com
C-class hotel halfway up the hill, with oblique sea views from most rooms. Rooms are typical pine-and-white-tile decor. No package allotment so good chance of vacancies. €€

Ostria
North approach road, Ágios Nikítas
Tel: 26450 97483
Fax: 26450 97300
Email: aguikitasostria@e-lefkas.gr
The 1970s-built rooms of

this *pension* can be cell-like, but are enlivened by terracotta floor tiles, dried flowers and wall art. It's the balcony views of the Ionian (save from four rooms) and the cool, trendy common areas (including a terrace bar open to all) that make the place a delight. The breakfast isn't always up to scratch. €–€€

Panorama
Atháni
Tel: 26450 33291
Fax: 26450 33476
One of the island's true getaways. The rooms are simple but clean, above an excellent restaurant. There are superb views and you are as close as you can stay to the stunning beaches of Gialós, Egremní and Pórto Katsíki – although you still need your own transport to reach them. €

Rouda Bay
Mikrós Gialós
Tel: 26450 95634
Fax: 26450 29285
www.roudabay.com
Spacious apartments, arranged around a well tended garden, back on to a fine restaurant where the buffet breakfasts are served, just a few metres from the smooth pebble beach. €€

Santa Maura/Ayia Mavra
Spyridónos Viánda 2, Lefkáda Town
Tel: 26450 21308
Fax: 26450 26253
Pagoda-like period piece: pre-earthquake ground floor, wood and corrugated tin upstairs. Rooms have air con, double glazing, traditional shutters, balconies. Lovely breakfast salon and garden patio. €€

Paxí

Paxos Beach Hotel
Gáios
Tel: 26620 31211
Fax: 26620 32695
www.paxosbeachhotel.gr
Hillside bungalow complex leading down through trees to its own small pebble beach about 2 km (1 mile) east of town. €€–€€€

Planos Tours
Lákka
Tel: 26620 31744
Fax: 26620 31010

Email: planos@otenet.gr
One of two agencies in this little port, efficiently handling everything from basic rooms to luxury villas.

Zákynthos

Contessa Estate
Akrotíri
A tranquil, stone-built aristocratic estate full of character and set in gorgeous surroundings. Accommodation is in either the large manor house, full of heirlooms of the Komoutou family, or the smaller but equally lovely garden cottage. The Comtessa Maria is a charming host, and the spectacular views and sense of history all add to the experience. €€

Hotel Palatino
Kolokotróni 10 and Kolivá, Zákynthos Town
Tel: 26950 27780
Fax: 26950 45400
www.palatinohotel.gr
One of Zákynthos Town's best-value options, stylish and well run. The rooms, designed for business travellers, are decent, with all the trimmings, and the hotel as a whole has been well cared for. A buffet breakfast is provided and there is also a restaurant. €€

Ionian Star Hotel
Alykés
Tel: 26950 83416/83658
Fax: 26950 83173
www.ionian-star.gr
A smallish and very well kept hotel. The spotless rooms are excellent value (breakfast is included) and there is a restaurant which concentrates on Greek food. €€

Levantino Studio Apartments
Kaminia beach, Vasilikós
Tel: 26950 35366
Fax: 26950 35173
www.levantino-apps.gr
Ten quiet and attractive apartments close to the sea at the Argási end of the Vasilikós Peninsula. All are equipped with a kitchen and some look out over the gardens and sea. Discounts available out of high season. €€

Nobelos Apartments
Ágios Nikólaos
Tel: 26950 27632/31400
Fax: 26950 31131/29277
www.nobelos.gr
These luxury apartments in the north of the island are expensive but lovely. The four tastefully decorated suites are in a traditional stone-built house, each with an individual character. Along with excellent service, breakfast is provided and a secluded bay is close by. €€€

Pansion Limni
Límni Kerioú
Tel: 26950 48716
www.pansionlimni.com
Friendly place at the quieter end of Laganás Bay, where guests are presented with home-made wine and olive oil. All rooms have fridges and cooking rings. There are two smart new blocks, one with huge family apartments, further behind the beach from the original *pension*. €–€€

Sirocco Hotel
Kalamáki
Tel: 26950 26083–6
Fax: 26950 26087
www.siroccohotel.gr
This is a good and reasonable quiet option for Kalamáki, the renovated and stylish standard rooms a bargain out of season. There is a large pool set in a garden, though the beach is not too far away. €€

Windmill
Korithí, Cape Skinári
Tel: 26950 31132
www.potamitisbros.gr
Two converted windmills and four spacious rooms in a stone house at the north end of the island, close to the Blue Caves. If you want to get away from it all this is a good option. €

Zante Palace
Tsiliví
Tel: 26950 490490
Fax: 26950 49092
www.zanteplace.com
This huge hotel is on the bluff overlooking Tsiliví bay, giving great views across to Kefalloniá. The rooms (which look out over the bay) are good value and if you can't be bothered to walk down to the beach there is a nicely sited pool. €€

CRETE

Agía Galíni

Neos Ikaros
Tel: 28320 91447
www.neosikaros.com
A bit out of the centre at the foot of a hillside, but still handy for the seafront, this amphitheatrically arrayed, smallish (29-room) hotel has large units with pine furniture, blue soft furnishings, air conditioning, fridge and phone, but best of all a lovely pool garden. €€

Agía Roúmeli

Tara Rooms/Hotel Calypso
Tel: 28250 91231
www.agiaroumeli.gr/tarra/index.html
Having hiked the Samarian Gorge, reward yourself with a beachside stay rather than pelting off immediately to Hóra Sfakíon. Two brothers offer either basic rooms, with a taverna underneath, or a somewhat more comfortable nearby hotel. Closed when the gorge is (typically Nov–Mar). €–€€

Ágios Nikólaos

Minos Beach Art Hotel
Aktí Ilía Sotírhou, Ammoúdi
Tel: 28410 22345
www.bluegr.com
Deluxe coastal resort: mostly bungalows plus a few suites amidst mature gardens, set on a small peninsula studded with specially commissioned contemporary sculpture. A five-star outfit – standard rates for seaview bungalows run from €400–600 for a double – with a half-dozen on-site restaurants. Dress code for supper. €€€

Ormos/Crystal
Órmos district, 1.5 km (1 mile) from centre
Tel: 28410 24407 or 28410 24094
www.ormos-crystal.gr
Two medium-sized sister hotels, set on a quiet bay looking towards town, each with a swimming pool. The buildings, 1980s concrete blocks, aren't wildly exciting but the rooms are fine and the price is right, often with seasonal offers online. €–€€

Sgouros Hotel
Aktí Pangaloú, Kitroplatía Beach
Tel: 28410 28931
www.sgourosgrouphotels.com
Small hotel right by the water's edge, with 22 stylish air-conditioned rooms with very nice bathrooms and tasteful common areas. Rooms pitched at the business as much as at the holiday trade. Open all year. €€

Ágios Geórgios Lasithíou

Rea Hotel
Tel: 28440 31209

Studio rooms rented up-stairs from one of the village's best, meat-orientated tavernas – proprietress Maria's husband is the local butcher. €

Eloúnda

Akti Olous
Skhísma
Tel: 28410 41270
www.eloundaaktiolous.gr
The 70 well-maintained rooms at this efficient, family-run shorefront hotel, which gets a broad mix of nationalities, were renovated in 2006. There's a roof pool, a tiny patch of beach (with amenities), and two restaurants, one of which is at the beach. €€

Elounda Beach Hotel
Tel: 28410 41812
www.eloundabeach.gr
One of the most luxurious resorts in Greece, over-looking Mirabello Bay; many of the villas have a private pool and gym, and main-wing rooms are a generous size. Private beach, spa, the usual complement of on-site bars/restaurants, and a high repeat-visit rate amongst the jet-set clientele. €€€

Elounda Mare Hotel
Tel: 28410 41102
www.eloundamare.gr
Rival to the Elounda Beach, its tone and emphasis are more homely and warmer – especially in the bungalows with their fireplaces, wood floors and private pools. The "Minoan Royalty Suites" have a more contemporary design, while standard rooms in the main building fall somewhere in between. The bungalows and suites are stratospherically expensive – which doesn't deter a Russian nouveau-riche clientele. On-site 9-hole golf course, spa and watersports, including scuba diving. Three restaurants on site. €€€

Georgioúpoli

Anna's House
300 metres/yds across the river bridge
Tel: 28250 61556
www.annashouse.gr
More accurately Anna's houses, or rather studios/apartments, these new, flawless units are in a peaceful rural garden setting around a large pool, and one of the few local establishments not (yet) in complete thrall to the package trade. €€

Haniá

All listings are near the old harbour and open all year.
Casa Delfino
Theofánous 7
Tel: 28210 93098
www.casadelfino.com
The most luxurious – and expensive – of the various restored Venetian-mansion boutique hotels in the old town. The 22 units, all different and ranging from one-bedroom to penthouse quad, are all suite-format. A copious buffet breakfast is served in the pebble-mosaic courtyard; there is also a roof terrace. €€€

BELOW: luxury at the Minos Beach Art Hotel, Crete.

PRICE CATEGORIES

Price categories are based on the cost of a double room for one night in the high season:
€ = under €60
€€ = €60–110
€€€ = over €110

Minoa Palace
West edge of "town", Plataniás
Tel: 28210 36500
www.minoapalace.gr
Well set out of the tatty main strip just before the river, though the beach is a walk away across the road. Rooms and suites are up to five-star standard but few have views. Good pools, a centrepiece basement spa and a half-dozen on-site restaurants and bars, the main one serving one of the best hotel buffet breakfasts in the country. Family-friendly, so published rates not always levied. €€€

Nostos
Zameblíou 42–6
Tel: 28210 94740
www.nostos-hotel.com
Superbly renovated 15th-century church on a pedestrianised lane, with 12 mostly galleried, balconied units (some with harbour views), and a roof terrace looking to the White Mountains. All units have mini-kitchen, phone, TV. €€

Porto del Colombo Hotel
Corner Theofános and Moskhón
Tel: 28210 70945
Fax: 28210 98467
Email: colompo@otenet.gr
This restored Venetian mansion had previously served – in the following order – as the Ottoman military commmand, the French consulate and

Eleftherios Venizelos' offices before becoming a 10-unit boutique hotel. All rooms have dark-wood floors and ceilings plus antique furnishings; two are two-room suites. €€

Selini Suites
Rapanianá district, Kolymbári
Tel: 28240 83033
www.selinisuites.com
A mix of large studios and 1-bed apartments in this beachfront holiday complex pitched at families, with plenty of children's amenities. €€

Theresa
Angelou 8, west side of old port near Naval Museum
Tel: 28210 92798
www.pensiontheresa.gr
Just seven idiosyncratic rooms (fitting up to three) with tasteful decor at this homely *pension* – one of several on this lane. Terrace with great view and communal kitchen. Loyal repeat clientele and new word-of-mouth introductions mean advance booking is essential from June to September. €€

Vranas Studios
Ayíon Deka, corner Kalliníkou Sarpáki, near cathedral
Tel: 28210 58618
www.vranas.gr
Set back a bit from the water, so quieter, and more "modern" than most old-town restoration projects,

but none the worse for it. Tile-floored, wood-ceilinged rooms are spacious and furnished in contemporary manner. Although the room sare self-catering, breakfast is available. €€

Ierápetra

Cretan Villa Hotel
Lakerdá 16
Tel: 28420 28522
www.cretan-villa.com
An 18th-century mansion restored as a hotel; rooms are simple but with nice touches like exposed stone pointing and arrayed around a pleasant courtyard. Free Wi-fi zone, friendly owner full of helpful local advice. €

Iráklio

Atrion Hotel
Hronáki 9
Tel: 2810 46000
www.atrion.gr
Suprisingly quiet but central B-class hotel, with balconied rooms redone in 2003, free ADSL, cheerful restaurant and a 2006-inaugurated conference centre for the business trade. €€

Kronos
Sofoklí Venizelou 2, corner Agaráthou
Tel: 2810 282240
www.kronoshotel.gr
Closest to the sea of all the city hotels, this C-class outfit represents excellent

value with about half the balconied rooms having a harbour view, though decor is decidedly 1980s. €€

Lato Hotel
Epimenídou 15
Tel: 2810 228103
www.lato.gr
The city's first self-styled boutique hotel, this features slightly clinically appointed standard rooms and suites (the latter worth the extra money), two restaurants (one on the roof), conference/function rooms, a sauna and "mini-gym" plus unbeatable views over the old Venetian harbour. €€€

Lena
Lahaná 10
Tel: 2810 223280
www.lena-hotel.gr
Small hotel renovated in 2003 – much of the effort went into the common areas, so rooms are still in two grades: bathroomless with fan, or en-suite and air-conditioned. Free Wi-fi access. €–€€

Mirabello
Theotokopoúlou 20
Tel: 2810 285052
www.mirabello-hotel.gr
Excellent location makes up in part for the dated quality of some of the rooms (the non-en-suite ones being budget territory) and the internet access (ISDN only). Balconies for all rooms, communal fridge, satellite TV lounge. €–€€

Rea
Kalimeráki 1, corner Hándakos
Tel: 2810 223638
www.hotelrea.gr
One of the best, central budget options, with a mix of en-suite and washbasin-only rooms, all with fans and some with balconies. Other perks include left-luggage service, book swop, on-site car hire, and long-hours breakfast. €

Kastéli-Kissámou

Galini Beach
East end of seafront near sports stadium
Tel: 28220 23288
www.galinibeach.com
Modern but well executed hotel with Art Deco touches, right behind pebbly Telonío beach. Air-conditioned,

BELOW: the Hotel Porto Loutro.

spotless rooms; full (not continental) breakfast served at sea-level terrace. €

Loútro

Blue House
Tel: 28250 91337
A mix of seafront, en-suite rooms and slightly more expensive upstairs units at this informal *pension*, as well as a very creditable on-site taverna. €

Porto Loutro Hotel
Tel: 28250 91433
www.hotelportoloutro.com
The largest hotel in this roadless, beachless settlement, spread over two premises (one is five steps from the water). Rooms have beam ceilings, slate floors, marble-trimmed bathrooms. Hospitable Anglo-Greek management. €€

Makrýgialos

White River Cottages
Aspropótamos district
Tel: 28430 51694
www.asprospotamos.com
The abandoned hamlet of Pefki, comprising a score of traditional stone cottages complete with original fireplaces, has been architect-restored since the 1980s as studio, 1-bedroom and 2-bedroom apartments around a swimming pool. Excellent opportunities for local gorge-walking and botany, especially in spring or autumn, and you're just inland from some of the best, most protected beaches of southeastern Crete. €

Mátala

Eva Marina Hotel
Tel: 28290 45125
www.evamarina.com
Small 1980s-vintage hotel with pale pine furniture and white-tile decor set in lush gardens just 100 metres/yds back from the sea. €

Matala Bay Hotel
Tel: 28920 45100
www.matalabay.gr
Good-value hotel just back from pebbly Kómos bay (not Mátala's main beach), with

a more recent annexe of family-orientated apartments. Welcoming staff, though the in-house restaurant gets very mixed reviews. €

Mýrtos

Myrtos Hotel
Mid-village
Tel: 28420 51227
www.myrtoshotel.com
Almost-all-white decor rooms, 1980s vintage but well kept, at this friendly hotel just five minutes' walk from the usually windless beach. Competent ground-floor restaurant, so half-board available. €

Omalós

Exari Hotel
Tel: 28210 67180
www.exari.gr
One of the best of a cluster of hotels in this hamlet, aimed at walkers wanting an early start down the Gorge of Samariá. The in-house restaurant relies in part on products of the managing family's cheese factory. The name comes from a famous six-man (*exári* in Greek) local raiding party during one of the 19th-century rebellions against the Ottomans. €

Paleohóra

Rea Hotel
Tel: 28230 41307
Fax: 28230 41605
Email: apap@cha.forthnet.gr
Small (14-room) family-run hotel in the backstreets with tile-floored, pastel-hued rooms and a garden bar where drinks and breakfast are provided. Just opposite is an annexe of more recently built apartments suitable for families. €

Sandy Beach
Tel: 28230 42138
Fax: 28230 42139
Cosy (12-room) hotel sited, as the name suggests, behind the town's main beach, near the castle, with balconied sea-view rooms. The overflow will be sent to the same family's simpler Castello Rooms (tel: 28230 41143). €

Plakiás

Just about every rented-room, studio or apartment establishment near the beach or in surrounding hamlets – some 150 of them – are found, complete with photos and contact details, on the community website www.plakias-filoxenia.gr.

Réthymno

Fortezza Hotel
Melissinoú 16
Tel: 28310 55551
www.fortezza.gr
Tastefully built hotel, inland under the shadow of the Venetian fortress. Medium-sized pool in the back (though beach is 10-minute walk away); rooms terracotta-tiled floors and simple but quality furnishings. Good value for the comfort offered. €€

Olga's Pension
Soulíou 57
Tel: 28310 54896
Fax: 28310 29851
A warren of eclectically decorated rooms and studios (en-suite and/or with sea view) on different levels, connected by flower-filled terraces and passageways; a good central budget option. Discounted breakfasts offered at the family-run ground-floor cafe. €

Palazzo Vecchio
Melissinoú corner Iróön Polytekhníou
Tel: 28310 35351
www.palazzovecchio.gr
A 15th-century Venetian building converted into a complex of studios and apartments with warm-toned soft furnishings. Patio pool with adjoining bar, but no restaurant. €€€

Sea Front
Arkadíou 159
Tel: 28310 51981
www.rethymnoatcrete.com
If you have to be on the beach, this – an old mansion converted into a *pension* with 10 well-equipped, wood-floored, en-suite rooms – is the closest spot, while still convenient for the centre. The same owners manage the modern Sea View Apartments

nearby, comprising four studios and two family units (which don't, however, have the eponymous views). €€

Veneto
Epimenídou 4
Tel: 28310 56634
www.veneto.gr
A Venetian-mansion conversion in the old town, more homely than the Sea Front with its arcaded courtyard, working wells and antique-furnished units which all vary (bathrooms are state-of-the-art). 10 studios and suites, and a restaurant with well stocked wine-cellar. A favourite honeymoon venue. €€€

Sitía

Arhontiko Hotel
Kondyláki 16
Tel: 28430 28172
An old neoclassical mansion converted into a basic (rooms are not en-suite) but atmospheric *pension*, with a garden out front. €€

Itanos
Platía Iróön Polytekhníou
Tel: 28430 22900
www.itanoshotel.com
Waterfront B-class hotel with a roof-garden, restaurant and some disabled-friendly units. Common areas have been refurbished but the rooms, while airy and bright, have dated furnishings. €€

Spíli

Heracles Rooms
Tel: 28320 22111
Fax: 28320 22411
Email: heraclespapadakis@hotmail.com
Superior "rooms" establishment just off the main road, with air-conditioned, bug-screened, balconied, white-walled units, some with hillside views. The geologist proprietor can advise on local walks, and rents out mountain bikes. €

PRICE CATEGORIES

Price categories are based on the cost of a double room for one night in the high season:
€ = under €60
€€ = €60–110
€€€ = over €110

E ATING OUT

RECOMMENDED RESTAURANTS, CAFÉS & BARS

What to Eat

There is considerable regional variety in Greek cuisine and you should keep an eye out for specialities of the house you haven't seen before. Another thing you'll quickly learn is how strikingly different the same dish can be when it is prepared well or badly. It is therefore worthwhile shopping around for your taverna (especially in heavily visited areas), asking the locals what they suggest. For experienced travellers, the term "tourist *mousakás*" is shorthand for an exploitative version of this standard dish, slathered with potatoes and poorly executed béchamel sauce, with nary a slice of aubergine or a crumb of mince.

Some tavernas, especially in rural areas or on non-touristy islands, may not have menus, in which case it is essential to establish the price of at least the most expensive main courses, particularly seafood.

Vegetarians are not well catered for in Greece: most main courses include fish or meat. Your best bet is to choose a selection of *mezédes*, many of which are vegetarian.

Many Greek specialities are cooked in the morning and left to stand, so food can be lukewarm (occasionally stone cold) but the Greeks believe this is better for the digestion and steeping of the flavours. For some vegetarian dishes, they are right; for dishes containing meat, this is a rather dubious practice.

Greek Salad

"Greek" salad is a staple of Greek cuisine. *Horiátiki*, the whole works with tomatoes, cucumber, green pepper, *féta* cheese and olives, is a lunch in itself with bread – and this is what you'll probably get if you ask for "salad". Some restaurateurs omit one or two of the vegetable ingredients – not all are available all summer – but by law *horiátiki* must contain a generous chunk of *féta*. If all you want is a small side salad, ask for *angourodomáta* (just tomatoes and cucumber).

Fish and Seafood

Seafood is now one of the most expensive dishes on the Greek menu (except for frozen squid and fresh octopus, which are widely available). Fish are usually in a tray of ice for you to choose from, and your dish is priced by the weight of the fish of your choice. It is strongly suggested that you watch the (uncleaned) fish being weighed, and reiterate the price you are quoted, as "fingers on

How much to pay

Greece is not the cheap deal it once was. A meal with bulk wine or local beer will cost at least €14 per person; €16–20 is a more realistic figure. If you dip into fish or bottled wine, then it's €25 minimum. Fancy restaurants run to €35–45 a head without wine. The restaurants on the following pages are mid-priced unless otherwise stated.

Eating out in Greece is above all a social affair, although the ritual of families and friends patronising tavernas twice a week is much less observed now thanks to hard economic times. Greeks have had to learn be careful with money – it is still considered an honour to snaffle the bill but this tends to be a less extravagant gesture these days.

the scales" and later misunderstandings are not unknown.

There is so much farmed and frozen seafood (often marked only in Greek with a "k" or "kat.", for *katapsygméno*, or just an asterisk) lying in ambush for the unwary traveller that the best strategy is to eat humbly and seasonally: far better grilled fresh sardines in August than swordfish frozen since June.

Where to Eat

The more casual eating establishments have more or less the same style and setup across Greece, and menus are similar in design and sequence (indeed, often pre-printed by drinks companies in return for including their logo).

However, the classical taverna is by no means the only kind of establishment. You will also encounter the *estiatório*, the traditional urban restaurant, which ranges from an *(ino)magírío*, trademan's lunch-hour hangout, with ready-cooked *(magirevtá)* food and bulk wine, up to pricey linentablecloth places with bow-tied staff.

The *psistariá* is a barbecue-style restaurant specialising in lamb, pork or chicken on a spit; the *psarotavérna* specialises in fish and shellfish; while the *gyrádiko* (*gýros* stall) and *souvlatzídiko* purvey *gýros* and *souvláki* respectively, sometimes to a sit-down trade, garnished with salads. Although the best *souvlákia* are made from lamb, most are pork nowadays.

Popular among the urban intelligentsia are *koultouriárika* restaurants, which serve nouvelle Greek cuisine based on updated traditional recipes, and *ouzerí* or *mezedopolío* (alternatively *tsipourádika* in the north), where the local tipple serves as accompaniment to *mezédes* or small plates of speciality dishes.

When to Eat

For Greeks the main meal of the day is eaten between 2pm and 3.30pm and, even in the cities, is usually followed by a siesta break lasting until 5.30pm or 6pm.

The evening meal can either be another full meal, or an assortment of *mezédes*. This is usually eaten between 9pm and 11pm.

Breakfast in Greece is traditionally small, usually bread and coffee. There are, however, wonderful *pítta* (pies) and turnover options available from bakeries, for snacking on the hoof.

Eating Out With Kids

Children regularly dine out with their parents until late at night, and (within their abilities) are expected to converse with the adults. There's no formality about this – kids are as likely to be racing round the taverna playing tag or under the table teasing the stray cats as sitting up at the table. The Greeks are extremely indulgent of their children, so don't be embarrassed to make any special food request for your own.

The Wines of Greece

While Greek wines have yet to obtain the status of their French counterparts, young oenologists trained abroad have opened micro-wineries on the mainland, and the results are impressive. Consult Kostas Lazarakis'*The Wines of Greece* for a guide to drinking and buying. A bottle will cost about €8–13 in a bottle shop, easily double that in a taverna.

Some of the better mainland labels include:

Boutari Nemea, a reliable, full-bodied mid-range red. There are other, premium versions of Nemea, such as

Olive Oil

The Greeks are more generous with olive oil in food than most northern European palates are used to. Although you can ask for no oil on a salad, for instance *(hóris ládi)*, most waiters will think this an odd request, as Greeks generally regard oil as good for the digestion. A whole category of slow-cooked vegetable stews are bluntly referred to as *laderá* or oil-cooked dishes.

Ktima Papaïoannou.

Tsantali Rapsani, a generally reliable red from a tiny viniculture area on the border between Thessaly and Macedonia.

Spyropoulou Orino Mantinea, a wonderful, smokily dry white made from moskhofílero grapes on the plateau near Trípoli, an increasingly popular taverna offering.

Averof Katoï, a smooth red from Métsovo, though quality isn't up to its legendary days of the mid-1990s.

Athanasiadi, premium red and white from central Greece, rather better than oft-cited rival **Hatzimihali**, and as readily available.

Lazaridi, these two rival wineries are run by cousins, in Dráma, in eastern Macedonia; their Merlots in particular are excellent.

Georgiadi, the subtlest bottled *retsína*, again produced by two rival cousins from Thessaloníki, far superior to the usually preferred **Kourtaki**. **Malamatina** is the classic half-litre bottled mainland strong *retsína*, especially enjoyable mixed with a glass of soda.

Island wines

Many islands produce excellent vintages that they can't or won't export, and which are sold only locally. Although barreled/bulk *(me to kiló, hýma)* wines tend to be rough and ready, they're cheap (€4–11 per litre) and certainly authentic.

In Corfu, **Theotoki** is the local wine (red or white); the speciality of the island is a very sweet liqueur called **Kumquat**, based on the tiny citrus fruit of that name. In Kefalloniá **Robola** is a delicate expensive white; **Gentilini** is reckoned the best label.

The lush green vineyards of Zákynthos produce **Comouto** rosé or the white **Verdea**. The grapes of Andípaxi are much appreciated; ask for wine from the barrel.

CAIR, the Rhodes cooperative originally founded in the 1920s by the Italians, has the ubiquitous white **Ilios** and red **Chevalier du Rhodes**, but the private Émbonas winery Emery is more esteemed for its **Mythiko** and **Villaré** red and white.

Sámos in the northeastern Aegean is one of the few islands to export wine, not only to the mainland but also abroad. The fortified Samos dessert wines **Anthemis** and **Vin de Liqueur** are esteemed world-wide. On Híos, particularly around Mestá, a heavy, sherry-like but very palatable wine is made from raisins. *Oúzo* is made here too – Tetteri Penindari is the best.

Lésvos is the undisputed *oúzo* capital of Greece, producing at least

15 varieties. **Varvagiannis** is the most celebrated, and expensive, but some prefer **Arvanitis**. EPOM is the principal cooperative, marketing among others the "Mini" brand, a staple of *ouzerí* across the country.

Like most volcanic islands, Límnos produces excellent whites (especially the oak-aged **Dryiino**), as well as a few good reds and rosés.

Thásos specialises in *tsípouro* – often flavoured with exotic spices or pear extract rather than the anise of *oúzo*. Homemade firewater gets lethally strong; anything over 50 percent alcohol must be barreled, not bottled, lest it explode.

Santoríni, a volcanic island like Límnos, is known for its upscale whites like **Boutari Nyhteri** and **Ktima Argyrou**.

In Crete, **Logado** plonk has been the delight of backpackers for years, but superior labels such as **Economou** (Sitía province) and **Lyrarakis** (Iráklio) have made an appearance.

Coffee, Chocolate and Tea

Greeks generally drink their coffee with lots of sugar. Essential phrases for those who like it without are *horís záhari*, "without sugar", or *skéto*, "plain". If you like some sugar ask for *métrio*. If you love sugar say nothing and they'll probably dump a few teaspoons into whatever you're drinking. *Me gála* means "with milk".

Espresso and cappuccino, when available, are exactly as in Italy, though not always so expertly made. *Freddoccino*, another resourceful Greek invention, is a cold, double cappuccino for the summer months.

Gallikós ("French"), in other words percolated coffee, is usually quite acceptable. *Fíltros* means the same thing. *Ellenikós kafés* is Greek coffee, boiled and served with the grounds in the cup. If you want a large cup, ask for a *diplós*. *Ellenikó cafés* is also known as *turkikós cafés* but this sometimes provokes patriotic objections.

Chocolate drinks *(tsokoláta)* can be very good indeed, served cold or hot according to season.

Britons will find it hard to get a decent cup of tea *(tsái)* and will usually have to make do with bagged tea of obscure origin, served either with milk or with lemon *(me lemóni)*.

Hamomíli is camomile tea, and *tsái (tou) vounoú* is "mountain tea", made with mountain sage leaves. Its cousin is called *alisfakiá* in some of the islands, especially in the Dodecanese and Cyclades.

ATHENS

Athinaïkon
Themistokéous 2, close to Omonia
Tel: 210 383 8485
An *ouzerí* established in 1932, with loyal lunchtime customers from the neighbouring offices. An extensive list of fresh fish and seafood, good Greek cheese and some interesting offal. Decent barreled wine.

Bakalarakia/O Damingos
Kydathinéon 41, Pláka
Tel: 210 322 5084
Excellent food dished up in a long-established cellar restaurant. Good things to order include *fáva*, *loukánika* and *saganáki*; the house speciality is *bakaliáro skordaliá* (salt cod with garlic). Excellent barreled wine.

Baïraktaris
Platía Monastirakíou 2
Tel: 210 321 3036
One of Athens' oldest restaurants dating back to 1879, known for its cheap and wholesome food, particularly *magirevtá*, with tasty *fasoláda* (bean soup), *domátes gemistés* (stuffed tomatoes) and *fáva*.

Benaki Museum Café
Koubári 1 and V, Sofías
Tel: 210 367 1030
Set on a lovely terrace on the second floor of the museum, this is a favourite with the more artistic Kolonáki crowd. As well as excellent coffee and retsina there are good salads, daily specials and puddings. The Thursday evening buffet (when the museum is open until midnight) is well worth booking for.

Dimos
Filoláou 148, Pangráti
Tel: 210 701 1260
A neighbourhood lodestar for *magirevtá* that's been going since 1970. Big portions at friendly prices. Unlike many such *inomageria*, the interior proves a very pleasant, updated environment in pastel shades.

Epirus/Monastiri/ Papandreou
These three cheap, basic eateries are all close together in the Central Meat Market off Athinás. Open 24 hours a day, they specialise in cooking up the more *recherché* parts of animals, in particular *patsás*. This tripe soup is much vaunted as a hangover cure.

Fasoli
Emmanouíl Benáki 45, Exárhia
Tel: 210 330 0010
Ippokrátous 22 corner Navarínou, midtown
Tel: 210 360 3626
Excellent value and trendy yet utilitarian decor make these two restaurants very popular. The food at both is solid Greek with creative twists: lentil salad, *biftéki* roulade, light pasta dishes, good bread, the usual starters. Closed Sun.

Filippou
Xenokrátous 19, Kolonáki
Tel: 210 721 6390
This *estiatório*, founded in 1923, remains a firm favourite with all sorts of diners for its honest, moderately priced fare, washed down by excellent white or red bulk wine. Service is low-key but efficient; the dining room retains a pleasantly retro air with proper table linen. Open continuously noon until late except closed Sat night, all day Sun, and part of Aug.

The Food Company
Anagnostopoúlou 47, Kolonáki
Tel: 210 363 0373
Just above Ágios Dionýsios, this is a good place for cheap, tasty food. The dishes are largely vegetarian, the portions large.

Ikonomou
Kydandídon 32, cnr Tróön, Áno Petrálona
Tel: 210 346 7555
This *inomagerío* does a handful of casseroles per day, with no menu per se: *laderá*, roast meat, a limited

repertoire of *orektiká* in big portions. The bulk retsina is cheap but average quality; the red wine is better. Supper only Mon–Sat.

Iy Kriti (O Takis)
Veranzérou 5, stoá off Platía Kánningos, near Platía Omónia
Tel: 210 382 6998
Popular little Cretan *stéki* (hangout) serving regional dishes such as *hiroméri* (smoked pork) and *marathópita* (fennel pie), along with more usual titbits like fresh *bakaliáros* and of course Cretan *rakí*. A bit pricey for the area, but portions are large. Open daily for lunch and supper.

Kalimarmaron
Evforíonos 13, Pangráti
Tel: 210 711 9727
This taverna stresses island and regional recipes. Several daily specials will be recited to you, though the permanent menu – stuffed baked sardines, sausages, and bean dishes – has broad appeal. Decent bulk wine from Neméa. Closed Sun eve and Mon.

O Thanassis
Mitropóleos 69, Monastiráki
Tel: 210 324 4705
Three hotly competing *souvláki* stalls cluster here where Mitropóleos meets Platía Monastiakíou, but this is the best. Thanassis' speciality is kebab, mincemeat blended with onion and spices. The side dish of chili peppers will blow your head off. Open daily noon–midnight except major holidays.

O Vlassis
Páster 8, Ambelókipi
Tel: 210 646 3060
Installed in an old house just off Platía Mavíli, *Vlassis* sticks to a time-tested formula of large-portioned, rich, "modern Greek" cooking. The place fills most evenings by 9.30pm, so booking is wise. Closed Sun eve and Aug.

Rakoumel
Emmanouíl Benáki 71, Exárhia
Tiny (30-seat) place

featuring Cretan *mezédes* and *rakí* at student-friendly prices. The menu (only in Greek) offers platters like skinny sausages, *gialodádika* (greens similar to lambs lettuce), and *paximádia* (dark rusks) rather than bread. Very much a local bohemian hangout. Open Mon–Sat 3pm–midnight.

To Diporto
Sokrátous 9, corner Theátrou; no sign out; metro Omónia;
Located at the western edge of the central market district, *To Diporto* attracts a varied clientele, from "suits" to market-stall-holders. They're here for the excellent, no-nonsense grub: grilled or fried fish of the day, a stew or two, and mountainous salads. Space is limited space, so you're expected to share tables with strangers. Open Mon–Sat noon–6pm.

To Tristrato
Dedálou 34, corner Angélou Géronda, Pláka
Tel: 210 324 4472
Excellent café/patisserie which specialises in unusual desserts. Drinks include *airáni* (diluted yogurt) in summer, *rakómelo* from Amorgós, homemade liqueurs and a wide range of herbal teas. Daily 9am–midnight.

Vasilenas
Etolikoú 72, Piraeus (Etolikoú runs north from Aktí Kondýli on the harbour)
Tel: 210 461 2457
In the 1950s, Thanasis Vasilenas was the first Greek to introduce the set-price *table d'hôte* to Greece, captivating his guests. His descendants continue the tradition, bringing on 16 platters in sequence, with meat choices and old standards like fish soup and *taramosaláta*. Charming decor. Supper only daily except Sun; closed a few weeks in Aug.

PELOPONNESE

Giálova

This tiny resort, on the northeast side of Navaríno Bay, north of Pýlos, has several good waterfront tavernas. They include:

Helonaki
Seafront
Tel: 27230 23080
The seaview "Little Turtle" offers home-style food, including well-prepared fish, plus a laid-back atmosphere attracting both locals and tourists. Occasional live music. They also rent rooms adjacent.

Spitiko
Highly recommended for its wonderful home-cooking.

Gýthion

Navtilia
Near main jetty
Tel: 27330 22137
This seafood *ouzerí* offers top-notch seafood, and unpretentious *mezédes*, at harbour-front tables served from a small kitchen across the road by traffic-dodging waiters. Views include fabulous sunsets over the Taygetos mountain ridge.

Kalamáta

Katófli
Salamínos 20, one block in from the marina on the city's western waterfront
A pleasant place to eat, with outdoor seating and a very wide-ranging menu.

Kardamýli

Léla's
Tel: 27210 73541
The oldest and most traditional taverna in the town, with only German draft beer as a concession to the predominant clientele. Terrace seating and occasional live music.

Kórinthos

Arhondiko
4 km (2½ miles) west of modern Kórinthos on coast road, opposite Léheo harbour
Tel: 27410 27968
The best food in this taverna is to be selected from the *mezédes*; there is also a good local rosé. It is open all year.

Koróni

Flisvos
Waterfront
The best of the quayside eating here, with seafood and fish, reasonably priced.

Kýthira

Platanos
Mylopótamos
Tel: 27360 33397
Venerable village *kafenío* in an old building on the *platía*; *magirevtá* for lunch, grills in the evening.

Sotíris
Avlémonas
All the classic elements for a Greek taverna: sea breezes, simplicity, and perfectly cooked fresh fish.

Methóni

Klimataria
Miaoúli Street
Tel: 27230 31544
A small, shady courtyard is the heart of this family-run establishment, which serves good vegetarian *mezédes* and *magireftá* Supper only May–Oct.

Monemvasiá

Matoula
Old Town
Tel: 27230 61660
Matoula has been going since 1950; it trades mostly on its lovely garden overlooking the sea, but the food – pasta and fish – is reasonable and well priced.

Návplio

Fanaria
Staikopoúlou 13
Tel: 27520 27141
Best at lunch time; good Mégara wine and reasonable prices, in a street known for tourist rip-offs.

Koutouki to Parelthon
Profítis Ilías 12
Tel: 27520 29930
Because it's in the unglamorous new town, prices for perfectly executed *mezédes* are much lower than in the old town, and service is friendlier.

Olympia

Kladíos
behind the train station on the riverside
Tel: 26240 23322
A find in tourist-clogged Olympia: real *mezédes*. Go early as seating is limited.

Pátra

For fish, there are two local favourites: **Ankyra**, by a beached boat at the fishing port (tel: 2610 333 778), with mostly outdoor seating, and **Kylikio Istioploïkos Omilos** (Sailing Club Canteen), Iróön Polytehníou 8 corner Terpsithéas (tel: 2610 435 905), a bit more formal with tables inside.

Pýlos

Gregory's
Georgíou Krasánou Street
Tel: 27230 22621
Old-fashioned *taverna* serving *magirevtá* such as *kokkinistó* (red-sauce stew) plus pasta, grilled meat and fish. Nice garden in summer.

Spárti

Akrolithi
Odós ton 118, No. 75
Tel: 27310 20123
Alfresco dining in summer; cosily indoors in winter. Excellent well-priced *mezédes*, popular with locals.

CENTRAL GREECE

Ágios Ioánnis

Posidonas
Central waterfront
Tel: 24260 31222
One of the best and cheapest fish tavernas here; a medium-sized fish, two starters and local wine will clock in at under €20. It is open most of the year.

Damoúhari

Barba Stergios
South side of Venetian port

A reliable, fairly inexpensive venue for non-farmed fish, as well as meat grills and a few *magirevtá* dishes. There is a lovely seaside terrace for eating during the summer, also a tasteful indoor salon for cooler months.

Galaxídi

Albatross
Inland street between two churches
Tel: 22650 42233

Lovely *magirío* with a handful of tables, a limited quantity of home-style food encompassing octopus, spinach/cheese pie, rabbit stew, pale *taramosaláta* and the house speciality *samári* (pancetta in savoury sauce).

Gávros

To Spiti tou Psara
Main valley-bottom road
Despite the name, lots else besides trout: excellent *hortópitta, kafterí* dip, own-made wine at reasonable prices.

Kalambáka

O Skaros (Papalexis)
Trikálon highway, 150 metres/yds past the Divani Hotel on the west edge of town
Tel: 24320 24152
Not many tourists find this spot, but locals certainly know about its meaty platters – particularly excellent *kebáb* (called *kondosoúvli* elsewhere) and

chops – plus home-grown vegetables. Open all year.

Kastráki Meteóron

O Paradisos
Through road
Tel: 24320 22723
The best all-rounder of a dozen local tavernas. Besides excellent *kokorétsi* and *biftéki* from the grill, there's *moussakás*, starters and *ravaní*.

Katigiórgis

Flisvos (Voulgaris)
Fishing port
Tel: 24230 71071
Folk from Vólos reckon the long trip out here worth it for the fresh fish and honest *magirevtá*, and you'll probably agree. Tables in the sand, weather and waves permitting.

Kissós

Makis
Just off the platía
Tel: 24260 31266
One of the oldest tavernas in Pílio: stress on *magirevtá* like rabbit stew, *gígandes*; bulk wine. Open all year.

Lamía

Ouzo Melathron
Aristotélous 3, up some steps from Platía Laoú
Tel: 22310 31502
Reasonably priced portions of Middle Eastern and Macedonian recipes are

washed down by Límnos bulk wine; tables in a courtyard or the stunning interior of an old house.

Mesolóngi

Filoxenos
Razikótsika 7
Tel: 26310 51660
The local speciality is smoked or grilled eel (*héli*), hunted with tridents in the lagoon. This is the priciest outlet on this pedestrian lane but worth it for the service and ambience.

Mikró Horió

Iy Kyra Maria
Ground floor of Helidona Hotel
Tel: 22370 41221
Atmospheric seating under the plane tree in the centre of the old village, with reasonable food.

Milína

O Sakis
South end of front
Tel: 24230 66078
This is one of the best tavernas in the south Pelion. A five-platter meal, including *gávros* (fresh anchovy), *hórta* and other *mezédes*, is about €20.

Mylopótamos

Angelika
Near end of the road into town
Tel: 24260 49588
The fish is a bit pricey but various *magirevtá* plates are

reasonable and service is kind and efficient. Easter to Oct open daily; Nov–Easter weekends and holidays .

Mýtikas

O Glaros
Northwest end of quay
Tel: 26460 81240
Busy fish taverna with fresh fare and terrace looking out to Kálamos island.

Návpaktos

Papoulis
Sismáni, corner Formíonos, Návpaktos
Tel: 26340 21578
The town's most accomplished eatery, comprising two premises – a *mezedopolío* and a standard taverna – the former more popular in summer. Big portions, willing service.

Pinakátes

Drosia (Taverna tou Papa)
West end of village
Tel: 24230 86772
Excellent leafy *dolmádes* and goat and lemon sauce as well as off-menu *mezédes*. May close random days Oct–May.

Portariá

Kritsa
Central *platía*
Tel: 22428 99121
Restaurant with tasteful environment, professional service and biggish

portions. Specialities include *tyropitákia*, *maïdanosaláta* (parsley dip) and of course Piliot *spétzofaï*.

Pórto Germenó

Akrotiri
Tel: 22630 41234
The best, friendliest and most consistently open of the tavernas on the esplanade. A good balance of meat and fish dishes,

Tríkala

Palia Istoria
Ypsilándou 3
Tel: 24310 77627
There are literally dozens of *ouzerí* in the old market district of Manávika. This one is open for lunch too, and has a light touch and attractive prices.

Vólos

Halambalias (Zafiris)
Orféos 8, corner Skýrou
Tel: 24210 20234
A shrine of *magirevtá* that attracts crowds to an uninspiring inland location; good bulk wine, baked seafood and meat dishes. Closed Sunday.
Monosandalos
Tsopótou 1, east waterfront by Ágios Konstandínos church
Tel: 24210 37525
The doyen of several *ouzerí*, with good prices. Shrimp croquettes a speciality.

EPIRUS

Amvrakikós Gulf

Myrtaria (Patendas)
Koronisía
Tel: 26810 24021
This end-of-the-line village on a sandspit has about half a dozen seafood tavernas; Myrtaria is last in line, most notable for its high-quality seafood from an admittedly limited menu.

Eláti

Sta Riza
centre of Eláti village

Tel: 69370 37544
Opened in 2005, this features Epirot turnovers, vegetarian and dairy starters plus a few cooked dishes of the day at moderate prices, accompanied by bulk wine. If it's not too cold or breezy, eat out on the balcony with an eyeful of Mt Gamíla. Closed Tues, also Thur in low season.

Ioánnina

Fysa Roufa
Averoff 55

Tel: 26510 26262
A 24-hour *magirío* whose slightly elevated prices for sustaining *magirevtá* like *patsás*, suckling pig and *spétzofaï* are justified by the careful cooking, polite service, big portions and a pleasant environment.
Stin Ithaki
Stratigoú Papágou 20A
Tel: 26510 73012
The most consistently good of a half-dozen eateries on the lakefront avenue. The ambitious menu includes Cypriot specialities and

Asia Minor recipes as well as Epirot staples like trout, turnovers, cheeses and mushrooms. Starters are big, and often better value than the main dishes.

Koukoúli

To Tritoxo
Koukoúli, Zagóri
Tel: 26530 71760
Named after the nearby three-arched bridge, this café-restaurant run by village priest Papa-Kosta and his wife serves up hearty,

reasonably priced meat dishes plus Epirot *píttes*, accompanied by good local bulk wine.

Limáni Lygiás

Skaloma (O Gios tou Foti)
Tel: 26820 56240
There's no sign, but it's the only eatery at this little fishing anchorage, and everybody for kilometres around comes here. Big portions and small prices.

Menídi

Vouliagmeni (Pandioras)
Between Árta and Amfilohía
Vouliagmeni, first place on left from main highway
Tel: 26810 88216
Where folk from Árta come for a big plate of the famous Amvrakian *garídes* (prawns, shrimp), as well

as scaly fish – budget over €25 per head.

Pápingo, Megálo

Kalliopi
South part of village
Tel: 26530 41081
Home-style cooking, good bulk wine, year-round operation and good music attract a lively crowd.

Nikos Tsoumanis
North part of village
Tel: 26530 41893
Huge salads, tasty lamb, regional dishes and assorted offal for the bold, plus unimpeded views of the famous *pýrgi* (rock towers) of Astráka from the terrace.

Párga

Golfo Beach
Southeast end of town
Tel: 26840 32336

One of the oldest tavernas in Párga, this has acquired a cult following for its seaside terrace and good-value oven-casserole food.

Taverna tou Khristou
Sarakíniko beach, 7 km (4 miles) northwest

Tel: 26840 35207 or 69779 82207
This old favourite features well-executed vegetable dishes, fresh seafood, a few select meat items, and limited bottlings from quality wineries in northern Greece.

THESSALONÍKI

Amanitis
D. Poliorkitoú 44
Tel: 2310 233513
A non-touristy eatery in the Kástra district that will appeal to vegetarians and carnivores alike.

Aristotelous
Aristotélous 8
Tel: 2310 233195
One of older *ouzerís* in the city centre, Aristotelous serves classic northern Greece cuisine with a twist alongside *ouzerí* standards. Excellent wine list.

The Barrister
Tsimiskí 103 and Výronos 2
Tel: 2310 253033
This smart top-of-the-range restaurant presents its European dishes with considerable flair. This is one of Thessaloníki's most sophisticated dining locales.

Mirovolos Smirni
Modiáno Market
Tel: 2310 274170
Doyenne of several *tsipourádika* at the market hall's west entrance: top-notch food that's strong on seafood and bags of atmosphere. Book ahead.

Ouzou Melathron
Karýpi 21
Tel: 2310 240043

Search for the small Greek sign for this cosy and popular *ouzerí*, tucked away down an alleyway. For your efforts you'll enjoy a wide range of moderately priced *mezédes*.

Parakath
Konstantinoupóleos 114
Tel: 2310 653705
Parakath is Thessaloníki's only Pontian-Greek restaurant and features a range of pasta and yoghurt dishes from Turkey's Pontus region. There are the usual grills as well. Live music and dancing from midnight till dawn.

Pyrgos
Venizélou 13
Tel: 2310 207769
Pyrgos is one of those quietly successful places that rely in its repeat clientele and its consistently quality fare. Up in the Kástra, this place dishes up a mixed Greek international cuisine with particular emphasis on its fine wine list. The food is well presented and the service friendly.

Ta Adelfia tis Pyxarias
Platía Navarínou 7
Tel: 2310 266432

This is one of the best among several tavernas operating around a pedestrianised square to the east of the city centre. Dine outside or inside among photos on the wall of an old Macedonian home. Succulent kebabs as well as a range of ready-made oven-cooked dishes.

Ta Kioupia
Platía Morihóvou 3-5
Tel: 2310 553239
The owners of this smart, businesslike restaurant in the heart of the city attempt to represent all areas of Greece in their extensive menu, which also features many of the less common Greek wines.

To Rema
Pasalídi 2, Káto Toúmba
Tel: 2310 901286
You'll need a cab to find this little out-of-the-way place to the east of the city centre, but it's worth the effort. Popular with students and youngish trendies, the food is unusual in that each dish has a "political" or "historical" name such as *perestroika* or Colossus of Rhodes.

Dishes are a mixture or French and Greek and are well prepared and presented.

Toumbourlika
Kalapotháki 11
Tel: 2310 282174
Yet another of the city's famous *ouzerí*, hidden away in a narrow street off Platía Dimokratías, this consists of a couple of small cosy rooms with a few outside tables. It specialises in fish *mezédes*. Some live music on weekends.

To Yedi
I. Paparéska 13, Kastra
Tel: 2310 246495
High up next to the Eptapýrgio fortress, this laid-back and friendly *ouzerí* serves up no-nonsense high-quality *mezédes*.

Zythos
Katoúni 5, Ladádika
Tel: 2310 540284
This is a great spot for people-watching while you dine on a variety of dishes featuring Greek, Asian and western European elements. Zythos is a restaurant-cum-pub and apart from its inventive cuisine serves up draft Irish and German beers.

TRANSPORT ACCOMMODATION EATING OUT ACTIVITIES A – Z LANGUAGE

MACEDONIA AND THRACE

Alexandroúpoli

To Nisiotiko
Zarífi 1
Tel: 2551 020990
To Nisiotiko stands out for its well prepared and not overly expensive food. Fish predominate though there's a range of grills and imaginative *mezédes*.

Flórina

Prespes
Tyrnovou 12
Tel: 23850 23973
A local favourite in the town centre, with grills and salads. Popular for lunch.

Foe

Gavaliotissa
Tel: 23810 28860
There are surprisingly few good places to eat in this bar-filled town, but this restaurant is a good place to settle on, with large terraces looking out over the Longos valley.

Kastoriá

Doltso
Tsakáli 2
Tel: 2467 024670
This classy dining venue on Doltso Square is a local

favourite, set in a lovely restored mansion. The top-class food includes many traditional Macedonian dishes.

Kavála

Tembelhanio
Poulídou 33b
Tel: 2510 232501
A Macedonian-style *ouzerí*: the *mezédes* are mainly fish, with shellfish taking pride of place, and you wash it all down with small carafes of *tsípouro* – the fiery grape spirit that is drunk throughout Macedonia. Tourists are noticeable by their absence. Dine in the company of knowledgable and appreciative locals.

Komotiní

Ta Adelfia
Orféos 25
Tel: 2531 020201
The food here is simple staples, cooked in the old-fashioned way. Go for the daily specials listed on a blackboard outside.

Litóhoro

To Bereketi
Agíou Nikoláou 40
Tel: 2352 082213

To Bereketi specialises in kebabs, roasted over a charcoal grill in the restaurant window. Good local draft wine.

Nikiti

Kazanis
Tel: 23750 23333
Typical seashore restaurant in this attractive resort. Kazanis has been in the family since 1952 and the fish is always fresh. Open year-round.

Préspa

Akrolimnia
The lakefront, Psarádes village
Tel: 2385 046260
If you eat in the Préspa Lake region, you should sample famous local produce – namely *fasoláda*, a rich bean soup, or the local lake trout, *péstrofa*. This busy lakefront taverna is one of the best places to enjoy them.

Véria

To Katafygi
Kondogeorgáki 18
Tel: 2331 027227
The impressive and cosy Katafygi (the name means "refuge", as in mountain shelter) dishes up a wide

range of game from quail to wild boar. Vegetarians are well catered for too.

Xánthi

Myrovolos
Platía Hristídi
Tel: 2541 072720
The atmospheric streets of Xánthi's old town is home to a rash of similar tavernas. Myrovolos is one of the better ones and specialises in *tsipouro-mézedes* (*mezédes* for *tsípouro*). On weekends you may catch live *rembétika* music.

Paparéska 13
Kastra
Tel: 2310 246495
High up next to the Eptapýrgio fortress, this laid-back *ouzerí* serves up no-nonsense high quality *mezédes* in a friendly, unfussy environment.

Zythos
Katoúni 5, Ladádika
Tel: 2310 540284
This is a great spot for people-watching while you dine on dishes featuring Greek, Asian and western European elements. Zythos is a restaurant-cum-pub and apart from its inventive cuisine serves up draft Irish and German beers.

SARONIC GULF

Égina

Agora (Geladakis)
Behind fish market
Tel: 22970 27308
One of the oldest (founded *c.*1960) seafood outfits in town, offering good value without airs and graces – you'll likely have to wait for a table. Summer seating on the cobbles outside, winter tables inside. Bulk wine or *oúzo* for refreshment.

Lekkas
Kazantzáki 4, northerly waterfront
Renowned for its good vegetable platters and hygienic meat grills, washed down by excellent bulk wine. Very inexpensive for Égina.

Póros

Taverna Karavolos
Póros Town
Tel: 22980 26158
Meaning a type of snail in Greek, Karavolos is a very popular taverna in the back streets of Póros town. Yes, the restaurant does serve snails, served with a rich sauce. There's a selection of ready made *magirevtá* (home cooked) dishes as well as grills. Dine indoors or on a leafy patio. Reservations recommended.

Taverna Platanos
Póros Town
Tel: 22980 24249
High up in the back streets of Póros town under a

plane tree *(plátanos)*, the speciality here is grills ranging from regular steaks to *kokorétsi*, mixed offal grilled on a long skewer. The atmosphere is relaxed and laid-back; evening dining is the best time to enjoy this place.

Spétses

Exedra
Old Harbour
Tel: 22980 73497
One of several classy tavernas in the Old Harbour, Exedra is a fish taverna, and you can see them swimming about as you dine on a platform extending into the harbour.

The house speciality is fish cooked in garlic and tomato and baked in the oven. You'll also find prawns and lobster, prepared with cheese or with spaghetti.

Liotrívi
Old Harbour
Tel: 22980 72269
Close to the Exedra is a restaurant in an old olive press *(liotrívi)*. This is also a fish taverna in a very attractive location near the old boatyards. Mainly Greek clientele enjoy all kinds of variations on fish and other seafood. Best for evening dining.

Patralis
Kounoupítsa waterfront
The most upmarket, white-

tablecloth venue away from the Dápia, with excellent service. Their *psári ala Spetsióta* (fish in ratatouille sauce) is made with fresh, not frozen, fish, as in many other places. The bulk wine is satisfactory, and baked-apple dessert rounds off the experience. Open all year.

Ydra

Taverna Gitoniko
Ýdra Town
Tel: 22980 53615
Popular with locals and foreigners alike, the Taverna Gitoniko (aka Kristina's) offers discreet rooftop dining as well as indoor tables downstairs.

Good-value dishes range from simple island vegetarian fare to hearty grilled meats and fish. Veal in quince or red wine sauce is a house speciality. Excellent draft wine.
To Steki
Ýdra Town
Tel: 22980 53517
A simple taverna-cum-*ouzerí*

just a short step back from the harbour front. Locals come here to sip wine and gossip. The food is simple and unadorned and consists in the main of ready-cooked dishes with a smattering of grills and fries. The lamb fricassée is worth tasting as are the tasty *píttes* (small triangular pastry turnovers).

CYCLADES

Amorgós

O Nikos
Langáda
Tel: 22850 73310
Polished taverna specialising in platters like beets with greens, dips, goat-based dishes, fish and some *magirevtá*. Not cheap for Amorgós but the quality is high, with seating on perhaps the island's loveliest vine-shaded terrace.
To Hyma
Hóra, main commercial street
Tel: 69747 86376
Excellent, genuine *ouzerí* in an ex-grocery store. Strong points are salads and seafood dishes, plus a few meat casseroles. *hýma* (in bulk) is your wine. Open all year, off-season by arrangement.
To Limani tis Kyra Katinas
Órmos Egiális
Tel: 22850 73269
Strong contender for best all-round eatery on the island; strengths are seafood, pulses, vegetable casseroles and local cheese. Very reasonably priced for the quality. Open from just before Easter–mid-Oct.

Anáfi

To Steki
Hóra
Simple, friendly all-round taverna with a terrace and bulk wine; in spring you might get flash-fried *hános*, a boney but tasty fish typical of the Cyclades.

Mýkonos

Efthimios' Patisserie
Fl. Zouganeli, Hóra

For over 40 years, Efthimios has sold his famed *kalathakiá* ("little baskets") and almond milk from this immaculate sweet shop. (Takeaway only.)
Katrin's
Ágios Gerásimos district, Hóra
Tel: 22890 26946
Since the 1980s, Katrin's Greek cuisine with a French accent has made this restaurant, on a back alley, extremely popular. Fairly pricey, reservations recommended.
Nikola's Taverna
Agía Ánna Beach (after Platýs Gialós)
A locals' favourite: an authentic Greek taverna on a pretty, tiny beach.
Niko's
just off the harbour, Hóra
For a quarter-century, Niko's has made fresh fish and lobster a speciality. Also try homemade *mousakás*, salads with capers and rocket. Slow service, moderate prices.
Sea Satin Market – Caprice
Alevhándra quarter, directly below the windmills, Hóra
Unique waveside restaurant, where Greeks often party after a baptism or wedding. Eat fish and shellfish. Easter–Oct.

Náxos

Gorgona
Agía Ánna
Tel: 22850 41007
This longtime beach taverna has grown more elaborate, but the prices are still good, as is the traditional Greek food. The fresh fish is bought at the

dock out front. Try the *kakaviá* (fish stew). Locals eat here year-round.
Meltemi Restaurant
Extreme southern end of Hóra's waterfront
The Meltemi has been here for 50 years, serving inexpensive traditional Greek cuisine, including fresh fish. It's authentic and popular with locals. Easter till end October, all day till midnight.
The Old Inn
Boúrgos, Hóra
Tel: 22850 26093
In a charming garden, Berlin chef Dieter von Ranizewski, who has spent most of his life on Naxos, serves Greek and international cuisine. He makes everything, even the smoked ham.

Paros

Boudaraki
Harbour road, Parikía
This is a typical Greek *ouzerí* with drinks and *mezédes* such as grilled octopus and fresh sea urchins. Open Easter–early Oct.
Levantis
Market Street, Parikía
Tel: 22840 23613
Inventive Mediterranean cuisine in a pretty, quiet garden. Moderate to expensive.
O Christos
Opposite the Church of the Panagía Pantanássa, Naoússa
Tel: 22840 51442
Paros' most elegant restaurant (and one of the more expensive) offers Mediterranean food, perfect service and great attention to detail.
Porphyra
Parikía
Tel: 22840 23410

Some of the fresh fish and shellfish, including oysters, are caught by the owners themselves. And there are daily specialities, such as sea-urchin salad. Open off season.

Santorini

1800
Ía
Tel: 22860 71485
In an old captain's mansion on main street, 1800 is one of Greece's best for elegant Mediterranean cuisine. Expensive; reservations essential.
Aktaion
Firostéfani
This taverna, on the caldera edge, has served traditional Greek food for 60 years. This is how *mousakás* is supposed to taste – Mum's recipes are still in use. Inexpensive.
Camille Stefani
Kamári
This restaurant, right on the black beach, has been serving seafood and Greek cuisine for 25 years. Locals favour it even in summer. Reasonable prices.
Restaurant Nicholas
Firá
On Stavros Street, parallel to the caldera road, Nikolas is Firá's oldest taverna. It serves all the usual Greek dishes. Open year round, lunch and dinner. Inexpensive.
Taverna Katina
Ammoúdi, Ía
On the right at the bottom of the steps leading down from Ía. In many people's eyes, the fresh, grilled fish, prawns and Santorini specialities make this the

island's best taverna, all helped along by the excellent, friendly service. Easter–October; from lunch until late.
Taverna Pyrgos
Pýrgos Village
An elegant, moderately priced restaurant with an unusual view. The best plan is to order a table-full of their excellent *mezédes*.

Sífnos

Liotriví (O Manganas)
Apollonía
Tel: 22840 31246
One of the oldest *koultouriárika* on the island. Maybe resting on its laurels a bit, and not cheap, but good for a special meal in atmospheric setting.

Odos Oniron

Apollonía
Tel: 22840 32002
Upscale, *koultouriárika* restaurant with eclectic but tasteful decor, featuring mostly baked, strongly herb-flavoured seafood, as well as beef and pasta dishes. There is delicious home-made walnut pie to finish off.

Sýros

Lilís
Áno Sýros
Tel: 22810 88087
Huge place, where the food is almost incidental to the live *rebétika* music at weekends; *rebétika* great, Markos Vamvakaris, was born in this village and is said to have played here.

RHODES

Rhodes Town

Marco Polo Café
Ayíou Fanouríou 42, Old Town
Tel: 22410 25562
One of the best old-town restaurants. The constantly changing menu is a mixture of traditional mainland and Cretan recipes. Kitchen shuts at 11pm for the sake of hotel guests.
Mavrikos
Líndos
Tel: 22440 31232
Founded in 1933 in the fig-tree square, and owned by the same family ever since, Mavrikos serves accomplished *mezédes* such as manoúri cheese with basil and pine-nuts; dipping into the excellent (and expensive) Greek wine list will double a basic bill of about €30 each.
Meltemi
Platía Koundourióti 8, east end of Élli beach
Tel: 22410 30480
Unbeatably set, locally attended beachside *ouzerí* specialising in *karavi-dópsyha* (crayfish nuggets), *oktapodokeftédes* (octopus croquettes) and

flavoursome starters. Inside there's a wintertime salon with old prints and photos on the wall. Open all day for food and drink.
Paragadi
Avstralías cnr Claude Pepper, Zéfyros district
Tel: 22410 37775
Slightly high fish prices at this seafood specialist are offset by a reasonable wine list; there are also the usual vegetarian starters. On Saturday night the place fills with the Rhodian *beau monde*, and you must book then. Closed Sun eve and Mon noon.
Sakis
Kanadá 95, Zéfyros district
Tel: 22410 35626
Indoor-outdoor spot known for its prime meats; there are also some shellfish plus the usual starter platters. Prices are a bit higher than usual but worth it for good, friendly service. Open all year for supper plus Sun lunch.
Sea Star
Sofokléous 24
Tel: 22410 22117
The least expensive quality fish outlet in the Old Town.

A limited menu – only scaly fish and a few shellfish and simple, *mezédes* – is all to the good. Inside seating during cool weather, otherwise out on the square under the vines.
Ta Marasia
Agíou Ioánnou 155, New Town
Tel: 22410 30745
Occupying the patio and (in winter) interior of a 1923-vintage house, this is one of the more creative *ouzerí* on the island. There's plenty for vegetarians, as well as seafood titbits and a full meat list.

Around Rhodes Island

Avandis
south end, Paralía Afándou
Tel: 22440 51280
Fish, grilled or fried to perfection, is accompanied by excellent *ambelofásola* (autumn beans) with garlic chips, and chunky *tzatzíki*. It's pricey for the remote locale but there are nice touches like table linen and chilled beer glasses.
Panorama Tsambikas
highway above Tsambíka beach

Tel: 22440 23153
The family patriarch mans the outside grill, turning out excellent if somewhat pricey fish and meat. Attentive service, and unbeatable views. Very popular weekend afternoons with Rhodians.
Perigiali
by fishing anchorage, Stegná
Tel: 22440 23444
Where islanders go at weekends for the sake of seafood, homemade *dolmádes* and unusually good bread. Slightly pricey.
Pigi Fasouli
Psínthos outskirts
Tel: 22410 50071
The best of several tavernas in this village, in a prime position overlooking plane trees and the namesake spring.
Platanos
Lahaniá village
Tel: 22440 46027
Arguably the most exquisite setting on the island, with outdoor tables between two gushing Ottoman fountains under the plane tree of the name. *Mezédes* are top-drawer and inexpensive, as are meat entrees, but the fish is pricey.

DODECANESE

Astypálea

Australia
Just inland from the head of the bay, Skála
Tel: 22430 61275
Kyria Maria presides over the oldest and most wholesome taverna here, with fresh seafood and island wine. Open Apr–Nov.

Maïstrali (Tou Penindara)
head of the harbour, Skála
The best spot for a local lobster banquet, or less extravagantly a scaly-fish meal or *magirevtá* from a broad menu. Open all year for dinner, lunch as per demand.
To Yerani
In the streambed just behind

Livádia beach
Tel: 22430 61484
The most consistently good taverna here, renowned for its excellent *magirevtá*. Open (May–Oct)

Hálki

Ftenayia
Tel: 69459 98333

Good seafood platters, vegetable *mezédes* and of course *oúzo* served above its own patch of pebble lido at the eponymous Ftenáyia cove.
Remezzo (Takis)
Emborió waterfront
Tel: 22460 45061
Excellent for *magirevtá* and pizzas.

TRANSPORT

Kálymnos

Kafenes
Platía Hristoú, opposite municipal "palace", Póthia
Tel: 22430 28727
Going since 1950, this hole-in-the-wall purveys seafood *mezédes*, great local cheese and salads, with *laïká* music cranked up loud. Throw in very low prices, and it's easy to see why you always wait for a table.

Pandelis
behind Olympic Hotel, Ágios Nikólaos district
Tel: 22430 51508
The menu only mentions the ubiquitous Kalymnian *mermizéli* salad (like Cretan *dákos*) and a few grills or *magireviá*; you have to ask after scaly fish, and fresh shellfish such as *kalógnomes* (like big mussels), *strídia* (round oysters) and *foúskes* (indescribable).

Kárpathos

L'Angolo-ly Gorgona
South end of quay, Diafáni
A versatile café with offerings including real Italian-standard coffees, *soumáda* (almond drink), lovely pies and limoncello liqueur.

Dramoundana
Mesohóri
Remarkably reasonably priced for Kárpathos, this features local caper greens, village sausages and marinated fish.

ly Orea Karpathos
Southeast end of main quay, Pigádia
Tel: 22450 22501
The best all-round taverna, with palatable local bulk wine, *trahanádes* soup and great spinach pie. The locals treat it as an *ouzerí*, so it's OK to order just a few *orektiká* to accompany a *karafáki* (small pitcher).

Pine Tree
Ádia, 7 km (4 miles) north of Finíki
Tel: 69773 69948
Sustaining, reasonable rural taverna with country fare like lentils and *htapodoma-karonáda* (octopus in pasta), washed down by sweet Óthos wine. Sea-view terrace under the trees of the name, plus a few rooms to rent.

Kastellórizo

Akrothalassi
Southwest corner of quay
Tel: 22460 49052
The most consistently salubrious fish and meat grills, reliably open at lunch too (unusual here), owing to shade from its arbour.

Ypomoni
mid-quay, Megísti
Tel: 22460 49224
Supper-only seafood specialists (plus a few meat grills) with minimalist presentation, minimalist prices, minimal seating and maximum freshness – so expect to wait for a table.

Kós

Ambavris
Ambávris hamlet, 800 metres (½ mile) south of Kós Town
Tel: 22420 25696
Ignore the perfunctory English-language menu in favour of the constantly changing *mezédes pikilía* or house medley – six platters for about €25 can encompass such delights as *pihtí* (brawn), stuffed squash blossoms, *fáva* dip, *loukán-ika*. Courtyard seating. Open for supper May–Oct.

Ambeli
1 km (½ mile) east of Tingáki resort
Tel: 22420 69682
Best policy here is to avoid the mains and order a variety of the excellent starters. Plates are fair priced and deceptively large, so don't over-order. Seating indoors and out in the vineyard; open daily lunch/dinner May–Oct, winter Fri and Sat eve, Sun lunch.

Makis
One lane in from front, Mastihári
Tel: 22420 51592
Currently the best – and best-priced – fish on the island outside of Kós Town, and an excellent spot to wait for the ro-ro ferry to Kálymnos. No *magireviá*, just a few salads and dips, and oblique sea views at best mean relatively few tourists.

Oromedon
Zía approach road
Tel: 22420 69983
One of the few tavernas here that doesn't need to rely on picture-menus and

other gimmicks, thanks to the prime view from its roof terrace, and the good, local food. Open all year.

Ouzeri Limni (Karamolengos)
Linopótis, below Pylí on main road
Tel: 22420 41579
If you're tired of being stuffed like a foie gras goose at Greek tavernas, then this *ouzerí* is perfect for you: all items are available in small, medium and large platters. Choose from a huge number of different *oúzo*, *tsikoudiá* and *tsípouro*. Open all year noon–11pm except Tuesday, though best at supper when road noise is less.

Platáni village
Central junction
Ethnic Turkish management at several clustered establishments dish out tasty Anatolian-style *mezédes* and kebabs; best go in a group so that you can pass the little platters around. The most popular, if the most touristy, is **Arap** (tel: 22420 28442); if you can't get in, head across the way to **Asklipios** or **Serif** (tel: 22420 23784), which fills with locals later in the evening. Between November and April these close, leaving **Gin's Place** a few steps further inland (tel: 22420 25166) – where the food is often even better – as the sole option. At any season, finish off with an Anatolian ice cream, best on the island, at **Zaharoplastio ly Paradosi** opposite the three summer restaurants.

Pote tin Kyriaki
Pissándrou 9, Kós Town
Tel: 22420 27872
The island's only genuine *ouzerí*, with fair prices and patio seating in summer, indoors in the converted old house otherwise. Supper only, Mon–Sat; winter Thur–Sat lunch and supper.

Léros

Mezedopolio Dimitris
Spiliá district, on road between Pandélli and Vromólithos
Tel: 22470 25626
The heartiest food on the island, hands down, and the best view of

Vromólithos. Stars include chunky, herby Lerian sausages, potato salad, *hanoúm bórek* (stuffed with cheese and *pastourmás* or cured meat). Moderate prices and large portions. Open most of the year.

Ouzeri Neromylos
out by the sea-marooned windmill, Agía Marína
Tel: 22470 24894
The most romantic setting on the island, whether for lunch or supper. Specialities include *garidopílafo* (shrimp-rice), baked four-cheese casserole and *kolokythokeftédes* (courgette patties). Open mid-Mar–late Oct; reservations mandatory July–Aug.

Psaropoula (Apostolis)
Pandélli beach
Tel: 22470 25200
A good balance of fresh seafood and *magireviá*, especially popular with locals at weekends. Open and enclosed sea-view terraces, so open most of the year.

Lipsí

Dilaila
Katsadiá, left-hand bay
Tel: 22470 41041
Incongruously classy for the rural surroundings, with platters such as fish with rosemary, saffron rice, excellent *fáva*. Open June–Sept.

O Giannis
Mid-quay
Tel: 22470 41395
Excellent all-rounder, with meat and seafood grills but plenty of salads and *laderá* dishes for vegetarians too. The only taverna open for lunch as well as supper all season long. Early May–early Oct.

Marathi

To Marathi
southeast end of Maráthi beach
Tel: 22470 31580
The more welcoming of two establishments here, with simple fish and free-range goat served up by piratically garbed Mihalis Kavouras, at attractive prices. Open all day, according to Mihalis' whim.

ACCOMMODATION
EATING OUT
ACTIVITIES
A – Z
LANGUAGE

Nísyros

Apyria (Triandafyllos)
Emborió
Tel: 22420 31377
The former *kafenío* of this all-but-abandoned village has been transformed into the best meat taverna on the island – *gouronópoulo* on the spit during summer, otherwise just a few *mezédes* and select meat platters daily at very fair prices, with local *halvás* for dessert. Indoor/outdoor seating; open all year (weekends only winter).

Limenari
Limenari cove west of Pálli
Tel: 22420 31023
Expect fair prices and portions for salads, fish, a few dishes of the day, and made-to-order *tyrokafterí* (which takes a while to arrive). A lovely spot in terraced valley above the bay. Islanders and conscript soldiers go all year, always a good sign.

To Ankyrovoli
Ágios Sávvas cove, Mandráki
Tel: 22420 31552
The reincarnation of the late lamented Fabrika, this *ouzerí* features *pittiá* (courgette and chickpea patties), *boukouniés* (fried pork), bulk wine from Attica, taped Greek sounds and big portions at moderate prices.

Pátmos

Benetos
Sápsila cove, 2 km (1 mile) southeast of Skála
Tel: 22470 33089
This eatery has a reputation as one of the best spots on the island for Mediterranean/Pacific Rim fusion cuisine, with a stress on seafood. Count on €36 for drinks and three courses. Open June–early Oct, supper only except Mon; best to reserve in summer.

Ktima Petra
Pétra beach, south of Grikou
Tel: 22470 33207
Hands down the best beach taverna on the island. Chunky *melitzanosaláta*, lush rocket salad, and pork *giovétsi* are typical of lunchtime offerings, with excellent retsina from Thebes; at sunset the grill is lit, and still later the place becomes a full-on bar. Open Easter–Oct.

Livadi Geranou
above eponymous beach
Tel: 69724 97426
Doesn't look like much, but this taverna has a cult following for the sake of its coarse-cut *hórta*, roast goat and seafood dishes – plus views over the entire island.

O Panagos tou Sarandi
upper Kámbos
Tel: 22470 31570
A beacon of *magirevtá* for the whole island. The autumn menu might feature baked *palamídi* (North Aegean tuna), chickpea hotpot, good bulk wine, yogurt dessert on the house. Very reasonably priced, open all year. A museum's worth of old photos inside.

Sými

Dimitris
South quay near ferry dock, Gialós
Tel: 22460 72207
Excellent, family-run, seafood-strong *ouzerí* with exotic items such as *hohlióalo* (sea snails), *foúskes* (mock oysters), *spinóalo* (pinna-shell flesh) and the indigenous miniature shrimps, as well as more usual platters. Lunch and supper.

Georgios
Top of Kalí Stráta, Horió
Tel: 22460 71984
An island institution; nouvelle Greek cuisine in large, non-nouvelle portions, served on the pebbled courtyard. Informal live music some nights.

Mythos
South quay, Gialós
Tel: 22460 71488
A supper-only *ouzerí* that is reckoned among the best-value cooking on the island. Ignore the menu and let chef Stavros deliver a Frenchified medley which may well include salad, seafood starters, meat followed by home-made desserts. Open Easter–Oct.

Tílos

Kastro
Megálo Horió
Tel: 22460 44116
The managing family can be a bit dour, but it's worth putting up with them for their excellent own-raised meat, goat cheese and *dolmádes*, served at the best terrace on the island.

Omonia (Mihalis')
Just above the harbour square
Tel: 22460 44287
Sit under the trees strung with fairy lights and enjoy the closest thing to an authentic *ouzerí* on the island by night; filling breakfasts in the morning.

To Armenon (Nikos')
On the shore road, Livádia
Tel: 22460 44134
Excellent and salubrious beach-taverna-cum-*ouzerí*; Alfa beer on tap.

NORTHEASTERN AEGEAN

Híos

Makellos
Pityós
Tel: 22720 23364
On the west edge of the village, this is a shrine of local creative cuisine; daily June–Sept, Fri–Sun eve Oct–May.

Mylarakia
Tambákika district, by Híos Town Hospital
Tel: 22710 41412
All eight brands of Hiot *oúzo* available to accompany starters, seafood and some meat dishes. Romantic setting. Supper all year; lunch on occasion.

O Hotzas
Georgíou Kondýli 3, Híos Town
Tel: 22710 42787
Oldest and arguably the best taverna in the city. Fare varies seasonally, but expect a mix of vegetarian dishes, sausages and fish. Open all year, supper only (not Sun).

To Mageirio tis Kyrarinis
Kipouriés
Tel: 22740 22016
The more accomplished of two tavernas here on this oasis-hamlet's square, with home-style casserole dishes, sweets and starters. June–Sept daily, winter weekends only.

To Talimi
central Thymianá
Tel: 22710 32940
A lodestar for unusual *magirevtá* and home-style platters, dished up by a very pleasant family. The name recalls a local sword dance representing the locals' ambush of medieval pirates. Open all year.
Tou Koupelou (Stelios)
Langáda harbour
Tel: 22710 74813
One of the best places on the island for a seafood supper. Best ring in advance with your party's special requirements, otherwise it will just be the standard *kalamári*, *barboúni* and *gávros*.

Ikaría

Delfini
Armenistís
Tel: 22750 71254
Popular venue for the sake of the waves lapping the terrace – and the food (fish, meat, grills and a few casseroles).
Thea
Nás
Tel: 22750 71491
Returned Ohio-Ikarian lady oversees the best *magirevtá* this end of the island, with lots of vegetarian dishes. Service can suffer a bit during the crush. Daily June–Sept, Sat–Sun in winter.

Lésvos

Anemoessa
Skála Sykaminiás, closest to the harbour chapel
Tel: 22530 55360
Tops for fresh fish, and good *mezédes*. Open all year (weekends only Nov–Apr).
Balouhanas
Géra Gulf seafront, Pérama
Tel: 22510 51948
Seafood *ouzerí* with wood-kiosk seating overhanging the water; interesting *mezédes* and home-made desserts too. Open all year.
Captain's Table
Fishing harbour, Mólyvos
Tel: 22530 71241
As the name suggests, a strong line in seafood but also meat and vegetable specialities such as their "Ukrainian" aubergine dip,

as well as good own-label wine. Open May–late Oct.
Ermis
Kornárou 2, corner Ermoú, Mytilíni Town
Tel: 22510 26232
The best and most atmospheric *ouzerí* of a cluster in Páno Skálo district. Special strengths are sardines, sausages and, Smyrna-style meatballs.
Taverna tou Panaï
Ágios Isídoros, north edge of village
Tel: 22520 31920
Plainly presented but tasty food: vegetarian *mezédes*, grills, cheese and so on. Mostly Greek clientele; open all year.
To Petri
Petrí village, in the hills above Pétra/Mólyvos
Tel: 22530 41239
Friendly, family-run taverna serving *magirevtá* and grills; unbeatable terrace. Open May–mid-Oct.

Límnos

Iy Glaropoula
Néa Koútali
Tel: 22540 92325
This is *the* place for a seafood blowout, with bay views from the terrace.
Iy Kali Kardia
Platía of Tsimándria
Tel: 22540 51278
Very cheap, very cheerful, with a nice, quiet location. From amongst grills and a few *magireftá*, tick your choices off on the menu-bill combo. Open all year.
Man-Tella
Sardés centre
Tel: 22540 61349
Cult taverna doubling as the central *kafenío* (thus open all year) of this highest hill village on Límnos. Big portions off a meat-strong menu; good service.
Tzitzifies
Rihá Nerá beach
Tel: 22540 23756
A proper taverna at this town beach, with tables on the sand. Good *ímam baildí*, dips and baked dishes.

Sámos

Aeolos
West end of quay, Ágios Konstandínos

Best-value fish and grills here, plus a few oven dishes of the day; unbeatable seating by the pebble shore.
Ammos Plaz
start of west beach, Kokkári
Tel: 22730 92463
Top outlet in this resort for *magirevtá* – especially *moussakás* or *pastítsio* – and fish. Their beach-facing conservatory is so popular you have to book days in advance in high season.
Ankyra
Iréon
Tel: 22730 95255
Maybe because it's on an inland lane away from sea, this excellent *ouzerí* tries a little bit harder and is a tad less expensive, with polite service and all the standard platters, well presented.
Artemis (Tou Karathanasi)
Kefalopoúlou 4, ferry dock, Vathý
Tel: 22730 23639
Currently the best *taverna* in town, with good *hórta* and *fáva*, excellent seafood platters, plus standard meat mains. The smooth red bulk wine from Manolátes won't leave you hung over.
Iy Byra
opposite main church
Tel: 22730 92350
The oldest (founded 1925) *kafenío* here, now transformed into a very good *mezedopolío*. Crowds of tourists don't seem to compromise quality.
Iy Psarades
Ágios Nikólaos Kondakeïkon
Tel: 22730 32489
Long reckoned the best fish taverna on the island, at surprisingly reasonable prices, plus the usual *orektiká*. In season you have to book. Open Easter–Oct.
Kryfi Folia
Platanákia district of Kérveli
Tel: 22730 25194
Near the east tip of Sámos in an isolated olive grove, a 1970s-style taverna in best sense dominated by Stavros your host. Starters precede the best (and cheapest) lamb chops on the island. Open Easter–late Oct.
Tarsanas
Little lane 100 metres/yds in from west beach Kokkári
Tel: 22730 92337
The stock-in-trade here are

pizzas and perhaps two vegetarian dishes of the day at bargain prices. Catch the sea breeze on the tiny terrace.
To Delfini
Avlákia
Tel: 22730 94279
The tables are right at water level in this tiny, Greeks-only resort, giving the best coastal view on the island. Come here for fresh fish platters and large veggie starters. The bulk wine isn't so good – choose a bottle instead.

Samothráki

Fengari Restaurant
Loutrá Thermá
Tel: 25510 98321
The Fengari serves a range of traditional island dishes as well as meat and fish grills. Very pleasant ambience and very good value for money.
I Klimataria
Kamariótissa
Tel: 25510 41535
On the waterfront just north of the ferry quay, this unassuming taverna puts out a range of good *magirevtá* dishes and grills to order. Twice a week the chef makes *gianniótiko* – a rich dish of pork, egg, potatoes, onions and garlic.

Thásos

Iy Pigi
central platía, Liménas
Tel: 25930 22941
Old standby dishing out dependable *magirevtá* next to the spring of the name; best at supper.
O Platanos
under the central tree, Sotíros village
Tel: 25930 71234
Summer-only taverna run by a young couple from neary Rahóni village. Elaborate *magirevtá* when trade justifies it, otherwise simple grills and home-made *tsípouro* if you ask.
Simi
east waterfront, Liménas
Tel: 25930 22517
Despite the touristy cadre, Simi serves decent fish and *mezédes*. Open all year.

SPORADES AND EVIA

Alónissos

Elaionas
Leftós Gialós beach
Tel: 24240 66066
The better of two decent tavernas here, with unusual platters like *tsitsírava*, *xynógalos*, other chunky dips and daily specials prepared by three generations of family ladies toiling in the kitchen. Outdoor seating in a gravel court under the olives of the name. May–Sept only.
Iy Mouria
harbour end of the access road, Vótsi
Tel: 24240 65273
Friendly, family-run, inexpensive option with big salads, a couple of *magirevtá* of the day, ace squid, and bulk wine. They rent rooms upstairs too.

Évia

Apanemo
shoreline at Fanári district, Halkída
Tel: 22210 22614
Halkída is famous for its seafood, so there's no excuse for tolerating the hit-and-miss performance of certain midtown outfits. This seafood taverna has one of the best settings, easiest parking and some of the best food – on the pricey side but worth it.
To Pyrofani (Livadítis)
Límni, northwest end of quay
Tel: 22270 31640
Slightly bumped-up prices

for average portions at this seafood-strong *ouzerí* are justified by the quality, with nice touches like sweet-cabbage marinade as a side dish, and big salads. Stick to their *oúzo*, as the bulk wine is not a strong point.

Skiáthos

Amfiliki
south edge of town by clinic
Tel: 24270 22839
Good smells wafting out the kitchen up front are the clue you've arrived. Out back, limited seating – about 40 places – with unlimited views of Mégas Gialós bay. The food lives up to the setting, especially off-menu seafood specials like *bráska kípo* (monkfish in spicy tomato sauce), and seafood salad. It's open winter too, with the fireplace going.
Alexandros
Old Town, 2 blocks in from fishing port
Tel: 24270 22431
Good grills (especially the lamb chops) and oven dishes, home-made crème caramel for dessert – so it's a shame about the poor bulk wine. Greeks in attendance provide singalongs with acoustic bouzouki and guitar. There's winter seating in a small house opposite, otherwise outside under the mulberry bushes.

Sklithri
Kalamáki
Tel: 24270 21494
Blink and you'll miss this tiny eatery almost hidden by the roadside a few kilometres from Skiáthos town. Most tourists do, so you'll find mainly locals dining on sardines or other fish dishes. It's cheap unassuming and genuine. Best of all, it's right on the beach.

Skópelos

In Hóra (the main harbour), the west quay is the place to eat and where locals go.
Englezos
west quay near *dimarhío*
Tel: 24240 22230
The creative Greek menu varies by the year but might include aubergine croquettes with mint and cheese, rock samphire, and a variety of lamb dishes, all done with panache. To drink, bulk wine from the Anhíalos co-op, and delicately perfumed brandy.
Klimataria
right next to *dimarhío*
Tel: 24240 22273
The best place for reasonable (for Skópelos) fish by weight, plus a few cooked dishes and *mezédes* – locals conspicuously in attendance.
Pavlos
Agnóndas port
Tel: 24240 22409
Reliable fish specialist with

fair prices, also doing unusual *mezédes* like *tsitsírava* (wild pistachio sprouts); good bulk wine from Apostolakis, a local Thessalian vintner. The best of three choices here; waterside seating under trees. Open Mar–Oct.
Ta Kymata
far north end of quay, Hóra
Tel: 24240 22381
About the oldest taverna here, run by an engaging family and renowned for its elaborate *magirevtá* such as lamb and vegetables in phyllo triangles; also, good eggplant salad and real beets with greens attached.

Skýros

O Lambros
Aspoús, through road
Tel: 22220 91388
Efficient, polite service, pleasant interior or the terrace in fine weather, grilled fish, chops and al dente vegetables make this a natural all-year favourite for locals and visitors.
To Perasma
start of airport slip road
Tel: 22220 92911
The airport staff and seemingly half the air force personnel on the island eat here, knowing a good thing: succulent own-raised meat and cheese, at reasonable prices. Seating outdoors or in, according to weather. Open all year.

CORFU

Kérkyra Town

Hryssomallis (Babis)
Nikifórou Theotókou 6, Kérkyra
Tel: 26610 30342
The sign says it's a *zythopsitopolío* ("beer-hall-grill"), but it's also almost the last traditional oven-food place in the old town: stews, *hórta*, *mousakás*, lamb offal and so forth. A typical bill won't be more than €15 each. The Durrells ate here during their 1930s stay, but the restaurant has been around a lot longer.

La Cucina
Guildford 15
Tel: 26610 45029
You'll usually have to wait for a table outside at this competent Italian eatery, which does excellent pizzas and handmade pasta dishes, as well as antipasti and seafood – though the interior is extremely pleasant in the cooler months. Open daily 7pm–midnight, Feb–Nov.
Mouragia
Arseníou 15, north quay, Kérkyra Town

Tel: 26610 33815
A good mix of seafood (with fresh and frozen items clearly indicated) and Corfiot *magirevtá* such as *sofríto* and *pastitsáda*. Inexpensive for any island, let alone Corfu, and great sea views in the bargain. Open daily noon–12.30am.
Theotoki Brothers (Kerkyraïki Paradosiaki Taverna)
Alkiviádi Dári 69, Garítsa Bay
By far the best of half-a-dozen tavernas with tables out in the eucalyptus park

here. A full range of *magirevtá* dishes and grills, plus some seafood, at very reasonable prices. Service can be leisurely, even by Corfu standards. Open lunch and dinner.
Venetian Well
Platía Kremastí, northwest of Cathedral, Kérkyra Town
Tel: 26610 44761
Tucked away through an arch, with tables around the well, is some of the town's most innovative and expensive cooking, generic Aegean with interesting

twists. Excellent (and pricey) wine list. Supper only Mon–Sat, Mar–Oct.

Around the Island

Agni
Agní cove, between Nissáki and Kassiópi
Tel: 26630 91142
Well-known restaurant run by Anglo-Greek couple, serving very good food. Open for lunch and dinner Apr–Oct.

Alonaki Bay
Paralía Alonáki, near Korissíon lagoon
Tel: 26610 75872
Good country recipes, strong on vegetables and seafood served at shady tables on a terrace overlooking the sea.

Boukari Beach
Boúkari
Tel: 26620 51791

The less commercial of two seafood tavernas at this seashore hamlet, in an idyllic setting, with great-value fresh fare. Open all day Apr–Oct.

Cavo Barbaro (Fotis)
Avláki
Tel: 26630 81905
An unusually good beach taverna, with welcoming service. A few magirevtá dishes at lunch, more grills after dark). Seating on the lawn, and plenty of parking. The only thing "barbarous" here can be the wind, as there's no shelter.

Etrusco
just outside Káto Korakiána village, on the Dassiá road
Tel: 26610 93342
Top-calibre nouvelle Italian cooking – budget a minimum €37 each before drinks. Early booking

essential. Open Apr–Oct, supper only.

Ftelia (Elm Tree)
Strinýlas village
Tel: 26630 71454
An almost mandatory stop on the way to or from the summit of Mt Pandokrátor, this taverna specialises in game. Open lunch and dinner May–Oct, random days in winter.

Kouloura
Kouloúra cove
Tel: 26630 91253
Fairly priced seafood or fish, large selection of mezédes and salads, plus great views. Open daily all day Apr–Oct; reservations needed at peak season.

Mitsos
Nissáki
Tel: 26630 91240
This ordinary-looking beachside taverna stands

out for the cheerful service and the freshness of the inexpensive fare.

7th Heaven Bar/Panorama Restaurant
Longás Beach cliff, Perouládes
Tel: 26630 95035
The place to watch Corfu's most majestic sunset; by half an hour before the event, it's standing-room only. The restaurant is better than you'd think. Open all day May–Oct.

Toula
Agní cove
Tel: 26630 91350
Worth a special mention for its professional demeanour, nice line in hot mezédes and the house special garídes (prawns, shrimp) grilled with spicy mixed-rice pilaff. Excellent bulk white wine; budget about €28 each; lunch and supper.

THE IONIANS

Itháki

To Paliocaravo
Around east quay, Vathý
Tel: 26740 32573
This well-established favourite with locals and visitors alike offers a fine range of mezédes, salads, meat and fish dishes, which can all be washed down with their light, refreshing bulk wine.

Ulysses
Fríkes
Tel: 26740 31733
Dine on reasonably priced fish and succulent meat dishes like rabbit stifádo or lamb kléftiko, whilst watching the gentle activity in the harbour.

Kefalloniá

Akrogiali
Lixoúri quay, towards south end
Tel: 26710 92613
An enduring, budget-priced institution, with largely local clientele. Tasty food with a stress on oven-casserole food, and fish and grills in the evening, plus excellent bulk wine.

Blue Sea (Spyros')
Káto Katélios
Tel: 26710 81353

The speciality here is superb grilled fish from the little anchorage adjacent. Budget about €30 each for a large portion with mezédes and bulk wine.

Kyani Akti
A. Trítsi 1, far end of the quay
Tel: 26710 26680
A superb, if expensive, psarotavérna built out over the sea. The speciality is fresh fish and seafood, all of which is sold by weight. There is also a range of mezédes and salads, and some tasty house wine.

Nirides
Ásos, the far end of the harbour
Tel: 26710 51467
This little estiatório in a great spot overlooking the harbour has the usual range of salads and a few grilled and oven dishes, as well as fresh fish by the kilo.

Odisseas
Agía Ierousalím nr Mánganos
Tel: 6937 714982
A hidden gem, tucked behind a small little-visited beach. The proprietors serve up delicious home-spun recipes such as lamb stew, made with free range meat and organic vege-tables. They also sell preserves and sweets.

Patsouras
A. Trítsi 32 (north quay), Argostóli
Tel: 26710 22779
Popular magirevtá specialist just along from the Lixoúri ferry. Good rib-sticking food with especially tasty bámies (okra), a few grills, big portions and a velvety red house wine. Open all year and inexpensive.

Romantza
Póros
Tel: 26740 72294
This estiatório is in a charming position, built into the headland at the end of the town beach. You eat on a first-storey balcony which has views over the sea to Itháki. The focus of the menu is on a large range of fresh fish (priced by weight), but there are also good mezédes and salads.

To Foki
at the head of Fóki Bay
This is a very pleasant taverna, friendly and just opposite the beach. It serves simple but tasty food which is much better, and far cheaper, than anything to be found in Fiskárdo.

To Pefko
Andipáta Erísou, by the turn for Dafnoúdi beach
Tel: 26740 41360

A serious contender for the best place to eat on the island, with seating outside under a huge pine tree. A mouthwatering selection of mezédes, oven-cooked dishes and some grilled meat and fish.

Xouras
Petaní
Tel: 26710 97128
The location halfway along the best beach on the Lixoúri peninsula is ideal and the Greek-American lady owner offers a warm welcome and dishes up an good assortment of meat, fish and veggie dishes, which can be washed down with decent bulk wine.

Lefkáda

Iy Palia Apothiki
Sývota
Tel: 26450 31895
A favourite among yachters, this lovingly converted 1710 storeroom (hence the name) is the place to enjoy imaginative fare such as giant prawns wrapped in bacon. Good bulk wine.

Pantazis
Nikián
Tel: 26450 71211
Appealingly set at the far

end of the yacht harbour, this locally patronised taverna does fresh seafood at very reasonable prices – though salad trimmings could sometimes be fresher. *Magirevtá* in high-season evenings; open all day.

Regantos
Dimárhou Verrióti 17, Levkáda Town
Tel: 26450 22855
Supper-only taverna with a good balance of grills (especially spit-roasted chicken), oven food and fish; inexpensive and colourful. Sometimes hosts live *kandádes* singing.

T'Agnandio
west hillside, Ágios Nikítas
Tel: 26450 97383
Tucked away up a lane with views to rival Sapfo's, one of the friendliest, least expensive home-style tavernas on the west coast; stress on *magirevtá* and fresh seafood such as *garídes* from the Amvrákikos gulf. Creditable barrel wine; supper only low season.

Ta Platania
central platía, Karyá
Seating under the giant plane trees of the name, and fresh wholesome grills, salads and beers at budget prices. Tables for two other eateries share the square.

Paxí

Alexandros
Platía Edward Kennedy, Lákka
Tel: 26620 30045
The most authentic island cooking and most atmospheric setting in town; own-produced grilled meat and chicken,

specialities like rabbit *sofríto* and mushroom pie, a few seafood dishes, but avoid the barrel wine.

Lilas
Magaziá
Tel: 26620 31102
Inexpensive little meat grill with good bulk wine in an ex-grocery shop at the centre of the island; usually live accordion or stringed music at weekends.

Vassilis
Longós quay
Tel: 26620 31587
Now often known as Kostakis after the son who's taken it over, this has grown from a grilled fish specialist to an all-round taverna with imaginative recipes for *magirevtá*, like stuffed mushrooms and peppers, baked meat dishes and various oven pies.

Zákynthos

Akrotiri Taverna
Akrotíri, 4 km (2½ miles) north of Zákynthos Town
Tel: 26950 45712
A pleasant summer-only taverna with a large garden. Grilled meats are a speciality here, but they also bring round large trays of very tempting *mezédes* from which you pick and choose. The house wine is very acceptable.

Alitzerini
entrance to Kiloméno
Tel: 26950 48552
Housed in one of the few surviving 17th-century Venetian village houses, this little *inomagerío* offers hearty, meat-based country cooking and its own wine;

kandádes some evenings. Evenings only: June–Sept daily, Oct–May Fri–Sun. Reservations essential.

Arekia
Dionysíou Romá, Zákynthos Town
Tel: 26950 26346
A smoky and unpretentious hole-in-the-wall, fitting perhaps 70 diners cosily on bench seats; open evenings only all year round. The food's decent but incidental to the main event: *kandádes* and *arékia* singing after 10pm.

Kakia Rahi
Pigadakia
Tel: 26950 63670
Set by a tiny stream in a leafy village a few kilometres inland from Alykés, this taverna serves far more authentic island food, both baked and grilled, in its rambling courtyard than you would find in the resort itself.

Kalas
Kambí
By far the best taverna in Kambí, Kalas is set in a pretty garden, shaded by large trees, and serves up all the usual favourites (*fáva*, *loukánika*, *horiátiki* and *patátes*), all tasty and freshly cooked. Good bulk wine as well.

Komis
Bastoúni tou Agíou, Zákynthos Town
Tel: 26950 26915
A lovely *psarotavérna* tucked into a rather unlikely spot behind the port authority building. The emphasis is on slightly pricey but fresh and inventive fish and seafood dishes, but there is a good list of *mezédes*, good wine and tempting desserts.

Mikrinisi
Kokkínou, 1 km (½ mile) beyond Makrýs Gialós
Tel: 26950 31566
Standard, but reasonable, taverna food – *horiátiki*, *kalamarákia*, *souvláki* and other such offerings – but the situation is lovely, on the edge of a headland overlooking a tiny harbour.

Porto Limnionas
Pórto Limniónas, near Ágios Léon
Tel: 26950 48650
Location can count for a lot. The food here is relatively expensive, standard taverna fare, but it is served on a promontory overlooking an idyllic rocky bay and facing west to the sunset.

Roulis
Kypséli Beach, near Drosiá
Tel: 26950 61628
This is a friendly place overlooking the sea. Popular with islanders, Roulis gets very fresh fish – one of its main attractions – but also does the usual salads and vegetables well. The house wine is drinkable and the freshness of all the ingredients make it worth the detour from the main coast road.

To Fanari tou Keriou
1½ km (1 mile) beyond Kerí village
Tel: 26950 43384
Watch the moon rise over the Myzíthres sea-stacks below the Kerí cliffs. The food's on the expensive side, but portions are fair size and quality is high – try the daily-made *galakto-boúreko* or vegetable-stuffed *pantsétta*, redolent of nutmeg. Reservations essential.

CRETE

Ágios Nikólaos

Pelagos
Stratigoú Kóraka 10
Tel: 28410 25737
Ensconced in one of the few surviving old houses in the town, this expensive taverna specialising in fish dishes has attractive garden seating out the back for dining in fine weather.

Argyroúpoli

O Kipos tis Arkoudenas
on road towards Episkopí
Tel: 28310 61607
Lamb and pork specialists, serving good food under the trees of the rear garden of the name. This is a better option than the cluster of tavernas at the famous springs in the village.

Eloúnda

Myli
Káto Pinés
Tel: 28410 41961
In the hills above Eloúnda; traditional, tasty, well-prepared Cretan food, very reasonable prices.

Vritómartis
Tel: 28410 41325
On its own little island, moored in the centre of the

harbour. Excellent fish, caught by the owner.

Frangokástello

Kali Kardia
Tel: 28250 92123
Old-fashioned taverna where the best tack is to eat what the proprietors are eating: perhaps a fry-up of the very fresh local fish, good *hýma* wine.

Haniá

Ask the locals where they eat when they're tired of the overpriced scene on the two Venetian harbours, and they'll tell you to go to Aktí Papanikolí just west of the walls at Néa Hóra, with its ten seafront tavernas.

Faka
Arholéon 15, back from inner harbour
Because of its location Faka is significantly less expensive and touristy than waterfront spots. All the traditional Cretan standards with good ingredients; occasional live music sessions a bonus.

Karnagio
Platía Kateháki 8
Tel: 28210 53366
Set back from the harbour, and set in an old *hamám* (steam-baths), this is a superb restaurant. Loved by the locals, it serves up fish and vegetarian dishes.

Katofli
Aktí Papanikolí 13
Tel: 28210 98621
As much *ouzerí* – or rather, *rakádiko* – as taverna, this has local dishes like *stamnagáthi* (an unusual autumn *hórta*). A bargain, with a €20 note covering a *karafáki* (small pitcher) of *rakí* and three platters of fishy and vegetarian fare. Open all year.

Ouzythino
Aktí Papanikolí 6
Tel: 28210 73315
Down-to-earth *ouzerí* with tables out on the jetty. The seafood is fair-priced and very fresh; three can eat well for under €40. Best in summer; open in winter too.

Iráklio

Giakoumis
Fotíou Theodosáki, in the market
Tel: 2810 284039
The city's oldest taverna, specialising in succulent lamb chops, washed down by bulk wine from the local Lyrarakis vintners.

Ippokambos
Sofoklí Venizélou
Tel: 2810 280240
A superb establishment overlooking the old harbour famed for its meticulously

prepared *mezédes* and reasonable fish. It gets busy, so go early. Open lunch and evenings.

Kalathás Beach (Akrotíri)

Kalathas Estiatorio
Tel: 28210 64729
Decent beachfront taverna with friendly service and reasonable, savoury *mezédes* platters – pity about the store-bought, defrosted *kalitsoúna*, though. Open Easter–Oct.

Kalýves

Alexis Zorbas
Tel: 28250 31363
A family-run taverna; open all year. Large portions, tasty food.

Kastéli-Kissámou (Kíssamos)

Kelari
beachfront promenade
Tel: 28220 23883
Stelios takes great pride in his local cuisine.

Káto Zákros

Akrogiali
by the beach
Tel: 28430 26893
Friendly service and a good reputation for fresh fish and meat.

Kournás

Kali Kardia
Kournás village, 3 km (2 miles) above the eponymous lake
Excellent local cooking, especially lamb and sausages.

Lassíthi Plateau

Andonis
between Psyhró and Pláti
Tel: 28440 31581
Set in quiet and attractive surroundings, this taverna offers a good selection of charcoal-grilled meats.

Lefkógia

Stelios
Tel: 28320 31866
Fine meat dishes, tasty home cooking and fresh

orange juice at very reasonable prices.

Makrýgialos

Oasis
west end of strip
Tel: 28430 51918
Taverna known for using only fresh ingredients.

Margarítes

Vrysi
outskirts of Margarítes village (32 km/20 miles east of Réthymno)
Very pleasant, with typical Cretan food.

Nída Plateau, (above Anógia)

Taverna Nida
Tel: 28340 31141
At the base of Psilorítis, Crete's highest mountain, this country taverna serves hearty meat- and chicken-based oven dishes and grills. Daily Apr–Oct; weekends otherwise.

Palékastro-Angathía-Hióna

Kakavia
on Hióna beach, just beyond Palékastro (20 km/12 miles east of Sitía)
Tel: 28430 61227
Named after its speciality, fish soup.

Nikolas O Psaras
Angathía village, 1 km (½ mile) from Palékastro
Tel: 28430 61598
An excellent taverna; fresh fish and Cretan specialities; beautiful view.

Paleohóra

Caravella
harbour quay
The top local seafood restaurant, with bulk wine from nearby Kastélli Kissámou.

Third Eye
between the centre and the beach
Tel: 28230 41234
This excellent vegetarian restaurant also offers Asian and Indian dishes.

Pánormos

Sofoklis
Pánormos harbour (22 km/13

miles east of Réthymno)
Tel: 28340 51297
A good place to try Greek and Cretan cooking.

Plakiás

Medousa
Plakiás, inland from the pharmacy
Tel: 28320 31521
Fine home cooking accompanied by shots of excellent *rakí*.

Plateia
Mýrthios village, overlooking Plakiás Bay
Tasty food, with good vegetarian options and fantastic views from the balcony.

Polyrrínia

Odysseas
7 km (4 miles) south of Kastéli-Kissámou
Tel: 28220 23331
A taste of the Cretan countryside, all dishes made from very fresh home-grown ingredients.

Réthymno

Mesostrati
Gerakári 1, off Platía Martýron
Neighbourhood *ouzerí* serving Cretan dishes; occasional excellent live music.

Thalassografia
Kefalogiannídon 33
Tel: 28310 52569
Clifftop, cutting-edge taverna near the Fortezza with a modern take on traditional Cretan dishes; reserve at weekends.

Veneto
Epimenídou 4
Tel: 28310 56634
An upmarket restaurant, serving refined Greek and Mediterranean cuisine.

Sitía–Agía Fotiá

Neromylos
5 km (3 miles) east of Sitía
Tel: 28430 25576
Simple grilled food and wonderful views.

Stalós

Levendis
in Áno Stalós, 6 km (4 miles) west of Haniá
Tel: 28210 68155
Excellent home cooking.

TRANSPORT
ACCOMMODATION
EATING OUT
ACTIVITIES
A – Z
LANGUAGE

A CTIVITIES

FESTIVALS, THE ARTS, NIGHTLIFE, SHOPPING AND SPECTATOR SPORTS

THE ARTS

Theatre

Athens has an active theatre life but, as most productions are in Greek, options for English-speakers are limited. Most productions in English take place during festivals *(see Cultural Events, below)*. One recent cultural initiative has provided some excellent productions of both modern and ancient drama in English at one of Greece's most striking open-air theatres – the Stone (Pétra) Theatre in Petropolis in the suburbs of Athens. In summer, plays are produced under the auspices of the Stones and Rocks Festival.

Cinema

Going to the cinema in Greece during the summer is a special pleasure not to be missed. Nearly all the movie theatres that run in the summer (the others shut down unless they have air-conditioning) are open-air, sometimes tucked among apartment buildings (whose tenants watch the film from their balconies); in other areas, they are perched on a seaside promontory under the stars. Tickets, at €6–8, are slightly cheaper than indoor cinemas and soundtracks are in the original language (with Greek subtitles). On smaller islands there may be only one showing, at around 9.30pm, while elsewhere there will be two screenings, at 9 and 11pm.

Music and Dance

Most of the best music and dance performances take place during festivals which occur across the country *(see Cultural Events)*. It is also worth looking out for other events in Athens and Thessaloníki.

In Athens, outstanding Greek and foreign musicians often perform at the **Lykavittós Theatre** on Mt Lykavittós, not to mention the larger concerts that take place in the soccer stadiums. Opera can be seen at the Olympia Theatre, performed by the **Lyrikí Skiní** (the National Opera Company), while classical music, from national and international ensembles, is typically performed at the **Mégaron Musikís** near the American Embassy.

In Thessaloníki, summertime venues include the **Théatro Dássos**, on the slopes beyond Kástra, and **Théatro Kípou**, near the archeological museum; in winter, performances of music, opera, dance and theatre move indoors to the nearly adjacent **State Theatre** and **Royal Theatre**, near the White Tower. More cutting-edge are the events at the cultural centre, **Mylos**, a converted flour mill 2 km (1 mile) southeast of the centre, comprising cinemas, concert halls, exhibition space, music clubs and a theatre. This complex has spawned numerous imitators across Greece.

There is an active dance scene in Athens, catering to all tastes, with ballet, folk, modern, jazz and experimental dance troupes.

Cultural Events

April–October Sound and Light performances in Athens at the Pnyx; on Corfu at the Páleo Froúrio; Rhodes at Grand Master's Palace.
May–September Folk dancing by the Dora Stratou Group in Athens, and Nelly Dimoglou Group in Rhodes Old Town.
June Rhodes-Ecofilms, a mixture of new and archival features and documentaries.
June Jazz and Blues Festival, Lykavittós Theatre, Athens.
June–July Athens Festival at the Herod Atticus Odeon, among other venues in the city: events include ballet, opera, jazz, and experimental music, plus modern and classical plays performed by world-ranking artists.
July Music Festival on the island of Itháki (Ithaca).
July–August Epídavros Festival: performances of ancient drama in the open-air Epidaurus main amphitheatre and little theatre.

July–August Réthymnon Renaissance Fair: cultural activities at the Venetian Fort.
July–September Pátra International Festival: ancient and modern drama and classical music in the castle grounds and the Odeon.
August Iráklio Festival: concerts, theatre, opera and so on.
August Lefkáda Festival of Music, Folklore and Theatre, with overseas groups.
August Kavala Festival: ancient drama performed at Philippi.
August–September Santorini Music Festival: mostly classical events.
August–September Sými Festival: a mix of classical and Greek pop performances.
August–October Rhodes Festival.
October Thessaloníki Dhimitria Festival: theatre, music, ballet, followed by a self-contained film-festival (November).
November International Thessaloníki Film Festival.

Greek Music

Thanks to Greece's geographical position and the vast number of cultures that have called it home, there is astonishing regional variety in folk music. Crete has one of the more vital traditions, characterised by the *lýra* (three-string spike fiddle) and *laoúto* (mandolin-like lute). In the Dodecanese, these are often joined by either *tsamboúna*, a goatskin bagpipe, *violí* (violin) *or sandoúri*, the hammer dulcimer popularised in the islands by refugees from Asia Minor.

Nisiótika is the general name for island music; that of the Ionians is the most Italian-influenced and Western in scale. Mainland music is also unmistakable, characterised by the extensive use of the *klaríno* (clarinet) and, in Epirus, an extraordinary, disappearing tradition of polyphonic singing.

Contemporary sounds include original syntheses or derivations of the traditional and rebetic traditions by such artists such as Thessalonian Dionysis Savvopoulos, who first challenged the supremacy of *bouzoúki* in the mid-1960s with his guitar and orchestral-based compositions, and who spawned a whole generation of disciples and protegés such as the rock-influenced Nikos Papazoglou, Nikos Xydakis and Heimerinoi Kolymvites.

Each region (and sometimes island) of Greece has its own particular folk dances. These ranges from the basic *sta tría* – three steps to one side, followed by a kick (growing gradually faster and faster) – to a frenzied combination of complicated footwork, jumps,

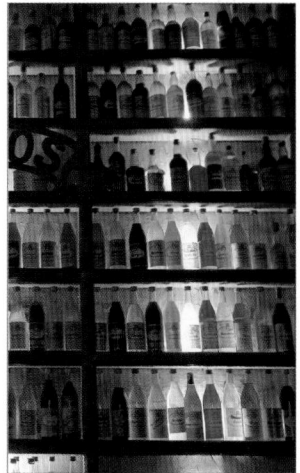

Religious and Other Festivals

1 January Feast of *Ágios Vasílios* (St Basil): celebrated all over Greece.

6 January Epiphany/*Agía Theofánia* – Blessing of the waters: all over Greece.

8 January Feast of *Agía Domníki* (St Domenica), patron saint of midwives: men and women switch roles in the villages around Xánthi, Komotiní, Kilkís and Sérres.

February–March Carnival season for three weeks before Lent: all over Greece. Some places with celebrations of special interest are: Náoussa, Kozáni, Zákynthos, Skýros, Thíva, Xánthi, Híos (Mestá, Olýmbi), Messíni, Ámfissa, Lésvos (Agiássos), Galaxídi, Lamía, Agía Anna (Évvia), Polýgyros, Thymianá, Kefalloniá, Sérres, Kárpathos, Iráklio, Evxinoúpolis (Vólos), Réthymno and (best of all) Pátra.

"Clean" Monday Beginning of fast for Lent. Picnics in the countryside and kite-flying: all over Greece.

25 March Feast of Annunciation/Independence Day: military parades in all main towns, pilgrimage to Tínos.

Easter weekend Good Friday, Holy Saturday and Easter Sunday are celebrated throughout Greece.

23 April Feast of St George: celebrated especially in Kaliópi (Límnos), Aráhova, Así Goniá (near Haniá) and Pylí (Kos).

1 May Labour Day: picnics in the countryside all over Greece.

21 May Anastenárides: fire-walking ritual at Agía Eléni (near Sérres) and Langáda (near Thessaloníki).

15 August Assumption of the Virgin: festivals all over Greece. Major pilgrimage to Tínos.

28 October Ohi (No) Day: anniversary of Greek defeat of Italian army in 1940 and Metaxas' supposed one-word response to Italy's ultimatum. Military parades in major cities.

Christmas season All over Greece. In a dwindling number of places, children sing *kálenda* (carols) from door to door for a small gratuity.

31 December New Year's Eve. Many Greeks play cards for money on this occasion, and cut the *vasilópitta* with a lucky coin hidden in it. Special celebration in the town of Híos.

slaps and kicks. Troupes, dressed in traditional Greek costume, are most likely to be performing on public holidays (you may also see them on TV). Probably the best-known professional group is Dora Stratou Greek Folk Dances, which holds regular shows from May to September at the Dora Stratou Theatre, Filopáppou Hill (southwest slope), Athens.

NIGHTLIFE

Metropolitan nightlife in Greece (essentially Athens, Thessaloníki, Iráklio, Haniá, Vólos, Lárissa, Kérkyra, Ródos Town and Pátra) can be roughly divided into four categories: bars; live music clubs with jazz, Greek music (most likely *laïki*, or a watered-down version of *rebétika*) or rock; dance clubs, mostly with a techno, house or ambient soundtrack; and musical *tavérnes* where food prices reflect the live entertainment.

For most Greeks, however, the simple *tavérna* remains the most popular site for a night out spent eating, drinking and, sometimes, singing and dancing. In general, younger Greeks frequent the bars and dance clubs, while the locales

for popular Greek music are more patronised by the older generations.

In Athens, the weekly *Athinorama* (in Greek) has an extensive listing of all the various venues and events. If you really want to find out what's going on in the city, ask a Greek friend to help you sort through the listings.

During the summer (late June–early September) many clubs and music halls close down, with musicians of all stripes touring the countryside for the summer festival season, or performing in the islands and coastal resorts.

Casinos

For a more sophisticated – and potentially more expensive – night out, there are casinos in numerous Greek cities and resorts, including Néos Marmarás (Halkidikí), Corfu, Rhodes, Ermoúpoli (Sýros), Loutráki, Párnes and at Thessaloníki airport.

SPORT

Participant Sports

Hiking and Mountaineering

Greece has long been a magnet for hikers and mountain climbers, with

TRANSPORT

ACCOMMODATION

EATING OUT

ACTIVITIES

A – Z

LANGUAGE

ABOVE: fishing is popular all over Greece.

many footpaths in the mainland mountains and on certain islands, threading through forested areas untouched by the tourist masses. Big-wall climbing is currently growing in popularity, both on the mainland and on islands such as Kálymnos. For information on trails, maps and excursions, consult one of the specialist guides in the booklist, or if you'd prefer an organised excursion, see the list of tour operators on page 377.

Caving

Greece is honeycombed with caves, though many are locked to protect delicate formations or archaeological artefacts, and are only opened to qualified spelunkers on an expedition. The following, however, have set hours and facilities for public visits: Koutoúki, Peanía, Attica; Pérama, near Ioánnina; Drogaráti and Melissáni, Kefaloniá; Andíparos, in the Cyclades; the Cave of the Lakes, near Kalávryta in the Peloponnese; Glyfáda and Alepótripa at Pýrgos Dyroú, Máni, Peloponnese; Petrálona, at Kókkines Pétres, Halkidikí; and the cave of Sykiás Olýmbon on Híos.

Scuba diving

Diving in Greece was for a long time tightly controlled, with the aim of preserving the nation's heritage of submerged antiquities. However, the laws on it were liberalised in 2007, with a corresponding eruption of new centres. Dive centres of long standing operate on Rhodes, Kálymnos, Lóros, Mýkonos, Sámos, Skiáthos, Corfu, Alónisos and Halkidikí. Consult your nearest EOT/ GNTO branch for an updated list *(see page 376)*.

Although there is a lot to see around the coast, do not expect undersea fauna and flora of Caribbean splendour; snorkelling in Greek waters is likely to be just as rewarding as scuba-diving.

Fishing

There are plenty of places where you can fish in Greece. In the villages of most islands you will find boats and fishing tackle for hire. If you'd like some suggestions contact the **Amateur Anglers and Maritime Sports Club**, Aktí Moutsopoúlou, in Piraeus; tel: 210 451 5731.

Horse Riding

Many small riding schools offer horse riding. For information, contact the **Riding Club of Greece**, Paradissos; tel: 210 682 6128, or in the capital the **Riding Club of Athens**, tel: 210 661 1088.

Skiing

Most Greek mountains above 2,400 metres (7,800 ft) high have good snow cover for skiing from January to April, with some of the higher mountains (Kaïmaktsalán and Parnassós) skiable in a good year until May.

These are the best downhill resorts, and most have some sort of cross-country/nordic pistes as well: **Mt Parnassós** (14 lifts, 16 runs); **Mt Vérmio** near Naoússa (8 lifts, 21 runs); **Mt Helmós**, near Kalávryta in the Peloponnese (7 lifts, 12 runs); **Vórras** on Mt Kaïmaktsalán (2 lifts, 7 runs); and **Veloúhi** on Mt Tymfristós near Karpenísi (6 lifts, 10 runs).

There are perhaps a dozen other tiny centres across Greece, but those cited above are the only ones with any sort of reputation. The GNTO sporadically issues a brochure listing all ski centres, but descriptions of facilities and runs tend to be some years out of date.

Tennis

Although there are tennis clubs in most larger cities, few are open to non-members/non-residents. Public courts are equally rare. But most island hotels and inclusive complexes of A or Luxury class have tennis facilities, where you may be able to book court space by the hour.

Waterskiing

Waterskiing (and in some places parasailing as well) is far cheaper in Greece than in most Mediterranean resorts. You will find waterskiing facilities at: Vouliagméni (southeast of Athens); Agrínio (Lake Trihonída); Vólos; Édessa (Lake Vegorítida); Thessaloníki; numerous locations on

Corfu; Haniá, Crete; Eloúnda, Crete; Pórto Héli; Rhodes; Párga (Váltos beach); Skiáthos; Ioánnina (Lake Pamvótida); and Halkidikí.

Windsurfing

Greece is ideal for windsurfing, with gentle breezes blowing around many small coves. Boards can be rented, and lessons are available (at very reasonable rates) at many popular Greek beaches, and at most of the beaches maintained by the GNTO.

The premier resorts dedicated to the sport, where people come from overseas just to windsurf, are: Prasonísi, Rhodes; southern Kárpathos; Kokkári, Sámos; Ágios Geórgios, Náxos; and Vasilikí, Lefkáda.

Spectator Sports

Football (soccer) is the main spectator sport, with matches played nearly every Wednesday night and Sunday afternoon during the season. The top teams are AEK (Athens), Olympiakós (Piraeus), Panathanaïkós (Athens) and PAOK (Thessaloníki).

Basketball is the second most popular sport since the national team won the European Championship in 1987, and the national league is followed keenly. Local Greek-language newspapers have details of games.

Sailing

Numerous companies offer sailing packages and cruises round the coast of Greece that can be booked from home – an internet search will be very productive. One useful website is: www.sailingissues.com.

Much of the sailing is in flotillas helmed by the hire companies, but experienced sailors can charter their own yacht. Alternatively, once you're in Greece you can hire boats by the day or week at many marinas. Either way, you can rely on the Port Authorty Harbour Police in your area for up-to-the-minute information on conditions.

The best times to sail are spring and autumn, as winds can be high through the summer months and prices are hiked up to many times that of the cooler seasons.

There are sailing schools, housed in the naval clubs of the following towns: Athens (Paleó Fáliro); Thessaloníki; Corfu; Vólos; Rhodes; Sýros; Kalamáta; Alexandroúpolis. Further information can be obtained from: Hellenic Yachting Federation, 51 Posidonos Avenue, Piraeus; tel: 210 940 4825; fax: 210 940 4829.

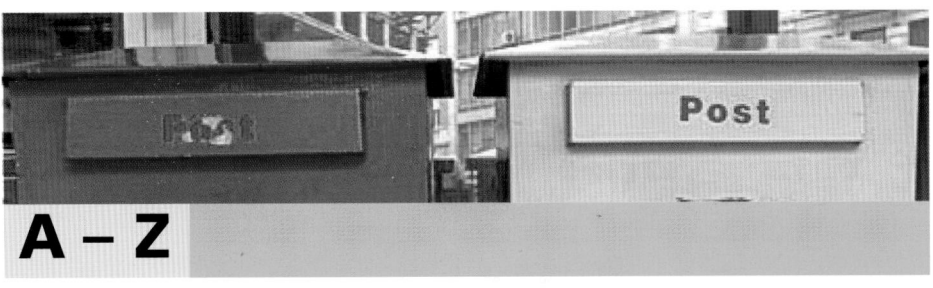

A – Z

A HANDY SUMMARY OF PRACTICAL INFORMATION, ARRANGED ALPHABETICALLY

A dmission Charges

Most archaeological sites and museums, public or private, have admission charges varying from €2 for minor affairs up to €12 for stellar attractions. Occasionally (as in Athens) you can get a joint ticket covering several sites and museums at an advantageous price. From November to March, most state-run sites give free admission to EU nationals on Sunday; Monday or Tuesday are the typical days of closure. Students with valid ID get one-third to one-half off entry fees, as do certified teachers, archaeology students and persons 60 or over.

B udgeting for Your Trip

Especially since the advent of the euro, Greece is no longer by any stretch of the imagination an inexpensive country. Travelling as one of a couple, allow a minimum of €30 for a share of accommodation (budget €40–50 each minimum in Athens or Thessaloníki), €15–20 for your half of a meal, €6–10 each for

site admissions, and €15–17 for your share of the cheapest small rental car – before petrol costs, which have risen steeply in recent months, in line with the rest of Europe.

Business Travellers

Business travellers are well catered for; most good-standard hotels now have some sort of "business person's corner" with a computer terminal and printer, as well as Wi-fi

signal for laptops (in the common areas if not in all the rooms). The same hotels tend to have multiple conference/event rooms as well as lounges suitable for semi-formal meetings.

C hildren

Children are adored in Greece, and many families are still highly super-stitious about their welfare – don't be surprised to see toddlers with amulets pinned to their clothes to ward off the evil eye. So expect your own kids to be the centre of attention. Children are given quite a bit of leeway in Greece and treated very indugently. They are allowed to stay up late and are routinely taken out to eat in tavernas. You may have to put your foot down when shop owners offer free sweets or strangers are over-indulgent towards your own children.

Climate

The Greece seen in tourist posters is a perennially warm and sunny place – and it is, by European standards. But

CLIMATE CHART

Athens

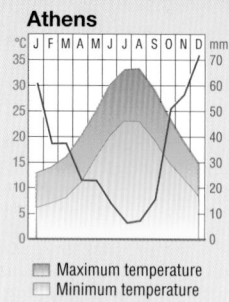

- Maximum temperature
- Minimum temperature
- — Rainfall

this picture does not reflect the considerable climatic variety. The north and inland regions have a modified continental climate, so winters are quite cold and summers extremely hot. In Ioánnina, Trípoli and Kastoriá, for example, snow and freezing temperatures are not uncommon. In mountainous regions, winters are even more inclement.

The southern islands, the coastal Peloponnese and the Attic Peninsula conform more to the traditional Mediterranean image: a long, warm season of rainless, sunny days extending roughly from late May to mid-October. But here too the winters can be cool, with rain falling in unpredictable spells between December and April.

In general, late spring (late April–June) and autumn (September–October) are the best times to visit. During these periods, you will find mild to warm temperatures, sunny days and fewer tourists. Throughout July and August, Greece is at its most hot and sticky, and most crowded. Still, millions of tourists seem to prefer the heat and the company, choosing this busiest period for their holiday.

Crime and Safety

Greece is still one of the safest countries in Europe. Despite the luridly publicised antics of certain Albanians and Romanians, violent crime remains relatively rare. Sadly, however, petty theft does occur, and it is now the norm to lock cars and front doors in the countryside.

Because of security considerations after the September 11 attacks in New York, and the Olympics, it is unwise to leave luggage unattended anywhere except perhaps in a hotel lobby, under the gaze of the desk staff. Belongings inadvertently left

behind in a café will still usually be put aside for you to collect.

Customs Regulations

There are no official restrictions on the movement of goods within the European Union, provided the goods were purchased within the EU. It is no longer necessary for EU nationals to exit their home-country Customs through a red or green channel.

Duty-paid goods

If you buy goods in Greece for which you pay tax, there are no restrictions on the amounts you can take home. EU law has set "guidance levels", however, on the following:
- **Tobacco** 3,200 cigarettes, or 400 cigarillos, or 200 cigars or 3kg of tobacco.
- **Spirits** 10 litres
- **Fortified wine/wine** 90 litres
- **Beer** 110 litres
   If you exceed these amounts you must be able to prove the goods are for personal use.

Duty-free goods

Since the abolition of duty-free concession within the European Union, all goods brought into Greece from EU countries must be duty-paid. In theory there are no limitations to the amount of duty-paid goods that can be brought into the country. However, cigarettes and most spirits are much cheaper in Greece than in Britain and Ireland (government duty is much lower), so waiting until you reach your destination to buy these goods will save you money.

For travellers from non-EU countries, allowances for duty-free goods brought into Greece are:
- **Tobacco** 200 cigarettes, or 100

cigarillos, or 50 cigars, or 250g of tobacco.
- **Alcohol** 1 litre of spirits or liqueurs over 22 percent volume, or 2 litres of fortified, sparkling wine or other liqueurs.
- **Perfume** 60cc of perfume, plus 250cc of *eau de toilette*.
   Non-EU residents can claim back Value Added Tax (currently between 6 and 19 percent) on any items costing over €120, provided they export the item within 90 days of purchase. Tax-free forms are available at tourist shops and department stores. Keep the receipt and form. Make your claim at the customs area of the airport when departing.

Currency restrictions

There are no limits on the amount of euros visitors can import or export. There are no restrictions on travellers' cheques, but cash sums of more than €10,000 or its equivalent should be declared on entry.

Importing cars

Visitors arriving with their own car are allowed to circulate for up to six months without formality; after that the bureaucratic fun begins, and people intending to establish residence will find that it's usually cheaper and easier to buy a Greek-registered car than try to import their overseas motor. Cars detected circulating after the initial six-month period without valid road tax are liable to seizure by customs/tax undercover agents.

Disabled Travellers

Despite nudging from the EU, Greece has some way to go before becoming fully compliant with regulations on facilities for disabled people.

Athens, with lifts in the metro, "kneeling" buses on many routes, recorded announcements of upcoming stops on the metro plus some buses, and ramps (when not blocked by illegally parked cars) at kerbside, is furthest ahead.

Elsewhere, amenities can be poor – there are few or no sound pips for the sight-impaired at pedestrian crossings, and it is common to see the wheelchair-bound tooling down the middle of the asphalt rather than risk the obstacle course of a pedestrian pavement.

Few hotels in the provinces are disabled-friendly, though things are improving slowly, and some are setting aside a few rooms with wide doors and safety handles in the bath – ask when booking.

Electricity

220 volts out of double round-pin sockets.

E mbassies and Consulates

Foreign Embassies in Athens

All embassies are open from Monday to Friday only, usually from 8am until 2pm, except for their own national holidays (as well as Greek ones). **Australia** Anastasíou Tsohá 24, corner Soútsou (Ambelókipi metro); tel: 210 64 50 404. **Canada** Gennadíou 4, Kolonáki, (Evangelismós metro); tel: 210 72 73 400. **Ireland** Vassiléos Konstandínou 7 (by National Gardens); tel: 210 72 32 771. **South Africa** Kifissiás 60, Maroússi; tel: 210 61 06 645. **UK** Ploutárhou 1, Kolonáki (Evangelismós metro); tel: 210 72 72 600. **US** Vasilísis Sofías 91, Ambelókipi (Mégaro Mousikís metro); tel: 210 72 12 951.

Entry Requirements

Citizens of EU nations, as well as Switzerland and EEA countries, have unlimited visitation rights to Greece; your passport will not be stamped on entry or exit. With a valid passport, citizens of the USA, Canada, Australia and New Zealand can stay in the country for up to three months (cumulative) within any six-month period, with no visa necessary. To stay longer, you must obtain a permit from the nearest Aliens' Bureau; however, this is lately proving nearly impossible (and very expensive) to do. Citizens of all non-EU/EEA countries should contact the nearest Greek embassy or consulate about visa and permitted length-of-stay requirements, which are liable to change again in future.

Emergency Numbers

The following numbers work country-wide:
• **Police** 100
• **Ambulance** 166
• **Fire brigade, urban** 199
• **Forest fire reporting** 191
• **Tourist police 171** (Athens only; in other parts of Greece, ring 210 171)
  Elsewhere, hotel staff will give you details of the nearest hospital or English-speaking doctor.

Etiquette

The Greeks are at heart a very traditional nation, protective of their families and their customs. So to avoid giving offence it is essential to follow their codes of conduct.
  Locals rarely drink to excess, so drunken and/or lewd behaviour is treated with at best bewilderment, at worse severe distaste (or criminal prosecution, as many young louts on Rhodes, Zákynthos, Corfu and Crete have learned to their cost).
  Nude bathing is legal at only a few beaches (such as on the island of Mýkonos), but it is deeply offensive to most Greeks. Even topless sunbathing is sometimes not sanctioned, so watch for signs forbidding it on beaches. The main rule of thumb is this: if it is a secluded beach and/or a beach that has become a commonly accepted locale for nude bathing, you probably won't offend anyone.
  Despite assorted scandals and embarrassing espousal of retrograde issues in recent years, the Greek Orthodox Church still commands considerable respect in Greece, so keep any unfavourable comments about the clergy or even Greek civil servants to yourself.

G ay and Lesbian Travellers

Overt gay behaviour is not a feature of Greek society. Homosexuality is legal at the age of 17, and bisexual activity fairly common among younger men, but few couples (male or female) are openly gay. Mýkonos is famous as a gay Mecca, and Skála Eressoú on Lésvos (where the poetess Sappho was born) for lesbians. But elsewhere in Greece single-sex couples are liable to be regarded as odd, although usually as welcome as any other tourists. If discreet, you will attract no attention asking for a double room and will find most people tolerant.

H ealth and Medical Care

Greece has few serious diseases apart from those that you can contract in the US or the rest of Europe. Citizens of the USA, Canada and the EU do not need any immunisations to enter the country.

Drugs and Medicines

Greek pharmacies stock most over-the-counter drugs. The Greeks themselves are enthusiastic hypochondriacs and potion-poppers, and all manner of homeopathic and herbal remedies and premium-ingredient dietary supplements are available. Many formulas that would be obtainable only on prescription elsewhere, if at all, are freely obtainable in Greece. So you should have no problem obtaining most medicines (except in remote areas and islands).
  Essential drugs, made locally under licence, are price-controlled, with uniform rates all over the country – e.g. a tube of 1 percent hydrocortisone cream costs less than €4 – but discretional sundries and anything imported can be pricey (eg a packet of four water-resistant French-made bandages for €3.50). If you want to be absolutely sure, pack a supply of your favourite remedies to last out the trip.
  Greek authorities take the unauthorised use of drugs very seriously indeed; this is not the country in which to carry cannabis.

Medical Treatment

For minor ailments your best port of call is a pharmacy. Greek chemists usually speak good English and are well-trained and helpful, and pharmacies stock a good range of medicines (including contraceptives) as well as bandages and dressings for minor wounds.
  Certain pharmacies are open outside of normal shop hours and at weekends, on a rotating basis. You can find out which are open either by looking at the bilingual (Greek/English) card posted in pharmacy windows or by consulting a local newspaper. In big cities, and major tourist resorts such as Crete or Rhodes, one or two pharmacies will be open 24 hours a day.
  There are English-speaking GPs in all the bigger towns and resorts, whose rates are usually reasonable. Ask your hotel or the tourist office for details. In Athens, the doctors' roster can be obtained by dialling 105; get the 24-hour pharmacy roster by dialling 107.
  Treatment for broken bones and similar mishaps is given free of charge in the state-run Greek hospitals – go straight to the casualty/emergency ward (epígon peristatiká). Have on you your European Health Insurance Card, obtainable from UK post offices or online (www.ehic.org).
  For more serious problems you should have private medical insurance. If you have a serious injury or illness, you are better off travelling home for treatment if you can. Greek public hospitals lag behind northern Europe and the US in both their hygiene and standard of care; the Greeks bring food and bedding when visiting sick relatives, and must bribe nurses for anything beyond the bare minimum in care.

TRANSPORT

ACCOMMODATION

EATING OUT

ACTIVITIES

A–Z

LANGUAGE

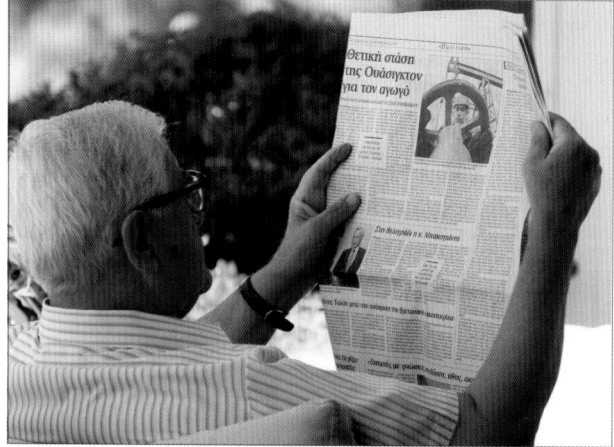

condemning many in the provinces to slow dial-up services. Also, some internet cafés – there will be at least one in every resort – that claim to have ADSL offer only the slowest speeds. Rates at cafés have dropped to €3–4 an hour as a rule, charged in fractional increments, though they tend to be smoky places full of spotty teenagers playing computer games. It's worth bringing a lightweight laptop, as Wi-fi zones are multiplying at the better hotels and at many ordinary, pleasant cafés that strictly speaking aren't internet ones.

M edia
Print

Many kiosks throughout Athens and other major resorts receive British newspapers, plus the *International Herald Tribune*, either late the same afternoon or, more usually, the next *Athens News* in colour (online at www.athensnews.gr) is interesting and informative, with both international and local news, particularly good for the Balkans, and complete TV and cinema listings. *Odyssey* is a glossy, bi-monthly magazine created by and for the wealthy Greek diaspora, somewhat more interesting than the usual airline in-flight mag.

Radio and TV

ER 1 and ER 2 are the two Greek state-owned radio channels. ER 1 is divided into three different "programmes". The First (728 KHz) and Second (1385 KHz) both have abundant Greek popular music and news, some foreign pop and occasional jazz and blues. Third (665 KHz) plays a lot of Western classical

Drinking Water

People carrying a large plastic bottle of mineral water is a common sight in Greece, but it is not the best way of keeping hydrated, as sunlight releases toxic chemicals from the plastic into the water, and the spent bottles contribute enormously to Greece's litter problem. Buy a sturdy, porcelain-lined canteen and fill it from the cool-water supply of bars and restaurants you've patronised; nobody will begrudge you this. Although unfiltered tap water is generally safe to drink, it may be brackish, and having a private water supply is much handier. On the mainland and larger islands, certain springs are particularly esteemed by the locals – queues of cars, and people with jerry-cans, tip you off. If you do want bottled water, it can be bought almost anywhere that sells food, even in beach cafés and tavernas.

Animal Hazards

Nearly half the stray dogs in rural areas carry echinococcosis (treatable by surgery only) or kala-azar disease (leishmaniasis), a potentially fatal protozoan blood disease spread by sandflies.

Mosquitos can be a nuisance in some areas of Greece, but topical repellents are readily available in pharmacies. For safeguarding rooms, accommodation proprietors often supply a plug-in electric pad, which vapourises smokeless, odourless rectangular tablets. If you see them by the bed, it's a good bet they'll be needed; refills can be found in any supermarket.

On the islands, poisonous baby pit vipers and scorpions are a problem in spring and summer. They will not strike you unless disturbed, but do

not put your hands or feet in places (such as drystone walls) that you haven't checked first. If you swim in the sea, beware jellyfish whose sting is usually harmless but which can swell and hurt for days.

On beaches, it is worth wearing plastic or trekking sandals to avoid sea urchins (those little black pincushions on rocks that can embed their very sharp and tiny spines into unwary feet). A local Greek remedy is to douse the wound with olive oil and then gently massage the foot until the spines pop out, but this rarely works unless you're willing to perform minor surgery with pen-knife and sewing needle – which should be done, as spine fragments tend to go septic.

I nsurance

British and EU residents are entitled to free medical treatment in Greece as long as they carry a European Health Insurance Card (obtainable from post offices). However, this guarantees only the most basic health care: you are only entitled to use one of the lowest-grade state hospitals, and will have to pay for your own medicine. So it is advisable to take out private medical insurance. You will have to pay for private treatment up front, so you must keep receipts for any bills or medicines you pay for to make a claim. If you plan to hire a motor scooter in Greece, you may have to pay extra to cover you for accidents.

Internet

Greece is slowly becoming wired, though nearly half the country geographically is not provided with exchanges compatible with ADSL,

Left Luggage

Airport At Level 0 of Arrivals at Eleftherios Venizelos airport, Pacific Left Luggage offers service; tel: 210 35 30 352. **Hotels** Most hotels in Greece are willing to store locked suitcases for up to a week if you want to take any short excursions. This is usually a free service, provided you've stayed a night or two, but the hotel will accept no responsibility in the highly unlikely event of theft. **Commercial offices** On the islands there are left-luggage offices in many harbour towns. For a small charge space can be hired by the hour, day, week or longer. Although the contents will probably be safe, take small valuables with you.

music. ER 2 (98 KHz) is much like the first two programmes.

The BBC World Service offers news on the hour (plus other interesting programmes and features). The best short-wave (MHz) frequencies to pick up the BBC in Athens are as follows: 3–7.30am GMT: 9.41 (31 m), 6.05 (49 m), 15.07 (19 m); 7.30am–6pm GMT: 15.07 (19 m); 6.30–11.15pm GMT: 9.41 (31 m), 6.05 (49 m).

Additionally, a plethora of private stations broadcast locally from just about every island or provincial town, no matter how tiny.

There are three state-owned and operated television channels (ET1 and NET in Athens, ET3 in Thessaloniki) and a half-dozen private television channels (Antenna, Net, Mega, Star, Alpha and Alter). Often they transmit foreign movies and programmes with Greek subtitles rather than being dubbed. Several cable and satellite channels are also broadcast, including Sky and CNN.

Money

The Greek currency is the euro (*evró* in Greek), which comes in coins of 1, 2, 5, 10, 20 and 50 cents (*leptá*), plus 1 and 2 euro, as well as notes of 5, 10, 20, 50, 100, 200 and 500 euro (the latter two denominations rarely seen).

All banks and most hotels buy foreign currency at the official rate of exchange fixed by the Bank of Greece. Though it's safer to carry most of your currency in travellers' cheques, it is also worth carrying a limited sum in US dollars or sterling. When you can't find a place to cash cheques, there will usually be a shop or post office able to convert those currencies into euros. Exchange rates go up or down daily. To find the current rate, check displays in bank windows, or the newspapers; you can read the tables even in Greek.

Credit/debit cards

Many of the better-established hotels, restaurants and shops accept major credit cards, as does Olympic Airways and the larger ferry companies or travel agents. The average pension or taverna does not, however, so be sure to enquire if that is how you intend to pay. You will find that most brands of card are accepted by the numerous autoteller machines, upon entry of your PIN number. However, use debit rather than credit cards in ATMs, as the latter tend to have ruinous surcharges, often amounting to over five percent of the transaction value. This caveat aside, you will find that this is the most convenient and least expensive

"Greek Time"

Beware Greek schedules. Although shops and businesses generally operate the hours indicated below, there is no guarantee that when you want to book a ferry or buy a gift, the office or shop will actually be open.

Siesta (*mikró ýpno* in Greek) is observed throughout Greece, and even in Athens the majority of people retire behind closed doors between the hours of 3pm and 6pm. Shops and businesses also close, and it is usually impossible to get much done that day until late-afternoon or early evening. To avoid frustration and disappointment, shop and book things between 10am and 1pm Monday to Friday.

Since 1994 Athens has experimented with "straight" hours

way of getting funds, and many of the machines operate around the clock.

Opening Hours

All banks are open 8am–2.30pm Monday to Thursday, and close at 2pm on Friday. ATMs are now everywhere – even the smaller islands will have at least one – and this is how most people obtain cash nowadays.

The schedule for business and shop hours is more complicated. Business hours vary according to the type of business and the day of the week. The main thing to remember is that businesses generally open at 8.30 or 9am and close on Monday, Wednesday and Saturday at 2.30pm. On Tuesday, Thursday and Friday most businesses close at 2pm and reopen in the afternoon from 5pm to 8.30pm (winter), 5.30 or 6pm to 9pm (summer).

You'll soon learn that schedules are very flexible in Greece (both in business and personal affairs). To avoid disappointment, allow ample time when shopping and doing business. That way, you may also enter into the Greek spirit of negotiation, in which a good chat can be as important as the matter of business itself.

Photography

Although Greece is a photographer's paradise, taking photographs at will is not recommended. Cameras are not allowed in museums, and you may have to pay a fee to take photographs or use your camcorder at archaeological sites. Watch out for signs showing a bellows camera with

during the winter to bring the country more in line with the EU, but this seems to be discretionary rather than obligatory, with some stores observing the hours and others adhering to traditional schedules – which can be rather confusing. So far it has not caught on across the rest of the country.

The shops in Athens' Pláka district remain open until 10pm or longer to take advantage of browsers, and tourist shops throughout the country usually trade well into the evening in summer. But butchers and fishmongers are not allowed to open on summer evenings (although a few disregard the law), and pharmacies (except for those on rota duty) are never open on Saturday mornings.

a red "X" through it, and do not point your camera at anything in or near airports – most of which double as military bases.

Memory chips and other supplies for all sorts of digital cameras are widely available.

Postal Services

Most local post offices are open weekdays from 7.30am until 2pm. However, the main post offices in central Athens (on Eólou near Omónia Square and on Sýndagma Square at the corner of Mitropóleos Street) are open longer hours on weekdays, as well as for a few hours on Saturday.

Postal rates are subject to fairly frequent change; currently a postcard or light letter costs 67 euro-cents to any overseas destination. Stamps are available from the post office or from many kiosks (*períptera*) and hotels, which may charge a 10–15 percent commission. But make sure you know how much it is to send a letter or postcard, as kiosk owners tend not to be up to date with latest international postal rates.

If you want to send a parcel from Greece, do not to wrap it until a post office clerk has inspected it, unless it's going to another EU country, in which case you can present it sealed. Major post offices stock various sizes of cardboard boxes for sale in which you can pack your material, as well as twine, but you had best bring your own tape and scissors.

Letters from abroad can be sent Post Restante to any post office. Take your passport or other ID when you go to pick up mail.

Public Holidays

The Greeks like their festivals and celebrate them in style, so most business and shops close during the afternoon before and the morning after a religious holiday, as well as the day itself.

- **1 January** *Protohroniá/*New Year's Day
- **6 January** *Agía Theofánia/* Epiphany
- **Moveable** *Katharí Deftéra* Clean Monday (First Day of Lent)
- **25 March** *Evangelismós/* Annunciation
- **1 May** Labour Day
- **Moveable** *Megáli Paraskeví/* Good Friday
- **Moveable** Orthodox Easter *(Pásha),* Easter Monday
- **Moveable** *Agíou Pnévmatos/* Pentecost Monday (50 days after Easter)
- **15 August** Assumption *(Kímisis)* of the Holy Virgin
- **28 October** "*Ohi*" Day, National Holiday
- **25 December** *Hristoúgenna/* Christmas Day
- **26 December** *Sýnaxis tis Theotókou/*Gathering of the Virgin's Entourage

R eligious Services

Most major towns and resort areas with significant foreign patronage or a large expat community – most obviously Corfu, Rhodes, Crete, Sámos, Santoríni, Athens and Thessaloníki – have at least one church dedicated to the Catholic, Anglican or other Protestant (eg Swedish Lutheran) rites, or an agreement for part-time use of an Orthodox premises. There are functioning Catholic parishes for locals on Sýros and Tinos, where foreigners are welcome. Placards posted on the churches themselves, or handouts at the nearest tourist office, give current info on schedules (anything from two Sundays a month to 2 or 3 times weekly).

S tudent Travellers

Other than the museum and archaeological site discounts noted on page 371, students and under-26s are eligible for discounted fares and youth passes on OSE (the Greek train network) and on some shipping lines, including those operating to and from Italy. Domestic airlines no longer appear to offer any youth

fares – they certainly do not advertise them on their websites.

T elecommunications

For local calls, including to mobiles, buy an OTE (Greek telecoms) telephone card from a kiosk and use a (usually noisy) street-corner booth. Cards come in 100-unit, 500-unit and 1,000-unit denominations; the Hronokarta species is slightly better value. Calls from hotel rooms typically have 200–300 percent surcharges on top of the basic rates – to be avoided for anything other than brief local calls. For overseas calls, almost everyone avoids the truly outrageous OTE rates by buying a code-card, whereby you scratch to reveal a 12-digit code, then ring an 807-prefixed number to enter said code, then the number you want. It may all sound a hassle, but savings can amount to about 70 percent. If you have a laptop, it's worth bringing a Skype headset along to take advantage of Wi-fi zones for calling abroad.

Greece has one of the highest per-capita mobile-phone usage rates in the world, and a mobile is an essential fashion accessory for any self-respecting Greek. Foreign mobile owners will find themselves well catered for, with thorough coverage and reciprocal agreements for most UK-based services. Calls within Greece are affordable, but the cost of overseas calls mounts up quickly. North American users will have to bring a tri-band apparatus to get any joy. If you're staying for any amount of time, you will find it better to either buy a pay-as-you-go phone from one of the three Greek providers (Vodaphone, Cosmote, tim) or, if feasible, buy just a SIM card for the apparatus you've brought along.

Tipping

Menu prices at most cafés, restaurants and *tavérnes* include a service charge, but it is still customary to leave an extra 5–10 percent on the table for the waiters.

Just as important as any such gratuity, however, is your appreciation

Time Zone

Greece is 2 hours ahead of GMT and, like the rest of Europe, observes Daylight Savings from 3am on the last Sunday in March until 3am on the last Sunday in October.

of the food you eat. Greek waiters and restaurant owners are proud when you tell them you like a particular dish.

Toilets

Public conveniences, often subterranean in parks or plazas, or perched on a harbour jetty, are of variable cleanliness and rarely have any paper. Most people just buy a drink in a café and use their facilities. In busy tourist areas, put-upon cafés may post signs saying "toilets for customers only". Elsewhere, establishments are a bit more lenient about those caught short just popping in.

Tourist Information

Tourist offices

If you would like tourist information about Greece during your trip, visit the nearest Greek National Tourist Organisation – GNTO, or EOT in Greek. They provide information on public transport, as well as leaflets and details about sites and museums. There are over a dozen regional GNTO offices across the country. The head office in Athens can be found at Amalías 26; tel: 210 33 10 392.

In some tourist areas, especially many of the islands, there are semi-official municipal tourist information centres open from June to September. These are usually prominently sited near the centre of the main town, and provide all the local information you might need. Some can even help with finding accommodation.

Tourist Police

The Greek Tourist Police are often a mine of information too. A branch of the local police and found in most large towns, they can be helpful in providing information about hotels as well as fielding a wide variety of travel questions.

Greek National Tourist Organisation Offices
UK
4 Conduit Street, London WIR 0DJ
Tel: 020 7495 9300
Fax: 020 7287 1369
Email: EOT-greektouristoffice@btinternet.com
US
Olympic Tower, 645 Fifth Avenue,
9th Floor, New York, NY 10022
Tel: 212 421 5777
Fax: 212 826 6940
E-mail: info@greektourism.com
Australia
51 Pitt Street, Sydney NSW 2000

Tour Operators

Your local overseas branch of the Greek National Tourist Organisation (see below) can usually provide a list of that country's tour operators and specialist agents offering holidays in Greece. Otherwise, here are a few suggestions for something unusual:

• **Bicycle tours**
Classic Adventures, USA; tel: 1 800 777 8090; www.classicadventures.com
• **Botanical tours**
Marengo Guided Walks, Hunstanton, UK; tel: 01485 532710; www.marengowalks.com
• **Sail-and-trek mixed tours**
Explore!, Aldershot, UK;

tel: 0845 013 1537; www.explore.co.uk
Hellenic Adventures, USA;
tel: 1 800 851 6349;
www.hellenicadventures.com
• **Walking holidays**
ATG Oxford, UK; tel: 01865 315678; www.atg-oxford.co.uk
Exodus London, UK;
tel: 020 8675 5550;
www.exodus.co.uk
Ramblers Holidays, Welwyn Garden City, UK; tel: 01707 331133; www.ramblersholidays.co.uk
• **Writing workshops/holistic holidays**
Skyros Centre, London, UK;
tel: 020 7267 4424; www.skyros.com

Tel: 02 9241 1663/5
Fax: 02 9235 2174
Email: hto@tpg.com.au
Canada
91 Scollard Street, 2nd Floor, Toronto, ON M5R 1G4
Tel: 416 968 2220
Fax: 416 968 6533
E-mail: grnto.tor@sympatico.can
www.greektourism.com

Websites

Greek weather forecasts are available at:
www.meteo.gr
www.poseidon.ncmr.gr
For local journalism in English try the sites of:
www.eKathimerini.com
www.athensnews.gr
Reviews and sales of books on all aspects of Greece can be found at:
www.hellenicbookservice.com
Seagoing schedules are available at:
www.gtp.gr
For general tourist information and links have a look at:
www.greektravel.com
www.travel-greece.com
The Ministry of Culture site has impressive coverage of most of the country's museums, archeological sites and remote monuments on:
www.culture.gr
Excellent window into contemporary Greek music, with videos, playlists and artist profiles, maintained by a clued-up lady DJ at New Jersey station WPRB:
http://musicalodyssey.blogspot.com

Weights and Measures

Greece is completely metric, though land is measured and sold in strémmata (1,000 sq. metres/ 10,764 sq. ft).

What to Bring

Clothes

If you visit Greece during the summer, you will need lightweight, casual clothing. Add a pullover or jacket and you will be prepared for the occasional cool night breeze. Lightweight shoes and sandals are ideal in the summer, but you will also need a pair of comfortable walking shoes that have already been broken in. If you plan to do any hiking in the mountains or on the islands, bring sturdy, over-the-ankle boots with a good tread; leather will be more comfortable in the summer heat than synthetic materials.

In general, both Greeks and tourists dine in casual dress but even in the hottest weather Athenian men won't wear shorts. You will only need formal dress if you plan to go to fancy establishments, casinos or formal affairs. If you visit Greece during the winter, which can be surprisingly cold, bring the kind of clothes you would wear during spring in the northern US or central Europe.

Toiletries

Most international brands are widely available, except on the smallest islands. Feminine hygiene products are more likely to be sold in supermarkets than pharmacies.

Sun protection

A hat, sun cream and sunglasses are highly recommended for protection from the intense midday sun (sophisticated sun creams of up to SPF50 are widely available).

Adaptors

220v AC is the standard household electric current throughout Greece. Non-dual-voltage shavers and hair dryers from North America should be left at home in favour of versatile travel models – they can be bought on the spot in Greece. Greek plugs are the standard round, two-pin European continental type, different from those in North America and the UK; plug adaptors for American appliances are easy to find, three-to-two-pin adaptors for UK appliances much less so, so these are best purchased before departure.

Universal plug

Greek basins often aren't equipped with plugs, so if you want water in your sink a universal plug is essential.

Torch

If you're planning a trip to one of the islands, pack a torch, as walking home from the taverna can be tricky if there's no moon.

What to Wear

The Greeks will not expect you as a tourist to dress as they do, but scuffed shoes, ripped jeans or visibly out-of-date clothing are considered offensive.

In certain places and regions, you will encounter explicit requirements or conventions concerning dress. To enter a church, men must wear long trousers, and women sleeved dresses. Often dresses or wraps will be provided at the church entrance. Not complying with this code will be taken as insulting irreverence.

Some specific areas have their own dress codes. On Mýkonos, for example, tourists will shock no one by wearing shorts or a swimsuit in most public places. But this same apparel will be severely alienating in a mountain village in Epirus or Crete. The best approach is to observe what other people are wearing and dress accordingly.

Women Travellers

Lone female visitors may still be targeted for attention by predatory Greek males, especially around beach bars and after-hours discos, but, in general, machismo is no more a problem here than anywhere else in southern Europe. Greek women have much more sexual freedom than previously, especially in the cities. There is now little controversy in their spending time with their male counterparts, up to and including cohabiting before (or instead of) marriage.

In remote areas, many Greeks are still highly traditional and may find it hard to understand why you are travelling alone. You will not feel comfortable in their all-male cafés.

L ANGUAGE

UNDERSTANDING THE LANGUAGE

The Greek Language

Modern Greek is the outcome of gradual evolution undergone by the Greek language since the Classical period (5th–4th centuries BC). The language is still relatively close to Ancient Greek: it uses the same alphabet and much of the same vocabulary, though the grammar – other than the retention of the three genders – is considerably streamlined. Many people speak English, some very well, but even just a few words in their native language will always be appreciated.

Pronunciation tips

Most of the sounds of Greek aren't difficult to pronounce for English speakers. There are only six vowel sounds: *a, e, i, o, u,* and *y* are consistently pronounced as shown in the table opposite. The letter *s* is usually pronounced "s", but "z" before an *m* or *g*. The sound represented here as *th* is always pronounced as in "thin", not "that"; the first sound in "that" is represented by *d*.

The only difficult sounds are *h*, which is pronounced like the "ch" in Scottish "loch" (we render this as *kh* before "s" so that you don't generate "sh"), and *g* before *e* or *i*, which has no equivalent in English – it's somewhere between the "y" in "yet" and the "g" in "get".

The position of the stress in words is of critical importance, as homonyms abound, and Greeks will often fail to understand you if you don't stress the right syllable (compare *psýllos,* "flea" with *psilós,* "tall"). In this guide, stress is marked by a simple accent mark (´), except for single-syllable words, which are, however, still stressed.

Greek word order is flexible, so you may often hear phrases in a different order from the one in which they are given here. Like the French, the Greeks use the plural of the second person when addressing someone politely. We have used the polite (formal) form throughout this language section, except where an expression is specified as "informal".

Communication

Good morning *kaliméra*
Good evening *kalispéra*
Good night *kaliníhta*
Hello/Goodbye *giásas*
(informal: *giásou*)
Pleased to meet you *hárika polý*
Yes *ne*
No *óhi*
Thank you *efharistó*
You're welcome *parakaló*
Please *parakaló*
Okay/All right *endáxi*
Excuse me (to get attention)
me synhoríte

Emergencies

Help! *Voíthia!*
Stop! *Stamatíste!*
I've had an accident *Íha éna atíhima*
Call a doctor *Fonáxte éna giatró*
Call an ambulance *Fonáxte éna asthenofóro*
Call the police *Fonáxte tin astinomía*
Call the fire brigade *Fonáxte tous pirozvéstes*
Where's the telephone? *Pou íne to tiléfono?*
Where's the nearest hospital?
Pou íne to pio kondinó nosokomío?
I would like to report a theft
Égine mia klopí

Excuse me (to get past) *syngnómi*
Please write it down for me
Na mou to gráfete parakaló?
How are you? *Ti kánete?*
(informal: *Ti kánis?*)
Fine, and you? *Kalá, esís?*
(informal: *Kalá, esí?*)
Cheers/Your health! (when drinking)
Giámas!
Could you help me? *Boríte na me voithísete?*
Can you show me *Boríte na mou díxete…*
I want… *Thélo…*
I don't know *Den xéro*
I don't understand *Den katálava*
Do you speak English? *Xérete angliká?*
Can you please speak more slowly?
Parakaló, miláte sigá-sigá
Please say that again *Parakaló, xanapésteto*
Here *edó*
There *ekí*
What? *ti?*
When? *póte?*
Why? *giatí?*
Where? *pou?*
How? *pos?*

Telephone Calls

the telephone *to tiléfono*
phonecard *tilekárta*
May I use the phone, please? *Boró na tilefoníso, parakaló?*
Hello (on the phone) *Embrós/Oríste*
My name is… *Légome…*
Could I speak to… *Boró na milíso me…*
Wait a moment *Periménete mía stigmí*
I didn't hear *Den ákousa*

In the Hotel

Do you have a vacant room? *Éhete domátio?*

Our Transliteration System

In Greece, all town and village names on road signs, as well as most street names, are written in Greek and the Roman alphabets. There's no universally accepted system of transliteration into Roman, and in any case the Greek authorities are gradually replacing old signs with new ones that use a slightly different system. This means you will have to get used to seeing different spellings of the same place on maps and signs and in this book.

Below is the transliteration scheme we have used in this book: beside each Greek letter or pair of letters is the Roman letter(s) we have used. Next to that is a rough approximation of the sound in an English word.

A	α	a	father
B	β	v	vote
Γ	γ	g	got except before "e" or "i", when it is nearer to yacht, but rougher
Δ	δ	d	then
E	ε	e	egg
Z	ζ	z	zoo
H	η	i	ski
Θ	θ	th	thin
I	ι	i	ski
K	κ	k	kiss
Λ	λ	l	long

M	μ	m	man
N	ν	n	no
Ξ	ξ	x	taxi
O	o	o	toad
Π	π	p	pen
P	ρ	r	room
Σ	σ/ς	s	set
		or	charisma
T	τ	t	tea
Y	υ	y	ski
Φ	φ	f	fish
X	χ	h	loch
Ψ	ψ	ps	maps
Ω	ω	o	toad

AI	αι (ai)	e	hay
AY	αυ(au)	av	lava
EI	ει (ei)	i	ski
EY	ευ (eu)	ev	ever
OI	οι (oi)	i	ski
OY	ου (ou)	ou	tourist
ΓΓ	γγ (gg)	ng	long
ΓΚ	γκ (gk)	ng	long
ΓΞ	γξ (gx)	nx	anxious
ΜΠ	μπ (mp)	b	beg
		or mb	limber
NT	ντ (nt)	d	dog
		or nd	under
TZ	τζ (tz)	tz	adze

I've booked a room Ého kratísi éna domátio
I'd like... Tha íthela...
a single/double room éna monóklino/díklino
double bed dipló kreváti
a room with a bath/shower éna domátio me bánio/dous
One night éna vrádi
Two nights dyo vradiá
How much is it? Póso káni?
Do you have a room with a sea-view? Éhete domátio me théa pros ti thálassa?
Is there a balcony? Éhi balkóni?
Is the room heated/air-conditioned? To domátio éhi thérmansi/klimatismós?
Is breakfast included? Mazí me to proinó?
Can I see the room please? Boró na do to domátio, parakaló?
The room is too hot/cold/small To domátio íne polý zestó/krýo/mikró
It's too noisy Éhi polý thóryvo
Could you show me another room, please? Boríte na mou díxete állo domátio, parakaló?
I'll take it Tha to páro
Can I have the bill, please? Na mou kánete to logariasmó, parakaló?
key klidí
towel petséta
sheet sedóni
blanket kouvérta
pillow maxilári
soap sapoúni
hot water zestó neró
toilet paper hartí toualéttas

At a Bar or Café

bar/café bar/kafenío (or kafetéria)
patisserie zaharoplastío

I'd like... Tha íthela...
a (Greek) coffee éna (ellinikó) kafé
filter coffee gallikó kafé/kafé fíltro
instant coffee neskafé (or nes)
cappuccino kapoutsíno
white (with milk) me gála
black (without milk) horís gála
with sugar me záhari
without sugar horís záhari
a cup of tea éna tsäi
tea with lemon éna tsái me lemóni
orange/lemon soda mía portokaláda/lemonáda
fresh orange juice éna hymó portokáli
a glass/bottle of water éna potíri/ boukáli neró
with ice me pagáki
an ouzo/brandy éna oúzo/koniák
a beer (draught) mía býra (apó varélli)
an ice-cream éna pagotó
a pastry, cake mía pásta
oriental pastries baklavá/kataïfi

In a Restaurant

Have you got a table for... Éhete trapézi giá...
There are (four) of us ímaste (tésseres)
I'm a vegetarian íme hortofágos
Can we see the menu? Boroúme na doúme ton katálogo?
We would like to order Théloume na parangíloume
Have you got wine by the carafe? Éhete krasí hýma?
a litre/half-litre éna kiló/misó kilo **of white/red wine** áspro/kókkino krasí
Would you like anything else? Thélete típot' állo?
No, thank you óhi, efharistó

glass potíri
knife/fork/ spoon mahéri/piroúni/ koutáli
plate piáto
napkin hartopetséta
Where is the toilet? Pou íne i toualétta?
The bill, please to logariasmó, parakaló

Food

Mezédes/Orektiká

taramosaláta **fish-roe dip**
tzatzíki **yoghurt-garlic cucumber dip**
melitzánes **aubergines**
kafterí **tomato and féta dip**
kolokythákia **courgettes**
loukánika **sausages**
tyrokaftéri **soft cheese seasoned with hot peppers**
tyropitákia **small cheese pies**
antsoúgies **anchovies**
eliés **olives**
dolmádes **rice-stuffed vine leaves**
saganáki **fried cheese**
fáva **puréed fava beans**

Meat Dishes

kréas **any meat**
arní **lamb**
hirinó **pork**
gourounópoulo **suckling pig**
kotópoulo **chicken**
moskhári **veal, beef**
psitó **roast or grilled**
sto foúrno **roast**
sta kárvouna **grilled**
soúvlas **on the spit**
souvláki **brochettes on skewers**
kokinistó **stewed in tomato sauce**
avgolémono **egg-lemon sauce**
tiganitó **fried**
kapnistó **smoked**

Ordering Drinks

býra **beer**
krasí **wine**
áspro **white wine**
kokkinélli **rosé wine**
mávro **red wine**
me to kiló **wine by the kilo**
hýma **bulk, from the barrel**
neró **water**
retsína **resin-flavoured wine**
oúzo **aniseed-flavoured grape-pressing distillate**
rakí **another distilled spirit from vintage crushings**
tsípouro **north-mainland version of** rakí
tsikoudiá **Cretan version of** rakí, **flavoured with terebinth**
portokaláda **orange juice**
lemonáda **lemon juice**

brizóla **(pork or veal) chop**
païdákia **lamb chops**
pantsétta **spare ribs**
sykóti **liver**
kymás **mince**
biftéki **burger (without bun)**
keftédes **meat-balls**
kokorétsi **grilled sheep's entrails**
soutzoukákia **rissoles baked in red sauce**
giouvarlákia **mince-and-rice balls in egg lemon sauce**
makarónia **spaghetti**
mousakás **lamb and aubergine bake**
piláfi **rice**
me kymá **with minced meat**
me sáltsa **with tomato sauce**
kléftiko **baked lamb**
pastitsáda **braised beef (or cockerel) in spiced tomato sauce**
pastítsio **macaroni with minced meat**
sofríto **veal (or rabbit) in white wine**
spétzofäi **sausage, aubergine and green pepper dish**
stifádo **beef stewed with small onions**
gýros me pítta **doner kebab**
domátes gemistés **stuffed tomatoes**
piperiés gemistés **stuffed peppers**

Seafood

frésko **fresh**
katapsygméno **frozen**
psári **fish**
óstraka **shellfish**
xifías **swordfish**
koliós **mackerel**
barboúnia **red mullet**
sardélles **sardines**
gávros **fresh anchovy**
marídes **picarel**
mýdia **mussels**
strýdia **oysters**
kalamarákia **squid**
soupiés **cuttlefish**
htapódi **octopus**
garídes **prawns**
astakós **lobster**

Vegetables

anginåres **artichokes**
arakádes **peas**
domátes **tomatoes**
fakés **brown lentils**
fasólia/fasoláda **stewed white beans**
fasolákia (fréska) **green beans, in tomato sauce**
gígandes **stewed butter-beans**
hórta **misc. boiled greens**
hortópitta **vegetable pie**
karóta **carrot**
kolokythákia **courgettes**
kounoupídi **cauliflower**
koukiá **broad beans**
kremídi **onion**
láhano **cabbage**
maroúli **lettuce**
pandzária **beetroot**
patátes(tiganités/sto foúrno) **potatoes (chips/roast)**
radíkia **dandelion leaves**
revýthia **chickpeas**
skórdo **garlic**
spanáki **spinach**
spanakópitta **spinach pie**
vlíta **boiled greens**
saláta **salad**
domatosaláta **tomato salad**
angourodomáta **tomato and cucumber salad**
horiátiki **Greek salad**

Fruit

míla **apples**
veríkoka **apricots**
banánes **bananas**
kerásia **cherries**
sýka **figs**
stafýlia **grapes**
lemónia **lemons**
pepónia **melons**
portokália **oranges**
rodákina **peaches**
ahládia **pears**
fráoules **strawberries**
karpoúzi **watermelon**

Basic Foods/Desserts

psomí **bread**
aláti **salt**
pipéri **pepper**
ládi **(olive) oil**
xýdi **vinegar**
moustárda **mustard**
voútyro **butter**
tyrí **cheese**
avgá (tiganitá) **(fried) eggs**
omelétta **omelette**
marmeláda **jam, marmelade**
rýzi **rice**
giaoúrti **yoghurt**
méli **honey**
záhari **sugar**
galaktoboúreko **custard pastry**
halvás **semolina and walnut pudding**
kalitsoúnia **sweet cheese and cinnamon pastry**
ravaní **semolina and syrup cake**

Sightseeing

information pliroforíes
open/closed anihtó/klistó
Is it possible to see the church/archaeological site? Boroúme na doúme tin eklisía/ta arhéa?
Where can I find the custodian/key? Pou boró na vro to fílaka/klidí?

At the Shops

shop magazí/katástima
What time do you open/close? ti óra aníyete/klínete?
What would you like? Oríste/ti thélete?
I'm just looking Aplós kitázo
How much is it? Póso kání?
Do you take credit cards? Déheste pistotikés kártes?
Have you got...? éhete...?
size (for clothes) noúmero
Can I try it on? Boró na to dokimáso?
This is faulty; can I have a replacement? Aftó éhi éna elátoma. Boró na to aláxo?
Can I have a refund? Boró na páro píso ta leftá?
a kilo éna kiló
half a kilo misókilo
a quarter éna tétarto
two kilos dío kilá
100 grams ekató gramária
200 grams dyakósa gramária
more perisótero
less ligótero
a little/very little lígo/polý lígo
with/without me/horís
That's enough ftáni
That's all tipot'álo

Travelling

airport aerodrómio
boarding card kárta epivívasis
boat plío/karávi
bus leoforío
bus station stathmós leoforíon
bus stop stási
coach púlman
ferry feribót
first/second class próti/défteri thési
flight ptísi
hydrofoil iptámeno
motorway ethnikí odós
port limáni
return ticket isitírio me epistrofí
single ticket aplo isitírio
station stathmós
taxi taxí
train tréno

Public Transport

Can you help me, please? Boríte na me voithísete, parakaló?
Where can I buy tickets? Pou na kópso isitírio?

At the counter *sto tamío*
Does it stop at... *Káni stási sto...*
You need to change at... *Tha prépi n'aláxete sto...*
When is the next train/bus/ferry to... *Póte févyi to tréno/leoforío/feribót gia...*
How long does the journey take? *Pósi óra káni to taxídi?*
What time will we arrive? *Ti óra tha ftásoume?*
How much is the fare? *Póso íne to isitírio*
Next stop please *Epómeni stási parakaló*
Can you tell me where to get off? *Tha mou píte pou na katévo?*
Should I get off here? *Edó na katévo?*
delay *kathistérisi*

Directions

right/left *dexiá/aristerá*
Take the first/second right *Párte ton próto/déftero drómo dexiá*
Turn right/left *strípste dexiá/aristerá*
Go straight on *Tha páte ísia/efthía*
after the traffic lights *metá ta fanária*
Is it near/far away? *Íne kondá/makriá?*

Numbers

1 *énas/mía/éna* (masc/fem/neut)
2 *dýo*
3 *tris/tría*
4 *tésseres/téssera*
5 *pénde*
6 *éxi*
7 *eptá*
8 *októ*
9 *ennéa*
10 *déka*
11 *éndeka*
12 *dódeka*
13 *dekatrís/dekatría*
14 *dekatésseres/dekatéssera*
15 *dekapénde*
16 *dekaéxi*
17 *dekaeptá*
18 *dekaoktó*
19 *dekaennéa*
20 *íkosi*
30 *triánda*
40 *saránda*
50 *penínda*
60 *exínda*
70 *evdomínda*
80 *ogdónda*
90 *enenínda*
100 *ekató*
200 *dyakósa*
300 *trakósies/trakósa*
400 *tetrakósies/tetrakósa*
500 *pendakósa*
1,000 *hílies/hília*
2,000 *dýo hiliádes*
1 million *éna ekatomírio*

How far is it? *Póso makriá íne?*
It's five minutes' walk *Íne pénde leptá me ta pódia*
It's ten minutes by car *Íne déka leptá me to avtokínito*
100 metres *ekató métra*
opposite/next to *apénandi/dípla*
junction *diastávrosi*
Where is/are... *Pou íne...*
Where can I find... *Pou boró na vro...*
a petrol station *éna venzinádiko*
a bank *mia trápeza*
a bus stop *mia stási*
a hotel? *éna xenodohío?*
How do I get there? *Pos na páo ekí?*
Can you show me where I am on the map? *Boríte na mou díhete sto hárti pou íme?*
Am I on the right road for... *Gia... kalá páo?*
No, you're on the wrong road *Óhi, pírate láthos drómo*

On the Road

Where can I hire a car? *Pou boró na nikiázo avtokínito?*
What is it insured for? *Ti asfália éhi?*
By what time must I return it? *Méhri ti óra prépi na to epistrépso?*
driving licence *díploma*
petrol *venzíni*
unleaded *amólyvdi*
oil *ládi*
Fill it up *Óso pérni*
My car has broken down *Hálase to avtokinitó mou*
I've had an accident *Íha éna atíhima*
Can you check... *Boríte na elénhete...*
the brakes *ta fréna*
the clutch *to ambrayáz*
the engine *i mihaní*
the exhaust *i exátmisi*
the fanbelt *to imánda*
the gearbox *i tahítites*
the headlights *ta fanárga*
the radiator *to psigío*
the spark plugs *ta boúzi*
the tyre(s) *ta lástiha*

Times and Dates

(in the) morning/afternoon/evening *to proí/to apógevma/to vrádi*
(at) night *(ti) níhta*
yesterday *htes*
today *símera*
tomorrow *ávrio*
now *tóra*
early *norís*
late *argá*
a minute *éna leptó*
five/ten *pénde/déka*
minutes *leptá*
an hour *mia óra*
half an hour *misí óra*
a quarter of an hour *éna tétarto*
at one/ two (o'clock) *sti mia/stis dýo (i óra)*

Notices

ΤΟΥΑΛΕΤΕΣ	toilets
ΑΝΔΡΩΝ	gentlemen
ΓΥΝΑΙΚΩΝ	ladies
ΑΝΟΙΚΤΟ	open
ΚΛΕΙΣΤΟ	closed
ΕΙΣΟΔΟΣ	entrance
ΕΞΟΔΟΣ	exit
ΑΠΑΓΟΡΕΥΤΑΙ	no entry
ΕΙΣΙΤΗΡΙΑ	tickets
ΑΠΑΓΟΡΕΥΤΑΙ ΤΟ ΚΑΠΝΙΣΜΑ	no smoking
ΠΛΗΡΟΦΟΡΙΕΣ	information
ΠΡΟΣΟΧΗ	caution
ΚΙΝΔΥΝΟΣ	danger
ΑΡΓΑ	slow
ΔΗΜΟΣΙΑ ΕΡΓΑ	road works
ΠΑΡΚΙΝΓ	parking
ΧΩΡΟΣ ΣΤΑΘΜΕΥΣΕΩΣ	car park
ΑΠΑΓΟΡΕΥΤΑΙ Η ΣΤΑΘΜΕΥΣΗ	no parking
ΤΑΞΙ	taxi
ΤΡΑΠΕΖΑ	bank
ΤΗΛΕΦΩΝΟ	telephone
ΤΗΛΕΚΑΡΤΕΣ	phone cards
ΕΚΤΟΣ ΛΕΙΤΟΥΡΓΙΑΣ	out of order

a day *mia méra*
a week *mia vdomáda*
(on) Monday *(ti) deftéra*
(on) Tuesday *(tin) tríti*
(on) Wednesday *(tin) tetárti*
(on) Thursday *(tin) pémpti*
(on) Friday *(tin) paraskeví*
(on) Saturday *(to) sávato*
(on) Sunday *(tin) kyriakí*

Health

Is there a chemist's nearby? *Ypárhi éna farmakío edó kondá?*
Which chemist is open all night? *Pio farmakío dianikterévi?*
I don't feel well *Den esthénome kalá*
I'm ill *Íme árostos* (feminine *árosti*)
He/she's ill *Íne árostos/árosti*
Where does it hurt? *Pou ponái?*
It hurts here *Ponái edó*
I suffer from... *Páskho apo...*
I have a... *Éxo...*
 headache *ponokéfalo*
 sore throat *ponólemo*
 stomach ache *kiliópono*
Have you got something for travel sickness? *Éhete típota gia ti navtía?*
It's not serious *Den íne sovaró*
Do I need a prescription? *Hriázete syndagí?*
It bit me (of an animal) *Me dángose*
It stung me *Me kéndrise*
 bee *mélisa*
 wasp *sfíka*
 mosquito *kounoúpi*
sticking plaster *lefkoplástis*
diarrhoea pills *hápia gia ti diária*

FURTHER READING

Books go in and out of print, or change imprints, with such rapidity of late that we've elected not to list the pubishers, except for obscure Greek publishers with no internet presence, or one-off presses with only internet presence. For most titles, conducting a web search with the author and title should suffice to dredge up its current incarnation.

Ancient History and Culture

Burkert, Walter **Greek Religion: Archaic and Classical**. Excellent overview of the gods and goddesses, their attributes, worship and the meaning of major festivals.
Burn, A.R. **The Penguin History of Greece**. A good, single-volume introduction to ancient Greece.
Davidson, James **The Greeks and Greek Love**. This "radical reappraisal of homosexuality in ancient Greece" tries to put queerness back at the centre of the ancient social equation and, despite too many bouts of special pleading, gets some way there.
Finley, M.I. **The World of Odysseus**. Reissued 1954 standard on just how well (or not) the Homeric sagas are borne out by archaelogical facts.
Fox, Robin Lane **Alexander the Great**. A psychobiography wedded to a conventional history.
Grimal, Pierre, ed **Dictionary of Classical Mythology**. Still considered to be tops among a handful of available alphabetical gazetteers.
Hornblower, Simon **The Greek World, 479–323 BC**. The eventful period from the end of the Persian Wars to Alexander's demise; the standard university text.

Byzantine History and Culture

Norwich, John Julius Byzantium (3 vols): **The Early Centuries, The Apogee** and **The Decline**. The most readable and masterful popular history, by the noted Byzantinologist; also available as one massive volume, **A Short History of Byantium**.
Psellus, Michael **Fourteen Byzantine Rulers**. That many changes of rule in a single century (10th–11th), as told

by a near-contemporary historian.
Rice, David Talbot **Art of the Byzantine Era**. Shows how Byzantine sacred craftsmanship extended from the Caucausus into northern Italy, in a variety of media.
Runciman, Steven **The Fall of Constantinople, 1453**. Still the definitive study of an event which continues to exercise modern Greek minds. His **Byzantine Style and Civilization** covers art, culture and monuments.
Ware, Archbishop Kallistos **The Orthodox Church**. Good introduction to what was, until recently, the de facto established religion of modern Greece.

Anthropology and Culture

Campbell, John **Honor, family and patronage: A study of institutions and moral values in a Greek mountain community** Classic study of Sarakatsáni shepherds in the Zagorian Píndos, with much wider application to Greece in general, which got the author banned from the area by touchy officialdom.
Danforth, Loring H. and Tsiaras, Alexander **The Death Rituals of Rural Greece**. Riveting, annotated photo essay on Greek funeral customs.
Du Boulay, Juliet **Portrait of a Greek Mountain Village**. Ambéli, a mountain village in Évvia, as it was in the mid-1960s.
Holst, Gail **Road to Rembetika: Songs of Love, Sorrow and Hashish** (Denise Harvey, Límni, Évvia). Introduction to the enduringly popular musical form; with translated lyrics and discographies.
Mackridge, Peter **The Modern Greek Language**. In-depth analysis by one of the foremost scholars of the tongue's evolution.
Tomkinson, John L. **Festive Greece: A Calendar of Tradition**. Copiously photographed calendar of all the extant rites of the Orthodox Church, their pagan substrata erupting frequently and vividly at popular *paniyíria*.

Cuisine

Dalby, Andrew **Siren Feasts**. Analysis

of Classical and Byzantine texts shows just how little Greek food has changed in three millennia.
Davidson, Alan **Mediterranean Seafood**. 1972 classic that's still the standard reference, guaranteed to end every argument as to just what that fish is on your *tavérna* plate. Complete with recipes.
Kyriakou, Theodore **A Culinary Voyage Around the Greek Islands**. The latest cookery book from the founder of London's Real Greek and Souvlaki restaurants. Beautifully illustrated.
Lazarakis, Konstantinos **The Wines of Greece** An overview, current to late 2005, of what's happening in Greece's eleven recognized wine-producing regions.

Modern History

Clogg, Richard **A Concise History of Greece**. Clear and lively account of Greece from Byzantine times to 2002, with helpful maps and well-captioned artwork. The best single-volume summary.
Koliopoulos, John and Thanos Veremis **Greece, the Modern Sequel: From 1831 to the Present**. Thematic and psycho-history of the independent nation, tracing trends, first principles and setbacks.
Mazower, Mark **Salonica: City of Ghosts**. A lucid account of this extraordinary city from 1430 to 1950, as Christians, Muslims and Jews came together and prospered, before man and nature tore it apart.
Mercouri, Melina **I Was Born Greek**. The tumultuous life and times of Greece's most famous actress, written in 1971 while she was in exile from the junta.
Pettifer, James **The Greeks: the Land and People since the War**. Useful general introduction to politics, family life, food, tourism and other contemporary topics.
Woodouse, C.M. **Modern Greece: A Short History**. Spans the period from early Byzantium to the early 1980s. His classic **The Struggle for Greece, 1941–1949**, reissued by C. Hurst (London), is perhaps the best overview of that turbulent decade.

Modern Greek Literature

Beaton, Roderick **An Introduction to Modern Greek**. Readable survey of Greek literature since independence.

Peter Bien, Peter Constantine, Edmund Keeley, Karen Van Dyck, eds **A Century of Greek Poetry, 1900–2000**. Well produced bilingual volume, with some lesser-known surprises alongside the big names.

Cavafy, C.P. **Collected Poems**, trans. by Edmund Keeley and Philip Sherrard or **The Complete Poems of Cavafy**, translated by Rae Dalven. The two "standard" versions available in English; newer 2007 translations by Evangelos Sachperoglou and Stratis Haviaris will also be of interest but don't break radically new ground.

Elytis, Odysseus **The Axion Esti**, **Selected Poems** and **The Sovereign Sun**. Pretty much the complete works of the Nobel laureate, in translation.

Karnezis, Panos. Karnezis grew up in Greece, but lives in London, writing in English; however, his concerns remain resolutely Greek. **Little Infamies** is a collection of short stories set in his native Peloponnese during the late 1950s and early 1960s; **The Maze** is a darker, more successful novel concerning the Asia Minor Catastrophe. Both display a penchant for old-fashioned plot twists – or excessive whimsical magical realism, depending on point of view. His most recent **The Birthday Party** is based on the life of Aristotle Onassis and daughter Christina.

Kazantzakis, Nikos. Nobel laureate, woolly Marxist and self-imposed exile, Kazantzakis embodies the old maxim that classics are books praised but generally unread. Whether in intricate, untranslatable Greek or wooden English, Kazantzakis can be hard going. **Zorba the Greek** is a surprisingly dark and nihilistic work, worlds away from the crude, two-dimensional character of the film; **The Last Temptation of Christ** provoked riots by Orthodox fanatics in Athens in 1989; **Report to Greco** explores his Cretanness/Greekness; while **Christ Recrucified** (published in the US as *The Greek Passion*) encompasses the Easter drama within Christian-Muslim dynamics on Crete.

Mourselas, Kostas **Red Dyed Hair** (Kedros, Athens). Politically incorrect picaresque saga of urban life from the 1950s to the 1970s among a particularly feckless paréa; the Greek original still sells well, and formed the basis of popular TV series.

Papadiamantis, Alexandros; trans. Peter Levi **The Murderess**. Landmark novel, set on Skiáthos at the turn of the 19th/20th centuries.

Papandreou, Nick **Father Dancing** (published as *A Crowded Heart* in the US). Thinly disguised, page-turning roman-à-clef by the late prime minister's younger son; Papandreou *père* comes across as an egotistical monster.

Ritsos, Yannis **Exile and Return, Selected Poems 1967–74**. The outcome of junta-era internal exile on Sámos for Greece's foremost communist poet.

Seferis, George; trans. Edmund Keeley **Collected Poems 1924–55**; **Complete Poems**. The former has Greek-English texts on facing pages and is preferable to the so-called "complete" works of Greece's other Nobel literary laureate.

Sotiriou, Dido **Farewell Anatolia** (Kedros, Athens). A best-selling classic since its appearance in 1962, this traces the end of the Greeks in Asia Minor from 1914 to 1922, using a character based on the author's father.

Tsirkas, Stratis; trans. Kay Cicellis **Drifting Cities**. (Kedros, Athens). Welcome paperback re-issue of this epic novel on wartime leftist intrigue in Alexandria, Cairo and Jerusalem.

Valaoritis, Nanos and Maskaleris, Thanasis, eds **An Anthology of Modern Greek Poetry**. English-only text, but excellent biographical info on the poets and good renditions by two native Greek speakers.

Vassilikos, Vassilis. **Z**. Based closely enough on the assassination of leftist MP Grigoris Lambrakis in 1963 by royalist thugs to get the book – and author – banned by the colonels' junta.

Foreign Writers in/on Greece

Andrews, Kevin **The Flight of Ikaros**. An educated, sensitive, Anglo-American archaeologist wanders the back-country in surprising freedom as the civil war winds down. Despite the massive changes since, still one of the best books on the country.

Bookshops in Athens

Athens has various bookshops that carry quality books in English: **Compendium**, Níkis 28, just behind Sýndagma Square (tel: 210 322 6931). **Eleftheroudakis**, Panepistimíou 17 (tel: 210 331 4180), plus three other midtown branches. **Iy Folia tou Vivlíou/The Book Nest**, Panepistimíou 25-29, Stoa Megárou Athinón (tel: 210 322 5209).

Bouras, Gillian **A Foreign Wife**, **A Fair Exchange** *and* **Aphrodite and the Others**. Scottish-Australian marries Greek-Australian, then consents to return to the "mother" country; the resulting trilogy is about the best of many chronicles of the acculturation experience.

De Bernières, Louis **Captain Corelli's Mandolin**. Heart-rending tragicomedy set on occupied Kefalloniá during World War II which has acquired cult status and long-term best-seller-list tenancy since its appearance in 1994.

Durrell, Lawrence **Prospero's Cell** and **Reflections on a Marine Venus**. Corfu in the 1930s, and Rhodes in 1945–47, now looking rather old-fashioned, alcohol-fogged and patronising of the "natives", but still entertaining enough.

Fowles, John **The Magus**. Best-seller, inspired by author's spell teaching on Spétses during the 1950s, of post-adolescent manipulation, conspiracy and cock-teasing (ie, the usual Fowles obsessions).

Gage, Eleni **North of Ithaka**. Eleni is the namesake and granddaughter of the Eleni whose murder her son Nicholas set out to avenge (*see below*). A New York journalist, she "took leave" for most of 2002 in her grandmother's village in Epirus, rebuilding the family house and more.

Gage, Nicholas **Eleni**. Epirus-born American correspondent returns to Greece to avenge the death of his mother at the hands of an ELAS firing squad in 1948.

Leigh Fermor, Patrick. **Roumeli: Travels in Northern Greece and Mani**. Written during the late 1950s and early 1960s, before the advent of mass tourism, these remain some of the best compendia of the then already-vanishing customs and relict communities of the mainland.

Manus, Willard **This Way to Paradise: Dancing on the Tables** (Lycabettus Press, Athens). An American expatriate's affectionate summing-up of 40-plus years living in Líndos, from its innocence to its corruption. Wonderful anecdotes of the hippie days, and walk-on parts for the famous and infamous.

Miller, Henry **The Colossus of Maroussi**. Miller takes to Corfu, the Argolid, Athens and Crete of 1939 with the enthusiasm of a first-timer in Greece who's found his element; deserted archaeological sites and larger-than-life personalities.

Salmon, Tim **The Unwritten Places** (Lycabettus Press, Athens). Veteran Hellenophile describes his love affair with the Greek mountains, and the Vlach pastoral communities of Epirus in particular.

Stone, Tom **The Summer of my Greek Taverna**. Set in a thinly disguised Kámbos of early-1980s Pátmos, this is a poignant cautionary tale for all who've ever fantasised about leasing a taverna (or buying a property) in the islands. **Zeus: A Journey Through Greece in the Footsteps of a God**. As the title says – part spirit-of-place travelogue (a very big spirit in this case), part unpicking of the myths surrounding the chief ancient deity by treating Him as a biographical subject. Storace, Patricia **Dinner with Persephone**. New York poet resident a year in Athens successfully takes the pulse of modern Greece, with all its shibboleths, foundation myths, carefully nurtured self-image and rampant misogyny. Very funny, and spot-on. Tomkinson, John L., ed **Traveller's Greece: Memories of an Enchanted Land** (www.anagnosis.gr). 17th–19th-century traveller's impressions of islands and mainland, ranging from the enraptured to the appalled. Zinovieff, Sofka **Eurydice Street**. An anthropologist and journalist by training, Zinovieff first came to Greece in the early 1980s (contributing to the first *Insight Guide Greece*), then returned in 2001 with her Greek husband and two daughters to live in Athens. With sharp insights on nationalism, Orthodoxy, politics, 17 November and leisure (among various topics), this is the best single account of life in contemporary urban Greece – tellingly, translated into Greek.

Regional and Archaelogical Guides

Anagnosis Guides (www.anagnosis.gr) Several well-illustrated guides to Athens and surroundings that highlight the obscure, unorthdox and over-looked, with directions to cited sites. Burn, A.R. and Mary **The Living Past of Greece**. Worth toting its oversized format around for the sake of lively text and clear plans; covers most major sites from Minoan to medieval. Hetherington, Paul **Byzantine and Medieval Greece**. Erudite and authoritative dissection of the castles and churches of the mainland. Chilton, Lance **Various walking guides** Short but detailed guidelets to the best walks around various mainland and island charter destinations, accompanied by maps. See the full list and order from: www.marengowalks.com Wilson, Loraine **The White Mountains of Crete**. The best of several guides to the range, with nearly sixty hikes of all levels,

Send Us Your Thoughts

We do our best to ensure the information in our books is as accurate and up-to-date as possible. The books are updated on a regular basis using local contacts, who painstakingly add, amend and correct as required. However, some details (such as telephone numbers and opening times) are liable to change, and we are ultimately reliant on our readers to put us in the picture.

We welcome your feedback, especially your experience of using the book "on the road". Maybe we recommended a hotel that you liked (or another that you didn't), or you came across a great bar or new attraction we missed.

We will acknowledge all contributions, and we'll offer an Insight Guide to the best letters received.

Please write to us at:
**Insight Guides
PO Box 7910
London SE1 1WE**
Or email us at:
insight@apaguide.co.uk

described by the most experienced foreign trek leader.

Botanical Field Guides

Baumann, Helmut **Greek Wildflowers and Plant Lore in Ancient Greece**. As the title says; lots of interesting ethnobotanical trivia, useful photos. Huxley, Anthony, and William Taylor **Flowers of Greece and the Aegean**. The only volume dedicated to both islands and mainland, with good photos, though taxonomy is now a bit obsolete. Polunin, Oleg **Flowers of Greece and the Balkans**. This book is also showing its age, but again has lots of colour photos to aid identification. Polunin, Oleg and Anthony Huxley **Flowers of the Mediterranean**. Lots of colour plates to aid in identification, and includes flowering shrubs; recent printings have a table of taxonomic changes.

Other Insight Guides

Insight Guides cover nearly 200 destinations, providing information on culture and all the top sights, as well as superb photography and detailed maps. Other Insight Guides to destinations in the region include: *Mediterranean Cruises*, *Greek Islands* and *Turkey*, Complementing the main Insight

series is the Insight **City Guides** series. *Insight City Guide: Athens* is the ideal guidebook to the city. As well as a detailed and lavishly illustrated Places section, with photo essays on key sights such as the Benaki Museum, the Archaeological Museum, Neoclassical architecture, and the best beaches, it provides detailed maps and floor plans, and a fact-packed practical information section. There is also a pull-out map plotting the city's best restaurants.

The new Insight **Step by Step** guide books contain personal recommendations from a local host, a programme of carefully timed itineraries and a fold-out map. They are particularly useful for the short-stay visitor intent on making the best use of every moment. Titles include Barcelona, Copenhagen, London, Marrakesh, Paris.

Insight **Smart Guides** are handy listings guides arranged in an A–Z format for easy use. They include an atlas section Titles include Bruges, Hong Kong, New York, Orlando and Venice.

Insight **FlexiMaps** are designed to complement our guidebooks. They provide full mapping of major destinations, and their easy-to-fold, laminated finish gives them ease of use and durability. The range of titles include Athens, Istanbul, Greek Islands, Corfu, Crete, Cyprus and Turkey.

Art & Photo Credits

INSIGHT GUIDE
GREECE

Cartographic Editor **Zoë Goodwin**
Production **Linton Donaldson**
Design Consultants
Carlotta Junger, Graham Mitchener
Picture Research **Celia Stern**

INDEX

Numbers in italics refer to photographs

INSIGHT GUIDES

The classic series that puts you in the picture

www.insightguides.com

Insight Guides Website

www.insightguides.com

Don't travel the
planet alone.
Keep in step with
Insight Guides'
walking eye,
just a click away

Athens Metro